ARRIAN
II

269

ARRIAN

WITH AN ENGLISH TRANSLATION

BY

P. A. BRUNT

FORMERLY

CAMDEN PROFESSOR OF ANCIENT HISTORY

UNIVERSITY OF OXFORD

IN TWO VOLUMES

II

ANABASIS ALEXANDRI

BOOKS V–VII

INDICA

CAMBRIDGE, MASSACHUSETTS

HARVARD UNIVERSITY PRESS

LONDON

WILLIAM HEINEMANN LTD

MCMLXXXIII

American ISBN 0–674–99297–0
British ISBN 0–434–99269–0

Edition by E. Iliff Robson first published 1933
*Revised text and translation with new introduction,
notes and appendixes by P. A. Brunt,* 1983

Printed in Great Britain

CONTENTS

PREFACE

The Greek text is again that of A. G. Roos, revised by G. Wirth (Teubner, 1967), reprinted by kind permission of B. G. Teubner Verlagsgesellschaft, Leipzig, with a few changes signalized in the apparatus at v 2, 6; 6, 7; 7, 3; 20, 10; vi 6, 1; 15, 1 and 5; 20, 3; 21, 3; 23, 1; 25, 5; 28, 1; 29, 4, 6 and 9; vii 4, 1; 8, 1 and 2; 11, 3; 20, 3; *Ind.* 1, 5; 4, 8; 18, 7; 27, 5; 32, 4; 37, 3.

Publication of this volume has been delayed since 1977 for reasons outside my control. I have not been able to revise the text systematically in the light of other works, which have appeared since it was first prepared for the press. Of these the most notable are N. G. L. Hammond and G. T. Griffith, *A History of Macedonia*, ii, 550–336 (Oxford 1979), and A. B. Bosworth, *Historical Commentary on Arrian's History of Alexander*, I–III (Oxford 1980). The latter incorporates the findings of earlier articles (of which that in *CQ* 1974 was misdated in vol. I to 1975 in notes on ii 13, 7, iii 6, 9; 16, 11 and iv 7, 2) and is supplemented for later books by his important essays in *JHS* 1980 and 1981. It need hardly be said that my own commentary cannot compete with this magisterial work. I would not tax Arrian with quite so many *sottises* as he does, but our estimates of Arrian do not widely differ.

My first volume contained some unintentional errors, and various points in translation and commentary have been challenged in works that have appeared since. After reflection I do not think this the place for a full list of *errata*. Students will be able

PREFACE

to see for themselves where I have been convicted of mistakes. On various matters, relevant to books v-vii and to the *Indica*, my own views have sometimes changed. The account I gave of Arrian and his sources in Introduction 1–6 and 10–23 is modified in App. XXVIII. My notes sometimes assigned passages too dogmatically to the vulgate. I withdraw Introd. n. 25, cf. App. XVIII, and would change the translation of i 12, 5, cf. App. XXVIII 5. On military matters Introd. 56–65 and App. XIII must now be taken with App. XIX. A few misleading references demand correction. In Introd. n. 43 read *Ind*. 18.; in App. X 2 the cross-reference is to App. IX 6, and in App. X 3 substitute A. iii 19, 7 for 20, 7. On p. 357 n. 3 belongs to iv 6, 7. Note also two inexplicable slips: Introd. 11 misdates Ipsus from 301 to 306, and iii 2, 7 n. refers to ' Chios' decree' instead of ' Alexander's decree about Chios'.

My thanks are again due to Professor E. H. Warmington for assistance with the translation and to Professor Philippa Goold, Associate Editor of the Loeb Classical Library, for assistance with the proofs.

Brasenose College   P. A. Brunt
Oxford

ABBREVIATIONS AND SHORT TITLES

A.	= Arrian	N.	= Nearchus
Al.	= Alexander	O.	= Onesicritus
Ar.	= Aristobulus	P.	= Plutarch, *Alexander*
D.	= Diodorus	Pt.	= Ptolemy
E.	= Eratosthenes	QC.	= Quintus Curtius
J.	= Justin	S.	= Strabo
Meg.	= Megasthenes		

Where no other author is indicated, references in the form iii 2, 3 are to Arrian's *Anabasis*; *Ind.* refers to *Indica*.

Book numbers for all authors are in Roman numerals, and are omitted where the context shows what book is intended.

All references to D. are to book xvii, unless otherwise specified.

Anspach	A. E. Anspach, *De Alexandri Magni Expeditione Indica*, 1903
Beloch	K. J. Beloch, *Griechische Geschichte* ²
Berve	H. Berve, *Das Alexanderreich* (see Introd. n. 110)
Bosworth	A. B. Bosworth, *Historical Commentary on Arrian's History of Alexander*, I, 1980
CHI	*Cambridge History of India*, I, 1935
CQ	*Classical Quarterly*
Engels	D. W. Engels, *Alexander the Great and the Logistics of the Macedonian Army*, 1978
Fuller	Major-General J. F. C. Fuller, *The Generalship of Alexander the Great*, 1958

ABBREVIATIONS AND SHORT TITLES

GR	*Greece and Rome*, vol. XII, 2, 1965 (*Alexander the Great*)
Griffith	see Hammond
Hamilton	J. R. Hamilton, *Plutarch, Alexander*, 1969
Hammond *or* Griffith	N. G. L. Hammond and G. T. Griffith, *History of Macedonia*, II, 1979
Jacoby	F. Jacoby, *Die Fragmente der griechischen Historiker*. The historians are numbered, and I refer to them by these numbers, e.g. no. 124 (Callisthenes) T[estimonium] 1 or F[ragmentum] 1; Jacoby's numbering of volumes is confusing.
JHS	*Journal of Hellenic Studies*
Lane Fox	R. Lane Fox, *Alexander the Great*, 1973
Pearson, *LH* *or* Pearson	L. Pearson, *The Lost Histories of Alexander the Great*, 1960
Pliny	*Natural History*
RE	Pauly-Wissowa, *Real-Encyclopädie der classischen Altertumswissenschaft*
Schiwek	H. Schiwek, *Bonner Jahrbücher*, 1962, 43 ff.
Tarn	W. W. Tarn, *Alexander the Great* (2 vols.), 1948
Tod	M. N. Tod, *Greek Historical Incriptions*, II

ARRIAN

ANABASIS OF ALEXANDER

BOOK V

ΑΡΡΙΑΝΟΥ

ΑΛΕΞΑΝΔΡΟΥ ΑΝΑΒΑΣΕΩΣ

ΒΙΒΛΙΟΝ ΠΕΜΠΤΟΝ

1. Ἐν δὲ τῇ χώρᾳ ταύτῃ, ἥντινα μεταξὺ τοῦ τε Κωφῆνος καὶ τοῦ Ἰνδοῦ ποταμοῦ ἐπῆλθεν Ἀλέξανδρος, καὶ Νῦσαν πόλιν ᾠκίσθαι λέγουσι· τὸ δὲ κτίσμα εἶναι Διονύσου· Διόνυσον δὲ κτίσαι τὴν Νῦσαν ἐπεί τε Ἰνδοὺς ἐχειρώσατο, ὅστις δὴ οὗτος ὁ Διόνυσος καὶ ὁπότε ἢ ὅθεν ἐπ᾽ Ἰνδοὺς ἐστράτευ-
2 σεν· οὐ γὰρ ἔχω συμβαλεῖν εἰ ὁ Θηβαῖος Διόνυσος [ὃς] ἐκ Θηβῶν ἢ ἐκ Τμώλου τοῦ Λυδίου ὁρμηθεὶς ἐπὶ Ἰνδοὺς ἧκε στρατιὰν ἄγων, τοσαῦτα μὲν ἔθνη μάχιμα καὶ ἄγνωστα τοῖς τότε Ἕλλησιν ἐπελθών, οὐδὲν δὲ αὐτῶν ἄλλο ὅτι μὴ τὸ Ἰνδῶν βίᾳ χειρωσάμενος· πλήν γε δὴ ὅτι οὐκ ἀκριβῆ ἐξεταστὴν χρὴ εἶναι τῶν ὑπὲρ τοῦ θείου ἐκ παλαιοῦ μεμυθευμένων. τὰ γάρ τοι κατὰ τὸ εἰκὸς ξυντιθέντι οὐ πιστά, ἐπειδὰν τὸ θεῖόν τις προσθῇ τῷ λόγῳ, οὐ πάντη ἄπιστα φαίνεται.
3 Ὡς δὲ ἐπέβη τῇ Νύσῃ Ἀλέξανδρος, ἐκπέμπουσι παρ᾽ αὐτὸν οἱ Νυσαῖοι τὸν κρατιστεύοντα σφῶν, ὄνομα δὲ ἦν αὐτῷ Ἄκουφις, καὶ ξὺν αὐτῷ πρέσβεις τῶν δοκιμωτάτων τριάκοντα, δεησομένους Ἀλεξ-
4 άνδρου ἀφεῖναι τῷ θεῷ τὴν πόλιν. παρελθεῖν τε δὴ ἐς τὴν σκηνὴν τὴν Ἀλεξάνδρου τοὺς πρέσβεις καὶ καταλαβεῖν καθήμενον κεκονιμένον ἔτι ἐκ τῆς ὁδοῦ ξὺν τοῖς ὅπλοις τοῖς τε ἄλλοις καὶ τὸ κράνος [αὐτῷ] περικείμενον καὶ τὸ δόρυ ἔχοντα· θαμβῆ-

ARRIAN

ANABASIS OF ALEXANDER

BOOK V

1. In this country between the rivers Cophen and 326 B.C. Indus which Alexander invaded it is said that a city called Nysa was also situated, a foundation of Dionysus in the time when he subdued the Indians, whoever this Dionysus was, and whenever or whence he marched against the Indians; for my part I can- 2 not gather whether the Theban Dionysus, starting from Thebes or from the Lydian Tmolus, led an army against the Indians, after assailing so many warlike peoples, unknown to the Greeks of that time, and yet subduing none of them by force but the Indians; still, one must not be a precise critic of ancient legends that concern the divine. For things which are incredible if you consider them on the basis of probability appear not wholly incredible, when one adds the divine element to the story.[1]

When Alexander approached Nysa, the people of 3 Nysa sent out to meet him the man of greatest power among them, whose name was Acuphis, with thirty envoys of the highest repute, to beg Alex- ander to leave the city to the god. The envoys, it is 4 said, came into Alexander's tent, and found him sitting still all dusty from the journey with his ordin- ary armour on and wearing his helmet and carrying his spear; they were amazed at the sight and fell to

---

[1] Cf. 3, 1-4; App. XVII 7 f. on E.; XVI on the Nysa story.

ARRIAN

σαί τε ἰδόντας τὴν ὄψιν καὶ πεσόντας ἐς γῆν ἐπὶ
πολὺ σιγὴν ἔχειν. ὡς δὲ ἐξανέστησέ τε αὐτοὺς
Ἀλέξανδρος καὶ θαρρεῖν ἐκέλευσε, τότε δὴ τὸν
Ἄκουφιν ἀρξάμενον λέγειν ὧδε.

5 Ὦ βασιλεῦ, δέονταί σου Νυσαῖοι ἐᾶσαι σφᾶς
ἐλευθέρους τε καὶ αὐτονόμους αἰδοῖ τοῦ Διονύσου.
Διόνυσος γὰρ ἐπειδὴ χειρωσάμενος τὸ Ἰνδῶν
ἔθνος ἐπὶ θάλασσαν ὀπίσω κατῄει τὴν Ἑλληνικήν,
ἐκ τῶν ἀπομάχων στρατιωτῶν, οἳ δὴ αὐτῷ καὶ
βάκχοι ἦσαν, κτίζει τὴν πόλιν τήνδε μνημόσυνον
τῆς αὑτοῦ πλάνης τε καὶ νίκης τοῖς ἔπειτα ἐσομέ-
νον, καθάπερ οὖν καὶ σὺ αὐτὸς Ἀλεξάνδρειάν τε
ἔκτισας τὴν πρὸς Καυκάσῳ ὄρει καὶ ἄλλην
Ἀλεξάνδρειαν ἐν τῇ Αἰγυπτίων γῇ, καὶ ἄλλας
πολλὰς τὰς μὲν ἔκτικας ἤδη, τὰς δὲ καὶ κτίσεις ἀνὰ
χρόνον, οἷα δὴ πλείονα Διονύσου ἔργα ἀποδειξ-
6 άμενος. Νῦσάν τε οὖν ἐκάλεσε τὴν πόλιν Διόνυσος
ἐπὶ τῆς τροφοῦ τῆς Νύσης καὶ τὴν χώραν Νυσαίαν·
τὸ δὲ ὄρος ὅ τι περ πλησίον ἐστὶ τῆς πόλεως καὶ
τοῦτο Μηρὸν ἐπωνόμασε Διόνυσος, ὅτι δὴ κατὰ τὸν
μῦθον ἐν μηρῷ τῷ τοῦ Διὸς ηὐξήθη. καὶ ἐκ
τούτου ἐλευθέραν τε οἰκοῦμεν τὴν Νῦσαν καὶ αὐτοὶ
αὐτόνομοι καὶ ἐν κόσμῳ πολιτεύοντες· τῆς δὲ ἐκ
Διονύσου οἰκίσεως καὶ τόδε σοι γενέσθω τεκμή-
ριον· κιττὸς γὰρ οὐκ ἄλλῃ τῆς Ἰνδῶν γῆς φυό-
μενος παρ' ἡμῖν φύεται.

2. Καὶ ταῦτα πάντα Ἀλεξάνδρῳ πρὸς θυμοῦ
ἐγίγνετο ἀκούειν καὶ ἤθελε πιστὰ εἶναι τὰ ὑπὲρ τοῦ
Διονύσου τῆς πλάνης μυθευόμενα· καὶ κτίσμα
εἶναι Διονύσου τὴν Νῦσαν ἤθελεν, ὡς ἤδη τε ἥκειν

---

[2] In Greek legend Dionysus was concealed from Hera by

326
B.C.

the ground and for a long time kept silent. But when Alexander raised them up and told them to take heart, then Acuphis began and spoke as follows:

' Sire, the people of Nysa beg you to leave them 5 free and independent, out of reverence for Dionysus. For when Dionysus had subdued the nation of the Indians, and was returning towards the Greek Sea, he founded this city with the men unfit for service among his soldiers, who were also his Bacchi, to be a memorial to posterity of his wanderings and victory, just as you have yourself founded Alexandria by Mount Caucasus and another Alexandria in Egypt, and as there are many other cities you have founded already or will found in course of time and thus give proof of more achievements than those of Dionysus. Now Dionysus called this city Nysa in honour of his 6 nurse Nyse, and the territory Nysaean; and he named the mountain near the city Merus, since according to the legend he grew in the thigh of Zeus.² From that time this city of Nysa in which we dwell has been free, and we ourselves independent, with an orderly civic life. And it should also be a proof that Dionysus was our founder that ivy grows nowhere else in India, but only with us.'

2. To hear all this was congenial to Alexander and he wanted to believe the tale about the wandering of Dionysus; he also wanted Nysa to be founded by Dionysus, in which case he had already reached the

---

Zeus in his thigh (*mēros*) and then reared by nymphs in Nysa, a place that had been located in various remote lands. QC. viii 10, 12 derives the legend from the name of the mountain; so too probably Meg., whence *Ind.* 1, 5 (which should not be amended) and D. ii 38, 4. Acuphis' speech: App. XXVII 4.

αὐτὸς ἔνθα ἦλθε Διόνυσος καὶ ἐπέκεινα ⟨ἂν⟩
ἐλθεῖν Διονύσου· οὐδ' ἂν Μακεδόνας τὸ πρόσω
ἀπαξιῶσαι συμπονεῖν οἱ ἔτι κατὰ ζῆλον τῶν
2 Διονύσου ἔργων. καὶ δίδωσιν ἐλευθέρους τε εἶναι
τοὺς οἰκήτορας τῆς Νύσης καὶ αὐτονόμους. ὡς δὲ
καὶ τοὺς νόμους ἐπύθετο αὐτῶν καὶ ὅτι πρὸς τῶν
ἀρίστων τὸ πολίτευμα ἔχεται, ταῦτά τε ἐπήνεσε καὶ
ἠξίωσε τῶν τε ἱππέων οἱ ξυμπέμψαι ἐς τριακοσίους καὶ τῶν προεστώτων τοῦ πολιτεύματος, ἦσαν
δὲ καὶ αὐτοὶ τριακόσιοι, ἑκατὸν τοὺς ἀρίστους ἐπι-
λεξαμένους· Ἄκουφιν δὲ εἶναι τὸν ἐπιλεγόμενον,
ὅντινα καὶ ὕπαρχον τῆς χώρας τῆς Νυσαίας
3 κατέστησεν αὐτός. τὸν δὲ Ἄκουφιν ταῦτα ἀκούσαντα ἐπιμειδιᾶσαι λέγεται τῷ λόγῳ· καὶ Ἀλέξανδρον ἐρέσθαι ἐφ' ὅτῳ ἐγέλασεν· ὑποκρίνασθαι
δ' Ἄκουφιν· καὶ πῶς ἄν, ὦ βασιλεῦ, μία πόλις
ἑκατὸν ἀνδρῶν ἀγαθῶν ἐρημωθεῖσα ἔτι καλῶς
πολιτεύοιτο; ἀλλὰ σύ, εἴ σοι μέλει Νυσαίων, τοὺς
ἱππέας μὲν ἄγεσθαι τοὺς τριακοσίους καὶ εἰ βούλει
ἔτι τούτων πλείονας, ἀντὶ δὲ τῶν ἑκατόν, οὕστινας
τοὺς ἀρίστους ἐπιλέξαι σὺ κελεύεις, διπλασίους
τῶν ἄλλων τῶν κακῶν ἄγεσθαι, ἵ⟨να⟩ σοι καὶ
αὖθις ἀφικομένῳ δεῦρο ἐν τῷ αὐτῷ τούτῳ κόσμῳ
4 φανείη ἡ πόλις. ταῦτα λέγοντα, λέγειν γὰρ δόξαι
φρόνιμα, πεῖσαι Ἀλέξανδρον. καὶ τοὺς μὲν ἱππέας
ξυμπέμπειν οἱ ἐκέλευσε, τοὺς δὲ ἑκατὸν τοὺς ἐπιλέκτους μηκέτι αἰτῆσαι, ἀλλὰ μηδὲ ἀντ' αὐτῶν
ἄλλους· τὸν δὲ παῖδα ἄρα τοῦ Ἀκούφιος καὶ τῆς
θυγατρὸς τὸν παῖδα ξυμπέμψαι αὐτῷ Ἄκουφιν.
5 Ἀλέξανδρον δὲ πόθος ἔλαβεν ἰδεῖν τὸν χῶρον,
ὅπου τινὰ ὑπομνήματα τοῦ Διονύσου οἱ Νυσαῖοι
ἐκόμπαζον. ἐλθεῖν τε ἐς τὸ ὄρος τὸν Μηρὸν ξὺν

point Dionysus reached, and would go even farther.
He also thought that the Macedonians would not
refuse to join him in still further efforts, in emulation
of Dionysus' achievements. He granted freedom 2
and independence to the settlers of Nysa. And
when he inquired about their laws and found that
their government was in the hands of the best
people,[1] he expressed approval of this, at the same
time demanding that they should send some three
hundred horsemen to accompany him, and also
select and send a hundred of the foremost men in the
government (they were also three hundred in
number). Acuphis was to select them, and Alexander appointed him hyparch of the territory of
Nysa. Acuphis is said to have smiled on hearing 3
hearing Alexander's words; when Alexander asked
why he laughed, he replied: ' How, Sire, could a
single city be deprived of a hundred good citizens and
still be well governed ? But if you have the interest
of Nysaeans at heart, have the three hundred horsemen sent, or still more, if you wish; but instead of
the hundred men, whom you tell me to choose as the
best, take twice as many of the inferior citizens, so
that on your return here you may think the city to
be in the same good order as now.' These words, 4
which appeared wise, won Alexander's consent. He
ordered Acuphis to send the horsemen to accompany
him, but no longer to demand the select hundred,
nor even any substitutes; however, Acuphis was to
send him his son and daughter's son.
Alexander was seized with a yearning [2] to see the 5
place where the Nysaeans proudly displayed certain
memorials of Dionysus. It is said that he went to

[1] Indian republics: *Ind.* 12, 7 n.
[2] App. V 3; vii 1, 1 n.

ARRIAN

τοῖς ἑταίροις τοῖς ἱππεῦσι καὶ τῷ πεζικῷ ἀγήματι
καὶ ἰδεῖν κισσοῦ τε ἀνάπλεων καὶ δάφνης τὸ ὄρος
καὶ ἄλση παντοῖα· καὶ ἰδεῖν σύσκιον, καὶ θήρας ἐν
6 αὐτῷ εἶναι θηρίων παντοδαπῶν. καὶ τοὺς Μακεδόνας ἡδέως τὸν κισσὸν ἰδόντας, οἷα δὴ διὰ μακροῦ
ὀφθέντα (οὐ γὰρ εἶναι ἐν τῇ Ἰνδῶν χώρᾳ κισσόν,
οὐδὲ ἵναπερ αὐτοῖς ἄμπελοι ἦσαν) στεφάνους
σπουδῇ ἀπ᾽ αὐτοῦ ποιεῖσθαι, καὶ στεφανώσασθαι
ὡς εἶχον,[1] ἐφυμνοῦντας τὸν Διόνυσόν τε καὶ τὰς
ἐπωνυμίας τοῦ θεοῦ ἀνακαλοῦντας. θῦσαί τε αὐτοῦ
Ἀλέξανδρον τῷ Διονύσῳ καὶ εὐωχηθῆναι ὁμοῦ
7 τοῖς ἑταίροις. οἱ δὲ καὶ τάδε ἀνέγραψαν, εἰ δή τῳ
πιστὰ καὶ ταῦτα, πολλοὺς τῶν ἀμφ᾽ αὐτὸν τῶν οὐκ
ἠμελημένων Μακεδόνων τῷ τε κισσῷ στεφανω-
σαμένους καὶ ὑπὸ τῇ κατακλήσει τοῦ θεοῦ κατα-
σχεθῆναί τε πρὸς τοῦ Διονύσου καὶ ἀνευάσαι τὸν
θεὸν καὶ βακχεῦσαι.

3. Καὶ ταῦτα ὅπως τις ἐθέλει ὑπολαβὼν ἀπισ-
τείτω ἢ πιστευέτω. οὐ γὰρ ἔγωγε Ἐρατοσθένει
τῷ Κυρηναίῳ πάντῃ ξυμφέρομαι, ὃς λέγει πάντα
ὅσα ἐς τὸ θεῖον ἀναφέρεται ἐκ Μακεδόνων πρὸς
χάριν τὴν Ἀλεξάνδρου ἐς τὸ ὑπέρογκον ἐπιφημισ-
2 θῆναι. καὶ γὰρ καὶ σπήλαιον λέγει ἰδόντας ἐν
Παραπαμισάδαις τοὺς Μακεδόνας καί τινα μῦθον
ἐπιχώριον ἀκούσαντας ἢ καὶ αὐτοὺς ξυνθέντας
φημίσαι, ὅτι τοῦτο ἄρα ἦν τοῦ Προμηθέως τὸ
ἄντρον ἵνα ἐδέδετο, καὶ ὁ ἀετὸς ὅτι ἐκεῖσε ἐφοίτα
δαισόμενος τῶν σπλάγχνων τοῦ Προμηθέως, καὶ ὁ
Ἡρακλῆς ὅτι ἐκεῖσε ἀφικόμενος τόν τε ἀετὸν
ἀπέκτεινε καὶ τὸν Προμηθέα τῶν δεσμῶν ἀπέλυσε.

---

[1] ὡς καὶ στεφανώσασθαι εἶχον codd. I have adopted
Vulcanius' transposition.

326
B.C.

Mount Merus with the Companion cavalry and the *agema* of foot, and saw the mountain full of ivy and laurel, with all sorts of groves; he saw how shady it was, and that there was hunting in it for game of every kind. The Macedonians were delighted to see 6 the ivy, since they had seen none for a long time; for there is no ivy in the Indians' country, not even where they have vines; and they eagerly made wreaths of it and crowned themselves there and then, singing hymns to Dionysus and calling on the various names of the god. Then Alexander sacrificed there to Dionysus, and feasted with his Companions. Some have also related [3] (if anyone can believe this 7 story) that many Macedonians of distinction in his company, after crowning themselves with the ivy and invoking the god, were possessed by Dionysus, raised the Dionysiac cry, and were transported with Bacchic frenzy.

3. However, these tales anyone may believe or not, taking them as he thinks fit. For my part I do not wholly agree with Eratosthenes the Cyrenaean, who says that all the Macedonians ascribe to the divine influence was magnified in this way to please Alexander. He says for instance that the Mace- 2 donians saw a cave among the Parapamisadae, and on hearing some local legend about it, or making it up themselves, declared that it was Prometheus' cave, where he had been chained, and that it was there that the eagle used to go, to feed on Prometheus' liver, and that Heracles, arriving at this same spot, killed the eagle and released Prometheus from

[3] ' Vulgate.'

3 τὸν δὲ Καύκασον τὸ ὄρος ἐκ τοῦ Πόντου ἐς τὰ
πρὸς ἔω μέρη τῆς γῆς καὶ τὴν Παραπαμισαδῶν
χώραν ὡς ἐπὶ Ἰνδοὺς μετάγειν τῷ λόγῳ τοὺς
Μακεδόνας, Παραπάμισον ὄντα τὸ ὄρος αὐτοὺς
καλοῦντας Καύκασον τῆς Ἀλεξάνδρου ἕνεκα δόξης,
ὡς ὑπὲρ τὸν Καύκασον ἄρα ἐλθόντα Ἀλέξανδρον.
4 ἔν τε αὐτῇ τῇ Ἰνδῶν γῇ βοῦς ἰδόντας ἐγκεκαυμένας
ῥόπαλον τεκμηριοῦσθαι ἐπὶ τῷδε, ὅτι Ἡρακλῆς ἐς
Ἰνδοὺς ἀφίκετο. ὅμοια δὲ καὶ ὑπὲρ Διονύσου τῆς
πλάνης ἀπιστεῖ Ἐρατοσθένης· ἐμοὶ δ᾽ ἐν μέσῳ
κείσθων οἱ ὑπὲρ τούτων λόγοι.

5 Ἀλέξανδρος δὲ ὡς ἀφίκετο ἐπὶ τὸν Ἰνδὸν ποταμόν, καταλαμβάνει γέφυράν τε ἐπ᾽ αὐτῷ πεποιη-
μένην πρὸς Ἡφαιστίωνος καὶ πλοῖα πολλὰ μὲν
σμικρότερα, δύο δὲ τριακοντόρους, καὶ παρὰ
Ταξίλου τοῦ Ἰνδοῦ δῶρα ἥκοντα ἀργυρίου μὲν
τάλαντα ἐς διακόσια, ἱερεῖα δὲ βοῦς μὲν τρισχιλίας,
πρόβατα δὲ ὑπὲρ μύρια, ἐλέφαντας δὲ ἐς τριάκοντα·
6 καὶ ἱππεῖς δὲ ἑπτακόσιοι αὐτῷ Ἰνδῶν ἐς ξυμ-
μαχίαν παρὰ Ταξίλου ἧκον· καὶ τὴν πόλιν Τάξιλα,
τὴν μεγίστην μεταξὺ Ἰνδοῦ τε ποταμοῦ καὶ
Ὑδάσπου, ὅτι αὐτῷ Ταξίλης ἐνδίδωσιν. ἐνταῦθα
θύει Ἀλέξανδρος τοῖς θεοῖς ὅσοις αὐτῷ νόμος καὶ
ἀγῶνα ποιεῖ γυμνικὸν καὶ ἱππικὸν ἐπὶ τῷ ποταμῷ·
καὶ γίγνεται αὐτῷ ἐπὶ τῇ διαβάσει τὰ ἱερά.

4. Ὁ δὲ Ἰνδὸς ποταμὸς ὅτι μέγιστος ποταμῶν
ἐστι τῶν κατὰ τὴν Ἀσίαν τε καὶ τὴν Εὐρώπην,
πλὴν Γάγγου, καὶ τούτου Ἰνδοῦ ποταμοῦ, καὶ ὅτι
αἱ πηγαί εἰσιν αὐτῷ ἐπὶ τάδε τοῦ ὄρους τοῦ
Παραπαμίσου ἢ Καυκάσου, καὶ ὅτι ἐκδίδωσιν ἐς

---

[1] Sibae: *Ind.* 5, 12; S. xv 1, 8; App. XVII 26.

his chains; that the Macedonians in their account **3**
transferred Mount Caucasus from the Pontus to the
eastern parts of the world and the country of the
Parapamisadae as far as India, and called Mount
Parapamisus Mount Caucasus, all for the glory of
Alexander, suggesting that he actually crossed
Mount Caucasus; while in India itself, when they **4**
saw cattle branded with a club,[1] they deduced from
this that Heracles had reached India. Eratosthenes
is similarly incredulous about the wandering of
Dionysus. As far as I am concerned, the stories
about these things must rest open.

On arriving at the river Indus, Alexander found a **5**
bridge made over it by Hephaestion, and many
smaller boats as well as two *triacontoroi*; also that
Taxilas the Indian had sent gifts of two hundred silver
Talents, and for sacrificial offering three thousand
cattle and over ten thousand sheep, with thirty
elephants. Seven hundred Indian cavalry also came **6**
from Taxilas as an auxiliary force, and Taxilas surrendered to him the city of Taxila, the greatest city
between the river Indus and the Hydaspes. There
Alexander sacrificed to the gods to whom it was his
custom, and held athletic and equestrian games by
the river; the sacrifices were favourable to the
crossing.[2]

4. The river Indus is the greatest river of Asia and
Europe except the Ganges, which is also an Indian
river. Its springs are on this side of Mount Parapamisus or Caucasus, it runs into the great sea where

---

[2] A. takes up the narrative from iv 30, 9. Route and
chronology: App. XVII 13. Taxilas: ib. 31. *Triacontoroi*:
ships of 30 oars, some perhaps in two tiers (vi 5, 2); *hemioliai*
had one and a half tiers; see L. Casson, *Ships and Seamanship
in the Anc. World*, 1971, 54 f.; 125; 128 ff.; 136; ibid. 1–6 for
rafts made of skins, which were doubtless used too (cf. 9, 3).

τὴν μεγάλην θάλασσαν τὴν κατὰ Ἰνδοὺς ὡς ἐπὶ
νότον ἄνεμον, καὶ ὅτι δίστομός ἐστιν ὁ Ἰνδὸς καὶ
αἱ ἐκβολαὶ αὐτοῦ ἀμφότεραι τεναγώδεις, καθάπερ αἱ πέντε τοῦ Ἴστρου, καὶ ὅτι Δέλτα ποιεῖ
καὶ αὐτὸς ἐν τῇ Ἰνδῶν γῇ τῷ Αἰγυπτίῳ Δέλτα
παραπλήσιον καὶ τοῦτο Πάταλα καλεῖται τῇ Ἰνδῶν
φωνῇ, ταῦτα μὲν ὑπὲρ τοῦ Ἰνδοῦ τὰ μάλιστα οὐκ
2 ἀμφίλογα καὶ ἐμοὶ ἀναγεγράφθω. ἐπεὶ καὶ ὁ
Ὑδάσπης καὶ Ἀκεσίνης καὶ Ὑδραώτης καὶ
Ὕφασις, καὶ οὗτοι Ἰνδοὶ ποταμοὶ ὄντες, τῶν μὲν
ἄλλων τῶν Ἀσιανῶν ποταμῶν πολύ τι κατὰ
μέγεθος ὑπερφέρουσι, τοῦ Ἰνδοῦ δὲ μείονές εἰσιν
καὶ πολὺ δὴ μείονες, ὅπου καὶ αὐτὸς ὁ Ἰνδὸς τοῦ
Γάγγου. Κτησίας μὲν δή, εἰ δή τῳ ἱκανὸς καὶ
Κτησίας ἐς τεκμηρίωσιν, ἵνα μὲν στενότατος αὐτὸς
αὐτοῦ ὁ Ἰνδός ἐστι, τεσσαράκοντα σταδίους
⟨λέγει⟩ ὅτι διέχουσιν αὐτῷ αἱ ὄχθαι, ἵνα δὲ
πλατύτατος, καὶ ἑκατόν· τὸ πολὺ δὲ εἶναι αὐτοῦ
τὸ μέσον τούτοιν.

3 Τοῦτον τὸν ποταμὸν τὸν Ἰνδὸν ὑπὸ τὴν ἕω
διέβαινε ξὺν τῇ στρατιᾷ Ἀλέξανδρος ἐς τῶν Ἰνδῶν
τὴν γῆν· ὑπὲρ ὧν ἐγὼ οὔτε οἷστισι νόμοις δια-
χρῶνται ἐν τῇδε τῇ συγγραφῇ ἀνέγραψα, οὔτε ζῷα
εἰ δή τινα ἄτοπα ἡ χώρα αὐτοῖς ἐκφέρει, οὔτε
ἰχθύας ἢ κήτη ὅσα ἢ οἷα ὁ Ἰνδὸς ἢ ὁ Ὑδάσπης ἢ ὁ
Γάγγης ἢ οἱ ἄλλοι Ἰνδῶν ποταμοὶ φέρουσιν, οὐδὲ
τοὺς μύρμηκας τοὺς τὸν χρυσόν σφισιν ἐργαζομέ-
νους, οὐδὲ τοὺς γρῦπας τοὺς φύλακας, οὐδὲ ὅσα
ἄλλα ἐφ᾽ ἡδονῇ μᾶλλόν τι πεποίηται ἢ ἐς ἀφήγησιν

---

[1] The greatness of Indian rivers (App. XVII 10; 18a) was

it washes India to the south, it has two mouths and
both its outlets are marshy, like the five outlets of the
Ister [Danube], and it too forms a delta in the land of
India analogous to the delta in Egypt and called
Patala in the Indian language. So much on the Indus
is absolutely beyond dispute; so let me set it down
here. In fact the Hydaspes [Jhelum], Acesines 2
[Chenab], Hydraotis [Ravi], and Hyphasis [Beas],
which are also all rivers of India, are much greater
than the other rivers of Asia; yet they are smaller, in
fact much smaller, than the Indus, as the Indus itself
is smaller than the Ganges.[1] Ctesias, if indeed any
one thinks him adequate as a witness, says that where
the Indus is narrowest, its banks are forty stades apart,
and at its broadest actually a hundred, though for the
greater part of its course the distance is the mean
between these figures.[2]

This river Indus Alexander crossed at dawn with 3
his army, so entering the land of the Indians.[3] In
this history I have not recorded their customs, nor
whether their country produces any strange animals,
nor the size or kinds of fishes or water monsters which
the Indus, Hydaspes, Ganges or other Indian rivers
produce, nor the ants that mine their gold, nor the
griffons that guard it, nor all the other stories which
have been made up for amusement rather than as a

judged by breadth, volume and speed, length being unknown;
the Indus, which rises north of the Himalayas 800 miles from
the Indian plain, was thought to rise near Aornos (S. xv 1, 8).
Patala (' ship-station,' cf. App. XXV 2); vi 18 ff.; *Ind.* 2, 5;
6, whence Patalene (e.g. S. xv 1, 13), the Indus delta, for which
see App. XVII 25. A. was unaware that by his time the Indus
had seven outlets (*RE* ix 1370).

  [2] A. cites from E. this Greek doctor at the Persian court c.
400 (Jacoby no. 688), justly thought unreliable in antiquity,
see App. XVII 7.

  [3] E's view: *Ind.* 1, 1 n.

τῶν ὄντων, ὡς τά γε κατ᾿ Ἰνδοὺς ὅσα ἂν ἄτοπα
ψεύσωνται, οὐκ ἐξελεγχθησόμενα πρὸς οὐδαμῶν.
4 ἀλλὰ Ἀλέξανδρος γὰρ καὶ οἱ ξὺν τούτῳ στρατεύσαντες τὰ πολλὰ ἐξήλεγξαν, ὅσα γε μὴ καὶ αὐτῶν
ἔστιν οἳ ἐψεύσαντο· ἀχρύσους τε εἶναι Ἰνδοὺς
ἐξήλεγξαν, ὅσους γε δὴ Ἀλέξανδρος ξὺν τῇ
στρατιᾷ ἐπῆλθε, πολλοὺς δὲ ἐπῆλθε, καὶ ἥκιστα
χλιδῶντας κατὰ τὴν δίαιταν, ἀλλὰ μεγάλους μὲν τὰ
σώματα, οἵους μεγίστους τῶν κατὰ τὴν Ἀσίαν,
πενταπήχεις τοὺς πολλοὺς ἢ ὀλίγον ἀποδέοντας,
καὶ μελαντέρους τῶν ἄλλων ἀνθρώπων, πλὴν
Αἰθιόπων, καὶ τὰ πολέμια πολύ τι γενναιοτάτους
5 τῶν γε δὴ τότε ἐποίκων τῆς Ἀσίας. τὸ γὰρ
Περσῶν τῶν πάλαι, ξὺν οἷς ὁρμηθεὶς Κῦρος ὁ
Καμβύσου Μήδους τε τὴν ἀρχὴν τῆς Ἀσίας
ἀφείλετο καὶ ἄλλα ἔθνη τὰ μὲν κατεστρέψατο, τὰ
δὲ προσχωρήσαντά οἱ ἑκόντα κατέσχεν, οὐκ ἔχω
ἀτρεκῶς ὥς γε δὴ πρὸς τὰ Ἰνδῶν ξυμβαλεῖν. καὶ
γὰρ καὶ Πέρσαι τότε πένητές τε ἦσαν καὶ χώρας
τραχείας οἰκήτορες, καὶ νόμιμά σφισιν ἦν οἷα
ἐγγυτάτω εἶναι τῇ Λακωνικῇ παιδεύσει. τὸ δὲ
τραῦμα τὸ γενόμενον Πέρσαις ἐν τῇ Σκυθικῇ γῇ
οὐδὲ τοῦτο ἔχω ἀτρεκῶς ξυμβαλεῖν πότερα δυσχω-
ρίαις ξυνενεχθεῖσιν ἢ τινι ἄλλῃ Κύρου ἁμαρτίᾳ
ξυνέβη ἢ Σκυθῶν γε τῶν ταύτῃ κακίους τὰ πολέμια
Πέρσαι ἦσαν.

5. Ἀλλὰ ὑπὲρ Ἰνδῶν ἰδίᾳ μοι γεγράψεται ὅσα

----

[4] A's scepticism comes from E. (App. XVII 8). Ants:
Ind. 15, 4 n. River animals: vi 1, 1; *Ind.* 6, 8. Other
marvels: e.g. S. ii 1, 9; xv 1, 21 f., 35, 37, 45 and 56 f.; Ctesias
F. 45, 26.

[5] Probably against Meg. *ap.* S. xv 1, 57 and 69 (gold dust in

326
B.C.

description of reality, on the basis that whatever
ridiculous lies men may tell about the Indians will
not be refuted by anyone.[4] Yet Alexander and his
fellow-soldiers did refute the greater number, except
that some were actually their inventions; they proved
that the Indians had no gold,[5] at least not the numerous peoples they encountered, and that they were
not at all luxurious in their way of living, but tall of
stature, in fact the tallest men in Asia, mostly five
cubits,[6] or very little less, darker-skinned than all
other men except the Ethiopians,[7] and much the
finest fighters of the inhabitants of Asia at that time.
I cannot accurately compare the Indians with the
ancient Persians, who followed Cyrus son of Cambyses
at the start when he deprived the Medes of the
sovereignty of Asia and subdued other peoples or
received their voluntary surrender; in fact the
Persians then were poor and dwelt in rough country,[8]
and their customs were as close as could be to the
Spartan discipline. As for the blow dealt the Persians in Scythia, I am again unable to assess with
accuracy whether it was due to the difficulty of the
country or to some other error of Cyrus, or whether
they were inferior in warfare to the Scythians in this
particular region.[9]

5. However, I shall write a special monograph

rivers). In fact, gold, but not silver, was abundant in India
(*CHI* 101; 213; 342 f.).

[6] $7\frac{1}{2}$ or perhaps 6 feet (Tarn ii 169 f.). A. discounts tales of
Indian pygmies (S. ii 1, 9) and falls into the opposite absurdity.

[7] Comparisons of India (Punjab and Sind) with Egypt (or
Ethiopia) were common and apt, cf. v 6, 5 ff.; vi 1; *Ind.* 2, 6;
6, 6 ff.; Hdt. iii 101; S. xv 1, 13, 16, 18 f.; 24-6; 33 (citing
Ar., N. and Onesicritus); App. XXV 1.

[8] A. perhaps recalls Hdt. ix 122.

[9] Hdt. i 208 ff.

πιστότατα ἐς ἀφήγησιν οἵ τε ξὺν Ἀλεξάνδρῳ
στρατεύσαντες καὶ ὁ ἐκπεριπλεύσας τῆς μεγάλης
θαλάσσης τὸ κατ' Ἰνδοὺς Νέαρχος, ἐπὶ δὲ ὅσα
Μεγασθένης τε καὶ Ἐρατοσθένης, δοκίμω ἄνδρε,
ξυνεγραψάτην, καὶ νόμιμα ἄττα Ἰνδοῖς ἐστι καὶ εἰ
δή τινα ἄτοπα ζῷα αὐτόθι φύεται καὶ τὸν παρά-
2 πλουν αὐτὸν τῆς ἔξω θαλάσσης. νῦν δὲ ὅσον ἐς τὰ
Ἀλεξάνδρου ἔργα ἀποχρῶν ἐφαίνετο, τοσόνδε μοι
ἀναγεγράφθω· τὸν Ταῦρον τὸ ὄρος ἀπείργειν τὴν
Ἀσίαν, ἀρχόμενον μὲν ἀπὸ Μυκάλης τοῦ καταντικρὺ Σάμου τῆς νήσου ὄρους, ἀποτεμνόμενον δὲ
τήν τε Παμφύλων καὶ Κιλίκων γῆν ἔνθεν μὲν ὡς
ἐς Ἀρμενίαν παρήκειν, ἀπὸ δὲ Ἀρμενίων ὡς ἐπὶ
Μηδίαν παρὰ Παρθυ⟨α⟩ίους τε καὶ Χορασμίους,
3 κατὰ δὲ Βακτρίους ξυμβάλλειν τῷ Παραπαμίσῳ
ὄρει, ὃ δὴ Καύκασον ἐκάλουν οἱ Ἀλεξάνδρῳ
ξυστρατεύσαντες Μακεδόνες, ὡς μὲν λέγεται τὰ
Ἀλεξάνδρου αὔξοντες, ὅτι δὴ καὶ ἐπέκεινα ἄρα τοῦ
Καυκάσου κρατῶν τοῖς ὅπλοις ἦλθεν Ἀλέξανδρος·
τυχὸν δὲ καὶ ξυνεχὲς τυγχάνει ὂν τοῦτο τὸ ὄρος τῷ
ἄλλῳ τῷ Σκυθικῷ Καυκάσῳ, καθάπερ οὖν αὐτῷ
τούτῳ ὁ Ταῦρος· καὶ ἐμοὶ αὐτῷ πρότερόν ποτε ἐπὶ
τῷδε λέλεκται Καύκασος τὸ ὄρος τοῦτο καὶ
4 ὕστερον τῷδε τῷ ὀνόματι κληθήσεται· τὸν δὲ
Καύκασον τοῦτον καθήκειν ἔστε ἐπὶ ⟨τὴν⟩ μεγάλην
τὴν πρὸς ἔω τε καὶ Ἰνδοὺς θάλασσαν. τοὺς οὖν
ποταμούς, ὅσοι κατὰ τὴν Ἀσίαν λόγου ἄξιοι, ἐκ
τοῦ Ταύρου τε καὶ τοῦ Καυκάσου ἀνίσχοντας τοὺς
μὲν ὡς ἐπ' ἄρκτον τετραμμένον ἔχειν τὸ ὕδωρ, καὶ
τούτων τοὺς μὲν ἐς τὴν λίμνην ἐκδιδόναι τὴν
Μαιῶτιν, τοὺς δὲ ἐς τὴν Ὑρκανίαν καλουμένην
θάλασσαν, καὶ ταύτην κόλπον οὖσαν τῆς μεγάλης

about India including the most reliable descriptions
given by Alexander's fellow-campaigners, especially
Nearchus, who coasted along the entire Indian part
of the Great Sea, and further all that Megasthenes
and Eratosthenes, both men of repute, have written,
and I shall record the customs of India, any strange
beasts which are bred there and the actual voyage
along the coast of the Outer Sea.[1]   But the present   2
record must be restricted to what appears sufficient
to explain Alexander's achievements.   Mount Taurus
is the boundary of Asia, beginning from Mycale, the
mountain opposite the island of Samos, then cutting
through between the land of Pamphylia and Lycia it
reaches Armenia, and from Armenia runs to Media
past the Parthyaean and Chorasmian country, and in   3
Bactria joins Mount Parapamisus [Hindu-Kush],
which the Macedonians who served with Alexander
called Caucasus, with a view (so it is said) of glorifying
Alexander, to make out that Alexander actually
reached the farther side of Mount Caucasus, victorious
in arms.   But perhaps this mountain is continuous
with the other Caucasus, that is, the Scythian, just
as Mount Taurus is continuous with this Caucasus.
For this reason I myself have on occasion previously
called this mountain Caucasus, and shall continue to
use this name later.   This Caucasus extends to the   4
great sea on the east and the Indian side.   Thus all
the important rivers of Asia rise from Taurus and
Caucasus; some of them flow northward, and empty
either into Lake Maeotis [Sea of Azov], or into the
sea called Hyrcanian [Caspian], itself a gulf of the

[1] App. XVII 1-9.   What follows comes from E., cf. S. xv 1,
10-14; App. XII.

5 θαλάσσης, τοὺς δὲ ὡς ἐπὶ νότον ἄνεμον τὸν
Εὐφράτην τε εἶναι καὶ τὸν Τίγρητα καὶ τὸν Ἰνδόν
τε καὶ τὸν Ὑδάσπην καὶ Ἀκεσίνην καὶ Ὑδραώτην
καὶ Ὕφασιν καὶ ὅσοι ἐν μέσῳ τούτων τε καὶ τοῦ
Γάγγου ποταμοῦ ἐς θάλασσαν καὶ οὗτοι ἐσβάλλου-
σιν ἢ εἰς τενάγη ἀναχεόμενοι ἀφανίζονται, καθάπερ
ὁ Εὐφράτης ποταμὸς ἀφανίζεται.

6. Ὅτῳ δὴ τὰ τῆς Ἀσίας ὧδε ἔχει ὡς πρὸς τοῦ
Ταύρου τε καὶ τοῦ Καυκάσου τέμνεσθαι ἀπὸ
ἀνέμου ζεφύρου ὡς ἐπὶ ἀπηλιώτην ἄνεμον τὴν
Ἀσίαν, τούτῳ δύο μὲν αὗται μέγισται πρὸς αὐτοῦ
τοῦ Ταύρου τῆς Ἀσίας μοῖραι γίγνονται, ἡ μὲν ἐς
μεσημβρίαν τε καὶ πρὸς νότον ἄνεμον [τοῦ
Ταύρου] κεκλιμένη, ἡ δὲ ἐπ᾽ ἄρκτον τε καὶ
2 ἄνεμον βορρᾶν. τῆς δὲ ὡς ἐπὶ νότον Ἀσίας
τετραχῇ αὖ τεμνομένης μεγίστην μὲν μοῖραν τὴν
Ἰνδῶν γῆν ποιεῖ Ἐρατοσθένης τε καὶ Μεγασθένης,
ὃς ξυνὴν μὲν Σιβυρτίῳ τῷ σατράπῃ τῆς Ἀραχω-
σίας, πολλάκις δὲ λέγει ἀφικέσθαι παρὰ Σανδρά-
κοττον τὸν Ἰνδῶν βασιλέα, ἐλαχίστην δὲ ὅσην ὁ
Εὐφράτης ποταμὸς ἀπείργει ὡς πρὸς τὴν ἐντὸς τὴν
ἡμετέραν θάλασσαν. δύο δὲ αἱ μεταξὺ Εὐφράτου
τε ποταμοῦ καὶ τοῦ Ἰνδοῦ ἀπειργόμεναι αἱ δύο
ξυντεθεῖσαι μόλις ἄξιαι τῇ Ἰνδῶν γῇ ξυμβαλεῖν.
3 ἀπείργεσθαι δὲ τὴν Ἰνδῶν χώραν πρὸς μὲν ἔω τε
καὶ ἀπηλιώτην ἄνεμον ἔστε ἐπὶ μεσημβρίαν τῇ
μεγάλῃ θαλάσσῃ· τὸ πρὸς βορρᾶν δὲ αὐτῆς
ἀπείργειν τὸν Καύκασον τὸ ὄρος ἔστε ἐπὶ τοῦ
Ταύρου τὴν ξυμβολήν· τὴν δὲ ὡς πρὸς ἑσπέραν τε
καὶ ἄνεμον Ἰάπυγα ἔστε ἐπὶ τὴν μεγάλην θάλασσαν
ὁ Ἰνδὸς ποταμὸς ἀποτέμνεται. καὶ ἔστι πεδίον ἡ
πολλὴ αὐτῆς, καὶ τοῦτο, ὡς εἰκάζουσιν, ἐκ τῶν

Great Sea; others flow southward, that is, the   5   326 B.C.
Euphrates, Tigris, Indus, Hydaspes [Jhelum],
Acesines [Chenab], Hydraotes [Ravi], and Hyphasis
[Beas], and all between these and the Ganges, and run
out into the sea, or are broken and disappear in
marshes, like the Euphrates.[2]

6. Anyone who treats Asia as divided by Mounts
Taurus and Caucasus from west to east will find that
the two greatest divisions of Asia are formed by
Mount Taurus itself, the one looking south and south
west, the other north and north east. If the southern   2
part of Asia is again divided into four, Eratosthenes
and Megasthenes regard the region of India as the
greatest part (Megasthenes lived with Sibyrtius,
satrap of Arachosia, and often speaks of his visiting
Sandracottus, the king of the Indians).[1] The
smallest part is, in their view, that bounded by
the Euphrates, looking towards our inland sea. The
other two parts lie between the Euphrates and the
Indus, and these two put together can hardly be
compared with the Indian land. India on the east is   3
bounded down to the south by the Great Sea, on its
northern part by Mount Caucasus up to its junction
with Mount Taurus; then to the west and north west
the Indus forms its boundary as far as the Great Sea.
The greater part of it is level plain which, they con-

---

[2] App. XXVI 3.
[1] 'Andracottus' in P. 62. The Greek does not mean that he
'often visited Sandracottus.' For this ch. see App. XVII
6–8.

4 ποταμῶν προ⟨σ⟩κεχωσμένον. εἶναι γὰρ οὖν καὶ
τῆς ἄλλης χώρας ὅσα πεδία οὐ πρόσω θαλάσσης τὰ
πολλὰ τῶν ποταμῶν παρ' ἑκάστοις ποιήματα· ὡς
δὲ καὶ τῆς χώρας τὴν ἐπωνυμίαν τοῖς ποταμοῖς ἐκ
παλαιοῦ προσκεῖσθαι, καθάπερ Ἕρμου τέ τι πεδίον
λέγεσθαι, ὃς κατὰ τὴν Ἀσίαν γῆν ἀνίσχων ἐξ
ὄρους Μητρὸς Δινδυμήνης παρὰ Σμύρναν πόλιν
Αἰολικὴν ἐκδιδοῖ ἐς θάλασσαν, καὶ ἄλλο Καΰστρου,
πεδίον Λύδιον καὶ Λυδίου ποταμοῦ, καὶ Καΐκου
ἄλλο ἐν Μυσίᾳ καὶ Μαιάνδρου τὸ Καρικὸν ἔστε ἐπὶ
5 Μίλητον πόλιν Ἰωνικήν. Αἴγυπτόν τε Ἡρόδοτός
τε καὶ Ἑκαταῖος οἱ λογοποιοί, ἢ εἰ δή του ἄλλου
ἢ Ἑκαταίου ἐστὶ τὰ ἀμφὶ τῇ γῇ τῇ Αἰγυπτίᾳ
ποιήματα, δῶρόν τε τοῦ ποταμοῦ ἀμφότεροι ὡσαύτως ὀνομάζουσιν καὶ οὐκ ἀμαυροῖς τεκμηρίοις ὅτι
ταύτῃ ἔχει Ἡροδότῳ ἐπιδέδεικται, ὡς καὶ τὴν γῆν
αὐτὴν τυχὸν τοῦ ποταμοῦ εἶναι ἐπώνυμον. Αἴγυπτος γὰρ τὸ παλαιὸν ὁ ποταμὸς ὅτι ἐκαλεῖτο,
ὅντινα νῦν Νεῖλον Αἰγύπτιοί τε καὶ οἱ ἔξω Αἰγύπτου ἄνθρωποι ὀνομάζουσιν, ἱκανὸς τεκμηριῶσαι
Ὅμηρος, λέγων ἐπὶ τῇ ἐκβολῇ τοῦ Αἰγύπτου
6 ποταμοῦ τὸν Μενέλεων στῆσαι τὰς νέας. εἰ δὴ
οὖν εἷς τε ποταμὸς παρ' ἑκάστοις καὶ οὐ μεγάλοι
οὗτοι ποταμοὶ ἱκανοὶ γῆν πολλὴν ποιῆσαι ἐς
θάλασσαν προχεόμενοι, ὁπότε ἰλὺν καταφέροιεν καὶ
πηλὸν ἐκ τῶν ἄνω τόπων ἔνθενπερ αὐτοῖς αἱ πηγαί
εἰσιν, οὐδὲ ὑπὲρ τῆς Ἰνδῶν ἄρα χώρας ἐς ἀπιστίαν
ἰέναι ἄξιον, ὅπως πεδίον τε ἡ πολλή ἐστι καὶ ἐκ
τῶν ποταμῶν τὸ πεδίον ἔχει προσκεχωσμένον.
7 Ἕρμον μὲν γὰρ καὶ Κάϋστρον καὶ Κάϊκόν τε καὶ
Μαίανδρον ἢ ὅσοι [πολλοὶ] [1] ποταμοὶ τῆς Ἀσίας

[1] Bracketed by Castiglioni.

jecture, was deposited by the rivers, for in other
country too plains near the sea are each generally the
creations of the neighbouring rivers; so too the country
from ancient times was given its name from the
rivers.[2] Thus men speak of a plain of Hermus, which
rises in Asia from the mountain of Mother Dindymene
and runs into the sea near the Aeolic city of Smyrna,
and again of the plain of Caÿster, a Lydian plain from
a Lydian river, and of Caïcus in Mysia, and of the
Carian plain of Maeander, stretching to Miletus, an
Ionian city. And as for Egypt, the historians Herodotus and Hecataeus (though possibly the work on
Egypt is not by Hecataeus) both call it similarly
' the gift of the river,' and Herodotus has shown
by very clear proofs that this is so, as the country
itself is actually called after the river. For that
Aegyptus was the old name of the river which
the Egyptians and men outside Egypt now call the
Nile, Homer is ample evidence, when he says that
Menelaus stationed his ships at the mouth of the
river Aegyptus.[3] If then a single river in each
country, and not great rivers either, can, while pouring into the sea, create a large amount of land, by
bringing down mud and deposits from the upper
country where they rise, there is no reason to doubt
how the Indian country too comes to be mostly plain,
and that its plain is deposited by the rivers; as for the
Hermus, Caÿster, Caïcus, Maeander or all the rivers

4

5

6

7

---

[2] Cf. vi 1, 3 n. Indus (Sanskrit, Sindhu = river) gave its
name first to the adjoining country (modern Sind, Persian
satrapy of Hindu), which classical writers extended to the sub-
continent. Punjab means the land of the five doabs (lands
between rivers).

[3] *Odyssey* iv 281, not adduced by Hdt. ii 5 ff.

ἐς τήνδε τὴν ἐντὸς θάλασσαν ἐκδιδοῦσιν οὐδὲ
σύμπαντας ξυντεθέντας ἑνὶ τῶν Ἰνδῶν ποταμῶν
ἄξιον ξυμβαλεῖν πλήθους ἕνεκα τοῦ ὕδατος, μὴ ὅτι
τῷ Γάγγῃ τῷ μεγίστῳ, ὅτῳ οὔτε ⟨τὸ⟩ τοῦ Νείλου
ὕδωρ τοῦ Αἰγυπτίου οὔτε ὁ Ἴστρος ὁ κατὰ τὴν
8 Εὐρώπην ῥέων ἄξιοι ξυμβαλεῖν, ἀλλ' οὐδὲ τῷ
Ἰνδῷ ποταμῷ ἐκεῖνοί γε πάντες ξυμμιχθέντες ἐς
ἴσον ἔρχονται, ὃς μέγας τε εὐθὺς ἀπὸ τῶν πηγῶν
ἀνίσχει καὶ πεντεκαίδεκα ποταμοὺς πάντας τῶν
Ἀσιανῶν μείζονας παραλαβὼν καὶ τῇ ἐπωνυμίᾳ
κρατήσας οὕτως ἐκδιδοῖ ἐς θάλασσαν. ταῦτά μοι
ἐν τῷ παρόντι περὶ Ἰνδῶν τῆς χώρας λελέχθω· τὰ
δὲ ἄλλα ἀποκείσθω ἐς τὴν Ἰνδικὴν ξυγγραφήν.

7. Τὸ δὲ ζεῦγμα τὸ ἐπὶ τοῦ Ἰνδοῦ ποταμοῦ
ὅπως μὲν ἐποιήθη Ἀλεξάνδρῳ οὔτε Ἀριστόβουλος
οὔτε Πτολεμαῖος, οἷς μάλιστα ἐγὼ ἕπομαι, λέγου-
σιν· οὐδὲ αὐτὸς ἔχω ἀτρεκῶς εἰκάσαι, πότερα
πλοίοις ἐζεύχθη ὁ πόρος, καθάπερ οὖν ὁ Ἑλλήσπον-
τός τε πρὸς Ξέρξου καὶ ὁ Βόσπορός τε καὶ ὁ
Ἴστρος πρὸς Δαρείου, ἢ γέφυρα κατὰ τοῦ ποταμοῦ
διηνεκὴς ἐποιήθη αὐτῷ· δοκεῖ δ' ἔμοιγε πλοίοις
μᾶλλον ζευχθῆναι· οὐ γὰρ ἂν δέξασθαι γέφυραν τὸ
βάθος τοῦ ὕδατος, οὐδ' ἂν ἐν τοσῷδε χρόνῳ ἔργον
2 οὕτως ἄτοπον ξυντελεσθῆναι. εἰ δὲ δὴ πλοίοις
ἐζεύχθη ὁ πόρος, πότερα ξυντεθεῖσαι αἱ νῆες
σχοίνοις καὶ κατὰ στοῖχον ὁρμισθεῖσαι ἐς τὸ ζεῦγμα
ἀπήρκεσαν, ὡς λέγει Ἡρόδοτος ζευχθῆναι τὸν
Ἑλλήσποντον, ἢ ὅτῳ τρόπῳ Ῥωμαίοις ἐπὶ τῷ
Ἴστρῳ ποταμῷ ζεῦγμα ποιεῖται καὶ ἐπὶ τῷ Ῥήνῳ
τῷ Κελτικῷ, καὶ τὸν Εὐφράτην καὶ τὸν Τίγρητα,

---

[4] E. followed Meg. (*Ind.* 4).

326
B.C.

of Asia which run out into this inner sea, put them all together, and you cannot properly compare them for volume of water with one of the rivers of India—to say nothing of the largest, Ganges,[4] with which not even the volume of the Nile in Egypt nor the Ister [Danube], which flows through Europe, is comparable; in fact all of them put together do not equal 8 even the Indus, which is already a great river at the very springs where it rises, and which takes in fifteen rivers [5] all greater than the Asian and, imposing its name on them as it goes, runs out to join the sea. For the present this must be all I have to say about the land of the Indians; the rest must be kept for my Indian treatise.

7. As for the method by which Alexander bridged the Indus, neither Aristobulus nor Ptolemy, the authors whom I chiefly follow, describes it; nor can I myself conjecture with certainty whether the passage was bridged with boats,[1] as was the Hellespont by Xerxes and the Bosporus and Ister by Darius,[2] or whether a bridge was built right across the stream. I am inclined to think it was spanned by boats, since the depth of the water would not admit of a bridge, nor could so extraordinary a work have been completed in so little time. But if the stream was spanned with 2 boats, were they lashed together by ropes and then moored in line across so as to form the bridge, as Herodotus of Halicarnassus says that the Hellespont was spanned, or was the method that which the Romans used to bridge the Ister and Celtic Rhine, or

---

[5] List in *Ind.* 4. Source: v 4, 2 n. 2.

[1] So D. 86, **3**; QC. viii 10, 2 f.; implicit in A. v **3**, 5; 8, 4. A. read his sources carelessly.

[2] Hdt. vii **33**–6; iv 89 and 97. Cf. vii 33–6 (Xerxes).

ὁσάκις κατέλαβεν αὐτοὺς ἀνάγκη, ἐγεφύρωσαν,
3 οὐδὲ τοῦτο ἔχω ξυμβαλεῖν. καίτοι ταχυτάτη γε
ὧν ἐγὼ οἶδα Ῥωμαίοις ἡ γεφύρωσις ἡ διὰ τῶν
νεῶν γίγνεται, καὶ ταύτην ἐγὼ ἀφηγήσομαι ἐν τῷ
παρόντι, ὅτι λόγου ἀξία. αἱ νῆες αὐτοῖς κατὰ
τοῦ ῥοῦ [1] ἀφίενται ἀπὸ ξυνθήματος, οὐκ ἐπ᾽ εὐθύ,
ἀλλὰ καθάπερ αἱ πρύμναν κρουόμεναι. ταύτας
ὑποφέρει μέν, οἷα εἰκός, ὁ ῥοῦς, ἀνέχει δὲ κελήτιον
ἐπῆρες, ἔστ᾽ ἂν καταστήσῃ ἐς τὸ τεταγμένον
χωρίον· καὶ ἐνταῦθα ἤδη καθίεται πλέγματα ἐκ
λύγου πυραμοειδῆ πλήρη λίθων λογάδων ἀπὸ
πρῴρας ἑκάστης νεώς, τοῦ ἀνέχειν τὴν ναῦν πρὸς
4 τὸν ῥοῦν. ἅμα δὲ δὴ μία τις τῶν νεῶν [ἅμα δὲ δὴ]
ἐσχέθη, καὶ ἄλλη ἀπὸ ταύτης διέχουσα ὅσον ξύμμετρον πρὸς ἰσχὺν τῶν ἐπιβαλλομένων ἀντίπρωρος
πρὸς τὸ ῥεῦμα ὁρμίζεται· καὶ ἀπ᾽ ἀμφοῖν ξύλα τε
ἐς εὐθὺ ὀξέως ἐπιβάλλεται καὶ σανίδες ἐγκάρσιαι ἐς
τὸ ξυνδεῖν· καὶ διὰ πασῶν οὕτω τῶν νεῶν, ὅσαι
ἱκαναὶ γεφυρῶσαι τὸν πόρον, χωρεῖ τὸ ἔργον.
5 ἑκατέρωθεν δὲ τοῦ ζεύγματος κλίμακες προβάλλονται καταπηγνύμεναι, τοῦ ἀσφαλεστέραν τοῖς τε
ἵπποις καὶ τοῖς ζεύγεσι τὴν ἔφοδον γίγνεσθαι, καὶ
ἅμα ὡς σύνδεσμος εἶναι τοῦ ζεύγματος. δι᾽ ὀλίγου
τε ξυντελεῖται ἅπαν καὶ ξὺν πολλῷ θορύβῳ, καὶ τὸ
τεταγμένον ἐν τῷ δρωμένῳ ὅμως οὐκ ἄπεστιν, οἵ
τε παρακελευσμοὶ ὡς τύχοιεν κατὰ ναῦν ἑκάστην
καὶ αἱ ἐπιτιμήσεις τοῦ ἐκλιποῦς οὔτε τὴν κατά-
κουσιν τῶν παραγγελμάτων οὔτε τὴν ὀξύτητα τοῦ
ἔργου ἀφαιροῦνται.

8. Ῥωμαίοις μὲν δὴ οὕτω ταῦτα ἐκ παλαιοῦ

---

[1] τοῦ ῥοῦ Krüger: πόρου A, kept by Roos.

the Euphrates and Tigris, whenever they were obliged to do so? This too I cannot decide, yet the **3** quickest way of bridging I know is the Roman use of boats, and I shall here describe it, for it merits description.[3] Their boats are at a signal allowed to float downstream, yet not bows on, but as if backing. The stream, naturally, carries them down, but a rowing skiff holds them up till it manoeuvres them into the appointed place and at that point wicker crates of pyramid shape full of unhewn stones are let down from the bows of each ship to hold it against the stream. No sooner has one ship thus been made fast **4** than another, just at the right interval to carry the superstructure safely, is anchored upstream and from both boats timbers are accurately and smartly laid and planks crosswise to bind them together. The work goes on in this way for all the boats needed for the bridging. On either side of the bridge gangways **5** are laid and fastened down, so that the passage may be safer for horses and baggage animals, and also to bind the bridge together; and in quite a short time the whole work is completed with much bustle, and yet there is good order in the course of the work; the cheers that may go up on each ship and reproofs for shirking work do not prevent the hearing of the orders nor the speed of the operation.

8. This then is the long-established method of the

---

[3] Cf. Cassius Dio's complementary account (lxxi 3); perhaps there was a common source. Cf. App. XXVIII 2.

ἐπήσκηται· Ἀλεξάνδρῳ δὲ ὅπως ἐζεύχθη ὁ Ἰνδὸς
ποταμὸς οὐκ ἔχω εἰπεῖν, ὅτι μηδὲ οἱ συστρατεύ-
σαντες αὐτῷ εἶπον. ἀλλά μοι δοκεῖ ὡς ἐγγυτάτω
τούτων ἐζεῦχθαι, ἢ εἰ δή τινι ἄλλῃ μηχανῇ, ἐκείνη
2 ἐχέτω. ὡς δὲ διέβη πέραν τοῦ Ἰνδοῦ ποταμοῦ,
καὶ ἐνταῦθα αὖ θύει κατὰ νόμον Ἀλέξανδρος.
ἄρας δὲ ἀπὸ τοῦ Ἰνδοῦ ἐς Τάξιλα ἀφίκετο, πόλιν
μεγάλην καὶ εὐδαίμονα, τὴν μεγίστην τῶν μεταξὺ
Ἰνδοῦ τε ποταμοῦ καὶ Ὑδάσπου. καὶ ἐδέχετο
αὐτὸν Ταξίλης ὁ ὕπαρχος τῆς πόλεως καὶ αὐτοὶ οἱ
τῇδε Ἰνδοὶ φιλίως. καὶ Ἀλέξανδρος προστίθησιν
3 αὐτοῖς χώραν τῆς ὁμόρου ὅσης ἐδέοντο. ἧκον δὲ
ἐνταῦθα παρ' αὐτὸν καὶ παρὰ Ἀβισάρου πρέσβεις
τοῦ τῶν ὀρείων Ἰνδῶν βασιλέως ὅ τε ἀδελφὸς τοῦ
Ἀβισάρου καὶ ἄλλοι ξὺν αὐτῷ οἱ δοκιμώτατοι, καὶ
παρὰ Δοξάρεως νομάρχου ἄλλοι, δῶρα φέροντες.
καὶ ἐνταῦθα αὖ Ἀλέξανδρος ἐν Ταξίλοις θύει ὅσα
οἱ νόμος καὶ ἀγῶνα ποιεῖ γυμνικόν τε καὶ ἱππικόν.
καὶ ἀποδείξας σατράπην τῶν ταύτῃ Ἰνδῶν Φίλιππον
τὸν Μαχάτα φρουράν τε ἀπολείπει ἐν Ταξίλοις
καὶ τοὺς ἀπομάχους τῶν στρατιωτῶν διὰ νόσον·
αὐτὸς δὲ ἦγεν ὡς ἐπὶ τὸν Ὑδάσπην ποταμόν.
4 Ἐπέκεινα γὰρ τοῦ Ὑδάσπου Πῶρος αὐτῷ
εἶναι ἐξηγγέλλετο ξὺν τῇ στρατιᾷ πάσῃ ἐγνωκὼς
εἴργειν τοῦ πόρου αὐτὸν ἢ περῶντι ἐπιτίθεσθαι.
ταῦτα ὡς ἔγνω Ἀλέξανδρος, Κοῖνον μὲν τὸν Πολεμοκράτους πέμψας ὀπίσω ἐπὶ τὸν Ἰνδὸν ποταμὸν τὰ
πλοῖα ὅσα παρεσκεύαστο αὐτῷ ἐπὶ τοῦ πόρου τοῦ
Ἰνδοῦ ξυντεμόντα κελεύει φέρειν ὡς ἐπὶ τὸν
5 Ὑδάσπην ποταμόν. καὶ ξυνετμήθη τε τὰ πλοῖα

---

[1] Campaign and battle: App. XVII 13–17.   Taxilas, Porus

Romans; but how Alexander bridged the Indus I cannot say, as even those who served under him did not tell us. I think that he must have approximated to this way of bridging, but if he employed some other means, let it pass. After taking his army 2 across, Alexander sacrificed there once more, according to custom. Then, leaving the Indus, he marched to Taxila, a great and prosperous city, the largest of all between the Indus and the Hydaspes. He was received there by Taxilas, the hyparch of the city, and the Indians of this district in a friendly manner; and Alexander gave them as much more of the neighbouring territory as they requested. Here he 3 was met by envoys from Abisares, the king of the Indians of the hills, his brother with others of the most note, as well as by other envoys from Doxareus the nomarch, bringing gifts. There again at Taxila Alexander offered the customary sacrifices, and held athletic and equestrian games. He appointed Philip son of Machatas satrap of the Indians of this region, and left behind a garrison in Taxila with the soldiers too sick for fighting; then he marched on towards the Hydaspes.[1]

For he had learnt that Porus was on the far side of 4 the Hydaspes with his whole army, determined to prevent his crossing, or at least to attack him, should he attempt it. On learning this, Alexander sent Coenus son of Polemocrates back to the river Indus, ordering him to take to pieces the boats that had been got ready at the crossing of the Indus and bring them to the Hydaspes. The boats were duly dis- 5

and Abisares: ib. 31–3. QC. viii 13, 3 f. puts the death of Barsaentes (iii 25, 8) here.

καὶ ἐκομίσθη αὐτῷ, ὅσα μὲν βραχύτερα διχῇ διατμηθέντα, αἱ τριακόντοροι δὲ τριχῇ ἐτμήθησαν, καὶ τὰ τμήματα ἐπὶ ζευγῶν διεκομίσθη ἔστε ἐπὶ τὴν ὄχθην τοῦ Ὑδάσπου κἀκεῖ ξυμπηχθέντα ναυτικὸν αὖθις δὴ ὁμοῦ ὤφθη ἐν τῷ Ὑδάσπῃ. αὐτὸς δὲ ἀναλαβὼν ἥν τε δύναμιν ἔχων ἧκεν ἐς Τάξιλα καὶ πεντακισχιλίους τῶν Ἰνδῶν, οὓς Ταξίλης τε καὶ οἱ ταύτῃ ὕπαρχοι ἦγον, ᾔει ὡς ἐπὶ τὸν Ὑδάσπην ποταμόν.

9. Καὶ Ἀλέξανδρός τε κατεστρατοπέδευσεν ἐπὶ τῇ ὄχθῃ τοῦ Ὑδάσπου, καὶ Πῶρος κατὰ τὴν ἀντιπέρας ὄχθην ὤφθη ξὺν πάσῃ τῇ στρατιᾷ καὶ τῶν ἐλεφάντων τῷ στίφει. ταύτῃ μὲν δὴ ᾗ κατεστρατοπεδευκότα εἶδεν Ἀλέξανδρον αὐτὸς μένων ἐφύλαττε τὸν πόρον· ὅσα δὲ ἄλλα τοῦ ποταμοῦ εὐπορώτερα, ἐπὶ ταῦτα φρουρὰς διαπέμψας καὶ ἡγεμόνας ἐπιστήσας ἑκάστοις εἴργειν ἐπενόει [ἀπὸ]
2 τοῦ πόρου τοὺς Μακεδόνας. ταῦτα δὲ ὁρῶντι Ἀλεξάνδρῳ κινητέα καὶ αὐτῷ ἐδόκει ἡ στρατιὰ πολλαχῇ, ὡς τὸν Πῶρον ἀμφίβολον γίνεσθαι. διελὼν δὴ ἐς πολλὰ τὸν στρατὸν τοὺς μὲν αὐτὸς ἄλλῃ καὶ ἄλλῃ ἦγε τῆς χώρας τὰ μὲν πορθῶν ὅσα πολέμια, τὰ δὲ σκοπῶν ὅπῃ εὐπορώτερος αὐτῷ ὁ ποταμὸς φανεῖται, τοὺς δὲ τῶν ἡγεμόνων ἄλλοις [καὶ] ἄλλους ἐπιτάξας, καὶ αὐτοὺς πολλαχῇ
3 διέπεμπε. σῖτος δὲ αὐτῷ πάντοθεν ἐκ τῆς ἐπὶ τάδε τοῦ Ὑδάσπου χώρας ἐς τὸ στρατόπεδον ξυνεκομίζετο, ὡς δῆλον εἶναι τῷ Πώρῳ ὅτι ἐγνωκὼς εἴη προσλιπαρεῖν τῇ ὄχθῃ, ἔστε τὸ ὕδωρ τοῦ ποταμοῦ

---

[1] QC. 13, 6 here gives Porus' battle array. D. omits the

membered and transported, the shorter ones in two sections, the *triacontoroi* in three, and the sections were brought in carts to the banks of the Hydaspes. There the flotilla was put together again, and once again seen in full force, now on the Hydaspes. Alexander himself, taking the force with which he arrived at Taxila and also five thousand Indians, led by Taxilas and the hyparchs of the district, marched to the Hydaspes.

9. Alexander pitched his camp on the bank of the Hydaspes, and Porus was observed on the opposite bank with all his forces and his mass of elephants.[1] In the place where Porus saw that Alexander had encamped, he guarded the crossing himself, while at the other parts of the river where a crossing was easier he posted guards, appointing commanders to each guard, with the intention of preventing the Macedonians from crossing. Seeing this, Alexander thought it well himself to move his army about in different directions, so as to keep Porus in uncertainty.[2] He therefore broke up his army into several detachments, some of which he himself led hither and thither over the country, ravaging enemy territory or reconnoitring for places to cross the river which looked easier, while he attached other troops to different commanders and kept sending them too in different directions. Grain was being transported into his camp from all parts of the country this side of the Hydaspes, so that it was evident to Porus that he had determined to stay on the bank, until the

whole story of the crossing, which must have stood in Clitarchus.

[2] Cf. P. 60, 1; Polyaenus iv **3**, 9. So the vulgate had these alarms, though omitted by QC., who tells of skirmishes on small islands.

μεῖον γενόμενον τοῦ χειμῶνος πολλαχῇ παραδοῦναί
οἱ τὸν πόρον· τά τε πλοῖα αὐτῷ ἄλλῃ καὶ ἄλλῃ
παραπλέοντα καὶ αἱ διφθέραι τῆς κάρφης ἐμπι-
πλάμεναι καὶ ἡ ὄχθη πᾶσα πλήρης φαινομένη τῇ μὲν
ἱππέων, τῇ δὲ πεζῶν, οὐκ εἴα ἠρεμεῖν τὸν Πῶρον,
οὐδὲ ἕν τι ἐπιλεξάμενον ἐς φυλακὴν ξύμφορον ἐς τοῦτο
4 ἐκ πάντων παρασκευάζεσθαι. ἄλλως τε ἐν μὲν τῷ
τότε οἱ ποταμοὶ πάντες οἱ Ἰνδικοὶ πολλοῦ τε ὕδατος
καὶ θολεροῦ ἔρρεον καὶ ὀξέος τοῦ ῥεύματος· ἦν γὰρ
ὥρα ἔτους ᾗ μετὰ τροπὰς μάλιστα ⟨τὰς⟩ ἐν θέρει
τρέπεται ὁ ἥλιος· ταύτῃ δὲ τῇ ὥρᾳ ὕδατά τε ἐξ
οὐρανοῦ ἀθρόα τε καταφέρεται ἐς τὴν γῆν τὴν
Ἰνδικὴν καὶ αἱ χιόνες αἱ τοῦ Καυκάσου, ἔνθενπερ
τῶν πολλῶν ποταμῶν αἱ πηγαί εἰσι, κατατηκόμεναι αὔξουσιν αὐτοῖς τὸ ὕδωρ ἐπὶ μέγα· χειμῶνος δὲ ἔμπαλιν ἴσχουσιν ὀλίγοι τε γίγνονται καὶ
καθαροὶ ἰδεῖν καὶ ἔστιν ὅπου περάσιμοι, πλήν γε
δὴ τοῦ Ἰνδοῦ καὶ Γάγγου καὶ τυχὸν καὶ ἄλλου του·
ἀλλ' ὅ γε Ὑδάσπης περατὸς γίνεται.

10. Ταύτην οὖν τὴν ὥραν τοῦ ἔτους προσμένειν
ἐς τὸ φανερὸν ἔφασκεν, εἰ ἐν τῷ τότε εἴργοιτο·
ὁ δὲ οὐδὲν μεῖον ἐφεδρεύων ἔμενεν, εἴ πῃ λάθοι
ὑφαρπάσας ὀξέως τὸν πόρον. ᾗ μὲν δὴ αὐτὸς
Πῶρος κατεστρατοπεδεύκει πρὸς τῇ ὄχθῃ τοῦ
Ὑδάσπου, ἔγνω ἀδύνατος ὢν περᾶσαι ὑπὸ πλήθους
τε τῶν ἐλεφάντων καὶ ὅτι πολλὴ στρατιὰ καὶ
αὐτὴ τεταγμένη τε καὶ ἀκριβῶς ὡπλισμένη ἐκβαί-
2 νουσιν αὐτοῖς ἐπιθήσεσθαι ἔμελλεν· οἵ τε ἵπποι
οὐκ ἂν ἐδόκουν αὐτῷ ἐθελῆσαι οὐδὲ ἐπιβῆναι τῆς
ὄχθης τῆς πέραν, προσκειμένων σφίσιν εὐθὺς τῶν

level of the river fell during the winter and gave him
a chance of crossing the river at several points.[3]   His
boats sailing along in this and that direction, the
filling with chaff of the rafts made of skins, and the
spectacle of the whole bank filled with troops, cavalry
here and infantry there, gave Porus no rest, and did
not permit him to choose a single position suitable for
keeping watch and to concentrate upon that alone.
Besides, at that time all the rivers of India were run-   4
ning deep and turbulent with a swift current; for it
was the season when the sun is first turning after the
summer solstice, and when heavy rains come down on
the land of India, and the snows of the Caucasus,
where most of the rivers rise, are melting and greatly
increase the volume of water; but in winter the flow
is checked and the rivers become smaller, clear in
appearance, and except for the Indus, Ganges, and
possibly some others, fordable in places; the Hydaspes at any rate can be forded.[4]

10. Alexander then announced in public that he
would wait in this summer season, if he were prevented from crossing for the time; but none the less
he stayed there watching, if by any chance he might
quickly streak across without being seen.   He recognized that it was impossible to cross in the place
where Porus himself had encamped on the bank of
the Hydaspes, owing to the number of the elephants,
and because there was a great army, well ordered
and carefully armed, ready to assail his troops as they
landed.   He thought that the horses would not be   2
willing even to set foot on the other bank, as the
elephants would immediately advance to attack them

[3] Veith, *Klio* 1908, 131 ff., shows that this need not come
from an authority who did not record the alarms.
[4] The river was four stades wide and flowing fast, QC. 13, 8 f.

ἐλεφάντων καὶ τῇ τε ὄψει ἅμα καὶ τῇ φωνῇ φοβ-
ούντων, οὐδ' ἂν ἔτι πρόσθεν μεῖναι ἐπὶ τῶν διφθερῶν
κατὰ τὸν πόρον, ἀλλ' ἐκπηδᾶν γὰρ ἐς τὸ ὕδωρ
ἀφορῶντες πέραν τοὺς ἐλέφαντας [καὶ] ἔκφρονες
3 γιγνόμενοι. κλέψαι οὖν ἐπενόει τὴν διάβασιν ὧδε
πράττων. νύκτωρ παραγαγὼν ἄλλῃ καὶ ἄλλῃ
τῆς ὄχθης τοὺς πολλοὺς τῶν ἱππέων βοήν τε ἐποίει
καὶ ἠλαλάζετο τῷ Ἐννᾱλίῳ καὶ τἆλλα ὅσα ἐπὶ
διαβάσει συσκευαζομένων θόρυβος παντοδαπὸς
ἐγίγνετο. καὶ ὁ Πῶρός τε ἀντιπαρῄει πρὸς τὴν
βοὴν ἐπάγων τοὺς ἐλέφαντας καὶ Ἀλέξανδρος ἐς
4 ἔθος αὐτὸν τῆς ἀντιπαραγωγῆς καθίστη. ὡς δὲ
ἐπὶ πολὺ τοῦτο ἐγίγνετο καὶ βοὴ μόνον καὶ ἀλαλαγ-
μός ἦν, οὐκέτι ὁ Πῶρος μετεκινεῖτο πρὸς τὰς
ἐκδρομὰς τῶν ἱππέων, ἀλλὰ κενὸν γὰρ γνοὺς τὸν
φόβον κατὰ χώραν ἐπὶ στρατοπέδου ἔμενε·
σκοποὶ δὲ αὐτῷ πολλαχοῦ τῆς ὄχθης καθε⟨ι⟩στήκε-
σαν. Ἀλέξανδρος δὲ ὡς ἐξείργαστο αὐτῷ ἄφοβον
τὸ τοῦ Πώρου εἰς τὰς νυκτερινὰς ἐπιχειρήσεις
μηχανᾶταί τι τοιόνδε.

11. Ἄκρα ἦν ἀνέχουσα τῆς ὄχθης τοῦ Ὑδάσπου,
ἵνα ἐπέκαμπτεν ὁ ποταμὸς λόγου ἀξίως, αὐτή τε
δασεῖα ἴδῃ παντοίων δένδρων καὶ κατ' αὐτὴν
νῆσος ἐν τῷ ποταμῷ ὑλώδης τε καὶ ἀστιβὴς
ὑπ' ἐρημίας. ταύτην καταμαθὼν τὴν νῆσον καταντικρὺ τῆς ἄκρας, ἀμφότερα ὑλώδη τὰ χωρία καὶ
οἷα κρύψαι τῆς διαβάσεως τὴν ἐπιχείρησιν, ταύτῃ
2 ἔγνω διαβιβάζειν τὸν στρατόν. ἀπέχει δὲ ἥ τε
ἄκρα καὶ ἡ νῆσος τοῦ μεγάλου στρατοπέδου ἐς
πεντήκοντα καὶ ἑκατὸν σταδίους. παρὰ πᾶσαν δὴ
τὴν ὄχθην φυλακαί τε αὐτῷ καθεστηκυῖαι ἦσαν,

326
B.C.

and scare them both by their appearance and their
trumpeting, and that even before this they would not
stay during the crossing on the rafts made of skins,
but would jump off into the water, once frenzied by
sight of the elephants on the other side. So he de- 3
termined to steal across in the following way. At
night he used to take the greater part of his cavalry in
this and that direction along the bank, with shouts
and war-cries, and to make every other sort of disturbance which was to be expected when an army
was preparing to cross. Porus then kept moving
parallel with the shouts, bringing up his elephants, and
Alexander led him on to make a habit of this counter-
movement. But when this had been going on some 4
time, and there was nothing but shouting and raising
of the war-cry, Porus no longer kept following the
directions in which the cavalry moved, but realizing
that the alarm was false, would remain in camp where
he was, though he had set scouts at various points of
the bank. When he had calmed Porus' nervousness
at these nightly manoeuvres, Alexander contrived
the following stratagem.

11. From the bank of the Hydaspes a headland
projected, where the river made a considerable bend;
the headland itself was densely forested with every
sort of tree, and opposite it was an island in the river,
wooded and pathless, as it was uninhabited. Observing this island opposite the headland, both places
being wooded and suited to hide the attempt at crossing, Alexander determined to take his army over at
this point. The headland and island were about a 2
hundred and fifty stades distant from the great camp.
Alexander had posted guards all along the bank, at

διαλείπουσαι ὅσον ξύμμετρον ἐς τὸ ξυνορᾶν τε
ἀλλήλους καὶ κατακούειν εὐπετῶς ὁπόθεν τι παρ-
αγγέλλοιτο, καὶ πανταχόθεν βοαί τε νύκτωρ ἐπὶ
πολλὰς νύκτας ἐγίγνοντο καὶ πυρὰ ἐκαίετο.

3   Ἐπειδὴ δὲ ἔγνω ἐπιχειρεῖν τῷ πόρῳ, κατὰ μὲν
τὸ στρατόπεδον φανερῶς αὐτῷ τὰ τῆς διαβάσεως
παρεσκευάζετο. καὶ Κρατερὸς ὑπελέλειπτο ἐπὶ
στρατοπέδου τήν τε αὑτοῦ ἔχων ἱππαρχίαν καὶ τοὺς
ἐξ Ἀραχωτῶν καὶ Παραπαμισαδῶν ἱππέας καὶ
τῆς φάλαγγος τῶν Μακεδόνων τήν τε Ἀλκέτου
καὶ τὴν Πολυπέρχοντος τάξιν καὶ τοὺς νομάρχας
τῶν ἐπὶ τάδε [1] Ἰνδῶν καὶ τοὺς ἅμα τούτοις τοὺς
4   πεντακισχιλίους. παρηγγέλλετο δὲ Κρατερῷ μὴ
πρὶν διαβαίνειν τὸν πόρον πρὶν ἀπαλλαγῆναι
Πῶρον ξὺν τῇ δυνάμει ὡς ἐπὶ σφᾶς ἢ φεύγοντα
μαθεῖν, αὐτοὺς δὲ νικῶντας· ἢν δὲ μέρος μέν τι τῆς
στρατιᾶς ἀναλαβὼν Πῶρος ἐπ᾽ ἐμὲ ἄγῃ, μέρος
δέ τι ὑπολειφθῇ αὐτῷ ἐπὶ στρατοπέδου καὶ
ἐλέφαντες, σὺ δὲ δὴ καὶ ὡς μένειν κατὰ χώραν·
εἰ δὲ τοὺς ἐλέφαντας ξύμπαντας ἅμα οἷ ἄγοι
Πῶρος ἐπ᾽ ἐμέ, τῆς δὲ ἄλλης στρατιᾶς ὑπολείποιτό
τι ἐπὶ στρατοπέδου, σὺ δὲ διαβαίνειν σπουδῇ· οἱ
γὰρ ἐλέφαντες μόνοι, ἔφη, ἄποροί εἰσι πρὸς τοὺς
ἐκβαίνοντας ἵππους, ἡ δὲ ἄλλη στρατιὰ εὔπορος.

12. Ταῦτα μὲν Κρατερῷ ἐνετέλλετο. ἐν μέσῳ
δὲ τῆς νήσου τε καὶ τοῦ μεγάλου στρατοπέδου,
ἵνα αὐτῷ Κρατερὸς ὑπελέλειπτο, Μελέαγρός τε καὶ
Ἄτταλος καὶ Γοργίας ξὺν τοῖς μισθοφόροις ἱπ-
πεῦσί τε καὶ πεζοῖς ἐτετάχατο· καὶ τούτοις διαβαίνειν παρηγγέλλετο κατὰ μέρος, διελόντας τὸν

---

[1] Perhaps insert τοῦ Ὑδάσπου (Roos).

326
B.C.

intervals at which they could see one another and hear easily, from whatever point an order was passed on; and from all sides shouts at night were raised over several nights and fires kept burning.

When he had determined to attempt the passage, **3** in the camp preparations for crossing were made openly; and Craterus was left in charge of the camp, with his own hipparchy, the cavalry of the Arachotians and Parapamisadae and from the Macedonian phalanx the battalions of Alcetas and Polyperchon, together with the nomarchs of the Indians of these districts [1] and their five thousand men. Craterus was **4** ordered not to attempt a crossing till Porus and his army had left his camp to attack Alexander's forces, or till he had learnt that Porus was in flight and his own side conquerors; ' but should Porus take a part of his army and lead it against me ' (Alexander continued) ' and leave another part behind at his camp with elephants, still stay where you are; if, however, Porus takes all his elephants with him against me, but leaves some part of his army behind at the camp, cross with all dispatch; for it is only the elephants which make it impracticable to disembark horses; the rest of the force will not trouble them.'

12. Such were Craterus' orders. Between the island and the great camp, where Craterus had been left, Meleager and Attalus and Gorgias were posted with the mercenary cavalry and infantry; and they too were instructed to cross in sections, dividing the

---

[1] Perhaps read ' Indians on the near side of the Hydaspes ' (cf. 8, 5). Variant and self-contradictory information in QC. **13**, 18–21 and **23**, where the importance of Pt's role may be Clitarchus' invention (vi 11, 8 n.).

στρατόν, ὁπότε ξυνεχομένους ἤδη ἐν τῇ μάχῃ τοὺς
Ἰνδοὺς ἴδοιεν.

2 Αὐτὸς δὲ ἐπιλεξάμενος τῶν τε ἑταίρων τὸ
ἄγημα καὶ τὴν Ἡφαιστίωνος ἱππαρχίαν καὶ τὴν
Περδίκκου τε καὶ Δημητρίου καὶ τοὺς ἐκ Βάκτρων
καὶ Σογδιανῶν καὶ τοὺς Σκύθας ἱππέας καὶ Δάας
τοὺς ἱπποτοξότας καὶ τῆς φάλαγγος τούς τε
ὑπασπιστὰς καὶ τὴν Κλείτου τε καὶ Κοίνου τάξιν
καὶ τοὺς τοξότας τε καὶ τοὺς Ἀγριᾶνας ἦγεν
ἀφανῶς πολύ τι ἀπέχων τῆς ὄχθης, τοῦ μὴ καταφανὴς εἶναι ἄγων ἐπὶ τὴν νῆσον καὶ τὴν ἄκραν,
3 ἔνθεν διαβαίνειν αὐτῷ ἦν ἐγνωσμένον. καὶ ἐνταῦθα
ἐπληροῦντο τῆς νυκτὸς αἱ διφθέραι τῆς κάρφης, ἐκ
πολλοῦ ἤδη παρενηνεγμέναι, καὶ κατερράπτοντο
ἐς ἀκρίβειαν· ὕδωρ τε ἐξ οὐρανοῦ τῆς νυκτὸς
λάβρον ἐπιγίγνεται. ταύτῃ καὶ μᾶλλόν τι ἡ
παρασκευή τε αὐτῷ καὶ ἡ ἐπιχείρησις ἡ ἐς τὴν
διάβασιν οὐ φανερὰ κατέστη, τῷ κτύπῳ τῷ ἀπὸ
τῶν ὅπλων καὶ τῷ θορύβῳ τῷ ἀπὸ τῶν παραγγελμάτων τῶν τε βροντῶν καὶ τοῦ ὄμβρου ἀντιπατα-
4 γούντων. καὶ τῶν πλοίων δὲ τὰ πολλὰ αὐτῷ ξυν-
τετμημένα παρεκεκόμιστο ἐς τὸν χῶρον τοῦτον καὶ
ἀφανῶς αὖθις ξυμπεπηγμένα ἐν τῇ ὕλῃ ἐκρύπτετο,
τά τε ἄλλα καὶ αἱ τριακόντοροι. ὑπὸ δὲ τὴν ἕω ὅ τε
ἄνεμος καὶ ὁ ὄμβρος κεκοίμητο. καὶ ἡ μὲν ἄλλη
στρατιὰ αὐτῷ ἡ ἱππικὴ τῶν διφθερῶν ἐπιβᾶσα καὶ
ὅσους τῶν πεζῶν τὰ πλοῖα ἐδέχετο ἐπέρα κατὰ τὴν
νῆσον, ὡς μὴ πρόσθεν ὀφθεῖεν πρὸς τῶν σκοπῶν τῶν
ἐκ Πώρου καθεστηκότων πρὶν παραλλάξαντας τὴν
νῆσον ὀλίγον ἔτι ἀπέχειν τῆς ὄχθης.

---

[1] These regiments are never mentioned in the fighting, but

force, as soon as they saw the Indians already engaged in battle.[1]

Alexander himself selected the *agema* of the Companions, the hipparchies of Hephaestion, Perdiccas and Demetrius, the cavalry from Bactria and Sogdiana and the Scythian horsemen, with the Dahae, mounted archers, and from the phalanx, the hypaspists and the battalions of Clitus and Coenus, the archers and the Agrianians [2]; he led this force where it could not be seen, keeping some distance from the bank, so that he might not be detected marching towards the island and headland, where he had determined to cross. And there, during the night, the rafts made of skins, which had already been brought along some time before, were filled with chaff and carefully sewn together. Violent rain came on in the night, and helped to conceal Alexander's preparations and his attempt to make the crossing; the thunder-claps and the rain counteracted the clatter of the arms and the commotion arising from the commands. Most of the boats, which had been broken into sections, had been duly transported to this place, put together again out of sight and hidden in the wood, including the *triacontoroi*. But towards dawn the wind and rain had quieted down,[3] and his cavalry embarked on the rafts with all the infantry the boats could take, and crossed by the island, so that they might not be seen by the scouts posted by Porus before they had passed the island and were already near the bank.

2

3

4

A. must have failed to record that they crossed after Al. and came up for the battle (Tarn ii 190). The mercenary force, if all stationed here, would have been large (App. XIII).

[2] App. XIX 3 f. on 11, 3–12, 2.

[3] Cf. 13, 3; QC. 13, 24; *contra* P. 60, 2 (Onesicritus?).

13. Αὐτὸς δὲ ἐπιβὰς τριακοντόρου ἐπέρα καὶ ἅμα αὐτῷ Πτολεμαῖός τε καὶ Περδίκκας καὶ Λυσίμαχος οἱ σωματοφύλακες καὶ Σέλευκος τῶν ἑταίρων, ὁ βασιλεύσας ὕστερον, καὶ τῶν ὑπασπιστῶν οἱ ἡμίσεες· τοὺς δὲ ἄλλους ὑπασπιστὰς ἄλλαι τριακόντοροι ἔφερον. ὡς δὲ τὴν νῆσον παρήλλαξεν ἡ στρατιά, φανερῶς ἤδη ἐπεῖχον τῇ ὄχθῃ· καὶ οἱ σκοποὶ κατιδόντες αὐτῶν τὴν ὁρμὴν ὡς ἑκάστοις τάχους οἱ ἵπποι εἶχον ἤλαυνον ὡς ἐπὶ τὸν Πῶρον.

2 ἐν τούτῳ δὲ Ἀλέξανδρος πρῶτος αὐτὸς ἐκβὰς καὶ τοὺς ἀπὸ τῶν ἄλλων τριακοντόρων ἀναλαβὼν ξυνέταττε τοὺς ἀεὶ ἐκβαίνοντας τῶν ἱππέων. οἱ γὰρ ἱππεῖς πρῶτοι ἐτετάχατο αὐτῷ ἐκβαίνειν· καὶ τούτους ἄγων προῄει ἐν τάξει. ἔλαθε δὲ οὐκ ἐς βέβαιον χωρίον ἐκβὰς ἀγνοίᾳ τῶν τόπων, ἀλλὰ ἐς νῆσον γὰρ καὶ αὐτὴν μὲν μεγάλην, ᾗ δὴ καὶ μᾶλλον νῆσος οὖσα ἔλαθεν, οὐ πολλῷ δὲ ὕδατι πρὸς

3 τοῦ ποταμοῦ ἀποτεμνομένην ἀπὸ τῆς ἄλλης γῆς. καὶ ἅμα ηὐξήκει τὸ ὕδωρ ὁ ὄμβρος λάβρος τε καὶ ἐπὶ πολὺ τῆς νυκτὸς κατασχών, ὥστε οὐκ ἐξεύρισκον αὐτῷ οἱ ἱππεῖς τὸν πόρον, καὶ δέος ἦν αὖθις ἄλλου δεῆσαι αὐτῷ ἐπὶ τῇ διαβάσει ἴσου τῷ πρώτῳ πόνῳ. ὡς δὲ ἐξευρέθη ποτὲ ὁ πόρος, ἦγε κατ' αὐτὸν χαλεπῶς· ἦν γὰρ τῶν μὲν πεζῶν ὑπὲρ τοὺς μαστοὺς τὸ ὕδωρ ἵναπερ τὸ βαθύτατον αὐτοῦ, τῶν δὲ ἵππων ὅσον τὰς κεφαλὰς ὑπερίσχειν τοῦ

4 ποταμοῦ. ὡς δὲ καὶ τοῦτο ἐπεπέρατο αὐτῷ τὸ

---

[1] Why does A. not name the other bodyguards (it would not be Pt. who singled out Perdiccas, App. XXIV 1) or note that Seleucus (but not Lysimachus) took the title of king (in 305)? He was perhaps influenced by the same late authority as he used in vii 22, 5. See n. on § 4.

13. Alexander in person embarked on a *triacon-toros* and began the passage, and with him were Ptolemy, Perdiccas and Lysimachus, bodyguards, and Seleucus, one of the Companions, who afterwards became king,[1] and half the hypaspists.[2] The rest were taken by other *triacontoroi*. Once the force passed the island, they were plainly attacking the bank; the scouts, observing their oncoming, rode to Porus as fast as each man's horse could carry him. Meanwhile Alexander disembarked first himself, and 2 taking over the men from the other *triacontoroi*, he marshalled the cavalry in order as they kept disembarking, for he had instructed the cavalry to disembark first; taking them with him, he advanced in fighting array. However, without being aware of it, he had disembarked through want of local knowledge not on solid land but on an island; it too was large,[3] and this was chiefly why he had not noticed that it was an island; still it was parted from the other side by a small stream of the river. At the same time the 3 rain, which was violent and kept on most of the night, had swollen the river, so that his cavalry did not find the ford, and there was apprehension that to complete the crossing he must repeat all the former effort. But when at last the ford was found, Alexander led them across it, though with difficulty, for the water at its deepest was above the breasts of the foot-soldiers, while the horses kept only their heads above the river. But when even this water had also been 4

---

[2] As one boat could not carry some 1500 men, A. has probably garbled a statement that half the hypaspists crossed at first, and that the boats returned for the rest.

[3] Not the island of 11, 1.

ὕδωρ, ἐπὶ μὲν τὸ δεξιὸν κέρας παρήγαγε τό τε
ἄγημα τῶν ἱππέων καὶ τῶν ἄλλων ἱππαρχιῶν
τοὺς κρατίστους ἐπιλεξάμενος· τοὺς δὲ ἱπποτοξότας τῆς πάσης ἵππου προέταξε· τῶν δὲ πεζῶν
πρώτους μὲν τοὺς ὑπασπιστὰς τοὺς βασιλικούς, ὧν
ἡγεῖτο Σέλευκος, ἐπέταξε τῇ ἵππῳ· ἐπὶ δὲ τούτοις
τὸ ἄγημα τὸ βασιλικόν· ἐχομένους δὲ τούτων
τοὺς ἄλλους ὑπασπιστάς, ὡς ἑκάστοις αἱ ἡγεμονίαι
ἐν τῷ τότε ξυνέβαινον· κατὰ δὲ τὰ ἄκρα τῆς
φάλαγγος οἱ τοξόται αὐτῷ καὶ οἱ Ἀγριᾶνες [καὶ]
οἱ ἀκοντισταὶ ἑκατέρωθεν ἐπέστησαν.

14. Οὕτως ἐκτάξας τὸν μὲν πεζὸν στρατὸν ἐν
κόσμῳ βάδην ἕπεσθαι ἐκέλευσεν, οὐ πολὺ ἀποδέοντας τῶν ἑξακισχιλίων· αὐτὸς δέ, ὅτι κρατεῖν
ἐδόκει τῇ ἵππῳ, τοὺς ἱππέας μόνους ἀναλαβὼν
σπουδῇ ἡγεῖτο, ὄντας ἐς πεντακισχιλίους. Ταύρωνι δὲ τῷ τοξάρχῃ προσέταξε τοὺς τοξότας
2 ἐπάγειν τῇ ἵππῳ καὶ αὐτοὺς σπουδῇ. γνώμην δὲ
ἐπεποίητο, ὡς εἰ μὲν προσμίξειαν αὐτῷ οἱ ἀμφὶ
τὸν Πῶρον ξὺν τῇ δυνάμει ἁπάσῃ, ἢ κρατήσειν
αὐτῶν οὐ χαλεπῶς τῇ ἵππῳ προσβαλὼν ἢ ἀπομα-
χεῖσθαί γε ἔστε τοὺς πεζοὺς ἐν τῷ ἔργῳ ἐπιγενέσ-
θαι· εἰ δὲ πρὸς τὴν τόλμαν τῆς διαβάσεως ἄτοπον
γενομένην οἱ Ἰνδοὶ ἐκπλαγέντες φεύγοιεν, οὐ
πόρρωθεν ἕξεσθαι αὐτῶν κατὰ τὴν φυγήν, ὡς
πλείονα ἐν τῇ ἀποχωρήσει τὸν φόνον γενόμενον
ὀλίγον ἔτι ὑπολείπεσθαι αὐτῷ τὸ ἔργον.

3 Ἀριστόβουλος δὲ λέγει τὸν Πώρου παῖδα φθάσαι ἀφικόμενον σὺν ἅρμασιν ὡς ἑξήκοντα πρὶν τὸ

---

[4] For A's errors and omissions see App. XIX 3. QC. 14, 15
makes Antigenes, Leonnatus and Tauron (cf. A. 16, 3) command all the foot, and does not mention Seleucus.

crossed, he led the *agema* of the cavalry round to his right wing, with the best men of the other hipparchies; the mounted archers were set in front of the whole line of cavalry; next to the cavalry he marshalled from the infantry the royal hypaspists under Seleucus, then the royal *agema*, and next the rest of the hypaspists, in order determined by the precedence of the commanders for that day; on the wings of the phalanx on either side he stationed the archers, the Agrianians and the javelin-throwers.[4]

14. With his army thus marshalled, Alexander ordered the infantry forces to follow in good order at a marching pace, their number being nearly six thousand, while, as he seemed to be superior in cavalry, he took the cavalry only in person and advanced at speed, the cavalry numbering about five thousand.[1] He directed Tauron the commander of the archers to lead them on with the cavalry, and also at full speed. He determined that if Porus and his 2 people were to attack him with their full force, he would either easily overcome them by charging with his cavalry, or he would fight them off till his infantry joined in the action. If, however, the Indians were panic-stricken by the extraordinary boldness of the crossing and fled, he would keep close up to them in the flight; and the greater the slaughter in the retreat, the less trouble there would be for him in the future.

Aristobulus says that Porus' son arrived with sixty 3 chariots before Alexander made his last crossing from

---

[1] Probably A's source gave a total (3000 hypaspists and 3000 other phalangites) for those who crossed with Al. But at the battle he had much larger forces (12, 1 n.). The figure for cavalry must include Orientals (Brunt, *JHS* 1963, 41 against Tarn ii 193). All figures are for paper strength.

ὕστερον ἐκ τῆς νήσου τῆς μικρᾶς [1] περᾶσαι Ἀλέξ-
ανδρον· καὶ τοῦτον δυνηθῆναι ἂν εἶρξαι Ἀλέξανδρον
τῆς διαβάσεως χαλεπῶς καὶ μηδενὸς εἴργοντος περαι-
ωθέντα, εἴπερ οὖν καταπηδήσαντες οἱ Ἰνδοὶ ἐκ τῶν
ἁρμάτων προσέκειντο τοῖς πρώτοις τῶν ἐκβαινόν-
των· ἀλλὰ παραλλάξαι γὰρ ξὺν τοῖς ἅρμασι καὶ
ἀκίνδυνον ποιῆσαι Ἀλεξάνδρῳ τὴν διάβασιν· καὶ
ἐπὶ τούτους ἀφεῖναι Ἀλέξανδρον τοὺς ἱπποτοξότας,
καὶ τραπῆναι αὐτοὺς οὐ χαλεπῶς, πληγὰς λαμ-
4 βάνοντας. οἱ δὲ καὶ μάχην λέγουσιν ἐν τῇ ἐκβάσει
γενέσθαι τῶν Ἰνδῶν τῶν ξὺν τῷ παιδὶ τῷ Πώρου
ἀφιγμένων πρὸς Ἀλέξανδρόν τε καὶ τοὺς ξὺν
αὐτῷ ἱππέας. καὶ γὰρ καὶ ἀφικέσθαι ξὺν μείζονι
δυνάμει τὸν Πώρου παῖδα, καὶ αὐτόν τε Ἀλέξανδρον τρωθῆναι πρὸς αὐτοῦ καὶ τὸν ἵππον αὐτοῦ
ἀποθανεῖν τὸν Βουκεφάλαν, φίλτατον Ἀλεξάνδρῳ
ὄντα τὸν ἵππον, καὶ τοῦτον τρωθέντα ὑπὸ τοῦ
παιδὸς τοῦ Πώρου. ἀλλὰ Πτολεμαῖος ὁ Λάγου,
5 ὅτῳ καὶ ἐγὼ ξυμφέρομαι, ἄλλως λέγει. ἐκπεμφ-
θῆναι μὲν γὰρ τὸν παῖδα ὑπὸ τοῦ Πώρου λέγει καὶ
οὗτος, ἀλλ' οὐχ ἑξήκοντα μόνα ἅρματα ἄγοντα.
οὐδὲ γὰρ εἰκὸς Πῶρον ἀκούσαντα ἐκ τῶν σκοπῶν,
ὅτι δὴ αὐτὸς Ἀλέξανδρος διαβέβηκεν τοῦ Ὑδάσπου
τὸν πόρον ἢ μέρος γέ τι τῆς στρατιᾶς, ξὺν ἑξήκοντα
6 ἅρμασι μόνοις ἐκπέμψαι τὸν αὑτοῦ παῖδα· ἃ δὴ
ὡς μὲν ἐπὶ κατασκοπὴν ἐκπεμπόμενα πολλά τε καὶ
οὐκ εὔζωνα ἐς τὴν ἀποχώρησιν ἦν, ὡς δὲ εἰς τὸ

---

[1] Schmieder proposed to substitute μακρᾶς or delete τῆς
μικρᾶς, cf. 13, 2.

326
B.C.

the small island,[2] and that he could have prevented Alexander's crossing, difficult as it was even when unopposed, if only the Indians had leapt from their chariots and attacked the foremost of those coming to land. However, he drove past with his chariots, and thus allowed Alexander to cross without danger; and Alexander launched his mounted archers against this force, and easily turned them to flight, inflicting casualties. Others say that there was actually a 4 battle at the landing between the Indians who had arrived with Porus' son and Alexander and his cavalry. For Porus' son actually did arrive (they say) with a superior force, and Alexander was wounded by him and his horse Bucephalas killed, his favourite horse, which was actually wounded by Porus' son.[3] But Ptolemy son of Lagus, with whom I too agree, gives a different account. He too states that Porus sent his 5 son, but not with only sixty chariots. Nor was it likely [4] that Porus, on learning from his scouts that the Hydaspes had been crossed either by Alexander in person or at least by a part of his army, would have sent out his own son with no more than sixty chariots. If these were sent for reconnaissance, they were too 6 many, as well as too cumbrous for withdrawal, but if

---

[2] See critical note. Unless we delete ' small ' or substitute ' large ' (the second emendation is easy), Ar. must have differed from Pt. on the size of the island in 13, 2.

[3] D. 95, 5 and probably QC. 14, 34 on Bucephalas. But QC. substitutes Porus' brother, Spitaces (cf. A. 18, 2), for his son and gives him 100 chariots and 4000 horse; this version (Clitarchus?) is not A's vulgate: P. 60, 5 (1000 horse and 60 chariots) is different again.

[4] The use of *oratio recta* shows (*contra* Jacoby etc.) that this is the comment of A., not Pt., who recorded what he saw and had no cause to resort to reasoning.

εἶρξαί τε τοὺς οὔπω πεπερακότας τῶν πολεμίων
καὶ τοῖς ἤδη ἐκβεβηκόσιν ἐπιθέσθαι οὐδαμῇ
ἀξιόμαχα. ἀλλὰ δισχιλίους γὰρ λέγει ἱππέας
ἄγοντα ἀφικέσθαι τοῦ Πώρου τὸν παῖδα, ἅρματα δὲ
ἑκατὸν καὶ εἴκοσι· φθάσαι δὲ περάσαντα Ἀλέξανδρον καὶ τὸν ἐκ τῆς νήσου τὸν τελευταῖον πόρον.

15. Καὶ ἐπὶ τούτους τὰ μὲν πρῶτα ἐκπέμψαι
Ἀλέξανδρον καὶ οὗτος λέγει τοὺς ἱπποτοξότας,
αὐτὸν δὲ ἄγειν τοὺς ἱππέας· προσάγειν γὰρ
οἰηθῆναι Πῶρον ξὺν τῇ πάσῃ δυνάμει· τὴν δὲ
ἵππον ταύτην προτεταγμένην αὐτῷ προπορεύεσθαι
2 πρὸ τοῦ ἄλλου στρατοῦ. ὡς δὲ κατέμαθεν ἀτρεκῶς
τὸ πλῆθος τὸ τῶν Ἰνδῶν, ἐνταῦθα δὴ ὀξέως ἐπιπεσεῖν αὐτοῖς ξὺν τῇ ἀμφ' αὑτὸν ἵππῳ τοὺς δὲ
ἐγκλῖναι, ὡς Ἀλέξανδρόν τε αὐτὸν κατεῖδον καὶ τὸ
στῖφος ἀμφ' αὑτὸν τῶν ἱππέων οὐκ ἐπὶ μετώπου,
ἀλλὰ κατ' ἴλας ἐμβεβληκός. καὶ τούτων ἱππέας
μὲν πεσεῖν ἐς τετρακοσίους, πεσεῖν δὲ καὶ τοῦ
Πώρου τὸν παῖδα· τὰ δὲ ἅρματα αὐτοῖς ἵπποις
ἁλῶναι ἔν τε τῇ ἀποχωρήσει βαρέα γενόμενα καὶ
ἐν αὐτῷ τῷ ἔργῳ ὑπὸ πηλοῦ ἀχρεῖα.

3 Πῶρος δέ, ὡς αὐτῷ ὅσοι ἱππεῖς ἐκ τῆς φυγῆς
διεσώζοντο Ἀλέξανδρόν τε αὐτὸν πεπερακότα ξὺν
τῇ στρατιᾷ ἐς τὸ καρτερώτατον καὶ τὸν παῖδα ἐν
τῇ μάχῃ τετελευτηκότα ἤγγειλαν, ἐγίγνετο μὲν
καὶ ὣς ἀμφίβολος τῇ γνώμῃ, ὅτι καὶ οἱ ἀπὸ τοῦ
καταντικρὺ τοῦ μεγάλου στρατοπέδου οἱ ξὺν
Κρατερῷ ὑπολελειμμένοι ἐπιχειροῦντες τῇ δια-
4 βάσει ἐφαίνοντο· εἵλετο δ' οὖν ἐπ' αὐτὸν Ἀλέξανδρον ἐλάσας ξὺν τῇ στρατιᾷ πάσῃ πρὸς τὸ καρτε-
ρώτατόν τε τῶν Μακεδόνων καὶ αὐτὸν τὸν βασιλέα
διαγωνίσασθαι. ἀλλὰ καὶ ὡς ὀλίγους τῶν ἐλεφάν-

the aim was to keep the enemy who had not yet
crossed from doing so and to attack those who had
already landed, they were altogether unequal to the
task. In fact Ptolemy says that Porus' son had with
him when he reached the place two thousand cavalry
and a hundred and twenty chariots; but that Alexander was too quick and had by then actually made
his final crossing from the island.

15. Ptolemy also says that Alexander at first sent
the mounted archers against them, while he himself
led on the cavalry, in the belief that Porus was coming up with all his army, and that this cavalry, marshalled in his van, preceded the rest of the army, but 2
that, on obtaining accurate information on the number of the Indians, he fell upon them sharply with the
cavalry he had with him; they gave way when they
saw that Alexander in person and the serried mass of
cavalry round him were attacking not in line but
squadron (*ilê*) by squadron; about four hundred of
their horsemen fell, as did Porus' son; and the
chariots with their teams were captured, as they
proved too heavy in retreat, and were useless in the
action itself because of mud.[1]

When the horsemen who had escaped in the flight 3
had reported to Porus that Alexander himself had
crossed with his army in full force and that his son
had fallen in the fight, he was still in two minds, all
the more because the forces in the camp opposite,
who had been left behind with Craterus, were now
seen to be attempting the passage. In fact, he chose 4
to advance against Alexander himself with all his
force, and fight to a finish against the strongest part
of the Macedonians and their king himself. Even so

---

[1] QC. 14, 2 ff. merges this fight into the main battle.

των σὺν οὐ πολλῇ στρατιᾷ αὑτοῦ ἐπὶ τοῦ στρατοπέδου ἀπέλιπεν, ὡς φοβεῖν ἀπὸ τῆς ὄχθης τοὺς
ξὺν Κρατερῷ ἱππέας. αὐτὸς δὲ τήν τε ἵππον
ἀναλαβὼν πᾶσαν, ἐς τετρακισχιλίους ἱππέας, καὶ
τὰ ἅρματα πάντα, τριακόσια ὄντα, καὶ τῶν ἐλεφάντων διακοσίους καὶ τῶν πεζῶν ὅ τι περ ὄφελος,
5 ἐς τρισμυρίους ἤλαυνεν ὡς ἐπ' Ἀλέξανδρον. ὡς
δὲ ἐνέτυχε χωρίῳ, ἵνα οὐ πηλὸς αὐτῷ ἐφαίνετο,
ἀλλὰ ὑπὸ ψάμμου γὰρ ξύμπαν ἦν ἄπεδον καὶ
στερεὸν ἐς τὰς ἐφόδους τε καὶ ἀναστροφὰς τῶν
ἵππων, ἐνταῦθα ἔτασσε τὴν στρατιάν, πρώτους
μὲν τοὺς ἐλέφαντας ἐπὶ μετώπου, διέχοντα ἐλέφαντα ἐλέφαντος οὐ μεῖον πλέθρου, ὡς πρὸ πάσης τε
τῆς φάλαγγος τῶν πεζῶν παραταθῆναι αὐτῷ τοὺς
ἐλέφαντας ἐπὶ μετώπου καὶ φόβον πάντῃ παρέχειν
6 τοῖς ἀμφ' Ἀλέξανδρον ἱππεῦσιν. ἄλλως τε οὐδὲ
ἠξίου ἐς τὰ διαλείποντα τῶν ἐλεφάντων τολμῆσαι
ἄν τινα ὤσασθαι τῶν πολεμίων, οὔτε ξὺν ἵπποις
διὰ τὸν φόβον τῶν ἵππων, πεζούς τε ἔτι μεῖον·
κατὰ στόμα τε γὰρ ἂν πρὸς τῶν ὁπλιτῶν προσβαλ-
λόντων εἴργεσθαι καὶ καταπατηθήσεσθαι ἐπιστρεψ-
7 άντων ἐπ' αὐτοὺς τῶν ἐλεφάντων. ἐπὶ τούτοις δὲ
οἱ πεζοὶ αὐτῷ ἐτετάχατο, οὐκ ἴσον τὸ μέτωπον
τοῖς θηρίοις ἐπέχοντες, ἀλλ' ἐν δευτέρῳ μετώπῳ
μετὰ τοὺς ἐλέφαντας, ὅσον ἐς τὰ διαλείποντα ἐπ'
ὀλίγον ἐμβεβλῆσθαι τοὺς λόχους. ἦσαν δὲ αὐτῷ
καὶ κατὰ τὰ κέρατα ἔτι ὑπὲρ τοὺς ἐλέφαντας πεζοὶ
ἐφεστηκότες, ἑκατέρωθεν δὲ τῶν πεζῶν ἡ ἵππος αὐτῷ
ἐτέτακτο καὶ πρὸ ταύτης τὰ ἅρματα ἑκατέρωθεν.

16. Αὕτη μὲν ἡ Πώρου τάξις ἦν. Ἀλέξανδρος
δὲ ὡς ἤδη καθεώρα τοὺς Ἰνδοὺς ἐκτασσομένους,

---

[2] Variant and mutually contradictory figures in D. and QC.

he left a few elephants behind with a small force there by the camp, to scare the cavalry under Craterus away from the bank. He himself, taking all his cavalry, about four thousand horse, all the three hundred chariots, two hundred of the elephants, and any serviceable infantry, about thirty thousand, advanced against Alexander.[2] When he found a place that he did not think muddy—it was sandy and therefore all level and solid for cavalry to charge and retire—he drew up his army there, putting the elephants on the front line, not less than a hundred feet apart,[3] so as to form a line in front of the whole phalanx of infantry, and terrify the cavalry of Alexander at all points. He did not in any case expect that any of the enemy would dare force a way through the gaps between the elephants on horseback, since the horses would take fright; still less did he fear the foot-soldiers, who would be kept back by the heavy armed troops advancing frontally and trampled down by the elephants turning upon them. Next the elephants he stationed his foot-soldiers, not on the same front as the beasts, but in a second line behind them, so that the companies were fitted more or less into the intervals. He also had foot-soldiers stationed on the wings stretching even beyond the line of elephants; on each flank of the infantry the cavalry were posted, and in front of them the chariots on both flanks.

16. This then was the disposition of Porus' battle-order. But as he already saw the Indians getting

---

13, 6 with 14, 2. None are reliable, cf. App. I 1; III 5; IX 3.

[3] With 200 elephants (130 in D., 85 in QC. and 50 in Polyaenus iv **3**, 22), the line would then have stretched for over 6 km! ' Phalanx ' is misleading, cf. *Ind.* 16, 6–9. Here A. does not allude to Indian archers, for whom see also QC. 14, 10 and 19; his statement that the mud prevented use of their bows is credible, cf. *Ind.* 16.

ἐπέστησε τοὺς ἱππέας τοῦ πρόσω, ὡς ἀναλαμβάν-
ειν τῶν πεζῶν τοὺς ἀεὶ προσάγοντας. ὡς δὲ καὶ
ἡ φάλαγξ αὐτῷ δρόμῳ συνάψασα ὁμοῦ ἤδη ἦν, ὁ δὲ
οὐκ εὐθὺς ἐκτάξας ἐπῆγεν, ὡς μὴ καματηρούς τε
καὶ πνευστιῶντας ἀκμῆσι παραδοῦναι τοῖς βαρβάροις, ἀλλὰ ἐς κύκλους παριππεύων ἀνέπαυε τοὺς
2 πεζοὺς ἔστε καταστῆναι αὐτοῖς τὸν θυμόν. ὡς δὲ
τὴν τάξιν κατεῖδε τῶν Ἰνδῶν, κατὰ μέσον μέν,
ἵνα οἱ ἐλέφαντες προεβέβληντο καὶ πυκνὴ ἡ φάλαγξ
κατὰ τὰ διαλείποντα αὐτῶν ἐπετέτακτο, οὐκ ἔγνω
προάγειν, αὐτὰ ἐκεῖνα ὀκνήσας ἅπερ ὁ Πῶρος τῷ
λογισμῷ ξυνθεὶς ταύτῃ ἔταξεν· ἀλλὰ αὐτὸς μὲν
ἅτε ἱπποκρατῶν τὴν πολλὴν τῆς ἵππου ἀναλαβὼν
ἐπὶ τὸ εὐώνυμον κέρας τῶν πολεμίων παρήλαυνεν,
3 ὡς ταύτῃ ἐπιθησόμενος. Κοῖνον δὲ πέμπει ὡς ἐπὶ τὸ
δεξιόν, τὴν Δημητρίου καὶ τὴν αὑτοῦ ἔχοντα ἱππαρχίαν, κελεύσας, ἐπειδὰν τὸ κατὰ σφᾶς στῖφος τῶν
ἱππέων ἰδόντες οἱ βάρβαροι ἀντιπαριππεύσωσιν, αὐτὸν
κατόπιν ἔχεσθαι αὐτῶν· τῶν πεζῶν δὲ τὴν φάλαγγα
Σελεύκῳ καὶ Ἀντιγένει καὶ Ταύρωνι προσέταξεν
ἄγειν, μὴ πρόσθεν δὲ ἅπτεσθαι τοῦ ἔργου πρὶν ὑπὸ
τῆς ἵππου τῆς ἀμφ' αὑτὸν τεταραγμένην τήν τε
φάλαγγα τῶν πεζῶν καὶ τοὺς ἱππέας κατίδωσιν.
4 Ἤδη τε ἐντὸς βέλους ἐγίγνετο καὶ ἐφῆκεν ἐπὶ τὸ

---

[1] P. 60, 6 says that the battle ended at the eighth hour.
The crossing had begun towards dawn (12, 4).

[2] ' To Al's right ' or ' against the enemy right '? On the
second and usual view the cavalry on Porus' right must have
moved in front or rear of his centre to reinforce his left, expos-
ing their own rear to Coenus' force behind them. Is this
credible, unless Coenus' force was kept out of sight? On the
first view, with the same Indian manoeuvre, Coenus might
have been held back on Al's extreme right (cf. perhaps Polyaenus iv 3, 22) and have ridden round the enemy left when their

326
B.C.

into line, Alexander halted his cavalry from any further advance, so as to await the infantry who were coming up behind in succession.[1] And when the phalanx had joined him at the double and was now all present, he did not put them in battle order at once and lead them forward, so as to deliver them tired and out of breath to the barbarians who were fresh, but wheeled his cavalry round and round, and rested his infantry till they had recovered their fighting spirit. On examining the Indian battle-order, 2 however, he decided not to advance in the centre, where the elephants had been thrown forward, and where the phalanx in close formation had been posted in the intervals between them; he was alarmed by the very points which Porus had taken into account when making this disposition; but since his superiority lay in cavalry, he took with him personally most of his cavalry and rode against the enemy's left wing, intending to make his attack there. Coenus was sent 3 to the right,[2] with the hipparchy of Demetrius and his own, and ordered to close on the barbarians from behind when the latter saw the solid body of cavalry opposite to them and began to ride out parallel with them; Seleucus and Antigenes and Tauron were put in command of the infantry phalanx, with orders not to take part in the action till they observed the enemy's phalanx of infantry and their cavalry thrown into confusion by his own cavalry force.

By now they were within missile range, and Alex- 4

line was already fully extended (cf. perhaps QC. 14, 14–17, which is equally ambiguous on the orders given to Coenus; conceivably this reflects an ambiguity in Pt., on whose account QC. might also have drawn, perhaps indirectly). P. 60, 5 makes Coenus attack the right, but with no mention of any manoeuvres. As there can be no certainty on this vital detail, the course of the battle is hopelessly obscure.

κέρας τὸ εὐώνυμον τῶν Ἰνδῶν τοὺς ἱπποτοξότας,
ὄντας ἐς χιλίους, ὡς ταράξαι τοὺς ταύτῃ ἐφεστηκό-
τας τῶν πολεμίων τῇ πυκνότητί τε τῶν τοξευμάτων καὶ τῶν ἵππων τῇ ἐπελάσει. καὶ αὐτὸς δὲ τοὺς
ἑταίρους ἔχων τοὺς ἱππέας παρήλαυνεν ὀξέως ἐπὶ
τὸ εὐώνυμον τῶν βαρβάρων, κατὰ κέρας ἔτι
τεταραγμένοις ἐμβαλεῖν σπουδὴν ποιούμενος, πρὶν
ἐπὶ φάλαγγος ἐκταθῆναι αὐτοῖς τὴν ἵππον.

17. Ἐν τούτῳ δὲ οἵ τε Ἰνδοὶ τοὺς ἱππέας
πάντοθεν ξυναλίσαντες παρίππευον Ἀλεξάνδρῳ
ἀντιπαρεξάγοντες τῇ ἐλάσει, καὶ οἱ περὶ Κοῖνον,
ὡς παρήγγελτο, κατόπιν αὐτοῖς ἐπεφαίνοντο.
ταῦτα ξυνιδόντες οἱ Ἰνδοὶ ἀμφίστομον ἠναγκάσ-
θησαν ποιῆσαι τὴν τάξιν τῆς ἵππου, τὴν μὲν ὡς ἐπ'
Ἀλέξανδρον τὴν πολλήν τε καὶ κρατίστην, οἱ δὲ
ἐπὶ Κοῖνόν τε καὶ τοὺς ἅμα τούτῳ ἐπέστρεφον.
2 τοῦτό τε οὖν εὐθὺς ἐτάραξε τὰς τάξεις τε καὶ τὰς
γνώμας τῶν Ἰνδῶν καὶ Ἀλέξανδρος ἰδὼν τὸν καιρὸν ἐν αὐτῇ τῇ ἐπὶ θάτερα ἐπιστροφῇ τῆς ἵππου
ἐπιτίθεται τοῖς καθ' αὑτόν, ὥστε οὐδὲ τὴν ἐμβολὴν
ἐδέξαντο τῶν ἀμφ' Ἀλέξανδρον ἱππέων οἱ Ἰνδοί,
ἀλλὰ κατηρ[ρ]άχθησαν ὥσπερ εἰς τεῖχός τι φίλιον
3 τοὺς ἐλέφαντας. καὶ ἐν τούτῳ οἱ ἐπιστάται τῶν
ἐλεφάντων ἀντεπῆγον τῇ ἵππῳ τὰ θηρία, καὶ ἡ
φάλαγξ αὐτὴ τῶν Μακεδόνων ἀντεπῄει πρὸς τοὺς
ἐλέφαντας, ἔς τε τοὺς ἐπιβάτας αὐτῶν ἀκοντίζοντες
καὶ αὐτὰ τὰ θηρία περισταδὸν πάντοθεν βάλλοντες.
καὶ ἦν τὸ ἔργον οὐδενὶ τῶν πρόσθεν ἀγώνων

---

[3] Porus' foot extending beyond the elephants (15, 7, *contra*
D. 87, 4; QC. 14, 10) or his cavalry? We do not know.

[4] *Or* 'to attack them on the flank, while they were still
confused, before the cavalry could be deployed in line.'

[1] ' Phalanx ' is misleading; the Macedonian foot could not

326
B.C.

ander launched his mounted archers, about a thousand strong, at the Indians' left wing,[3] to throw into confusion the enemy stationed there by the density of the volleys as well as by the horses charging. He himself with the Companions' cavalry rode at full speed against the enemy left, as he was anxious to attack them in their confusion, while they were still in column formation, before their cavalry could be deployed in line.[4]

17. Meantime the Indians, concentrating all their cavalry from every quarter, kept riding parallel to Alexander to match and oppose his movement, and Coenus and his troops, according to orders, began to appear in their rear. Seeing this, the Indians were compelled to form their cavalry so that it faced both ways; the more numerous and strongest part confronted Alexander, the rest wheeled against Coenus and his force. This of course at once upset both the 2 lines and the minds of the Indians, and Alexander, seeing his opportunity exactly in this redeployment of the cavalry, attacked those on his front, with such effect that the Indians did not even wait to receive the charge of his cavalry, but were broken and driven back to their elephants, as if to some friendly wall. At this point the drivers of the elephants brought up 3 their animals against the cavalry, and the Macedonian phalanx for its part boldly advanced to meet the elephants, hurling javelins at their drivers, and, forming a ring round the animals, volleyed upon them from all sides.[1] And the action was now without

have kept their dense formation if they had formed rings round the elephants, and they had no javelins; QC. 14, 24 rightly refers to Agrianians and Thracians. D. 88 and QC. 14, 18 ff. emphasize the confusion. (In 23, 2 A. means by 'phalanx' soldiers normally arrayed in phalanx-formation, even though they had lost that formation.)

ἐοικός· τά τε γὰρ θηρία ἐπεκθέοντα ἐς τὰς τάξεις τῶν πεζῶν, ὅπῃ ἐπιστρέψειεν, ἐκεράϊζε καίπερ πυκνὴν οὖσαν τὴν τῶν Μακεδόνων φάλαγγα, καὶ οἱ ἱππεῖς οἱ τῶν Ἰνδῶν τοῖς πεζοῖς ἰδόντες ξυνεστηκὸς τὸ ἔργον ἐπιστρέψαντες αὖθις καὶ αὐτοὶ
4 ἐπήλαυνον τῇ ἵππῳ. ὡς δὲ πάλιν ἐκράτησαν αὐτῶν οἱ ἀμφ᾽ Ἀλέξανδρον τῇ τε ῥώμῃ καὶ τῇ ἐμπειρίᾳ πολὺ προέχοντες, ὡς ⟨ἐπὶ⟩ τοὺς ἐλέφαντας αὖθις κατειλήθησαν. καὶ ἐν τούτῳ πᾶσα ἡ ἵππος Ἀλεξάνδρῳ ἐς μίαν ἴλην ἤδη ξυνηγμένη, οὐκ ἐκ παραγγέλματος, ἀλλὰ ἐν τῷ ἀγῶνι αὐτῷ ἐς τήνδε τὴν τάξιν καταστᾶσα, ὅπῃ προσπέσοι τῶν Ἰνδῶν ταῖς τάξεσι, ξὺν πολλῷ φόνῳ ἀπελύοντο.
5 καὶ ἐς στενὸν ἤδη κατειλημ[μ]ένων τῶν θηρίων οὐ μείω πρὸς αὐτῶν οἱ φίλιοι ἤπερ οἱ πολέμιοι ἐβλάπτοντο ἐν ταῖς ἐπιστροφαῖς τε καὶ τοῖς ὠθισμοῖς καταπατούμενοι. τῶν τε οὖν ἱππέων, οἷα δὴ ἐν στενῷ περὶ τοὺς ἐλέφαντας εἰλουμένων, πολὺς φόνος ἐγίγνετο καὶ οἱ ἡγεμόνες τῶν ἐλεφάντων οἱ πολλοὶ κατηκοντισμένοι ἦσαν, καὶ αὐτοὶ οἱ ἐλέφαντες τὰ μὲν τιτρωσκόμενοι, τὰ δὲ ὑπό τε τῶν πόνων καὶ ἐρημίᾳ ἡγεμόνων οὐκέτι διακεκριμένοι ἐν
6 τῇ μάχῃ ἦσαν, ἀλλ᾽ οἷα δὴ ὑπὸ τοῦ κακοῦ ἔκφρονες φιλίοις τε ὁμοῦ καὶ πολεμίοις προσφερόμενοι πάντα τρόπον ἐξώθουν τε καὶ κατεπάτουν καὶ κατέκαινον. ἀλλ᾽ οἱ μὲν Μακεδόνες, ἅτε ἐν εὐρυχωρίᾳ τε καὶ κατὰ γνώμην τὴν σφῶν προσφερόμενοι τοῖς θηρίοις, ὅπῃ μὲν ἐπιφέροιντο εἶκον, ἀποστραφέντων δὲ εἴχοντο ἐσακοντίζοντες· οἱ δὲ Ἰνδοὶ ἐν αὐτοῖς ἀναστρεφόμενοι τὰ πλείω ἤδη πρὸς ἐκείνων
7 ἐβλάπτοντο. ὡς δὲ καματηρά τε ἦν τὰ θηρία καὶ οὐκέτι αὐτοῖς ἐρρωμέναι αἱ ἐκδρομαὶ ἐγίγνοντο,

326
B.C.

parallel in any previous contest, for the beasts charged
into the line of infantry and, whichever way they
turned, began to devastate the Macedonian phalanx,
dense though it was, while the Indian cavalry, seeing
the infantry fully engaged, wheeled again and themselves charged the cavalry. But when Alexander's 4
forces had the mastery over them a second time, as
they were much superior both in strength and
experience, they were again pressed back on to the
elephants. At this point all Alexander's cavalry had
become concentrated in one squadron, not under
orders but forced into this concentration in the very
conflict, and wherever it fell upon the Indian ranks
they escaped only with heavy slaughter. The ele- 5
phants were now crowded into a narrow space, and
their own side were as much damaged by them as the
enemy, and trodden down in their turnings and
jostlings. Among the Indian cavalry, cramped
round the elephants in a narrow space, there was great
carnage; and most of the drivers of the elephants
had been shot down, some of the elephants had been
wounded, others were weary and had lost their
drivers; they no longer kept their separate formation in the battle but, as if maddened by suffering, 6
attacked friends and foes alike and in all sorts of ways
kept pushing, trampling, and destroying. The
Macedonians, however, had plenty of room, and
attacked the animals at their own judgement, giving
way wherever they charged, but following close as
they turned round, and shooting at them with javelins, whereas the Indians who were retreating
among the elephants were now receiving most
damage from them. As the beasts wearied and no 7
longer made vigorous charges, but merely trumpeted

ἀλλὰ συριγμῷ μόνον διαχρώμενα ὥσπερ αἱ
πρύμναν κρουόμεναι νῆες ἐπὶ πόδα ὑπεχώρουν,
αὐτὸς μὲν ᾿Αλέξανδρος περιβάλλει ἐν κύκλῳ τὴν
ἵππον τῇ πάσῃ τάξει, τοὺς πεζοὺς δὲ ξυνασπίσαντας
ὡς ἐς πυκνοτάτην ξύγκλεισιν ἐπάγειν τὴν φάλαγγα
ἐσήμηνε. καὶ οὕτως οἱ μὲν ἱππεῖς τῶν ᾿Ινδῶν
πλὴν ὀλίγων κατεκόπησαν ἐν τῷ ἔργῳ· ἐκόπτοντο
δὲ καὶ οἱ πεζοὶ πανταχόθεν ἤδη προσκειμένων σφίσι
τῶν Μακεδόνων. καὶ ἐν τούτῳ ἵνα διέσχεν ἡ
ἵππος ἡ ᾿Αλεξάνδρου ἐς φυγὴν πάντες ἐπεστράφησαν.
18. Καὶ ἐν τῷ αὐτῷ Κρατερός τε καὶ οἱ ἄλλοι
ὅσοι τῆς στρατιᾶς [τε] τῆς ᾿Αλεξάνδρου ἐπὶ τῇ
ὄχθῃ τοῦ ῾Υδάσπου ὑπολελειμμένοι ἡγεμόνες
ἦσαν, ὡς νικῶντα λαμπρῶς κατεῖδον ᾿Αλέξανδρον,
ἐπέρων καὶ αὐτοὶ τὸν πόρον. καὶ οὗτοι οὐ μείονα
τὸν φόνον ἐν τῇ ἀποχωρήσει τῶν ᾿Ινδῶν ἐποίησαν,
ἀκμῆτες ἀντὶ κεκμηκότων τῶν ἀμφ᾿ ᾿Αλέξανδρον
ἐπιγενόμενοι τῇ διώξει.

2   ᾿Απέθανον δὲ τῶν ᾿Ινδῶν πεζοὶ μὲν ὀλίγον ἀποδέοντες τῶν δισμυρίων, ἱππεῖς δὲ ἐς τρισχιλίους,
τὰ δὲ ἅρματα ξύμπαντα κατεκόπη· καὶ Πώρου
δύο παῖδες ἀπέθανον καὶ Σπιτάκης ὁ νομάρχης
τῶν ταύτῃ ᾿Ινδῶν καὶ τῶν ἐλεφάντων καὶ ἁρμάτων οἱ
ἡγεμόνες καὶ οἱ ἱππάρχαι καὶ οἱ στρατηγοὶ τῆς
στρατιᾶς τῆς Πώρου ξύμπαντες..... ἐλήφθησαν
δὲ καὶ οἱ ἐλέφαντες, ὅσοι γε αὐτῶν μὴ αὐτοῦ

3   ἀπέθανον. τῶν δὲ ἀμφ᾿ ᾿Αλέξανδρον πεζοὶ μὲν ἀπὸ
ἑξακισχιλίων τῶν ἐν τῇ πρώτῃ προσβολῇ γενο-
μένων ἐς ὀγδοήκοντα μάλιστα ἀπέθανον· ἱππεῖς
δὲ τῶν μὲν ἱπποτοξοτῶν, οἳ δὴ καὶ πρῶτοι τοῦ
ἔργου ἥψαντο, δέκα· τῆς δὲ ἑταιρικῆς ἵππου ἀμφὶ
τοὺς εἴκοσι· τῶν δὲ ἄλλων ἱππέων ὡς διακόσιοι.

and gradually retired like ships backing water, Alex- 326 B.C.
ander himself threw his cavalry in a circle around their
whole division, and then gave a signal for the infantry
to lock shields, concentrate into the most compact
mass possible and advance the phalanx. In this way
the Indian cavalry were cut down in the action with
few exceptions, while their infantry too were falling,
as the Macedonians were by this time pressing them
on all sides. At this point, where a gap appeared in
Alexander's cavalry, they all turned and fled.

18. At the same time Craterus and the others who
had been left behind as commanders of Alexander's
army on the bank of the Hydaspes, seeing Alexander
carrying off a brilliant victory, themselves began to
cross the river, and wrought equal slaughter in the
Indian retreat, coming fresh to join in the pursuit, in
place of Alexander's wearied troops.[1]

The Indians lost nearly twenty thousand foot, and 2
up to three thousand horsemen; all the chariots were
broken to pieces; two sons of Porus perished, with
Spitaces,[2] the nomarch of the Indians of this district,
the commanders of the elephants and the cavalry and
the generals of Porus' army to a man . . . and all the
surviving elephants were captured. Alexander's 3
army lost about eighty foot-soldiers at most out of a
force which had been six thousand strong in the first
attack; as for the cavalry, ten of the mounted archers,
who were the first to engage, and about twenty of the
Companions' cavalry with two hundred other troopers
were killed.[3]

[1] Only A. records this.
[2] 14, 4 n.; App. XVII 16.
[3] But cf. 14, 1 n. Variant casualty figures in D. 89.

4 Πῶρος δὲ μεγάλα ἔργα ἐν τῇ μάχῃ ἀποδειξά-
μενος μὴ ὅτι στρατηγοῦ, ἀλλὰ καὶ στρατιώτου
γενναίου, ὡς τῶν τε ἱππέων τὸν φόνον κατεῖδε καὶ
τῶν ἐλεφάντων τοὺς μὲν αὐτοῦ πεπτωκότας, τοὺς
δὲ ἐρήμους τῶν ἡγεμόνων λυπηροὺς πλανωμένους,
τῶν δὲ πεζῶν αὐτῷ οἱ πλείους ἀπολώλεσαν, οὐχ
ᾗπερ Δαρεῖος ὁ μέγας βασιλεὺς ἐξάρχων τοῖς ἀμφ'
5 αὐτὸν τῆς φυγῆς ἀπεχώρει, ἀλλὰ ἔστε γὰρ ὑπέμενέ
τι τῶν Ἰνδῶν ἐν τῇ μάχῃ ξυνεστηκός, ἐς τοσόνδε
ἀγωνισάμενος, τετρωμένος δὲ τὸν δεξιὸν ὦμον, ὃν
δὴ γυμνὸν μόνον ἔχων ἐν τῇ μάχῃ ἀνεστρέφετο
(ἀπὸ γὰρ τοῦ ἄλλου σώματος ἤρκει αὐτῷ τὰ βέλη
ὁ θώραξ περιττὸς ὢν κατά τε τὴν ἰσχὺν καὶ τὴν
ἁρμονίαν, ὡς ὕστερον καταμαθεῖν θεωμένοις ἦν),
τότε δὴ καὶ αὐτὸς ἀπεχώρει ἐπιστρέψας τὸν ἐλέφαν-
6 τα. καὶ Ἀλέξανδρος μέγαν τε αὐτὸν καὶ γενναῖον
ἄνδρα ἰδὼν ἐν τῇ μάχῃ σῶσαι ἐπεθύμησε. πέμπει
δὴ παρ' αὐτὸν πρῶτα μὲν Ταξίλην τὸν Ἰνδόν· καὶ
Ταξίλης προσιππεύσας ἐφ' ὅσον οἱ ἀσφαλὲς
ἐφαίνετο τῷ ἐλέφαντι ὃς ἔφερε τὸν Πῶρον ἐπι-
στῆσαί τε ἠξίου τὸ θηρίον, οὐ γὰρ εἶναί οἱ ἔτι
φεύγειν, καὶ ἀκοῦσαι τῶν παρ' Ἀλεξάνδρου λόγων.
7 ὁ δὲ ἰδὼν ἄνδρα ἐχθρὸν ἐκ παλαιοῦ τὸν Ταξίλην
ἐπιστρέψας ἀνήγετο ὡς ἀκοντίσων· καὶ ἂν καὶ
κατέκανε τυχόν, εἰ μὴ ὑποφθάσας ἐκεῖνος ἀπήλασεν
ἀπὸ τοῦ Πώρου πρόσω τὸν ἵππον. Ἀλέξανδρος
δὲ οὐδὲ ἐπὶ τῷδε τῷ Πώρῳ χαλεπὸς ἐγένετο, ἀλλ'
ἄλλους τε ἐν μέρει ἔπεμπε καὶ δὴ καὶ Μερόην
ἄνδρα Ἰνδόν, ὅτι φίλον εἶναι ἐκ παλαιοῦ τῷ Πώρῳ
τὸν Μερόην ἔμαθεν. Πῶρος δὲ ὡς τὰ παρὰ τοῦ
Μερόου ἤκουσε καὶ ἐκ τοῦ δίψους ἅμα ἐκρατεῖτο,
ἐπέστησέ τε τὸν ἐλέφαντα καὶ κατέβη ἀπ' αὐτοῦ·

Porus had acquitted himself manfully in the battle not only as a commander-in-chief but also as a brave soldier; but when he saw the slaughter of his cavalry, some of the elephants fallen on the field and others wandering in distress after losing their riders, and when most of his infantry had perished, unlike the great king Darius, he still did not set his own men an example of flight, but battled on, so long as any part of the Indian troops held their ground in the fight as an organized unit; only when wounded in the right shoulder (the one part of his body unprotected as he moved about in the battle, for the missiles were kept off the rest of his body by his corslet which was unusually strong and well fitted, as those who saw afterwards could observe) did he too at last wheel his elephant round and retreat. Alexander, having seen him play a great and gallant part in the battle, desired to save his life. So he sent to him first Taxilas the Indian, who rode up as near as he thought safe to the elephant carrying Porus and required him to halt the beast, since further flight was unavailing, and to hear Alexander's message. But Porus saw in Taxilas an old enemy, turned his elephant and rode up to pierce him with a javelin; and he might perhaps have killed him, had not Taxilas in anticipation wheeled his horse further away from Porus. Even then Alexander did not show anger against Porus, but sent others one after another, and finally an Indian, Meroes, as he learnt that Meroes was an old friend of Porus. On hearing Meroes' message, Porus, who was also overcome by thirst, halted his elephant and dis-

4 _{326 B.C.}

5

6

7

ὡς δὲ ἔπιέ τε καὶ ἀνέψυξεν, ἄγειν αὐτὸν σπουδῇ
ἐκέλευσεν παρὰ ᾿Αλέξανδρον.

19. Καὶ ὁ μὲν ἤγετο· ᾿Αλέξανδρος δὲ ὡς προσάγοντα ἐπύθετο, προσιππεύσας πρὸ τῆς τάξεως ξὺν
ὀλίγοις τῶν ἑταίρων ἀπαντᾷ τῷ Πώρῳ· καὶ
ἐπιστήσας τὸν ἵππον τό τε μέγεθος ἐθαύμαζεν,
ὑπὲρ πέντε πήχεις μάλιστα ξυμβαῖνον, καὶ τὸ
κάλλος τοῦ Πώρου καὶ ὅτι οὐ δεδουλωμένος τῇ
γνώμῃ ἐφαίνετο, ἀλλ᾿ ὥσπερ ⟨ἂν⟩ ἀνὴρ ἀγαθὸς
ἀνδρὶ ἀγαθῷ προσέλθοι ὑπὲρ βασιλείας τῆς αὑτοῦ
2 πρὸς βασιλέα ἄλλον καλῶς ἠγωνισμένος. ἔνθα δὴ
᾿Αλέξανδρος πρῶτος προσειπὼν αὐτὸν λέγειν ἐκέλευσεν ὅ τι οἱ γενέσθαι ἐθέλοι. Πῶρον δὲ ἀπο-
κρίνασθαι λόγος ὅτι· βασιλικῶς μοι χρῆσαι, ὦ
᾿Αλέξανδρε. καὶ ᾿Αλέξανδρος ἡσθεὶς τῷ λόγῳ,
τοῦτο μὲν ἔσται σοι, ἔφη, ὦ Πῶρε, ἐμοῦ ἕνεκα·
σὺ δὲ σαυτοῦ ἕνεκα ὅ τι σοὶ φίλον ἀξίου. ὁ δὲ
3 πάντα ἔφη ἐν τούτῳ ἐνεῖναι. καὶ ᾿Αλέξανδρος
τούτῳ ἔτι μᾶλλον τῷ λόγῳ ἡσθεὶς τήν τε ἀρχὴν
τῷ Πώρῳ τῶν τε αὐτῶν ᾿Ινδῶν ἔδωκεν καὶ ἄλλην
ἔτι χώραν πρὸς τῇ πάλαι οὔσῃ πλείονα τῆς πρόσθεν
προσέθηκεν· καὶ οὕτως αὐτός τε βασιλικῶς κεχρημένος ἦν ἀνδρὶ ἀγαθῷ καὶ ἐκείνῳ ἐκ τούτου ἐς
ἅπαντα πιστῷ ἐχρήσατο. τοῦτο τὸ τέλος τῇ μάχῃ
τῇ πρὸς Πῶρόν τε καὶ τοὺς ἐπέκεινα τοῦ ῾Υδάσ-
που ποταμοῦ ᾿Ινδοὺς ᾿Αλεξάνδρῳ ἐγένετο ἐπ᾿
ἄρχοντος ᾿Αθηναίοις ῾Ηγήμονος μηνὸς Μουνυχιῶνος.
4 ῞Ινα δὲ ἡ μάχη ξυνέβη καὶ ἔνθεν ὁρμηθεὶς ἐπέ-
ρασε τὸν ῾Υδάσπην ποταμὸν πόλεις ἔκτισεν ᾿Αλέξ-

---

[4] The stories of Porus' valour and capture in D., QC. and P.
diverge from A. and *inter se.*

mounted, and after refreshing himself by drinking, told Meroes to conduct him at once to Alexander.[4]

19. Meroes did so. Learning of his approach, Alexander rode and met him in advance of the line with a few of the Companions; halting his horse, he admired the stature of Porus, who was approximately over five cubits in height,[1] his beauty, and the appearance he gave of a spirit not enslaved, but of one man of honour meeting another after a fine struggle against another king for his own kingdom. Then Alexander 2 spoke to him first and urged him to say what he desired to be done with him. Porus is said to have replied: ' Treat me, Alexander, like a king,' and Alexander, pleased with the reply, answered: ' That you shall have, Porus, for my own sake; now demand what you would wish for yours.' He replied that everything was comprised in this one request.[2] Alexander was all the more pleased with this reply, 3 and gave Porus the government of his Indians and added still further territory even greater in extent to his old realm.[3] In this way he himself acted like a king in his treatment of a man of honour, while in Porus he found from this time entire fidelity. This then was the issue of the battle of Alexander against Porus and the Indians on the far side of the Hydaspes in the archonship of Hegemon at Athens and the month Munychion.[4]

In the place where the battle was fought and in that 4 from which he set out to cross the Hydaspes Alexander

---

[1] Hamilton on P. 60, 6 for divergent estimates; cf. Tarn ii 169 f., who takes them too seriously.

[2] So too P. 60, 7, embellished in QC. 14, 41 ff. A. follows Pt./Ar. Other romantic incidents in their works: ii 12, 3–6 (both); iii 17, 6; 30, 4 and S. vii 3, 8 (Pt.); Ar. F 2. Cf. § 4–6.

[3] App. XVII 32.

[4] App. XVII 14 f.

ανδρος. καὶ τὴν μὲν Νίκαιαν τῆς νίκης τῆς κατ'
Ἰνδῶν ἐπώνυμον ὠνόμασε, τὴν δὲ Βουκεφάλαν ἐς
τοῦ ἵππου τοῦ Βουκεφάλα τὴν μνήμην, ὃς ἀπέθανεν
5 αὐτοῦ, οὐ βληθεὶς πρὸς οὐδενός, ἀλλὰ ὑπὸ καύματος
τε καὶ ἡλικίας (ἦν γὰρ ἀμφὶ τὰ τριάκοντα ἔτη)
καματηρὸς γενόμενος, πολλὰ δὲ πρόσθεν ξυγκαμών
τε καὶ συγκινδυνεύσας Ἀλεξάνδρῳ, ἀναβαινόμενός
τε πρὸς μόνου Ἀλεξάνδρου [ὁ Βουκεφάλας οὗτος],
ὅτι τοὺς ἄλλους πάντας ἀπηξίου ἀμβάτας, καὶ
μεγέθει μέγας καὶ τῷ θυμῷ γενναῖος. σημεῖον δέ
οἱ ἦν βοὸς κεφαλὴ ἐγκεχαραγμένη, ἐφ' ὅτῳ καὶ τὸ
ὄνομα τοῦτο λέγουσιν ὅτι ἔφερεν· οἱ δὲ λέγουσιν
ὅτι λευκὸν σῆμα εἶχεν ἐπὶ τῆς κεφαλῆς, μέλας ὢν
6 αὐτός, ἐς βοὸς κεφαλὴν μάλιστα εἰκασμένον. οὗτος
ὁ ἵππος ἐν τῇ Οὐξίων χώρᾳ ἀφανὴς ἐγένετο
Ἀλεξάνδρῳ, καὶ Ἀλέξανδρος προεκήρυξεν ἀνὰ τὴν
χώραν πάντας ἀποκτενεῖν Οὐξίους, εἰ μὴ ἀπάξουσιν
αὐτῷ τὸν ἵππον· καὶ ἀπήχθη εὐθὺς ἐπὶ τῷ
κηρύγματι. τοσήδε μὲν σπουδὴ Ἀλεξάνδρῳ ἀμφ'
αὐτὸν ἦν, τόσος δὲ Ἀλεξάνδρου φόβος τοῖς βαρβάροις. καὶ ἐμοὶ ἐς τοσόνδε τετιμήσθω ὁ Βουκεφάλας οὗτος Ἀλεξάνδρου ἕνεκα.

20. Ἀλεξάνδρῳ δὲ ἐπειδὴ οἱ ἀποθανόντες ἐν τῇ
μάχῃ κεκόσμηντο τῷ πρέποντι κόσμῳ, ὁ δὲ τοῖς
θεοῖς τὰ νομιζόμενα ἐπινίκια ἔθυε, καὶ ἀγὼν ἐποιεῖτο
αὐτῷ γυμνικὸς καὶ ἱππικὸς αὐτοῦ ἐπὶ τῇ ὄχθῃ
τοῦ Ὑδάσπου, ἵναπερ τὸ πρῶτον διέβη ἅμα τῷ
2 στρατῷ. Κρατερὸν μὲν δὴ ξὺν μέρει τῆς στρατιᾶς
ὑπελείπετο τὰς πόλεις ἅστινας ταύτῃ ἔκτιζεν ἀνα-
στήσοντά τε καὶ ἐκτειχιοῦντα· αὐτὸς δὲ ἤλαυνεν ὡς

---

[5] *Contra* Tarn ii 236 f., A. like QC. ix 1, 6 places the cities on

founded cities. One was called Nicaea from the victory (*nikê*) over the Indians, the other Bucephala,[5] in memory of his horse Bucephalas which died there, not wounded by anyone, but worn out by heat and age; he was about thirty years old; up to then 5 he had shared Alexander's numerous exertions and dangers and had never been mounted by anyone but Alexander himself, since he would brook no other rider; his size was large and his spirit noble. His mark was an ox-head (*boos kephale*) branded upon him; hence, they say, his name Bucephalas; others, however, say that he was black except for a white mark on his head, which was exactly like an ox-head. In the Uxian country Alexander once lost him, and 6 issued a proclamation throughout the country that he would kill every Uxian unless they brought him back his horse; he was brought back immediately after the proclamation.[6] Such was Alexander's devotion to him, and such was the terror he inspired in the barbarians. So much I had to say in praise of this Bucephalas for Alexander's sake.

20. As soon as the due tributes of respect had been paid to those who fell in the battle, Alexander sacrificed to the gods the customary thanksgivings of victory, and held athletic and equestrian games on the bank of the Hydaspes where he first crossed with his army. Craterus, with part of the forces, was left 2 behind to build and fortify the cities he was founding there. He himself advanced towards the Indians

---

opposite banks (D. 89, 6, who does not, is muddled), and as Nicaea commemorates the victory, Bucephala must be on the west bank.

[6] Clitarchus evidently located this in the Mardian land (D. 76, 3 ff.; QC. vi 5, 11 ff.); P. 44 is vague.

ἐπὶ τοὺς προσχώρους τῇ Πώρου ἀρχῇ Ἰνδούς. ὄνομα δὲ ἦν τῷ ἔθνει Γλαυγανῖκαι, ὡς λέγει Ἀριστόβουλος, ὡς δὲ Πτολεμαῖος, Γλαῦσαι. ὁπο-
3 τέρως δὲ ἔχει τὸ ὄνομα οὔ μοι μέλει. ἐπῄει δὲ τὴν χώραν αὐτῶν Ἀλέξανδρος τῶν τε ἑταίρων ἱππέων ἔχων τοὺς ἡμίσεας καὶ τῶν πεζῶν ἀπὸ φάλαγγος ἑκάστης ἐπιλέκτους καὶ τοὺς ἱπποτοξότας σύμπαντας καὶ τοὺς Ἀγριᾶνας καὶ τοὺς τοξότας·
4 καὶ προσεχώρουν αὐτῷ ὁμολογίᾳ πάντες. καὶ ἔλαβε πόλεις μὲν ἐς τριάκοντα καὶ ἑπτά, ὧν ἵνα ὀλίγιστοι ἦσαν οἰκήτορες πεντακισχιλίων οὐκ ἐλάττους ἦσαν, πολλῶν δὲ καὶ ὑπὲρ τοὺς μυρίους· καὶ κώμας πλήθει τε πολλὰς ἔλαβε καὶ πολυανθρώπους οὐ μεῖον τῶν πόλεων. καὶ ταύτης τῆς χώρας Πώρῳ ἄρχειν ἔδωκεν. καὶ Ταξίλῃ δὲ διαλλάττει Πῶρον καὶ Ταξίλην ἀποπέμπει ὀπίσω ἐς τὰ ἤθη τὰ αὑτοῦ.

5 Ἐν τούτῳ δὲ παρά τε Ἀβισάρου πρέσβεις ἧκον, ἐνδιδόντες αὐτόν τε Ἀλεξάνδρῳ Ἀβισάρην καὶ τὴν χώραν ὅσης ἦρχε. καίτοι πρό γε τῆς μάχης τῆς πρὸς Πῶρον γενομένης Ἀλεξάνδρῳ ἐπενόει Ἀβι-σάρης καὶ αὐτὸς ξὺν Πώρῳ τάττεσθαι· τότε δὲ καὶ τὸν ἀδελφὸν τὸν αὑτοῦ ξὺν τοῖς ἄλλοις πρέσ-βεσι παρ' Ἀλέξανδρον ἔπεμψε, χρήματά τε κομί-ζοντα καὶ ἐλέφαντας τεσσαράκοντα δῶρον Ἀλεξ-
6 άνδρῳ. ἧκον δὲ καὶ παρὰ τῶν αὐτονόμων Ἰνδῶν πρέσβεις παρ' Ἀλέξανδρον καὶ παρὰ Πώρου ἄλλου του ὑπάρχου Ἰνδῶν. Ἀλέξανδρος δὲ Ἀβισάρην διὰ τάχους ἰέναι παρ' αὐτὸν κελεύει ἐπαπειλήσας,

---

[1] App. XVII 18 f.
[2] Probably it was mere caprice in A. to mention this par-

who bordered on Porus' realm.[1] The name of the
tribe was Glauganicae, as Aristobulus says, but
Ptolemy calls them Glausae; I do not mind which
was the name.[2] Alexander invaded their country 3
with half of the Companions' cavalry and picked men
of the infantry from each phalanx,[3] all the mounted
archers, the Agrianians, and the (unmounted) archers; and the tribesmen all came over to him by
agreement. So he acquired some thirty-seven cities, 4
of which the least had above five thousand inhabitants, and many over ten thousand. The villages he
acquired were numerous and not less populous than
the cities.[4] He gave the government of this country
to Porus, whom he reconciled to Taxilas, and then
sent Taxilas back to his own lands.

At this point [5] envoys came from Abisares, offering 5
to surrender to Alexander his own person and the
country over which he ruled. And yet before the
battle with Porus, Abisares too had the intention of
ranging himself on Porus' side. But now he sent his
own brother with the other envoys to Alexander, con-
veying money and forty elephants as a gift to him.
Envoys also came to Alexander from the self-govern- 6
ing Indians, and from another Porus, a hyparch of
Indians.[6] Alexander ordered Abisares to come to
him quickly, threatening, if he did not appear, that

ticular discrepancy in nomenclature, cf. App. XVII 18a;
XXVIII 25.

[3] ' Phalanx ' for the more usual ' taxis ' or regiment of
Macedonian foot, cf. i 14, 2; iii 9, 6; v 21, 5. If it is Ar's
term (Bosworth, *Harv. St. Class. Phil.* 1977, 249), evidence from
Ar. is deeply imbedded in A's military narratives. Cf. Bosworth on i 14, 2; 24, 3.

[4] Such figures need not be believed.

[5] But before Al. left the Hydaspes in D. 90, 4; QC. ix 1, 7.

[6] ' Hyparch ' does not mean that he was a rebel subordinate
of the good Porus, cf. App. XIV 2.

εἰ μὴ ἔλθοι, ὅτι αὐτὸν ὄψεται ἥκοντα ξὺν τῇ στρατιᾷ
ἵνα οὐ χαιρήσει ἰδών.

7 Ἐν τούτῳ δὲ Φραταφέρνης τε ὁ Παρθυαίων καὶ
Ὑρκανίας σατράπης τοὺς καταλειφθέντας παρὰ οἷ
Θρᾷκας ἄγων ἧκεν ὡς Ἀλέξανδρον καὶ παρὰ
Σισικόττου τοῦ Ἀσσακηνῶν σατράπου ἄγγελοι,
ὅτι τόν τε ὕπαρχον σφῶν ἀπεκτονότες εἶεν οἱ Ἀσσα-
κηνοὶ καὶ ἀπ᾿ Ἀλεξάνδρου ἀφεστηκότες. καὶ ἐπὶ
τούτους Φίλιππον ἐκπέμπει καὶ Τυρίεσπιν σὺν
στρατιᾷ τὰ περὶ τὴν Ἀσσακηνῶν χώραν καταστη-
σομένους καὶ κοσμήσοντας.

8 Αὐτὸς δὲ ὡς ἐπὶ τὸν Ἀκεσίνην ποταμὸν προὔ-
χώρει. τούτου τοῦ Ἀκεσίνου τὸ μέγεθος μόνου
τῶν Ἰνδῶν ποταμῶν Πτολεμαῖος ὁ Λάγου ἀνέγρα-
ψεν· εἶναι γὰρ ἵνα ἐπέρασεν αὐτὸν Ἀλέξανδρος
ἐπὶ τῶν πλοίων τε καὶ τῶν διφθερῶν ξὺν τῇ στρατιᾷ
τὸ μὲν ῥεῦμα ὀξὺ τοῦ Ἀκεσίνου πέτραις μεγάλαις
καὶ ὀξείαις, καθ᾿ ὧν φερόμενον βίᾳ τὸ ὕδωρ κυμαί-
νεσθαί τε καὶ καχλάζειν, τὸ δὲ εὖρος σταδίους
9 ἐπέχειν πεντεκαίδεκα. τοῖς μὲν δὴ ἐπὶ τῶν
διφθερῶν περῶσιν εὐμαρῆ γενέσθαι τὸν πόρον, τοὺς
δὲ ἐν τοῖς πλοίοις διαβάλλοντας ἐποκειλάντων
πολλῶν πλοίων ἐπὶ ταῖς πέτραις καὶ συναρ[ρ]αχθέν-
των οὐκ ὀλίγους αὐτοῦ ἐν τῷ ὕδατι διαφθαρῆναι.
10 εἴη ἂν οὖν ἐκ τοῦδε τοῦ λόγου ξυντιθέντι τεκμηριοῦσθαι, ὅτι οὐ πόρρω τοῦ ἀληθοῦς ἀναγέγραπται
τοῦ Ἰνδοῦ ποταμοῦ τὸ μέγεθος, ὅσοις ἐς τεσσαράκοντα σταδίους δοκεῖ τοῦ Ἰνδοῦ εἶναι τὸ εὖρος,
ἵνα μέσως ἔχει αὐτὸς αὐτοῦ [ὁ Ἰνδός]·[1] ἵνα δὲ

---

[1] Roos suggested deletion.

Abisares would see him come with his army, and would rue the sight.

At this point Phrataphernes, the satrap of Parthyaea and Hyrcania, came to Alexander, bringing the Thracians left behind with him [7]; messengers also arrived from Sisicottus, satrap of the Assacenians,[8] to say that they had assassinated their hyparch and had revolted from Alexander. Alexander sent Philippus and Tyriespis against them with an army, to settle affairs round the Assacenian country and establish order.

He himself moved towards the Acesines [Chenab]. The river Acesines is the only river of India whose size Ptolemy son of Lagus has described; its stream, he says, at the point where Alexander crossed it with his army on the boats and hides is very swift, with great, sharp rocks; the water rushes down over them, billowing and roaring; the breadth is fifteen stades. For those who crossed on the hides, he says, the crossing was easy; but many of those who made the transit in the boats were lost in the stream, since several boats ran upon the rocks and were dashed to pieces. If then one draws inferences from this account one may show that writers are not far from the truth who have given the apparent size of the river Indus as above forty stades wide at its mean width, but that where it is narrowest, and for that reason deepest, it

[7] Nothing of Autophradates' fate (cf. iv 18, 2), for which see QC. x 1, 39.

[8] In fact commandant at Aornos (iv 30, 1); Nicanor was satrap (iv 28, 6) and is presumably the 'hyparch' killed. Philip, son of Machatas (Berve no. 780), seems to have taken over Nicanor's satrapy in addition to his own (v 8, 3; vi 2, 3); after his death (vi 27, 2) Taxilas succeeded him, and in the division of satrapies in 323 and 321 (D. xviii 3 and 39), we hear nothing of any separate satrapy corresponding to that of Nicanor.

στενότατός τε καὶ διὰ στενότητα βαθύτατος ἐς τοὺς
πεντεκαίδεκα ξυνάγεσθαι· καὶ ταῦτα πολλαχῇ
εἶναι τοῦ Ἰνδοῦ. καὶ γὰρ καὶ τοῦ Ἀκεσίνου
τεκμαίρομαι ἐπιλέξασθαι Ἀλέξανδρον, ἵναπερ τὸ
πλατύτατον ἦν τοῦ πόρου, ὡς σχολαιτέρῳ χρήσασθαι τῷ ῥεύματι.

21. Περάσας δὲ τὸν ποταμὸν Κοῖνον μὲν ξὺν τῇ
αὑτοῦ τάξει ἀπολείπει αὐτοῦ ἐπὶ τῇ ὄχθῃ προστάξας
ἐπιμελεῖσθαι τῆς ὑπολελειμμένης στρατιᾶς τῆς
διαβάσεως, οἳ τόν τε σῖτον αὐτῷ τὸν ἐκ τῆς ἤδη
ὑπηκόου τῶν Ἰνδῶν χώρας καὶ τὰ ἄλλα ἐπιτήδεια
2 παρακομίζειν ἔμελλον. Πῶρον δὲ ἐς τὰ αὑτοῦ
ἤθη ἀποπέμπει, κελεύσας Ἰνδῶν τε τοὺς μαχιμωτάτους ἐπιλεξάμενον καὶ εἴ τινας παρ' αὑτῷ
ἔχοι ἐλέφαντας, τούτους δὲ ἀναλαβόντα [s] ἰέναι
παρ' αὑτόν. αὐτὸς δὲ Πῶρον τὸν ἕτερον τὸν κακόν,
ὅτι ἐξηγγέλθη πεφευγέναι ἀπολιπὼν τὴν χώραν
ἧς ἦρχεν, ἐπενόει διώκειν σὺν τοῖς κουφοτάτοις
3 τῆς στρατιᾶς. ὁ γὰρ Πῶρος οὗτος, ἔστε μὲν
πολέμια ξυνειστήκει Ἀλεξάνδρῳ τὰ πρὸς τὸν
ἄλλον Πῶρον, πρέσβεις παρ' Ἀλέξανδρον πέμπων
αὐτόν τε καὶ τὴν ὑπὸ οἷ χώραν ἐνεδίδου Ἀλεξάνδρῳ,
κατὰ ἔχθος τὸ Πώρου μᾶλλον ἢ φιλίᾳ τῇ Ἀλεξ-
άνδρου· ὡς δὲ ἀφειμένον τε ἐκεῖνον καὶ πρὸς
τῇ αὑτοῦ καὶ ἄλλης πολλῆς ἄρχοντα ἔμαθε, τότε
δὴ φοβηθείς, οὐχ οὕτω τι Ἀλέξανδρον, ὡς τὸν
Πῶρον ἐκεῖνον τὸν ὁμώνυμον, φεύγει τὴν ἑαυτοῦ
ἀναλαβὼν ὅσους τῶν μαχίμων ξυμπεῖσαι ἠδυνήθη
μετασχεῖν οἱ τῆς φυγῆς.

[9] App. XVII 10 and 18, cf. S. xv 1, 18 (N. and Ar.) and 32.
H. T. Lambrick, *Sind*, 1964, 104 thinks S's estimates of maxi-

326
B.C.

contracts to some fifteen stades, and that this is its breadth in many places. And I conjecture that Alexander again chose the widest part of the river Acesines to cross, so that he might find the current slower.[9]

21. When he had crossed the river, Alexander left Coenus with his battalion [1] on the bank, there bidding him supervise the crossing by the army which had been left behind, who were to convoy to him the corn and all other supplies from the part of India already subject. Porus was sent back to his own lands, with 2 orders to select the most warlike of the Indians and any elephants at his disposal, and bring them to join him. Alexander purposed to pursue with the nimblest of his troops the other Porus, the bad one, because he was reported to have left his realm. For as 3 long as Alexander's relations had remained unfriendly towards the first Porus, this Porus had been sending envoys to Alexander, offering to surrender himself and the country under his rule, rather from hatred of the other Porus than from friendship for Alexander; but on learning that the latter had been released and was now ruler of much new territory besides his own, he was seized with fear not so much of Alexander as of his namesake, and fled from his country, taking with him as many of the warlike tribesmen as he could persuade to share his flight.

mum and minimum breadth as 40 and 7 stades, rejecting the maximum of 100, given by Ctesias (v 4, 2), and inconsistently accepted by A. in vi 14, 5, ' near the truth, if we allot (them) to the peak of the swell and to the slack season respectively.'

[1] 27, 1 n.; App. XIX 3. For operations in chapters 21–24 see App. XVII 20.

4 Ἐπὶ τοῦτον ἐλαύνων Ἀλέξανδρος ἀφικνεῖται
ἐπὶ τὸν Ὑδραώτην ποταμόν, ἄλλον αὖ τοῦτον
Ἰνδὸν ποταμόν, τὸ μὲν εὖρος οὐ μείονα τοῦ Ἀκεσίνου, ὀξύτητι δὲ τοῦ ῥοῦ μείονα. ὅσην δὲ τῆς
χώρας ἔστε ἐπὶ τὸν Ὑδραώτην ἐπῆλθε, φυλακὰς
ὑπέλιπεν ἐν τοῖς ἐπικαιροτάτοις χωρίοις, ὅπως οἱ
ἀμφὶ Κρατερόν τε καὶ Κοῖνον δι' ἀσφαλείας ἐπέρ-
χοιντο τῆς χώρας τὴν πολλὴν προνομεύοντες.
5 ἐνταῦθα Ἡφαιστίωνα μὲν ἐκπέμπει δοὺς αὐτῷ
μέρος τῆς στρατιᾶς, πεζῶν μὲν φάλαγγας δύο,
ἱππέων δὲ τήν τε αὐτοῦ καὶ τὴν Δημητρίου ἱππαρχίαν καὶ τῶν τοξοτῶν τοὺς ἡμίσεας, ἐς τὴν
Πώρου τοῦ ἀφεστηκότος χώραν, κελεύσας παρα-
διδόναι ταύτην Πώρῳ τῷ ἄλλῳ, καὶ εἰ δή τινα
πρὸς ταῖς ὄχθαις τοῦ Ὑδραώτου ποταμοῦ αὐτόνομα
ἔθνη Ἰνδῶν νέμεται, καὶ ταῦτα προσαγαγόμενον
6 τῷ Πώρῳ ἄρχειν ἐγχειρίσαι. αὐτὸς δ' ἐπέρα τὸν
Ὑδραώτην ποταμόν, οὐ καθάπερ τὸν Ἀκεσίνην
χαλεπῶς. προχωροῦντι δὲ αὐτῷ ἐπέκεινα τῆς
ὄχθης τοῦ Ὑδραώτου τοὺς μὲν πολλοὺς καθ'
ὁμολογίαν προσχωρεῖν ξυνέβαινεν, ἤδη δέ τινας
ξὺν ὅπλοις ἀπαντήσαντας, τοὺς δὲ καὶ ὑποφεύ-
γοντας ἑλὼν βίᾳ κατεστρέψατο.

22. Ἐν τούτῳ δὲ ἐξαγγέλλεται Ἀλεξάνδρῳ τῶν
αὐτονόμων Ἰνδῶν ἄλλους τέ τινας καὶ τοὺς καλου-
μένους Καθαίους αὐτούς τε παρασκευάζεσθαι ὡς
πρὸς μάχην, εἰ προσάγοι τῇ χώρᾳ αὐτῶν Ἀλέξανδρος, καὶ ὅσα ὅμορά σφισιν ⟨ἔθνη⟩ ὡσαύτως
αὐτόνομα, καὶ ταῦτα παρακαλεῖν ἐς τὸ ἔργον·
2 εἶναι δὲ τήν τε πόλιν ὀχυρὰν πρὸς ᾗ ἐπενόουν
ἀγωνίσασθαι, Σάγγαλα ἦν τῇ πόλει ὄνομα, καὶ
αὐτοὶ οἱ Καθαῖοι εὐτολμότατοί τε καὶ τὰ πολέμια

In his pursuit Alexander arrived at the river 4 $\begin{smallmatrix}326\\ \text{B.C.}\end{smallmatrix}$
Hydraotes [Ravi], another Indian river, as broad as
the Acesines but not so swift in current. In all the
country he traversed as far as the Hydraotes, he left
guards in the most advantageous places, so that the
troops with Craterus and Coenus might safely traverse
the greater part of the country when foraging. Here 5
he despatched Hephaestion, giving him part of the
army, two phalanxes of foot-soldiers and his own and
Demetrius' hipparchies of cavalry with half the
archers, to the country of the rebellious Porus, with
orders to hand it over to the other Porus, together
with any independent Indian tribes dwelling by the
banks of the Hydaspes; these too he was to win over
and entrust them to Porus to govern.[2] Then he him- 6
self crossed the Hydraotes, without the difficulties
which the Acesines had caused. As he advanced on
the farther bank of the Hydraotes, most of the people
came over to him by agreement, including some who
actually met him under arms; others were taken in
flight and subdued by force.

22. At this point it was reported to Alexander that
some of the self-governing Indians, in particular the
people called Cathaeans, were getting themselves
ready for battle, in case Alexander should approach
their country, and were urging to the same enterprise
all self-governing tribes on their borders; they had a 2
strong city near which they proposed to make their
stand, named Sangala. The Cathaeans themselves

---

[2] 29, 3 n.; App. XVII 32.

κράτιστοι ἐνομίζοντο, καὶ τούτοις κατὰ τὰ αὐτὰ
Ὀξυδράκαι, ἄλλο Ἰνδῶν ἔθνος, καὶ Μαλλοί, ἄλλο
καὶ τοῦτο· ἐπεὶ καὶ ὀλίγῳ πρόσθεν στρατεύσαντας
ἐπ᾽ αὐτοὺς Πῶρόν τε καὶ Ἀβισάρην ξύν τε τῇ
σφετέρᾳ δυνάμει καὶ πολλὰ ἄλλα ἔθνη τῶν αὐτονόμων Ἰνδῶν ἀναστήσαντας οὐδὲν πράξαντας τῆς
παρασκευῆς ἄξιον ξυνέβη ἀπελθεῖν.

3   Ταῦτα ὡς ἐξηγγέλθη Ἀλεξάνδρῳ, σπουδῇ ἤλαυνεν ὡς ἐπὶ τοὺς Καθαίους. καὶ δευτεραῖος μὲν
ἀπὸ τοῦ ποταμοῦ τοῦ Ὑδραώτου πρὸς πόλιν ἦκεν
ᾗ ὄνομα Πίμπραμα· τὸ δὲ ἔθνος τοῦτο τῶν Ἰνδῶν
4   Ἀδραῖσται ἐκαλοῦντο. οὗτοι μὲν δὴ προσεχώρησαν ὁμολογίᾳ Ἀλεξάνδρῳ. καὶ Ἀλέξανδρος ἀναπαύσας τῇ ὑστεραίᾳ τὴν στρατιὰν τῇ τρίτῃ
προὐχώρει ἐπὶ τὰ Σάγγαλα, ἵνα οἱ Καθαῖοί τε καὶ
οἱ ἄλλοι πρόσχωροι αὐτοῖς ξυνεληλυθότες πρὸ τῆς
πόλεως παρατεταγμένοι ἦσαν ἐπὶ γηλόφου οὐ
πάντῃ ἀποτόμου· κύκλῳ δὲ τοῦ γηλόφου ἁμάξας
περιστήσαντες ἐντὸς αὐτῶν ἐστρατοπέδευον, ὡς
τριπλοῦν χάρακα προβεβλῆσθαι [πρὸ] τῶν ἁμαξῶν.
5   Ἀλέξανδρος δὲ τό τε πλῆθος κατιδὼν τῶν βαρβάρων καὶ τοῦ χωρίου τὴν φύσιν, ὡς μάλιστα πρὸς τὰ
παρόντα ἐν καιρῷ οἱ ἐφαίνετο παρετάσσετο· καὶ
τοὺς μὲν ἱπποτοξότας εὐθὺς ὡς εἶχεν ἐκπέμπει ἐπ᾽
αὐτούς, ἀκροβολίζεσθαι κελεύσας παριππεύοντας,
ὡς μήτε ἐκδρομήν τινα ποιήσασθαι τοὺς Ἰνδοὺς
πρὶν ξυνταχθῆναι αὐτῷ τὴν στρατιὰν καὶ ὡς
πληγὰς γίγνεσθαι αὐτοῖς καὶ πρὸ τῆς μάχης ἐντὸς
6   τοῦ ὀχυρώματος. αὐτὸς δὲ ἐπὶ μὲν τοῦ δεξιοῦ κέρως
τῶν ἱππέων τὸ ἄγημα κατέστησε καὶ τὴν Κλείτου
ἱππαρχίαν, ἐχομένους δὲ τούτων τοὺς ὑπασπιστάς,
καὶ ἐπὶ τούτοις τοὺς Ἀγριᾶνας· κατὰ δὲ τὸ

were considered to excel in daring and military qualities, as were two other Indian tribes, the Oxydracae and the Mallians [1]; not long before, in fact, Porus and Abisares had marched against them with their own forces and had also stirred up many other self-governing Indian tribes against them, but had achieved nothing commensurate with their resources, and had withdrawn.

When this was reported to Alexander he marched 3 at full speed against the Cathaeans. On the second day after leaving the river Hydraotes he came to a city called Pimprama; this tribe of Indians is called the Adraïstae. They came over by agreement to 4 Alexander. The next day Alexander rested his troops, and on the third advanced on Sangala, where the Cathaeans and their neighbours who had joined them were drawn up in front of the city on a hill not sheer on all sides; round about the hill they had placed their waggons and were camping within them in such a way that the waggons formed a triple palisade. Seeing the large number of the barbarians 5 and the nature of the place, Alexander made counter dispositions he thought best for the exigencies of the moment; he despatched the mounted archers without delay against them, with orders to ride along the front and shoot at long range, so that the Indians should not make any sally before he had marshalled his forces and that they might suffer casualties within their stronghold, even before the battle began. On 6 the right wing (his own station) he posted the *agema* of cavalry and Clitus' hipparchy, next to them the hypaspists, and then the Agrianians; Perdiccas was

---

[1] Cf. vi 4 ff. The text does not justify a common statement that the Cathaeans were allied with these peoples. S. and others write ' Sydracae ' for Oxydracae.

εὐώνυμον Περδίκκας αὐτῷ ἐτέτακτο τήν τε αὐτοῦ
ἔχων ἱππαρχίαν καὶ τὰς τῶν πεζεταίρων τάξεις·
ἐπὶ κέρως δὲ ἑκατέρου οἱ τοξόται αὐτῷ διχῇ
7 διακριθέντες ἐτάχθησαν. ἐκτάσσοντι δὲ αὐτῷ παρ-
εγένοντο καὶ οἱ ἀπὸ τῆς ὀπισθοφυλακίας πεζοί τε
καὶ ἱππεῖς. καὶ τούτων τοὺς μὲν ἱππέας ἐπὶ τὰ
κέρατα διελὼν παρήγαγεν, ἀπὸ δὲ τῶν πεζῶν τῶν
προσγενομένων πυκνοτέραν τὴν ξύγκλεισιν τῆς
φάλαγγος ποιήσας αὐτὸς ἀναλαβὼν τὴν ἵππον
τὴν ἐπὶ τοῦ δεξιοῦ τεταγμένην πασήγαγεν ἐπὶ τὰς
κατὰ τὸ εὐώνυμον τῶν Ἰνδῶν ἁμάξας. ταύτῃ γὰρ
εὐπροσοδώτερον αὐτῷ ἐφαίνετο τὸ χωρίον καὶ οὐ
πυκναὶ ὡσαύτως αἱ ἅμαξαι ἐφειστήκεσαν.

23. Ὡς δὲ ἐπὶ τὴν ἵππον προσαγαγοῦσαν οὐκ
ἐξέδραμον οἱ Ἰνδοὶ ἔξω τῶν ἁμαξῶν, ἀλλ' ἐπιβε-
βηκότες αὐτῶν ἀφ' ὑψηλοῦ ἠκροβολίζοντο, γνοὺς
Ἀλέξανδρος ὅτι οὐκ εἴη τῶν ἱππέων τὸ ἔργον καταπηδήσας ἀπὸ τοῦ ἵππου πεζὸς ἐπῆγε τῶν πεζῶν
2 τὴν φάλαγγα. καὶ ἀπὸ μὲν τῶν πρώτων ἁμαξῶν
οὐ χαλεπῶς ἐβιάσαντο οἱ Μακεδόνες τοὺς Ἰνδούς·
πρὸ δὲ τῶν δευτέρων οἱ Ἰνδοὶ παραταξάμενοι ῥᾶον
ἀπεμάχοντο, οἷα δὴ πυκνότεροί τε ἐφεστηκότες
ἐλάττονι τῷ κύκλῳ καὶ τῶν Μακεδόνων οὐ κατ'
εὐρυχωρίαν ὡσαύτως προσαγόντων σφίσιν, ἐν ᾧ
τάς τε πρώτας ἁμάξας ὑπεξῆγον καὶ κατὰ τὰ
διαλείμματα αὐτῶν ὡς ἑκάστοις προὐχώρει ἀτάκ-
τως προσέβαλλον· ἀλλὰ καὶ ἀπὸ τούτων ὅμως
ἐξώσθησαν οἱ Ἰνδοὶ βιασθέντες πρὸς τῆς φάλαγγος.
3 οἱ δὲ οὐκέτι ἐπὶ τῶν τρίτων ἔμενον, ἀλλὰ ὡς
τάχους εἶχον φυγῇ εἰς τὴν πόλιν κατεκλείσθησαν.
καὶ Ἀλέξανδρος ταύτην μὲν τὴν ἡμέραν περιεστρα-
τοπέδευσε τοῖς πεζοῖς τὴν πόλιν ὅσα γε ἠδυνήθη

326
B.C.

posted on his left with his own hipparchy and the battalions of the *asthetairoi*.[2] On either wing were
stationed the archers in two separate divisions.
While Alexander was thus arranging his troops, the 7
infantry and cavalry of the rearguard came up. He
divided up their cavalry and sent them off to either
wing, and used the infantry who also had come up to
increase the solidity of his phalanx. Personally
taking the cavalry posted on the right, he led them
against the waggons on the Indians' left, for on this
side the place seemed easier of access, and the waggons were not packed so closely together.

23. Since the Indians did not sally out beyond the
waggons upon the cavalry as it rode up, but stood on
them shooting from the top, Alexander, recognizing
that the action was not work for cavalry, leapt down
from his horse and led on the phalanx of foot-soldiers
on foot. The Macedonians easily forced the Indians 2
from the first line of waggons, but before the second
line the Indians drew themselves up in order and
defended themselves more easily as they were
standing in denser formation in a smaller circle, while
the Macedonians were not attacking, as before, in an
open space, but were now removing the first row of
waggons out of the way and charging in without order
through the spaces between, just as each man found a
path. Yet even from this second line the Indians
were forced back by the phalanx. They no longer 3
attempted to stand at the third line, but with all
speed retreated and shut themselves into the city.
Alexander camped this day with his infantry round

---

[2] Introd. n. 99 (vol. I); App. XIX 9.

αὐτῷ περιβαλεῖν ἡ φάλαγξ· ἐπὶ πολὺ γὰρ ἐπέχον
τὸ τεῖχος τῷ στρατοπέδῳ κυκλώσασθαι οὐ δυνατὸς
4 ἐγένετο· κατὰ δὲ τὰ διαλείποντα αὐτοῦ, ἵνα καὶ
λίμνη οὐ μακρὰν τοῦ τείχους ἦν, τοὺς ἱππέας ἐπέ-
ταξεν ἐν κύκλῳ τῆς λίμνης, γνοὺς οὐ βαθεῖαν
οὖσαν τὴν λίμνην καὶ ἅμα εἰκάσας ὅτι φοβεροὶ
γενόμενοι οἱ Ἰνδοὶ ἀπὸ τῆς προτέρας ἥττης ἀπο-
5 λείψουσι τῆς νυκτὸς τὴν πόλιν. καὶ συνέβη οὕτως
ὅπως εἴκασεν· ἀμφὶ γὰρ δευτέραν φυλακὴν ἐκπίπτ-
οντες ἐκ τοῦ τείχους οἱ πολλοὶ αὐτῶν ἐνέκυρσαν
ταῖς προφυλακαῖς τῶν ἱππέων· καὶ οἱ μὲν πρῶτοι
αὐτῶν κατεκόπησαν πρὸς τῶν ἱππέων, οἱ δὲ ἐπὶ
τούτοις αἰσθόμενοι ὅτι φυλάσσεται ἐν κύκλῳ ἡ
λίμνη ἐς τὴν πόλιν αὖθις ἀνεχώρησαν.
6   Ἀλέξανδρος δὲ χάρακί τε διπλῷ περιβάλλει
ἵναπερ μὴ εἶργεν ἡ λίμνη τὴν πόλιν καὶ φυλακὰς ἐν
κύκλῳ τῆς λίμνης ἀκριβεστέρας κατέστησεν.
αὐτὸς δὲ μηχανὰς προσάγειν τῷ τείχει ἐπενόει, ὡς
κατασείειν τὸ τεῖχος. αὐτομολήσαντες δὲ αὐτῷ
τῶν ἐκ τῆς πόλεώς τινες φράζουσιν, ὅτι ἐν νῷ
ἔχοιεν αὐτῆς ἐκείνης τῆς νυκτὸς ἐκπίπτειν ἐκ τῆς
πόλεως οἱ Ἰνδοὶ κατὰ τὴν λίμνην, ἵναπερ τὸ
7 ἐκλιπὲς ἦν τοῦ χάρακος. ὁ δὲ Πτολεμαῖον τὸν
Λάγου ἐπιτάττει ἐνταῦθα, τῶν τε ὑπασπιστῶν
αὐτῷ δοὺς χιλιαρχίας τρεῖς καὶ τοὺς Ἀγριᾶνας
ξύμπαντας καὶ μίαν τάξιν τῶν τοξοτῶν, ἀποδείξας
τὸ χωρίον, ᾗπερ μάλιστα εἴκαζε βιάσεσθαι τοὺς βαρ-
βάρους· σὺ δὲ ἐπειδὰν αἴσθῃ, ἔφη, βιαζομένους
ταύτῃ, αὐτὸς μὲν ξὺν τῇ στρατιᾷ εἶργειν τοὺς
βαρβάρους τοῦ πρόσω, τὸν δὲ σαλπιγκτὴν κέλευε
σημαίνειν· ὑμεῖς δέ, ἄνδρες ἡγεμόνες, ἐπειδὰν
σημανθῇ, ξὺν τοῖς καθ᾽ αὑτοὺς ἕκαστοι ξυντεταγ-

the city, so far at least as his phalanx could surround
it; for since the wall stretched a considerable distance
he could not encircle it with his camp, but in the re- 4
maining space, where there was also a lake not far
from the wall, he posted his cavalry around the lake,
as he noticed that it was shallow, and also conjectured
that the Indians, terrified by the previous defeat,
would desert the city at night. It happened exactly 5
as he conjectured; about the second watch most of
them emerged from the wall and fell in with the
cavalry outposts; the firstcomers were cut down by
the cavalry; those behind, perceiving that the lake
was guarded all round, retired again into the city.

Alexander threw a double stockade all round, 6
where the lake did not enclose the city, and placed
outposts round about the lake more carefully. He
planned himself to bring up engines against the wall,
to batter it down. But some of the inhabitants of
the city deserted to him and told him that the Indians
proposed to escape from the city that night by the
lake, where there was the gap in the stockade. He 7
posted Ptolemy son of Lagus there, giving him three
chiliarchies of the hypaspists,[1] all the Agrianians, and
one battalion of archers, and, pointing out the place
where he guessed the tribesmen would probably try
to break out, ' as soon,' he said, ' as you observe them
breaking out here, you yourself will, with your army,
prevent their going further and will tell the bugler to
sound an alarm; and you, officers, on this signal, will
each with his appointed forces make in the direction

---

[1] Pt. is no doubt the source; the narrative is more precise,
where he is personally concerned.

μένοι ἰέναι ἐπὶ τὸν θόρυβον, ἵνα ἂν ἡ σάλπιγξ
παρακαλῇ. ἀποστατήσω δὲ οὐδὲ ἐγὼ τοῦ ἔργου.

24. Ὁ μὲν ταῦτα παρήγγειλεν· Πτολεμαῖος δὲ
ἁμάξας τε ἐκ τῶν ἀπολελειμμένων ἐν τῇ πρώτῃ
φυγῇ ἁμαξῶν ταύτῃ ξυναγαγὼν ὡς πλείστας
κατέστησεν ἐγκαρσίας, ἵνα πολλὰ ἐν νυκτὶ τὰ
ἄπορα φαίνηται τοῖς φεύγουσι, καὶ τοῦ χάρακος τοῦ
κεκομμένου τε καὶ οὐ καταπηχθέντος συννῆσαι
ἄλλῃ καὶ ἄλλῃ ἐκέλευσεν ἐν μέσῳ τῆς τε λίμνης
καὶ τοῦ τείχους. καὶ ταῦτ' αὐτῷ οἱ στρατιῶται ἐν τῇ
2 νυκτὶ ἐξειργάσαντο. ἤδη τε ἦν ἀμφὶ τετάρτην
φυλακὴν καὶ οἱ βάρβαροι, καθάπερ ἐξηγγέλλετο
Ἀλεξάνδρῳ, ἀνοίξαντες τὰς ὡς ἐπὶ τὴν λίμνην
πύλας δρόμῳ ἐπ' αὐτὴν ἐφέροντο. οὐ μὴν ἔλαθον
τὰς ταύτῃ φυλακὰς οὐδὲ Πτολεμαῖον τὸν ἐπ'
αὐταῖς τεταγμένον, ἀλλὰ ἐν τούτῳ οἵ τε σαλπιγκταὶ
ἐσήμαινον αὐτῷ καὶ αὐτὸς τὴν στρατιὰν ὡπλισμέ-
νην τε καὶ συντεταγμένην ἔχων ἐχώρει ἐπὶ τοὺς
3 βαρβάρους. τοῖς δὲ αἵ τε ἅμαξαι ἐμποδὼν ἦσαν καὶ
ὁ χάραξ ἐν μέσῳ καταβεβλημένος· ὡς δὲ ἥ τε
σάλπιγξ ἐφθέγξατο καὶ οἱ ἀμφὶ Πτολεμαῖον προσέκειντο αὐτοῖς τοὺς ἀεὶ ἐκπίπτοντας διὰ τῶν ἁμαξῶν
κατακαίνοντες, ἐνταῦθα δὴ ἀποστρέφονται αὖθις ἐς
τὴν πόλιν. καὶ ἀπέθανον αὐτῶν ἐν τῇ ἀποχωρήσει
ἐς πεντακοσίους.

4   Ἐν τούτῳ δὲ καὶ Πῶρος ἀφίκετο τούς τε ὑπολοί-
πους ἐλέφαντας ἅμα οἷ ἄγων καὶ τῶν Ἰνδῶν ἐς
πεντακισχιλίους, αἵ τε μηχαναὶ Ἀλεξάνδρῳ ξυμπε-
πηγμέναι ἦσαν καὶ προσήγοντο ἤδη τῷ τείχει.
ἀλλὰ οἱ Μακεδόνες, πρὶν καὶ κατασεισθῆναί τι τοῦ
τείχους, ὑπορύττοντές τε αὐτοὶ πλίνθινον ὂν τὸ
τεῖχος καὶ τὰς κλίμακας ἐν κύκλῳ πάντῃ προσθέν-

326
B.C.

of the hubbub, wherever the bugle calls you. I shall be present in person at the action.'

24. These were Alexander's orders. Ptolemy, after gathering together as many as possible of the waggons left behind in the first flight, set them crosswise, in order that the difficulties might seem numerous to the fugitives at night; he ordered parts of the stockade which had been cut but not yet fixed down to be joined up at different points between the lake and the wall. His men completed this work in the night. It was now about the fourth watch, and 2 the tribesmen, as Alexander had been informed, opened the gates leading to the lake and ran towards it. Yet they did not escape detection by the guards on this side, nor by Ptolemy, who had been put in charge of them; but at once his buglers sounded the alarm, and he moved with his forces fully armed and in good order against the tribesmen, who found 3 obstacles in the waggons and the stockade thrown in the intervening space. And when the bugle sounded and Ptolemy and his troops assailed them, cutting them down as fast as they emerged between the waggons, they turned and fled back into the city. Some five hundred perished in this withdrawal.

At this point too Porus arrived, bringing with him 4 the rest of the elephants and some five thousand Indians, and Alexander had his siege engines put together, and they were already being brought up to the wall. But before any part of the wall was battered, the Macedonians themselves began to undermine it, as it was of brick, and then, setting up their ladders all round, captured the city by assault.

5 τες αἱροῦσι κατὰ κράτος τὴν πόλιν. καὶ ἀποθνήσκουσι μὲν ἐν τῇ καταλήψει τῶν Ἰνδῶν ἐς μυρίους
καὶ ἑπτακισχιλίους, ἑάλωσαν δὲ ὑπὲρ τὰς ἑπτὰ
μυριάδας καὶ ἅρματα τριακόσια καὶ ἵπποι πεντα-
κόσιοι. τῆς δὲ ξὺν Ἀλεξάνδρῳ στρατιᾶς ἀπέθανον
μὲν ὀλίγον ἀποδέοντες τῶν ἑκατὸν ἐν τῇ πάσῃ
πολιορκίᾳ, τραυματίαι δὲ οὐ κατὰ τὸ πλῆθος τῶν
νεκρῶν ἐγένοντο, ἀλλὰ ὑπὲρ τοὺς χιλίους καὶ
διακοσίους, καὶ ἐν τούτοις τῶν ἡγεμόνων ἄλλοι
τε καὶ Λυσίμαχος ὁ σωματοφύλαξ.

6 Θάψας δὲ ὡς νόμος αὐτῷ τοὺς τελευτήσαντας
Εὐμενῆ τὸν γραμματέα ἐκπέμπει ἐς τὰς δύο πόλεις
τὰς ξυναφεστώσας τοῖς Σαγγάλοις δοὺς αὐτῷ τῶν
ἱππέων ἐς τριακοσίους, φράσοντα [ς] τοῖς ἔχουσι
τὰς πόλεις τῶν τε Σαγγάλων τὴν ἅλωσιν καὶ ὅτι
αὐτοῖς οὐδὲν ἔσται χαλεπὸν ⟨ἐξ⟩ Ἀλεξάνδρου
ὑπομένουσί τε καὶ δεχομένοις φιλίως Ἀλέξανδρον·
οὐδὲ γὰρ οὐδὲ ἄλλοις τισὶ γενέσθαι τῶν αὐτονόμων
7 Ἰνδῶν ὅσοι ἑκόντες σφᾶς ἐνέδοσαν. οἱ δὲ (ἤδη
γὰρ ἐξήγγελτο αὐτοῖς κατὰ κράτος ἑαλωκότα πρὸς
Ἀλεξάνδρου τὰ Σάγγαλα) φοβεροὶ γενόμενοι ἔφευγον ἀπολιπόντες τὰς πόλεις. καὶ Ἀλέξανδρος,
ἐπειδὴ ἐξηγγέλθη αὐτῶν ἡ φυγή, σπουδῇ ἐδίωκεν·
ἀλλὰ οἱ πολλοὶ μὲν αὐτῶν ἔφθασαν ἀποφυγόντες,
διὰ μακροῦ γὰρ ἡ δίωξις ἐγίγνετο, ὅσοι δὲ κατὰ
τὴν ἀποχώρησιν ἀσθενείᾳ ὑπελείποντο, οὗτοι
ἐγκαταληφθέντες πρὸς τῆς στρατιᾶς ἀπέθανον ἐς
8 πεντακοσίους μάλιστα. ὡς δὲ ἀπέγνω διώκειν τοῦ
πρόσω τοὺς φεύγοντας, ἐπανελθὼν ἐς τὰ Σάγγαλα
τὴν πόλιν μὲν κατέσκαψε, τὴν χώραν δὲ τῶν
Ἰνδῶν τοῖς πάλαι μὲν αὐτονόμοις, τότε δὲ ἑκουσίως
προσχωρήσασι προσέθηκεν. καὶ Πῶρον μὲν ξὺν

Some seventeen thousand of the Indians perished in the capture and over seventy thousand were captured with three hundred waggons and five hundred horses.[1] Of Alexander's forces rather under a hundred were lost in the entire siege; the wounded were out of proportion to the dead, over twelve hundred including officers, notably Lysimachus the bodyguard.

When he had buried the dead according to his custom, Alexander sent Eumenes his secretary [2] to the two cities which had rebelled at the same time as Sangala, giving him about three hundred cavalry, to to tell those holding the cities of the capture of Sangala and to say that Alexander would not treat them harshly if they stayed where they were and received him in a friendly way, just as he had shown no harshness to any of the other self-governing Indians who had voluntarily surrendered. But as they had 7 already heard that Alexander had captured Sangala by assault, they were terrified and left their cities in flight. Alexander pursued them hotly as soon as their flight was reported to him, but most of them had got safe away, for the pursuit began after a long interval. All who had been left behind in the retreat through infirmity were captured and put to death by the army, to the number of about five hundred. After deciding not to pursue the fugitives 8 further, Alexander returned to Sangala, razed the city to the ground, and annexed its territory to those Indians who had formerly been self-governing but at this time came over voluntarily. Porus was sent

---

[1] Obviously exaggerated numbers.
[2] Cf. vii 4, 6; 13, 1; 14, 9, foreshadowing the importance of this Greek from Cardia after Al's death (see Plutarch, *Eumenes*). A. omits mention of an independent mission for Perdiccas and of Hephaestion's return and substantial successes (QC. ix 1, 19 and 35).

ARRIAN

τῇ δυνάμει τῇ ἀμφ' αὐτὸν ἐκπέμπει ἐπὶ τὰς πόλεις
αἳ προσκεχωρήκεσαν, φρουρὰς εἰσάξοντα εἰς
αὐτάς, αὐτὸς δὲ ξὺν τῇ στρατιᾷ ἐπὶ τὸν Ὕφασιν
ποταμὸν προὐχώρει, ὡς καὶ τοὺς ἐπέκεινα Ἰνδοὺς
καταστρέψαιτο. οὐδὲ ἐφαίνετο αὐτῷ πέρας τι τοῦ
πολέμου ἔστε ὑπελείπετό τι πολέμιον.

25. Τὰ δὲ δὴ πέραν τοῦ Ὑφάσιος εὐδαίμονά τε
τὴν χώραν εἶναι ἐξηγγέλλετο καὶ ἀνθρώπους ἀγα-
θοὺς μὲν γῆς ἐργάτας, γενναίους δὲ τὰ πολέμια καὶ
ἐς τὰ ἴδια δὲ σφῶν ἐν κόσμῳ πολιτεύοντας (πρὸς
γὰρ τῶν ἀρίστων ἄρχεσθαι τοὺς πολλούς, τοὺς δὲ
οὐδὲν ἔξω τοῦ ἐπιεικοῦς ἐξηγεῖσθαι), πλῆθός τε
ἐλεφάντων εἶναι τοῖς ταύτῃ ἀνθρώποις πολύ τι ὑπὲρ
τοὺς ἄλλους Ἰνδούς, καὶ μεγέθει μεγίστους καὶ
2 ἀνδρείᾳ. ταῦτα δὲ ἐξαγγελλόμενα Ἀλέξανδρον
μὲν παρώξυνεν ἐς ἐπιθυμίαν τοῦ πρόσω ἰέναι· οἱ
Μακεδόνες δὲ ἐξέκαμνον ἤδη ταῖς γνώμαις, πόνους
τε ἐκ πόνων καὶ κινδύνους ἐκ κινδύνων ἐπαναιρού-
μενον ὁρῶντες τὸν βασιλέα· ξύλλογοί τε ἐγίγνοντο
κατὰ τὸ στρατόπεδον τῶν μὲν τὰ σφέτερα ὀδυρο-
μένων, ὅσοι ἐπιεικέστατοι, τῶν δὲ οὐκ ἀκολουθήσειν, οὐδ' ἢν ἄγῃ Ἀλέξανδρος, ἀπισχυριζομένων.
ταῦτα ὡς ἐπύθετο Ἀλέξανδρος, πρὶν καὶ ἐπὶ
μεῖζον προελθεῖν τὴν ταραχὴν τοῖς στρατιώταις καὶ
τὴν ἀθυμίαν, ξυγκαλέσας τοὺς ἡγεμόνας τῶν
τάξεων ἔλεξεν ὧδε.

3 Ὁρῶν ὑμᾶς, ὦ ἄνδρες Μακεδόνες τε καὶ ξύμμαχοι, οὐχ ὁμοίᾳ ἔτι τῇ γνώμῃ ἑπομένους μοι ἐς
τοὺς κινδύνους, ξυνήγαγον ἐς ταὐτό, ὡς ἢ πείσας
ἄγειν τοῦ πρόσω ἢ πεισθεὶς ὀπίσω ἀποστρέφεσθαι.
εἰ μὲν δὴ μεμπτοί εἰσιν ὑμῖν οἱ μέχρι δεῦρο πονηθέν-
τες πόνοι καὶ αὐτὸς ἐγὼ ἡγούμενος, οὐδὲν ἔτι

326
B.C.

back with his force to the cities which had come over, to set garrisons in them while Alexander himself advanced with his army to the Hyphasis, to subdue the Indians beyond as well. For he thought there could be no end of the war as long as any enemy was left.

25. The country beyond the Hyphasis was reported to be fertile, and the inhabitants good farmers and excellent fighting men, with their affairs under orderly government, for the masses were ruled by the best men, who did not exercise leadership unfairly. These people also had a far greater number of elephants than the other Indians, and the best for size and courage. This report stirred Alexander to a desire 2 for further advance; but the Macedonians' spirits were flagging by now, as they saw the king taking on one hard and dangerous task after another; meetings took place in the camp among men who complained of their own plight—they were the most moderate kind—or who flatly denied that they would follow Alexander's leadership any farther. When Alexander heard of this, before indiscipline and despair grew worse among the troops, he summoned the regimental commanders and addressed them thus [1]:

' I observe that you, Macedonians and allies,[2] are 3 not following me into dangers any longer with your old spirit. I have summoned you together, either to persuade you to go forward, or to be persuaded by you to turn back. If indeed you have any fault to find with the exertions you have hitherto endured, and with me as your leader, there is no object in my

[1] Cf. D. 93 f.; QC. ix 2, 8 ff., with a fictitious speech, addressed to the whole army. See App. XVII 11; 22 f.; XXVII 5.

[2] Literally ' partners in fighting,' the word could perhaps apply honorifically to Greek mercenary officers.

ARRIAN

4 προὔργου λέγειν μοί ἐστιν. εἰ δὲ Ἰωνία τε πρὸς
ἡμῶν διὰ τούσδε τοὺς πόνους ἔχεται καὶ Ἑλλήσπον-
τος καὶ Φρύγες ἀμφότεροι καὶ Καππαδόκαι καὶ
Παφλαγόνες καὶ Λυδοὶ καὶ Κᾶρες καὶ Λύκιοι καὶ
Παμφυλία δὲ καὶ Φοινίκη καὶ Αἴγυπτος ξὺν τῇ
Λιβύῃ τῇ Ἑλληνικῇ καὶ Ἀραβίας ἔστιν ἃ καὶ
5 Συρία ἥ τε κοίλη καὶ ἡ μέση τῶν ποταμῶν, καὶ
Βαβυλὼν δὲ ἔχεται καὶ τὸ Σουσίων ἔθνος καὶ
Πέρσαι καὶ Μῆδοι καὶ ὅσων Πέρσαι καὶ Μῆδοι
ἐπῆρχον, καὶ ὅσων δὲ οὐκ ἦρχον, τὰ ὑπὲρ τὰς
Κασπίας πύλας, τὰ ἐπέκεινα τοῦ Καυκάσου, ὁ
Τάναϊς, τὰ πρόσω ἔτι τοῦ Τανάϊδος, Βακτριανοί,
Ὑρκάνιοι, ἡ θάλασσα ἡ Ὑρκανία, Σκύθας τε
ἀνεστείλαμεν ἔστε ἐπὶ τὴν ἔρημον, ἐπὶ τούτοις
μέντοι καὶ ὁ Ἰνδὸς ποταμὸς διὰ τῆς ἡμετέρας ῥεῖ,
ὁ Ὑδάσπης διὰ τῆς ἡμετέρας, ὁ Ἀκεσίνης, ὁ
Ὑδραώτης, τί ὀκνεῖτε καὶ τὸν Ὕφασιν καὶ τὰ
ἐπέκεινα τοῦ Ὑφάσιος γένη προσθεῖναι τῇ ἡμετέρᾳ
6 Μακεδόνων τε ἀρχῇ; ἢ δέδιτε μὴ δέξωνται ὑμᾶς ἔτι
ἄλλοι βάρβαροι ἐπιόντας; ὧν γε οἱ μὲν προσχω-
ροῦσιν ἑκόντες, οἱ δὲ φεύγοντες ἁλίσκονται, οἱ δὲ
ἀποφυγόντες τὴν χώραν ἡμῖν ἔρημον παραδιδόασιν,
ἢ δὴ τοῖς ξυμμάχοις τε καὶ τοῖς ἑκοῦσι προσχωρήσασι προστίθεται.

26. Πέρας δὲ τῶν πόνων γενναίῳ μὲν ἀνδρὶ
οὐδὲν δοκῶ ἔγωγε ὅτι μὴ αὐτοὺς τοὺς πόνους,
ὅσοι αὐτῶν ἐς καλὰ ἔργα φέρουσιν. εἰ δέ τις
καὶ αὐτῷ τῷ πολεμεῖν ποθεῖ ἀκοῦσαι ὅ τι περ
ἔσται πέρας, μαθέτω ὅτι οὐ πολλὴ ἔτι ἡμῖν ἡ
λοιπή ἐστιν ἔστε ἐπὶ ποταμόν τε Γάγγην καὶ τὴν

---

[3] I.e. Cyrene (vii 9, 7 n.).

speaking further. If, however, it is through these 4 326
exertions that Ionia is now in our hands, and the   B.C.
Hellespont, both Phrygian peoples, the Cappado-
cians, Paphlagonians, Lydians, Carians, Lycians,
Pamphylia, Phoenicia, Egypt, with the Greek part of
Libya,[3] part of Arabia, Syria, both the ' hollow ' land
and that between the rivers, Babylonia, the Susian 5
nation, the Persians and Medes, with all the nations
subject to Persia and Media, and those which were
not,[4] the regions beyond the Caspian gates, beyond the
Caucasus, on the other side of the Tanais, Bactrians,
Hyrcanians, the Hyrcanian Sea; if we have driven the
Scythians into the desert[5]; if, besides all this, it is
through territory now our own that the Indus flows,
and the Hydaspes, the Acesines, and the Hydraotes,
why do you hesitate to add the Hyphasis and the
peoples beyond the Hyphasis to this Macedonian empire of ours ? Do you fear lest other barbarians may 6
yet withstand your approach ? Why, some of them
come over readily, some are captured in flight, some
desert their country and leave it vacant for us; this
land we have indeed annexed to our allies and those
who have voluntarily come over to us.

26. ' For my part, I set no limit to exertions for a
man of noble spirit, save that the exertions themselves should lead to deeds of prowess. Yet if any
one longs to hear what will be the limit of the actual
fighting, he should understand that there remains no
great stretch of land before us up to the river Ganges [1]

---

[4] E.g. in India, App. XV.
[5] iv 1–5 and 15; Pharasmanes could be held to have submitted. It is idle to analyse the rhetoric here or in vii 10, 5 ff.,
as Tarn does (App. 15).
[1] App. XVII 22 f.

ἑῴαν θάλασσαν· ταύτῃ δέ, λέγω ὑμῖν, ξυναφὴς
φανεῖται ἡ Ὑρκανία θάλασσα· ἐκπεριέρχεται γὰρ
2 γῆν πέρι πᾶσαν ἡ μεγάλη θάλασσα. καὶ ἐγὼ
ἐπιδείξω Μακεδόσι τε καὶ τοῖς ξυμμάχοις τὸν
μὲν Ἰνδικὸν κόλπον ξύρρουν ὄντα τῷ Περσικῷ,
τὴν δὲ Ὑρκανίαν ⟨θάλασσαν⟩ τῷ Ἰνδικῷ· ἀπὸ
δὲ τοῦ Περσικοῦ εἰς Λιβύην περιπλευσθήσεται
στόλῳ ἡμετέρῳ τὰ μέχρι Ἡρακλέους Στηλῶν·
ἀπὸ δὲ Στηλῶν ἡ ἐντὸς Λιβύη πᾶσα ἡμετέρα
γίγνεται καὶ ἡ Ἀσία δὴ οὕτω πᾶσα, καὶ ὅροι τῆς
ταύτῃ ἀρχῆς οὕσπερ καὶ τῆς γῆς ὅρους ὁ θεὸς
3 ἐποίησε. νῦν δὲ δὴ ἀποτρεπομένων πολλὰ μὲν
μάχιμα ὑπολείπεται γένη ἐπέκεινα τοῦ Ὑφάσιος
ἔστε ἐπὶ τὴν ἑῴαν θάλασσαν, πολλὰ δὲ ἀπὸ τούτων
ἔτι ἐπὶ τὴν Ὑρκανίαν ὡς ἐπὶ βορρᾶν ἄνεμον, καὶ τὰ
Σκυθικὰ γένη οὐ πόρρω τούτων, ὥστε δέος μὴ
ἀπελθόντων ὀπίσω καὶ τὰ νῦν κατεχόμενα οὐ
βέβαια ὄντα ἐπαρθῇ πρὸς ἀπόστασιν πρὸς τῶν
4 μήπω ἐχομένων. καὶ τότε δὴ ἀνόνητοι ἡμῖν ἔσονται οἱ πολλοὶ πόνοι ἢ ἄλλων αὖθις ἐξ ἀρχῆς δεήσει
πόνων τε καὶ κινδύνων. ἀλλὰ παραμείνατε, ἄνδρες
Μακεδόνες καὶ ξύμμαχοι. πονούντων τοι καὶ
κινδυνευόντων τὰ καλὰ ἔργα, καὶ ζῆν τε ξὺν
ἀρετῇ ἡδὺ καὶ ἀποθνήσκειν κλέος ἀθάνατον ὑπο-
5 λειπομένους. ἢ οὐκ ἴστε ὅτι ὁ πρόγονος ὁ ἡμέτε-
ρος οὐκ ἐν Τίρυνθι οὐδὲ Ἄργει, ἀλλ’ οὐδὲ ἐν Πελο-
ποννήσῳ ἢ Θήβαις μένων ἐς τοσόνδε κλέος ἦλθεν
ὡς θεὸς ἐξ ἀνθρώπου γενέσθαι ἢ δοκεῖν; οὐ μὲν
δὴ οὐδὲ Διονύσου, ἁβροτέρου τούτου θεοῦ ἢ καθ’
Ἡρακλέα, ὀλίγοι πόνοι. ἀλλὰ ἡμεῖς γε καὶ ἐπ-

---

² App. XII 2; XXVII 5.

326
B.C.

and the eastern sea. This sea, I assure you, will prove to be joined to the Hyrcanian sea[2]; for the great sea encircles all the land. And it will be for me 2 to show Macedonians and allies alike that the Indian gulf [Arabian Sea] forms but one stretch of water with the Persian gulf, and the Hyrcanian Sea with the Indian gulf. From the Persian gulf our fleet shall sail round to Libya, as far as the Pillars of Heracles [Straits of Gibraltar]; from the Pillars all the interior of Libya then becomes ours, just as Asia is in fact becoming ours in its entirety, and the boundaries of our Empire here are becoming those which God set for the whole continent.[3] But if we flinch now, there 3 will be many warlike races left behind on the far side of the Hyphasis up to the Eastern Sea, and many too stretching from these to the Hyrcanian Sea to the north, and the Scythian tribes not far from these, so that there is reason to fear that if we turn back, even our present possessions, which are not held securely, may be stirred to revolt by those who are not yet under our control. Then our numerous exertions 4 will indeed be profitless, or we shall have to start again with fresh exertions and dangers. But you must persevere, Macedonians and allies. Exertions and dangers are the price of deeds of prowess, and it is sweet for men to live bravely, and die leaving behind them immortal renown. Or do you not know that it 5 was not by remaining in Tiryns or in Argos or even in the Peloponnese or Thebes that our ancestor attained such renown that from a man he became, or was held, a god? Even Dionysus, a more delicate god than Heracles, had not a few labours to perform. And

[3] Cf. vii 1, 2 f.

ἐκεῖνα τῆς Νύσης ἀφίγμεθα καὶ ἡ "Αορνος πέτρα ἡ
6 τῷ Ἡρακλεῖ ἀνάλωτος πρὸς ἡμῶν ἔχεται. ὑμεῖς
δὲ καὶ τὰ ἔτι ὑπόλοιπα τῆς Ἀσίας πρόσθετε
τοῖς ἤδη ἐκτημένοις καὶ τὰ ὀλίγα τοῖς πολλοῖς.
ἐπεὶ καὶ ἡμῖν αὐτοῖς τί ἂν μέγα καὶ καλὸν κατεπέ-
πρακτο, εἰ ἐν Μακεδονίᾳ καθήμενοι ἱκανὸν ἐποιού-
μεθα ἀπόνως τὴν οἰκείαν διασώζειν, Θρᾳκας τοὺς
ὁμόρους ἢ Ἰλλυριοὺς ἢ Τριβαλλοὺς ἢ καὶ τῶν
Ἑλλήνων, ὅσοι οὐκ ἐπιτήδειοι ἐς τὰ ἡμέτερα,
ἀναστέλλοντες;
7   Εἰ μὲν δὴ ὑμᾶς πονοῦντας καὶ κινδυνεύοντας
αὐτὸς ἀπόνως καὶ ἀκινδύνως ἐξηγούμενος ἦγον,
οὐκ ἀπεικότως ἂν προεκάμνετε ταῖς γνώμαις, τῶν
μὲν πόνων μόνοις ὑμῖν μετόν, τὰ δὲ ἆθλα αὐτῶν
ἄλλοις περιποιοῦντες· νῦν δὲ κοινοὶ μὲν ἡμῖν
οἱ πόνοι, ἴσον δὲ μέτεστι τῶν κινδύνων, τὰ δὲ
8 ἆθλα ἐν μέσῳ κεῖται ξύμπασιν. ἥ τε χώρα ὑμετέρα
καὶ ὑμεῖς αὐτῆς σατραπεύετε. καὶ τῶν χρημάτων
τὸ μέρος νῦν τε ἐς ὑμᾶς τὸ πολὺ ἔρχεται καὶ
ἐπειδὰν ἐπεξέλθωμεν τὴν Ἀσίαν, τότε οὐκ ἐμπλή-
σας μὰ Δι' ὑμᾶς, ἀλλὰ καὶ ὑπερβαλὼν ὅσα ἕκαστος ἐλπίζει ἀγαθὰ ἔσεσθαι τοὺς μὲν ἀπιέναι
οἴκαδε ἐθέλοντας εἰς τὴν οἰκείαν ἀποπέμψω ἢ
ἐπανάξω αὐτός, τοὺς δὲ αὐτοῦ μένοντας ζηλωτοὺς
τοῖς ἀπερχομένοις ποιήσω.
    27. Ταῦτα καὶ τοιαῦτα εἰπόντος Ἀλεξάνδρου
πολὺν μὲν χρόνον σιωπὴ ἦν οὔτε ἀντιλέγειν τολ-
μώντων πρὸς τὸν βασιλέα ἐκ τοῦ εὐθέος οὔτε
ξυγχωρεῖν ἐθελόντων. ἐν δὲ τούτῳ πολλάκις μὲν

---

⁴ App. V 10; XVI.

326
B.C.

yet we have actually passed beyond Nysa and taken the rock Aornos, which Heracles could not take.[4] Let it be your task to add what yet remains of Asia to the possessions already won, a small conquest in comparison.   For that matter what great or noble success could we ourselves have achieved, had we sat still in Macedonia and thought it enough to guard our own home without effort, merely keeping in check the Thracians on our borders or Illyrians or Triballians, or those Greeks too, who were not well disposed to us [5]?

' Now if the exertions and dangers had been yours, and I had personally escaped them, while issuing commands as your leader, it would not have been unreasonable for you to have grown weary in spirit before me, when you alone were taking part in the exertions, while the prizes they procured went to others; but as it is, we undergo the exertions in common, our share in the dangers is equal, and the prizes are open to all alike.   For the land is yours; it is you who are its satraps [6]; the greater part of the treasure is now coming to you, and, when we overrun all Asia, then by Heaven I will not merely satisfy you, but will surpass the utmost hope of good things each man has, I will send all who desire to go home back to their own country or will myself lead them back, while those who remain behind I shall make the envy of those who depart.'

27. After Alexander had spoken these words or in this sense, for a long time there was silence; no one either dared to oppose the King on the spur of the moment, or was yet willing to agree.   In this interval

---

[5] The insecurity of Macedonian frontiers and control of Greece emerges better here than in vii 9, 3–5.

[6] Less absurd, as addressed to officers, than vii 9, 8.

'Αλέξανδρος ἐκέλευε λέγειν τὸν βουλόμενον, εἰ δή
τις τὰ ἐναντία τοῖς ὑπ' αὐτοῦ λεχθεῖσι γιγνώσκει·
ἔμενε δὲ καὶ ὡς ἐπὶ πολὺ ἡ σιωπή· ὀψὲ δέ ποτε
θαρσήσας Κοῖνος ὁ Πολεμοκράτους ἔλεξε τοιάδε.

2 Ἐπειδὴ αὐτός, ὦ βασιλεῦ, οὐ κατὰ πρόσταγμα
ἐθέλεις Μακεδόνων ἐξηγεῖσθαι, ἀλλὰ πείσας μὲν
ἄξειν φής, πεισθεὶς δὲ οὐ βιάσεσθαι, οὐχ ὑπὲρ
ἡμῶν τῶνδε ποιήσομαι ἐγὼ τοὺς λόγους, οἳ καὶ
προτιμώμενοι τῶν ἄλλων καὶ τὰ ἆθλα τῶν πόνων
οἱ πολλοὶ ἤδη κεκομισμένοι καὶ τῷ κρατιστεύειν
παρά τοὺς ἄλλους πρόθυμοί σοι ἐς πάντα
3 ἐσμέν, ἀλλ' ὑπὲρ τῆς στρατιᾶς τῆς πολλῆς. οὐδὲ
ὑπὲρ ταύτης τὰ καθ' ἡδονὴν ἐκείνοις ἐρῶ, ἀλλὰ
ἃ νομίζω σύμφορά τέ σοι ἐς τὰ παρόντα καὶ ἐς
τὰ μέλλοντα μάλιστα ἀσφαλῆ εἶναι. δίκαιος δέ
εἰμι καθ' ἡλικίαν τε μὴ ἀποκρύπτεσθαι τὰ δοκοῦν-
τα βέλτιστα καὶ κατὰ τὴν ἐκ σοῦ μοι οὖσαν καὶ
ἐς τοὺς ἄλλους ἀξίωσιν καὶ κατὰ τὴν ἐν τοῖς πόνοις
τε καὶ κινδύνοις ἐς τόδε ἀπροφάσιστον τόλμαν.
4 ὅσῳ γάρ τοι πλεῖστα καὶ μέγιστα σοί τε ἡγουμένῳ
καταπέπρακται καὶ τοῖς ἅμα σοὶ οἴκοθεν ὁρμηθεῖσι,
τοσῷδε μᾶλλόν τι ξύμφορόν μοι δοκεῖ πέρας τι ἐπιθεῖναι τοῖς πόνοις καὶ κινδύνοις. αὐτὸς γάρ τοι
ὁρᾷς, ὅσοι μὲν Μακεδόνων τε καὶ Ἑλλήνων ἅμα
5 σοὶ ὡρμήθημεν, ὅσοι δὲ ὑπολελείμμεθα· ὧν
Θετταλοὺς μὲν ἀπὸ Βάκτρων εὐθὺς οὐ προθύμους
ἔτι ἐς τοὺς πόνους αἰσθόμενος οἴκαδε, καλῶς
ποιῶν, ἀπέπεμψας· τῶν δὲ ἄλλων Ἑλλήνων οἱ μὲν

---

[1] QC. ix 3 also has a fictitious speech by Coenus. There is
no reason to doubt that he spoke (*contra* Tarn). 21, 4 suggests
that he and Craterus were not expected to remain at the

Alexander often invited any who wished to speak, if he really held opposite views to those he had expressed himself; yet even so silence reigned long, and only after some time Coenus, Polemocrates' son, plucked up his courage and spoke thus [1]:

' Seeing that you, Sire, do not yourself desire to 2 lead the Macedonians as a dictator, but say that you will lead them by persuasion, and that, if they persuade you, you will not coerce them, I shall speak not on behalf of those here present among us, who are held in honour beyond the rest and have mostly already received the prizes of our exertions, and, in virtue of our eminence in comparison with the rest, are zealous to serve you in every way, but on behalf of the majority in the army. And even in their cause 3 I shall not speak to gratify them, but say what I consider useful to yourself in present circumstances and most conducive to safety for the future. My age entitles me not to conceal the views I think best and so does the superior rank you have granted me, and the unhesitating daring I have shown up to now in exertions and dangers.

' The successes achieved by you as our leader and 4 by those who set out with you from our homes have been so numerous and splendid that for that very reason I think it more in our interest to set some limit to exertions and dangers. Surely you see yourself how many Macedonians and Greeks we were when we set forth with you, and how many survive. The 5 Thessalians you sent straight home from Bactria,[2] observing that they had little heart left for further exertions, and you were right. As for the other

Hydaspes (21, 1), and his rejoining the main army could have been overlooked by A., like that of Hephaestion (24, 8 n.).

[2] Misleading, cf. iii 19, 5; 29, 5.

ἐν ταῖς πόλεσι ταῖς πρὸς σοῦ οἰκισθείσαις κατῳκισ-
μένοι οὐδὲ οὗτοι πάντῃ ἑκόντες μένουσιν· οἱ δὲ
ξυμπονοῦντές τε ἔτι καὶ ξυγκινδυνεύοντες, αὐτοί
τε καὶ ἡ Μακεδονικὴ στρατιά, τοὺς μὲν ἐν ταῖς
μάχαις ἀπολωλέκασιν, οἱ δὲ ἐκ τραυμάτων ἀπόμαχοι γεγενημένοι ἄλλοι ἄλλῃ τῆς Ἀσίας ὑπολελειμ-
6 μένοι εἰσίν, οἱ πλείους δὲ νόσῳ ἀπολώλασιν, ὀλίγοι
δὲ ἐκ πολλῶν ὑπολείπονται, καὶ οὔτε τοῖς σώμασιν
ἔτι ὡσαύτως ἐρρωμένοι, ταῖς τε γνώμαις πολὺ
ἔτι μᾶλλον προκεκμηκότες. καὶ τούτοις ξύμπασιν
πόθος μὲν γονέων ἐστίν, ὅσοις ἔτι σῴζονται, πόθος
δὲ γυναικῶν καὶ παίδων, πόθος δὲ δὴ τῆς γῆς
αὐτῆς τῆς οἰκείας, ἣν ξὺν τῷ ἐκ σοῦ πορισθέντι
σφίσιν κόσμῳ μεγάλοι τε ἀντὶ μικρῶν καὶ πλούσιοι
ἐκ πενήτων ἀναστρέφοντες ξύγγνωστοί εἰσιν ἐπιδεῖν
7 ποθοῦντες. σὺ δὲ νῦν μὴ ἄγειν ἄκοντας· οὐδὲ
γὰρ ὁμοίοις ἔτι χρήσῃ ἐς τοὺς κινδύνους, οἷς τὸ ἑκού-
σιον ἐν τοῖς ἀγῶσιν ἀπέσται· ἐπανελθὼν δὲ αὐτός
[τε], εἰ δοκεῖ, ἐς τὴν οἰκ⟨ε⟩ίαν καὶ τὴν μητέρα
τὴν σαυτοῦ ἰδὼν καὶ τῶν Ἑλλήνων καταστησά-
μενος καὶ τὰς νίκας ταύτας τὰς πολλὰς καὶ μεγάλας
ἐς τὸν πατρῷον οἶκον κομίσας οὕτω δὴ ἐξ ἀρχῆς
ἄλλον στόλον στέλλεσθαι, εἰ μὲν βούλει, ἐπ᾽ αὐτὰ
ταῦτα τὰ πρὸς τὴν ἕω ᾠκισμένα Ἰνδῶν γένη, εἰ δὲ
βούλει, ἐς τὸν Εὔξεινον πόντον, εἰ δέ, ἐπὶ Καρχηδόνα καὶ τὰ ἐπέκεινα Καρχηδονίων τῆς Λιβύης.
8 ταῦτα δὲ σὸν ἤδη ἐξηγεῖσθαι. ἔψονται δέ σοι ἄλλοι
Μακεδόνες καὶ ἄλλοι Ἕλληνες, νέοι τε ἀντὶ γερόν-
των καὶ ἀκμῆτες ἀντὶ κεκμηκότων, καὶ οἷς τὰ

---

[3] Cf. iv 22, 3 n.; App. XXIII 7. The discontent that led
to revolt *might* have been known already.

Greeks, some have been settled in the cities you have
founded, and even they do not remain there entirely
of their own free will[3]; others are still sharing in
your exertions and dangers, but they and the
Macedonian forces have lost part of their number in
battle; others have been invalided from wounds, and
have been left behind in different parts of Asia; but 6
most have died of sickness, and of all that host few
survive, and even they no longer enjoy their bodily
strength, while their spirit is far more wearied out.
One and all, they long to see their parents, if they are
still alive, their wives and children, and indeed their
own homeland, which they may pardonably long to
look on once more, for with the honour of the provision you have made for them, they will return great
and wealthy, instead of being humble and poor. It 7
is not for you now to be a leader of unwilling troops.
For you will no longer find men meeting dangers as
they once did, when it is not by their own choice that
they engage in conflicts. But if it please you, return
in person to your own country, look on your own
mother, settle the affairs of the Greeks and, after
bringing these victories, numerous and splendid, to
your father's house, then indeed begin again and fit
out another expedition, if you wish, against the very
same Indian peoples settled in the east or, if you wish,
one to the Euxine [Black] Sea, or alternatively
against Carthage and the part of Libya beyond
Carthage.[4]   These decisions it will then be for you to 8
take as leader, but your followers will be other Macedonians, other Greeks, young men in place of old,
men who are fresh and not worn out, who will have no

[4] Cf. vii 1; 8, 1.

τοῦ πολέμου διὰ τὸ ἀπείρατον ἔς τε τὸ παραυτίκα
οὐ φοβερὰ καὶ κατὰ τὴν τοῦ μέλλοντος ἐλπίδα ἐν
σπουδῇ ἔσται· οὓς καὶ ταύτῃ ἔτι προθυμότερον
ἀκολουθήσειν σοι εἰκός, ὁρῶντας τοὺς πρότερον
ξυμπονήσαντάς τε καὶ ξυγκινδυνεύσαντας ἐς τὰ
σφέτερα ἤθη ἐπανεληλυθότας, πλουσίους τε ἀντὶ
πενήτων καὶ ἀντὶ ἀφανῶν τῶν πάλαι εὐκλεεῖς.
9 καλὸν δέ, ὦ βασιλεῦ, εἴπερ τι καὶ ἄλλο, καὶ ἡ ἐν τῷ
εὐτυχεῖν σωφροσύνη. σοὶ γὰρ αὐτῷ ἡγουμένῳ καὶ
στρατιὰν τοιαύτην ἄγοντι ἐκ μὲν πολεμίων δέος
οὐδέν, τὰ δὲ ἐκ τοῦ δαιμονίου ἀδόκητά τε καὶ
ταύτῃ καὶ ἀφύλακτα τοῖς ἀνθρώποις ἐστί.

28. Τοιαῦτα εἰπόντος τοῦ Κοίνου θόρυβον γενέσθαι ἐκ τῶν παρόντων ἐπὶ τοῖς λόγοις· πολλοῖς δὲ
δὴ καὶ δάκρυα προχυθέντα ἔτι μᾶλλον δηλῶσαι τό
τε ἀκούσιον τῆς γνώμης ἐς τοὺς πρόσω κινδύνους
καὶ τὸ καθ' ἡδονήν σφισιν εἶναι τὴν ἀποχώρησιν.
Ἀλέξανδρος δὲ τότε μὲν ἀχθεσθεὶς τοῦ τε Κοίνου
τῇ παρρησίᾳ καὶ τῷ ὄκνῳ τῶν ἄλλων ἡγεμόνων
2 διέλυσε τὸν ξύλλογον· ἐς δὲ τὴν ὑστεραίαν ξυγκαλέσας αὖθις ξὺν ὀργῇ τοὺς αὐτοὺς αὐτὸς μὲν ἰέναι
ἔφη τοῦ πρόσω, βιάσεσθαι δὲ οὐδένα ἄκοντα Μακεδόνων ξυνέπεσθαι· ἕξειν γὰρ τοὺς ἀκολουθήσοντας
τῷ βασιλεῖ σφῶν ἑκόντας· τοῖς δὲ καὶ ἀπιέναι
οἴκαδε ἐθέλουσιν ὑπάρχειν ἀπιέναι καὶ ἐξαγγέλλειν
τοῖς οἰκείοις, ὅτι τὸν βασιλέα σφῶν ἐν μέσοις τοῖς
3 πολεμίοις ἐπανήκουσιν ἀπολιπόντες. ταῦτα εἰπόντα ἀπελθεῖν ἐς τὴν σκηνὴν μηδέ τινα τῶν ἑταίρων

---

[1] QC. ix 3, 16 ff., who omits this second meeting, ascribes
similar statements to Al. at the first (2, 31 ff.). Cf. vii 10, 5 ff.
If a substantial number of men had been ready to follow Al.,

immediate fear of war, having no experience of it, and whose warlike ardour will be excited by their hopes of the future; it is likely that they will follow you with all the more enthusiasm, because they see the partners in your earlier exertions and dangers returned to their own lands and raised from poverty to riches and from obscurity to high renown. Nothing, Sire, is so unquestionably good as a sound mind in good fortune and, though with you as commander and such an army to lead our enemies can inspire no fear, the strokes of divine power are beyond the foresight and therefore beyond the precautions of human beings.'

28. After Coenus had spoken in this way, it is said that his speech produced uproar among the audience and that many even shed tears, still further proof that their minds did not go with further dangers and that what they wanted was to return home, and of the joy with which they would hail a retreat. At the time Alexander, irritated at Coenus' freedom of language and at the timidity of the other officers, dismissed the conference, but next day he convened the same men once more and angrily affirmed that he himself was going on, but that he would compel no Macedonian to go with him against his will; he would have volunteers as followers of their king. As for those who wished to return home, they might do so, and might tell it abroad to their friends that they had come back, leaving their king surrounded by enemies.[1] After these words it is said that he went back to his tent, and did not admit even any of the Companions

the rest might have succumbed to pressure and their fears of being left leaderless; *pace* Tarn, this sort of bluff could have been tried; if so, it was called!

προσέσθαι αὐτῆς τε ἐκείνης τῆς ἡμέρας καὶ ἐς
τὴν τρίτην ἔτι ἀπ' ἐκείνης, ὑπομένοντα, εἰ δή τις
τροπὴ ταῖς γνώμαις τῶν Μακεδόνων τε καὶ ξυμμά-
χων, οἷα δὴ ἐν ὄχλῳ στρατιωτῶν τὰ πολλὰ φιλεῖ
γίγνεσθαι, ἐμπεσοῦσα εὐπειθεστέρους παρέξει αὐ-
4 τούς. ὡς δὲ σιγὴ αὖ πολλὴ ⟨ἦν⟩ ἀνὰ τὸ στρατόπεδον καὶ ἀχθόμενοι μὲν τῇ ὀργῇ αὐτοῦ δῆλοι
ἦσαν, οὐ μὴν μεταβαλλόμενοί γε ὑπ' αὐτῆς,
ἐνταῦθα δὴ λέγει Πτολεμαῖος ὁ Λάγου, ὅτι ἐπὶ
τῇ διαβάσει οὐδὲν μεῖον ἐθύετο, θυομένῳ δὲ οὐκ
ἐγίγνετο αὐτῷ τὰ ἱερά. τότε δὴ τοὺς πρεσβυτά-
τους τε τῶν ἑταίρων καὶ τοὺς μάλιστα ἐπιτηδείους
αὐτῷ συναγαγών, ὡς πάντα ἐς τὴν ὀπίσω ἀναχώ-
ρησιν αὐτῷ ἔφερεν, ἐκφαίνει ἐς τὴν στρατιάν, ὅτι
ἔγνωσται ὀπίσω ἀποστρέφειν.

29. Οἱ δὲ ἐβόων τε οἷα ἂν ὄχλος ξυμμιγὴς χαίρων
βοήσειε καὶ ἐδάκρυον οἱ πολλοὶ αὐτῶν· οἱ δὲ καὶ τῇ
σκηνῇ τῇ βασιλικῇ πελάζοντες ηὔχοντο Ἀλεξάνδρῳ
πολλὰ καὶ ἀγαθά, ὅτι πρὸς σφῶν μόνων νικηθῆναι
ἠνέσχετο. ἔνθα δὴ διελὼν κατὰ τάξεις τὴν στρατιὰν
δώδεκα βωμοὺς κατασκευάζειν προστάττει, ὕψος μὲν
κατὰ τοὺς μεγίστους πύργους, εὖρος δὲ μείζονας ἔτι
ἢ κατὰ πύργους, χαριστήρια τοῖς θεοῖς τοῖς ἐς τοσόνδε ἀγαγοῦσιν αὐτὸν νικῶντα καὶ μνημεῖα τῶν αὐτοῦ
2 πόνων. ὡς δὲ κατεσκευασμένοι αὐτῷ οἱ βωμοὶ
ἦσαν, θύει δὴ ἐπ' αὐτῶν ὡς νόμος καὶ ἀγῶνα ποιεῖ
γυμνικόν τε καὶ ἱππικόν. καὶ τὴν μὲν χώραν τὴν
μέχρι τοῦ Ὑφάσιος ποταμοῦ Πώρῳ ἄρχειν προσέθηκεν, αὐτὸς δὲ ἐπὶ τὸν Ὑδραώτην ἀνέστρεφε.

---

² So QC. ix 3, 18 f.; P. 62, 3.   Both omit the sacrifices, Pt's

326
B.C.

that day nor till the third day after,[2] waiting to see if any change of mind on the part of the Macedonians and allies, such as often occurs in a crowd of soldiers, would come over them and make them easier to persuade. But when dead silence again persisted in the 4 camp and it was clear that the men resented his anger but were not at all converted by it, Ptolemy, son of Lagus, tells us that then he none the less offered sacrifices with a view to crossing the river, but that as he sacrificed the victims proved unfavourable. Then 5 he called together the eldest of the Companions and especially his particular friends and, since everything was now contributing to make him withdraw, he proclaimed openly to the army that he had decided to turn back.

29. They shouted in the way a heterogeneous crowd would do in joy, and most of them began to weep; others drew near the royal tent and invoked blessings on Alexander, since he had submitted to defeat at their hands alone. Then he divided the army into twelve parts and ordered each to set up an altar as high as the greatest towers, and in breadth even greater than towers would be, as thank-offerings to the gods who had brought him so far as a conqueror, and as memorials of his own exertions.[1]

When the altars had been built for him, he per- 2 formed the customary sacrifices on them, and held athletic and equestrian games. He added the territory as far as the river Hyphasis to Porus' dominion,[2] and he himself began to return towards the Hydraotes.

---

excuse for Al's acceptance of defeat (App. XXVII 5); for these see Bosworth on i 4, 5.

[1] D. 95; P. 62; QC. ix 3, 19. Pliny, *NH* vi 62 implausibly puts the altars on the east bank. Cf. App. XVI 5.

[2] App. XVII 32.

διαβὰς δὲ τὸν Ὑδραώτην, ἐπὶ τὸν Ἀκεσίνην αὖ
3 ἐπανήει ὀπίσω. καὶ ἐνταῦθα καταλαμβάνει τὴν
πόλιν ἐξῳκοδομημένην, ἥντινα Ἡφαιστίων αὐτῷ
ἐκτειχίσαι ἐτάχθη· καὶ ἐς ταύτην ξυνοικίσας
τῶν τε προσχώρων ὅσοι ἐθελονταὶ κατῳκίζοντο
καὶ τῶν μισθοφόρων ὅ τι περ ἀπόμαχον, αὐτὸς τὰ
ἐπὶ τῷ κατάπλῳ παρεσκευάζετο τῷ ἐς τὴν μεγάλην
θάλασσαν.
4 Ἐν τούτῳ δὲ ἀφίκοντο πρὸς αὐτὸν Ἀρσάκης τε
ὁ τῆς ὁμόρου Ἀβισάρῃ χώρας ὕπαρχος καὶ ὁ
ἀδελφὸς Ἀβισάρου καὶ οἱ ἄλλοι οἰκεῖοι, δῶρά τε
κομίζοντες ἃ μέγιστα παρ’ Ἰνδοῖς καὶ τοὺς παρ’
Ἀβισάρου ἐλέφαντας, ἀριθμὸν ἐς τριάκοντα· Ἀβισάρην γὰρ νόσῳ ἀδύνατον γενέσθαι ἐλθεῖν. ξυν-
έβαινον δὲ τούτοις καὶ οἱ παρὰ Ἀλεξάνδρου ἐκπεμ-
5 φθέντες πρέσβεις πρὸς Ἀβισάρην. καὶ ταῦτα οὐ
χαλεπῶς πιστεύσας οὕτως ἔχειν Ἀβισάρῃ τε τῆς
αὑτοῦ χώρας σατραπεύειν ἔδωκεν καὶ Ἀρσάκην τῇ
Ἀβισάρου ἐπικρατείᾳ προσέθηκεν· καὶ φόρους
οὕστινας ἀποίσουσι τάξας θύει αὖ καὶ ἐπὶ τῷ
Ἀκεσίνῃ ποταμῷ. καὶ τὸν Ἀκεσίνην αὖ διαβὰς
ἐπὶ τὸν Ὑδάσπην ἧκεν, ἵνα καὶ τῶν πόλεων τῆς τε
Νικαίας καὶ τῶν Βουκεφάλων ὅσα πρὸς τῶν
ὄμβρων πεπονηκότα ἦν ξὺν τῇ στρατιᾷ ἐπεσκεύασε
καὶ τὰ ἄλλα τὰ κατὰ τὴν χώραν ἐκόσμει.

After crossing it, he went back again to the Acesines, and there he found the city already built which he 3 had instructed Hephaestion to fortify [3]; as its inhabitants he settled any of the tribesmen who volunteered to settle there and mercenaries no longer fit for service, while he himself made preparations for the voyage down to the Great Sea.[4]

At this point Arsaces the hyparch of the territory 4 next to Abisares came to him with Abisares' brother and his other relatives, bringing gifts which Indians account of chief value and the elephants from Abisares, numbering about thirty; Abisares (they said) had been unable through illness to attend. The envoys sent by Alexander to Abisares arrived at the same time. Thus, being easily convinced that the facts 5 were as stated, he gave Abisares the satrapy of his own land, and attached Arsaces to Abisares' dominion, and, having fixed the tribute they should bring, he sacrificed at the river Acesines.[5] Then crossing the Acesines again, he came to the Hydaspes, where with the help of his troops he restored the parts of the cities of Nicaea and Bucephala which had been damaged by heavy rains,[6] and settled all other affairs in the country.

---

[3] A. probably forgot that he had not recorded the instructions (21, 5). The site is unknown.

[4] D. 95 and QC. ix 3, 20 ff. made the voyage to the Indus mouth begin on the Acesines, *contra* all A's main sources (cf. *Ind.* 18, 1 for N., and S. xv 1, 17 and 32, following Ar.; see App. XVII 18); hence they misplace there events on the Hydaspes. They alone record large reinforcements (App. XIII 8, cf. XIX 7). Preparations for the voyage: App. XXV 1 f.

[5] App. XVII 33.

[6] Cf. 19, 4.

BOOK VI

ΒΙΒΛΙΟΝ ΕΚΤΟΝ

1. Ἀλέξανδρος δέ, ἐπειδὴ παρεσκευάσθησαν
αὐτῷ ἐπὶ τοῦ Ὑδάσπου ταῖς ὄχθαις πολλαὶ μὲν
τριακόντοροι καὶ ἡμιόλιαι, πολλὰ δὲ καὶ ἱππαγωγὰ
πλοῖα καὶ ἄλλα ὅσα ἐς παρακομιδὴν στρατιᾶς
ποταμῷ εὔπορα, ἔγνω καταπλεῖν κατὰ τὸν Ὑδάσπην
2 ὡς ἐπὶ τὴν μεγάλην θάλασσαν. πρότερον μέν γε
ἐν τῷ Ἰνδῷ ποταμῷ κροκοδείλους ἰδών, μόνῳ τῶν
ἄλλων ποταμῶν πλὴν Νείλου, πρὸς δὲ ταῖς ὄχθαις
τοῦ Ἀκεσίνου κυάμους πεφυκότας ὁποίους ἡ γῆ
ἐκφέρει ἡ Αἰγυπτία, καὶ [ὁ] ἀκούσας ὅτι ὁ
Ἀκεσίνης ἐμβάλλει ἐς τὸν Ἰνδόν, ἔδοξεν ἐξευρη-
3 κέναι τοῦ Νείλου τὰς ἀρχάς, ὡς τὸν Νεῖλον ἐνθένδε
ποθὲν ἐξ Ἰνδῶν ἀνίσχοντα καὶ δι' ἐρήμου πολλῆς
γῆς ῥέοντα καὶ ταύτῃ ἀπολλύοντα τὸν Ἰνδὸν τὸ
ὄνομα, ἔπειτα, ὁπόθεν ἄρχεται διὰ τῆς οἰκουμένης
χώρας ῥεῖν, Νεῖλον ἤδη πρὸς Αἰθιόπων τε τῶν
ταύτῃ καὶ Αἰγυπτίων καλούμενον ⟨ἢ⟩,[1] ὡς Ὅμηρος
ἐποίησεν, ἐπώνυμον τῆς Αἰγύπτου Αἴγυπτον, οὕτω
4 δὴ ἐσδιδόναι ἐς τὴν ἐντὸς θάλασσαν. καὶ δὴ
καὶ πρὸς Ὀλυμπιάδα γράφοντα ὑπὲρ τῶν Ἰνδῶν
τῆς γῆς ἄλλα τε γράψαι καὶ ὅτι δοκοίη αὐτῷ
ἐξευρηκέναι τοῦ Νείλου τὰς πηγάς, μικροῖς δή τισι
καὶ φαύλοις ὑπὲρ τῶν τηλικούτων τεκμαιρόμενον.

[1] Roos inserted ἤ, cf. v 6, 5.

[1] See v 3, 5 n. For the voyage *Ind*. 18 f.; D. 96–104; QC.
ix 3, 24–10, 4; P. 63–6; App. XVII 5 (on Nearchus); 24–8
(chronology and topography); XXV 1 f. (Al's plan and fleet
construction).

BOOK VI

1. Since Alexander had ready for him on the banks of the Hydaspes many *triacontoroi* and *hemioliai* [1] and many transports for horses and other vessels useful for the conveyance of an army by river, he determined to sail down the Hydaspes to the Great Sea. He had 2 already seen crocodiles on the Indus, as on no other river except the Nile, and beans growing on the banks of the Acesines of the same sort as the land of Egypt produces and, having heard that the Acesines runs into the Indus, he thought he had found the origin of the Nile; his idea was that the Nile rose somewhere 3 thereabouts in India, flowed through a great expanse of desert, and there lost the name of Indus, and then, where it began to flow through inhabited country, got the name of Nile from the Ethiopians in those parts and the Egyptians, or that of Aegyptus, which Homer gave in his poem,[2] whence the name of the land [Egypt], and that it then issued into the inner sea [Mediterranean]. In fact it is reported that, when 4 writing to Olympias about the Indian country, Alexander wrote among other things that he thought that he had discovered the springs of the Nile, drawing a conclusion about matters of so much importance from

[2] *Odyssey* iv 581, cf. v 6, 5. Homer as geographical authority: Strabo i *passim*. N. as A's source here: S. xv 1, 25. Crocodiles: S. xv 1, 45 (Ar.). Comparisons with Nile valley: v 4, 4 n. Contemporary discussions of Nile floods: S. xvii 1, 5 (Aristotle and Callisthenes); *Ind.* 6, 7 (Meg.?).

5 ἐπεὶ μέντοι ἀτρεκέστερον ἐξήλεγξε τὰ ἀμφὶ τῷ
ποταμῷ τῷ Ἰνδῷ, οὕτω δὴ μαθεῖν παρὰ τῶν
ἐπιχωρίων τὸν μὲν Ὑδάσπην τῷ Ἀκεσίνῃ, τὸν
Ἀκεσίνην δὲ τῷ Ἰνδῷ τό τε ὕδωρ ξυμβάλλοντας
καὶ τῷ ὀνόματι ξυγχωροῦντας, τὸν Ἰνδὸν δὲ ἐκδιδόντα ἤδη ἐς τὴν μεγάλην θάλασσαν, δίστομον τὸν
Ἰνδὸν ὄντα, οὐδέ⟨ν⟩ τι αὐτῷ προσῆκον τῆς γῆς τῆς
Αἰγυπτίας· τηνικαῦτα δὲ τῆς ἐπιστολῆς τῆς πρὸς
τὴν μητέρα τοῦτο ⟨τὸ⟩ ἀμφὶ τῷ Νείλῳ γραφὲν
6 ἀφελεῖν. καὶ τὸν κατάπλουν τὸν κατὰ τοὺς ποταμοὺς ἔστε ἐπὶ τὴν μεγάλην θάλασσαν ἐπινοοῦντα
παρασκευασθῆναί οἱ ἐπὶ τῷδε κελεῦσαι τὰς ναῦς.
αἱ δὲ ὑπηρεσίαι αὐτῷ ἐς τὰς ναῦς ξυνεπληρώθησαν
ἐκ τῶν ξυνεπομένων τῇ στρατιᾷ Φοινίκων καὶ
Κυπρίων καὶ Καρῶν καὶ Αἰγυπτίων.

2. Ἐν δὲ τούτῳ Κοῖνος μὲν ἐν τοῖς πιστοτάτοις
Ἀλεξάνδρῳ ὢν τῶν ἑταίρων νόσῳ τελευτᾷ· καὶ
τοῦτον θάπτει ἐκ τῶν παρόντων μεγαλοπρεπῶς.
αὐτὸς δὲ ξυναγαγὼν τούς τε ἑταίρους καὶ ὅσοι
Ἰνδῶν πρέσβεις παρ᾽ αὐτὸν ἀφιγμένοι ἦσαν βασιλέα μὲν τῆς ἑαλωκυίας ἤδη Ἰνδῶν γῆς ἀπέδειξε
Πῶρον, ἑπτὰ μὲν ἐθνῶν τῶν ξυμπάντων, πόλεων
ἐν τοῖς ἔθνεσιν ὑπὲρ τὰς δισχιλίας. τὴν στρατιὰν
2 δὲ διένειμεν ὧδε· αὐτὸς μὲν τοὺς ὑπασπιστάς τε
ἅμα οἷ ξύμπαντας ἐπὶ τὰς ναῦς ἀνεβίβασε καὶ
τοὺς τοξότας καὶ τοὺς Ἀγριᾶνας καὶ τὸ ἄγημα
τῶν ἱππέων. Κρατερὸς δὲ αὐτῷ μοῖράν τε τῶν
πεζῶν καὶ τῶν ἱππέων παρὰ τὴν ὄχθην τοῦ Ὑδάσπου τὴν ἐν δεξιᾷ ἦγεν· κατὰ δὲ τὴν ἑτέραν ὄχθην
τὸ πλεῖστόν τε καὶ κράτιστον τῆς στρατιᾶς καὶ
τοὺς ἐλέφαντας Ἡφαιστίων προὐχώρει ἄγων, ἤδη
ὄντας ἐς διακοσίους· τούτοις δὲ ἦν παρηγγελμένον

very slender indications; but that, when he had more 5 326 B.C.
accurately investigated the geography of the river
Indus, he learnt from the inhabitants that the Hydaspes joins its stream to the Acesines and the Acesines
to the Indus, and that they resign their names, while
the Indus then flows out into the Great Sea by two
mouths and has nothing whatever to do with Egypt,
and as a result he cancelled the part of the letter to
his mother which dealt with the Nile,[3] and that, with 6
the idea of sailing down the rivers to the great sea, he
ordered the boats to be made ready for him for this
purpose. The crews of his boats were made up from
the Phoenicians, Cyprians, Carians and Egyptians
who accompanied the expedition.[4]

2. At this time Coenus, one of the most trusty of
the Companions of Alexander, died of disease.[1] So
far as circumstances allowed, Alexander gave him a
magnificent funeral. He himself convened the Companions and all the Indian envoys who had come to
visit him, and proclaimed Porus king of the Indian
land so far acquired, seven nations in all, including
more than two thousand cities.[2] He divided the army 2
as follows. He embarked on the ships with himself
all the hypaspists, the archers, the Agrianians, and
the *agema* of cavalry.[3] Craterus led a division of the
infantry and the cavalry along the right bank of the
Hydaspes. Hephaestion advanced along the other
bank in command of the largest and strongest part
of the army and the elephants, of which there were
now some two hundred; this force was under orders

---

[3] N's report of a *draft* letter.
[4] *Ind.* 18, 1 omits Carians and mentions Greeks.
[1] QC. ix **3**, 20 (inaccurate).
[2] App. XVII **32**.
[3] *Ind.* 19, 5 n.

ὡς τάχιστα ἄγειν ἵναπερ τὰ Σωπείθου βασίλεια.
3 Φιλίππῳ δὲ τῷ σατράπῃ τῆς ἐπέκεινα τοῦ Ἰνδοῦ
ὡς ἐπὶ Βακτρίους γῆς διαλιπόντι τρεῖς ἡμέρας
παρήγγελτο ἕπεσθαι ξὺν τοῖς ἀμφ' αὐτόν. τοὺς
ἱππέας δὲ τοὺς Νυσαίους ὀπίσω ἀποπέμπει ἐς
τὴν Νῦσαν. τοῦ μὲν δὴ ναυτικοῦ παντὸς Νέαρχος
αὐτῷ ἐξηγεῖτο, τῆς δὲ αὐτοῦ νεὼς κυβερνήτης
⟨ἦν⟩ Ὀνησίκριτος, ὃς ἐν τῇ ξυγγραφῇ, ἥντινα
ὑπὲρ Ἀλεξάνδρου ξυνέγραψε, καὶ τοῦτο ἐψεύσατο,
ναύαρχον ἑαυτὸν εἶναι γράψας, κυβερνήτην ὄντα.
4 ἦν δὲ τὸ ξύμπαν πλῆθος τῶν νεῶν, ὡς λέγει
Πτολεμαῖος ὁ Λάγου, ᾧ μάλιστα ἐγὼ ἕπομαι,
τριακόντοροι μὲν ἐς ὀγδοήκοντα, τὰ δὲ πάντα
πλοῖα σὺν τοῖς ἱππαγωγοῖς τε καὶ κερκούροις καὶ
ὅσα ἄλλα ποτάμια ἢ τῶν πάλαι πλεόντων κατὰ
τοὺς ποταμοὺς ἢ ἐν τῷ τότε ποιηθέντων οὐ πολὺ
ἀποδέοντα τῶν δισχιλίων.

3. Ὡς δὲ ξύμπαντα αὐτῷ παρεσκεύαστο, ὑπὸ
τὴν ἕω ὁ μὲν στρατὸς ἐπέβαινε τῶν νεῶν, αὐτὸς
δὲ ἔθυε τοῖς θεοῖς ὡς νόμος καὶ τῷ ποταμῷ Ὑδάσπῃ ὅπως οἱ μάντεις ἐξηγοῦντο. καὶ ἐπιβὰς τῆς
νεὼς ἀπὸ τῆς πρώρας ἐκ χρυσῆς φιάλης ἔσπενδεν ἐς
τὸν ποταμόν, τόν τε Ἀκεσίνην ξυνεπικαλούμενος
τῷ Ὑδάσπῃ, ὅντινα μέγιστον αὖ τῶν ἄλλων ποταμῶν ξυμβάλλειν τῷ Ὑδάσπῃ ἐπέπυστο καὶ οὐ
πόρρω αὐτῶν εἶναι τὰς ξυμβολάς, καὶ τὸν Ἰνδόν,
ἐς ὅντινα ὁ Ἀκεσίνης ξὺν τῷ Ὑδάσπῃ ἐμβάλλει.
2 ἐπὶ δὲ Ἡρακλεῖ τε τῷ προπάτορι σπείσας καὶ
Ἄμμωνι καὶ τοῖς ἄλλοις θεοῖς ὅσοις αὐτῷ νόμος

---

[4] App. XVII 20: presumably 'Sophytes,' whose name in
Greek script occurs on Indian coins (*CHI* 388).

to make at full speed for the capital of Sopithes.[4]
Philip, the satrap of the country west of the Indus 3
towards Bactria, had orders to follow with his forces
after waiting three days.[5] The cavalry of Nysa were
sent back home.[6] Nearchus was appointed admiral
of the whole fleet, and the steersman of Alexander's
own vessel was Onesicritus, who in the history he
wrote of Alexander told this falsehood among others,
that he was its captain, though a mere steersman.[7]
The entire number of ships, according to Ptolemy son 4
of Lagus, whom for my part I am chiefly following,[8]
was eighty *triacontoroi*, while all the boats including
the horse transports, *kerkouroi*, and all the other craft
that had been long plying on the rivers or that had
been constructed at the time came to nearly two
thousand.

3. When everything had been got ready by Alexander, at dawn the army began its embarkation, and
Alexander sacrificed to the gods according to custom,
and to the river Hydaspes according to the instructions
of the seers. After embarking he poured a libation
into the river out of a golden bowl from the bows, calling upon the Acesines as well as the Hydaspes, since he
had learned that it was the largest of the other rivers
and joined the Hydaspes, and also that the meeting
of the waters was not far away; and he also called
upon the Indus, into which the Acesines runs with the
Hydaspes. When he had poured a libation to 2
Heracles his ancestor, to Ammon and to the other

---

[5] N. diverges, but rightly, in making him also satrap of
'this country' (cf. v 8, 3; 20, 7 n.).

[6] App. XVI 6. From Ar.?

[7] App. XVII 4.

[8] This applies at least to the surrounding narrative. Numbers: App. XXV 2. *Kerkouroi*: large oared cargo carriers
according to Casson (v 3, 6 n.) 163 ff.

σημῆναι ἐς ἀναγωγὴν κελεύει τῇ σάλπιγγι. ἅμα τε
δὴ ἐσημάνθη καὶ ἀνήγοντο ἐν κόσμῳ. παρήγγελτο
γὰρ ἐφ᾽ ὅσων τε τὰ σκευοφόρα πλοῖα ἐχρῆν τετάχ-
θαι καὶ ἐφ᾽ ὅσων τὰ ἱππαγωγά, ἐφ᾽ ὅσων τε τὰς
μαχίμους τῶν νεῶν, ὡς μὴ συμπίπτειν ἀλλήλαις
κατὰ τὸν πόρον εἰκῇ πλεούσας· καὶ ταῖς ταχυναυ-
3 τούσαις φθάνειν οὐκ ἐφίετο ἔξω τῆς τάξεως. ἦν
δὲ ὅ τε κτύπος τῆς εἰρεσίας οὐδενὶ ἄλλῳ ἐοικώς,
ἅτε ἀπὸ πολλῶν νεῶν ἐν ταὐτῷ ἐρεσσομένων, καὶ
βοὴ ἀπό τε τῶν κελευστῶν ἐνδιδόντων τὰς ἀρχάς
τε καὶ ἀναπαύλας τῇ εἰρεσίᾳ καὶ τῶν ἐρετῶν ὁπότε
ἀθρόοι ἐμπίπτοντες τῷ ῥοθίῳ ἐπαλαλάξειαν· αἵ
τε ὄχθαι, ὑψηλότεραι τῶν νεῶν πολλαχῇ οὖσαι, ἐς
στενόν τε τὴν βοὴν ξυνάγουσαι καὶ τῇ ξυναγωγῇ
αὐτῇ ἐπὶ μέγα ηὐξημένην ἐς ἀλλήλας ἀντέπεμπον,
καί που καὶ νάπαι ἑκατέρωθεν τοῦ ποταμοῦ τῇ τε
ἐρημίᾳ καὶ τῇ ἀντιπέμψει τοῦ κτύπου καὶ αὐται
4 ξυνεπελάμβανον· οἵ τε ἵπποι διαφαινόμενοι διὰ τῶν
ἱππαγωγῶν πλοίων, οὐ πρόσθεν ἵπποι ἐπὶ νεῶν
ὀφθέντες ἐν τῇ Ἰνδῶν γῇ (καὶ γὰρ καὶ τὸν
Διονύσου ἐπ᾽ Ἰνδοὺς στόλον οὐκ ἐμέμνηντο γενέσθαι ναυτικόν), ἔκπληξιν παρεῖχον τοῖς θεωμένοις
τῶν βαρβάρων, ὥστε οἱ μὲν αὐτόθεν τῇ ἀναγωγῇ
5 παραγενόμενοι ἐπὶ πολὺ ἐφωμάρτουν, ἐς ὅσους δὲ
τῶν ἤδη Ἀλεξάνδρῳ προσκεχωρηκότων Ἰνδῶν
ἡ βοὴ τῶν ἐρετῶν ἢ ὁ κτύπος τῆς εἰρεσίας ἐξίκετο,
καὶ οὗτοι ἐπὶ τῇ ὄχθῃ κατέθεον καὶ ξυνείποντο
ἐπᾴδοντες βαρβαρικῶς. φιλῳδοὶ γάρ, εἴπερ τινὲς
ἄλλοι, Ἰνδοὶ καὶ φιλορχήμονες ἀπὸ Διονύσου

---

[1] *Ind.* 18, 11 f. is complementary. Al's reverence for
Ammon: vi 19, 4; vii 14, 7; 23, 6; *Ind.* 35, 8; App. V 10; cf.

326
B.C.

gods to whom he usually made offering, he bade the
bugle sound for departure. On the sound of the
bugle they started in due order.[1] For instructions
had been given how far apart the baggage vessels,
the horse transports and the warships should be, so
that they should not collide with each other by sailing
irregularly down the stream. Even the fast sailing
ships were not allowed to move ahead out of formation.
There was nothing like the sound of the rowing, with **3**
so many ships rowing at one and the same moment,
and the shouts of the boatswains giving the time for
every stroke, and of the rowers when they struck the
foaming water all together and huzza'd. The banks,
which were often higher than the ships, enclosed the
shouts into a narrow funnel, and this compression
made them even more resonant, as they reverberated
from side to side, and here and there on either side of
the river glens helped to swell the sound, as they
echoed it from their empty spaces. No horses had **4**
hitherto been seen on shipboard in India (for the
Indians had no recollection that Dionysus [2] had also
made his expedition against them by ship); hence
the sight of the horses in the transports astonished
the barbarian onlookers, so that those present at the
departure of the fleet escorted it a long way, and **5**
Indians who had come over to Alexander and were in
earshot of the shouting of the oarsmen and the beat
of the oars also came running down to the bank and
followed, singing barbarian incantations. For none
have more love of song and dance than the Indians

Bosworth, *Greece and the Eastern Mediterranean*, ed. K. H.
Kinzl, 51 ff.
   [2] App. XVI, esp. 8. From Ar.?

ἔτι καὶ τῶν ἅμα Διονύσῳ βακχευσάντων κατὰ τὴν
Ἰνδῶν γῆν.

4. Οὕτω δὴ πλέων τρίτῃ ἡμέρᾳ κατέσχεν,
ἵναπερ Ἡφαιστίωνί τε καὶ Κρατερῷ κατὰ τὸ αὐτὸ
στρατοπεδεύειν ἐπὶ ταῖς ἀντιπέρας ὄχθαις παρήγγελτο. μείνας δὲ ἐνταῦθα ἡμέρας δύο, ὡς καὶ
Φίλιππος αὐτῷ ξὺν τῇ λοιπῇ στρατιᾷ ἀφίκετο,
τοῦτον μὲν ἐπὶ τὸν Ἀκεσίνην ποταμὸν ἐκπέμπει
ξὺν οἷς ἔχων ἧκε, τάξας παρὰ τοῦ Ἀκεσίνου
ποταμοῦ τὴν ὄχθην πορεύεσθαι· τοὺς δὲ ἀμφὶ
Κρατερόν τε καὶ Ἡφαιστίωνα αὖθις ἐκπέμπει,
παραγγείλας ὅπως χρὴ τὴν πορείαν ποιεῖσθαι.
2 αὐτὸς δὲ ἔπλει κατὰ τὸν Ὑδάσπην ποταμὸν οὐδαμοῦ
μείονα ἐν τῷ κατάπλῳ εἴκοσι σταδίων τὸ εὖρος.
προσορμιζόμενος δὲ ὅπῃ τύχοι ταῖς ὄχθαις τοὺς
προσοικοῦντας τῷ Ὑδάσπῃ Ἰνδοὺς τοὺς μὲν
ἐνδιδόντας σφᾶς ὁμολογίαις παρελάμβανεν, ἤδη δέ
τινας καὶ ἐς ἀλκὴν χωρήσαντας βίᾳ κατεστρέψατο.
3 αὐτὸς δὲ ὡς ἐπὶ τὴν Μαλλῶν τε καὶ Ὀξυδρακῶν γῆν
σπουδῇ ἔπλει, πλείστους τε καὶ μαχιμωτάτους
τῶν ταύτῃ Ἰνδῶν πυνθανόμενος καὶ ὅτι ἐξηγγέλλοντο αὐτῷ παῖδας μὲν καὶ γυναῖκας ἀποτεθεῖσθαι
εἰς τὰς ὀχυρωτάτας τῶν πόλεων, αὐτοὶ δὲ ἐγνωκέναι
διὰ μάχης ἰέναι πρὸς αὐτόν. ἐφ᾽ ὅτῳ δὴ καὶ σπουδῇ
πλείονι ἐποιεῖτο τὸν πλοῦν, ὅπως μὴ καθεστηκόσιν
αὐτοῖς, ἀλλὰ ἐν τῷ ἐνδεεῖ τε ἔτι τῆς παρασκευῆς
4 καὶ τεταραγμένῳ προσφέρεται. ἔνθεν δὲ ὡρμήθη
τὸ δεύτερον, [καὶ] πέμπτῃ ἡμέρᾳ ἀφίκετο ἐπὶ τὴν
ξυμβολὴν τοῦ τε Ὑδάσπου καὶ τοῦ Ἀκεσίνου. ἵνα
δὲ ξυμβάλλουσιν οἱ ποταμοὶ οὗτοι, στενότατος εἰς
ποταμὸς ἐκ τοῖν δυοῖν γίγνεται καὶ τὸ ῥεῦμα αὐτῷ
ὀξὺ ἐπὶ τῇ στενότητι καὶ δῖναι ἄτοποι ὑποστρέφον-

ever since the days of Dionysus and of those who shared his revels in India.

4. Sailing in this way, on the third day Alexander put in at a place where orders had been given to both Hephaestion and Craterus to camp, though on opposite banks. There he stayed two days, and when Philip joined him with the rest of the army, he sent him to the river Acesines with the troops he had brought, with orders to march along the bank of the Acesines. The troops with Craterus and Hephaestion were sent on again with instructions as to their route, while he himself sailed on down the river Hydaspes, which was never narrower during the descent than twenty stades. He put in to the banks where chance determined, and would grant terms of submission to the Indians living by the Hydaspes who surrendered; some who resorted to resistance he had already subdued by force. He himself was set on sailing against the land of the Mallians and the Oxydracae, as he was informed that they were the most numerous and the most warlike of the Indians in these parts, and because it was reported to him that they had removed their wives and children to the strongest of their cities and were themselves determined to do battle with him; for this reason he urged on his voyage with the greater speed, so that he might attack them when they had not yet made their arrangements but were still short in their preparations and in a state of confusion. On the fifth [1] day from his second start he came to the meeting of the Hydaspes and the Acesines. Where these two rivers meet, they form one very narrow river; its current is rapid because of the narrows, and the

[1] Perhaps amend to ' fifteenth', though QC. ix 3, 24 makes the daily distance covered only 40 stades.

τος τοῦ ῥοῦ, καὶ τὸ ὕδωρ κυμαίνεταί τε καὶ καχλά-
ζει ἐπὶ μέγα, ὡς καὶ πόρρω ἔτι ὄντων ἐξακούεσθαι
5 τὸν κτύπον τοῦ κύματος. καὶ ἦν μὲν προεξηγ-
γελμένα ταῦτα Ἀλεξάνδρῳ ἐκ τῶν ἐγχωρίων καὶ
⟨ἐξ⟩ Ἀλεξάνδρου τῇ στρατιᾷ· ὅμως δὲ ἐπειδὴ
ἐπέλαζεν αὐτῷ ταῖς ξυμβολαῖς ὁ στρατός, ἐς τοσόνδε
ὁ ἀπὸ τοῦ ῥοῦ κτύπος κατεῖχεν, ὥστε ἐπέστησαν
τὰς εἰρεσίας οἱ ναῦται, οὐκ ἐκ παραγγέλματος,
ἀλλὰ τῶν τε κελευστῶν ὑπὸ θαύματος ἐκσιωπησάν-
των καὶ αὐτοὶ μετέωροι πρὸς τὸν κτύπον γενόμενοι.
5. Ὡς δὲ οὐ πόρρω τῶν ξυμβολῶν ἦσαν,
ἐνταῦθα δὴ οἱ κυβερνῆται παραγγέλλουσιν ὡς
βιαιοτάτῃ εἰρεσίᾳ χρωμένους ἐξελαύνειν ἐκ τῶν
στενῶν, τοῦ μὴ ἐμπιπτούσας τὰς ναῦς ἐς τὰς δίνας
ἀναστρέφεσθαι πρὸς αὐτῶν, ἀλλὰ κρατεῖν γὰρ τῇ
2 εἰρεσίᾳ τῶν ἐπιστροφῶν τοῦ ὕδατος. τὰ μὲν δὴ
στρογγύλα πλοῖα ὅσα καὶ ἔτυχεν αὐτῶν περιστρα-
φέντα πρὸς τοῦ ῥοῦ, οὐδέν τι παθόντα ἐν τῇ
ἐπιστροφῇ ὅτι μὴ ταράξαντα τοὺς ἐμπλέοντας,
κατέστη ἐς εὐθύ, πρὸς αὐτοῦ τοῦ ῥοῦ ὀρθωθέντα·
αἱ δὲ μακραὶ νῆες οὐχ ὡσαύτως ἀπαθεῖς ἀπῆλθον
ἐν τῇ ἐπιστροφῇ, οὔτε μετέωροι ἐπὶ τοῦ ἐπικαχλά-
ζοντος κύματος ὡσαύτως οὖσαι, ὅσαι τε δίκροτοι
αὐτῶν τὰς κάτω κώπας οὐκ ἐπὶ πολὺ ἔξω ἔχουσαι τοῦ
3 ὕδατος· καὶ αἱ κῶπαι δὲ αὐτοῖς πλαγίοις ἐν ταῖς
δίναις γενομένοις συνετρίβοντο, ὅσων γε ἐγκατ-
ελήφθησαν ὑπὸ τοῦ ὕδατος οὐ φθασάντων αὐτὰς
μετεωρίσαι, ὡς πολλὰς μὲν πονῆσαι τῶν νεῶν,
δύο δὲ δὴ περιπεσούσας ἀλλήλαις αὐτάς τε διαφθαρῆναι καὶ τῶν ἐμπλεόντων ἐν αὐταῖς πολλούς.
ὡς δὲ ἐς πλάτος ἤδη ὁ ποταμὸς διέσχεν, ἐνταῦθα δὴ ὅ τε ῥοῦς οὐκέτι ὡσαύτως χαλεπὸς ἦν καὶ

326
B.C.

swirling of the stream produces extraordinary whirlpools; the water billows and roars loudly, so that from
far off one can hear the din of the waves.   All this had 5
been told to Alexander beforehand by the inhabitants, and he had warned his men; yet when they
got near the meeting waters, the din of the stream
was so loud that the sailors stopped their rowing, not
by order, but because the boatswains were struck
dumb with amazement and the sailors themselves
were confused by the din.

5. But when they were not far from the meeting of
the waters, the steersmen directed them to row as
strenuously as possible and get out of the narrows, so
that the ships might not be caught in the whirlpools
and be capsized by them, but that they should master
the eddies of the water by their rowing.   The round 2
boats in their service, though actually twisted about
by the stream, suffered nothing serious in the swirl,
though they caused much anxiety to those aboard;
they kept a straight course, righted by the current
itself, but the long ships did not come off so scathless
in the swirl; they did not ride so high over the roaring
waters; and those with two tiers of oars hardly kept
their lower tier clear of the stream; and when the 3
boats were brought broadside on in the eddies their
oars were broken, at any rate if they were caught
by the water and did not first lift their oars in anticipation, so that many ships were in distress, and two
collided and were themselves wrecked, and many
of those aboard lost.   But when the river broadened
out, at least the stream no longer ran so roughly;

4 αἱ δῖναι οὐχ ὁμοίᾳ τῇ βίᾳ ἐπέστρεφον. προσορμίσας οὖν τῇ ἐν δεξιᾷ ὄχθῃ ᾿Αλέξανδρος τὸν στρατόν, ἵνα σκέπη τε ἦν τοῦ ῥοῦ καὶ προσβολὴ ταῖς ναυσὶν καί τις καὶ ἄκρα τοῦ ποταμοῦ ἐπιτηδείως ἀνεῖχεν ἐς τῶν ναυαγίων τε τὴν ξυναγωγὴν καὶ εἴ τινες ἐπ' αὐτῶν ζῶντες ἔτι ἐφέροντο, τούτους τε διέσωσε καὶ ἐπισκευάσας τὰς πεπονηκυίας τῶν νεῶν Νέαρχον μὲν καταπλεῖν κελεύει ἔστ' ἂν ἀφίκηται ἐπὶ τὰ ὅρια τοῦ Μαλλῶν ἔθνους, αὐτὸς δὲ τῶν βαρβάρων τῶν οὐ προσχωρούντων καταδρομὴν τῆς χώρας ποιησάμενος καὶ κωλύσας ἐπικουρῆσαι αὐτοὺς τοῖς Μαλλοῖς, οὕτω δὴ αὖθις ξυνέμιξε τῷ ναυτικῷ.

5 Καὶ ἐνταῦθα ῾Ηφαιστίων τε αὐτῷ καὶ Κρατερὸς καὶ Φίλιππος ξὺν τοῖς ἀμφ' αὐτοὺς ὁμοῦ ἤδη ἦσαν. ὁ δὲ τοὺς μὲν ἐλέφαντας καὶ τὴν Πολυπέρχοντος τάξιν καὶ τοὺς ἱπποτοξότας καὶ Φίλιππον ξὺν τῇ ἀμφ' αὐτὸν στρατιᾷ διαβιβάσας τὸν ῾Υδάσπην ποταμὸν Κρατερῷ ἄγειν προσέταξε· Νέαρχον δὲ ξὺν τῷ ναυτικῷ πέμπει τρισὶν ἡμέραις τὴν στρατιὰν 6 κελεύσας φθάνειν κατὰ τὸν πλοῦν. τὸν δὲ ἄλλον στρατὸν τριχῇ διένειμε· καὶ ῾Ηφαιστίωνα μὲν πέντε ἡμέραις προϊέναι ἔταξεν, ὡς εἴ τινες τοὺς ξὺν αὐτῷ τεταγμένους φεύγοντες ἐς τὸ πρόσω κατὰ σπουδὴν ἴοιεν, τοῖς ἀμφὶ ῾Ηφαιστίωνα ἐμπίπτοντες ἁλίσκωνται· Πτολεμαῖον δὲ τὸν Λάγου δοὺς καὶ τούτῳ τῆς στρατιᾶς μέρος τρισὶν ἡμέραις ὑπολειπόμενον ἕπεσθαι ἐκέλευσεν, ὡς ὅσοι τὸ ἔμπαλιν ὑποστρέφοιεν αὐτὸν φεύγοντες, οὗτοι δὲ ἐς τοὺς 7 ἀμφὶ τὸν Πτολεμαῖον ἐμπίπτοιεν. ἐπὰν δὲ ἀφίκωνται ἐς τὰς ξυμβολὰς τοῦ τε ᾿Ακεσίνου καὶ τοῦ

and the eddies did not whirl the ships about with so
much violence.[1]   Alexander then brought his fleet to   4
land on the right bank, where there was shelter from
the current and a landing place for the ships, and
where a headland ran out into the river conveniently
for gathering in the wrecks and anyone still alive on
them, and so saved the survivors and repaired the
damaged ships.   After this he ordered Nearchus to
sail down till he reached the boundaries of the Mallian
people, while he himself raided the country of the
tribesmen who had not submitted to him, and so prevented them from bringing help to the Mallians.
Then he again joined the flotilla.

Here Hephaestion and Craterus and Philip with   5
their troops joined him again.   Alexander put the
elephants, Polyperchon's battalion, the mounted
archers [2] and Philip with his army across the river
Hydaspes, and ordered Craterus to take command
of them; Nearchus was sent with the fleet and
ordered to proceed three days in advance of the army
down stream.   Alexander divided the remaining   6
forces into three parts; Hephaestion was ordered to
go on five days ahead, so that any who fled from his
own force and moved rapidly ahead would fall in with
Hephaestion's troops and be captured, while Ptolemy
son of Lagus, to whom he also handed over part of
the army, was told to follow him at an interval of
three days, so that any who turned back again, fleeing from himself, might fall in with Ptolemy and his
troops.   The advance guard was ordered as soon as   7
they arrived at the junction of the Acesines and

---

[1] D. 97. QC. 4, 8 ff. reserves the terrors (with Al. almost
drowning) to other confluences and inserts an outbreak of
mutinous feeling.

[2] Here, or in 6, 1, the mounted javelin men must be meant.

Ὑδραώτου ποταμοῦ, ἐνταῦθα δὴ τούς τε φθάνοντας
ὑπομένειν ἐκέλευσεν, ἔστ' ἂν ἥκῃ αὐτός, καὶ τοὺς
ἀμφὶ Κρατερὸν καὶ Πτολεμαῖον αὐτῷ ξυμβαλεῖν.

6. Αὐτὸς δὲ ἀναλαβὼν τοὺς ὑπασπιστάς τε καὶ
τοὺς τοξότας καὶ τοὺς Ἀγριᾶνας καὶ τῶν ἀσθεταίρων [1] καλουμένων τὴν Πείθωνος τάξιν καὶ τοὺς
ἱπποτοξότας τε πάντας καὶ τῶν ἱππέων τῶν ἑταίρων τοὺς ἡμίσεας διὰ γῆς ἀνύδρου ὡς ἐπὶ Μαλλοὺς
2 ἦγεν, ἔθνος Ἰνδικὸν Ἰνδῶν τῶν αὐτονόμων. καὶ
τῇ μὲν πρώτῃ κατεστρατοπέδευσε πρὸς ὕδατι οὐ
πολλῷ, ὃ δὴ ἀπεῖχε τοῦ Ἀκεσίνου ποταμοῦ σταδίους ἐς ἑκατόν· δειπνοποιησάμενος δὲ καὶ ἀναπαύσας τὴν στρατιὰν οὐ πολὺν χρόνον παραγγέλλει
ὅ τι τις ἔχοι ἄγγος ἐμπλῆσαι ὕδατος. διελθὼν δὲ
τῆς τε ἡμέρας τὸ ἔτι ὑπολ⟨ε⟩ιπόμενον καὶ τὴν
νύκτα ὅλην ἐς τετρακοσίους μάλιστα σταδίους
ἅμα ἡμέρᾳ πρὸς πόλιν ἀφίκετο, ἐς ἣν ξυμπε-
3 φεύγεσαν πολλοὶ τῶν Μαλλῶν. οἱ δὲ οὔποτ' ἂν
οἰηθέντες διὰ τῆς ἀνύδρου ἐλθεῖν ἐπὶ σφᾶς Ἀλέξανδρον ἔξω τε τῆς πόλεως οἱ πολλοὶ καὶ ἄνοπλοι
ἦσαν· ἐφ' ὅτῳ καὶ δῆλος ἐγένετο ταύτην ἀγαγὼν
Ἀλέξανδρος, ἣν ὅτι αὐτῷ ἀγαγεῖν χαλεπὸν ἦν, ἐπὶ
τῷδε οὐδὲ τοῖς πολεμίοις ὅτι ἄξει πιστὸν ἐφαίνετο.
τούτοις μὲν δὴ οὐ προσδοκήσασιν ἐπιπεσὼν τοὺς
μὲν πολλοὺς ἀπέκτεινεν αὐτῶν οὐδὲ ἐς ἀλκὴν οἷα
δὴ ἀνόπλους τραπέντας· τῶν δὲ ἄλλων εἰς τὴν πόλιν
κατειληθέντων κύκλῳ περιστήσας τῷ τείχει τοὺς
ἱππέας, ὅτι μήπω ἡ φάλαγξ τῶν πεζῶν ἠκολουθήκει
4 αὐτῷ, ἀντὶ χάρακος ἐχρήσατο τῇ ἵππῳ. ὡς δὲ
τάχιστα οἱ πεζοὶ ἀφίκοντο, Περδίκκαν μὲν τήν τε
αὑτοῦ ἱππαρχίαν ἔχοντα καὶ τὴν Κλείτου καὶ τοὺς

[1] See Introduction n. 99.

Hydraotes to wait there till he arrived in person and till the forces of Craterus and Ptolemy joined him.

6. Then he himself took with him the hypaspists, the archers, the Agrianians and Pithon's battalion of the so-called *asthetairoi*, with all the mounted archers and half the Companion cavalry,[1] and led them through a waterless country against the Mallians, an Indian tribe, one of those which were self-governing. On the first day he camped about a hundred stades 2 from the river Acesines where there was a small supply of water, and, after dining and resting his army a short time, he passed the word along that every vessel any one had was to be filled with water. Marching about four hundred stades during the remainder of that day and through the night, at daybreak he arrived at a city into which many of the Mallians had congregated in flight; never supposing 3 that Alexander would attack them through this waterless region, they were mostly outside the city and unarmed; even his enemies did not think it credible that he would take this route, for the very reason (as it was now plain) that he had taken it, the mere fact of its difficulty. As then his attack was unexpected, he killed most of them without their attempting resistance, unarmed as they were. The rest were cooped in the city, and Alexander stationed his cavalry round the wall in a cordon, using them like a palisade, since his infantry phalanx had not yet come up with him. But as soon as the infantry 4 arrived, he sent Perdiccas with his own hipparchy, that of Clitus, and the Agrianians, against another

---

[1] Cf. 5, 5 n.; App. XIX 3. Divergent accounts of subsequent operations with exaggerated enemy numbers in D. and QC., see App. XVII 25–7. *Asthetairoi*: v 22 n.2.

Ἀγριᾶνας πρὸς ἄλλην πόλιν ἐκπέμπει τῶν Μαλλῶν, οἳ ξυμπεφευγότες ἦσαν πολλοὶ τῶν ταύτῃ
Ἰνδῶν, φυλάσσειν τοὺς ἐν τῇ πόλει κελεύσας,
ἔργου δὲ μὴ ἔχεσθαι ἔστ' ἂν ἀφίκηται αὐτός, ὡς
μηδὲ ἀπὸ ταύτης τῆς πόλεως διαφυγόντας τινὰς
αὐτῶν ἀγγέλους γενέσθαι τοῖς ἄλλοις βαρβάροις ὅτι
προσάγει ἤδη Ἀλέξανδρος· αὐτὸς δὲ προσέβαλλεν
5 τῷ τείχει. οἱ δὲ βάρβαροι τὸ μὲν τεῖχος ἐκλείπουσιν, ὡς οὐκ ἂν διαφυλάξαντες αὐτὸ ἔτι, πολλῶν
ἐν τῇ καταλήψει τεθνηκότων, τῶν δὲ καὶ ἀπὸ
τραυμάτων ἀπομάχων γεγενημένων· ἐς δὲ τὴν
ἄκραν ξυμφυγόντες χρόνον μέν τινα ἠμύνοντο ἐξ
ὑπερδεξίου τε χωρίου καὶ χαλεποῦ ἐς προσβολήν,
προσκειμένων δὲ πάντοθεν εὐρώστως τῶν Μακεδόνων καὶ αὐτοῦ Ἀλεξάνδρου ἄλλοτε ἄλλῃ ἐπιφαιν-
ομένου τῷ ἔργῳ ἥ τε ἄκρα κατὰ κράτος ἑάλω καὶ
οἱ ξυμφυγόντες ἐς αὐτὴν πάντες ἀπέθανον· ἦσαν
δὲ ἐς δισχιλίους.

6 Περδίκκας δὲ ἐς τὴν πόλιν ἐφ' ἥντινα ἐστάλη
ἀφικόμενος τὴν μὲν πόλιν ἐρήμην καταλαμβάνει,
μαθὼν δὲ ὅτι οὐ πρὸ πολλοῦ πεφεύγεσαν ἐξ αὐτῆς
οἱ ἐνοικοῦντες δρόμῳ ἤλαυνε κατὰ στίβον τῶν
φευγόντων· οἱ δὲ ψιλοὶ ὡς τάχους ποδῶν εἶχον
αὐτῷ ἐφείποντο. καταλαβὼν δὲ τῶν φευγόντων
κατέκοψεν ὅσοι γε μὴ ἔφθασαν ἐς τὰ ἕλη ξυμφυγόντες.

7. Ἀλέξανδρος δὲ δειπνοποιησάμενός τε καὶ
ἀναπαύσας τοὺς ἀμφ' αὐτὸν ἔστε ἐπὶ πρώτην
φυλακὴν ᾔει τοῦ πρόσω· καὶ τὴν νύκτα διελθὼν
πολλὴν ὁδὸν ἅμα ἡμέρᾳ ἀφίκετο πρὸς τὸν Ὑδραώτην ποταμόν. ἔνθα δὴ τῶν Μαλλῶν τοὺς μὲν
πολλοὺς διαβεβηκότας ἤδη ἔμαθεν, τοῖς δὲ καὶ

city of the Mallians, where many Indians of the
district had taken refuge, with orders to watch the
men in the city, but not to engage in action till he
arrived himself; thus they were to prevent anyone
from this city escaping to tell the other barbarians
that Alexander was already close at hand. He himself attacked the city wall. The barbarians deserted 5
it, in despair of defending it further, many having
perished in the assault, while others had been in-
capacitated for service from wounds. Taking refuge
in the citadel, for some time they continued to defend
themselves from a commanding position, difficult
to assail. But as the Macedonians pressed on
vigorously from all sides, and as Alexander himself
appeared here, there and everywhere in the action,
the citadel was taken by assault, and all who had
taken refuge there perished, to the number of about
two thousand.

Perdiccas arrived at the city which he had been 6
sent against, and found it empty, but, learning that
the inhabitants had not long fled, he rode at full speed
on the track of the fugitives, and the light-armed followed with the best speed they could make on foot.
He caught up with and massacred all the fugitives who
had not first found refuge in the marshes.[2]

7. After seeing that his troops had dined and
rested, Alexander began his advance again about the
first watch. He marched a considerable distance in
the night and at daybreak arrived at the river
Hydraotes. There he learned that most of the
Mallians had already crossed, but he fell in with

---

[2] Presumably Perdiccas rejoined Al. (cf. 9, 1) before Pithon
was detached with two hipparchies (7, 2); cf. App. XIX 3.

διαβαίνουσιν ἐπιγενόμενος περὶ αὐτὸν τὸν πόρον
2 πολλοὺς αὐτῶν διέφθειρε. καὶ αὐτὸς ὡς εἶχε
ξυνδιαβὰς κατὰ τὸν αὐτὸν πόρον διώκων εἴχετο
τῶν φθασάντων ἐς τὴν ἀποχώρησιν. καὶ πολλοὺς
μὲν ἀπέκτεινεν αὐτῶν, τοὺς δὲ καὶ ζῶντας ἔλαβεν,
οἱ πλείους δὲ κατέφυγον ἔς τι χωρίον ὀχυρὸν καὶ
τετειχισμένον. Ἀλέξανδρος δέ, ὡς οἱ πεζοὶ ἀφίκοντο αὐτῷ, ἀποστέλλει ἐπὶ τούτους Πείθωνα τήν
τε αὐτοῦ τάξιν ἔχοντα καὶ τῶν ἱππέων δύο ἱππ-
3 αρχίας. καὶ οὗτοι δὴ ἐξ ἐφόδου προσβαλόντες
λαμβάνουσι τὸ χωρίον καὶ τοὺς καταπεφευγότας
ἐς αὐτὸ ἠνδραπόδισαν, ὅσοι γε μὴ ἐν τῇ προσβολῇ
διεφθάρησαν. ταῦτα δὲ οἱ ἀμφὶ τὸν Πείθωνα
διαπραξάμενοι ἐπανῆλθον αὖθις ἐς τὸ στρατόπεδον.
4 Αὐτὸς δὲ Ἀλέξανδρος ὡς ἐπὶ τῶν Βραχμάνων τινὰ
πόλιν ἦγεν, ὅτι καὶ ἐς ταύτην ξυμπεφευγέναι τινὰς
τῶν Μαλλῶν ἔμαθεν. ὡς δὲ ἀφίκετο πρὸς αὐτήν,
ἐπῆγε τῷ τείχει πάντοθεν πυκνὴν τὴν φάλαγγα.
οἱ δὲ ὑπορυσσόμενα τὰ τείχη ἰδόντες καὶ ἐκ τῶν
βελῶν ἀναστελλόμενοι τὰ μὲν τείχη καὶ οὗτοι
ἐκλείπουσιν, ἐς δὲ τὴν ἄκραν ξυμφυγόντες ἐκεῖθεν
ἠμύνοντο· ξυνεισπεσόντων δὲ αὐτοῖς ὀλίγων
Μακεδόνων μεταβαλλόμενοι καὶ ξυστραφέντες τοὺς
μὲν ἐξέωσαν αὐτῶν, ἀπέκτειναν δὲ ἐν τῇ ὑποστροφῇ
5 ἐς πέντε καὶ εἴκοσι. καὶ ἐν τούτῳ Ἀλέξανδρος τάς
τε κλίμακας πάντοθεν κελεύει προστιθέναι τῇ ἄκρᾳ

---

¹ But for 16, 5 and 17, 2 one would take Brachmanes to
denote a people (so D. 102, 6). The term was used by Ar. and
N. (S. xv 1, 61 and 66) for the class A. normally calls 'sophists'
(vii 1, 5; 2 f.; *Ind.* 11, from Meg., cf. S. xv 1, 39). Meg.
restricted it to one sect of 'philosophers,' contrasted with
Garmanes (ib. 58 ff.), and distinguished warriors (47). Neither

others who were actually crossing, and destroyed many of them during the passage. He himself with 2 no more ado crossed along with them by the same ford, and continued to pursue and hold on to those who had got away in their retreat. Many were killed, some captured alive, but the greater number took refuge in a strong, fortified position. But as soon as his infantry came up with him, Alexander sent Pithon against them with his own battalion and two hipparchies of cavalry. They attacked without 3 a pause, captured the place, and enslaved all those who had taken refuge there, except for those who had fallen in the assault. Then Pithon and his detachment, having finished all this, returned back again to the camp.

Alexander himself was now advancing against a 4 city of the Brachmanes,[1] as he had learned that some of the Mallians had taken refuge there too. On arrival, he led his phalanx in close formation on all sides up to the wall. When they saw their walls undermined, and were pushed back by the missiles, they too deserted the walls and took refuge in the citadel where they continued their defence. A few Macedonians broke in with them, whereupon they turned round, formed a solid mass and drove out the attackers, killing about twenty-five while they attempted to withdraw. At this point Alexander 5 ordered ladders to be set up on all sides against the

he nor any writer except A. (perhaps following Pt.) referred to them as warriors (J. W. McCrindle, *Anc. India as described in Class. Lit.* 1901, 167–86 collects later evidence). Perhaps Pt. meant that they controlled the government, but cf. Meg. (S. xvi 49 ff.).

ARRIAN

καὶ ὑπορύττειν τὸ τεῖχος. ὡς δὲ πύργος τε ἔπεσεν
ὑπορυσσόμενος καὶ τοῦ μεταπυργίου τι παρραγὲν
ἐπιμαχωτέραν ταύτῃ ἐποίησε τὴν ἄκραν, πρῶτος
Ἀλέξανδρος ἐπιβὰς τοῦ τείχους ὤφθη ἔχων τὸ
6 τεῖχος. καὶ τοῦτον ἰδόντες οἱ ἄλλοι Μακεδόνες
αἰσχυνθέντες ἄλλος ἄλλῃ ἀνῄεσαν. εἴχετό τε ἤδη
ἡ ἄκρα, καὶ τῶν Ἰνδῶν οἱ μὲν τὰς οἰκίας ἐνεπίμ-
πρασαν καὶ ἐν αὐταῖς ἐγκαταλαμβανόμενοι ἀπέ-
θνησκον, οἱ πολλοὶ δὲ μαθόμενοι αὐτῶν. ἀπέθανον
δὲ οἱ πάντες ἐς πεντακισχιλίους, ζῶντες δὲ δι᾽
ἀνδρ⟨ε⟩ίαν ὀλίγοι ἐλήφθησαν.

8. Μείνας δὲ αὐτοῦ μίαν ἡμέραν καὶ ἀναπαύσας
τὴν στρατιὰν τῇ ὑστεραίᾳ προὐχώρει ὡς ἐπὶ τοὺς
ἄλλους Μαλλούς. καὶ τὰς μὲν πόλεις ἐκλελοιπό-
τας καταλαμβάνει, αὐτοὺς δὲ ἔμαθεν ὅτι πεφευγότες
2 εἶεν ἐς τὴν ἔρημον. καὶ ἐνταῦθα αὖθις μίαν ἡμέραν
ἀναπαύσας τὴν στρατιὰν ἐς τὴν ἐπιοῦσαν Πείθωνα
μὲν καὶ Δημήτριον τὸν ἱππάρχην πρὸς τὸν ποταμὸν
ὀπίσω ἀπέπεμψεν, ὧν τε αὐτοὶ ἡγοῦντο ἄγοντας
καὶ πρὸς τούτοις ψιλῶν τάξεις δοὺς αὐτοῖς ὅσαι
3 ἱκαναὶ πρὸς τὸ ἔργον. προσέταξε δὲ παρὰ τῇ ὄχθῃ
τοῦ ποταμοῦ ἰόντας, εἴ τισι περιτυγχάνοιεν τῶν ἐς
τὰς ὕλας ξυμπεφευγότων, αἳ δὴ πολλαὶ πρὸς τῇ
ὄχθῃ τοῦ ποταμοῦ ἦσαν, τούτους κτείνειν, ὅσοι
μὴ ἐθελονταὶ σφᾶς ἐνδιδοῖεν. καὶ πολλοὺς κατα-
λαβόντες ἐν ταῖς ὕλαις οἱ ἀμφὶ Πείθωνά τε καὶ
Δημήτριον ἀπέκτειναν.

4 Αὐτὸς δὲ ἦγεν ἐπὶ τὴν μεγίστην τῶν Μαλλῶν πόλιν,
ἵνα καὶ ἐκ τῶν ἄλλων πόλεων πολλοὺς ξυμπεφευγέναι
αὐτῷ ἐξηγγέλλετο. ἀλλὰ καὶ ταύτην ἐξέλιπον οἱ
Ἰνδοὶ ὡς προσάγοντα Ἀλέξανδρον ἔμαθον. δια-
βάντες δὲ τὸν Ὑδραώτην ποταμὸν ἐπὶ ταῖς ὄχθαις

citadel, and the wall to be undermined. When a tower was undermined and fell, and a breach in part of the curtain wall made the citadel easier of assault on that side, Alexander was first to mount the wall and was seen holding it. At the sight, the rest of 6 the Macedonians mounted, out of shame, one here and one there. And by this time the citadel was in their hands; some of the Indians set fire to their houses, and perished imprisoned in them, but most of them died fighting. Up to five thousand in all fell, but such was their courage that few were captured alive.

8. Alexander remained there one day and rested his army, and on the next day went on against the remaining Mallians. He found the cities abandoned and learned that the inhabitants had fled into the desert. There again he rested his army one day, 2 and on the next day sent Pithon and Demetrius the hipparch back to the river with the troops they themselves commanded [1] and, in addition, as many battalions of light troops as were enough for their task. He directed them to go along the river bank 3 and, if they should come across any of those who had taken refuge together in the woods, of which there were many along the river bank, to kill all who did not voluntarily surrender. Pithon's and Demetrius' troops did, in fact, find and kill many in the woods.

Alexander himself marched against the greatest 4 city of the Mallians, where he was told many from the other cities had taken refuge together. But even this city was deserted by the Indians when they learned of Alexander's approach; they crossed the Hydraotes and stood their ground, marshalled on the

[1] Presumably Pithon's foot battalion and Demetrius' hipparchy.

ARRIAN

αὐτοῦ, ὅτι ὑψηλαὶ αἱ ὄχθαι ἦσαν, παρατεταγμένοι
5 ἔμενον, ὡς εἴρξοντες τοῦ πόρου Ἀλέξανδρον. καὶ
ταῦτα ὡς ἤκουσεν, ἀναλαβὼν τὴν ἵππον τὴν ἅμα
αὐτῷ πᾶσαν ᾔει ὡς ἐπὶ τὸν Ὑδραώτην, ἵναπερ
παρατετάχθαι τοὺς Μαλλοὺς ἐξηγγέλλετο. οἱ
δὲ πεζοὶ ἕπεσθαι αὐτῷ ἐτάχθησαν. ὡς δὲ ἀφίκετό
τε ἐπ᾽ αὐτὸν καὶ ἐν τῷ πέραν τοὺς πολεμίους τεταγμένους κατεῖδεν, ὡς εἶχεν ἐκ τῆς ὁδοῦ ἐμβάλλει
6 ἐς τὸν πόρον ξὺν τῇ ἵππῳ μόνῃ. οἱ δὲ ἰδόντες ἐν
μέσῳ τοῦ ποταμοῦ ὄντα ἤδη Ἀλέξανδρον κατὰ
σπουδὴν μέν, ξυντεταγμένοι δὲ ὅμως ἀπεχώρουν
ἀπὸ τῆς ὄχθης· καὶ Ἀλέξανδρος ξὺν μόνῃ τῇ ἵππῳ
εἵπετο. ὡς δὲ κατεῖδον ἱππέας μόνους, ἐπιστρέψαντες οἱ Ἰνδοὶ καρτερῶς ἐμάχοντο πλῆθος ὄντες
ἐς πέντε μυριάδας. καὶ Ἀλέξανδρος ὡς τήν τε
φάλαγγα αὐτῶν πυκνὴν κατεῖδε καὶ αὐτῷ οἱ πεζοὶ
ἀπῆσαν, προσβολὰς μὲν ἐποιεῖτο ἐς κύκλους
παριππεύων, ἐς χεῖρας δὲ οὐκ ᾔει τοῖς Ἰνδοῖς.
7 καὶ ἐν τούτῳ παραγίγνονται αὐτῷ οἵ τε Ἀγριᾶνες
καὶ ἄλλαι τάξεις τῶν ψιλῶν, ἃς δὴ ἐπιλέκτους ἅμα
οἷ ἦγε, καὶ οἱ τοξόται· οὐ πόρρω δὲ οὐδὲ ἡ
φάλαγξ ἐφαίνετο τῶν πεζῶν. καὶ οἱ Ἰνδοὶ ὁμοῦ
σφισι πάντων τῶν δεινῶν προσκειμένων ἀποστρέ-
ψαντες ἤδη προτροπάδην ἔφευγον ἐς πόλιν ὀχυρω-
8 τάτην τῶν πλησίον. καὶ Ἀλέξανδρος ἑπόμενός
τε αὐτοῖς πολλοὺς ἔκτεινε καὶ ὡς ἐς τὴν πόλιν οἱ
διαφυγόντες κατειλήθησαν, πρῶτα μὲν τοῖς ἱππεῦσιν ἐξ ἐφόδου ἐκυκλώσατο τὴν πόλιν· ὡς δὲ οἱ
πεζοὶ αὐτῷ παρῆσαν, ταύτῃ μὲν τῇ ἡμέρᾳ περιστρα-
τοπεδεύει ἐν κύκλῳ τοῦ τείχους, ὅτι οὐ πολύ τε
τῆς ἡμέρας ὑπελείπετο ἐς τὴν προσβολὴν καὶ ἡ
στρατιὰ αὐτῷ ὑπό τε πορείας μακρᾶς οἱ πεζοὶ καὶ

326/5
B.C.

banks, since the banks were high, to prevent Alexander from crossing. When he heard this, he took 5
all the cavalry he had with him and made for the
Hydraotes, where it was reported that the Mallians
were marshalled; the infantry were ordered to
follow. When he reached the river and saw the
enemy in battle order on the far side, he plunged
just as he was from the road into the ford with the
cavalry only. Seeing Alexander already in mid- 6
stream, the enemy retired from the bank rapidly,
but in good order. Alexander followed with only
his cavalry. But when the Indians saw cavalry by
themselves, they turned about and offered a vigorous
resistance, in number about fifty thousand. Alexander saw that their infantry formation was solid and,
with his own foot not yet on the field, kept circling
round and making charges, without coming to close
quarters with the Indians. And now he was joined 7
by the Agrianians and other battalions of the light
troops, picked units he had in his own force, and by
the archers. Not far off the phalanx of infantry was
visible. The Indians with all these terrors converg-
ing upon them turned and, now in full flight, sought
refuge in a city which was the strongest in the
neighbourhood. Alexander followed them and 8
killed many, and when the fugitives had been cooped
up in the city he first, without a pause, threw his
cavalry in a circle round the city. When his infantry
came up, for this day he encamped all round the wall,
since little daylight was left for the attack, and his
army was much fatigued, the infantry from their long

ὑπὸ διώξεως συνεχοῦς οἱ ἵπποι καὶ οὐχ ἥκιστα
κατὰ τὸν πόρον τοῦ ποταμοῦ τεταλαιπωρήκεσαν.

9. Τῇ δὲ ὑστεραίᾳ διχῇ διελὼν τὸν στρατὸν τοῦ
μὲν ἑτέρου αὐτὸς ἡγούμενος προσέβαλλε τῷ τείχει,
τὸ δὲ ἕτερον Περδίκκας προσῆγε. καὶ ἐν τούτῳ
οὐ δεξάμενοι οἱ Ἰνδοὶ τῶν Μακεδόνων τὴν ὁρμὴν
τὰ μὲν τείχη τῆς πόλεως λείπουσιν, αὐτοὶ δὲ ἐς
τὴν ἄκραν ξυνέφευγον. Ἀλέξανδρος μὲν οὖν καὶ
οἱ ἀμφ’ αὐτὸν πυλίδα τινὰ κατασχίσαντες παρῆλθον
2 ἐς τὴν πόλιν πολὺ πρὸ τῶν ἄλλων. οἱ δὲ ὁμοῦ
Περδίκκᾳ τεταγμένοι ὑστέρησαν ὑπερβαίνοντες
κατὰ τὰ τείχη οὐκ εὐπετῶς, οὐδὲ τὰς κλίμακας οἱ
πολλοὶ αὐτῶν φέροντες, ὅτι ἑαλωκέναι αὐτοῖς
ἐδόκει ἡ πόλις, ἐρημούμενα τῶν προμαχομένων τὰ
τείχη ὡς κατεῖδον. ὡς δὲ ἡ ἄκρα ἐχομένη πρὸς
τῶν πολεμίων καὶ πρὸ ταύτης τεταγμένοι εἰς τὸ
ἀπομάχεσθαι πολλοὶ ἐφάνησαν, ἐνταῦθα δὴ οἱ μὲν
ὑπορύσσοντες τὸ τεῖχος, οἱ δὲ προσθέσει ὅπῃ παρ-
είκοι τῶν κλιμάκων βιάσασθαι ἐπειρῶντο ἐς τὴν
3 ἄκραν. Ἀλέξανδρος δέ, ὡς βλακεύειν αὐτῷ ἐδόκουν τῶν Μακεδόνων οἱ φέροντες τὰς κλίμακας,
ἁρπάσας κλίμακα ἑνὸς τῶν φερόντων προσέθηκε τῷ
τείχει αὐτὸς καὶ εἰληθεὶς ὑπὸ τῇ ἀσπίδι ἀνέβαινεν·
ἐπὶ δὲ αὐτῷ Πευκέστας ὁ τὴν ἱερὰν ἀσπίδα φέρων,
ἣν ἐκ τοῦ νεὼ τῆς Ἀθηνᾶς τῆς Ἰλιάδος λαβὼν ἅμα
οἱ εἶχεν Ἀλέξανδρος καὶ πρὸ αὐτοῦ ἐφέρετο ἐν ταῖς
μάχαις· ἐπὶ δὲ τούτῳ Λεοννάτος ἀνῄει κατὰ τὴν
αὐτὴν κλίμακα ὁ σωματοφύλαξ· κατὰ δὲ ἄλλην
κλίμακα Ἀβρέας τῶν διμοιριτῶν τις στρατευομέ-
4 νων. ἤδη τε πρὸς τῇ ἐπάλξει τοῦ τείχους ὁ
βασιλεὺς ἦν καὶ ἐρείσας ἐπ’ αὐτῇ τὴν ἀσπίδα τοὺς
μὲν ὤθει εἴσω τοῦ τείχους τῶν Ἰνδῶν, τοὺς δὲ καὶ

march, the cavalry from their continuous pursuit; worst of all was the crossing of the river.

9. Next day Alexander divided his army in two and, taking the command of one part himself, began to attack the wall. Perdiccas brought up the other half. At this point the Indians did not withstand the onslaught of the Macedonians, but deserted the walls of the city, and sought their own safety in mass flight to the citadel. Now Alexander and his troops tore down a small gate and penetrated into the city far in advance of the rest, whereas those under Perdiccas' 2 command fell behind, finding difficulty in getting over the wall; most of them were not even carrying ladders, since they thought the city had actually been captured when they saw the walls deserted by their defenders. When, however, the citadel was seen to be in the enemy's hands and large numbers drawn up for its protection, some at once began undermining the wall, others set ladders wherever opportunity offered and tried to force a way into the citadel. Thinking that the Macedonians who were 3 bringing the ladders were laggard, Alexander seized a ladder from one of the bearers, set it up himself against the wall, huddled under his shield and mounted up; next went Peucestas, carrying the sacred shield, which Alexander had taken from the temple of Athena of Ilium and always kept by him, and which was carried before him in battle, then Leonnatus, the bodyguard, went up by the same ladder, and by another ladder Abreas, one of the soldiers with double pay.[1] By this time the king was 4 by the battlement of the wall and, propping his shield on it, he pushed off some of the Indians within

---

[1] Perhaps an N.C.O.; cf. vii 23, 3.

αὐτοῦ τῷ ξίφει ἀποκτείνας γεγύμνωκει τὸ ταύτῃ
τεῖχος· καὶ οἱ ὑπασπισταὶ ὑπέρφοβοι γενόμενοι
ὑπὲρ τοῦ βασιλέως σπουδῇ ὠθούμενοι κατὰ τὴν
αὐτὴν κλίμακα συντρίβουσιν αὐτήν, ὥστε οἱ μὲν
ἤδη ἀνιόντες αὐτῶν κάτω ἔπεσον, τοῖς δὲ ἄλλοις
ἄπορον ἐποίησαν τὴν ἄνοδον.

5 Ἀλέξανδρος δὲ ὡς ἐπὶ τοῦ τείχους στὰς κύκλῳ
τε ἀπὸ τῶν πλησίον πύργων ἐβάλλετο, οὐ γὰρ
πελάσαι γε ἐτόλμα τις αὐτῷ τῶν Ἰνδῶν, καὶ ὑπὸ
τῶν ἐκ τῆς πόλεως, οὐδὲ πόρρω τούτων γε ἐσακον-
τιζόντων (ἔτυχε γάρ τι καὶ προσκεχωσμένον
ταύτῃ πρὸς τὸ τεῖχος), δῆλος μὲν ἦν Ἀλέξανδρος
ὢν τῶν τε ὅπλων τῇ λαμπρότητι καὶ τῷ ἀτόπῳ
τῆς τόλμης, ἔγνω δὲ ὅτι αὐτοῦ μὲν μένων κινδυ-
νεύσει μηδὲν ὅ τι καὶ λόγου ἄξιον ἀποδεικνύμενος,
καταπηδήσας δὲ εἴσω τοῦ τείχους τυχὸν μὲν αὐτῷ
τούτῳ ἐκπλήξει τοὺς Ἰνδούς, εἰ δὲ μή, καὶ κινδυνεύειν δέοι, μεγάλα ἔργα καὶ τοῖς ἔπειτα πυθέσθαι
ἄξια ἐργασάμενος οὐκ ἀσπουδεὶ ἀποθανεῖται —
ταῦτα γνοὺς καταπηδᾷ ἀπὸ τοῦ τείχους ἐς τὴν
6 ἄκραν. ἔνθα δὴ ἐρεισθεὶς πρὸς τῷ τείχει τοὺς
μέν τινας ἐς χεῖρας ἐλθόντας καὶ τόν γε ἡγεμόνα
τῶν Ἰνδῶν προσφερόμενόν οἱ θρασύτερον παίσας τῷ
ξίφει ἀποκτείνει· ἄλλον δὲ πελάζοντα λίθῳ βαλὼν
ἔσχε καὶ ἄλλον λίθῳ, τὸν δὲ ἐγγυτέρω προσάγοντα
τῷ ξίφει αὖθις. οἱ δὲ βάρβαροι πελάζειν μὲν αὐτῷ
οὐκέτι ἤθελον, ἔβαλλον δὲ πάντοθεν περιεστηκότες
ὅ τι τις ἔχων βέλος ἐτύγχανεν ἢ ἐν τῷ τότε
ἔλαβεν.

10. Ἐν τούτῳ δὲ Πευκέστας τε καὶ ὁ διμοιρίτης
Ἀβρέας καὶ ἐπ’ αὐτοῖς Λεοννάτος, οἳ δὴ μόνοι
ἔτυχον πρὶν ξυντριβῆναι τὰς κλίμακας ἀναβεβηκότες

326/5
B.C.

the wall, there and then killed others with his sword, and had thus cleared that part of the wall; but the hypaspists became over-anxious for the king, hurriedly jostled up the same ladder and broke it, so that the men already mounting fell down, and as a result the rest had no way up.

Standing as he was upon the wall, Alexander was 5 shot at all round from the neighbouring towers (for none of the Indians dared approach him) and also by the men in the citadel, and they were actually within short range, as at this point there happened to be a mound near the wall. Conspicuous as Alexander was both by the splendour of his arms and by his extraordinary audacity, he decided that by remaining where he was he would be in danger, while not even performing any deed of note, but that if he leapt down within the wall he might perhaps by this very action strike the Indians with panic but, if not and danger was inevitable, he might do great deeds, worth hearing to men of later generations, and that glory would attend his death. On this decision he leapt down from the wall into the citadel. There he 6 propped himself against the wall and, when some Indians came to close quarters and their commander set on him rather boldly, he struck and killed them with his sword. He checked the approach of others, one after another, by hurling stones, but any one who moved too close was again struck with the sword, till the barbarians were unwilling to approach him, but surrounding him on all sides threw any missiles they happened to have or could at the moment lay their hands on.

10. At this point Peucestas and Abreas, ' the double-pay man ', and on their heels Leonnatus, the only men who had actually got on to the wall before

ἐπὶ τὸ τεῖχος, καταπηδήσαντες καὶ αὐτοὶ πρὸ τοῦ
βασιλέως ἐμάχοντο. καὶ Ἀβρέας μὲν ὁ διμοιρίτης πίπτει αὐτοῦ τοξευθεὶς ἐς τὸ πρόσωπον,
Ἀλέξανδρος ⟨δὲ⟩ βάλλεται καὶ αὐτὸς διὰ τοῦ
θώρακος ἐς τὸ στῆθος τοξεύματι ὑπὲρ τὸν μαστόν,
ὥστε λέγει Πτολεμαῖος ὅτι καὶ πνεῦμα ὁμοῦ τῷ
2 αἵματι ἐκ τοῦ τραύματος ἐξεπνεῖτο. ὁ δέ, ἔστε
μὲν ἔτι θερμὸν ἦν αὐτῷ τὸ αἷμα, καίπερ κακῶς
ἔχων ἠμύνετο· πολλοῦ δὲ δὴ τοῦ αἵματος καὶ
ἀθρόου οἷα δὴ ξὺν πνεύματι ἐκρυέντος, ἴλιγγός τε
αὐτὸν καὶ λειποψυχία κατέσχε καὶ πίπτει αὐτοῦ
ἐπὶ τὴν ἀσπίδα ξυννεύσας. Πευκέστας δὲ περιβὰς
πεπτωκότι καὶ ὑπερσχὼν τὴν ἱερὰν τὴν ἐξ Ἰλίου
ἀσπίδα πρὸ αὐτοῦ [εἶχε], καὶ Λεοννάτος ἐς τὰ ἐπὶ
θάτερα, οὗτοί τε·βάλλονται ἀμφότεροι καὶ Ἀλέξανδρος ἐγγὺς ἦν ἤδη ὑπὸ τοῦ αἵματος ἐκλιπεῖν.
3 τοῖς γὰρ Μακεδόσι καὶ ταύτῃ ἐν ἀπόρῳ γεγένητο τὰ
τῆς προσβολῆς, ὅτι οἱ τὸν Ἀλέξανδρον βαλλόμενόν
τε ἐπὶ τῷ τείχει ἰδόντες καὶ πηδῶντα ἔσω ἐς τὴν
ἄκραν, ὑπὸ σπουδῆς τε καὶ φόβου μή τι αὐτοῖς ὁ
βασιλεὺς πάθῃ οὐ ξὺν νόῳ κινδυνεύων, τὰς κλίμακας
ξυντετριφότες ἄλλοι ἄλλας μηχανὰς ἐς τὸ ἀνελθεῖν
ἐπὶ τὸ τεῖχος ὡς ἐν ἀπόροις ἐμηχανῶντο, οἱ μὲν
πασσάλους ἐμπηγνύοντες ἐς τὸ τεῖχος γήινον ὄν, καὶ
κατὰ τούτους ἐκκρεμαννύμενοι χαλεπῶς ἀνεῖρπον,
4 οἱ δὲ ἄλλοι ἐπ' ἄλλους ἐπιβαίνοντες. ὁ δὲ πρῶτος
ἀνελθὼν ἐνρίπτει αὐτὸν κατὰ τοῦ τείχους ἐς τὴν
πόλιν, ἵναπερ τὸν βασιλέα ἑώρων κείμενον, ξὺν
οἰμωγῇ καὶ ἀλαλαγμῷ πάντες. ἤδη τε ἀμφ' αὐτῷ
πεπτωκότι καρτερὰ μάχη ξυνειστήκει ἄλλου ἐπ'
ἄλλῳ τῶν Μακεδόνων προασπίζοντος, καὶ ἐν
τούτῳ οἱ μὲν τὸν μοχλὸν ὅτῳ εἴχετο ἡ κατὰ τὸ

326/5
B.C.

the ladders broke, also leapt down and fought to
defend the king. Abreas the double-pay man fell
there, shot with an arrow in the face, and Alexander
himself was struck, right through the corslet into his
chest above the breast, so that, according to Ptolemy,
breath as well as blood spouted from the wound.
Yet as long as his blood was still warm, he continued 2
to defend himself, though distressed, but when a good
deal of blood poured out all at once, which naturally
happened as he breathed out, he was overcome with
dizziness and faintness, and fell there bending over
his shield. Peucestas stepped astride him as he lay
there, and held over him the sacred shield from Ilium
to protect him, Leonnatus was on the other side, and
they two received the showers of missiles while Alexander from loss of blood was near to death. For the 3
Macedonian assault had also come into great difficulties at this point. Those who saw Alexander
exposed to missiles on the wall and leaping inside
into the citadel were impelled by ardour and fear
that their king should come to harm by his thought-
less daring and, as they had broken the ladders to
pieces, they contrived various expedients in this
difficulty for scaling the wall; some fixed pegs in the
wall, which was of earth, and clinging to them crept
up with difficulty; others mounted on their comrades'
shoulders. The first to ascend threw himself down 4
from the wall into the citadel, where he saw the king
lying; and all groaned and raised their battle-cry.
Already a fierce battle had been joined round the
fallen king, with now one, now another of the Macedonians holding his shield over him, when some
severed the bar with which the gate in the curtain

μεταπύργιον πύλη κατασχίσαντες ἐπ' ὀλίγους
παρῄεσαν, οἱ δὲ καθ' ὅ τι ἡ πύλη διέσχε τοὺς
ὤμους ὑποθέντες καὶ ὤσαντες ἐς τὸ ἔσω τὸ τεῖχος
ἀνεπέτασαν ταύτῃ τὴν ἄκραν.

11. Ἐν τούτῳ δὲ οἱ μὲν ἔκτεινον τοὺς Ἰνδούς,
καὶ ἀπέκτεινάν γε πάντας οὐδὲ γυναῖκα ἢ παῖδα
ὑπελείποντο, οἱ δὲ ἐξέφερον τὸν βασιλέα ἐπὶ τῆς
ἀσπίδος κακῶς ἔχοντα, οὔπω γιγνώσκοντες βιώσιμον ὄντα. τὸ δὲ βέλος ἐξελκύσαι ἐκ τοῦ τραύματος ἐπιτεμόντα τὴν πληγὴν οἱ μὲν Κριτόδημον
ἀνέγραψαν, ἰατρὸν Κῶον, τὸ γένος τῶν Ἀσκληπια-
δῶν, οἱ δὲ Περδίκκαν τὸν σωματοφύλακα, οὐ
παρόντος ἐν τῷ δεινῷ ἰατροῦ, ἐγκελευσαμένου
Ἀλεξάνδρου τῷ ξίφει ἐπιτεμεῖν τὴν πληγὴν καὶ
2 κομίσασθαι τὸ βέλος. ἐν δὲ τῇ κομιδῇ φορὰ
αἵματος πολλοῦ γίγνεται, ὥστε λειποψυχῆσαι
αὖθις Ἀλέξανδρον καὶ οὕτω σχεθῆναι αὐτῷ τὸ
αἷμα ὑπὸ τῇ λειποψυχίᾳ. πολλὰ δὲ καὶ ἄλλα
ἀναγέγραπται τοῖς ξυγγραφεῦσιν ὑπὲρ τοῦ παθήματος, καὶ ἡ φήμη παραδεξαμένη αὐτὰ κατὰ τοὺς
πρώτους ψευσαμένους ἔτι καὶ εἰς ἡμᾶς διασῴζει,
οὐδὲ ἀφήσει παραδιδοῦσα καὶ ἐφεξῆς ἄλλοις τὰ
ψευδῆ, εἰ μὴ ὑπὸ τῆσδε τῆς ξυγγραφῆς παύσεται.
3 Αὐτίκα ἐν Ὀξυδράκαις τὸ πάθημα τοῦτο
γενέσθαι Ἀλεξάνδρῳ ὁ πᾶς λόγος κατέχει· τὸ δὲ
ἐν Μαλλοῖς ἔθνει αὐτονόμῳ Ἰνδικῷ ξυνέβη, καὶ ἥ
τε πόλις Μαλλῶν ἦν καὶ οἱ βαλόντες Ἀλέξανδρον
Μαλλοί, οἳ δὴ ἐγνώκεσαν μὲν ξυμμίξαντες τοῖς
Ὀξυδράκαις οὕτω διαγωνίζεσθαι, ἔφθη δὲ διὰ τῆς
ἀνύδρου ἐπ' αὐτοὺς ἐλάσας πρίν τινα ὠφέλειαν

---

[1] ' Vulgate.'   QC. ix 5, 25 writes ' Critobulus.'

wall was fastened, and got through a few at a time, while others put their shoulders to the place where the gate provided an aperture, pushed it back within the wall, and opened up the citadel on this side.

11. At this point, while some were slaughtering the Indians, and they killed all, leaving neither woman nor child, others carried off the king on his shield, in such bad condition that they did not yet know if he could live. Some authorities [1] recorded that Critodemus, a physician of Cos, of the family of the Asclepiads, drew out the arrow from the wound, cutting the part it had struck; others that Perdiccas the bodyguard, no surgeon being at hand in the emergency, cut the wound with his sword at Alexander's express command, and so extracted the missile. In the extraction there was a great flow of blood, so that 2 Alexander fainted again and the haemorrhage was thus checked by his fainting. Many other stories have been written by the historians about the misfortune, and tradition has received them as the first falsifiers told them, and still keeps them alive to this day, nor indeed will it ever cease handing on the falsehoods to others in turn, unless it is checked by this history.

To begin with, it is universally told and believed 3 that the misfortune happened to Alexander among the Oxydracae,[2] whereas it took place among the Mallians, an independent Indian tribe; the city was a Mallian city, and it was Mallians who wounded Alexander; to be sure, they had determined to join the Oxydracae and so fight together, but Alexander reached them too quickly, marching through the desert, before any help could reach them from the

[2] So QC. ix 4, 26 ff. (D. is vague), but not P. 63 nor S. xv 1, 33 (on which see App. XVII 18).

αὐτοῖς παρὰ τῶν Ὀξυδρακῶν γενέσθαι ἢ αὐτοὺς
4 ἐκείνοις τι ἐπωφελῆσαι. ἐπεὶ καὶ τὴν τελευταίαν
μάχην τὴν πρὸς Δαρεῖον γενομένην, καθ' ἥντινα
ἔφυγε Δαρεῖος οὐδὲ πρόσθεν ἔληξε τῆς φυγῆς πρὶν
ξυλληφθῆναι ὑπὸ τῶν ἀμφὶ Βῆσσον καὶ προσάγον-
τος ἤδη Ἀλεξάνδρου ἀποθανεῖν, πρὸς Ἀρβήλοις
γενέσθαι ὁ πᾶς λόγος κατέχει, καθάπερ οὖν καὶ
τὴν πρὸ ταύτης ἐν Ἰσσῷ καὶ τὴν πρώτην ἱππο-
5 μαχίαν πρὸς Γρανίκῳ. ἀλλὰ πρὸς Γρανίκῳ μὲν
ξυνέβη ⟨ἡ⟩ μάχη ἡ ἱππικὴ καὶ πρὸς Ἰσσῷ ἡ
αὖθις πρὸς Δαρεῖον μάχη, Ἄρβηλα δὲ τοῦ χώρου,
ἐν ᾧ τὴν ἐσχάτην μάχην Δαρεῖός τε καὶ Ἀλέξανδρος ἐμαχέσαντο, οἱ μὲν τὰ πλεῖστα ξυγγράψαντες
λέγουσιν ὅτι ἑξακοσίους σταδίους ἀπέχει, οἱ δὲ τὰ
ἐλάχιστα, ὅτι ἐς πεντακοσίους. ἀλλὰ ἐν Γαυγαμή-
λοις γὰρ γενέσθαι τὴν μάχην πρὸς ποταμῷ Βουμή-
6 λῳ λέγει Πτολεμαῖος καὶ Ἀριστόβουλος. πόλις
δὲ οὐκ ἦν τὰ Γαυγάμηλα, ἀλλὰ κώμη μεγάλη, οὐδὲ
ὀνομαστὸς ὁ χῶρος οὐδὲ ἐς ἀκοὴν ἡδὺ τὸ ὄνομα·
ἔνθεν δή μοι δοκεῖ πόλις οὖσα τὰ Ἄρβηλα ἀπηνέγ-
κατο τὴν δόξαν τῆς μεγάλης μάχης. εἰ δὲ πρὸς
Ἀρβήλοις χρὴ οἴεσθαι γενέσθαι τὸ ἔργον ἐκεῖνο ἐς
τοσόνδε Ἀρβήλων ἀπέχον, καὶ τὴν ἐν Σαλαμῖνι
γενομένην ναυμαχίαν πρὸς ἰσθμῷ τῷ Κορινθίων ἔξεστι λέγειν ὅτι ἐγένετο, καὶ τὴν ἐπ' Ἀρτεμισίῳ
τῆς Εὐβοίας πρὸς Αἰγίνῃ ἢ Σουνίῳ.
7 Καὶ μὴν ὑπὲρ τῶν ὑπερασπισάντων ἐν τῷ
κινδύνῳ Ἀλεξάνδρου, Πευκέσταν μὲν γενέσθαι
ξύμπαντες ὁμολογοῦσιν, ὑπὲρ Λεοννάτου δὲ οὐκέτι
ξυμφέρονται οὐδὲ ὑπὲρ Ἀβρέου τοῦ διμοιρίτου.
καὶ οἱ μὲν ξύλῳ πληγέντα κατὰ τοῦ κράνους Ἀλέξανδρον καὶ ἰλιγγιάσαντα πεσεῖν, αὖθις δὲ ἀναστάν-

326/5
B.C.

Oxydracae, and indeed before they gave any to the
Oxydracae. In the same way, it is universally told 4
and believed that the last battle with Darius, in which
Darius fled, never ceasing his flight until he was
arrested by Bessus and his followers, and perished
when Alexander was already close at hand, took
place at Arbela, and the battle before this at Issus,
and the first cavalry battle by Granicus. But while 5
a cavalry battle did take place by Granicus, and the
second battle against Darius near Issus, Arbela is six
hundred stades distant from the place where Darius
and Alexander fought their last battle, according to
writers who give the highest figure, five hundred
stades on the lowest figure. But Ptolemy and
Aristobulus state that the battle took place at
Gaugamela by the river Bumodus. Gaugamela was 6
not a city but a large village; it was not a famous
place, and the name has an unpleasing sound; and so
I suppose Arbela, as a city, carried off the glory of the
great battle,[3] though, if we must ascribe this action
to Arbela, it is legitimate to say that the naval battle
at Salamis took place by the Isthmus of Corinth, and
the battle of Euboean Artemisium near Aegina or
Sunium.

Then again, as to those who protected Alexander 7
in his danger with their shields, one and all agree that
Peucestas was there, but agreement ceases about
Leonnatus as well as about Abreas, the double-pay
man. Then some say that Alexander was struck on
the helmet with a club, became dizzy and fell, but
rose up again and was then struck by a missile in the

---

[3] Here A., S. xvi 1, **3** (with the same explanation) and P.
31, 3 probably follow Ar., whom all three had read. Cf. App.
V 2.

τα βληθῆναι βέλει διὰ τοῦ θώρακος ἐς τὸ στῆθος·
Πτολεμαῖος δὲ ὁ Λάγου ταύτην μόνην τὴν πληγὴν
8 πληγῆναι λέγει τὴν ἐς τὸ στῆθος. τὸ δὲ δὴ
μέγιστον πλημμέλημα τῶν ξυγγραψάντων τὰ ἀμφὶ
Ἀλέξανδρον ἐκεῖνο τίθεμαι ἔγωγε. Πτολεμαῖον
γὰρ τὸν Λάγου ἔστιν οἳ ἀνέγραψαν ξυναναβῆναί τε
Ἀλεξάνδρῳ κατὰ τὴν κλίμακα ὁμοῦ Πευκέστᾳ καὶ
ὑπερασπίσαι κειμένου, καὶ ἐπὶ τῷδε Σωτῆρα ἐπικληθῆναι τὸν Πτολεμαῖον· καίτοι αὐτὸς Πτολεμαῖος ἀναγέγραφεν οὐδὲ παραγενέσθαι τούτῳ τῷ
ἔργῳ, ἀλλὰ στρατιᾶς γὰρ αὐτὸς ἡγούμενος ἄλλας
μάχεσθαι μάχας καὶ πρὸς ἄλλους βαρβάρους.
ταῦτα μὲν δὴ ἐν ἐκβολῇ τοῦ λόγου ἀναγεγράφθω
μοι, ὡς μὴ ἀταλαίπωρον γίγνεσθαι τοῖς ἔπειτα
ἀνθρώποις τὴν ὑπὲρ τῶν τηλικούτων ἔργων τε καὶ
παθημάτων ἀφήγησιν.

12. Ἐν ᾧ δὲ Ἀλέξανδρος αὐτοῦ μένων τὸ τραῦμα
ἐθεραπεύετο, ἐς τὸ στρατόπεδον, ἔνθενπερ ὡρμήθη
ἐπὶ τοὺς Μαλλούς, ὁ μὲν πρῶτος λόγος ἧκεν ὅτι
τεθνηκὼς εἴη ἐκ τοῦ τραύματος. καὶ τὰ μὲν πρῶτα
οἰμωγὴ ἦν τῆς στρατιᾶς ξυμπάσης ἄλλου ἄλλῳ
παραδιδόντος τὴν φήμην· παυσάμενοι δὲ τῆς οἰμω-
γῆς ἄθυμοί τε καὶ ἄποροι ἦσαν, ὅστις μὲν ἐξηγού-
2 μενος ἔσται τῆς στρατιᾶς (πολλοῖς γὰρ δὴ ἐν ἴσῳ
τὰ τῆς ἀξιώσεως ἐδόκει πρός τε αὐτοῦ Ἀλεξάν-

---

[4] Leonnatus is named alone, D. 99 (cf. A vii 5, 5 from
Pt./Ar.); with Timaeus and Aristonus, QC. 5, 14; with
Limnaeus, P. 63. Ar. put the wound in the neck (Plut. *Mor.*
341 C). The club wound is not attested elsewhere. Hamilton
on P. 63 notes other minute divergencies.

[5] E.g. Clitarchus (Plut. 327 B), cf. v 11, 3; vi, 16, 5 nn.

[6] QC. ix 5, 21 notes that Pt., though no detractor of his own

chest through his breastplate. But Ptolemy son of
Lagus states that there was only the one wound, in
the chest.[4] But in my own estimation the greatest 8
error of the historians of Alexander is this: some
recorded [5] that Ptolemy son of Lagus mounted with
Alexander up the ladder together with Peucestas,
and held his shield over him when he had fallen, and
that for this reason he was surnamed Saviour, and yet
Ptolemy himself has recorded that he was not so much
as present in this action, but was at the head of his
own force, fighting other battles against other
barbarians.[6] This I had to write, by way of digression, so that later generations may take some care in
the narration of such great deeds and misfortunes.

12. While Alexander stayed here getting treatment for his wound, the first report at the camp from
which he had set out against the Mallians suggested
that he had died from the wound. And first lament
was raised by the army as a whole, as one passed on
the report to another; when they ceased the lament,
they were disheartened and could not see who would
be the future leader of the army (for in fact in the 2
opinion both of Alexander and of the Macedonians

glory, recorded that he was absent on an expedition, and
castigates Clitarchus and Timagenes (Jacoby no. 88) for alleg-
ing his presence: did he and A. have a common source? Pt.
was called ' Saviour ' first by the Rhodians for aiding them in
304, and in Egypt (so far as we know) only after his death
(*RE* xxiii 1623; 1638). As a contemporary Alexandrian,
Clitarchus would have known the origin of the name, and
whenever he wrote (App. XXVIII 20) could not have gone
wrong on that. So A. is refuting an embellished version of
Clitarchus' story. It is not clear that Pt. *expressly* contradicted him.

δρου καὶ πρὸς Μακεδόνων καθεστηκέναι), ὅπως δὲ
ἀποσωθήσονται ἐς τὴν οἰκείαν, τοσούτων μὲν
ἐθνῶν μαχίμων περιειργόντων σφᾶς ἐν κύκλῳ, τῶν
μὲν οὔπω προσκεχωρηκότων, ἃ δὴ ὑπὲρ τῆς ἐλευθερίας εἴκαζον ἀγωνιεῖσθαι καρτερῶς, τῶν δὲ
ἀποστησομένων ἀφαιρεθέντος αὐτοῖς τοῦ Ἀλεξάνδρου φόβου, ποταμῶν τε ἐν μέσῳ ἀδιαβάτων
τότε δὴ ἐδόκουν εἶναι καὶ πάντα σφίσιν ἄπορα καὶ
3 ἀμήχανα ἐρήμοις Ἀλεξάνδρου ἐφαίνετο. ὡς δὲ ἧκέ
ποτε λόγος ὅτι ζῇ Ἀλέξανδρος, τούτῳ μὲν μόγις
ξυνεχώρησαν, εἰ δὲ καὶ βιώσιμός ἐστιν, οὔπω ἐπισ-
τεύετο. ὡς δὲ καὶ γράμματα παρ' αὐτοῦ ἧκεν ὅτι
ὅσον οὔπω κατελεύσεται ἐπὶ τὸ στρατόπεδον,
οὐδὲ ταῦτα τοῖς πολλοῖς ὑπὸ τοῦ ἄγαν δέους πιστὰ
ἐφαίνετο, ἀλλὰ πλάττεσθαι γὰρ πρὸς τῶν ἀμφ'
αὐτὸν σωματοφυλάκων τε καὶ στρατηγῶν εἰκάζετο.

13. Καὶ ταῦτα ἐννοήσας Ἀλέξανδρος, μή τι
νεωτερισθείη ἐν τῇ στρατιᾷ, ὅτε πρῶτον ἠδυνήθη
κομίζεται ἐπὶ τοῦ ποταμοῦ τοῦ Ὑδραώτου τὰς
ὄχθας· καὶ πλέων κατὰ τὸν ποταμόν (ἦν γὰρ τὸ
στρατόπεδον ἐπὶ ταῖς ξυμβολαῖς τοῦ τε Ὑδραώτου
καὶ τοῦ Ἀκεσίνου, ἵνα Ἡφαιστίων τε ἐπὶ τῆς
στρατιᾶς ἦν καὶ Νέαρχος τὸ ναυτικὸν αὐτῷ εἶχεν),
ὡς [δὲ] ἐπέλαζεν ἡ ναῦς ἤδη τῷ στρατοπέδῳ τὸν
βασιλέα φέρουσα, κελεύει δὴ ἀφελεῖν τὴν σκηνὴν
2 ἀπὸ τῆς πρύμνης, ὡς καταφανὴς εἶναι πᾶσιν. οἱ δὲ ἔτι
ἠπίστουν, ὡς νεκροῦ δῆθεν κομιζομένου Ἀλεξάνδρου, πρίν γε δὴ προσχούσης τῆς νεὼς τῇ ὄχθῃ
ὁ μὲν τὴν χεῖρα ἀνέτεινεν ἐς τὸ πλῆθος· οἱ δὲ
ἀνεβόησαν, ἐς τὸν οὐρανὸν ἀνασχόντες τὰς χεῖρας,
οἱ δὲ πρὸς αὐτὸν Ἀλέξανδρον· πολλοῖς δὲ καὶ
δάκρυα ἐπὶ τῷ ἀνελπίστῳ προεχύθη ἀκούσια. καὶ

326/5
B.C.

many possessed an equal reputation), and how they would get back safe to their own homes, with so many warlike nations hemming them in all round, some of whom had not yet come over, and were in their view likely to fight vigorously for their freedom, while others would revolt, once their dread of Alexander was removed. Then they believed that they were in the midst of impassable rivers. Everything seemed to them impracticable and hopeless if they were bereft of Alexander. When news eventually came 3 that Alexander was alive, they hardly believed it; and they still had no confidence that he would yet survive. But when a letter came from him that he would very shortly come to the camp, most of them could not believe it for excess of fear, but they guessed that it was forged by his bodyguards and generals.

13. On consideration of this, to prevent any disturbance in the army, Alexander was conveyed as soon as he was able to the bank of the river Hydraotes, and sailed downstream, as the camp was at the junction of the Hydraotes and Acesines, where Hephaestion was in command of the army and where Nearchus had his fleet; as soon as the boat with the king on board drew near to the camp, he ordered the awning to be taken off the stern, so that everyone might see him. Yet they were still incredulous, as 2 they thought Alexander's dead body was being brought down, until the moment when the ship actually put in to the bank, and Alexander held up his hand to the crowd, and they shouted, holding up their hands to heaven, others towards Alexander himself; many even wept involuntarily in surprise.

οἱ μὲν τῶν ὑπασπιστῶν κλίνην προσέφερον αὐτῷ
ἐκκομιζομένῳ ἐκ τῆς νεώς, ὁ δὲ τὸν ἵππον προσ-
3 αγαγεῖν ἐκέλευσεν. ὡς δὲ ἐπιβὰς τοῦ ἵππου
ὤφθη αὖθις, κρότῳ δὴ πολλῷ ἐπεκτύπησεν ἡ
στρατιὰ πᾶσα, ἐπήχησαν δὲ αἵ τε ὄχθαι καὶ αἱ
πλησίον αὐτῶν νάπαι. προσάγων δὲ ἤδη τῇ σκηνῇ
καταβαίνει ἀπὸ τοῦ ἵππου, ὥστε καὶ βαδίζων
ὀφθῆναι. οἱ δὲ ἐπέλαζον ἄλλος ἄλλοθεν, οἱ μὲν
χειρῶν, οἱ δὲ γονάτων, οἱ δὲ τῆς ἐσθῆτος αὐτῆς
ἁπτόμενοι, οἱ δὲ καὶ ἰδεῖν ἐγγύθεν καί τι καὶ
ἐπευφημήσαντες ἀπελθεῖν· οἱ δὲ ταινίαις ἔβαλλον,
οἱ δὲ ἄνθεσιν, ὅσα ἐν τῷ τότε ἡ Ἰνδῶν γῆ παρεῖχε.
4   Νέαρχος δὲ λέγει, ὅτι χαλεποὶ αὐτῷ τῶν φίλων
ἐγένοντο ὅσοι ἐκάκιζον, ὅτι αὐτὸς πρὸ τῆς στρατιᾶς
κινδυνεύοι· οὐ γὰρ στρατηγοῦ ταῦτα, ἀλλὰ στρατιώτου εἶναι. καί μοι δοκεῖ ἄχθεσθαι Ἀλέξανδρος
τοῖσδε τοῖς λόγοις, ὅτι ἀληθεῖς τε ὄντας ἐγίγνωσκε
καὶ αὐτὸν ὑπαίτιον τῇ ἐπιτιμήσει. καὶ ὅμως ὑπὸ
μένους τε τοῦ ἐν ταῖς μάχαις καὶ τοῦ ἔρωτος τῆς
δόξης, καθάπερ οἱ ἄλλης τινὸς ἡδονῆς ἐξηττώμενοι,
5   οὐ καρτερὸς ἦν ἀπέχεσθαι τῶν κινδύνων. ἄνθρωπον
δέ τινα πρεσβύτερον λέγει Βοιώτιον, τὸ δὲ ὄνομα
τοῦ ἀνθρώπου οὐ λέγει, ὡς ἀχθόμενόν τε πρὸς τὰς
ἐπιτιμήσεις τῶν φίλων κατέμαθεν Ἀλέξανδρον καὶ
ἐσκυθρωπακότα, προσελθόντα τοῦτον βοιωτιάζοντα
ἅμα τῇ φωνῇ ταῦτα φάναι· ὦ Ἀλέξανδρε, ἀνδρῶν
τὰ ἔργα· καί τι καὶ ἰαμβεῖον ὑπειπεῖν, τὸν δὲ νοῦν
εἶναι τοῦ ἰαμβείου ὅτι τῷ τι δρῶντι καὶ παθεῖν
ἐστιν ὀφειλόμενον. καὶ τοῦτον ἔν τε τῷ παραυτίκα
εὐδοκιμῆσαι καὶ ἐπιτηδειότερον ἐς τὸ ἔπειτα Ἀλεξάνδρῳ γενέσθαι.

14. Ἐν τούτῳ δὲ ἀφίκοντο παρὰ Ἀλέξανδρον

326/5
B.C.

Some of the hypaspists brought a litter for him as he was being carried out of the ship; but he ordered his horse to be brought alongside. When he was seen 3 once more to have mounted the horse, the whole army clapped their hands again and again, and the banks and glens nearby echoed the sound. As Alexander drew near his tent, he dismounted from his horse, so as to be seen walking too. Then they got near to him on this side and that, touching his hands, knees or clothing, or just to look at him close at hand, cast a blessing upon him and go away; some showered wreaths upon him or the flowers the country of India produced at that season.

Nearchus tells us that he was pained by some of his 4 friends who blamed him for running a personal risk in advance of his army; this, they said, was a soldier's part, not a commander's. My own idea is that Alexander was irritated with these remarks because he knew that they were true and that he had laid himself open to this censure. And yet his rage in battle and passion for glory made him like men overcome by any other form of pleasure, and he was not strong-minded enough to keep out of dangers. Nearchus says that an oldish man, a Boeotian—he 5 does not give his name—on learning of Alexander's anger with his friends' reproaches and sullen looks, came up to him and in his Boeotian dialect said: ' Alexander, deeds are men's work;' that he added an iambic verse of which the general tenor was that suffering too is the doer's due,[1] and won Alexander's immediate approval and thenceforward his close friendship.

14. At this time envoys from the rest of the

---

[1] Aeschylus fr. 444 Nauck[2]: δράσαντι γάρ τοι καὶ παθεῖν ὀφείλεται.

τῶν Μαλλῶν τῶν ὑπολειπομένων πρέσβεις ἐνδιδόντες τὸ ἔθνος, καὶ παρὰ 'Οξυδρακῶν οἵ τε ἡγεμόνες
τῶν πόλεων καὶ οἱ νομάρχαι αὐτοὶ καὶ ἄλλοι ἅμα
τούτοις ἑκατὸν καὶ πεντήκοντα οἱ γνωριμώτατοι
αὐτοκράτορες περὶ σπονδῶν· δῶρά τε ὅσα μέγιστα
παρ'. 'Ινδοῖς κομίζοντες καὶ τὸ ἔθνος καὶ οὗτοι
2 ἐνδιδόντες. συγγνωστὰ δὲ ἁμαρτεῖν ἔφασαν οὐ
πάλαι παρ'· αὐτὸν πρεσβευσάμενοι· ἐπιθυμεῖν γάρ,
ὥσπερ τινὲς ἄλλοι, ἔτι μᾶλλον αὐτοὶ ἐλευθερίας τε καὶ
αὐτόνομοι εἶναι, ἥντινα ἐλευθερίαν ἐξ ὅτου Διόνυσος
ἐς 'Ινδοὺς ἧκε σώαν σφίσιν ,εἶναι ἐς 'Αλέξανδρον·
εἰ δὲ 'Αλεξάνδρῳ δοκοῦν ἐστιν, ὅτι καὶ 'Αλέξανδρον ἀπὸ θεοῦ [1] γενέσθαι λόγος κατέχει, σατράπην
τε ἀναδέξεσθαι, ὅντινα τάττοι 'Αλέξανδρος, καὶ
φόρους ἀποίσειν τοὺς 'Αλεξάνδρῳ δόξαντας· διδόναι δὲ καὶ ὁμήρους ἐθέλειν ὅσους ἂν αἰτῇ 'Αλέξ-
3 ανδρος. ὁ δὲ χιλίους ᾔτησε τοὺς κρατιστεύοντας
τοῦ ἔθνους, οὕς, εἰ μὲν βούλοιτο, ἀντὶ ὁμήρων
καθέξειν, εἰ δὲ μή, ξυστρατεύοντας ἕξειν ἔστ' ἂν
διαπολεμηθῇ αὐτῷ πρὸς τοὺς ἄλλους 'Ινδούς. οἱ
δὲ τούς τε χιλίους ἔπεμψαν, τοὺς κρατίστους καὶ
μεγίστους σφῶν ἐπιλεξάμενοι, καὶ ἅρματα πεντακόσια οὐκ αἰτηθέντες καὶ τοὺς ἀμβάτας τῶν
ἁρμάτων. 'Αλέξανδρος δὲ σατράπην μὲν τούτοις
τε καὶ τῶν Μαλλῶν τοῖς ἔτι σωζομένοις ἐπέταξε
Φίλιππον· τοὺς ὁμήρους δὲ αὐτοῖς ἀφῆκεν, τὰ δὲ
ἅρματα ἔλαβεν.
4 'Ως δὲ ταῦτα αὐτῷ κεκόσμητο καὶ πλοῖα ἐπὶ
τῇ διατριβῇ τῇ ἐκ τοῦ τραύματος πολλὰ προσ-
εναυπήγητο, ἀναβιβάσας ἐς τὰς ναῦς τῶν μὲν

---

[1] θεοῦ is the reading of all MSS. of the *excerpta de legationibus*:
θεῶν A.

326/5
B.C.

Mallians reached Alexander offering the tribe's surrender, and the Oxydracae sent the governors of their cities and their nomarchs in person, along with one hundred and fifty others of their chief personages, as plenipotentiaries to discuss terms; they brought the most precious Indian gifts, and they too offered surrender of their tribe.[1] They urged that their 2 fault was pardonable in not sending envoys long before; like some other peoples but in a still higher degree, they desired freedom and self-government; that freedom they had preserved intact from the days when Dionysus came into India until Alexander's time, but, if it so pleased Alexander, since the story prevailed that Alexander too was born to a god,[2] they would accept a satrap whom Alexander might appoint, pay tribute determined by him, and also give as many hostages as he might require. He demanded a 3 thousand of the chief men of the tribe, to keep as hostages if he desired or, if not, to have them serving with his army, till he finished his wars against the rest of the Indians. They sent the thousand men, choosing the most important and greatest men of their people, with five hundred chariots which had not been demanded, and men to drive them. Alexander appointed Philip as satrap for them and the surviving Mallians,[3] returned the hostages to them, but took the chariots.

When he had settled these affairs, and a large 4 325 B.C.
number of additional boats had been constructed during the delay his convalescence occasioned, he

---

[1] With § 1–3 contrast QC. ix 7, 12–15; 8, 1 f.

[2] App. XVI, esp. 6–8. With a different reading (see critical note), we must render ' descended of gods,' but the Greek is less natural; cf. App. V 8.

[3] Cf. 15, 2 n.

ἑταίρων ἱππέας ἑπτακοσίους καὶ χιλίους, τῶν
ψιλῶν δὲ ὅσουσπερ καὶ πρότερον, πεζοὺς δὲ ἐς
μυρίους, ὀλίγον μέν τι τῷ Ὑδραώτῃ ποταμῷ
κατέπλευσεν, ὡς δὲ συνέμιξεν ὁ Ὑδραώτης τῷ
Ἀκεσίνῃ, ὅτι ὁ Ἀκεσίνης κρατεῖ τοῦ Ὑδραώτου
[ἐν] τῇ ἐπωνυμίᾳ, κατὰ τὸν Ἀκεσίνην αὖ ἔπλει,
ἔστε ἐπὶ τὴν ξυμβολὴν τοῦ Ἀκεσίνου καὶ τοῦ
5 Ἰνδοῦ ἧκεν. τέσσαρες γὰρ οὗτοι μεγάλοι ποταμοὶ
καὶ ναυσίποροι οἱ τέσσαρες εἰς τὸν Ἰνδὸν ποταμὸν
τὸ ὕδωρ ξυμβάλλουσιν, οὐ ξὺν τῇ σφετέρᾳ ἕκαστος
ἐπωνυμίᾳ, ἀλλὰ ὁ Ὑδάσπης μὲν ἐς τὸν Ἀκεσίνην
ἐμβάλλει, ἐμβαλὼν δὲ τὸ πᾶν ὕδωρ Ἀκεσίνην
παρέχεται καλούμενον· αὖθις δὲ ὁ Ἀκεσίνης
οὗτος ξυμβάλλει τῷ Ὑδραώτῃ, καὶ παραλαβὼν
τοῦτον ἔτι Ἀκεσίνης ἐστί· καὶ τὸν Ὕφασιν ἐπὶ
τούτῳ ὁ Ἀκεσίνης παραλαβὼν τῷ αὑτοῦ δὴ ὀνόματι
ἐς τὸν Ἰνδὸν ἐμβάλλει· ξυμβαλὼν δὲ ξυγχωρεῖ
δὴ τῷ Ἰνδῷ. ἔνθεν δὴ ὁ Ἰνδὸς πρὶν ἐς τὸ Δέλτα
σχισθῆναι οὐκ ἀπιστῶ ὅτι καὶ ἐς ἑκατὸν σταδίους
ἔρχεται καὶ ὑπὲρ τοὺς ἑκατὸν τυχόν, ἵναπερ
λιμνάζει μᾶλλον.

15. Ἐνταῦθα ἐπὶ ταῖς ξυμβολαῖς τοῦ Ἀκεσίνου
καὶ Ἰνδοῦ προσέμενεν ἔστε ἀφίκετο αὐτῷ ξὺν τῇ
στρατιᾷ Περδίκκας καταστρεψάμενος ἐν παρόδῳ τὸ
Ἀβαστανῶν ἔθνος αὐτόνομον. ἐν τούτῳ δὲ ἄλλαι
τε προσγίγνονται Ἀλεξάνδρῳ τριακόντοροι καὶ
πλοῖα στρογγύλα ἄλλα, ἃ δὴ ἐν Ξάθροις ἐναυπη-
γήθη αὐτῷ, καὶ ⟨Σόγδοι⟩ ἄλλο ἔθνος Ἰνδῶν αὐτόνομον προσεχώρησαν. καὶ παρὰ Ὀσσαδίων, καὶ
τούτου γένους αὐτονόμου Ἰνδικοῦ, πρέσβεις ἧκον,
2 ἐνδιδόντες καὶ οὗτοι τοὺς Ὀσσαδίους. Φιλίππῳ
μὲν δὴ τῆς σατραπείας ὅρους ἔταξε τὰς συμβολὰς

embarked on the ships seventeen hundred cavalry of
the Companions, the same number as before of the
light-armed troops, and up to ten thousand infantry,
and sailed a short way down the Hydraotes; but
where the Hydraotes joined the Acesines, since there
the name Acesines takes precedence over Hydraotes,
he sailed down the Acesines too till he came to its
meeting with the Indus. These four great, navigable 5
rivers pour their waters into the Indus, though they
do not all keep their original name; the Hydaspes
runs into the Acesines, and pouring in its whole
stream takes the name Acesines; then again the
Acesines meets the Hydraotes [4] and, taking in this
tributary, retains its own name; next it takes in the
Hyphasis, keeping its own name till it runs into the
Indus; after this confluence it loses its name to the
Indus. From this point until it splits into the delta,
the Indus, I do not question, is some hundred stades
broad, and perhaps more, where it becomes more like
a lake than a river.[5]

15. There at the junction of the Acesines and Indus
Alexander remained till Perdiccas reached him with
his army, after subduing on his march an independent
tribe of Abastanes. At this time also Alexander was
joined by more *triacontoroi* and round vessels, which
had been built for him among the Xathrians, and the
Sogdians,[1] another independent Indian tribe, came
over to him. Envoys came too from the Ossadians,[2]
also an independent tribe of Indians; they offered
their submission. Alexander then fixed as the 2
boundaries of Philip's satrapy the junction of the

---

[4] *Ind.* 4, 8 and 13 n.
[5] See v 20, 10 n.
[1] Conjecturally inserted by Roos, cf. § 4.
[2] On 15–17 cf. App. XVII 28.

τοῦ τε Ἀκεσίνου καὶ Ἰνδοῦ καὶ ἀπολείπει ξὺν
αὐτῷ τούς τε Θρᾷκας πάντας καὶ ἐκ τῶν τάξεων
ὅσοι ἐς φυλακὴν τῆς χώρας ἱκανοὶ ἐφαίνοντο,
πόλιν τε ἐνταῦθα κτίσαι ἐκέλευσεν ἐπ' αὐτῇ τῇ
ξυμβολῇ τοῖν ποταμοῖν, ἐλπίσας μεγάλην τε
ἔσεσθαι καὶ ἐπιφανῆ ἐς ἀνθρώπους, καὶ νεωσοίκους
3 ποιηθῆναι. ἐν τούτῳ δὲ καὶ Ὀξυάρτης ὁ Βάκτριος,
ὁ Ῥωξάνης τῆς γυναικὸς τῆς Ἀλεξάνδρου πατήρ,
ἧκε παρ' Ἀλέξανδρον· καὶ προστίθησιν αὐτῷ
Παραπαμισαδῶν σατραπεύειν, ἀπαλλάξας Τυρίεσπιν τὸν πρόσθεν σατράπην, ὅτι οὐκ ἐν κόσμῳ
ἐξηγεῖσθαι αὐτῷ ὁ Τυρίεσπις ἐξήγγελτο.

4 Ἔνθα δὴ διαβιβάσας Κρατερόν τε καὶ τῆς στρατιᾶς τὴν πολλὴν καὶ τοὺς ἐλέφαντας ἐπ' ἀριστερὰ
τοῦ Ἰνδοῦ ποταμοῦ, ὅτι εὐπορώτερά τε ταύτῃ τὰ
παρὰ τὸν ποταμὸν στρατιᾷ βαρείᾳ ἐφαίνετο καὶ τὰ
ἔθνη τὰ προσοικοῦντα οὐ πάντῃ φίλια ἦν, αὐτὸς
κατέπλει ἐς τῶν Σόγδων τὸ βασίλειον. καὶ ἐνταῦθα
πόλιν τε ἐτείχιζεν ἄλλην καὶ νεωσοίκους ἐποίει ἄλλους καὶ τὰ πλοῖα αὐτῷ τὰ πεπονηκότα ἐπεσκευ-
άσθη. τῆς δὲ ἀπὸ τῶν ξυμβολῶν τοῦ τε Ἰνδοῦ
καὶ Ἀκεσίνου χώρας ἔστε ἐπὶ θάλασσαν σατράπην
ἀπέδειξε[ν Ὀξυάρτην καὶ] Πείθωνα ξὺν τῇ παρα-
λίᾳ πάσῃ τῆς Ἰνδῶν γῆς.

5 Καὶ Κρατερὸν μὲν ἐκπέμπει αὖθις ξὺν τῇ στρα-

---

³ Cf. iii 1, 5 n. 4.   D. 102, 4 (10,000 inhabitants) and QC.
ix 8, 8 may refer to this city or that in § 4 (Tarn ii 237).   Philip
is son of Machatas (Berve no. 780).

⁴ In addition to being Al's father-in-law? QC. ix 8, 9, who
here records the execution of ' Terioltes ' (Tyriespis?   Cf. iv
22, 5) for greedy and arrogant acts and the acquittal of O. on
unspecified charges, calls him ' praetor Bactrianorum ' and
says he was now given a more extensive government, pre-

Acesines and the Indus, and left with him all the Thracians, and as many men from the (other) units as seemed enough to garrison the country. He ordered him to found a city there just at the meeting of the two rivers, as he expected it would be great and famous in the world, and dockyards to be built.[3] At 3 this time Oxyartes the Bactrian, father of Roxane, Alexander's wife, came to Alexander; and Alexander gave him in addition [4] the satrapy of the Parapamisadae, removing Tyriespis the former satrap, since he had heard reports that Tyriespis' conduct of affairs was outrageous.

Here he had Craterus and the greater part of the 4 army and the elephants ferried across to the left bank of the river Indus, since the route by the river seemed easier on that side to an army heavily encumbered, and not all the neighbouring tribes were friendly. He himself sailed down towards the royal city of Sogdia. There he fortified a new city, and constructed new ship-stations and had his damaged boats refitted. As satrap of the country from the meeting of the Indus and the Acesines up to the sea, with all the coastline of the country of India, he appointed [Oxyartes and] Pithon.

Craterus was again sent off with his army [through 5

sumably Parapamisus, of which he was satrap on Al's death (D. xviii 3, 7). But at that time Philip (Berve no. 785) was satrap of Bactria (ibid.) and if O. had replaced Amyntas (A. iv 22, 3) as a result of the mercenary revolt in Bactria (D. 99, 5 f.; QC. ix 7, 1-11) this is nowhere else attested, and O. must later have been removed from that satrapy.

τιᾷ διὰ τῆς Ἀραχωτῶν καὶ Δραγγῶν γῆς,[1] αὐτὸς
δὲ κατέπλει ἐς τὴν Μουσικανοῦ ἐπικράτειαν,
ἥντινα εὐδαιμονεστάτην τῆς Ἰνδῶν γῆς εἶναι
ἐξηγγέλλετο, ὅτι οὔπω οὔτε ἀπηντήκει αὐτῷ
Μουσικανὸς ἐνδιδοὺς αὐτόν τε καὶ τὴν χώραν οὔτε
πρέσβεις ἐπὶ φιλίᾳ ἐκπέμπει, οὐδέ τι οὔτε αὐτὸς
ἐπεπόμφει ἃ δὴ μεγάλῳ βασιλεῖ εἰκός, οὔτε τι
6 ᾐτήκει ἐξ Ἀλεξάνδρου. καὶ γίγνεται αὐτῷ ὁ
πλοῦς κατὰ τὸν ποταμὸν ἐς τοσόνδε ἐσπουδασ-
μένος ὥστε ἔφθη ἐπὶ τοῖς ὁρίοις γενέσθαι τῆς
Μουσικανοῦ χώρας, πρὶν πυθέσθαι Μουσικανὸν ὅτι
ὥρμηται ὡς ἐπ’ αὐτὸν Ἀλέξανδρος. οὕτω δὴ
ἐκπλαγεὶς κατὰ τάχος ἀπήντα Ἀλεξάνδρῳ, δῶρά
τε τὰ πλείστου ἄξια παρ’ Ἰνδοῖς κομίζων καὶ τοὺς
ἐλέφαντας ξύμπαντας ἄγων καὶ τὸ ἔθνος τε καὶ
αὐτὸν ἐνδιδοὺς καὶ ὁμολογῶν ἀδικεῖν, ὅπερ μέγιστον
παρ’ Ἀλεξάνδρῳ ἦν ἐς τὸ τυχεῖν ὧν τις δέοιτο.
7 καὶ οὖν καὶ Μουσικανῷ ἐπὶ τοῖσδε ἄδεια ἐδόθη
ἐξ Ἀλεξάνδρου, καὶ τὴν πόλιν ἐθαύμασεν Ἀλέξανδρος καὶ τὴν χώραν, καὶ ἄρχειν αὐτῆς Μουσικανῷ
ἔδωκεν· Κρατερὸς δὲ ἐν τῇ πόλει ἐτάχθη τὴν
ἄκραν ἐκτειχίσαι· καὶ παρόντος ἔτι ἐτειχίσθη
Ἀλεξάνδρου καὶ φυλακὴ κατεστάθη, ὅτι ἐπι-
τήδειον αὐτῷ ἐφάνη τὸ χωρίον ἐς τὸ κατέχεσθαι τὰ
κύκλῳ ἔθνη φυλαττόμενα.

[1] See note to translation.

[5] The words bracketed here and in 4 are usually regarded as
glosses, since the statement on O. is false (last note), and
Craterus is still with the main army in § 7, and his march to
Arachotia is dated later in 17, 3; wrongly according to Bosworth, *CQ* 1976, who argues that A. found incompatible
accounts in his main sources and inadvertently gave both.
He is surely right (in his note on iii 25, 7) that A's oscillation

325
B.C.

the Arachotian and Drangian country] 5 while he himself sailed downstream towards the kingdom of Musicanus, which was reported to be the richest of all India, since Musicanus had not yet met him to surrender himself and his country, nor had sent envoys to establish friendly relations, nor indeed any gifts suitable for a great king, nor had he made any request from Alexander. The voyage down the river proved 6 so swift that he arrived at the border of Musicanus' country before Musicanus learned that Alexander had started to move against him. He was so panic-stricken that he promptly went to meet Alexander, bringing gifts of the greatest value among the Indians, leading all his elephants, submitting himself and his people and acknowledging his error, the most potent method with Alexander for anyone to obtain what he might desire. And, sure enough, Musicanus 7 received pardon from Alexander, who much admired his city and country and granted the government to Musicanus. Craterus was ordered to fortify the citadel in the city, and it was fortified while Alexander was still there, and a garrison placed there, since the place seemed to him convenient for watching and keeping a hold over the tribes round about.

between Drangian and Zarangian, as here and in 17, 3, shows that Ar. and Pt. adopted different forms; A. used whichever he found in the source he was following (one indication that, whichever A. preferred, the military narrative sometimes follows Ar.). But ' Drangian ' was the usual Greek form, which a glossator too would naturally have used. In § 4 the singular ' satrap ' can surely stand in apposition to only one person, i.e. Pithon, son of Agenor (Berve no. 619), who is amply attested as satrap of Sind, and in 5 the word ' again ' suggests that (as in 4) Craterus was temporarily detached from Al., cf. 7, though A. characteristically omits details, and ignores his return (cf. v 27, 1; vi 6, 6 nn.). Parallel instances of the crass stupidity Bosworth imputes to A. are unconvincing.

16. Ἔνθεν δὲ ἀναλαβὼν τούς τε τοξότας καὶ τοὺς Ἀγριᾶνας καὶ τὴν ἵππον τὴν ἅμα οἳ πλέουσαν ἐξελαύνει ἐπὶ τὸν νομάρχην τῆς ταύτῃ γῆς, ὄνομα δὲ ἦν Ὀξικανός, ὅτι μήτε αὐτὸς ἀφῖκτο μήτε πρέσβεις παρ' αὐτοῦ ἧκον ἐνδιδόντες αὐτόν τε καὶ

2 τὴν χώραν. δύο μὲν δὴ τὰς μεγίστας πόλεις τῶν ὑπὸ τῷ Ὀξικανῷ ἐξ ἐφόδου κατὰ κράτος ἔλαβεν, ἐν δὲ τῇ ἑτέρᾳ τούτων καὶ αὐτὸς Ὀξικανὸς ἑάλω. ὁ δὲ τὴν μὲν λείαν τῇ στρατιᾷ δίδωσι, τοὺς ἐλέφαντας δὲ ἅμα οἳ ἧγε· καὶ ⟨αἱ⟩ ἄλλαι δὲ πόλεις αὐτῷ αἱ ἐν τῇ αὐτῇ χώρᾳ ἐνεδίδοντο ἐπιόντι οὐδέ τις ἐτρέπετο ἐς ἀλκήν· οὕτω καὶ Ἰνδοὶ πάντες ἐδεδούλωντο ἤδη τῇ γνώμῃ πρὸς Ἀλεξάνδρου τε καὶ τῆς Ἀλεξάνδρου τύχης.

3 Ὁ δὲ ἐπὶ Σάμβον αὖ ἦγε τῶν ὀρείων Ἰνδῶν σατράπην ὑπ' αὐτοῦ κατασταθέντα, ὃς πεφευγέναι αὐτῷ ἐξηγγέλλετο ὅτι Μουσικανὸν ἀφειμένον πρὸς Ἀλεξάνδρου ἐπύθετο καὶ τῆς χώρας τῆς ἑαυτοῦ ἄρχοντα· τὰ γὰρ πρὸς Μουσικανὸν αὐτῷ πολέμια

4 ἦν. ὡς δὲ ἐπέλαζεν ἤδη τῇ πόλει Ἀλέξανδρος, ἥντινα μητρόπολιν εἶχεν ἡ τοῦ Σάμβου χώρα, ὄνομα δὲ ἦν τῇ πόλει Σινδίμανα, αἵ τε πύλαι αὐτῷ ἀνοίγονται προσάγοντι καὶ οἱ οἰκεῖοι οἱ τοῦ Σάμβου τά τε χρήματα ἀπηρίθμησαν καὶ τοὺς ἐλέφαντας μετὰ σφῶν ἄγοντες ἀπήντων· οὐ γὰρ δὴ Ἀλεξάνδρῳ γε πολεμίως ἔχοντα Σάμβον

5 φυγεῖν, ἀλλὰ Μουσικανοῦ τὴν ἄφεσιν δείσαντα. ὁ δὲ καὶ ἄλλην πόλιν ἐν τούτῳ ἀποστᾶσαν εἷλεν καὶ τῶν Βραχμάνων, οἳ δὴ σοφισταὶ τοῖς Ἰνδοῖς εἰσιν, ὅσοι αἴτιοι τῆς ἀποστάσεως ἐγένοντο ἀπέκτεινεν. ὑπὲρ ὧν ἐγὼ τῆς σοφίας, εἰ δή τίς ἐστιν, ἐν τῇ Ἰνδικῇ ξυγγραφῇ δηλώσω.

16. From there Alexander, taking with him the archers, the Agrianians and the cavalry sailing with him, made an expedition against the nomarch of this district named Oxicanus, since he had neither come himself nor sent envoys, to surrender himself and his land. Two of the largest cities in Oxicanus' realm 2 were taken by assault without delay, and in the second of these Oxicanus himself was captured. Alexander handed over all the plunder to the army, but took away the elephants himself. The other cities in the same country surrendered on Alexander's approach, no one resisting, so completely had the spirit of all the Indians been broken by Alexander and Alexander's fortune.

Next Alexander advanced against Sambus, 3 appointed by himself satrap of the Indian hillmen; he was reported to have fled on learning that Alexander had released Musicanus and made him ruler of his own land, for Sambus and Musicanus were at enmity. But when Alexander was already close to 4 the capital city of Sambus' territory, named Sindimana, the gates were opened to him at his coming, and the relatives of Sambus counted out his treasure and went to meet Alexander with the elephants; they represented that Sambus' flight had not been due to enmity with Alexander, but to fear at his release of Musicanus. At this point Alexander captured yet another city which had rebelled, and put to death those of 5 the Brahmans, the Indian philosophers, who had been responsible for the revolt.[1] The wisdom of these men, if such it is, I shall explain in my Indian treatise.

---

[1] Cf. 7, 4 n.; Hamilton on P. 64. D. 102, 6 and QC. ix 8, 21 f. interpose a story of Al. curing Pt. of poison, flattering to Pt. (from Clitarchus, cf. 11, 8 n. 6), which S. xv 2, 7 locates in the Oritan country, perhaps following N. (App. XVIII).

ARRIAN

17. Καὶ ἐν τούτῳ Μουσικανὸς αὐτῷ ἀφεστάναι
ἐξηγγέλλετο. καὶ ἐπὶ τοῦτον μὲν ἐκπέμπει
Πείθωνα τὸν Ἀγήνορος σατράπην ξὺν στρατιᾷ
ἀποχρώσῃ, αὐτὸς δὲ τὰς πόλεις τὰς ὑπὸ Μουσικανῷ τεταγμένας ἐπελθὼν τὰς μὲν ἐξανδραποδίσας
αὐτῶν κατέσκαψεν, εἰς ἃς δὲ φρουρὰς εἰσήγαγε καὶ
ἄκρας ἐξετείχισε. ταῦτα δὲ διαπραξάμενος ἐπὶ τὸ
2 στρατόπεδόν τε ἐπανῆκε καὶ τὸν στόλον. ἔνθα δὴ
Μουσικανός τε ξυλληφθεὶς ἄγεται πρὸς Πείθωνος,
καὶ τοῦτον κρεμάσαι κελεύει Ἀλέξανδρος ἐν τῇ
αὐτοῦ γῇ, καὶ τῶν Βραχμάνων ὅσοι αἴτιοι τῆς
ἀποστάσεως τῷ Μουσικανῷ κατέστησαν. ἀφίκετο
δὲ αὐτῷ καὶ ὁ τῶν Παταλῶν τῆς χώρας ἄρχων, ὃ
δὴ τὸ Δέλτα ἔφην εἶναι τὸ πρὸς τοῦ ποταμοῦ
τοῦ Ἰνδοῦ ποιούμενον, μεῖζον ἔτι τοῦ Δέλτα τοῦ
Αἰγυπτίου, καὶ οὗτος τήν τε χώραν αὐτῷ ἐνεδίδου
πᾶσαν καὶ αὑτόν τε καὶ τὰ αὑτοῦ ἐπέτρεψεν.
3 τοῦτον μὲν δὴ ἐπὶ τῇ αὑτοῦ ἀρχῇ ἐκπέμπει αὖθις
παραγγείλας παρασκευάζειν ὅσα ἐς ὑποδοχὴν τῇ
στρατιᾷ· αὐτὸς δὲ Κρατερὸν μὲν τήν τε Ἀττάλου
τάξιν ἄγοντα καὶ τὴν Μελεάγρου καὶ Ἀντιγένους
καὶ τῶν τοξοτῶν ἔστιν οὓς καὶ τῶν ἑταίρων τε καὶ
ἄλλων Μακεδόνων ὅσους ἐς Μακεδονίαν ἀπομάχους
ὄντας ἤδη ἔστελλε τὴν ἐπ' Ἀραχωτῶν καὶ Ζαραγγῶν ἔπεμπεν ἐς Καρμανίαν, καὶ τοὺς ἐλέφαντας
4 τούτῳ ἄγειν ἔδωκεν· τὴν δὲ ἄλλην στρατιάν, ὅση
γε μὴ ξὺν αὑτῷ κατέπλει ὡς ἐπὶ θάλασσαν, ...
Ἡφαιστίων ἐπετάχθη,[1] Πείθωνα δὲ τούς τε ἱππ-
ακοντιστὰς ἄγοντα καὶ τοὺς Ἀγριᾶνας ἐς τὴν

[1] Roos suggested that the lacuna might be filled *exempli
gratia* ⟨διχῇ διένειμε· καὶ τῇ μὲν πλείστῃ μοίρᾳ⟩.

17. At this point the revolt of Musicanus was reported. Alexander sent against him Pithon son of Agenor the satrap with a sufficient force. He himself advanced against the cities subject to Musicanus, some of which he razed to the ground and sold their inhabitants into slavery; in others he established garrisons and fortified citadels. When he had completed this, he returned to the camp and fleet. Here 2 too Musicanus was brought as a captive by Pithon, and Alexander ordered him to be hanged in his own land, together with the Brahmans who had been the instigators of his revolt. There also arrived the ruler of the land of Patala,[1] which, as I said, is the delta made by the river Indus and is still larger than the Egyptian delta; he too surrendered all his territory and committed himself and all that he had to Alexander. Alexander sent him back to his own realm, 3 with orders to prepare everything for the reception of the army. He despatched Craterus with the battalions of Attalus, Meleager and Antigenes, some of the archers and all the Companions and other Macedonians that he had already decided to send back to Macedonia as being past service, to go by the road through the Arachotians and Zarangians[2] to Carmania; he also gave Craterus the elephants to take with him. The rest of his forces which were not 4 sailing in his company downstream to the sea were divided in two; the largest part was put under the command of Hephaestion[3]; Pithon with the mounted

---

[1] See v 4, 1 and 2 n. D. 104, 2 credits Patala with a dual kingship and elders; Onesicritus found other Spartan analogies in Musicanus' kingdom (S. xv 1, 34).

[2] Cf. 15, 5 n.; App. XVII 29.

[3] A lacuna is filled conjecturally; the text may also have specified on which bank H. was to march.

ἐπέκεινα ὄχθην τοῦ Ἰνδοῦ διαβιβάσας, οὐχ ᾗπερ
Ἡφαιστίων τὴν στρατιὰν ἄγειν ἤμελλε, τάς τε
ἐκτετειχισμένας ἤδη πόλεις ξυνοικίσαι ἐκέλευσε
καὶ εἰ δή τινα νεωτερίζοιτο πρὸς τῶν ταύτῃ
Ἰνδῶν καὶ ταῦτα ἐς κόσμον καταστήσαντα ξυμβάλλειν οἱ ἐς τὰ Πάταλα.

5 Ἤδη δὲ τρίτην ἡμέραν αὐτῷ τοῦ πλοῦ ἔχοντι
ἐξαγγέλλεται ὅτι ὁ τῶν Πατάλων ὕπαρχος ξυλλαβὼν τῶν Παταλέων τοὺς πολλοὺς ἀποδεδρακὼς
οἴχοιτο ἀπολιπὼν τὴν χώραν ἔρημον· καὶ ἐπὶ
τούτῳ πλείονι ἢ πρόσθεν σπουδῇ κατέπλει Ἀλέξανδρος. ὡς δὲ ἀφίκετο ἐς τὰ Πάταλα, τήν τε
πόλιν καὶ τὴν χώραν ἔρημον καταλαμβάνει τῶν
6 ἐνοικούντων τε καὶ ἐπεργαζομένων. ὁ δὲ κατὰ
δίωξιν τῶν φευγόντων ἐκπέμψας τῆς στρατιᾶς τοὺς
κουφοτάτους, ἐπεί τινες αὐτῶν ξυνελήφθησαν,
ἀποπέμπει τούτους παρὰ τοὺς ἄλλους, ἐντειλάμενος
ἐπανιέναι θαρροῦντας· εἶναι γὰρ αὐτοῖς τήν τε πόλιν οἰκεῖν ὡς πρόσθεν καὶ τὴν χώραν ἐργάζεσθαι.
καὶ ἐπανῆλθον οἱ πολλοὶ αὐτῶν.

18. Αὐτὸς δὲ Ἡφαιστίωνι προστάξας τειχίζειν
ἐν τοῖς Πατάλοις ἄκραν ἀποπέμπει ἐς τὴν ἄνυδρον
τῆς πλησίον γῆς φρέατά τε ὀρύξοντας καὶ οἰκήσιμον
τὴν χώραν κατασκευάσοντας. καὶ τούτοις ἐπέθεντο
τῶν προσχώρων τινὲς βαρβάρων, καὶ ἔστι μὲν
οὓς διέφθειραν αὐτῶν ἄφνω προσπεσόντες, πολλοὺς
δὲ καὶ σφῶν ἀποβαλόντες ἔφυγον ἐς τὴν ἔρημον,
ὥστε ἐπιτελεσθῆναι τοῖς ἐκπεμφθεῖσι τὰ ἔργα
προσγενομένης αὐτοῖς καὶ ἄλλης στρατιᾶς, ἣν
Ἀλέξανδρος πυθόμενος τῶν βαρβάρων τὴν ἐπίθεσιν
ἐστάλκει μεθέξοντας τοῦ ἔργου.

2 Περὶ δὲ τοῖς Πατάλοις σχίζεται τοῦ Ἰνδοῦ τὸ

javelin-men [4] and the Agrianians were put across on the side of the Indus opposite to that by which Hephaestion was to take his army, with orders to muster inhabitants for the cities already fortified and, if any rebellion were to break out among the Indians in these parts, to establish order and finally meet him at Patala.

On the third day of the voyage, he received news 5 that the hyparch of Patala had taken with him most of the tribesmen and had absconded, leaving his country deserted; on this Alexander sailed down with greater speed than before. When he arrived at Patala, he found the city and land empty of inhabitants and labourers. He despatched the nimblest of 6 his troops in pursuit of the fugitives and, when some had been captured, sent them off to enjoin the rest to come back without fear; for the city was theirs to dwell in as before, and the country to till. Most of them did come back.[5]

18. Alexander ordered Hephaestion to fortify the citadel in Patala, and sent out men to the desert in the adjoining country to dig wells and to make the country inhabitable. Some of the neighbouring tribesmen set upon them and destroyed a number by the suddenness of their attack, but they also lost many of their own people and fled into the desert, so that those who had been sent out completed the work, another force having joined them, which Alexander, on hearing of the barbarian attack, had sent to help with the work.

Round Patala the stream of the Indus parts into 2

---

[4] Bosworth, *JHS* 1980, conjecturally identifies them with the *prodromoi*, *contra* Introd. 60.

[5] Cities established in the delta (QC. ix 10, **3**) were probably refoundations.

ὕδωρ ἐς ⟨δύο⟩ ποταμοὺς μεγάλους, καὶ οὗτοι
ἀμφότεροι σώζουσι τοῦ Ἰνδοῦ τὸ ὄνομα ἔστε ἐπὶ
τὴν θάλασσαν. ἐνταῦθα ναύσταθμόν τε καὶ νεωσοίκους ἐποίει Ἀλέξανδρος· ὡς δὲ προὐκεχωρήκει
αὐτῷ τὰ ἔργα, ὁ δὲ καταπλεῖν ἐπενόει ἔστε ἐπὶ τὴν
ἐκβολὴν τοῦ ἐν δεξιᾷ ῥέοντος ποταμοῦ ἐς τὴν
3 θάλασσαν. Λεοννάτον μὲν δὴ δοὺς αὐτῷ τῶν τε
ἱππέων ἐς χιλίους καί τῶν ὁπλιτῶν τε καὶ ψιλῶν ἐς
ὀκτακισχιλίους κατὰ τὴν νῆσον τὰ Πάταλα ἐκπέμπει ἀντιπαράγειν τῷ στόλῳ, αὐτὸς δὲ τὰς μάλιστα
τῶν νεῶν ταχυναυτούσας ἀναλαβὼν ὅσαι τε ἡμιόλιαι καὶ τὰς τριακοντόρους πάσας καὶ τῶν κερκού-
ρων ἔστιν οὓς ἔπλει κατὰ τὸν ποταμὸν τὸν ἐν
4 δεξιᾷ. οὐκ ἔχοντι δὲ αὐτῷ ἡγεμόνα τοῦ πλοῦ, ὅτι
πεφεύγεσαν οἱ ταύτῃ Ἰνδοί, ἀπορώτερα τὰ τοῦ
κατάπλου ἦν· χειμών τε ἐπιγίγνεται ἐς τὴν ὑστεραίαν
ἀπὸ τῆς ἀναγωγῆς καὶ ὁ ἄνεμος τῷ ῥόῳ πνέων
ὑπεναντίος κοῖλόν τε ἐποίει τὸν ποταμὸν καὶ τὰ
σκάφη διέσειεν, ὥστε ἐπόνησαν αὐτῷ αἱ πλεῖσται
τῶν νεῶν, τῶν δὲ τριακοντόρων ἔστιν αἳ καὶ πάντῃ
διελύθησαν. ἔφθησαν δὲ ἐποκείλαντες αὐτὰς πρὶν
5 παντάπασιν διαπεσεῖν ἐν τῷ ὕδατι. ἕτεραι οὖν
ξυνεπήγνυντο. καὶ τῶν ψιλῶν τοὺς κουφοτάτους
ἐκπέμψας ἐς τὴν προσωτέρω τῆς ὄχθης χώραν
ξυλλαμβάνει τινὰς τῶν Ἰνδῶν, καὶ οὗτοι τὸ ἀπὸ
τοῦδε ἐξηγοῦντο αὐτῷ τὸν πόρον. ὡς δὲ ἧκον
ἵναπερ ἀναχεῖται ἐς εὖρος ὁ ποταμός, ὡς καὶ διακοσίους ταύτῃ σταδίους ἐπέχειν ᾗπερ εὐρύτατος αὐτὸς
αὑτοῦ ἦν, τό τε πνεῦμα κατήιει μέγα ἀπὸ τῆς ἔξω
θαλάσσης καὶ αἱ κῶπαι ἐν κλύδωνι χαλεπῶς ἀνε-
φέροντο, ξυμφεύγουσιν αὖ ἐς διώρυχα, ἐς ἥντινα
οἱ ἡγεμόνες αὐτῷ καθηγήσαντο.

two large rivers, both of these retaining the name
Indus till they reach the sea. Here Alexander
began to build a ship-station and dockyards, and,
when his works had advanced well, he planned to
sail down to the outlet of the right-hand stream into
the sea. He gave Leonnatus a thousand of the 3
cavalry and about eight thousand of the heavy and
light armed troops and sent him to the island of
Patala, to march alongside the fleet, while he himself, taking the swiftest sailers of his fleet, that is, the
hemioliai, all the *triacontoroi* and some of the *kerkouroi*,
sailed down the right-hand river.[1] But as he had no 4
pilot, since all the Indians of these parts had fled, there
were grave difficulties in the descent and, on the day
after the fleet weighed, a storm came on and the wind
blowing contrary to the current made troughs in the
stream and battered the hulls; most of the ships were
damaged, and some of the *triacontoroi* were actually
complete wrecks, though they were run ashore before
totally breaking up in the water. Other ships there- 5
fore were built, and he sent off the lightest of his light
armed troops to the country on the farther bank to
capture some of the Indians, and they showed him the
channel thereafter. When they came to the
broadening of the river, which makes it extend here
at its broadest to two hundred stades, the wind was
blowing violently from the ocean, the oars could
hardly be lifted in the surf, and they ran for shelter
into a canal, to which Alexander's pilots directed
them.

[1] v 3, 6; vi 2, 4 nn. Cf. D. 104; QC. ix 9, 1 ff. with other
useful information. H. T. Lambrick, *Sind*, Hyderabad, 1964,
gives an excellent account of the country from personal
knowledge. It seems unlikely that Leonnatus could have
carried out the plan, in the flooded delta. A. probably
follows N. in 18, 2–21, 2 (App. XVII 5); cf. 20, 2 n.

19. Ἐνταῦθα ὁρμισάντων τὸ πάθημα ἐπιγίγνεται τῆς μεγάλης θαλάσσης ἡ ἄμπωτις, ὥστε ἐπὶ ξηροῦ ἀπελήφθησαν αὐτοῖς αἱ νῆες. καὶ τοῦτο οὔπω πρότερον ἐγνωκόσι τοῖς ἀμφ᾽ Ἀλέξανδρον ἔκπληξιν μὲν καὶ αὐτὸ οὐ σμικρὰν παρέσχε, πολὺ δὲ δὴ ἔτι μείζονα, ὁπότε διελθούσης τῆς ὥρας προσῄει τε τὸ
2 ὕδωρ καὶ τὰ σκάφη ⟨ἐ⟩μετεωρίζοντο. ὅσας μὲν δὴ τῶν νεῶν ἐν τῷ πηλῷ ἑδραίας κατέλαβεν, αὗται δὲ ἀβλαβῶς τε ἐμετεωρίσθησαν καὶ οὐδὲν χαλεπὸν παθοῦσαι ἔπλεον αὖθις· ὅσαι δὲ ἐν ξηροτέρᾳ τε τῇ γῇ καὶ οὐ βεβαίως τὴν στάσιν ἔχουσαι ὑπελείφθησαν, αὗται δὲ ἀθρόου ἐπελθόντος τοῦ κύματος αἱ μὲν αὐτῶν ἐμπεσοῦσαι ἐς ἀλλήλας, αἱ δὲ πρὸς τῇ γῇ ἀρ[ρ]αχθεῖσαι συνετρίβησαν.
3 ταύτας τε οὖν ἐπεσκεύασεν Ἀλέξανδρος ἐκ τῶν παρόντων καὶ ἐν κερκούροιν δυοῖν προπέμπει κατὰ τὸν ποταμὸν τοὺς κατασκεψομένους τὴν νῆσον, ἐς ἥντινα οἱ ἐπιχώριοι ἔφασκον ὁρμιστέα εἶναι αὐτῷ κατὰ τὸν πλοῦν τὸν ἐς τὴν θάλασσαν· Κίλλουτα δὲ τῇ νήσῳ τὸ ὄνομα ἔλεγον. ὡς δὲ ἐξηγγέλθη ὅτι ὅρμοι τε ἐν τῇ νήσῳ εἰσὶ καὶ αὐτὴ μεγάλη καὶ ὕδωρ ἔχουσα, ὁ μὲν ἄλλος αὐτῷ στόλος ἐς τὴν νῆσον κατέσχεν, αὐτὸς δὲ ταῖς ἄριστα πλεούσαις τῶν νεῶν ἐπέκεινα προὐχώρει, ὡς ἀπιδεῖν τοῦ ποταμοῦ τὴν ἐκβολὴν τὴν ἐς τὴν θάλασ-
4 σαν, εἰ παρέχει τὸν ἔκπλουν εὔπορον. προελθόντες δὲ ἀπὸ τῆς νήσου σταδίους ὅσον διακοσίους ἀφορῶσιν ἄλλην νῆσον, ταύτην ἤδη ἐν τῇ θαλάσσῃ. τότε μὲν δὴ ἐπανῆλθον ἐς τὴν ἐν τῷ ποταμῷ νῆσον, καὶ πρὸς τοῖς ἄκροις αὐτῆς καθορμισθεὶς θύει τοῖς θεοῖς Ἀλέξανδρος ὅσοις ἔφασκεν ὅτι παρὰ τοῦ Ἄμμωνος ἐπηγγελμένον ἦν θῦσαι αὐτῷ. ἐς δὲ τὴν

19. When they had anchored there, the ebb-tide, characteristic of the great sea, followed; as a result their ships were left high and dry.[1] Alexander's men had not known of this before, and it was another thing that gave them a severe shock, repeated with still more force when the time passed and the tide came up again and the ships were lifted up. Ships which 2 the tide found comfortably settled on the mud were lifted off unharmed, and floated once more without sustaining damage; but those which were caught on a drier bottom and were not on an even keel, as the onrushing tide came in all together, either collided with each other or were dashed on the land and shattered. Alexander repaired them as best he 3 could, and despatched men jn two *kerkouroi* to explore the island which, they said, was called Cilluta, where the natives affirmed he must anchor on his voyage down to the sea. They reported that there was good anchorage on the island and that it was large and had fresh water; so the rest of his fleet put in at the island while Alexander himself with the best sailing ships went to its far side, to get a view of the outlet of the river into the sea, and discover if it offered a safe passage out. Going about two hundred stades beyond 4 the island, they sighted a second island, right out in the sea. For the time being they returned to the river island, and anchoring by its headland Alexander sacrificed to the gods to which, he used to say, Ammon had enjoined him to sacrifice. Next day he sailed

[1] Tides and tidal bores were unfamiliar to Mediterranean dwellers.

ὑστεραίαν κατέπλει ὡς ἐπὶ τὴν ἄλλην τὴν ἐν τῷ
πόντῳ νῆσον, καὶ προσχὼν καὶ ταύτῃ ἔθυε καὶ
ἐνταῦθα ἄλλας αὖ θυσίας ἄλλοις τε θεοῖς καὶ ἄλλῳ
τρόπῳ· καὶ ταύτας δὲ κατ' ἐπιθεσπισμὸν θύειν
5 ⟨ἔφασκε⟩ τοῦ Ἄμμωνος. αὐτὸς δὲ ὑπερβαλὼν
τοῦ Ἰνδοῦ ποταμοῦ τὰς ἐκβολὰς ἐς τὸ πέλαγος
ἀνέπλει, ὡς μὲν ἔλεγεν, ἀπιδεῖν εἴ πού τις χώρα
πλησίον ἀνίσχει ἐν τῷ πόντῳ, ἐμοὶ δὲ δοκεῖ, οὐχ
ἥκιστα ὡς πεπλευκέναι τὴν μεγάλην τὴν ἔξω
Ἰνδῶν θάλασσαν. ἐνταῦθα ταύρους τε σφάξας τῷ
Ποσειδῶνι ἀφῆκεν ἐς τὴν θάλασσαν καὶ σπείσας
ἐπὶ τῇ θυσίᾳ τήν τε φιάλην χρυσῆν οὖσαν καὶ
κρατῆρας χρυσοῦς ἐνέβαλεν ἐς τὸν πόντον χαριστήρια, εὐχόμενος σῶόν οἱ παραπέμψαι τὸν στρατὸν
τὸν ναυτικόν, ὅντινα ξὺν Νεάρχῳ ἐπενόει στέλλειν
ὡς ἐπὶ τὸν κόλπον τὸν Περσικὸν καὶ τὰς ἐκβολὰς τοῦ τε Εὐφράτου καὶ τοῦ Τίγρητος.
20. Ἐπανελθὼν δὲ ὀπίσω ἐς τὰ Πάταλα τήν
τε ἄκραν τετειχισμένην καταλαμβάνει καὶ Πείθωνα
ξὺν τῇ στρατιᾷ ἀφιγμένον καὶ τούτῳ ξύμπαντα
καταπεπραγμένα ἐφ' οἷσπερ ἐστάλη. Ἡφαιστίων μὲν δὴ ἐτάχθη παρασκευάζειν τὰ πρὸς
τὸν ἐκτειχισμόν τε τοῦ ναυστάθμου καὶ τῶν νεω-
σοίκων τὴν κατασκευήν· καὶ γὰρ καὶ ἐνταῦθα
ἐπενόει στόλον ὑπολείπεσθαι νεῶν οὐκ ὀλίγων
πρὸς τῇ πόλει τοῖς Πατάλοις, ἵναπερ ἐσχίζετο ὁ
ποταμὸς ὁ Ἰνδός.
2 Αὐτὸς δὲ κατὰ τὸ ἕτερον στόμα τοῦ Ἰνδοῦ κατέπλει αὖθις ἐς τὴν μεγάλην θάλασσαν, ὡς καταμαθεῖν, ὅπῃ εὐπορωτέρα ἡ ἐκβολὴ τοῦ Ἰνδοῦ ἐς τὸν
πόντον γίγνεται· ἀπέχει δὲ ἀλλήλων τὰ στόματα
τοῦ ποταμοῦ τοῦ Ἰνδοῦ ἐς σταδίους μάλιστα ὀκτα-

down to the other island in the sea, put in there, and
sacrificed there too, performing different sacrifices to
different gods with different ceremonial; these
sacrifices also, he said, he offered in accordance with
the oracle given by Ammon. Passing the mouths 5
of the river Indus, he sailed out in person to the sea,
to observe, as he said, if any country stood out nearby in the ocean, but in my own judgment chiefly
that he might have voyaged in the great sea outside India.[2] Then he sacrificed bulls to Posidon, and
cast them into the sea, and after the sacrifice poured
a libation and cast into the sea the cup made of gold
and golden bowls as thank-offerings, praying that
Posidon would safely convoy the naval force he intended to despatch with Nearchus towards the
Persian Gulf and the mouths of the Euphrates and
Tigris.

20. On return to Patala, he found the citadel
fortified, and Pithon arrived with his army, after
successfully accomplishing his whole mission.[1] Hephaestion was now ordered to get ready everything
necessary for fortifying the ship-station and building the dockyards; for he intended to leave behind
there a fleet of many ships, near the city of Patala,
where the river Indus divided.

He himself sailed down to the ocean again by the 2
other mouth of the Indus, to learn by which branch
the outlet of the Indus to the ocean was easier; the
mouths of the river Indus are above eighteen hundred

[2] Al. had achieved his purpose by sailing in the Ocean, cf.
Ind. 20, 2; vii 1; D. 104, 1; QC. ix 9, 27. Sacrifices: *Ind.*
20, 10, cf. vi 3, 2 n. and esp. Bosworth there cited.
[1] As usual, no particulars of a subordinate's mission.
Citadel: 18, 1.

3 κοσίους καὶ χιλίους. ἐν δὲ τῷ κατάπλῳ ἀφίκετο τῆς
ἐκβολῆς τοῦ ποταμοῦ ἐς λίμνην μεγάλην, ἥντινα
ἀναχεόμενος ὁ ποταμός, τυχὸν δὲ καὶ [ἐκ]¹ τῶν
πέριξ ὑδάτων ἐμβαλλόντων ἐς αὐτήν, μεγάλην τε
ποιεῖ καὶ κόλπῳ θαλάσσης μάλιστα ἐοικυῖαν· καὶ
γὰρ ἰχθύες ἤδη ἐν αὐτῇ τῶν ἀπὸ θαλάσσης ἐφαίνοντο, μείζονες τῶν ἐν τῇδε τῇ ἡμετέρᾳ θαλάσσῃ.
προσορμισθεὶς οὖν κατὰ τὴν λίμνην ἵναπερ οἱ
καθηγεμόνες ἐξηγοῦντο, τῶν μὲν στρατιωτῶν τοὺς
πολλοὺς καταλείπει σὺν Λεοννάτῳ αὐτοῦ καὶ τοὺς
4 κερκούρους ξύμπαντας, αὐτὸς δὲ ταῖς τριακοντό-
ροις τε καὶ ἡμιολίαις ὑπερβαλὼν τὴν ἐκβολὴν τοῦ
Ἰνδοῦ καὶ προελθὼν καὶ ταύτῃ ἐς τὴν θάλασσαν
εὐπορωτέραν τε κατέμαθεν τὴν ἐπὶ τάδε τοῦ Ἰνδοῦ
ἐκβολὴν καὶ αὐτὸς προσορμισθεὶς τῷ αἰγιαλῷ καὶ
τῶν ἱππέων τινὰς ἅμα οἷ ἔχων παρὰ θάλασσαν
ᾔει σταθμοὺς τρεῖς, τήν τε χώραν ὁποία τίς ἐστιν
ἡ ἐν τῷ παράπλῳ ἐπισκεπτόμενος καὶ φρέατα
ὀρύσσεσθαι κελεύων, ὅπως ἔχοιεν ὑδρεύεσθαι οἱ
5 πλέοντες. αὐτὸς μὲν δὴ ἐπανελθὼν ἐπὶ τὰς ναῦς
ἀνέπλει ἐς τὰ Πάταλα μέρος δέ τι τῆς στρατιᾶς τὰ
αὐτὰ ταῦτα ἐργασομένους κατὰ τὴν παραλίαν
ἔπεμψεν, ἐπανιέναι καὶ τούτοις προστάξας ἐς τὰ
Πάταλα. αὖθις δὲ ὡς ἐπὶ τὴν λίμνην καταπλεύσας
ἄλλον ναύσταθμον καὶ ἄλλους νεωσοίκους ἐνταῦθα
κατεσκεύασε, καὶ φυλακὴν καταλιπὼν τῷ χωρίῳ
σῖτόν τε ὅσον καὶ ἐς τέτταρας μῆνας ἐξαρκέσαι τῇ
στρατιᾷ ἐσηγάγετο καὶ τἄλλ' ὅσα [ἐν] τῷ παράπλῳ παρεσκεύαζεν.

¹ I adopt Sintenis' deletion.

² N's figure: Onesicritus gave 2000 and Ar. 1000 (about

stades apart from one another.[2] In the descent he   **3** 325
reached the point where the river debouches into a   B.C.
great lake; the river spreads out, and perhaps the
surrounding streams empty into it, and help to make
it large, very like a gulf of the sea; in fact sea fish were
already to be seen in it, bigger than those in our own
sea.   Anchoring then at a point in the lake where
the pilots directed, he left behind most of the troops
there with Leonnatus, and all the *kerkouroi*, while with   **4**
the *triacontoroi* and *hemioliai* he himself passed beyond
the outlet of the Indus, and proceeding by this
passage reached the sea again and discovered that
the outlet of the Indus on our side was easier to
navigate.[3] He then anchored by the shore and taking with him some of the cavalry went three days'
march along the coast, observing the nature of the
country for the coast voyage, and ordering wells to be
dug, so that the voyagers might be able to get water.
Then while he himself, after returning to his ships,   **5**
sailed back to Patala, he sent part of the army along
the foreshore to carry on this same work, with instructions also to return to Patala. He sailed once
more down to the lake, and built another ship-station
and other dockyards there; and leaving a garrison in
the place, brought in four months' grain for the army
and made all other preparations for the coast voyage.

right), cf. S. xv 1, **33**; all estimates were hearsay, as it was
impossible to traverse the flooded coast (Lambrick), and N.
did not sail along the coast (*Ind.* 21, 2 n.).
    [3] For the translation, Hammond, *CQ* 1980, 465–7; Lambrick
had already seen that N. actually sailed from the western outlet. But the next sentence (*pace* Hammond) now makes
nonsense; even if the cavalry could have marched along the
swampy foreshore (Ones. *ap.* S. xv 1, 20 and **34**, right), it was
not for the purpose A. gives, clearly misunderstanding his
source; perhaps he marched eastwards in exploration.

ARRIAN

21. Ἦν δὲ ἐν μὲν τῷ τότε ἄπορος ἡ ὥρα ἐς τὸν
πλοῦν· οἱ γὰρ ἐτησίαι ἄνεμοι κατεῖχον, οἳ δὴ τῇ
ὥρᾳ ἐκείνῃ οὐ καθάπερ παρ' ἡμῖν ἀπ' ἄρκτου, ἀλλ'
ἀπὸ τῆς μεγάλης θαλάσσης κατὰ νότον μάλιστα
2 ἄνεμον ἵστανται. ἀπὸ δὲ τοῦ χειμῶνος τῆς ἀρχῆς
τὸ ἀπὸ Πλειάδων δύσεως ἔστε ἐπὶ τροπάς, ἃς ἐν
χειμῶνι ὁ ἥλιος ἐπιστρέφει, πλόϊμα εἶναι ταύτῃ
ἐξηγγέλλετο. τότε γὰρ κατὰ γῆν μᾶλλον οἷα δὴ
πολλῷ ὕδατι ἐξ οὐρανοῦ βεβρεγμένην αὔρας ἵστασ-
θαι μαλθακὰς καὶ ἐς τὸν παράπλουν ταῖς τε κώπαις
καὶ τοῖς ἱστίοις ξυμμέτρους.

3 Νέαρχος μὲν δὴ ἐπιταχθεὶς τῷ ναυτικῷ προσ-
έμενε τὴν ὥραν τοῦ παράπλου, αὐτὸς δὲ ἄρας ἐκ
Πατάλων ἔστε μὲν ἐπὶ τὸν ποταμὸν τὸν Ἀράβιον
ξὺν τῇ στρατιᾷ πάσῃ προὐχώρει. ἐκεῖθεν δὲ
ἀναλαβὼν τῶν ὑπασπιστῶν τε καὶ τῶν τοξοτῶν
τοὺς ἡμίσεας καὶ τῶν ἀσθεταίρων [1] καλουμένων
τὰς τάξεις καὶ τῆς ἵππου τῆς ἑταιρικῆς τό τε
ἄγημα καὶ ἴλην ἀφ' ἑκάστης ἱππαρχίας καὶ τοὺς
ἱπποτοξότας ξύμπαντας ὡς ἐπὶ τὴν θάλασσαν ἐς
ἀριστερὰ ἐτράπετο, ὕδατά τε ὀρύσσειν, ὡς κατὰ
τὸν παράπλουν ἄφθονα εἴη τῇ στρατιᾷ τῇ παρα-
πλεούσῃ, καὶ ἅμα ὡς τοῖς Ὠρείταις [2] τοῖς ταύτῃ
Ἰνδοῖς αὐτονόμοις ἐκ πολλοῦ οὖσιν ἄφνω ἐπιπεσεῖν,
ὅτι μηδὲν φίλιον αὐτοῖς ἐς αὐτόν τε καὶ τὴν στρατιὰν ἐπέπρακτο. τῆς δὲ ὑπολειφθείσης δυνάμεως
4 Ἡφαιστίων αὐτῷ ἀφηγεῖτο. Ἀραβῖται μὲν δή,
ἔθνος καὶ τοῦτο αὐτόνομον τῶν περὶ τὸν Ἀράβιον
ποταμὸν νεμομένων, οὔτε ἀξιόμαχοι δόξαντες

---

[1] Introduction n. 99.
[2] Salmasius here inserted καὶ to produce agreement with
Ind. 22, 10, but see note *ad loc.*

21. The season, however, at that time was impracticable for sailing, for the trade winds were blowing continuously; in that season they blow not, as with us, from the north, but from the great sea and a roughly southerly quarter. But from the beginning 2 of winter, the setting of the Pleiads, to the winter solstice, navigation was reported to be possible here; for, as is natural when the land is drenched with heavy rains, there are light land breezes, convenient for the coast voyage whether by oars or sails.

Nearchus, the admiral of the fleet, awaited the 3 season for the voyage, while Alexander left Patala and advanced with his entire force as far as the river Arabius [1]; and thence, taking with him half of the hypaspists and the archers, the battalions of the so-called *asthetairoi*, the *agema* of the Companions' cavalry and a squadron from each hipparchy [2] and all the mounted archers, he turned left towards the sea, to dig wells, so that there might be plenty of water for the forces sailing along the coast, and also to make a surprise attack on the Oritans [3] and the Indians in these parts who had long been independent, since they had done no friendly services to Alexander and the army. Hephaestion was put in command of the force left behind. The Arabitae, another of the in- 4 dependent peoples who dwell about the river Arabius, did not think themselves capable of resisting Alex-

[1] In *Indica* A. writes 'Arabis' after N. (river Hab). For 21–26 see App. XVIII; cf. XVII 3–5; 24 on sources and chronology.

[2] On some views, each hipparchy had an Oriental squadron, cf. Introd. 59; App. XIX 2.

[3] *Ind.* 22, 10 n.

εἶναι Ἀλεξάνδρῳ οὔτε ὑποδῦναι ἐθελήσαντες, ὡς
προσάγοντα ἐπύθοντο Ἀλέξανδρον, φεύγουσιν ἐς
τὴν ἔρημον. Ἀλέξανδρος δὲ διαβὰς τὸν Ἀράβιον
ποταμὸν στενόν τε καὶ ὀλίγου ὕδατος καὶ διελθὼν
ἐν νυκτὶ τῆς ἐρήμου τὴν πολλὴν ὑπὸ τὴν ἔω πρὸς
τῇ οἰκουμένῃ ἦν· καὶ τοὺς μὲν πεζοὺς ἐν τάξει
ἐκέλευσεν ἕπεσθαι, τοὺς δὲ ἱππέας ἀναλαβὼν
αὐτὸς καὶ ἐς ἴλας κατανείμας, ὅπως ἐπὶ πλεῖστον
τοῦ πεδίου ἐπέχοιεν, ἐπῄει τὴν χώραν τῶν Ὠρειτῶν.
5 ὅσοι μὲν δὴ ἐς ἀλκὴν αὐτῶν ἐτράποντο κατεκόπησαν
πρὸς τῶν ἱππέων, πολλοὶ δὲ καὶ ζῶντες ἑάλωσαν.
ὁ δὲ τότε μὲν κατεστρατοπέδευσε πρὸς ὕδατι οὐ
πολλῷ, ὡς δὲ καὶ οἱ περὶ Ἡφαιστίωνα αὐτῷ ὁμοῦ
ἤδη ἦσαν, προὐχώρει ἐς τὸ πρόσω. ἀφικόμενος δὲ
εἰς κώμην, ἥπερ ἦν μεγίστη τοῦ ἔθνους τοῦ
Ὠρειτῶν, Ῥαμβακία ἐκαλεῖτο ἡ κώμη, τόν τε
χῶρον ἐπῄνεσε καὶ ἐδόκει ἂν αὐτῷ πόλις ξυνοικισ-
θεῖσα μεγάλη καὶ εὐδαίμων γενέσθαι. Ἡφαιστίωνα
μὲν δὴ ἐπὶ τούτοις ὑπελείπετο.

22. Αὐτὸς δὲ ἀναλαβὼν αὖθις τῶν ὑπασπιστῶν
καὶ τῶν Ἀγριάνων τοὺς ἡμίσεας καὶ τὸ ἄγημα τῶν
ἱππέων καὶ τοὺς ἱπποτοξότας προῄει ὡς ἐπὶ τὰ
ὅρια τῶν τε Γαδρωσῶν καὶ Ὠρειτῶν, ἵναπερ
στενή τε ἡ πάροδος αὐτῷ εἶναι ἐξηγγέλλετο καὶ οἱ
Ὠρεῖται τοῖς Γαδρωσοῖς ξυντεταγμένοι πρὸ τῶν
στενῶν στρατοπεδεύειν, ὡς εἴρξοντες τῆς παρ-
2 όδου Ἀλέξανδρον. καὶ ἦσαν μὲν ταύτῃ τεταγμένοι,
ὡς δὲ προάγων ἤδη ἐξηγγέλλετο, οἱ μὲν πολλοὶ
ἔφυγον ἐκ τῶν στενῶν λιπόντες τὴν φυλακήν, οἱ δὲ

---

4 Literally ' near water that was not large.'

5 Rhambacia should lie near the modern Las Bela, where
ancient remains have been found; even though the coast has

325
B.C.

ander, and yet did not choose to submit; when they
learned that Alexander was approaching, they fled
into the desolate country. Alexander crossed the
river Arabius, a narrow river with little water, traversed most of the desert by night, and at dawn was
close to the inhabited region. Here he ordered his
infantry to follow in marching order, but took the
cavalry with him and divided it into squadrons, in
order that they might cover the greatest extent of the
plain, and thus invaded the territory of the Oritans.
Those who offered resistance were cut down by the 5
cavalry; many were captured alive. For the time being, Alexander encamped near a small sheet of water,[4]
but when Hephaestion and his troops had come close
he advanced further. Arriving at the largest village
of the Oritans, called Rhambacia, he expressed
admiration of the site and thought that, if people
were settled together in a city there, it would become
great and prosperous. Hephaestion then was left
behind to attend to this.[5]

22. Alexander, taking with him again half of the
hypaspists and the Agrianians, the *agema* of the
cavalry and the mounted archers, advanced towards
the borders of the Gadrosians and Oritans, where it
was reported to him that the approach was by a defile, and that the Gadrosians and Oritans were drawn
up together encamped in front of the defile to bar his
approach. They were, in fact, arrayed there; but 2
when news was brought that he was advancing, most
of them fled from the defile, deserting their post; the

receded (Engels 139), it was inland, and D. 104, 8 must be
wrong in attributing to it a sheltered harbour; none is mentioned in *Ind.* 23. Onesicritus *ap.* Pliny, *NH* vi 97 called it
Alexandria founded by Leonnatus on Al's order; presumably
L. completed Hephaestion's work, cf. 22, 3.

ARRIAN

ἡγεμόνες τῶν Ὠρειτῶν ἀφίκοντο παρ' αὐτὸν σφᾶς
τε αὐτοὺς καὶ τὸ ἔθνος ἐνδιδόντες. τούτοις μὲν
δὴ προστάττει ξυγκαλέσαντας τὸ πλῆθος τῶν
Ὠρειτῶν πέμπειν ἐπὶ τὰ σφέτερα ἤθη, ὡς δεινὸν
οὐδὲν πεισομένους· σατράπην δὲ καὶ τούτοις
3 ἐπιτάσσει Ἀπολλοφάνη· καὶ ξὺν τούτῳ ἀπολείπει
Λεοννάτον τὸν σωματοφύλακα ἐν Ὤροις, ἔχοντα
τούς τε Ἀγριᾶνας ξύμπαντας καὶ τῶν τοξοτῶν
ἔστιν οὓς καὶ τῶν ἱππέων καὶ ἄλλους πεζούς τε καὶ
ἱππέας Ἕλληνας μισθοφόρους, τό τε ναυτικὸν
ὑπομένειν ἔστ' ἂν περιπλεύσῃ τὴν χώραν καὶ τὴν
πόλιν ξυνοικίζειν καὶ τὰ κατὰ τοὺς Ὠρείτας
κοσμεῖν, ὅπως μᾶλλόν τι προσέχοιεν τῷ σατράπῃ
τὸν νοῦν. αὐτὸς δὲ ξὺν τῇ στρατιᾷ τῇ πολλῇ, καὶ
γὰρ καὶ Ἡφαιστίων ἀφίκετο ἄγων αὐτῷ τοὺς
ὑπολειφθέντας, προὐχώρει ὡς ἐπὶ Γαδρωσοὺς
ἔρημον τὴν πολλήν.

4 Καὶ ἐν τῇ ἐρήμῳ ταύτῃ λέγει Ἀριστόβουλος
σμύρνης πολλὰ δένδρα πεφυκέναι μείζονα ἢ κατὰ
τὴν ἄλλην σμύρναν, καὶ τοὺς Φοίνικας τοὺς κατ'
ἐμπορ[ε]ίαν τῇ στρατιᾷ ξυνεπομένους ξυλλέγοντας
τὸ δάκρυον τῆς σμύρνης (πολὺ γὰρ εἶναι, οἷα δὴ
ἐκ μεγάλων τε τῶν πρέμνων καὶ οὔπω πρόσθεν
ξυλλελεγμένον) ἐμπλήσαντας τὰ ὑποζύγια ἄγειν.
5 ἔχειν δὲ τὴν ἔρημον ταύτην καὶ νάρδου ῥίζαν πολλήν τε καὶ εὔοδμον καὶ ταύτην ξυλλέγειν τοὺς
Φοίνικας· πολὺ δὲ εἶναι αὐτῆς τὸ καταπατούμενον
πρὸς τῆς στρατιᾶς, καὶ ἀπὸ τοῦ πατουμένου ὀδμὴν
ἡδεῖαν κατέχειν ἐπὶ πολὺ τῆς χώρας. τοσόνδε
6 εἶναι τὸ πλῆθος· εἶναι δὲ καὶ ἄλλα δένδρα ἐν τῇ
ἐρήμῳ, τὸ μέν τι δάφνῃ ἐοικὸς τὸ φύλλον, καὶ
τοῦτο ἐν τοῖς προσκλυζομένοις τῇ θαλάσσῃ χωρίοις

chiefs of the Oritans came to him to surrender themselves and their nation.   He commanded them to call together the mass of the Oritans and send them to their own homes with the assurance that they would suffer no harm;   as satrap over them he appointed Apollophanes.   With him Leonnatus, the 3 bodyguard, was left behind in Ora in command of all the Agrianians, some of the archers and cavalry, and other foot and horse, Greek mercenaries;   he was to await the fleet until it sailed past this district, to people the city, and to settle affairs in the country of the Oritans, so that they might be more obedient to the satrap.   Then Alexander himself with the larger part of his army, for Hephaestion had arrived with the men left behind, proceeded towards the Gadrosians, through country that was mostly desert.

In this desert Aristobulus says that many myrrh 4 trees grow, taller than the ordinary myrrh, and that the Phoenicians who followed the army as traders collected the gum of the myrrh, for it was abundant, coming from such large trunks and never having been collected before, and took it away, loading their packmules.   He adds that this desert also produces ginger 5 grass, plentiful and fragrant, which was also gathered by the Phoenicians;   much of it was trodden underfoot by the army, and this wafted a delightful fragrance for some distance over the country, such was its abundance.   According to Aristobulus there are 6 other trees in the desert,[1] one with a leaf like laurel, which grows in places washed by the sea;   the trees

---

[1] Mangroves, seen on the coastal stretch of the march (26, 5).

πεφυκέναι· καὶ ἀπολείπεσθαι μὲν τὰ δένδρα πρὸς
τῆς ἀμπώτεως ἐπὶ ξηροῦ, ἐπελθόντος δὲ τοῦ
ὕδατος ἐν τῇ θαλάσσῃ πεφυκότα φαίνεσθαι· τῶν
δὲ καὶ ἀεὶ τὰς ῥίζας τῇ θαλάσσῃ ἐπικλύζεσθαι, ὅσα
ἐν κοίλοις χωρίοις ἐπεφύκει, ἔνθενπερ οὐχ ὑπενόσ-
τει τὸ ὕδωρ, καὶ ὅμως οὐ διαφθείρεσθαι τὸ
7   δένδρον πρὸς τῆς θαλάσσης. εἶναι δὲ τὰ δένδρα
ταύτῃ πήχεων καὶ τριάκοντα ἔστιν ἃ αὐτῶν, τυχεῖν
τε ἀνθοῦντα ἐκείνῃ τῇ ὥρᾳ, καὶ τὸ ἄνθος εἶναι τῷ
λευκῷ μάλιστα ἴῳ προσφερές, τὴν ὀδμὴν δὲ πολύ τι
ὑπερφέρον. καὶ ἄλλον εἶναι καυλὸν ἐκ γῆς πεφυκότα ἀκάνθης, καὶ τούτῳ ἐπεῖναι ἰσχυρὰν τὴν
ἄκανθαν, ὥστε ἤδη τινῶν καὶ παριππευόντων
ἐμπλακεῖσαν τῇ ἐσθῆτι κατασπάσαι ἀπὸ τοῦ
ἵππου μᾶλλόν τι τὸν ἱππέα ἢ αὐτὴν ἀποσχισθῆναι
8   ἀπὸ τοῦ καυλοῦ. καὶ τῶν λαγῶν λέγεται ὅτι
παραθεόντων εἴχοντο ἐν ταῖς θριξὶν αἱ ἄκανθαι καὶ
ὅτι οὕτως ἡλίσκοντο οἱ λαγῶ, καθάπερ ὑπὸ ἰξοῦ αἱ
ὄρνιθες ἢ τοῖς ἀγκίστροις οἱ ἰχθύες, σιδήρῳ δὲ
ὅτι διακοπῆναι οὐ χαλεπὴ ἦν· καὶ ὀπὸν ὅτι ἀνίει πολὺν ὁ καυλὸς τῆς ἀκάνθης τεμνομένης, ἔτι πλείονα
ἢ αἱ συκαῖ τοῦ ἦρος καὶ δριμύτερον.

23. Ἔνθεν δὲ διὰ τῆς Γαδρωσῶν χώρας ᾔει
ὁδὸν χαλεπὴν καὶ ἄπορον τῶν ἐπιτηδείων, τῶν
τε ἄλλων καὶ ὕδωρ πολλαχοῦ τῇ στρατιᾷ οὐκ ἦν·
ἀλλὰ νύκτωρ ἠναγκάζοντο γῆν πολλὴν πορεύεσθαι
καὶ προσωτέρω ἀπὸ θαλάσσης, ἐπεὶ αὐτῷ γε ἐν
σπουδῇ ἦν ἐπελθεῖν [1] τὰ παρὰ τὴν θάλασσαν τῆς
χώρας καὶ λιμένας τε ἰδεῖν τοὺς ὄντας καὶ ὅσα γε
ἐν παρόδῳ δυνατὰ γένοιτο τῷ ναυτικῷ παρασκευά-
σαι, ἢ φρέατα ὀρύξαντας ἢ ἀγορᾶς που ἢ ὅρμου

[1] Krüger: ἐλθεῖν A, Roos.

are left high and dry by the ebb-tide, but when the
water has come in they appear to be growing in the
sea; indeed when they grow in hollow places where
the water does not recede the roots are washed by the
sea continuously, and yet the tree is not killed by the
sea water. By his account the trees here are some- 7
times thirty cubits high, and at that season they were
in flower, the flower being most like a white violet,
but of a very much sweeter perfume, and there is also
a stalk of thorn growing out of the soil, on which the
thorn is so strong that it actually tangled with the
clothes of a man just riding past, and pulled him from
his horse rather than come away from its stalk. It is 8
also said that the hares as they run through get their
fur caught in the thorns, and are captured in this way
just as birds are with bird-lime or fishes with hooks,
but that it was easy to cut it through with an axe, and
that the stalk of the thorn when cut emits juice more
abundant and sharper to the taste than figs in spring.

23. From there Alexander went through the
country of the Gadrosians by a difficult route, wholly
lacking in supplies; in particular, the army often
found no water; but they were obliged to traverse
much ground by night, and rather far from the sea.
And yet Alexander was anxious to traverse the land
by the coast, to see what harbours there were and on
his march through to get ready all he could for the
fleet either by digging wells or perhaps by providing

ARRIAN

2 ἐπιμεληθέντας. ἀλλὰ ἦν γὰρ ἔρημα παντάπασιν τὰ
πρὸς τῇ θαλάσσῃ τῆς Γαδρωσῶν γῆς, ὁ δὲ Θόαντα
τὸν Μανδροδώρου καταπέμπει ἐπὶ θάλασσαν ξὺν
ὀλίγοις ἱππεῦσιν, κατασκεψόμενον εἴ πού τις
ὅρμος ὢν τυγχάνει ταύτῃ ἢ ὕδωρ οὐ πόρρω ἀπὸ
3 θαλάσσης ἤ τι ἄλλο τῶν ἐπιτηδείων. καὶ οὗτος
ἐπανελθὼν ἀπήγγειλεν ἁλιέας τινὰς καταλαβεῖν
ἐπὶ τοῦ αἰγιαλοῦ ἐν καλύβαις πνιγηραῖς· πεποιῆσθαι δὲ τὰς καλύβας ξυνθέντας τὰς κόγχας·
στέγην δὲ εἶναι αὐταῖς τὰς ἀκάνθας τῶν ἰχθύων·
καὶ τούτους τοὺς ἁλιέας ὕδατι ὀλίγῳ διαχρῆσθαι
χαλεπῶς διαμωμένους τὸν κάχληκα, καὶ οὐδὲ
τούτῳ πάντῃ γλυκεῖ τῷ ὕδατι.
4 Ὡς δὲ ἀφίκετο Ἀλέξανδρος ἐς χῶρόν τινα τῆς
Γαδρωσίας ἵνα ἀφθονώτερος ἦν σῖτος, διανέμει ἐς
τὰ ὑποζύγια τὸν καταληφθέντα καὶ τοῦτον σημηνά-
μενος τῇ ἑαυτοῦ σφραγῖδι κατακομίζεσθαι κελεύει
ὡς ἐπὶ θάλασσαν. ἐν ᾧ δὲ ᾔει ὡς ἐπὶ τὸν σταθμόν,
ἔνθενπερ ἐγγυτάτω ἦν ἡ θάλασσα, ἐν τούτῳ
ὀλίγα φροντίσαντες οἱ στρατιῶται τῆς σφραγῖδος
αὐτοί τε οἱ φύλακες τῷ σίτῳ ἐχρήσαντο καὶ ὅσοι
μάλιστα λιμῷ ἐπιέζοντο καὶ τούτοις μετέδωκαν.
5 ἐς τοσόνδε γὰρ πρὸς τοῦ κακοῦ ἐνικῶντο, ὡς τὸν
πρόδηλον καὶ παρόντα ἤδη ὄλεθρον τοῦ ἀφανοῦς
τε καὶ πρόσω ἔτι ὄντος ἐκ τοῦ βασιλέως κινδύνου
ξὺν λογισμῷ ἔδοξέ σφισιν ἔμπροσθεν ποιήσασθαι.
καὶ Ἀλέξανδρος καταμαθὼν τὴν ἀνάγκην ξυνέγνω
τοῖς πράξασιν. αὐτὸς δέ, ὅσα ἐκ τῆς χώρας
ἐπιδραμὼν ξυναγαγεῖν ἠδυνήθη εἰς ἐπισιτισμὸν τῇ
στρατιᾷ τῇ περιπλεούσῃ ξὺν τῷ στόλῳ, ταῦτα
6 κομίσοντα πέμπει Κρηθέα τὸν Καλλατιανόν. καὶ
τοῖς ἐγχωρίοις προσετάχθη ἐκ τῶν ἄνω τόπων

170

for a market or an anchorage. But the Gadrosian 2 ^{325 B.C.}
country was entirely desert along the coast-line, and
he sent Thoas son of Mandrodorus down to the sea
with a few cavalry, to see if there was actually any
anchorage there, or water near the sea, or any other
supplies. He returned with the report that he had 3
found some fishermen on the beach in stifling cabins,
made out of shells fixed together, and roofed with the
backbones of fishes, but that these fishermen had
little fresh water for use, as they dug it with difficulty
from the shingle, and even then it was not always
fresh.[1]

Once Alexander had reached a place in Gadrosia 4
where food was more plentiful, he distributed what he
had seized among the baggage trains, sealed it with
his own seal, and ordered it to be conveyed to the sea.
But while he was going towards the halting-place
nearest the sea, the troops, including the guards
themselves, paying little regard to the seal, used the
food, sharing it out among those suffering most from
hunger. So far were they overcome by their distress 5
that in their calculations they took more account of
the death immediately before their eyes than of the
uncertain and still distant danger from the king.
Understanding the necessity, Alexander pardoned
the offenders. For his own part, he sent Cretheus of
Callatis to convey the supplies he had been able to
get together by forays from the country to provision
the force sailing round with the fleet. The inhabi- 6
tants also were commanded to grind and bring down

---

[1] Cf. *Ind.* 24-9, esp. 24, 9; 29, 9 ff.

σῖτόν τε ὅσον δυνατοὶ ἦσαν κατακομίσαι ἀλέσαντας
καὶ τὰς βαλάνους τὰς τῶν φοινίκων καὶ πρόβατα
ἐς ἀγορὰν τῷ στρατῷ. καὶ ἐς ἄλλον αὖ τόπον
Τήλεφον κατέπεμψε τῶν ἑταίρων σὺν σίτῳ οὐ πολλῷ ἀληλεσμένῳ.

24. Αὐτὸς δὲ προύχώρει ὡς ἐς τὰ βασίλεια τῶν
Γαδρωσῶν, ὁ δὲ χῶρος Ποῦρα ὀνομάζεται, ἵναπερ
ἀφίκετο ἐξ Ὤρων ὁρμηθεὶς ἐν ἡμέραις ταῖς
πάσαις ἑξήκοντα. καὶ λέγουσιν οἱ πολλοὶ τῶν
ξυγγραψάντων τὰ ἀμφ' Ἀλέξανδρον οὐδὲ τὰ
ξύμπαντα ὅσα ἐταλαιπώρησεν αὐτῷ κατὰ τὴν
Ἀσίαν ἡ στρατιὰ ξυμβληθῆναι ἄξια εἶναι τοῖς
2 τῇδε πονηθεῖσι πόνοις. οὐ μὴν ἀγνοήσαντα Ἀλέξανδρον τῆς ὁδοῦ τὴν χαλεπότητα ταύτῃ ἐλθεῖν,
τοῦτο μὲν μόνος Νέαρχος λέγει ὧδε, ἀλλὰ ἀκούσαντα γὰρ ὅτι οὔπω τις πρόσθεν διελθὼν ταύτῃ
ξὺν στρατιᾷ ἀπεσώθη, ὅτι μὴ Σεμίραμις ἐξ Ἰνδῶν
ἔφυγε. καὶ ταύτην δὲ ἔλεγον οἱ ἐπιχώριοι σὺν
εἴκοσι μόνοις τῆς στρατιᾶς ἀποσωθῆναι, Κῦρον
δὲ τὸν Καμβύσου σὺν ἑπτὰ μόνοις καὶ τοῦτον.
3 ἐλθεῖν γὰρ δὴ καὶ Κῦρον ἐς τοὺς χώρους τούτους
ὡς ἐσβαλοῦντα ἐς τὴν Ἰνδῶν γῆν, φθάσαι δὲ ὑπὸ
τῆς ἐρημίας τε καὶ ἀπορίας τῆς ὁδοῦ ταύτης
ἀπολέσαντα τὴν πολλὴν τῆς στρατιᾶς. καὶ ταῦτα
Ἀλεξάνδρῳ ἐξαγγελλόμενα ἔριν ἐμβαλεῖν πρὸς
Κῦρον καὶ Σεμίραμιν. τούτων τε οὖν ἕνεκα καὶ
ἅμα ὡς τῷ ναυτικῷ ἐγγύθεν ἐκπορίζεσθαι
τὰ ἀναγκαῖα, λέγει Νέαρχος ταύτην τραπῆναι
4 Ἀλέξανδρον. τό τε οὖν καῦμα ἐπιφλέγον καὶ
τοῦ ὕδατος τὴν ἀπορίαν πολλὴν τῆς στρατιᾶς
διαφθεῖραι καὶ μάλιστα δὴ τὰ ὑποζύγια· ταῦτα μὲν
πρὸς τοῦ βάθους τε τῆς ψάμμου καὶ τῆς θέρμης,

from the upper parts all the grain they could spare
for supplies for the fleet, with dates from the palm
trees, and sheep for the army market, and he sent
Telephus, one of the Companions, to yet another
place with a small supply of ground corn.

24. He himself advanced towards the Gadrosian
capital; the place is called Pura[1]; and he arrived
there from Ora in a total of sixty days. Most historians of Alexander say that all the trials that the army
endured for him in Asia were not comparable, taken
together, with the miseries they suffered here. In 2
their view, however, Alexander did not go that way
in ignorance of the difficulty of the route (Nearchus
alone makes this claim); but because he had heard
that no one yet had got through safely this way with
an army, except for Semiramis fleeing from India.
Even she, according to the local story, only escaped
with twenty of her whole force, and Cyrus son of
Cambyses with only seven; in most accounts Cyrus 3
too was said to have reached these parts, intending to
invade India, though before he could do so he lost the
greater part of his army from the barrenness and
difficulty of this route. The relation of these stories
to Alexander is said to have inspired him with
emulation of Cyrus and Semiramis.[2] It was then on
this account, and also to be close to the fleet, and
provide it with necessaries that according to Nearchus
he chose this route. It is said that the scorching 4
heat and want of water destroyed a great part of the
army and most particularly the baggage animals;
that the depth of the sand and its heat, burning as it

---

[1] In the Bampur basin.
[2] A. obscures the fact that N. said this (S. xv 1, 5). See
also *Ind.* 1, 1 n. and 5, 7 n. N. as the source for what follows:
App. XVIII.

ὅτι κεκαυμένη ἦν, τὰ πολλὰ δὲ καὶ δίψει ἀπόλ-
λυσθαι· καὶ γὰρ καὶ γηλόφοις ἐπιτυγχάνειν
ὑψηλοῖς ψάμμου βαθείας, οὐ νεναγμένης, ἀλλ' οἵας
δέχεσθαι καθάπερ ἐς πηλὸν ἢ ἔτι μᾶλλον ἐς χιόνα
5 ἀπάτητον ἐπιβαίνοντας. καὶ ἅμα ἐν ταῖς προσβά-
σεσί τε καὶ καταβαίνοντας τούς τε ἵππους καὶ τοὺς
ἡμιόνους ἔτι μᾶλλον κακοπαθεῖν τῷ ἀνωμάλῳ τῆς
ὁδοῦ καὶ ἅμα οὐ βεβαίῳ, τῶν τε σταθμῶν τὰ μήκη
πιέσαι οὐχ ἥκιστα τὴν στρατιάν· ἀπορία γὰρ
ὕδατος οὐ ξύμμετρος οὖσα μᾶλλόν τι ἦγε πρὸς
6 ἀνάγκην τὰς πορείας ποιεῖσθαι. ὁπότε μὲν δὴ τῆς
νυκτὸς ἐπελθόντες τὴν ὁδὸν ἥντινα ἀνύσαι ἐχρῆν
ἕωθεν πρὸς ὕδωρ ἔλθοιεν, οὐ πάντῃ ἐταλαιπωροῦν-
το· προχωρούσης δὲ τῆς ἡμέρας ὑπὸ μήκους τῆς
ὁδοῦ, εἰ ὁδοιποροῦντες ἔτι ἐγκαταληφθεῖεν, ἐνταῦθα ἂν ἐταλαιπώρουν πρὸς τοῦ καύματός τε καὶ
ἅμα δίψει ἀπαύστῳ συνεχόμενοι.

25. Τῶν δὲ δὴ ὑποζυγίων πολὺς ὁ φθόρος καὶ
ἑκούσιος τῇ στρατιᾷ ἐγίγνετο· ξυνιόντες γάρ,
ὁπότε ἐπιλίποι σφᾶς τὰ σιτία, καὶ τῶν ἵππων τοὺς
πολλοὺς ἀποσφάζοντες καὶ τῶν ἡμιόνων τὰ κρέα
ἐσιτοῦντο καὶ ἔλεγον δίψει ἀποθανεῖν αὐτοὺς ἢ
ὑπὸ καμάτου ἐκλιπόντας· καὶ ὁ τὴν ἀτρέκειαν
τοῦ ἔργου ἐξελέγξων ὑπό τε τοῦ πόνου οὐδεὶς ἦν
2 καὶ ὅτι ξύμπαντες τὰ αὐτὰ ἡμάρτανον. καὶ
Ἀλέξανδρον μὲν οὐκ ἐλελήθει τὰ γιγνόμενα,
ἴασιν δὲ τῶν παρόντων ἑώρα τὴν τῆς ἀγνοίας
προσποίησιν μᾶλλόν τι ἢ τὴν ὡς γιγνωσκομένων
ἐπιχώρησιν. οὔκουν οὐδὲ τοὺς νόσῳ κάμνοντας
τῆς στρατιᾶς οὐδὲ τοὺς διὰ κάματον ὑπολειπομένους
ἐν ταῖς ὁδοῖς ἄγειν ἔτι ἦν εὐμαρῶς ἀπορίᾳ τε τῶν
ὑποζυγίων καὶ ὅτι τὰς ἁμάξας αὐτοὶ κατέκοπτον,

was, and in most cases thirst as well brought about
their destruction, as they even came across high hills
of deep sand, not beaten down, but letting them sink
in as they stepped on it, like liquid mud or, to put it
better still, untrodden snow, that in addition in 5
ascents and descents the horses and mules suffered
still further from the uneven and unstable nature of
the road. Then the lengths [3] of the marches, it is
said, did most to distress the army; for want of water,
which was found at irregular intervals, drove them to
make their marches as necessity dictated. In fact 6
whenever they covered the distance which had to be
traversed at night and at dawn came upon water,
their misery was not total; but if the march was prolonged by its length into the day, and they were
caught still marching, then they were tormented in
the grip of heat combined with ceaseless thirst.

25. The loss of transport animals was heavy and
caused deliberately by the army; for whenever their
provisions failed them, they would club together and
kill off most of their horses and mules and eat their
flesh, saying that they had perished from thirst or
collapsed from fatigue; and there was no one to in-
vestigate the actual facts, because of the distress and
because they were all involved in the same offence.
Alexander was not unaware of these happenings, but 2
he saw that the remedy for the situation lay rather in
his pretending ignorance than in recognizing and
permitting the practice. Nor was it easy any longer
to bring along the troops who were suffering from
sickness, or left dying on the road from fatigue, as
there was a shortage of transport animals, and the
men themselves kept breaking up the waggons, which

[3] App. XVIII 6.

ἀπόρους οὔσας αὐτοῖς ὑπὸ βάθους τῆς ψάμμου
ἄγεσθαι καὶ ὅτι ἐν τοῖς πρώτοις σταθμοῖς
διὰ ταῦτα ἐξηναγκάζοντο οὐ τὰς βραχυτάτας
ἰέναι τῶν ὁδῶν, ἀλλὰ τὰς εὐπορωτάτας τοῖς ζεύγεσι.
3 καὶ οὕτως οἱ μὲν νόσῳ κατὰ τὰς ὁδοὺς ὑπελείποντο,
οἱ δὲ ὑπὸ καμάτου ἢ καύματος ἢ τῷ δίψει οὐκ
ἀντέχοντες, καὶ οὔτε οἱ ἄξοντες ἦσαν οὔτε οἱ
μένοντες θεραπεύσοντες· σπουδῇ γὰρ πολλῇ ἐγίγνετο ὁ στόλος, καὶ ἐν τῷ ὑπὲρ τοῦ παντὸς προθύμῳ
τὸ καθ' ἑκάστους ξὺν ἀνάγκῃ ἠμελεῖτο· οἱ δὲ καὶ
ὕπνῳ κάτοχοι κατὰ τὰς ὁδοὺς γενόμενοι οἷα δὴ
νυκτὸς τὸ πολὺ τὰς πορείας ποιούμενοι, ἔπειτα
ἐξαναστάντες, οἷς μὲν δύναμις ἔτι ἦν κατὰ τὰ
ἴχνη τῆς στρατιᾶς ἐφομαρτήσαντες ὀλίγοι ἀπὸ
πολλῶν ἐσώθησαν, οἱ πολλοὶ δὲ ὥσπερ ἐν πελάγει
ἐκπεσόντες ἐν τῇ ψάμμῳ ἀπώλλυντο.
4 Ξυνηνέχθη δὲ τῇ στρατιᾷ καὶ ἄλλο πάθημα, ὃ δὴ
οὐχ ἥκιστα ἐπίεσεν αὐτούς τε καὶ τοὺς ἵππους καὶ
τὰ ὑποζύγια. ὕεται γὰρ ἡ Γαδρωσίων γῆ ὑπ' ἀνέμων τῶν ἐτησίων, καθάπερ οὖν καὶ ἡ Ἰνδῶν γῆ, οὐ
τὰ πεδία τῶν Γαδρωσίων, ἀλλὰ τὰ ὄρη, ἵναπερ
προσφέρονταί τε αἱ νεφέλαι ἐκ τοῦ πνεύματος καὶ
ἀναχέονται, οὐχ ὑπερβάλλουσαι τῶν ὀρῶν τὰς
5 κορυφάς. ὡς δὲ ηὐλίσθη ἡ στρατιὰ πρὸς χειμάρρῳ
ὀλίγου ὕδατος, αὐτοῦ δὴ ἕνεκα τοῦ ὕδατος, ἀμφὶ
δευτέραν φυλακὴν τῆς νυκτὸς ἐμπλησθεὶς ὑπὸ τῶν
ὄμβρων ὁ χειμάρρους ὁ ταύτῃ ῥέων ἀφανῶν τῇ
στρατιᾷ γεγενημένων τῶν ὄμβρων τοσούτῳ ἐπῆλθε
τῷ ὕδατι, ὡς γύναια καὶ παιδάρια τὰ πολλὰ τῶν
ἑπομένων τῇ στρατιᾷ διαφθεῖραι καὶ τὴν κατα-
σκευὴν τὴν βασιλικὴν ξύμπασαν ἀφανίσαι καὶ τῶν

325
B.C.

it was impossible to drag along owing to the depth of
the sand, and because in the earlier marches they had
been compelled for this reason not to go by the
shortest routes but by those that were easiest for the
teams.   And so some were left behind on the roads 3
from sickness, others from weariness or heat or in-
ability to hold out against thirst; there was no one to
help them forward, and no one to stay behind and
take care of them; for the march was pressed hurriedly on, and in concern for the whole army the
welfare of individuals was necessarily neglected.
Sleep too overpowered men on the roads, since it was
by night that they generally made their stages.   In
that case on waking, if they still had the strength,
they would follow in the tracks of the army, but few
out of many were saved: most of them were lost in
the sand, like men who fall overboard at sea.

The army suffered also a further disaster, which 4
more than anything else distressed the troops, horses
and transport animals.   Rain is brought to Gadrosia,
just as it is to India, by the trade winds, but not to the
Gadrosian plains, only to the hills, where the clouds
borne by the breeze pour down without passing over
the mountain tops.   Now the army had bivouacked 5
near a torrent bed with a little water—it was actually
for the water that the site was chosen—when about
the second watch in the night the stream here, swollen
by rains of which the army had seen nothing, came
down with so great a spate of water that it killed most
of the women and children following the army and
swept away all the royal equipment and the sur-

ὑποζυγίων ὅσα ὑπελείπετο,[1] αὐτοὺς δὲ μόλις καὶ
χαλεπῶς ξὺν τοῖς ὅπλοις οὐδὲ τούτοις πᾶσιν
6 ἀποσωθῆναι. οἱ πολλοὶ δὲ καὶ πίνοντες, ὁπότε ἐκ
καύματός τε καὶ δίψους ὕδατι ἀθρόῳ ἐπιτύχοιεν,
πρὸς αὐτοῦ τοῦ ἀπαύστου ποτοῦ ἀπώλλυντο. καὶ
τούτων ἕνεκα ᾿Αλέξανδρος τὰς στρατοπεδείας οὐ
πρὸς τοῖς ὕδασιν αὐτοῖς τὸ πολὺ ἐποιεῖτο, ἀλλὰ
ἀπέχων ὅσον εἴκοσι σταδίους μάλιστα, ὡς μὴ
ἀθρόους ἐμπίπτοντας τῷ ὕδατι αὐτούς τε καὶ κτήνη
ἀπόλλυσθαι καὶ ἅμα τοὺς μάλιστα ἀκράτορας
σφῶν ἐπεμβαίνοντας ἐς τὰς πηγὰς ἢ τὰ ῥεύματα
διαφθείρειν καὶ τῇ ἄλλῃ στρατιᾷ τὸ ὕδωρ.
26. Ἔνθα δὴ ἔργον καλὸν εἴπερ τι ἄλλο τῶν
᾿Αλεξάνδρου οὐκ ἔδοξέ μοι ἀφανίσαι, ἢ ἐν τῇδε τῇ
χώρᾳ πραχθὲν ἢ ἔτι ἔμπροσθεν ἐν Παραπαμισάδαις,
ὡς μετεξέτεροι ἀνέγραψαν. ἰέναι μὲν τὴν στρατιὰν
διὰ ψάμμου τε καὶ τοῦ καύματος ἤδη ἐπιφλέγοντος,
ὅτι πρὸς ὕδωρ ἐχρῆν ἐξανύσαι· τὸ δὲ ἦν πρόσθεν
τῆς ὁδοῦ· καὶ αὐτόν τε ᾿Αλέξανδρον δίψει κατεχ-
όμενον μόλις μὲν καὶ χαλεπῶς, πεζὸν δὲ ὅμως
ἡγεῖσθαι· ὡς δὲ καὶ τοὺς ἄλλους στρατιώτας,
οἷάπερ φιλεῖ ἐν τῷ τοιῷδε, κουφοτέρως φέρειν τοὺς
2 πόνους ἐν ἰσότητι τῆς ταλαιπωρήσεως. ἐν δὲ
τούτῳ τῶν ψιλῶν τινας κατὰ ζήτησιν ὕδατος
ἀποτραπέντας ἀπὸ τῆς στρατιᾶς εὑρεῖν ὕδωρ
συλλελεγμένον ἔν τινι χαράδρᾳ οὐ βαθείᾳ, ὀλίγην
καὶ φαύλην πίδακα· καὶ τοῦτο οὐ χαλεπῶς συλ-
λέξαντας σπουδῇ ἰέναι παρ' ᾿Αλέξανδρον, ὡς μέγα
δή τι ἀγαθὸν φέροντας· ὡς δὲ ἐπέλαζον ἤδη,

―――――――――――――――

[1] Castiglioni: ἀπελείπετο codd.

―――――――――――――――

[1] App. XXV 7 f.

325
B.C.

viving transport animals; and indeed the troops themselves were only saved with great difficulty, with
their weapons only, and not even all of these. To 6
very many of them even drinking, whenever they
found abundant water, was fatal after the heat and
thirst, by reason of their intemperate draughts; and
for this reason Alexander did not, as a rule, camp
close to the watercourses, but about twenty stades
away,[1] to prevent a general rush to the stream, in
which they would perish themselves with their beasts;
so too those with least self-control would not step
into the springs or streams and spoil the water for the
rest of the army.

26. Now at this point a noble deed, as noble as any
of Alexander's, in my judgement is not to be left in
obscurity, whether it was performed in this country,
or still earlier among the Parapamisadae, as some
other accounts have it.[1] The story goes as follows.
The army was marching through sand with the heat
already burning, since they were obliged to get to
water at the end of the march, and this was some distance ahead. Alexander himself was in the grip of
thirst, and it was with much difficulty that he persisted in leading the way on foot, so that the rest of
the troops should (as usually happens in such a case)
bear their sufferings more easily, with all sharing the
distress equally. At this moment some light-armed 2
troops left the army to look for water, and found some,
collected in a shallow torrent-bed, a poor and wretched
water-hole; they easily collected it and hurried to
Alexander, feeling that they were bringing something of great value, and, when they came near,

[1] Probably ' vulgate,' but QC. vii 4, 19 locates the incident
in Sogdiana, so there were at least three versions.

ἐμβαλόντας ἐς κράνος τὸ ὕδωρ προσενεγκεῖν τῷ
3 βασιλεῖ. τὸν δὲ λαβεῖν μὲν καὶ ἐπαινέσαι τοὺς
κομίσαντας, λαβόντα δὲ ἐν ὄψει πάντων ἐκχέαι·
καὶ ἐπὶ τῷδε τῷ ἔργῳ ἐς τοσόνδε ἐπιρρωσθῆναι
τὴν στρατιὰν ξύμπασαν ὥστε εἰκάσαι ἄν τινα πότον
γενέσθαι πᾶσιν ἐκεῖνο τὸ ὕδωρ τὸ πρὸς Ἀλεξάνδρου
ἐκχυθέν. τοῦτο ἐγώ, εἴπερ τι ἄλλο, τὸ ἔργον εἰς
καρτερίαν τε καὶ ἅμα στρατηγίαν ἐπαινῶ Ἀλεξάνδρου.

4　Ξυνηνέχθη δέ τι καὶ τοιόνδε τῇ στρατιᾷ ἐν τῇ
γῇ ἐκείνῃ. οἱ γὰρ ἡγεμόνες τῆς ὁδοῦ τελευτῶν-
τες οὐκέτι μεμνῆσθαι ἔφασκον τὴν ὁδόν, ἀλλ'
ἀφανισθῆναι τὰ σημεῖα αὐτῆς πρὸς τοῦ ἀνέμου
ἐπιπνεύσαντος· καὶ — οὐ γὰρ εἶναι ἐν τῇ ψάμμῳ
πολλῇ τε καὶ ὁμοίᾳ πάντῃ νενημένῃ ὅτῳ τεκμηριώ-
σονται τὴν ὁδόν, οὔτ' οὖν δένδρα ξυνήθη παρ'
αὐτὴν πεφυκότα, οὔτε τινὰ γήλοφον βέβαιον
ἀνεστηκότα· οὐδὲ πρὸς τὰ ἄστρα ἐν νυκτὶ ἢ μεθ'
ἡμέραν πρὸς τὸν ἥλιον μεμελετῆσθαί σφισι τὰς
πορείας, καθάπερ τοῖς ναύταις πρὸς τῶν ἄρκτων
τὴν μὲν Φοίνιξι, τὴν ὀλίγην, τὴν δὲ τοῖς ἄλλοις
5　ἀνθρώποις, τὴν μείζονα. — ἔνθα δὴ Ἀλέξανδρον
ξυνέντα ὅτι ἐν ἀριστερᾷ ⟨δεῖ⟩ ἀποκλίναντα ἄγειν,
ἀναλαβόντα ὀλίγους ἅμα οἷ ἱππέας ⟨προχωρῆσαι⟩·
ὡς δὲ καὶ τούτων οἱ ἵπποι ἐξέκαμνον ὑπὸ τοῦ
καύματος, ἀπολιπεῖν καὶ τούτων τοὺς πολλούς,
αὐτὸν δὲ ξὺν πέντε τοῖς πᾶσιν ἀφιππάσα-
σθαι καὶ εὑρεῖν τὴν θάλασσαν, διαμησάμενόν τε
αὐτὸν ἐπὶ τοῦ αἰγιαλοῦ τὸν κάχληκα ἐπιτυχεῖν
ὕδατι γλυκεῖ καὶ καθαρῷ καὶ οὕτω μετελθεῖν τὴν
στρατιὰν πᾶσαν· καὶ ἐς ἑπτὰ ἡμέρας ἰέναι παρὰ
τὴν θάλασσαν ὑδρευομένους ἐκ τῆς ἠϊόνος. ἔνθεν

poured the water into a helmet and offered it to the
king. He took it and thanked them, but then poured 3
it out in the sight of every one; and at this action the
army was so much heartened that you would have
guessed that all had drunk what Alexander had
poured away. This deed of Alexander's I specially
commend as a proof of his endurance and also of his
generalship.

Another incident happened to the army in this 4
district as follows.[2] The guides finally said that they
could not remember the way, as the marks of direction had been obliterated by the blast of the wind;
and, of course, in the mass of sand which was all
alike, heaped up on all sides, there was nothing by
which one could determine the road, no ordinary trees
growing along it and no solid hillock standing up;
nor were they practised in making their marches by
the stars at night or the sun in the day in the way
that the Phoenician sailors go by the Little Bear and
other men at sea by the Great Bear. Then Alexander, 5
realizing that he ought to lead the army by a course
swerving to the left, took a few horsemen with him
and rode on ahead; and when even their horses began
to weary beneath the heat, he left most of them
behind, rode off with no more than five of them and
found the sea; by digging on the shingle shore, he
came on fresh, pure water. So the whole army followed and for seven days they marched by the sea,
getting water from the shore. From this point on,

---

[2] Perhaps from Ar. rather than N.

δέ, ἤδη γὰρ γιγνώσκειν τὴν ὁδὸν τοὺς ἡγεμόνας, ἐπὶ τῆς μεσογαίας ποιεῖσθαι τὸν στόλον.

27. Ὡς δὲ ἀφίκετο ἐς τῶν Γαδρωσίων τὰ βασίλεια, ἀναπαύει ἐνταῦθα τὴν στρατιάν. καὶ Ἀπολλοφάνην μὲν παύει τῆς σατραπείας, ὅτι οὐδενὸς ἔγνω ἐπιμεληθέντα τῶν προεπηγγελμένων, Θόαντα δὲ σατραπεύειν τῶν ταύτῃ ἔταξε· τούτου δὲ νόσῳ τελευτήσαντος Σιβύρτιος τὴν σατραπείαν ἐκδέχεται· ὁ αὐτὸς δὲ καὶ Καρμανίας σατράπης ἦν νεωστὶ ἐξ Ἀλεξάνδρου ταχθείς· τότε δὲ τούτῳ μὲν Ἀραχωτῶν τε καὶ τῶν Γαδρωσίων ἄρχειν ἐδόθη, Καρμανίαν δὲ ἔσχε Τληπόλεμος ὁ Πυθοφάνους.
2 ἤδη τε ἐπὶ Καρμανίας προὔχωρει ὁ βασιλεὺς καὶ ἀγγέλλεται αὐτῷ Φίλιππον τὸν σατράπην τῆς Ἰνδῶν γῆς ἐπιβουλευθέντα πρὸς τῶν μισθοφόρων δόλῳ ἀποθανεῖν, τοὺς δὲ ἀποκτείναντας ὅτι οἱ σωματοφύλακες τοῦ Φιλίππου οἱ Μακεδόνες τοὺς μὲν ἐν αὐτῷ τῷ ἔργῳ, τοὺς δὲ καὶ ὕστερον λαβόντες ἀπέκτειναν. ταῦτα δὲ ὡς ἔγνω, ἐκπέμπει γράμματα ἐς Ἰνδοὺς παρὰ Εὔδαμόν τε καὶ Ταξίλην ἐπιμελεῖσθαι τῆς χώρας τῆς πρόσθεν ὑπὸ Φιλίππῳ τεταγμένης ἔστ' ἂν αὐτὸς σατράπην ἐκπέμψῃ ἐπ' αὐτῆς.
3 Ἤδη δ' ἐς Καρμανίαν ἥκοντος Ἀλεξάνδρου Κρατερὸς ἀφικνεῖται, τήν τε ἄλλην στρατιὰν ἅμα οἷ ἄγων καὶ τοὺς ἐλέφαντας καὶ Ὀρδάνην τὸν

---

[1] Not for long, S. xv 2, 7 (Ar.?); *contra* QC. ix 10, 18?

[2] A. failed to note that N's account (*Ind.* 23, 5) shows that he was not to blame (presumably for not forwarding supplies). Al. cannot yet have heard of his death in battle. Cf. App. XXIII 9. Bosworth (*CQ* 1971, 124) conjectures that A. has confused Astaspes (next note) and Apollophanes: this would

as the guides now knew the way, he marched into the interior.

27. After arriving at the Gadrosian capital, Alexander rested his army there.[1] He removed Apollophanes from the satrapy, finding that he had neglected all his orders,[2] and appointed Thoas satrap in his stead; but as he died of sickness, Sibyrtius received the office. He had been recently appointed by Alexander satrap of Carmania, but now was given charge of both the Arachotians and the Gadrosians, and Tlepolemus son of Pythophanes took over Carmania.[3] Alexander was already on the way towards Carmania when it was reported to him that Philip, the satrap of the Indian land, had been treacherously killed in a plot against him by the mercenaries, but that Philip's Macedonian body-guards had killed the assassins, some in the act, and others after capture. On learning this, he despatched letters to India to Eudamus and Taxilas telling them to take charge of the district formerly under Philip, until he himself sent a satrap to govern it.[4]

When Alexander had reached Carmania,[5] Craterus arrived bringing with him the rest of the army and the elephants and Ordanes, who had revolted and caused

be a double error, as A. plainly refers to the satrap of Gadrosia.

[3] QC. ix 10, 21 f., cf. 29, says that Al. made Sibyrtius satrap of Arachosia *vice* Menon (iii 28, 1), and dissembled his suspicions of the loyalty of Astaspes, satrap of Carmania (never named by A.) till he reached the Carmanian capital, and then put him to death (cf. *Ind.* 36, 8); if so, A. has reported these appointments too early.

[4] v 8, 3; vi 14, 3; 15, 2; App. XVII 31.

[5] Cf. D. 106, QC. ix 10, 20 ff.; P. 67 for events here.

ἀποστάντα καὶ νεωτερίσαντα συνειληφώς. ἐνταῦθα
δὲ Στασάνωρ τε ὁ ᾿Αρείων καὶ ὁ Ζαραγγῶν σατράπης ἧκεν καὶ ξὺν αὐτοῖς Φαρισμάνης ὁ Φραταφέρνου
τοῦ Παρθυαίων καὶ ῾Υρκανίων σατράπου παῖς.
ἧκον δὲ καὶ οἱ στρατηγοὶ οἱ ὑπολειφθέντες ἅμα
Παρμενίωνι ἐπὶ τῆς στρατιᾶς τῆς ἐν Μηδίᾳ,
Κλέανδρός τε καὶ Σιτάλκης καὶ ῾Ηράκων, τὴν
4 πολλὴν τῆς στρατιᾶς καὶ οὗτοι ἄγοντες. τοὺς μὲν
δὴ ἀμφὶ Κλέανδρόν τε καὶ Σιτάλκην πολλὰ ἐπι-
καλούντων αὐτοῖς τῶν τε ἐγχωρίων καὶ τῆς
στρατιᾶς αὐτῆς, ὡς ἱερά τε πρὸς αὐτῶν σεσυλη-
μένα καὶ θήκας παλαιὰς κεκινημένας καὶ ἄλλα
ἄδικα ἔργα ⟨ἐς⟩ τοὺς ὑπηκόους τετολμημένα καὶ
ἀτάσθαλα, ταῦτα ὡς ἐξηγγέλθη,[1] τοὺς μὲν ἀπέκτεινεν, ὡς καὶ τοῖς ἄλλοις δέος εἶναι, ὅσοι σατράπαι
ἢ ὕπαρχοι ἢ νομάρχαι ἀπολείποιντο, τὰ ἴσα
5 ἐκείνοις πλημμελοῦντας πείσεσθαι· (καὶ τοῦτο,
εἴπερ τι ἄλλο, κατέσχεν ἐν κόσμῳ τὰ ἔθνη τὰ ἐξ
᾿Αλεξάνδρου δοριάλωτα ἢ ἑκόντα προσχωρήσαντα,
τοσαῦτα μὲν πλήθει ὄντα, τόσον δὲ ἀλλήλων
ἀφεστηκότα, ὅτι οὐκ ἐξῆν ὑπὸ τῇ ᾿Αλεξάνδρου
βασιλείᾳ ἀδικεῖσθαι τοὺς ἀρχομένους ὑπὸ τῶν
ἀρχόντων·) ῾Ηράκων δὲ τότε μὲν ἀφείθη τῆς
αἰτίας· ὀλίγον δὲ ὕστερον ἐξελεγχθεὶς πρὸς ἀνδρῶν
Σουσίων σεσυληκέναι τὸ ἐν Σούσοις ἱερὸν καὶ

---

[1] codd.: ἐξηλέγχθη Sintenis.

---

[6] Cf. App. XVII 29. A. suppresses explanatory details.
QC. ix 10, 19 says that Al. had heard at Pura of Craterus'
arrest of ' Ozines ' and Zariaspes, rebel Persian nobles; they
were now put to death (x 1, 9).
[7] Stasanor held both satrapies (iii 29, 5; iv 18,1 and 3; D.
xviii 3, 3).

trouble, but whom he had captured.[6]   There Alexander was also joined by Stasanor, satrap of the
Areians and the Zarangians,[7] along with Pharismanes,
son of Phrataphernes, satrap of Parthyaea and Hyrcania, and by the generals who had been left behind
with Parmenio in command of the army in Media,
Cleander, Sitalces and Heracon; they too brought
the greater part of their army.[8]   Both the natives and   4
the army itself brought many charges against
Cleander, Sitalces and their followers of having
plundered temples, disturbed ancient tombs, and
perpetrated other acts of injustice against the subjects with presumptuous audacity. On receiving
this report,[9] Alexander executed these two, to make
the other remaining satraps, hyparchs or nomarchs
fear that if they committed the like crimes they
would suffer the like fate. Nothing did more to keep   5
order among the peoples that Alexander had conquered by force or that had voluntarily come over to
him, numerous as they were and widely separated
from each other, than that in Alexander's realm the
rulers were not allowed to wrong the subjects.
Heracon was for the time acquitted of the charge;
but soon afterwards was convicted by men from Susa
of having plundered the temple of Susa, and paid the

[8] QC. x 1, 1 ff., who adds the name of Agathon (A. i 14, 3;
iii 12, 4), and says that they brought 5000 foot and 1000 horse
(App. XIII 5 f.), that they were hated for their part in killing
Parmenio (A. iii 26), that they had gravely oppressed the subjects, but that Al., who thought it their worst crime to have
despaired of his safety, put them in bonds, while executing 600
of their soldiers as instruments in their tyranny; he does not
record their own execution. Heracon, who had for some
time been at Susa (§ 5), had perhaps replaced Menidas (cf. iv
18, 3; vii 23, 1). Cleander was brother to Coenus, Al's
opponent at the Hyphasis.

[9] Emendation to ' on obtaining proof ' is wanton.

6 οὗτος ἔδωκεν δίκην. οἱ δὲ σὺν Στασάνορι καὶ
Φραταφέρνῃ πλῆθός τε ὑποζυγίων παρ' Ἀλέξανδρον ἄγοντες ἦλθον καὶ καμήλους πολλάς, ὡς
ἔμαθον ὅτι τὴν ἐπὶ Γαδρωσίων ἄγει, εἰκάσαντες
ὅτι τὰ αὐτὰ ἐκεῖνα πείσεται αὐτῷ ἡ στρατιὰ ἃ δὴ
ἔπαθε· καὶ οὖν καὶ ἐν καιρῷ μὲν καὶ οὗτοι ἀφίκοντο,
ἐν καιρῷ δὲ αἱ κάμηλοί τε καὶ τὰ ὑποζύγια·
διένειμε γὰρ ξύμπαντα Ἀλέξανδρος τοῖς μὲν
ἡγεμόσι κατ' ἄνδρα, τοῖς δὲ κατ' ἴλας τε καὶ
ἑκατοστύας, τοῖς δὲ κατὰ λόχους, ὅπως τὸ πλῆθος
τῶν ὑποζυγίων τε καὶ καμήλων αὐτῷ ξυνέβαινεν.

28. Ἤδη δέ τινες καὶ τοιάδε ἀνέγραψαν, οὐ
πιστὰ ἐμοὶ λέγοντες, ὡς συζεύξας δύο ἁρμαμάξας
κατακείμενος ξὺν τοῖς ἑταίροις ⟨καὶ⟩[1] καταυ-
λούμενος τὴν διὰ Καρμανίας ἦγεν, ἡ στρατιὰ δὲ
αὐτῷ ἐστεφανωμένη τε καὶ παίζουσα εἵπετο,
προὔκειτο δὲ αὐτῇ σῖτά τε καὶ ὅσα ἄλλα ἐς
τρυφὴν παρὰ τὰς ὁδοὺς συγκεκομισμένα πρὸς τῶν
Καρμανίων, καὶ ταῦτα πρὸς μίμησιν τῆς Διονύ-
2 σου βακχείας ἀπεικάσθη Ἀλεξάνδρῳ, ὅτι καὶ ὑπὲρ
ἐκείνου λόγος ἐλέγετο καταστρεψάμενον Ἰνδοὺς
Διόνυσον οὕτω τὴν πολλὴν τῆς Ἀσίας ἐπελθεῖν,
καὶ Θρίαμβόν τε αὐτὸν ἐπικληθῆναι τὸν Διόνυσον
καὶ τὰς ἐπὶ ταῖς νίκαις ταῖς ἐκ πολέμου πομπὰς
ἐπὶ τῷ αὐτῷ τούτῳ θριάμβους. ταῦτα δὲ οὔτε
Πτολεμαῖος ὁ Λάγου οὔτε Ἀριστόβουλος ὁ
Ἀριστοβούλου ἀνέγραψαν οὐδέ τις ἄλλος ὅντινα
ἱκανὸν ἄν τις ποιήσαιτο τεκμηριῶσαι ὑπὲρ τῶν
τοιῶνδε, καί μοι ὡς οὐ πιστὰ ἀναγεγράφθαι

[1] Inserted by Polak.

[10] Cf. P. 66, 3; App. XVIII 3.

penalty. Stasanor and Phrataphernes and their men 6   325 B.C.
brought Alexander a large number of transport
animals and many camels, having guessed, when they
learned of his march into Gadrosia, that his army
would undergo the very sufferings it did. Their
coming was indeed timely, as was that of the camels
and animals, for Alexander distributed them all, to
officers individually, to the others by squadrons and
centuries or companies in proportion to the total number of camels and transport animals he received.[10]

28. Some writers have recounted a story, which I
do not myself credit, that Alexander bound together
two war-chariots, and drove through Carmania re-
clining with his Companions to the sound of the pipes,
while his army followed behind, garlanded and
sporting; that provisions and everything else that
could make for luxury had been brought together
along their path by the Carmanians; and that this
pageantry was devised by Alexander in imitation of
the Bacchic revelry of Dionysus, since there was a 2
story about Dionysus that, after subduing India, he
traversed the greater part of Asia in this way, that he
himself was surnamed 'Triumph', and that pro-
cessions after victories in war were for this very
reason called 'triumphs'. This is not recorded by
Ptolemy son of Lagus or Aristobulus son of Aristobulus or any other author who could be regarded as
offering adequate evidence on such transactions.[1]
My own obligation has been adequately discharged
by including the story, unreliable though it is.

---

[1] Cf. Hamilton on P. 67; App. XV 4. Vines in Carmania:
S. xv 2, 14. 'Triumph' as a victory procession is purely
Roman; A. is thus citing a late version of the 'vulgate' (not
Clitarchus).

3 ἐξήρκεσαν. ἀλλὰ ἐκεῖνα ἤδη Ἀριστοβούλῳ ἑπόμενος ξυγγράφῳ, θῦσαι ἐν Καρμανίᾳ Ἀλέξανδρον
χαριστήρια τῆς κατ' Ἰνδῶν νίκης καὶ ὑπὲρ τῆς
στρατιᾶς, ὅτι ἀπεσώθη ἐκ Γαδρωσίων, καὶ ἀγῶνα
διαθεῖναι μουσικόν τε καὶ γυμνικόν· καταλέξαι δὲ
καὶ Πευκέσταν ἐς τοὺς σωματοφύλακας, ἤδη μὲν
ἐγνωκότα σατράπην καταστῆσαι τῆς Περσίδος,
ἐθέλοντα δὲ πρὸ τῆς σατραπείας μηδὲ ταύτης τῆς
τιμῆς καὶ πίστεως ἀπείρατον εἶναι ἐπὶ τῷ ἐν
4 Μαλλοῖς ἔργῳ· εἶναι δὲ αὐτῷ ἑπτὰ εἰς τότε σωματοφύλακας, Λεοννάτον † Ἀντέου,[1] Ἡφαιστίωνα
τὸν Ἀμύντορος, Λυσίμαχον Ἀγαθοκλέους, Ἀρι-
στόνουν Πεισαίου, τούτους μὲν Πελλαίους, Περδίκκαν δὲ Ὀρόντου ἐκ τῆς Ὀρεστίδος, Πτολεμαῖον δὲ
Λάγου καὶ Πείθωνα Κρατεύα Ἐορδαίους· ὄγδοον
δὲ προσγενέσθαι αὐτοῖς Πευκέσταν τὸν Ἀλεξάνδρου ὑπερασπίσαντα.

5 Ἐν τούτῳ δὲ καὶ Νέαρχος περιπλεύσας τὴν
Ὤρων τε καὶ Γαδρωσῶν γῆν καὶ τὴν τῶν Ἰχθυοφάγων κατῆρεν ἐς τῆς Καρμανίας τὰ πρὸς θάλασσαν
ᾠκισμένα· ἔνθεν δὲ ἀνελθὼν σὺν ὀλίγοις Ἀλεξάνδρῳ
ἀπήγγειλε τὰ ἀμφὶ τὸν περίπλουν τὸν γενόμενον
6 αὐτῷ κατὰ τὴν ἔξω θάλασσαν. τοῦτον μὲν δὴ
καταπέμπει αὖθις ἐκπεριπλεύσοντα ἔστε ἐπὶ τὴν
Σουσιανῶν τε γῆν καὶ τοῦ Τίγρητος ποταμοῦ τὰς
ἐκβολάς· ὅπως δὲ ἐπλεύσθη αὐτῷ τὰ ἀπὸ τοῦ

[1] See textual note on iii 5, 5.

---

[2] Evidently Ar., not Pt., was A's source for § 4 f.: he alone
recorded these games.

[3] See textual note on iii 5, 5.

[4] N. in *Ind*. 18 gives Aristonous and Pithon different origins;
perhaps they had fiefs in two places.

However, following Aristobulus, I do record that in **3** 325
Carmania Alexander sacrificed thank-offerings for his B.C.
conquest of India and his army's safe transit through
Gadrosia, that he conducted musical and athletic
games,[2] and that he enrolled Peucestas as an additional bodyguard; Aristobulus says that he had
already decided to make him satrap of Persia, but
wished him first to enjoy this honour and mark of confidence as well, because of his exploit among the
Mallians, and that, while up to this time Alexander's **4**
bodyguards were seven in number, Leonnatus son of
Anteas,[3] Hephaestion son of Amyntor, Lysimachus
son of Agathocles, Aristonous son of Pisaeus, all from
Pella, Perdiccas son of Orontes from Orestis, Ptolemy
son of Lagus and Pithon son of Crateuas from Eor-
daea, an eighth was now added—Peucestas who had
protected Alexander with his shield.[4]

Meanwhile [5] Nearchus, after completing his voyage **5**
round the country of the Oritans, the Gadrosians and
the Fish-Eaters, put in to the inhabited part of the
Carmanian seashore; thence he went up with a few
of his men to Alexander and reported his experiences
on the voyage in the outer ocean. Alexander sent **6** 324
him back again to continue his voyage along the B.C.
coast to the land of Susia and the mouths of the river
Tigris. But I shall record separately, following

---

[5] The Greek phrase often means this (e.g. i 7, 1). *Contra*
Badian, *Yale Cl. St.*, 1975, 162 ff., A. does not here belie N's
story (*Ind.* 33–6) that he arrived before the games; he is revert-
ing to Pt., who ignored the games and could not put N's arrival
before or after. As for other evidence, D. 106, 4 is wholly
inaccurate, P. 68, 1 vague chronologically, and QC. x 1, 10 ff.
does no more than put the arrival both of Cleander and of N.
after the Bacchic rout, not after Ar's games. Of course N.
falsely suggests that the games were held simply to celebrate
his own success.

Ἰνδοῦ ποταμοῦ ἐπὶ τὴν θάλασσαν τὴν Περσικὴν καὶ τὸ στόμα τοῦ Τίγρητος, ταῦτα ἰδίᾳ ἀναγράψω αὐτῷ Νεάρχῳ ἑπόμενος, ὡς καὶ τήνδε εἶναι ὑπὲρ Ἀλεξάνδρου Ἑλληνικὴν τὴν συγγραφήν. ταῦτα μὲν δὴ ἐν ὑστέρῳ ἔσται τυχόν, εἰ [ς] ὅ τε θυμός [τέ] με καὶ ὁ δαίμων ταύτῃ ἄγοι.

7   Ἀλέξανδρος δὲ Ἡφαιστίωνα μὲν σύν τε τῇ πλείστῃ μοίρᾳ τῆς στρατιᾶς καὶ τοῖς ὑποζυγίοις καὶ τοὺς ἐλέφαντας ἅμα οἷ ἔχοντα τὴν παρὰ θάλασσαν ἀπὸ Καρμανίας ὡς ἐπὶ τὴν Περσίδα ἄγειν ἐκέλευσεν, ὅτι χειμῶνος ὥρα γιγνομένου αὐτῷ τοῦ στόλου τὰ πρὸς τῇ θαλάσσῃ τῆς Περσίδος ἀλεεινά τε ἦν καὶ τῶν ἐπιτηδείων ἀφθόνως ἔχοντα.

29. Αὐτὸς δὲ ξὺν τοῖς κουφοτάτοις τῶν πεζῶν καὶ ξὺν τῶν ἱππέων τοῖς ἑταίροις καὶ μέρει τινὶ τῶν τοξοτῶν ᾔει τὴν ἐπὶ Πασαργάδας τῆς Περσί-δος. Στασάνορα δὲ καταπέμπει ἐπὶ τὴν ἀρχὴν
2   τὴν ἑαυτοῦ. ὡς δὲ ἐπὶ τοῖς ὅροις ἦν τῆς Περσίδος, Φρασαόρτην μὲν οὐ κατέλαβε σατραπεύοντα ἔτι (νόσῳ γὰρ τετελευτηκὼς ἐτύγχανεν ἐν Ἰνδοῖς ἔτι Ἀλεξάνδρου ὄντος), Ὀρξίνης δὲ ἐπεμέλετο τῆς Περσίδος, οὐ πρὸς Ἀλεξάνδρου κατασταθείς, ἀλλ' ὅτι οὐκ ἀπηξίωσεν αὐτὸν ἐν κόσμῳ Πέρσας διαφυλάξαι Ἀλεξάνδρῳ οὐκ ὄντος ἄλλου ἄρχοντος.
3   ἦλθε δὲ ἐς Πασαργάδας καὶ Ἀτροπάτης ὁ Μηδ[ε]ίας σατράπης, ἄγων Βαρυάξην ἄνδρα Μῆδον συνειλημμένον, ὅτι ὀρθὴν τὴν κίδαριν περι-θέμενος βασιλέα προσεῖπεν αὐτὸν Περσῶν καὶ Μήδων, καὶ ξὺν τούτῳ τοὺς μετασχόντας αὐτῷ τοῦ

---

[6] No coastal route was practicable (Herzfeld, *Klio*, 1908, 20); doubtless H. kept closer to the coast than Al., but A's source,

Nearchus himself, the incidents of his voyage from the river Indus to the Persian sea and the mouth of the Tigris, so that this too will be an account of Alexander in pure Greek, but it will be written later, maybe, if inclination and divine power should so move me.

Alexander despatched Hephaestion with the 7 largest part of the army, the baggage train and elephants along the sea-coast from Carmania to Persia; as his expedition was in winter, the coastal parts of Persia were then sunny and well supplied with all necessaries.[6]

29. Alexander himself with the nimblest of the infantry, the cavalry Companions and part of the archers proceeded towards Pasargadae in Persia; he despatched Stasanor to his own country.[1] When he 2 was on the Persian border, he found that Phrasaortes was no longer satrap, for he had actually died of sickness while Alexander was still in India, but Orxines[2] was in charge of Persia, not by appointment of Alexander, but because he felt that he was the right person, in the absence of any other governor, to keep the Persians in order for Alexander. Atropates, the 3 satrap of Media, also came to Pasargadae with Baryaxes a Mede, whom he had arrested, since he had worn the tiara upright[3] and assumed the title of king of the Persians and Medes; with him were his

---

no doubt Pt., was ignorant, cf. N. *ap. Ind.* 40, 2. Engels' notion (p. 118) that N's fleet provisioned Hephaestion is refuted by N's silence.

[1] The 'Testament of Alexander' (vii 27, 1 n.) makes Stasanor present at Babylon when Al. died; for his return cf. vii 6, 1 n.

[2] See iii 8, 5; QC. x 1, 22; cf. iv 12, 8.

[3] App. XIV 2.

νεωτερισμοῦ τε καὶ τῆς ἀποστάσεως. τούτους
μὲν δὴ ἀπέκτεινεν Ἀλέξανδρος.

4 Ἐλύπησε δὲ αὐτὸν ἡ παρανομία ἡ ἐς τὸν Κύρου τοῦ
Καμβύσου τάφον, ὅτι διορωρυγμένον τε καὶ σεσυλ-
ημένον κατέλαβε [τοῦ Κύρου τὸν τάφον],[1] ὡς λέγει
Ἀριστόβουλος. εἶναι γὰρ ἐν Πασαργάδαις ἐν τῷ
παραδείσῳ τῷ βασιλικῷ Κύρου ἐκείνου τάφον καὶ
περὶ αὐτὸν ἄλσος πεφυτεῦσθαι δένδρων παντοίων
καὶ ὕδατι εἶναι κατάρρυτον καὶ πόαν βαθεῖαν
5 πεφυκέναι ἐν τῷ λειμῶνι, καὶ αὐτὸν δὲ τὸν τάφον
τὰ κάτω λίθου τετραπέδου ἐς τετράγωνον σχῆμα
πεποιῆσθαι, ἄνωθεν δὲ οἴκημα ἐπεῖναι λίθινον
ἐστεγασμένον, θυρίδα ἔχον φέρουσαν ἔσω στενήν,
ὡς μόλις ἂν ⟨εἶναι⟩ ἑνὶ ἀνδρὶ οὐ μεγάλῳ πολλὰ κα-
κοπαθοῦντι παρελθεῖν. ἐν δὲ τῷ οἰκήματι πύελον
χρυσῆν κεῖσθαι, ἵνα τὸ σῶμα τοῦ Κύρου ἐτέθαπτο,
καὶ κλίνην παρὰ τῇ πυέλῳ· πόδας δὲ εἶναι τῇ
κλίνῃ χρυσοῦς σφυρηλάτους καὶ τάπητα ἐπίβλημα
τῶν Βαβυλωνίων καὶ καυνάκας πορφυροῦς ὑπο-
6 στρώματα. ἐπεῖναι δὲ καὶ κάνδυς καὶ ἄλλους
χιτῶνας τῆς Βαβυλωνίου ἐργασίας. καὶ ἀναξυρί-
δες Μηδικαὶ καὶ στολαὶ ὑακινθινοβαφεῖς λέγει ὅτι
ἔκειντο, αἱ δὲ πορφύρας αἱ δὲ ἄλλης καὶ ἄλλης χρόας,
καὶ στρεπτοὶ καὶ ἀκινάκαι καὶ ἐνώτια χρυσοῦ τε καὶ
λίθων κολλητά, καὶ τράπεζα ἔκειτο. ἐν μέσῳ δὲ
⟨τῆς τραπέζης καὶ⟩[2] τῆς κλίνης ἡ πύελος ἔκειτο
7 ἡ τὸ σῶμα τὸ Κύρου ἔχουσα. εἶναι δὲ ἐντὸς τοῦ
περιβόλου πρὸς τῇ ἀναβάσει τῇ ἐπὶ τὸν τάφον φερ-

---

[1] Deleted by Polak.

[2] Without the addition of such words, proposed by Polak,
the sentence seems either nonsensical or inconsistent with what
has been said before.

associates in revolution and rebellion. Alexander
put them to death.

He was distressed by the outrage on the tomb of 4
Cyrus son of Cambyses, since (as Aristobulus relates) [4]
he found it broken into and rifled. The tomb of the
famous Cyrus was in Pasargadae in the royal park;
a grove had been planted round it with all sorts of
trees and irrigated, and deep grass had grown in the
meadow; the tomb itself in the lower parts was built 5
of stones cut square and was rectangular in form.
Above, there was a stone chamber with a stone roof
and a door leading into it so narrow that it was hard
and caused much distress for a single man of low
stature to get through. In the chamber lay a
golden sarcophagus, in which Cyrus' body had been
buried; a couch stood by its side with feet of wrought
gold; a Babylonian tapestry served as a coverlet and
purple rugs as a carpet. There was placed on it a 6
sleeved mantle and other garments of Babylonian
workmanship. According to Aristobulus, Median
trousers and robes dyed blue lay there, some dark,
some of other varying shades, with necklaces,
scimitars and earrings of stones set in gold, and a
table stood there. It was between the table and the
couch that the sarcophagus containing Cyrus' body
was placed. Within the enclosure and by the ascent 7
to the tomb itself there was a small building put up

[4] Ar's first-hand evidence refutes the accounts of Onesicritus (but cf. Pearson 93 n. 38) and Aristos *ap.* S. xv 3, 7 (cf.
8), and of QC. x 1, 30 ff.

οὔσῃ οἴκημα σμικρὸν τοῖς Μάγοις πεποιημένον, οἳ
δὴ ἐφύλασσον τὸν Κύρου τάφον ἔτι ἀπὸ Καμβύσου
τοῦ Κύρου, παῖς παρὰ πατρὸς ἐκδεχόμενος τὴν
φυλακήν. καὶ τούτοις πρόβατόν τε ἐς ἡμέραν
ἐδίδοτο ἐκ βασιλέως καὶ ἀλεύρων τε καὶ οἴνου τεταγμένα καὶ ἵππος κατὰ μῆνα ἐς θυσίαν τῷ Κύρῳ.
8 ἐπεγέγραπτο δὲ ὁ τάφος Περσικοῖς γράμμασι· καὶ
ἐδήλου Περσιστὶ τάδε· ὦ ἄνθρωπε, ἐγὼ Κῦρός
εἰμι ὁ Καμβύσου ὁ τὴν ἀρχὴν Πέρσαις καταστησ-
άμενος καὶ τῆς Ἀσίας βασιλεύσας. μὴ οὖν φθον-
ήσῃς μοι τοῦ μνήματος.

9 Ἀλέξανδρος δὲ (ἐπιμελὲς γὰρ ἦν αὐτῷ, ὁπότε
ἔλθοι ⟨ἐς⟩ [1] Πέρσας, παριέναι ἐς τοῦ Κύρου τὸν
τάφον) τὰ μὲν ἄλλα καταλαμβάνει ἐκπεφορημένα
πλὴν τῆς πυέλου καὶ τῆς κλίνης· οἱ δὲ καὶ τὸ
σῶμα τοῦ Κύρου ἐλωβήσαντο ἀφελόντες τὸ πῶμα
τῆς πυέλου καὶ τὸν νεκρὸν ἐξέβαλον· αὐτὴν δὲ
τὴν πύελον ἐπειρῶντο εὔογκόν σφισι ποιήσασθαι
καὶ ταύτῃ εὔφορον τὰ μὲν παρακόπτοντες, τὰ δὲ
ξυνθλῶντες αὐτῆς. ὡς δὲ οὐ προὑ⟨ὐ⟩χώρει αὐτοῖς
τοῦτο τὸ ἔργον, οὕτω δὴ ἐάσαντες τὴν πύελον
10 ἀπῆλθον. καὶ λέγει Ἀριστόβουλος αὐτὸς ταχθῆναι πρὸς Ἀλεξάνδρου κοσμῆσαι ἐξ ὑπαρχῆς τῷ
Κύρῳ τὸν τάφον. καὶ τοῦ μὲν σώματος ὅσαπερ
ἔτι σῶα ἦν καταθεῖναι ἐς τὴν πύελον καὶ τὸ πῶμα
ἐπιθεῖναι, ὅσα δὲ λελώβητο αὐτῆς κατορθῶσαι· καὶ
τὴν κλίνην ἐντεῖναι ταινίαις καὶ τἆλλα ὅσα ἐς
κόσμον ἔκειτο κατὰ ἀριθμόν τε καὶ τοῖς πάλαι
ὅμοια ἀποθεῖναι καὶ τὴν θυρίδα δὲ ἀφανίσαι τὰ

[1] ἔλθοι ἐς Pflugk and A. Miller: ἔλοι codd. See note to
translation.

for the Magians who used to guard Cyrus' tomb, from as long ago as Cambyses, son of Cyrus, an office transmitted from father to son. The king used to give them a sheep a day, a fixed amount of meal and wine, and a horse each month to sacrifice to Cyrus. There was an inscription on the tomb in Persian 8 letters; it signified this in Persian: ' Mortal! I am Cyrus son of Cambyses, who founded the Persian empire, and was King of Asia. Grudge me not then my monument.'

Alexander, who made it his business to visit Cyrus' 9 tomb whenever he went to the Persian capital,[5] found everything else removed except the sarcophagus and the couch. The robbers had even violated the body of Cyrus, for they had removed the top of the sarcophagus and had thrown out the body; they had tried to reduce the size of the sarcophagus itself, chipping some parts away and crushing others, and so make it easy to carry away. Not succeeding in this attempt, they left the sarcophagus where it was and went off. Aristobulus says that he himself 10 received orders from Alexander to put the tomb in its pristine order, to deposit any whole parts of the body in the sarcophagus again, and put on the lid, to repair it where it was damaged, to spread the couch with ribands, to restore, just like the originals, everything else that had been placed there by way of ornament, piece by piece, to obliterate the door

---

[5] S's summary of Ar. (xv 3, 7) shows that both Al. and he visited the tomb in 331; hence I adopt an emendation; the manuscript reading makes Al. intend to visit it ' whenever he might conquer the Persians.'

μὲν αὐτῆς λίθῳ ἐνοικοδομήσαντα, τὰ δὲ πηλῷ
ἐμπλάσαντα, καὶ ἐπιβαλεῖν τῷ πηλῷ τὸ σημεῖον τὸ
11 βασιλικόν. Ἀλέξανδρος δὲ ξυλλαβὼν τοὺς Μάγους
τοὺς φύλακας τοῦ τάφου ἐστρέβλωσεν, ὡς κατειπεῖν τοὺς δράσαντας, οἱ δὲ οὐδὲν οὔτε σφῶν
οὔτε ἄλλου κατεῖπον στρεβλούμενοι, οὐδὲ ἄλλῃ πῃ
ἐξηλέγχοντο ξυνειδότες τῷ ἔργῳ· καὶ ἐπὶ τῷδε
ἀφείθησαν ἐξ Ἀλεξάνδρου.
  30. Ἔνθεν δὲ ἐς τὰ βασίλεια ᾔει τὰ Περσῶν, ἃ
δὴ πρόσθεν κατέφλεξεν αὐτός, ὥς μοι λέλεκται,
ὅτε οὐκ ἐπῄνουν τὸ ἔργον· ἀλλ' οὐδ' αὐτὸς Ἀλέξανδρος ἐπανελθὼν ἐπῄνει. καὶ μὲν δὴ καὶ κατὰ
Ὀρξίνου πολλοὶ λόγοι ἐλέχθησαν πρὸς Περσῶν,
ὃς ἦρξε Περσῶν ἐπειδὴ Φρασαόρτης ἐτελεύτησε.
2 καὶ ἐξηλέγχθη Ὀρξίνης ἱερά τε ὅτι σεσυλήκει καὶ
τάφους βασιλικούς, καὶ Περσῶν πολλοὺς ὅτι οὐ
ξὺν δίκῃ ἀπέκτεινε. τοῦτον μὲν δὴ οἷς ἐτάχθη
ὑπὸ Ἀλεξάνδρου ἐκρέμασαν, σατράπην δὲ Πέρσαις
ἔταξε Πευκέσταν τὸν σωματοφύλακα, πιστόν τέ
οἱ ἐς τὰ μάλιστα τιθέμενος τά τε ἄλλα καὶ ἐπὶ τῷ
ἐν Μαλλοῖς ἔργῳ, ἵνα προεκινδύνευσέ τε καὶ συν-
εξέσωσεν Ἀλέξανδρον, καὶ ἄλλως τῷ βαρβαρικῷ
3 τρόπῳ τῆς διαίτης οὐκ ἀξύμφορον· ἐδήλωσε
δὲ ἐσθῆτά τε εὐθὺς ὡς κατεστάθη σατραπεύειν
Περσῶν μόνος τῶν ἄλλων Μακεδόνων μεταβαλὼν
τὴν Μηδικὴν καὶ φωνὴν τὴν Περσικὴν ἐκμαθὼν καὶ
τἆλλα ξύμπαντα ἐς τρόπον τὸν Περσικὸν κατασκευ-
ασάμενος. ἐφ' οἷς Ἀλέξανδρός γε ἐπῄνει αὐτὸν καὶ

---

[6] S. says explicitly that this exonerated the satrap. Ar.
surely had in mind the charges against Orxines (30, 2).
[1] Cf. iii 18, 12.

partly by walling it up in stone and partly by plaster-
ing it with clay, and then to set the royal seal on the
clay.   Alexander seized the Magians who were the 11
guardians of the tomb and tortured them to make
them denounce the perpetrators, but under torture
they did not denounce themselves or anyone else,[6]
nor was any other proof found of their complicity;
and so Alexander let them go.

30. Then Alexander proceeded to the Persian
palace to which he himself had formerly set fire, as I
related while expressing my condemnation of his act.
In fact Alexander himself did not approve it on his
return.[1]   And now many allegations were made by
the Persians against Orxines too, who governed them
after the death of Phrasaortes.   It was proved that 2
he had rifled temples and royal tombs, and that he
used to put many Persians to death unjustly.   He
was hanged by persons Alexander appointed.   As
satrap of the Persians he appointed Peucestas the
bodyguard, whom he regarded as especially loyal to
him, chiefly on account of his exploit among the
Mallians, where he risked his life and helped to save
Alexander, and as otherwise well suited to the post
because of his barbarian mode of life, which he
publicly adopted as soon as he was made satrap of
Persia; he was the only Macedonian to change over 3
to the Median dress and learn the Persian language,
and in all other respects assimilated himself to Persian
ways.   This   brought   him   Alexander's   commen-

οἱ Πέρσαι ὡς τὰ παρὰ σφίσι πρὸ τῶν πατρίων πρεσβεύοντι ἔχαιρον.

dations, and the Persians were gratified that he preferred their ways to those of his own ancestors.[2]

[2] Acc. to Ar., Al. had decided to make Peucestas satrap
before he reached Persia (28, 3), i.e. before he could have known
of the charges brought against Orxines, who was guiltless on
at least one count (29, 11 n.); QC. x 1, 22 ff. says that Al's
favourite eunuch, Bagoas, falsely accused him of removing
3000 Talents of gold from Cyrus' tomb. A. is now following
Pt's apologetic version, cf. Badian, *CQ* 1958, 144 ff.; App.
XXIII 9. Peucestas sided with Pt's enemies after 323, and
Pt. did not necessarily approve of his Orientalism, cf. vii
6, 3; 23, 3; D. (Hieronymus) xix 14, 5 (who says that he alone
was permitted by Al. to dress in Persian style); 48, 5 (cf.
Bosworth, *JHS* 1980, 12).

BOOK VII

ΒΙΒΛΙΟΝ ΕΒΔΟΜΟΝ

1. Ὡς δὲ ἐς Πασαργάδας τε καὶ ἐς Περσέπολιν ἀφίκετο Ἀλέξανδρος, πόθος λαμβάνει αὐτὸν καταπλεῦσαι κατὰ τὸν Εὐφράτην τε καὶ κατὰ τὸν Τίγρητα ἐπὶ τὴν θάλασσαν τὴν Περσικὴν καὶ τῶν τε ποταμῶν ἰδεῖν τὰς ἐκβολὰς τὰς ἐς τὸν πόντον, καθάπερ τοῦ Ἰνδοῦ, καὶ τὴν ταύτῃ θάλασ-
2 σαν. οἱ δὲ καὶ τάδε ἀνέγραψαν, ὅτι ἐπενόει Ἀλέξανδρος περιπλεῦσαι τήν τε Ἀραβίαν τὴν πολλὴν καὶ τὴν Αἰθιόπων γῆν καὶ τὴν Λιβύην τε καὶ τοὺς Νομάδας ὑπὲρ τὸν Ἄτλαντα τὸ ὄρος ὡς ἐπὶ Γάδειρα ἔσω ἐς τὴν ἡμετέραν θάλασσαν καὶ τὴν Λιβύην τε καταστρεψάμενος καὶ Καρχηδόνα οὕτω δὴ τῆς Ἀσίας πάσης δικαίως ἂν βασιλεὺς καλεῖσ-
3 θαι· τοὺς γάρ τοι Περσῶν καὶ Μήδων βασιλέας οὐδὲ τοῦ πολλοστοῦ μέρους τῆς Ἀσίας ἐπάρχοντας οὐ σὺν δίκῃ καλεῖν σφᾶς μεγάλους βασιλέας. ἔνθεν δὲ οἱ μέν, ὅτι ἐς τὸν πόντον τὸν Εὔξεινον ἐσπλεῖν ἐπενόει ἐς Σκύθας τε καὶ τὴν λίμνην τὴν Μαιῶτιν, οἱ δέ, ὅτι ἐς Σικελίαν τε καὶ ἄκραν Ἰαπυγίαν· ἤδη γὰρ καὶ ὑποκινεῖν αὐτὸν τὸ Ῥωμαίων ὄνομα προχωροῦν ἐπὶ μέγα.
4 Ἐγὼ δὲ ὁποῖα μὲν ἦν Ἀλεξάνδρου τὰ ἐνθυμήματα οὔτε ἔχω ἀτρεκῶς ξυμβαλεῖν οὔτε μέλει ἔμοιγε εἰκάζειν, ἐκεῖνο δὲ καὶ αὐτὸς ἄν μοι δοκῶ ἰσχυρίσασθαι, οὔτε μικρόν τι καὶ φαῦλον ἐπινοεῖν Ἀλέξανδρον οὔτε μεῖναι ἂν ἀτρεμοῦντα ἐπ' οὐδενὶ τῶν ἤδη κεκτημένων, οὐδὲ εἰ τὴν Εὐρώπην

BOOK VII

1. After reaching Pasargadae and Persepolis Alexander was seized with a longing [1] to sail down the Euphrates and Tigris to the Persian Sea, and to see the outlets of the rivers into the sea, like that of the Indus, and the sea in that region. Some have also 2 recorded that Alexander was planning to sail round most of Arabia, Ethiopia, Libya and the Nomads beyond Mount Atlas, Gadeira [Cadiz] and into our sea and, after subduing Libya and Carthage, finally to earn the title of king of all Asia; as for the Persian 3 and Median kings, in his view they had not ruled even a fraction of Asia, and so had no right to call themselves Great Kings. Thereafter, in some accounts, he planned to sail into the Euxine [Black] Sea to Scythia [Russia] and Lake Maeotis [Sea of Azov], in others to make for Sicily and the Iapygian promontory [Capo S. Maria di Leuca], as he was already rather disturbed that Rome's fame was advancing to a great height.

For my part I cannot determine with certainty 4 what sort of plans Alexander had in mind, and it is no purpose of mine to make guesses, but there is one thing I think I can assert myself, that none of Alexander's plans were small and petty and that, no matter what he had already conquered, he would not have stopped there quietly, not even if he had

---

[1] App. V 3, cf. *Ind.* 20, 2 n.   On 1–4 see App. XXIII 2–5.

τῇ Ἀσίᾳ προσέθηκεν, οὐδ' εἰ τὰς Βρεττανῶν
νήσους τῇ Εὐρώπῃ, ἀλλὰ ἔτι ἂν ἐπέκεινα ζητεῖν τι
τῶν ἠγνοημένων, εἰ καὶ μὴ ἄλλῳ τῳ, ἀλλὰ αὐτόν
γε αὐτῷ ἐρίζοντα. καὶ ἐπὶ τῷδε ἐπαινῶ τοὺς
5 σοφιστὰς τῶν Ἰνδῶν, ὧν λέγουσιν ἔστιν οὓς κατα-
ληφθέντας ὑπ' Ἀλεξάνδρου ὑπαιθρίους ἐν λειμῶνι, ἵναπερ αὐτοῖς διατριβαὶ ἦσαν, ἄλλο μὲν
οὐδὲν ποιῆσαι πρὸς τὴν ὄψιν αὐτοῦ τε καὶ τῆς
στρατιᾶς, κρούειν δὲ τοῖς ποσὶ τὴν γῆν ἐφ' ἧς
βεβηκότες ἦσαν. ὡς δὲ ἤρετο Ἀλέξανδρος δι'
ἑρμηνέων ὅ τι νοοῖ αὐτοῖς τὸ ἔργον, τοὺς δὲ
6 ὑποκρίνασθαι ὧδε· βασιλεῦ Ἀλέξανδρε, ἄνθρωπος μὲν ἕκαστος τοσόνδε τῆς γῆς κατέχει ὅσονπερ
τοῦτό ἐστιν ἐφ' ὅτῳ βεβήκαμεν· σὺ δὲ ἄνθρωπος
ὢν παραπλήσιος τοῖς ἄλλοις, πλήν γε δὴ ὅτι
πολυπράγμων καὶ ἀτάσθαλος, ἀπὸ τῆς οἰκείας τοσαύτην γῆν ἐπεξέρχῃ πράγματα ἔχων τε καὶ
παρέχων ἄλλοις. καὶ οὖν καὶ ὀλίγον ὕστερον ἀπο-
θανὼν τοσοῦτον καθέξεις τῆς γῆς ὅσον ἐξαρκεῖ
ἐντεθάφθαι τῷ σώματι.

2. Κἀνταῦθα ἐπήνεσε μὲν Ἀλέξανδρος τούς τε
λόγους αὐτοὺς καὶ τοὺς εἰπόντας, ἔπρασσε δὲ
ὅμως ἄλλα καὶ τἀναντία οἷς ἐπήνεσεν. ἐπεὶ καὶ
Διογένην τὸν ἐκ Σινώπης θαυμάσαι λέγεται, ἐν
Ἰσθμῷ ἐντυχὼν τῷ Διογένει κατακειμένῳ ἐν
ἡλίῳ, ἐπιστὰς σὺν τοῖς ὑπασπισταῖς καὶ τοῖς
πεζεταίροις καὶ ἐρόμενος εἴ του δέοιτο· ὁ δὲ
Διογένης ἄλλου μὲν ἔφη δεῖσθαι οὐδενός, ἀπὸ τοῦ
ἡλίου δὲ ἀπελθεῖν ἐκέλευσεν αὐτόν τε καὶ τοὺς σὺν
2 αὐτῷ. οὕτω τοι οὐ πάντῃ ἔξω τοῦ ἐπινοεῖν τὰ

---

[2] App. XX, also on ch. 2 f.

added Europe to Asia and the Britannic Islands to
Europe, but that he would always have searched far
beyond for something unknown, in competition with
himself in default of any other rival. In this con- 5
nection I commend the Indian sophists, some of whom,
the story goes, were found by Alexander in the open
air in a meadow, where they used to have their dis-
putations; when they saw Alexander and his army,
they did nothing more than beat with their feet on
the ground they stood on. When Alexander enquired through interpreters what their action meant,
they replied: ' King Alexander, each man possesses 6
no more of this earth than the patch we stand on;
yet you, though a man like other men, except of course
that you are restless and presumptuous, are roaming
over so wide an area away from what is your own,
giving no rest to yourself or others. And very soon
you too will die, and will possess no more of the earth
than suffices for the burial of your body.' [2]

2. On that occasion Alexander commended their
remarks and the speakers, but his actions were
different from and contrary to what he commended.
So too he is said to have expressed surprise at Diogenes
of Sinope, when he found him on the Isthmus lying in
the sun; he halted with the hypaspists and infantry
Companions and asked if he needed anything.
Diogenes answered that he needed nothing else, but
told him and his followers to stand out of the sun-
light.[1] Thus, while Alexander was not wholly beyond 2

---

[1] As the date of Diogenes' death is unknown, a meeting
cannot be excluded on chronological grounds but, like other
anecdotes about Diogenes and Al. (*RE* v 767 f.), this is surely
late and apocryphal.

κρείττω ἦν Ἀλέξανδρος, ἀλλ' ἐκ δόξης γὰρ δεινῶς
ἐκρατεῖτο. ἐπεὶ καὶ ἐς Τάξιλα αὐτῷ ἀφικομένῳ
καὶ ἰδόντι τῶν σοφιστῶν ⟨τῶν⟩ Ἰνδῶν τοὺς
γυμνοὺς πόθος ἐγένετο ξυνεῖναί τινά οἱ τῶν ἀνδρῶν
τούτων, ὅτι τὴν καρτερίαν αὐτῶν ἐθαύμασε· καὶ
ὁ μὲν πρεσβύτατος τῶν σοφιστῶν, ὅτου ὁμιληταὶ
οἱ ἄλλοι ἦσαν, Δάνδαμις ὄνομα, οὔτε αὐτὸς ἔφη
παρ' Ἀλέξανδρον ἥξειν οὔτε τοὺς ἄλλους εἴα,
3 ἀλλὰ ὑποκρίνασθαι γὰρ λέγεται ὡς Διὸς υἱὸς καὶ
αὐτὸς εἴη, εἴπερ οὖν καὶ Ἀλέξανδρος, καὶ ὅτι
οὔτε δέοιτό του τῶν παρ' Ἀλεξάνδρου, ἔχει⟨ν⟩
γάρ οἱ εὖ τὰ παρόντα, καὶ ἅμα ὁρᾶν τοὺς ξὺν
αὐτῷ πλανωμένους τοσαύτην γῆν καὶ θάλασσαν
ἐπ' ἀγαθῷ οὐδενί, μηδὲ πέρας τι αὐτοῖς γινόμενον
τῶν πολλῶν πλανῶν. οὔτ' οὖν ποθεῖν τι αὐτὸς
ὅτου κύριος ἦν Ἀλέξανδρος δοῦναι, οὔτε αὖ δεδιέναι, ὅτου κρατοίη ἐκεῖνος, ἔστιν οὗ εἴργεσθαι·
4 ζῶντι μὲν γάρ οἱ τὴν Ἰνδῶν γῆν ἐξαρκεῖν φέρουσαν τὰ ὡραῖα, ἀποθανόντα δὲ ἀπαλλαγήσεσθαι
οὐκ ἐπιεικοῦς ξυνοίκου τοῦ σώματος. οὔκουν
οὐδὲ Ἀλέξανδρον ἐπιχειρῆσαι βιάσασθαι γνόντα
ἐλεύθερον ὄντα τὸν ἄνδρα, ἀλλὰ Κάλανον γὰρ
ἀναπεισθῆναι τῶν ταύτῃ σοφιστῶν, ὅντινα μάλιστα
δὴ αὐτοῦ ἀκράτορα Μεγασθένης ἀνέγραψεν αὐτούς
τοὺς σοφιστὰς λέγειν κακίζοντας τὸν Κάλανον,
ὅτι ἀπολιπὼν τὴν παρὰ σφίσιν εὐδαιμονίαν ὁ δὲ
δεσπότην ἄλλον ἢ τὸν θεὸν ἐθεράπευε.

3. Ταῦτα ἐγὼ ἀνέγραψα, ὅτι καὶ ὑπὲρ Καλάνου
ἐχρῆν εἰπεῖν ἐν τῇ περὶ Ἀλεξάνδρου συγγραφῇ·
μαλακισθῆναι γάρ τι τῷ σώματι τὸν Κάλανον ἐν
τῇ Περσίδι γῇ, οὔπω πρόσθεν νοσήσαντα· οὔκουν
οὐδὲ δίαιταν διαιτᾶσθαι θέλειν ἀρρώστου ἀνδρός,

comprehension of better courses, he was fearfully
mastered by love of fame.   For when on his arrival
at Taxila he saw those of the Indian sophists who go
naked, a longing came to him that one of these men
should live with him, since he admired their endurance.   The oldest of the sophists, called Dandamis
(the others were his disciples), said he would not join
Alexander nor let any of the others do so; in fact he **3**
is said to have replied that he himself was just as much
a son of Zeus [2] as Alexander, and that he had no need
of anything Alexander could give, since he was con-
tented with what he had; he saw, moreover, that
Alexander's companions were wandering about over
all that land and sea to no profit, and that there was
no limit to their many wanderings.   He did not then
yearn for anything that Alexander could give him,
and equally did not fear being denied anything Alexander might control.   So long as he lived, the land of **4**
India was all he needed, producing fruits in season;
and when he died, he would merely be released from
an uncomfortable companion, his body.   Nor indeed
did Alexander try to coerce him, realizing that the
man was free.   But a certain Calanus, one of the
sophists there, was over-persuaded into joining
Alexander; by Megasthenes' account, he was a man
they themselves regarded as specially lacking self-
control; they reproached Calanus because he deserted the happiness to be found with them and
served a master other than God.

3. All this I have narrated because it was impossible to write a history of Alexander without mention
of Calanus.   The story goes that his body grew en-
feebled in Persia, though he had never been ill
before; yet he would not submit to the regimen of an

[2] App. V 6 and 8.

ARRIAN

ἀλλὰ εἰπεῖν γὰρ πρὸς Ἀλέξανδρον, καλῶς αὐτῷ
ἔχειν ἐν τῷ τοιῷδε καταστρέψαι, πρίν τινος ἐς
πεῖραν ἐλθεῖν παθήματος ὅ τι περ ἐξαναγκάσει
2 αὐτὸν μεταβάλλειν τὴν πρόσθεν δίαιταν. καὶ
Ἀλέξανδρον ἀντειπεῖν μὲν αὐτῷ ἐπὶ πολύ· ὡς δ'
οὐχ ἡττησόμενον ἑώρα, ἀλλὰ ἄλλως ἂν ἀπαλλαγέν-
τα, εἰ μή τις ταύτῃ ὑπεικάθοι, οὕτω δὴ ὅπῃ ἐπήγ-
γελλεν αὐτός, κελεῦσαι νησθῆναι αὐτῷ πυράν, καὶ
ταύτης ἐπιμεληθῆναι Πτολεμαῖον τὸν Λάγου τὸν
σωματοφύλακα. οἱ δὲ καὶ πομπήν τινα προπομ-
πεῦσαι αὐτοῦ λέγουσιν ἵππους τε καὶ ἄνδρας, τοὺς
μὲν ὡπλισμένους, τοὺς δὲ θυμιάματα παντοῖα τῇ
πυρᾷ ἐπιφέροντας· οἱ δὲ καὶ ἐκπώματα χρυσᾶ καὶ
ἀργυρᾶ καὶ ἐσθῆτα βασιλικὴν λέγουσιν ὅτι ἔφερον.
3 αὐτῷ δὲ παρασκευασθῆναι μὲν ἵππον, ὅτι βαδίσαι
ἀδυνάτως εἶχεν ὑπὸ τῆς νόσου· οὐ μὴν δυνηθῆναί
γε οὐδὲ τοῦ ἵππου ἐπιβῆναι, ἀλλὰ ἐπὶ κλίνης γὰρ
κομισθῆναι φερόμενον, ἐστεφανωμένον τε τῷ
Ἰνδῶν νόμῳ καὶ ᾄδοντα τῇ Ἰνδῶν γλώσσῃ. οἱ
δὲ Ἰνδοὶ λέγουσιν ὅτι ὕμνοι θεῶν ἦσαν καὶ αὐτῶν
4 ἔπαινοι. καὶ τὸν μὲν ἵππον τοῦτον ὅτου ἐπιβήσεσ-
θαι ἔμελλε, βασιλικὸν ὄντα τῶν Νησαίων, πρὶν
ἀναβῆναι ἐπὶ τὴν πυρὰν Λυσιμάχῳ χαρίσασθαι,
τῶν τινι θεραπευόντων αὐτὸν ἐπὶ σοφίᾳ· τῶν δὲ
δὴ ἐκπωμάτων ἢ στρωμάτων ὅσα ἐμβληθῆναι
εἰς τὴν πυρὰν κόσμον αὐτῷ τετάχει Ἀλέξανδρος,
5 ἄλλα ἄλλοις δοῦναι τῶν ἀμφ' αὐτόν. οὕτω δὴ
ἐπιβάντα τῇ πυρᾷ κατακλιθῆναι μὲν ἐν κόσμῳ,
ὁρᾶσθαι δὲ πρὸς τῆς στρατιᾶς ξυμπάσης. Ἀλεξάνδρῳ δὲ οὐκ ἐπιεικὲς φανῆναι τὸ θέαμα ἐπὶ φίλῳ
ἀνδρὶ γιγνόμενον· ἀλλὰ τοῖς γὰρ ἄλλοις θαῦμα
παρασχέσθαι οὐδέν τι παρακινήσαντα ἐν τῷ πυρὶ

invalid, but told Alexander that he was glad to make an end as he was, before experiencing any suffering that would force him to change his old regimen. Alexander argued with him at some length; but when 2 he saw that Calanus would not give in, but would depart in another way, if baulked at this point, he ordered that in conformity with his own instructions a pyre should be built for him and that Ptolemy son of Lagus, the bodyguard, should be in charge of it. Some say that he also had a great procession formed, horses and men, some in full armour, others carrying all sorts of incense for the pyre; others again say that they carried gold and silver cups and royal raiment. For Calanus himself a horse was made ready, since he 3 could not walk because of his illness; and yet he could not even mount the horse, but was borne upon a litter, lying down, crowned with garlands in the Indian fashion and chanting in the Indian tongue. The Indians say that these chants were hymns of praise to gods. It is said that the horse on which he was to 4 have mounted was a royal horse belonging to the Nesaeans,[1] that before he climbed the pyre it was presented to Lysimachus, one of those who attended on him for instruction, and that he distributed among his associates the cups and rugs which Alexander had ordered to be heaped on the pyre in his honour. So 5 then according to the story he climbed the pyre and lay down with decorum in the sight of the whole army. Alexander did not approve of the spectacle afforded by a friend, but the rest were astonished to see that Calanus did not move any part of his body in the

[1] vii 13, 1.

ARRIAN

6 τοῦ σώματος. ὡς δὲ τὸ πῦρ ἐς τὴν πυρὰν ἐνέβαλον
οἷς προστεταγμένον ἦν, τάς τε σάλπιγγας φθέγξ-
ασθαι λέγει Νέαρχος, οὕτως ἐξ Ἀλεξάνδρου
προστεταγμένον, καὶ τὴν στρατιὰν ἐπαλαλάξαι
πᾶσαν ὁποῖόν τι καὶ ἐς τὰς μάχας ἰοῦσα ἐπηλάλαζε,
καὶ τοὺς ἐλέφαντας συνεπηχῆσαι τὸ ὀξὺ καὶ
πολεμικόν, τιμῶντας Κάλανον. ταῦτα καὶ τοιαῦτα
ὑπὲρ Καλάνου τοῦ Ἰνδοῦ ἱκανοὶ ἀναγεγράφασιν,
οὐκ ἀχρεῖα πάντα ἐς ἀνθρώπους, ὅτῳ γνῶναι
ἐπιμελές, [ὅτι] ὡς καρτερόν τέ ἐστι καὶ ἀνίκητον
γνώμη ἀνθρωπίνη ὅ τι περ ἐθέλοι ἐξεργάσασθαι.

4. Ἐν τούτῳ δὲ Ἀλέξανδρος Ἀτροπάτην μὲν
ἐπὶ τὴν αὐτοῦ σατραπείαν ἐκπέμπει παρελθὼν ἐς
Σοῦσα, Ἀβουλίτην δὲ καὶ τὸν τούτου παῖδα Ὀξά-
θρην, ὅτι κακῶς ἐπεμελοῦντο[1] τῶν Σουσίων,
2 συλλαβὼν ἀπέκτεινε. πολλὰ μὲν δὴ ἐπεπλημ-
μέλητο ἐκ τῶν κατεχόντων τὰς χώρας ὅσαι δορί-
κτητοι πρὸς Ἀλεξάνδρου ἐγένοντο ἔς τε τὰ ἱερὰ
καὶ τάφους καὶ αὐτοὺς τοὺς ὑπηκόους, ὅτι χρόνιος
ὁ εἰς Ἰνδοὺς στόλος ἐγεγένητο τῷ βασιλεῖ καὶ οὐ
πιστὸν ἐφαίνετο ἀπονοστήσειν αὐτὸν ἐκ τοσῶνδε
ἐθνῶν καὶ τοσῶνδε ἐλεφάντων, ὑπὲρ τὸν Ἰνδόν τε
καὶ Ὑδάσπην καὶ τὸν Ἀκεσίνην καὶ Ὕφασιν
3 φθειρόμενον. καὶ αἱ ἐν Γαδρωσίοις δὲ αὐτῷ ξυμ-
φοραὶ ξυνενεχθεῖσαι ἔτι μᾶλλον ἐπῆραν τοὺς [ἐν]
ταύτῃ σατραπεύοντας καταφρονῆσαι αὐτοῦ τῆς
οἴκοι ἀπονοστήσεως. οὐ μὴν ἀλλὰ καὶ αὐτὸς Ἀλέξανδρος ὀξύτερος λέγεται γενέσθαι ἐν τῷ τότε ἐς τὸ
πιστεῦσαί τε τοῖς ἐπικαλουμένοις ὡς πιθανοῖς δὴ
ἐν παντὶ οὖσι, καὶ ἐπὶ τὸ τιμωρήσασθαι μεγάλως

---

[1] Polak: ἐπεμελεῖτο codd.

flames. When the fire was lit by those detailed for 6 the task, the trumpets (says Nearchus) sounded, as Alexander had ordered, and the whole army raised the shout they would raise when entering battle, and the elephants trumpeted their shrill war-cry, in honour of Calanus. Competent authorities have recorded these and similar stories of Calanus the Indian, which are not altogether valueless to mankind, at least for anyone who cares to realize how strong and invincible is human resolution to carry out whatever it may desire.

4. At this time Alexander despatched Atropates to his satrapy, after reaching Susa.[1] There he arrested Abulites and his son Oxathres for bad administration of the Susians and put them to death. In fact many 2 offences had been committed by those in control of countries Alexander had conquered, against temples, tombs, and the subjects themselves, since the king had been a long time on his Indian expedition, and it did not seem credible that he would return, escaping so many peoples and elephants; he would perish beyond the Indus, Hydaspes, Acesines, and Hyphasis. The disasters too in which he was involved in Gadrosia 3 did still more to encourage the satraps on this side to scout any idea of his return. Not but what Alexander himself is said at this time to have grown quicker to give credit to accusations, as if they were reliable in all circumstances, and to punish severely

324
B.C.

---

[1] A. neglects to record the junction with N., probably at Ahvaz (*Ind.* 42), which is implied in 4, 6; 5, 5 and misleadingly mentioned in 7, 1; having deserted his main sources, he did not resume at the right point. Date: not earlier than late March, 324 (App. XXIII 1).

ARRIAN

τοὺς καὶ ἐπὶ μικροῖς ἐξελεγχθέντας, ὅτι καὶ τὰ
μεγάλα ἂν ἐδόκουν αὐτῷ τῇ αὐτῇ γνώμῃ ἐξεργάσασθαι.

4 Ὁ δὲ καὶ γάμους ἐποίησεν ἐν Σούσοις αὐτοῦ τε
καὶ τῶν ἑταίρων· αὐτὸς μὲν τῶν Δαρείου θυγατέρων τὴν πρεσβυτάτην Βαρσίνην ἠγάγετο, ὡς δὲ
λέγει Ἀριστόβουλος, καὶ ἄλλην πρὸς ταύτῃ, τῶν
Ὤχου θυγατέρων τὴν νεωτάτην Παρύσατιν. ἤδη
δὲ ἦν αὐτῷ ἠγμένη καὶ ἡ Ὀξυάρτου τοῦ Βακτρίου
5 παῖς Ῥωξάνη. Δρύπετιν δὲ Ἡφαιστίωνι δίδωσι,
Δαρείου παῖδα καὶ ταύτην, ἀδελφὴν τῆς αὑτοῦ
γυναικός· ἐθέλειν γάρ οἱ ἀνεψιοὺς τῶν παίδων
γενέσθαι τοὺς Ἡφαιστίωνος παῖδας· Κρατερῷ δὲ
Ἀμαστρίνην τὴν Ὀξυάτρου τοῦ Δαρείου ἀδελφοῦ
παῖδα· Περδίκκᾳ δὲ τὴν Ἀτροπάτου τοῦ Μηδίας
6 σατράπου παῖδα ἔδωκεν· Πτολεμαίῳ δὲ τῷ σωμα-
τοφύλακι καὶ Εὐμενεῖ τῷ γραμματεῖ τῷ βασιλικῷ τὰς Ἀρταβάζου παῖδας τῷ μὲν Ἀρτακάμαν,
τῷ δὲ Ἄρτωνιν· Νεάρχῳ δὲ τὴν Βαρσίνης τε καὶ
Μέντορος παῖδα· Σελεύκῳ δὲ τὴν Σπιταμένους τοῦ
Βακτρίου παῖδα· ὡσαύτως δὲ καὶ τοῖς ἄλλοις
ἑταίροις τὰς δοκιμωτάτας Περσῶν τε καὶ Μήδων
παῖδας ἐς ὀγδοήκοντα. οἱ γάμοι δὲ ἐποιήθησαν
7 νόμῳ τῷ Περσικῷ· θρόνοι ἐτέθησαν τοῖς νυμ-
φίοις ἐφεξῆς καὶ μετὰ τὸν πότον ἧκον αἱ γαμούμεναι

---

[2] P. 68 (before Al's arrival in Persepolis) says that Al.
arrested Abulites for supplying money instead of provisions
and killed his son with a spear (cf. 57, 2 for parallel). Oxathres: iii 19, 2. Cf. App. XXIII 9.

[3] Cf. Chares (Jacoby no. 125) F. 4 (92 marriages); D. 107, 6;
P. 70 with some variant details.

[4] Philip II had also practised polygamy (Athenaeus 557 DE).
Barsine, named Statira in all other sources, with her sister was

those who were convicted even of slight faults on the ground that in the same frame of mind they might commit grave crimes.[2]

He also held weddings at Susa for himself and for the Companions[3]; he himself married Darius' eldest daughter Barsine, and, as Aristobulus says, another wife as well, Parysatis, the youngest daughter of Ochus. He had already taken to wife Roxane, the daughter of Oxyartes the Bactrian.[4] To Hephaestion he gave Drypetis, another daughter of Darius, sister to his own wife (for he desired Hephaestion's children to be cousins to his own)[5]; to Craterus, Amastrine daughter of Oxyatres, Darius' brother; to Perdiccas, a daughter of Atropates, satrap of Media; to Ptolemy the bodyguard and Eumenes the royal secretary, the daughters of Artabazus, Artacama and Artonis respectively; to Nearchus the daughter of Barsine[6] and Mentor; to Seleucus the daughter of Spitamenes the Bactrian,[7] and similarly to the other Companions the noblest daughters of Persians and Medes, numbering about eighty. These weddings were solemnized in the Persian style; chairs were placed for the bridegrooms in order, then, after the healths had been

4

5

6

7

murdered after Al's death by Roxane, when she was 6 or 8 months with child (Berve no. 688). Ochus is Artaxerxes III (359–38). Either Pt. is the sole source for all other names, or on all others Ar. concurred. We cannot tell if A. had a complete list of marriages and selected for mention only the most important.

[5] App. XXIV 3.

[6] Another daughter of Artabazus, mother to Al's bastard son, Heracles (Brunt, *Riv. Fil.* 1975, 22 ff.).

[7] Apame, ancestress of the Seleucid dynasty. No other marriage is known to have lasted; some certainly did not. D. says that Al. 'persuaded' the bridegrooms, but cf. 6, 2. For his purpose cf. 11, 8; QC. x 3, 11 f.; Plut., *Moralia* 329 EF, but cf. Bosworth, *JHS* 1980, 11 f.

καὶ παρεκαθέζοντο ἑκάστη τῷ ἑαυτῆς· οἱ δὲ
ἐδεξιώσαντό τε αὐτὰς καὶ ἐφίλησαν· πρῶτος δὲ ὁ
βασιλεὺς ἦρξεν· ἐν τῷ αὐτῷ γὰρ πάντων ἐγίγνοντο
οἱ γάμοι. καὶ τοῦτο, εἴπερ τι ἄλλο, ἔδοξε δημοτι-
8 κόν τε καὶ φιλέταιρον πρᾶξαι Ἀλέξανδρον. οἱ δὲ
παραλαβόντες ἀπῆγον τὴν αὑτοῦ ἕκαστος· προῖκας
δὲ ξυμπάσαις ἐπέδωκεν Ἀλέξανδρος. καὶ ὅσοι δὲ
ἄλλοι ἠγμένοι ἦσαν Μακεδόνες τῶν Ἀσιανῶν τινας
γυναικῶν, ἀπογραφῆναι ἐκέλευσε καὶ τούτων τὰ
ὀνόματα, καὶ ἐγένοντο ὑπὲρ τοὺς μυρίους, καὶ
τούτοις δωρεαὶ Ἀλεξάνδρου ἐδόθησαν ἐπὶ τοῖς
γάμοις.

5. Καὶ τὰ χρέα ἐπιλύσασθαι τῆς στρατιᾶς ὅσοις
χρέα ἦν ἐν καιρῷ οἱ ἔδοξε, καὶ κελεύει ἀπογράφεσ-
θαι ὁπόσον ὀφείλει ἕκαστος, ὡς ληψομένους. καὶ
τὰ μὲν πρῶτα ὀλίγοι ἀπέγραψαν σφῶν τὰ ὀνόματα
δεδιότες ἐξ Ἀλεξάνδρου μὴ πεῖρα αὕτη εἴη καθει-
μένη, ὅτῳ οὐκ ἀποχρῶσα ἡ μισθοφορὰ τῶν στρα-
2 τιωτῶν ἐστι καὶ ὅτῳ πολυτελὴς ἡ δίαιτα. ὡς δὲ
ἐξήγγελτο ὅτι οὐκ ἀπογράφουσι σφᾶς οἱ πολλοί,
ἀλλ' ἐπικρύπτουσιν ὅτῳ τι εἴη συμβόλαιον, τὴν μὲν
ἀπιστίαν τῶν στρατιωτῶν ἐκάκισεν· οὐ γὰρ
χρῆναι οὔτ' οὖν τὸν βασιλέα ἄλλο τι ἢ ἀληθεύειν
πρὸς τοὺς ὑπηκόους, οὔτε τῶν ἀρχομένων τινὰ
3 ἄλλο τι ἢ ἀληθεύειν δοκεῖν τὸν βασιλέα. καταθεὶς
δὲ τραπέζας ἐν τῷ στρατοπέδῳ καὶ ἐπὶ τούτων
χρυσίον καὶ τοὺς ἐπιμελησομένους τῆς δόσεως
ἑκάστοις, ὅστις συμβόλαιον ἐπεδείκνυτο, ἐπιλύεσ-
θαι τὰ χρέα ἐκέλευεν οὐκ ἀπογραφομένους ἔτι τὰ

---

[8] P. 70 says that Al. spent 9870 Talents on paying the debts
of all soldiers who had taken Asian wives, QC. x 2, 8 has the

drunk, the brides came in and each sat down by the side of her bridegroom, and the men took them by the hand and kissed them, the king setting the example, for all the weddings took place together. None of Alexander's actions was thought to show more affability and comradeship. After receiving his bride each bridegroom led her home. Alexander gave them all dowries. All other Macedonians who had married Asian women had their names registered by Alexander's orders; they proved to be more than ten thousand, and Alexander gave them too wedding gifts.[8]

5. He thought this a convenient moment to discharge all the debts any of his soldiers had incurred and ordered each man to register what he owed, on the basis that they would receive the money. At first only a few registered their names in the fear that Alexander had merely tried an experiment, to see which soldiers had not lived on their pay and which had been extravagant; but when he was informed that most were not registering their names but concealing any bonds, he reproved the troops for not trusting him; the king, he said, must always speak the truth to his subjects, and none of the subjects must ever suppose that the king speaks anything but the truth.[1] He set up tables in the camp with gold on them and instructed the persons who were to administer the grants to discharge the debts to all who produced a bond, without any further registration

same sum for all soldiers' debts (20,000 in A. 5, 3; J. xii 11, 1 f.); D. 109, 2 has 10,000 for debts of those soldiers who were sent home to Macedon.

[1] Cf. A's preface 2; Bosworth *ad loc.* makes veracity a conventional virtue of the ideal king, but cf. Brunt, *JRS* 1974, 9.

ὀνόματα. καὶ οὕτω δὴ ἐπίστευσάν τε ἀληθεύειν
Ἀλέξανδρον καὶ σὺν χάριτι μείζονι ἐγίγνετο αὐτοῖς
τὸ μὴ γνωσθῆναι μᾶλλόν τι ἢ τὸ παύσασθαι ὀφεί-
λοντας. λέγεται δὲ γενέσθαι ἡ δόσις αὕτη τῇ
στρατιᾷ ἐς τάλαντα δισμύρια.

4 Ἔδωκεν δὲ καὶ δῶρα ἄλλοις ἄλλα, ὅπως τις κατ᾿
ἀξίωσιν ἐτιμᾶτο ἢ κατ᾿ ἀρετὴν εἴ τις ἐπιφανὴς
ἐγεγόνει ἐν τοῖς κινδύνοις. καὶ ἐστεφάνωσε χρυσοῖς στεφάνοις τοὺς ἀνδραγαθίᾳ διαπρέποντας,
πρῶτον μὲν Πευκέσταν τὸν ὑπερασπίσαντα, ἔπειτα
5 Λεοννάτον, καὶ τοῦτον ὑπερασπίσαντα, καὶ διὰ
τοὺς ἐν Ἰδοῖς κινδύνους καὶ τὴν ἐν Ὥροις νίκην
γενομένην, ὅτι παραταξάμενος σὺν τῇ ὑπολειφ-
θείσῃ δυνάμει πρὸς τοὺς νεωτερίζοντας τῶν τε
Ὠρειτῶν καὶ τῶν πλησίον τούτων ᾠκισμένων τῇ
τε μάχῃ ἐκράτησε καὶ τὰ ἄλλα καλῶς ἔδοξε τὰ ἐν
6 Ὥροις κοσμῆσαι. ἐπὶ τούτοις δὲ Νέαρχον ἐπὶ τῷ
περίπλῳ τῷ ἐκ τῆς Ἰνδῶν γῆς κατὰ τὴν μεγάλην
θάλασσαν ἐστεφάνωσε· καὶ γὰρ καὶ οὗτος ἤδη
ἀφιγμένος ἐς Σοῦσα ἦν· ἐπὶ τούτοις δὲ Ὀνησίκρι-
τον τὸν κυβερνήτην τῆς νεὼς τῆς βασιλικῆς· ἔτι δὲ
Ἡφαιστίωνα καὶ τοὺς ἄλλους τοὺς σωματοφύλακας.

6. Ἧκον δὲ αὐτῷ καὶ οἱ σατράπαι οἱ ἐκ τῶν
πόλεών τε τῶν νεοκτίστων καὶ τῆς ἄλλης γῆς τῆς
δοριαλώτου παῖδας ἡβάσκοντας ἤδη ἐς τρισμυρίους
ἄγοντες τὴν αὐτὴν ἡλικίαν γεγονότας, οὓς Ἐπι-
γόνους ἐκάλει Ἀλέξανδρος, κεκοσμημένους Μακε-
δονικοῖς ὅπλοις καὶ τὰ πολέμια ἐς τὸν τρόπον τὸν

of names. As a result they actually came to believe that Alexander was speaking the truth, and they were more gratified by the concealment of their names than by the extinction of the debts. This grant to the army is said to have amounted to twenty thousand Talents.[2]

He also gave presents to others, varying in proportion to the honour that rank conferred or to conspicuous courage displayed in dangers. He decorated with gold crowns those distinguished for bravery. Peucestas was first, for having shielded him; then came Leonnatus for the same service and for the risks he incurred in India and the victory he gained in Ora; with the force left him he had faced the rebel Oritans and neighbouring peoples, mastered them in the battle and was then held to have made a good settlement in general of affairs in Ora.[3] Next he decorated Nearchus for his coasting voyage from India by the great sea (Nearchus too had now arrived at Susa) and next, Onesicritus, the helmsman of the royal ship; and in addition Hephaestion and the other bodyguards.[4]

6. He was also joined by the satraps from the new cities he had founded, and the other land he had conquered, bringing about thirty thousand boys now growing up, all of the same age, whom Alexander called Epigoni (Successors), dressed in Macedonian dress and trained to warfare in the Macedonian

---

[2] 4, 7 n.
[3] Cf. vi 11, 7; *Ind.* 23, 5 ff.
[4] *Ind.* 42, 9 n.

2 Μακεδονικὸν ἠσκημένους. καὶ οὗτοι ἀφικόμενοι
λέγονται ἀνιᾶσαι Μακεδόνας, ὡς πάντα δὴ μηχα-
νωμένου Ἀλεξάνδρου ὑπὲρ τοῦ μηκέτι ὡσαύτως
δεῖσθαι Μακεδόνων· εἶναι γὰρ οὖν καὶ Μηδικὴν
τὴν Ἀλεξάνδρου στολὴν ἄλγος οὐ σμικρὸν Μακεδόσιν ὁρωμένην καὶ τοὺς γάμους ἐν τῷ νόμῳ τῷ
Περσικῷ ποιηθέντας οὐ πρὸς θυμοῦ γενέσθαι τοῖς
πολλοῖς αὐτῶν, οὐδὲ τῶν γημάντων ἔστιν οἷς,
καίτοι τῇ ἰσότητι τῇ ἐς τὸν βασιλέα μεγάλως
3 τετιμημένοις. Πευκέστας τε ὁ Περσῶν σατράπης
τῇ τε σκευῇ καὶ τῇ φωνῇ περσίζων ἐλύπει αὐτούς,
ὅτι τῷ βαρβαρισμῷ αὐτοῦ ἔχαιρεν Ἀλέξανδρος, καὶ
οἱ Βακτρίων δὲ καὶ οἱ Σογδιανῶν καὶ Ἀραχωτῶν
ἱππεῖς καὶ Ζαραγγῶν δὲ καὶ Ἀρείων καὶ Παρθυαίων καὶ ἐκ Περσῶν οἱ Εὐάκαι καλούμενοι ἱππεῖς
καταλοχισθέντες εἰς τὴν ἵππον τὴν ἑταιρικὴν
ὅσοι αὐτῶν κατ᾽ ἀξίωσιν καὶ κάλλει τοῦ σώματος
ἢ τῇ ἄλλῃ ἀρετῇ ὑπερφέροντες ἐφαίνοντο, καὶ

---

[1] Not previously mentioned by A. See D. 108, 1; P. 47, 3;
71, 1; QC. viii 5, 1; Bosworth, *JHS* 1980, 17 f., who seems to
think that by satraps A. here means ' city commandants ';
however, Stasanor at least had joined Al. by his death (vi 29, 1
n.). Various Alexandrias (Droysen, *Gesch. des Hellenismus*
iii² 187 ff.; Berve 291 ff.; Tarn ii 232 ff.) could have been
founded by satraps on Al's orders, not by Al. personally. D.
108 ff. places at Susa (*contra* A. 7, 1) the discharge of veterans
and mutiny with the sequel described by A. 12, as well as the
arrival of Peucestas and formation of mixed units described in
A. 23! Large lacunae in QC. obscure his account, but like J.
xii 11 f. he closely connected the discharge of veterans and the
payment of soldiers' debts (x 2, 8 ff.), and like D. he interposed
before the mutiny an account of Harpalus' doings, which A.
reported later, probably implying that Al. heard of it after the
mutiny (cf. App. XXIII 8).

style.[1] It is said[2] that their arrival aggrieved the Macedonians, as if Alexander was actually contriving every means of reducing his dependence on Macedonians in future, that in fact they were greatly pained to see Alexander wearing the Median dress,[3] while the marriages celebrated in the Persian style did not correspond to the desires of most of them, including even some of the bridegrooms, despite the great honour of being raised to equality with the king. They were also aggrieved at the adoption by Peucestas, satrap of Persia, of the Persian apparel and language because Alexander approved of him going barbarian[4]; at the incorporation of the Bactrian, Sogdianian, Arachotian, Zarangian, Areian and Parthyaean cavalrymen and of the Persian troopers called Euacae in the Companion cavalry, in so far as they seemed to be specially distinguished by rank,

---

[2] This might suggest use of vulgate, explaining the mutiny, which the vulgate placed at Susa; the causes are again recorded in 8, 2 at the proper place in A's narrative. Yet the return to direct speech in § 3–5 better fits derivation from one of A's chief sources; this is supported by the use of ' Zarangian ' in § 3 (cf. vi 15, 5 n.); in that case either Pharismenes (vi 27, 3 with ' Zarangian ') or Phradasmenes here is an error by A. or a scribe; Cophes (cf. QC. vii 11, 5) for Cophen (A. ii 15, 1; iii 23, 7) and perhaps Artiboles for Antibelus (iii 21, 1) could be explained by spelling discrepancies of Pt and Ar. So A. seems to report their accounts in succession (cf. iii 11, 3 n.); 8, 2 is summary but coherent with 6.

[3] App. XIV 1 f., cf. Bosworth, *JHS* 1980, 4 ff.

[4] Cf. vi 30, 2 f.

ARRIAN

4 πέμπτη ἐπὶ τούτοις ἱππαρχία προσγενομένη, οὐ
βαρβαρικὴ ἡ πᾶσα, ἀλλὰ ἐπαυξηθέντος γὰρ τοῦ
παντὸς ἱππικοῦ κατελέγησαν ἐς αὐτὸ τῶν βαρβάρων, τῷ τε ἀγήματι προσκαταλεγέντες Κωφῆς
τε ὁ Ἀρταβάζου καὶ Ὑδάρνης καὶ Ἀρτιβόλης οἱ
Μαζαίου, καὶ Σισίνης καὶ Φραδασμένης [καὶ] οἱ
Φραταφέρνου τοῦ Παρθυαίων καὶ Ὑρκανίας σατρά-
5 που παῖδες, καὶ Ἰτάνης Ὀξυάρτου μὲν παῖς,
Ῥωξάνης δὲ τῆς γυναικὸς Ἀλεξάνδρου ἀδελφός,
καὶ Αἰγοβάρης καὶ ὁ τούτου ἀδελφὸς Μιθροβαῖος,
καὶ ἡγεμὼν ἐπὶ τούτοις ἐπισταθεὶς Ὑστάσπης ὁ
Βάκτριος, καὶ τούτοις δόρατα Μακεδονικὰ ἀντὶ τῶν
βαρβαρικῶν μεσαγκύλων δοθέντα, — ταῦτα πάντα
ἐλύπει τοὺς Μακεδόνας, ὡς πάντῃ δὴ βαρβαρίζοντος
τῇ γνώμῃ Ἀλεξάνδρου, τὰ δὲ Μακεδονικὰ νόμιμά
τε καὶ αὐτοὺς Μακεδόνας ἐν ἀτίμῳ χώρᾳ ἄγοντος.

7. Ἀλέξανδρος δὲ τῆς μὲν πεζῆς στρατιᾶς τὴν
πολλὴν Ἡφαιστίωνα ἄγειν κελεύει ἔστε ἐπὶ τὴν
θάλασσαν τὴν Περσικήν, αὐτὸς δὲ ἀναπλεύσαντος
αὐτῷ τοῦ ναυτικοῦ ἐς τὴν Σουσίαν γῆν ἐπιβὰς τῶν
νεῶν ξὺν τοῖς ὑπασπισταῖς τε καὶ τῷ ἀγήματι καὶ
τῶν ἱππέων τῶν ἑταίρων ἀναβιβασάμενος οὐ πολλοὺς κατέπλει κατὰ τὸν Εὐλαῖον ποταμὸν ὡς ἐπὶ

---

⁵ See now Bosworth, *JHS* 1980, 14 ff. But whether ' incorporation ' means the formation of barbarian units (*lochoi*)
within the hipparchies or enrolment of individuals, it is incorporation in the Companion cavalry, and no reader of A.
could have taken this to mean, in the absence of an explicit
statement, that these cavalrymen formed their own barbarian
hipparchies distinct from the Companion cavalry of the past
who were Macedonians; the reference to the special qualities
of those enrolled also suggests that they were not very numerous, but an élite, though of lesser rank than those admitted to
the *agema* (§ 4), and therefore a minority in all hipparchies

physical beauty or any other good quality [5]; at the
addition to these of a fifth hipparchy, though it was
not entirely barbarian, but when the whole cavalry
force had been augmented, barbarians had been enrolled for the purpose [6]; at the further enrolment in
the *agema* of Cophen, son of Artabazus, Hydarnes and
Artiboles, sons of Mazaeus, Sisines and Phradasmenes, sons of Phrataphernes, satrap of Parthyaea
and Hyrcania, Itanes, son of Oxyartes and brother of
Alexander's wife, Roxane, and Aegobares and his
brother, Mithrobaeus, at the appointment of Hys-
taspes the Bactrian as their commander,[7] and at the
issue to them of Macedonian lances in place of barbarian thonged javelins. All this aggrieved the
Macedonians, as they thought that Alexander was
going utterly barbarian at heart, and treating Macedonian customs and Macedonians themselves without
respect.

7. Alexander ordered Hephaestion to take most of
the infantry force to the Persian Sea and, now that
his fleet had put in to Susian land, embarked himself
with the hypaspists, the *agema* and a few of the Companion cavalry, and sailed down the river Eulaeus to

4   324
    B.C.

5

---

except the fifth; 8, 2 also attests admission of Orientals to the
Companions.   Hipparchies: App. XIX 3.
  [6] The text is not sound, cf. Bosworth 20 f., but I would not
now confidently defend any emendation; the general sense is
that unlike the rest the fifth hipparchy was mostly barbarian,
no doubt with a Macedonian cadre (for parallel 23, 3). Whether
or not Orientals had been introduced into the Companions
before the Gadrosian march, we might guess that the losses
then sustained resulted first in the reduction of the number of
hipparchies from seven to four (cf. App. XIX 3), and that
somewhat later Al. then increased the number of his remaining
cavalry by creating the mainly Oriental fifth hipparchy.
  [7] Bosworth's assumption that the list is exhaustive need not
be accepted.

ARRIAN

2 θάλασσαν. ἤδη δὲ πλησίον ὢν τῆς ἐκβολῆς τῆς ἐς τὸν πόντον τὰς μὲν πλείονάς τε καὶ πεπονηκυίας τῶν νεῶν καταλείπει αὐτοῦ, αὐτὸς δὲ ταῖς μάλιστα ταχυναυτούσαις παρέπλει ἀπὸ τοῦ Εὐλαίου ποταμοῦ κατὰ τὴν θάλασσαν ὡς ἐπὶ τὰς ἐκβολὰς τοῦ Τίγρητος· αἱ δὲ ἄλλαι αὐτῷ νῆες ἀνακομισθεῖσαι κατὰ τὸν Εὐλαῖον ἔστε ἐπὶ τὴν διώρυχα, ἣ τέτμηται ἐκ τοῦ Τίγρητος ἐς τὸν Εὐλαῖον, ταύτῃ διεκομίσθησαν ἐς τὸν Τίγρητα.

3 Τῶν γὰρ δὴ ποταμῶν τοῦ τε Εὐφράτου καὶ τοῦ Τίγρητος, οἳ τὴν μέσην σφῶν Ἀσσυρίαν ἀπείργουσιν, ὅθεν καὶ τὸ ὄνομα Μεσοποταμία πρὸς τῶν ἐπιχωρίων κληΐζεται, ὁ μὲν Τίγρης πολύ τι ταπεινότερος ῥέων τοῦ Εὐφράτου διώρυχάς τε πολλὰς ἐκ τοῦ Εὐφράτου ἐς αὑτὸν δέχεται καὶ πολλοὺς ἄλλους ποταμοὺς παραλαβὼν καὶ ἐξ αὐτῶν αὐξηθεὶς ἐσβάλλει ἐς τὸν πόντον τὸν Περσικόν, μέγας τε καὶ οὐδαμοῦ διαβατὸς ἔστε ἐπὶ τὴν ἐκβολήν, καθότι

4 οὐ καταναλίσκεται αὐτοῦ οὐδὲν ἐς τὴν χώραν. ἔστι γὰρ μετεωροτέρα ἡ ταύτῃ γῆ τοῦ ὕδατος οὐδὲ ἐκδίδωσιν οὗτος κατὰ τὰς διώρυχας οὐδὲ ἐς ἄλλον ποταμόν, ἀλλὰ δέχεται γὰρ ἐκείνους μᾶλλον,

5 ἄρδεσθαί τε ἀπὸ οὗ τὴν χώραν οὐδαμῇ παρέχει. ὁ δὲ Εὐφράτης μετέωρός τε ῥεῖ καὶ ἰσοχείλης παντα-χῇ τῇ γῇ, καὶ διώρυχες δὲ πολλαὶ ἀπ' αὐτοῦ πεποίηνται, αἱ μὲν ἀέναοι, ἀφ' ὧν ὑδρεύονται οἱ παρ' ἑκάτερα ᾠκισμένοι, τὰς δὲ καὶ πρὸς καιρὸν ποιοῦνται, ὁπότε σφίσιν ὕδατος ἐνδεῶς ἔχοι, ἐς τὸ ἐπάρδειν τὴν χώραν· οὐ γὰρ ὕεται τὸ πολὺ ἡ γῆ αὕτη ἐξ οὐρανοῦ· καὶ οὕτως ἐς οὐ πολὺ ὕδωρ ὁ Εὐ-φράτης τελευτῶν καὶ τεναγῶδες [ἐς] τοῦτο οὕτως ἀποπαύεται.

the sea.[1] Once he was near the estuary, he left most **2** 324 B.C.
of his ships there including those which had been
damaged, and with the faster sailers coasted himself
by sea from the river Eulaeus to the mouths of the
Tigris, while the rest of his flotilla were brought back
by the Eulaeus as far as the canal cut between the
Tigris and Eulaeus, by which they entered the
Tigris.

Now of these rivers Euphrates and Tigris, which **3**
enclose Assyria between them—hence the name
Mesopotamia (' between-rivers land ')—the Tigris,
which runs through much lower ground, receives
many canals from the Euphrates, and takes in many
tributaries, thus increasing its volume, runs into the
Persian ocean and is large and cannot be crossed at
any point down to its mouth, since none of the water
is used up on the land. For the land is here higher **4**
than the river, and the Tigris does not empty its
water into canals or into any other river, but instead
receives theirs; hence it does not provide irrigation
for the land. The bed in which the Euphrates flows **5**
is, however, higher; its banks are level with the land
at all points, and many canals have been cut from it,
some of which are always running and supply water
to the inhabitants on either bank, while others are
constructed as occasion requires, whenever they are
short of water to irrigate the land; for in general this
country gets no rain. Thus the Euphrates, coming
to an end in little water, and that swampy, ceases to
flow.

---

[1] 4, 1 n. For the ch. see App. XXVI. A. perhaps follows
E. in § 3–5, and probably Ar. in 7 (cf. 19–21; S. xvi 1, 9–11;
App. XXVIII 23).

6 Ἀλέξανδρος δὲ περιπλεύσας κατὰ τὴν θάλασσαν ὅσον μεταξὺ τοῦ τε Εὐλαίου ποταμοῦ καὶ τοῦ
Τίγρητος ἐπεῖχεν ὁ αἰγιαλὸς τοῦ κόλπου τοῦ
Περσικοῦ ἀνέπλει κατὰ τὸν Τίγρητα ἔστε ἐπὶ τὸ
στρατόπεδον, ἵνα Ἡφαιστίων αὐτῷ τὴν δύναμιν
πᾶσαν ἔχων ἐστρατοπεδεύκει. ἐκεῖθεν δὲ αὖθις
ἔπλει ἐς Ὦπιν, πόλιν ἐπὶ τοῦ Τίγρητος ᾠκισμένην.
7 ἐν δὲ τῷ ἀνάπλῳ τοὺς καταρράκτας τοὺς κατὰ τὸν
ποταμὸν ἀφανίζων ὁμαλὸν πάντῃ ἐποίει τὸν ῥοῦν,
οἳ δὴ ἐκ Περσῶν πεποιημένοι ἦσαν τοῦ μή τινα
ἀπὸ θαλάσσης ἀναπλεῦσαι εἰς τὴν χώραν αὐτῶν
νηΐτῃ στόλῳ κρατήσαντα. ταῦτα δὲ μεμηχάνητο
ἅτε δὴ οὐ ναυτικοῖς τοῖς Πέρσαις· οὕτω δὴ συνεχεῖς
οἱ καταρράκται πεποιημένοι ἄπορον τὸν ἀνάπλουν
ἐποίουν τὸν κατὰ τὸν Τίγρητα. Ἀλέξανδρος δὲ
οὐκ ἔφη τῶν κρατούντων τοῖς ὅπλοις εἶναι τὰ
τοιαῦτα σοφίσματα· οὔκουν πρὸς αὑτοῦ ἐποιεῖτο
ταύτην τὴν ἀσφάλειαν, ἥντινα ἔργῳ οὐδὲ λόγου
ἀξίαν ἀπέφηνε οὐ χαλεπῶς διακόψας τῶν Περσῶν
τὰ σπουδάσματα.

8. Ὡς δὲ ἐς τὴν Ὦπιν ἀφίκετο, συναγαγὼν τοὺς
Μακεδόνας προεῖπεν ὅτι τοὺς ὑπὸ γήρως ἢ πηρώσ-
εως τοῦ σώματος ἀχρείους ἐς τὰ πολέμια ὄντας
παραλύει μὲν τῆς στρατιᾶς, ἀποπέμπει δὲ ἐς τὰ
σφέτερα ἤθη, ἐπιδώσει δὲ ⟨τοῖς⟩ μένουσιν [1] ὅσα
αὐτούς τε ζηλωτοτέρους ποιήσει τοῖς οἴκοι καὶ τοὺς
ἄλλους Μακεδόνας ἐξορμήσει ἐς τὸ ἐθέλειν τῶν
2 αὐτῶν κινδύνων τε καὶ πόνων μετέχειν. Ἀλέξανδρος μὲν ὡς χαριούμενος δῆθεν τοῖς Μακεδόσιν

[1] ⟨τοῖς⟩ Hammond.   Roos deleted μένουσιν.

After sailing by sea along the whole length of the   6   324
coast of the Persian gulf between the Eulaeus and the   B.C.
Tigris, Alexander sailed up the Tigris to the camp
where Hephaestion had encamped with all his force.
From there he sailed on to Opis, a city situated on the
Tigris.[2]   In the voyage upstream he removed the   7
weirs in the river and made the stream level throughout; these weirs had been made by the Persians to
prevent anyone sailing up to their country from the
sea and mastering it with a naval force.   The Persians
had constructed them because they had no naval
power, and the weirs, built up at such regular intervals, made the voyage on the Tigris impracticable.
Alexander, however, said that contrivances of this
kind were the work of men lacking military supremacy; he therefore regarded this precaution as of no
advantage to himself, and showed by his action in
destroying with ease works on which the Persians
had spent their energy that it was of no value.

8. On reaching Opis, he summoned his Macedonians and announced that he was discharging from
the army and sending home men unfit for active service because of old age or physical disability.[1]   He
would give those who remained with him [2] enough
to make them objects of envy to those at home, and
stir up the rest of the Macedonians to readiness for
sharing the same dangers and hardships.[3]   Alexander   2
said this, no doubt, to show his favour to the Macedo-

---

[2] A large place till supplanted by Seleucia close by.   The
Tigris was navigable up to Opis, where it was linked by a royal
canal with the Euphrates, 30 km. distant (S. xvi 1, 9;   *RE*
xviii 683).

[1] The vulgate misplaced the discharge and mutiny of troops
at Susa.

[2] For text see Hammond, *CQ* 1980.

[3] This implies that Al. had further conquests in mind.

ταῦτα ἔλεγεν· οἱ δὲ ὡς ὑπερορώμενοί τε ἤδη πρὸς
'Αλεξάνδρου καὶ ἀχρεῖοι πάντη ἐς τὰ πολέμια
νομιζόμενοι οὐκ ἀλόγως αὖ τῷ λόγῳ ἠχθέσθησαν
τῷ πρὸς 'Αλεξάνδρου λεχθέντι, κατὰ τὴν στρατιὰν ταύτην πᾶσαν πολλοῖς καὶ ἄλλοις ἀχθεσθέν-
τες, ὅτι πολλάκις ἤδη ἐλύπει αὐτοὺς ἥ τε ἐσθὴς ἡ
Περσικὴ ἐς ταὐτὸ² φέρουσα καὶ τῶν 'Επιγόνων
τῶν βαρβάρων ⟨ἡ ἐς⟩ τὰ Μακεδονικὰ ἤθη κόσμησις
καὶ ἀνάμιξις τῶν ἀλλοφύλων ἱππέων ἐς τὰς τῶν
3 ἑταίρων τάξεις. οὔκουν σιγῇ ἔχοντες ἐκαρτέρησαν,
ἀλλὰ πάντας γὰρ ἀπαλλάττειν στρατιᾶς ἐκέλευον,
αὐτὸν δὲ μετὰ τοῦ πατρὸς στρατεύεσθαι, τὸν
῎Αμμωνα δὴ τῷ λόγῳ ἐπικερτομοῦντες. ταῦτα
ἀκούσας 'Αλέξανδρος (ἦν γὰρ δὴ ὀξύτερός τε ἐν τῷ
τότε καὶ ἀπὸ τῆς βαρβαρικῆς θεραπείας οὐκέτι ὡς
πάλαι ἐπιεικὴς ἐς τοὺς Μακεδόνας) καταπηδήσας σὺν
τοῖς ἀμφ' αὑτὸν ἡγεμόσιν ἀπὸ τοῦ βήματος ξυλ-
λαβεῖν τοὺς ἐπιφανεστάτους τῶν ταραξάντων τὸ
πλῆθος κελεύει, αὐτὸς τῇ χειρὶ ἐπιδεικνύων τοῖς
ὑπασπισταῖς οὕστινας χρὴ συλλαμβάνειν· καὶ
ἐγένοντο οὗτοι ἐς τρισκαίδεκα. τούτους μὲν δὴ
ἀπάγειν κελεύει τὴν ἐπὶ θανάτῳ. ὡς δὲ κατε-
σιώπησαν οἱ ἄλλοι ἐκπλαγέντες, ἀναβὰς αὖθις
ἐπὶ τὸ βῆμα ἔλεξεν ὧδε.

9. Οὐχ ὑπὲρ τοῦ καταπαῦσαι ὑμῶν, ὦ Μακεδόνες, τὴν οἴκαδε ὁρμὴν λεχθήσεταί μοι ὅδε ὁ
λόγος, ἔξεστι γὰρ ὑμῖν ἀπιέναι ὅποι βούλεσθε
ἐμοῦ γε ἕνεκα, ἀλλὰ ὡς γνῶναι ὑμᾶς πρὸς ὁποίους
τινὰς ἡμᾶς ὄντας ὁποῖοί τινες αὐτοὶ γενόμενοι ἀπ-

---

² Polak: τοῦτο codd., Roos.

nians. But they supposed that they were by now objects of his contempt and that he thought them wholly useless in his wars; they were, not without reason, aggrieved once more by the speech he had delivered. In the whole of their expedition they had had many sources of discontent; on many previous occasions they had been vexed by his Persian dress, which suggested the same thing, by the equipment of the barbarian Epigoni in Macedonian style and the introduction of foreign horsemen in the ranks of the Companions.[4] Consequently, they did not en- 3 dure in silence, but called on him to discharge them all from the army, and to campaign himself in company with his father, referring in mockery to Ammon.[5] Hearing this Alexander, who had become by this time quicker-tempered and, courted as he now was in the barbarian manner, had ceased to be so kindly as in old times to the Macedonians, leapt down from the platform with the officers round him and ordered them to arrest the most conspicuous of the popular agitators, personally pointing out to the hypaspists with his finger whom they were to arrest; they numbered about thirteen. He ordered them to be led away to execution but, as the others were stunned and remained in dead silence, he remounted the platform and spoke as follows [6]:

9. 'It is not to put an end to your passion for home, Macedonians, that I shall deliver this speech, for you may depart wherever you wish for all I care, but to make you understand your own character and ours and the way you have behaved to us, at the time

[4] Cf. 6, 2–5 with nn. The policies complained of went back only to 330.

[5] App. V 8 ff.

[6] App. XXVI 6. QC. also inserts a speech.

2 ἀλλάσσεσθε. καὶ πρῶτά γε ἀπὸ Φιλίππου τοῦ πα-
τρός, ἧπερ καὶ εἰκός, τοῦ λόγου ἄρξομαι. Φίλιππος
γὰρ παραλαβὼν ὑμᾶς πλανήτας καὶ ἀπόρους, ἐν διφ-
θέραις τοὺς πολλοὺς νέμοντας ἀνὰ τὰ ὄρη πρόβατα
ὀλίγα καὶ ὑπὲρ τούτων κακῶς μαχομένους Ἰλλυ-
ριοῖς καὶ Τριβαλλοῖς καὶ τοῖς ὁμόροις Θραξίν,
χλαμύδας μὲν ὑμῖν ἀντὶ τῶν διφθερῶν φορεῖν
ἔδωκεν, κατήγαγε δὲ ἐκ τῶν ὀρῶν ἐς τὰ πεδία,
ἀξιομάχους καταστήσας τοῖς προσχώροις τῶν
βαρβάρων, ὡς μὴ χωρίων ἔτι ὀχυρότητι πιστεύ-
οντας μᾶλλον ἢ τῇ οἰκείᾳ ἀρετῇ σώζεσθαι, πόλεών
τε οἰκήτορας ἀπέφηνε καὶ νόμοις καὶ ἔθεσι χρησ-
3 τοῖς ἐκόσμησεν. αὐτῶν δὲ ἐκείνων τῶν βαρβάρων,
ὑφ' ὧν πρόσθεν ἤγεσθε καὶ ἐφέρεσθε αὐτοί τε καὶ
τὰ ὑμέτερα, ἡγεμόνας κατέστησεν ἐκ δούλων καὶ
ὑπηκόων, καὶ τῆς Θρᾴκης τὰ πολλὰ τῇ Μακεδονίᾳ
προσέθηκεν, καὶ τῶν ἐπὶ θαλάττῃ χωρίων τὰ
ἐπικαιρότατα καταλαβόμενος τὴν ἐμπορίαν τῇ
χώρᾳ ἀνεπέτασε, καὶ τῶν μετάλλων τὴν ἐργασίαν
4 ἀδεῆ παρέσχε, Θεσσαλῶν δὲ ἄρχοντας, οὓς πάλαι
ἐτεθνήκειτε τῷ δέει, ἀπέφηνε, καὶ τὸ Φωκέων
ἔθνος ταπεινώσας τὴν ἐς τὴν Ἑλλάδα πάροδον
πλατεῖαν καὶ εὔπορον ἀντὶ στενῆς τε καὶ ἀπόρου
ὑμῖν ἐποίησεν, Ἀθηναίους τε καὶ Θηβαίους
ἐφεδρεύοντας ἀεὶ τῇ Μακεδονίᾳ ἐς τοσόνδε ἐτα-
πείνωσεν, ἤδη ταῦτά γε καὶ ἡμῶν αὐτῷ ξυμπον-
ούντων, ὡς ἀντὶ τοῦ φόρους τελεῖν Ἀθηναίοις καὶ
ὑπακούειν Θηβαίων, παρ' ἡμῶν ἐν τῷ μέρει

---

[1] An exaggeration, see Hammond, *Hist. of Mac.* ii 647 ff.,
but also 657 ff. for Ph's solid improvements in military security
and material prosperity.

you leave. First of all, I shall begin my speech with 2 324
Philip, my father, as is only fair. Philip took you   B.C.
over when you were helpless vagabonds, mostly
clothed in skins, feeding a few animals on the
mountains and engaged in their defence in unsuccessful fighting with Illyrians, Triballians and the
neighbouring Thracians. He gave you cloaks to
wear instead of skins, he brought you down from the
mountains to the plains; he made you a match in
battle for the barbarians on your borders, so that you
no longer trusted for your safety to the strength of
your positions so much as to your natural courage.
He made you city dwellers and established the order
that comes from good laws and customs.[1] It was 3
due to him that you became masters and not slaves
and subjects of those very barbarians who used previously to plunder your possessions and carry off your
persons. He annexed the greater part of Thrace to
Macedonia [2] and, by capturing the best placed
positions by the sea, he opened up the country to
trade; he enabled you to work the mines in safety;
he made you the rulers of the Thessalians, who in the 4
old days made you dead with terror; he humbled the
Phocian people and gave you access into Greece that
was broad and easy instead of being narrow and hard.
The Athenians and Thebans were always lying in
wait to attack Macedonia; Philip reduced them so
low, at a time when we were actually sharing in his
exertions, that instead of our paying tribute to the
Athenians [3] and taking orders from the Thebans it

---

[2] Not all, cf. Hammond 656 f.; 672 ff.; A. i 25, 2; D 62, 5;
QC. x 1, 43.
[3] False Athenian propaganda (cf. Ps-Dem. vii 12), unlikely
ο come from Pt./Ar.

5 ἐκείνους τὴν ἀσφάλειάν σφισι πορίζεσθαι. ἐς
Πελοπόννησον δὲ παρελθὼν τὰ ἐκεῖ αὖ ἐκόσμησε
καὶ ἡγεμὼν αὐτοκράτωρ συμπάσης τῆς ἄλλης
Ἑλλάδος ἀποδειχθεὶς τῆς ἐπὶ τὸν Πέρσην στρατιᾶς οὐχ ἑαυτῷ μᾶλλόν τι τὴν δόξαν τήνδε ἢ τῷ
κοινῷ τῶν Μακεδόνων προσέθηκεν.

6 Ταῦτα μὲν τὰ ἐκ τοῦ πατρὸς τοῦ ἐμοῦ ἐς ὑμᾶς
ὑπηργμένα, ὡς μὲν αὐτὰ ἐφ' ἑαυτῶν σκέψασθαι
μεγάλα, μικρὰ δὲ ὥς γε δὴ πρὸς τὰ ἡμέτερα
ξυμβαλεῖν. ὃς παραλαβὼν παρὰ τοῦ πατρὸς
χρυσᾶ μὲν καὶ ἀργυρᾶ ἐκπώματα ὀλίγα, τάλαντα
δὲ οὐδὲ ἑξήκοντα ἐν τοῖς θησαυροῖς, χρεῶν
δὲ ὀφειλόμενα ὑπὸ Φιλίππου ἐς πεντακόσια
τάλαντα, δανεισάμενος ἐπὶ τούτοις αὐτὸς ἄλλα
ὀκτακόσια ὁρμηθεὶς ἐκ τῆς χώρας τῆς γε οὐδὲ
ὑμᾶς αὐτοὺς βοσκούσης καλῶς εὐθὺς μὲν τοῦ
Ἑλλησπόντου ὑμῖν τὸν πόρον θαλασσοκρατούντων

7 ἐν τῷ τότε Περσῶν ἀνεπέτασα· κρατήσας δὲ τῇ
ἵππῳ τοὺς σατράπας τοὺς Δαρείου τήν τε Ἰωνίαν
πᾶσαν τῇ ὑμετέρᾳ ἀρχῇ προσέθηκα καὶ τὴν
Αἰολίδα πᾶσαν καὶ Φρύγας ἀμφοτέρους καὶ
Λυδούς, καὶ Μίλητον εἷλον πολιορκίᾳ· τὰ δὲ
ἄλλα πάντα ἑκόντα προσχωρήσαντα λαβὼν ὑμῖν

8 καρποῦσθαι ἔδωκα· καὶ τὰ ἐξ Αἰγύπτου καὶ
Κυρήνης ἀγαθά, ὅσα ἀμαχεὶ ἐκτησάμην, ὑμῖν
ἔρχεται, ἥ τε κοίλη Συρία καὶ ἡ Παλαιστίνη καὶ ἡ
μέση τῶν ποταμῶν ὑμέτερον κτῆμά εἰσι, καὶ
Βαβυλὼν καὶ Βάκτρα καὶ Σοῦσα ὑμέτερα, καὶ ὁ

---

4 An exaggeration of which Al. was doubtless capable.
5 Xenophon's ' commonwealth of the Persians ' (*Cyrop.* i
5, 8) could have suggested this phrase; in any case Hammond,

was we in our turn who gave them security. He
entered the Peloponnese and there too he settled
affairs, and his recognition as leader with full powers [4]
over the whole of the rest of Greece in the expedition
against the Persians did not perhaps confer more
glory on himself than on the commonwealth of the
Macedonians.[5]

' These services which my father rendered you, 6
great as they are when considered by themselves
alone, are actually small in comparison with our own.
Inheriting from my father only a few gold and silver
cups and not so much as sixty Talents [6] in the treas-
ury, with debts Philip had contracted of about five
hundred Talents, I myself borrowed another eight
hundred in addition and, setting out from the land
from which you did not get a fair subsistence your-
selves, I at once opened up for you the Hellespontine
straits, although at that time the Persians controlled
the sea, and after my cavalry victory over the satraps 7
of Darius I added all Ionia to your empire and all
Aeolis, both Phrygias and Lydia; I captured Miletus
by siege, and gave you the enjoyment of all the other
countries that voluntarily surrendered to my power.
All the benefits from Egypt and Cyrene,[7] which I won 8
without a blow, go to you; " hollow " Syria, Pales-
tine, Mesopotamia, are your possessions; Babylon,
Bactria, Susa are yours, and yours are the wealth of

CQ 1980, 461–5 subverts my remarks in Introd. 28 to some
extent; in practice the Macedonian people could not control a
strong king.

[6] Ar. gave 70 (P. 15)—so A. is not following him—and
Onesicritus put the debt at 200 (ib.); A's first two figures are
those of QC. x 2, 24, the third is unique.

[7] D. 49; QC. iv 7, 9 for embassy from Cyrene (332/1), which
could have been construed as submission. A's silence does
not imply that Pt./Ar. ignored it.

Λυδῶν πλοῦτος καὶ οἱ Περσῶν θησαυροὶ καὶ τὰ
Ἰνδῶν ἀγαθὰ καὶ ἡ ἔξω θάλασσα ὑμέτερα· ὑμεῖς
9 σατράπαι, ὑμεῖς στρατηγοί, ὑμεῖς ταξιάρχαι. ὡς
ἔμοιγε αὐτῷ τί περίεστιν ἀπὸ τούτων τῶν πόνων
ὅτι μὴ αὕτη ἡ πορφύρα καὶ τὸ διάδημα τοῦτο;
κέκτημαι δὲ ἰδίᾳ οὐδέν, οὐδὲ ἔχει τις ἀποδεῖξαι
θησαυροὺς ἐμοὺς ὅτι μὴ ταῦτα, ὑμέτερα κτήματα ἢ
ὅσα ἕνεκα ὑμῶν φυλάττεται. ἐπεὶ οὐδὲ ἔστιν ἰδίᾳ
μοι ἐς ὅ τι φυλάξω αὐτούς, σιτουμένῳ τε τὰ αὐτὰ
ὑμῖν σιτία καὶ ὕπνον τὸν αὐτὸν αἱρουμένῳ·
καίτοι οὐδὲ σιτία ἐμοὶ δοκῶ τὰ αὐτὰ τοῖς τρυφῶσιν
ὑμῶν σιτεῖσθαι· προαγρυπνῶν δὲ ὑμῶν οἶδα, ὡς
καθεύδειν ἔχοιτε ὑμεῖς.

10. Ἀλλὰ ταῦτα γὰρ ὑμῶν πονούντων καὶ ταλαι-
πωρουμένων ἐκτησάμην αὐτὸς ἀπόνως καὶ ἀταλαι-
πώρως ἐξηγούμενος. καὶ τίς ὑμῶν ἢ πονήσας
οἶδεν ἐμοῦ μᾶλλον . . . . . ἢ ἐγὼ ὑπὲρ ἐκείνου;
ἄγε δὴ καὶ ὅτῳ τραύματα ὑμῶν ἐστι γυμνώσας
αὐτὰ ἐπιδειξάτω καὶ ἐγὼ τὰ ἐμὰ ἐπιδείξω ἐν μέρει·
2 ὡς ἔμοιγε οὐκ ἔστιν ὅ τι τοῦ σώματος τῶν γε δὴ
ἔμπροσθεν μερῶν ἄτρωτον ὑπολέλειπται, οὐδὲ
ὅπλον τι ἔστιν ἢ ἐκ χειρὸς ἢ τῶν ἀφιεμένων οὗ γε
οὐκ ἴχνη ἐν ἐμαυτῷ φέρω· ἀλλὰ καὶ ξίφει ἐκ
χειρὸς τέτρωμαι καὶ τετόξευμαι ἤδη καὶ ἀπὸ
μηχανῆς βέβλημαι, καὶ λίθοις πολλαχῇ καὶ ξύλοις
παιόμενος ὑπὲρ ὑμῶν καὶ τῆς ὑμετέρας δόξης καὶ
τοῦ ὑμετέρου πλούτου νικῶντας ὑμᾶς ἄγω διὰ
πάσης γῆς καὶ θαλάσσης καὶ πάντων ποταμῶν καὶ
3 ὀρῶν καὶ πεδίων πάντων, γάμους τε ὑμῖν τοὺς

---

[8] Tarn supposes that Al. here turned to the officers, but the
narrative does not suggest that they had manifested any

the Lydians, the treasures of the Persians, the
bounty of India and the outer sea. It is you who are
satraps, generals and taxiarchs.[8] If you consider 9
me, what is there still in my possession after these
exertions but this purple and diadem [9]? I have
acquired nothing for myself; no one can point to
treasures of mine, but only to your possessions or
what is kept in trust for you, for I have nothing to
gain by keeping them for my own use; I eat the same
food as you do, I sleep as you do, except that my food
is not, I think, as luxurious as some of you consume,
and that I know that on your behalf I am wakeful, so
that you may be able to slumber soundly.

10. ' But, you may say, the exertions and hardships were yours and all these acquisitions were mine,
while I direct you without any personal exertion or
hardship! Yet which of you is conscious that he
exerted himself more in my behalf than I in his?
Come then, let any of you strip and display his own
wounds, and I will display mine in turn; in my case 2
there is no part of the body, or none in front, that has
been left unwounded, and there is no weapon of close
combat, no missile whose scars I do not bear on my
person, but I have been wounded by the sword hand
to hand, shot by arrows and struck by a catapult, and
I am often struck by stones and clubs for your interest, your glory and your riches, while I lead you as
conquerors through every land and sea, river,
mountain and plain. I have made the same mar- 3

opposition; this is a point suitable for a rhetorician who had
forgotten the historic circumstances of the speech. Cf. 10, 3
nn.

[9] App. XIV 2. Bosworth, *JHS* 1980, 8 ff. shows that Al.
was now affecting more regal splendour, see e.g. 22, 2; 24, 2;
Athenaus xii 537 D–540 A.

αὐτοὺς γεγάμηκα καὶ πολλῶν ὑμῶν οἱ παῖδες
συγγενεῖς ἔσονται τοῖς παισὶ τοῖς ἐμοῖς. ἔτι δὲ ᾧ
χρέα ἦν, οὐ πολυπραγμονήσας ἐφ' ὅτῳ ἐγένετο, τοσαῦτα μὲν μισθοφορούντων, τοσαῦτα δὲ ἁρπαζόντων,
ὁπότε ἐκ πολιορκίας ἁρπαγὴ γίγνοιτο, διαλέλυ-
μαι ταῦτα. στέφανοί τε χρυσοῖ τοῖς πλείστοις
ὑμῶν εἰσι μνημεῖα τῆς τε ἀρετῆς τῆς ὑμετέρας καὶ
4 τῆς ἐξ ἐμοῦ τιμῆς ἀθάνατα. ὅστις δὲ δὴ καὶ ἀπέθανεν,
εὐκλεὴς μὲν αὐτῷ ἡ τελευτὴ ἐγένετο, περιφανὴς
δὲ ὁ τάφος, χαλκαῖ δὲ αἱ εἰκόνες τῶν πλείστων οἴκοι
ἑστᾶσιν, οἱ γονεῖς δ' ἔντιμοί εἰσι λειτουργίας τε
ξυμπάσης καὶ εἰσφορᾶς ἀπηλλαγμένοι· οὐ γάρ τίς
γε φεύγων ὑμῶν ἐτελεύτα ἐμοῦ ἄγοντος.

5 Καὶ νῦν τοὺς ἀπολέμους ὑμῶν ζηλωτοὺς τοῖς οἴκοι
ἀποπέμψειν ἤμελλον· ἀλλ' ἐπειδὴ πάντες ἀπιέναι
βούλεσθε, ἄπιτε πάντες, καὶ ἀπελθόντες οἴκοι
ἀπαγγείλατε ὅτι τὸν βασιλέα ὑμῶν 'Αλέξανδρον,
νικῶντα μὲν Πέρσας καὶ Μήδους καὶ Βακτρίους καὶ
6 Σάκας, καταστρεψάμενον δὲ Οὐξίους τε καὶ
'Αραχωτοὺς καὶ Δράγγας, κεκτημένον δὲ καὶ
Παρθυαίους καὶ Χορασμίους καὶ 'Υρκανίους ἔστε
ἐπὶ τὴν θάλασσαν τὴν Κασπίαν, ὑπερβάντα δὲ τὸν
Καύκασον ὑπὲρ τὰς Κασπίας πύλας, καὶ περάσαντα
"Οξον τε ποταμὸν καὶ Τάναϊν, ἔτι δὲ τὸν 'Ινδὸν
ποταμόν, οὐδενὶ ἄλλῳ ὅτι μὴ Διονύσῳ περαθέντα,
καὶ τὸν 'Υδάσπην καὶ τὸν 'Ακεσίνην καὶ τὸν
7 'Υδραώτην, καὶ τὸν "Υφασιν διαπεράσαντα ἄν, εἰ μὴ
ὑμεῖς ἀπωκνήσατε, καὶ ἐς τὴν μεγάλην θάλασσαν
κατ' ἀμφότερα τοῦ 'Ινδοῦ τὰ στόματα ἐμβαλόντα,

---

[1] Absurd in relation to the common soldiers: an invention
perhaps influenced by 11, 7.

riages as you, and many of your children will be the
kin of mine.[1]   Furthermore, if you contracted debts,
I did not make it my business to discover why,
despite the enormous sums you gained by pay and
plunder, whenever a besieged place was plundered,
but I discharged them all.   Most of you have gold
crowns [2] as memorials of your own courage, but also of
the honour that I have accorded you, and that will
last all time.   Indeed, when a man died, glory came   4
to him by his death, splendour in his funeral, and
brazen images have been erected for most of them at
home, while his parents enjoy the honour of being
freed from every public duty and tax [3]; of course not
a man of you died in flight under my command.

' And now it was my intention to send away only   5
men unfit for war, to be the envy of those at home
but, as you all desire to go, let all of you begone, return to your homes and report that your king,
Alexander, defeated Persians, Medes, Bactrians,
Sacae, subdued Uxians, Arachotians, Drangians,   6
conquered Parthyaeans, Chorasmians,[4] Hyrcanians
as far as the Caspian [5] sea, went over the Caucasus
beyond the Caspian gates,[6] crossed the river Oxus and
the Tanais, and even the river Indus which no one
but Dionysus had crossed before, and the Hydaspes
and Acesines and Hydraotes, and would have crossed   7
the Hyphasis as well but for your apprehensions, and
that he burst out on the great sea by both mouths of

[2] For officers, e.g. vii 5, 4 ff.
[3] Cf. i 16, 4 f. with Bosworth *ad loc*.
[4] Pharasmanes' visit (iv 15, 4) could have been taken as
submission.
[5] *Contra* Tarn ii 294, Al's contemporaries did use this name
as well as ' Hyrcanian sea,' cf. 16, 2 (so too Hdt. i 203).
[6] App. VIII 9; XII.

καὶ διὰ τῆς Γαδρωσίας τῆς ἐρήμου ἐλθόντα, ἧ
οὐδείς πω πρόσθεν σὺν στρατιᾷ ἦλθε, καὶ Καρμανίαν ἐν παρόδῳ προσκτησάμενον καὶ τὴν Ὠρειτῶν
γῆν, περιπεπλευκότος δὲ ἤδη αὐτῷ τοῦ ναυτικοῦ
τὴν ἀπ' Ἰνδῶν γῆς εἰς Πέρσας θάλασσαν, ὡς εἰς
Σοῦσα ἐπανηγάγετε, ἀπολιπόντες οἴχεσθε, παρα-
δόντες φυλάσσειν τοῖς νενικημένοις βαρβάροις. ταῦτα
ὑμῖν καὶ πρὸς ἀνθρώπων ἴσως εὐκλεᾶ καὶ πρὸς
θεῶν ὅσια δήπου ἔσται ἀπαγγελθέντα. ἄπιτε.

11. Ταῦτα εἰπὼν κατεπήδησέ τε ἀπὸ τοῦ
βήματος ὀξέως καὶ ἐς τὰ βασίλεια παρελθὼν οὔτε
ἐθεράπευσε τὸ σῶμα οὔτε τῳ ὤφθη τῶν ἑταίρων·
ἀλλ' οὐδὲ ἐς τὴν ὑστεραίαν ὤφθη. τῇ τρίτῃ δὲ
καλέσας εἴσω τῶν Περσῶν τοὺς ἐπιλέκτους τάς τε
ἡγεμονίας αὐτοῖς τῶν τάξεων διένειμε καὶ ὅσους
συγγενεῖς ἀπέφηνε, τούτοις δὲ νόμιμον ἐποίησε
2 φιλεῖν αὐτὸν μόνοις. οἱ δὲ Μακεδόνες ἔν τε τῷ
παραυτίκα ἀκούσαντες τῶν λόγων ἐκπεπληγμένοι
σιγῇ ἔμενον αὐτοῦ πρὸς τῷ βήματι οὐδέ τις
ἠκολούθησε τῷ βασιλεῖ ἀπαλλαττομένῳ ὅτι μὴ οἱ
ἀμφ' αὐτὸν ἑταῖροί τε καὶ οἱ σωματοφύλακες, οἱ
δὲ πολλοὶ οὔτε μένοντες ὅ τι πράττωσιν ἢ λέγωσιν
3 εἶχον, οὔτε ἀπαλλάσσεσθαι ἤθελον. ὡς δὲ τὰ
Περσῶν τε καὶ Μήδων αὐτοῖς ἐξηγγέλλετο, αἵ τε
ἡγεμονίαι Πέρσαις διδόμεναι καὶ ἡ στρατιὰ ἡ
βαρβαρικὴ ἐς λόχους τε καταλεγομένη καὶ τὰ
Μακεδονικὰ ὀνόματα ἄγημά τι Περσικὸν καλούμενον

---

[7] A. presupposes the accuracy of the vulgate, contradicting
his narrative.

[8] Tarn ii 295 thinks the ending (also imitated in QC's speech

the Indus, and came through the Gadrosian desert, where no one had ever before gone with an army, and acquired Carmania and the land of the Oritans as he passed through, while the fleet had already sailed along the coast from India to Persia, and that when you returned to Susa [7] you deserted him and went off, handing him over to the protection of the barbarians he had conquered. This is a report that will perhaps win you a fine reputation with men and will doubtless be holy in the sight of heaven. Begone!' [8]

11. After his speech he leapt down swiftly from his platform and, passing into the palace, paid no attention to his bodily needs, and was not seen by any of the Companions, not even on the following day.[1] But on the third day he summoned inside the picked men among the Persians and divided the commands of the battalions among them and restricted the right to kiss him to those he declared his kinsmen. The Macedonians had been immediately stunned by [2] his speech, and stayed in silence there by the platform, none following the king when he left except for the attendant Companions and bodyguards; but the mass, though they stayed behind, had nothing to say and yet were unwilling to depart. But when they [3] heard about the Persians and the Medes, and the commands given to the Persians, and the Oriental force being drafted into the units, and the Macedonian names—an *agema* called Persian,[2] and Persian

at the Beas, ix 2, 34) beyond a Greek rhetorician, and thus an authentic utterance of Àl. But cf. Lysias xi 18; xii 100.

[1] For what follows cf. D. 109; QC. x 3, 1 ff. (with a speech of Al. to the foreign troops); P. 71; J. xii 1, all with variant details.

[2] Cf. 29, 4; Bosworth, *JHS* 1980, 9, citing D. 110, 1 f.; xviii 27, 1; J. xii 12, 4, shows that the *agema* of hypaspists was to remain distinct and wholly Macedonian.

καὶ πεζέταιροι Πέρσαι καὶ ἀσθέτεροι ἄλλοι [1] καὶ
ἀργυρασπίδων τάξις Περσικὴ καὶ ἡ τῶν ἑταίρων
ἵππος καὶ ταύτης ἄλλο ἄγημα βασιλικόν, οὐκέτι
4 καρτεροὶ σφῶν ἦσαν, ἀλλὰ ξυνδραμόντες ὡς πρὸς
τὰ βασίλεια τὰ μὲν ὅπλα αὐτοῦ πρὸ τῶν θυρῶν
ἐρρίπτουν, ἱκετηρίας ταύτας τῷ βασιλεῖ, αὐτοὶ
δ' ἐβόων πρὸ τῶν θυρῶν ἑστηκότες δεόμενοι παρελθεῖν εἴσω· τούς τε αἰτίους τῆς ἐν τῷ τότε ταραχῆς
καὶ τοὺς ἄρξαντας τῆς βοῆς ἐκδιδόναι ἐθέλειν·
οὔκουν ἀπαλλαγήσεσθαι τῶν θυρῶν οὔτε ἡμέρας
οὔτε νυκτός, εἰ μή τινα οἶκτον σφῶν ἕξει Ἀλέξανδρος.
5   Ταῦτα ὡς ἀπηγγέλλετο αὐτῷ, ὁ δὲ σπουδῇ ἐξ-
έρχεται καὶ ἰδών τε ταπεινῶς διακειμένους καὶ
ἀκούσας σὺν οἰμωγῇ τῶν πολλῶν βοώντων καὶ
αὐτῷ προχεῖται δάκρυα. καὶ ὁ μὲν ἀνήγετο ὥς τι
6 ἐρῶν, οἱ δὲ ἔμενον λιπαροῦντες. καί τις αὐτῶν
καθ' ἡλικίαν τε καὶ ἱππαρχίαν τῆς ἵππου τῆς
ἑταιρικῆς οὐκ ἀφανής, Καλλίνης ὄνομα, τοιαῦτα
εἶπεν· ὦ βασιλεῦ, τὰ λυποῦντά ἐστι Μακεδόνας
ὅτι σὺ Περσῶν μέν τινας ἤδη πεποίησαι σαυτῷ συγγενεῖς καὶ καλοῦνται Πέρσαι συγγενεῖς Ἀλεξάνδρου
καὶ φιλοῦσί σε, Μακεδόνων δὲ οὔπω τις γέγευται
7 ταύτης τῆς τιμῆς. ἔνθα δὴ ὑπολαβὼν Ἀλέξανδρος, ἀλλ' ὑμᾶς τε, ἔφη, ξύμπαντας ἐμαυτῷ
τίθεμαι συγγενεῖς καὶ τό γε ἀπὸ τούτου οὕτως κα-
λέσω. ταῦτα εἰπόντα προσελθὼν ὁ Καλλίνης τε
ἐφίλησε καὶ ὅστις ἄλλος φιλῆσαι ἠθέλησε. καὶ
οὕτω δὴ ἀναλαβόντες τὰ ὅπλα βοῶντές τε καὶ παι-
8 ωνίζοντες ἐς τὸ στρατόπεδον ἀπῄεσαν. Ἀλέξανδρος

----

[1] See Introduction n. 99.

' foot-companions ', and *astheteroi* too, and a Persian
battalion of ' silver-shields',[3] and the cavalry of the
Companions which now included a new royal *agema*—
they could no longer contain themselves, but all ran   4
together to the palace and, throwing down their arms
there before the doors as signs of supplication to the
king, they themselves stood shouting before the
doors begging to be let in. They said they would
give up the instigators of the late disturbance and
those who began the clamour; they would depart
from the doors neither by day nor by night unless
Alexander would have some pity on them.

When this was reported to Alexander, he quickly   5
came out, and seeing them so humble, and hearing
most of them lamenting loudly, he too shed tears.
He came forward as if to say something, while they
stayed there in supplication. One of them called   6
Callines, a man distinguished by age and hipparchy [4]
in the Companions' cavalry, said something like this :
' What grieves the Macedonians, Sire, is that you
have now made some of the Persians your kinsmen
and that Persians are called " Alexander's kinsmen ", and permitted to kiss you, but no Macedonian
has yet enjoyed this privilege.' On this Alexander   7
broke in : ' But I regard all of you as my kinsmen, and
from this time forth I shall give you that name.'
When he had said this, Callines approached and
kissed him, and so did any other who wished.[5] So
they took up their arms again and returned to the
camp shouting and singing their victory song. On   8

---

[3] This name, applied after Al. to some or all of the hypaspists, could have come into use before his death, implying of
course an issue to them of silver shields, cf. Bosworth, *JHS*
1980 n. 64.

[4] A cavalry officer, but not a hipparch.

[5] Introd. 32, cf. iv 11, 3; 12, 3–5.

δὲ ἐπὶ τούτοις θυσίαν τε θύει τοῖς θεοῖς οἷς αὐτῷ
νόμος καὶ θοίνην δημοτελῆ ἐποίησε, καθήμενός τε
αὐτὸς καὶ πάντων καθημένων, ἀμφ' αὐτὸν μὲν
Μακεδόνων, ἐν δὲ τῷ ἐφεξῆς τούτων Περσῶν, ἐπὶ
δὲ τούτοις τῶν ἄλλων ἐθνῶν ὅσοι κατ' ἀξίωσιν ἤ
τινα ἄλλην ἀρετὴν πρεσβευόμενοι, καὶ ἀπὸ τοῦ
αὐτοῦ κρατῆρος αὐτός τε καὶ οἱ ἀμφ' αὐτὸν ἀρυό-
μενοι ἔσπενδον τὰς αὐτὰς σπονδὰς καταρχομένων
τῶν τε Ἑλλήνων μάντεων καὶ τῶν Μάγων.
9 εὔχετο δὲ τά τε ἄλλα [καὶ τὰ] ἀγαθὰ καὶ ὁμόνοιάν
τε καὶ κοινωνίαν τῆς ἀρχῆς Μακεδόσι καὶ Πέρσαις.
εἶναι δὲ κατέχει λόγος τοὺς μετασχόντας τῆς
θοίνης ἐννακισχιλίους, καὶ τούτους πάντας μίαν τε
σπονδὴν σπεῖσαι καὶ ἐπ' αὐτῇ παιωνίσαι.

12. Ἔνθα δὴ ἐθελονταὶ ἤδη αὐτῷ ἀπῄεσαν τῶν
Μακεδόνων ὅσοι διὰ γῆρας ἤ τινα ἄλλην ξυμφορὰν
ἀπόλεμοι ἦσαν· καὶ οὗτοι αὐτῷ ἐγένοντο ἐς τοὺς
μυρίους. τούτοις δὲ τήν τε μισθοφορὰν οὐ τοῦ
ἐξήκοντος ἤδη χρόνου ἔδωκεν Ἀλέξανδρος μόνον,
ἀλλὰ καὶ τοῦ ἐς τὴν ἀπονόστησιν τὴν οἴκαδε ξυμ-
2 βαίνοντος. ἐπέδωκεν δὲ καὶ τάλαντον ἑκάστῳ
ὑπὲρ τὴν μισθοφοράν· παῖδες δὲ εἴ τῳ ἦσαν ἐκ
τῶν Ἀσιανῶν γυναικῶν, παρὰ οἷ καταλιπεῖν
ἐκέλευσε μηδὲ στάσιν κατάγειν ἐς Μακεδονίαν
ἀλλοφύλους τε καὶ ἐκ τῶν βαρβάρων γυναικῶν
παῖδας τοῖς οἴκοι ὑπολελειμμένοις παισί τε καὶ
μητράσιν αὐτῶν· αὐτὸς δὲ ἐπιμελήσεσθαι ὡς ἐκτρέ-
φοιντο Μακεδονικῶς τά τε ἄλλα καὶ ἐς τὰ πολέμια

---

6 The Macedonians enjoy precedence.
7 Presumably Greeks and non-Persian Orientals.
8 Here 'Macedonians' doubtless includes Greek Compan-

324
B.C.

this Alexander sacrificed to the gods to whom it was his custom to sacrifice, and gave a public banquet, seated all the Macedonians round him, and next to them Persians,[6] and then any persons from the other peoples who took precedence for rank or any other high quality,[7] and he himself and those around him drank from the same bowl and poured the same libations, with the Greek soothsayers and Magi initiating the ceremony. Alexander prayed for 9 various blessings and especially that the Macedonians and Persians should enjoy harmony as partners in the government.[8] The story prevails that those who shared the banquet were nine thousand, and that they all poured the same libation and gave the one victory cry as they did so.[9]

12. And now such of the Macedonians as were unfit for service from old age or any other circumstance were ready to leave him; they numbered about ten thousand.[1] Alexander gave them the pay due not only for the time already served but also for that of their journey home; in addition he also gave each man a gratuity of a Talent. If they had children 2 by Asian wives, he ordered them to leave them behind with him, and not take home to Macedonia a source of conflict between foreigners and children of foreign wives and the children and mothers they had left behind them; he promised personally to see that they were brought up in the Macedonian way, particularly in military training; when they were grown to man-

ions (e.g. *Ind.* 18, 4 and 10) and ' Persians ' includes non-Persian notables like Roxane's father. Tarn, App. 25, was refuted by Badian, *Historia* 1958, 425 ff., cf. Bosworth, *JHS* 1980, 2 ff.

[9] Vulgate?

[1] App. XIX 8.

ARRIAN

κοσμούμενοι, γενομένους δὲ ἄνδρας ἄξειν αὐτὸς ἐς
3 Μακεδονίαν καὶ παραδώσειν τοῖς πατράσιν. ταῦτά
τε ἀπαλλαττομένοις ἀστάθμητα καὶ ἀτέκμαρτα
ἐπηγγέλλετο, καὶ ὅπως ἔχει φιλίας τε καὶ πόθου ἐς
αὐτοὺς τὸ ἀτρεκέσατον τεκμήριον ἐκεῖνο ποιεῖσθαι
ἠξίου, ὅτι τὸν πιστότατόν τε αὐτῷ καὶ ὅντινα
ἴσον τῇ ἑαυτοῦ κεφαλῇ ἄγει, Κρατερόν, ξυμπέμπει
αὐτοῖς φύλακά τε καὶ ἡγεμόνα τοῦ στόλου. οὕτω
δὴ ἀσπασάμενος ξύμπαντας αὐτός τε δακρύων καὶ
4 δακρύοντας ἐκείνους ἀπὸ οὗ ἀπήλλαξε. Κρατερῷ
δὲ τούτους τε ἄγειν ἐκέλευσε καὶ ἀπαγαγόντι
Μακεδονίας τε καὶ Θρᾴκης καὶ Θετταλῶν ἐξηγεῖσθαι καὶ τῶν Ἑλλήνων τῆς ἐλευθερίας· Ἀντίπατρον
δὲ διαδόχους τοῖς ἀποπεμπομένοις ἄγειν Μακεδόνας
τῶν ἀκμαζόντων ἐκέλευσεν. ἔστειλε δὲ καὶ Πολυ-
πέρχοντα ὁμοῦ τῷ Κρατερῷ, δεύτερον δὲ ἀπὸ
Κρατεροῦ ἡγεμόνα, ὡς εἴ τι κατὰ πορείαν Κρατερῷ
συμπίπτοι, ὅτι καὶ μαλακῶς τὸ σῶμα ἔχοντα
ἀπέπεμπεν αὐτόν, μὴ ποθῆσαι στρατηγὸν τοὺς
ἰόντας.
5 Λόγος δέ τις οὗτος ἐφοίτα ἀφανὴς παρὰ τοῖς τὰ
βασιλικὰ πράγατα, ὅσῳ ἐπικρύπτεται, τοσῷδε
φιλοτιμότερον ἐξηγουμένοις, καὶ τὸ πιστὸν ἐς τὸ
χεῖρον μᾶλλον, ἢ τὸ εἰκός τε καὶ ἡ αὐτῶν μοχθηρία
ἄγει, ἢ πρὸς τὸ ἀληθὲς ἐκτρέπουσιν, ἐξηττώμενον
Ἀλέξανδρον ἤδη τῆς μητρὸς τῶν διαβολῶν τῶν ἐς
Ἀντίπατρον ἀπαλλάξαι ἐθέλειν ἐκ Μακεδονίας
6 Ἀντίπατρον. καὶ τυχὸν οὐκ ἐς ἀτιμίαν τὴν
Ἀντιπάτρου ἡ μετάπεμψις αὐτοῦ ἔφερεν, ἀλλ' ὡς

___
² D. 110, 3; P. 71, 5.

hood, he would take them back himself to Macedonia
and hand them over to their fathers.[2]   While making 3
these vague and uncertain promises to them at their
departure, he also thought fit to give them the most
solid proof of his love and affection for them by sending
with them Craterus, his most loyal follower, whom
he loved as dearly as his own life, to protect and lead
them on their march.   So then having bidden them
all farewell, with tears in his eyes, and tears in theirs,
he dismissed them.   Craterus was not only appointed 4
to be their leader but, after conducting them back, he
was to take charge of Macedonia, Thrace, Thessaly
and the freedom of the Greeks,[3] while Antipater was
to bring drafts of Macedonians of full age to replace
the men being sent home.   He also despatched Polyperchon with Craterus, as the officer next in seniority
to Craterus, so that in case of harm coming to
Craterus on the way, since he was an invalid when
sent off, they should not want a general on their
route.

But a story [4] was going about surreptitiously among 5
those who explain the policies of kings all the more
eagerly the more they are kept secret, and perversely
put their faith in the more sinister interpretation, to
which conjecture and their own malice lead them,
rather than in the truth: it was said that Alexander
was already a victim of his mother's calumnies about
Antipater and wished to remove him from Macedonia.   Perhaps his recall was not meant in fact to 6
disgrace him, but to prevent mutual unpleasantness

---

[3] Introd. 39.   On 4–7 see App. XXIII 10.   Plut. *Eumenes*
6, 2 (Hieronymus) says that Craterus incurred Al's displeasure
and won popularity by opposition to Al's ' Orientalizing '
(Bosworth, *JHS* 1980, 7).
    [4] A rumour going about, which Pt./Ar. sought to discredit.

μή τι ἐκ τῆς διαφορᾶς αὐτοῖς γένοιτο ἄχαρι ἐς
ἀλλήλους καὶ οὐδὲ αὐτῷ ἰάσιμον. ἐπεὶ οὐδὲ ἐπαύ-
οντο Ἀλεξάνδρῳ γράφοντες ὁ μὲν τὴν αὐθάδειάν
τε τῆς Ὀλυμπιάδος καὶ ὀξύτητα καὶ πολυπραγμο-
σύνην, ἥκιστα δὴ τῇ Ἀλεξάνδρου μητρὶ εὐσχήμονα,
ὥστε καὶ λόγος τις τοιόσδε ἐφέρετο Ἀλεξάνδρου
ἐφ᾽ οἷς ὑπὲρ τῆς μητρὸς αὐτῷ ἐξηγγέλλετο, βαρὺ δὴ
τὸ ἐνοίκιον τῶν δέκα μηνῶν εἰσπράττεσθαι αὐτοῦ
7   τὴν μητέρα· ἡ δέ, ὑπέρογκον εἶναι τῇ τε ἀξιώσει
καὶ τῇ ἄλλῃ θεραπείᾳ Ἀντίπατρον οὐδὲ μεμνῆσθαι
τοῦ καταστήσαντος ἔτι, ἀλλ᾽ αὐτὸν γὰρ ἀξιοῦν τὰ
πρῶτα φέρεσθαι ἐν τοῖς ἄλλοις Μακεδόσι τε καὶ
Ἕλλησι. καὶ ταῦτα μᾶλλόν τι ἰσχύειν παρ᾽ Ἀλεξάνδρῳ ἐφαίνετο ὅσα ἐς τοῦ Ἀντιπάτρου τὴν δια-
βολὴν φέροντα ἦν, οἷα δὴ καὶ φοβερώτερα ἐν
βασιλείᾳ ὄντα. οὐ μέντοι καταφανές γέ τι ἢ
ἔργον ἢ λόγος ἐξηγγέλλετο Ἀλεξάνδρου ἐφ᾽ ὅτῳ
ἄν τις συνέθηκεν οὐχ ὡσαύτως εἶναι αὐτῷ πρὸς
θυμοῦ Ἀντίπατρον . . . .

. . . . Ἡφαιστίων.

13. Τούτῳ τῷ λόγῳ ὑποπτήξαντα Ἡφαιστίωνα
συναλλαγῆναι Εὐμενεῖ, οὐχ ἑκόντα ἑκόντι. ἐν ταύτῃ
τῇ ὁδῷ καὶ τὸ πεδίον λέγεται ἰδεῖν Ἀλέξανδρον
τὸ ἀνειμένον ταῖς ἵπποις ταῖς βασιλικαῖς, αὐτό τε
πεδίον Νησαῖον καλούμενον καὶ αἱ ἵπποι ὅτι
Νησαῖαι κληΐζονται λέγει Ἡρόδοτος· εἶναι δὲ
πάλαι μὲν ἐς πεντεκαίδεκα μυριάδας τῶν ἵππων,
τότε δὲ Ἀλέξανδρον οὐ πολὺ πλείονας τῶν πέντε

---

[5] D. 118, 1. A's source claimed to know only the general

arising out of their disagreement, beyond Alexander's own ability to heal. In fact they never ceased writing letters to Alexander: Antipater would describe the headstrong nature of Olympias, her sharp temper and interfering ways, most unfitting to the mother of Alexander, so that a remark was even imputed to Alexander in reference to the accounts of his mother's doings, to the effect that she was exacting a heavy price from him for housing him for ten months, while 7 Olympias accused Antipater of being swollen with dignity and the court paid to him and of forgetting who had appointed him and claiming for himself pre-eminence among the other Macedonians and Greeks.[5] And it appeared that these charges were gaining force with Alexander, tending as they did to discredit Antipater, since they were of just the kind to inspire apprehension in a monarchy. And yet no overt act or word was recorded of Alexander which might have led one to conclude that Antipater was not as high as ever in his regard . . .[6]

13. It is said that Hephaestion was prevailed on by this argument to make up his quarrel with Eumenes, though with a reluctance Eumenes did not share.[1] It was on this journey that Alexander is said to have also seen the plain in which the royal mares were pastured; the plain itself was called the Nesaean and the horses Nesaean, as Herodotus tells us; and there were originally about a hundred and fifty thousand mares, but at that time Alexander found no more

tenor of the letters; no allusion to the spurious collection (Introd. 15).
[6] For the lacuna see App. XXIII 8 f.
[1] Not necessarily from 'vulgate,' cf. 14, 9.

καταλαβεῖν· πρὸς λῃστῶν γὰρ διαρπαγῆναι τὰς πολλὰς αὐτῶν.

2 Ἐνταῦθα λέγουσιν ὅτι Ἀτροπάτης ὁ τῆς Μηδίας σατράπης γυναῖκας ἑκατὸν αὐτῷ ἔδωκεν, ταύτας φάσκων εἶναι τῶν Ἀμαζόνων, καὶ ταύτας σκευῇ ἀνδρῶν ἱππέων ἐσταλμένας, πλήν γε δὴ ὅτι πελέκεις ἀντὶ δοράτων ἐφόρουν καὶ ἀντὶ ἀσπίδων πέλτας· οἱ δὲ καὶ τὸν μαστὸν λέγουσιν ὅτι μείονα εἶχον τὸν δεξιόν, ὃν δὴ καὶ ἔξω εἶχον ἐν ταῖς μά-
3 χαις. ταύτας μὲν δὴ ἀπαλλάξαι τῆς στρατιᾶς Ἀλέξανδρον, μή τι νεωτερισθείη κατ' αὐτὰς ἐς ὕβριν πρὸς τῶν Μακεδόνων ἢ βαρβάρων· κελεῦσαι δὲ ἀπαγγεῖλαι πρὸς τὴν βασίλισσαν σφῶν ὅτι αὐτὸς ἥξει πρὸς αὐτὴν παιδοποιησόμενος. ταῦτα δὲ οὔτε Ἀριστόβουλος οὔτε Πτολεμαῖος οὔτε τις ἄλλος ἀνέγραψεν ὅστις ἱκανὸς ὑπὲρ τῶν τηλικούτων
4 τεκμηριῶσαι. οὐδὲ δοκεῖ μοι ἐν τῷ τότε σώζεσθαι τὸ γένος τῶν Ἀμαζόνων, οὐδ' ἔτι πρὸ Ἀλεξάνδρου, ἢ Ξενοφῶν ἂν ἐμνήσθη αὐτῶν, Φασιανῶν τε μνησθεὶς καὶ Κόλχων καὶ ὅσα ἄλλα ἀπὸ Τραπεζοῦντος ὁρμώμενοι ἢ πρὶν ἐς Τραπεζοῦντα κατελθεῖν οἱ Ἕλληνες ἐπῆλθον ἔθνη βαρβαρικά, ἵναπερ καὶ ταῖς Ἀμαζόσιν ἐντετυχήκεσαν ⟨ἄν⟩,
5 εἴπερ οὖν ἔτι ἦσαν Ἀμαζόνες. μὴ γενέσθαι μὲν γὰρ παντελῶς τὸ γένος τούτων τῶν γυναικῶν οὐ πιστὸν δοκεῖ ἔμοιγε, πρὸς τοσούτων καὶ τοιούτων ὑμνηθέν. ὡς Ἡρακλέα τε ἐπ' αὐτὰς λόγος κατέχει ὅτι ἐστάλη καὶ ζωστῆρά τινα Ἱππολύτης τῆς βασιλίσσης αὐτῶν ὅτι ἐς τὴν Ἑλλάδα ἐκόμισε, καὶ οἱ ξὺν Θησεῖ Ἀθηναῖοι ὅτι ἐπιούσας τὰς γυναῖκας ταύτας τὴν Εὐρώπην πρῶτοι μάχῃ νικήσαντες ἀνέστειλαν· καὶ γέγραπται ἡ Ἀθηναίων καὶ Ἀμα-

than fifty thousand, as most of them had been driven
off by robbers.[2]

They say that there Atropates, the satrap of Media, 2
gave him a hundred women, saying that they belonged to the Amazons; they were equipped like
cavalry troopers, except that they carried axes instead of spears, and small targets instead of shields.
Some say their right breast was smaller, and was un-
covered in battle.   According to the story [3] Alexander 3
sent them away from the army, in case they suffered
any outrage from the Macedonians or barbarian
troops, but he told them to inform their queen that
he would come to see her to get children by her.
This, however, neither Aristobulus nor Ptolemy nor
any other reliable author on such matters has attested.
Nor do I myself think that the race of Amazons sur- 4
vived at that time, or even before Alexander, or
Xenophon would have referred to them as he referred
to Phasians and Colchians and other barbarian races
which the Greeks met either when starting from
Trapezus or before they reached Trapezus, where
they certainly would have met Amazons too if any
had still remained.   And yet I do not think it credible 5
that this race of women never existed at all, as so
many eminent writers have descanted on them.   The
story prevails that Heracles was sent against them
and brought back to Greece the girdle of Hippo-
lyte their queen, and that the Athenians with Theseus
were the first to defeat these women in battle
and repel them when invading Europe; and Micon
painted the battle of the Athenians and Amazons,

---

[2] Perhaps from Ar. (App. XXVIII 22). Cf. D. 110, 6;
Hdt. iii 106; vii 40.

[3] App. XXI.

ζόνων μάχη πρὸς Μίκωνος οὐ μεῖον ἤπερ ἡ
6 Ἀθηναίων καὶ Περσῶν. καὶ Ἡροδότῳ πολλάκις
περὶ τῶν γυναικῶν τούτων πεποίηται, καὶ ὅσοι
Ἀθηναίων τοὺς ἐν πολέμῳ τελευτήσαντας λόγῳ
ἐκόσμησαν, καὶ τοῦ πρὸς Ἀμαζόνας ἔργου Ἀθηναίων ἐν τοῖς μάλιστα μνήμην ἐποιήσαντο. εἰ δὲ ἱππι-
κὰς δή τινας γυναῖκας Ἀτροπάτης ἔδειξεν Ἀλεξάνδρῳ, βαρβάρους τινὰς ἄλλας γυναῖκας ἱππεύειν
ἠσκημένας δοκῶ ὅτι ἔδειξεν ἐς τὸν λεγόμενον δὴ
τῶν Ἀμαζόνων κόσμον ἐσταλμένας.

14. Ἐν Ἐκβατάνοις δὲ θυσίαν τε ἔθυσεν Ἀλέξανδρος, ὥσπερ αὐτῷ ἐπὶ ξυμφοραῖς ἀγαθαῖς νόμος, καὶ
ἀγῶνα ἐπετέλει γυμνικόν τε καὶ μουσικόν, καὶ πότοι
αὐτῷ ἐγίνοντο παρὰ τοῖς ἑταίροις. καὶ ἐν τούτῳ
Ἡφαιστίων ἔκαμε τὸ σῶμα· ἑβδόμη τε ἡμέρα ἤδη
ἦν αὐτῷ τῆς νόσου καὶ λέγουσι τὸ μὲν στάδιον
πλῆρες εἶναι· παίδων γὰρ ἀγὼν ἦν ἐκείνῃ τῇ
ἡμέρᾳ γυμνικός· ἐπεὶ δὲ ἐξηγγέλλετο Ἀλεξάνδρῳ
ὅτι κακῶς ἔχοι Ἡφαιστίων, ὁ δὲ παρ' αὐτὸν
ἐλθὼν σπουδῇ οὐκέτι ζῶντα κατέλαβεν.

2 Ἔνθα δὴ καὶ ἄλλοι ἄλλα ἀνέγραψαν ὑπὲρ τοῦ
πένθους τοῦ Ἀλεξάνδρου· μέγα μὲν γενέσθαι
αὐτῷ τὸ πένθος, πάντες τοῦτο ἀνέγραψαν, τὰ δὲ
πραχθέντα ἐπ' αὐτῷ ἄλλοι ἄλλα, ὡς ἕκαστος ἢ
εὐνοίας πρὸς Ἡφαιστίωνα ἢ φθόνου εἶχεν ἢ καὶ
3 πρὸς αὐτὸν Ἀλέξανδρον. ὧν οἱ τὰ ἀτάσθαλα
ἀναγράψαντες οἱ μὲν ἐς κόσμον φέρει⟨ν⟩ μοι
δοκοῦσιν οἰηθῆναι Ἀλεξάνδρῳ ὅσα ὑπεραλγήσας
ἔδρασεν ἢ εἶπεν ἐπὶ τῷ πάντων δὴ ἀνθρώπων

---

[1] Perhaps Pt./Ar., though Ar. will hardly have mentioned
the drinking bouts (29, 4), for which see the hostile accounts

just as he did the battle of the Greeks and Persians.
Then Herodotus often mentions them, and all the   6
Athenians who pronounced eulogies on the war-dead
specially commemorated the Athenian action against
the Amazons.   But if Atropates did show Alexander
any women riders on horse, I think they were some
other barbarian women taught to ride, whom he ex-
hibited, dressed in the traditional Amazon fashion.

14. At Ecbatana [Hamadan] Alexander offered a
sacrifice, as he usually did after some successful event,
and held athletic and musical games and drinking
bouts with the Companions.   At this time Hephaestion fell ill, and his illness had run seven days, they
say,[1] when the race-course was filled with people, as
there were athletic sports that day for boys; but
when Alexander heard that Hephaestion was seriously ill, he left the course and hurried to him, but
found him no longer living.

At this point indeed historians have given varied   2
accounts of Alexander's grief.   That it was great,
all have related; as to the actions it occasioned, they
differ according to the good-will or malice each felt
towards Hephaestion or even towards Alexander
himself.   The writers who have recounted his ex-   3
cesses appear to me to have thought either that anything redounds to Alexander's credit that he did or
said in extremity of grief for the dearest of his

of Ephippus (iii 5, 3 n.; App. XIV 2) and Nicobule (Jacoby
nos. 126 f.).   Pt./Ar. must be among the authorities cited in §
7 f., cf. 23, 6 n.   Cf. D. 110, 7 f. and 114; P. 72 (with Hamilton's notes) and Tarn ii 4, 57 and 78 on the multiplicity of
variants.   Al's irrational grief was a count against him for
Stoics (Seneca, *ep.* 113, 29), not for A.   Hephaestion: App.
XXIV 4.

ARRIAN

φιλτάτῳ, οἱ δὲ ἐς αἰσχύνην μᾶλλόν τι ὡς οὐ πρέ-
ποντα οὔτ' οὖν βασιλεῖ οὔτε Ἀλεξάνδρῳ, οἱ μέν, τὸ
πολὺ μέρος τῆς ἡμέρας ἐκείνης ἐρριμμένον ἐπὶ τοῦ
σώματος τοῦ ἑταίρου ὀδύρεσθαι οὐδ' ἐθέλειν ἀπαλλαγῆναι, πρίν γε δὴ πρὸς βίαν ἀπηνέχθη πρὸς τῶν
4 ἑταίρων· οἱ δέ, τήν τε ἡμέραν ὅλην καὶ τὴν νύκτα
ὅλην ἐρρῖφθαι ἐπὶ τῷ σώματι· οἱ δὲ καί, τὸν ἰατρὸν
Γλαυκίαν ὅτι ἐκρέμασε, καὶ τοῦτο[ν] ὡς ἐπὶ
φαρμάκῳ κακῶς δοθέντι, οἱ δέ, ὅτι οἴνου περιεῖδεν
ἐμπλησθέντα θεωρῶν αὐτός· καὶ κείρασθαι Ἀλέξανδρον ἐπὶ τῷ νεκρῷ τὴν κόμην τά τε ἄλλα οὐκ
ἀπεικότα τίθεμαι καὶ κατὰ ζῆλον τὸν Ἀχιλλέως,
5 πρὸς ὅντινα ἐκ παιδὸς φιλοτιμία αὐτῷ ἦν· οἱ δὲ
καί, τὸ ἅρμα ἐφ' ὅτῳ τὸ σῶμα ἐφέρετο αὐτὸς
ἔστιν ὅτε ⟨ὅτι⟩ ἡνιόχει, τοῦτο οὐδαμῇ πιστὸν
ἔμοιγε λέγοντες· ἄλλοι δέ, ὅτι καὶ τοῦ Ἀσκληπιοῦ
τὸ ἕδος ἐν Ἐκβατάνοις κατασκάψαι ἐκέλευσε,
βαρβαρικὸν τοῦτό γε καὶ οὐδαμῇ Ἀλεξάνδρῳ πρόσ-
φορον, ἀλλὰ τῇ Ξέρξου μᾶλλόν τι ἀτασθαλίᾳ τῇ ἐς
τὸ θεῖον καὶ ταῖς πέδαις ἃς λέγουσιν ἐς τὸν Ἑλλήσποντον καθεῖναι Ξέρξην, τιμωρούμενον δῆθεν
6 τὸν Ἑλλήσποντον. ἀλλὰ καὶ ἐκεῖνο οὐ πάντῃ ἔξω
τοῦ εἰκότος ἀναγεγράφθαι μοι δοκεῖ, ὡς ἐπὶ Βαβυλῶνος ἤλαυνεν Ἀλέξανδρος, ἐντυχεῖν αὐτῷ κατὰ
τὴν ὁδὸν πολλὰς πρεσβείας ἀπὸ τῆς Ἑλλάδος,
εἶναι δὲ δὴ ἐν τούτοις Ἐπιδαυρίων πρέσβεις· καὶ
τούτους ὧν τε ἐδέοντο ἐξ Ἀλεξάνδρου τυχεῖν καὶ
ἀνάθημα δοῦναι αὐτοῖς Ἀλέξανδρον κομίζειν τῷ
Ἀσκληπιῷ, ἐπειπόντα ὅτι· καίπερ οὐκ ἐπιεικῶς

---

[2] As disreputable for Al. as for Nero (Tacitus, *Annals* xv
67)!

friends, or that all was to his discredit, since it was not becoming either for a king or for Alexander. Some say that for the greater part of that day he lay prostrate and weeping on his companion's body and would not be parted, till he was actually carried away by the Companions, others that he lay prostrate on the body all day and all night, others again that he hanged Glaucias the doctor, and that for a drug wrongly given, or alternatively because Glaucias had seen Hephaestion drinking most immoderately and had not stopped him. I regard it as not unlikely that Alexander cut off his hair over the corpse, especially considering his emulation of Achilles, with whom he had a rivalry from boyhood. Some add that Alexander himself for a time drove the car in which the body was borne, but I regard this statement as quite incredible.[2] Yet others tell us that he ordered the temple of Asclepius [3] at Ecbatana to be razed to the ground, but this would have been barbaric, and not at all characteristic of Alexander, but more suitable to Xerxes' presumption towards heaven and the fetters they say he let down into the Hellespont, in the belief he could punish it.[4] But there is also a story recorded which I think not wholly beyond the bounds of likelihood, that when Alexander was going to Babylon many emissaries from Greece met him on the way, including Epidaurian envoys; they obtained from Alexander what they sued for, and Alexander gave them a votive offering to take back to Asclepius, adding: ' Yet Asclepius has not been

---

[3] In the story some native god was identified with Asclepius, perhaps because his cult included incubation. Epictetus had heard that Al. ordered all temples of Asclepius to be burned (ii 22, 17).

[4] Hdt. vii 34 f.

κέχρηταί μοι ὁ Ἀσκληπιός, οὐ σώσας μοι τὸν
ἑταῖρον ὄντινα ἴσον τῇ ἐμαυτοῦ κεφαλῇ ἦγον.

7 ἐναγίζειν τε ὅτι ἀεὶ ἥρωϊ ἐκέλευεν Ἡφαιστίωνι,
τοῦτο μὲν πρὸς τῶν πλείστων ἀναγέγραπται· οἱ
δὲ λέγουσιν ὅτι καὶ εἰς Ἄμμωνος ἔπεμψεν ἐρησομένους τὸν θεὸν εἰ καὶ ὡς θεῷ θύειν συγχωρεῖ
Ἡφαιστίωνι, τὸν δὲ οὐ ξυγχωρῆσαι.

8 Ἐκεῖνα δὲ πρὸς πάντων ξυμφωνούμενα, ἐς τρίτην ἀπὸ τοῦ θανάτου τοῦ Ἡφαιστίωνος ἡμέραν
μήτε σίτου γεύσασθαι Ἀλέξανδρον μήτε τινὰ
θεραπείαν ἄλλην θεραπεῦσαι τὸ σῶμα, ἀλλὰ κεῖσθαι γὰρ ἢ ὀδυρόμενον ἢ πενθικῶς σιγῶντα· καὶ
πυρὰν κελεῦσαι αὐτῷ ἑτοιμάζεσθαι ἐν Βαβυλῶνι
ἀπὸ ταλάντων μυρίων, οἱ δὲ καὶ πλειόνων ἀνέγρα-

9 ψαν· καὶ ὅτι πένθος ποιεῖσθαι περιηγγέλη κατὰ
πᾶσαν τὴν χώραν τὴν βάρβαρον· καὶ ὅτι πολλοὶ τῶν
ἑταίρων τῶν Ἀλεξάνδρου ἐς θεραπείαν τὴν ἐκείνου
σφᾶς τε αὐτοὺς καὶ τὰ ὅπλα Ἡφαιστίωνι ἀνέθε-
σαν ἀποθανόντι· πρῶτον δὲ Εὐμενῆ ἄρξαι τοῦ
σοφίσματος, ὅντινα ὀλίγῳ πρόσθεν ἔφαμεν ὅτι διη-
νέχθη πρὸς Ἡφαιστίωνα· καὶ τοῦτο δὲ δρᾶσαι, τῷ
Ἀλεξάνδρῳ ὡς μὴ ἐφήδεσθαι δοκοίη τελευτήσαντι

10 Ἡφαιστίωνι. οὔκουν οὐδὲ ἄλλον τινὰ ἔταξεν ἀντὶ
Ἡφαιστίωνος χιλίαρχον ἐπὶ τῇ ἵππῳ τῇ ἑταιρικῇ
Ἀλέξανδρος, ὡς μὴ ἀπόλοιτο τὸ ὄνομα τοῦ Ἡφαιστίωνος ἐκ τῆς τάξεως, ἀλλὰ Ἡφαιστίωνός τε ἡ
χιλιαρχία ἐκαλεῖτο καὶ τὸ σημεῖον αὐτῆς ἡγεῖτο
⟨τὸ⟩ ἐξ Ἡφαιστίωνος πεποιημένον. ἀγῶνά τε
ἐπενόει ποιῆσαι γυμνικόν τε καὶ μουσικὸν πλήθει
τε τῶν ἀγωνιζομένων καὶ τῇ εἰς αὐτὸν χορηγίᾳ
πολύ τι τῶν ἄλλων τῶν πρόσθεν ἀριδηλότερον·

kind to me, in failing to save for me the comrade whom I valued as much as my life.' Most authorities 7 have recorded that he ordered that the kind of sacrifice appropriate to a hero should always be offered to Hephaestion; some say that he sent to the oracle of Ammon to enquire of the god if he permitted Hephaestion to receive the kind of sacrifice appropriate to a god, but that the oracle refused permission.

The following, however, harmonizes in all accounts, 8 that for two days after Hephaestion's death Alexander tasted no food and took no care of his body, but lay either moaning or in a sorrowful silence, that he ordered a pyre to be made ready for him in Babylon at a cost of ten thousand Talents (by some accounts, even more) [5] and commanded mourning throughout 9 the whole barbarian country; and that many of Alexander's Companions in respect for him dedicated themselves and their arms to the dead Hephaestion; and that the first to initiate this expedient was Eumenes, of whose quarrel with Hephaestion we spoke a little earlier, and that he did this to prevent Alexander thinking that he rejoiced at Hephaestion's death. At any rate Alexander never appointed any- 10 one in place of Hephaestion as chiliarch over the Companions' cavalry, so that the name of Hephaestion might never be lost to the unit; the chiliarchy was still called Hephaestion's, and the standard went before it which had been made by his order. Alexander also planned athletic and musical games far more splendid than any before in the number of competitions and the cost of production; he provided

---

[5] Details in D. 115.

τρισχιλίους γὰρ ἀγωνιστὰς τοὺς σύμπαντας παρε-
σκεύασε. καὶ οὗτοι ὀλίγον ὕστερον ἐπ' Ἀλεξάνδρου
τῷ τάφῳ λέγουσιν ὅτι ἠγωνίσαντο.

15. Χρόνος τε ἦν συχνὸς τῷ πένθει καὶ αὐτός
τε αὐτὸν ἤδη μετεκάλει ἀπ' αὐτοῦ καὶ οἱ ἑταῖροι
μᾶλλόν τι ἐν τῷ τοιῷδε ἤνυτον. ἔνθα δὴ ἐξέλασιν
ποιεῖται ἐπὶ Κοσσαίους, ἔθνος πολεμικὸν ὅμορον
2 τῷ Οὐξίων. εἰσὶ δὲ ὄρειοι οἱ Κοσσαῖοι καὶ χωρία
ὀχυρὰ κατὰ κώμας νέμονται, ὁπότε προσάγοι
δύναμις ἐς τὰ ἄκρα τῶν ὀρῶν ἀποχωροῦντες
ἀθρόοι ἢ ὅπως ἂν προχωρῇ ἑκάστοις οὕτω
διαφεύγουσιν, ἐς ἀπορίαν βάλλοντες τοὺς ξὺν
δυνάμει σφίσιν ἐπιχειροῦντας· ἀπελθόντων δὲ
αὖθις εἰς τὸ λῃστεύειν τρεπόμενοι ἀπὸ τούτου τὸν
3 βίον ποιοῦνται. Ἀλέξανδρος δὲ ἐξεῖλεν αὐτῶν τὸ
ἔθνος καίπερ χειμῶνος στρατεύσας. ἀλλ' οὔτε
⟨ὁ⟩ χειμὼν ἐμποδὼν ἐγένετο αὐτῷ οὔτε αἱ δυσ-
χωρίαι, οὔτε αὐτῷ οὔτε Πτολεμαίῳ τῷ Λάγου,
ὃς μέρος τῆς στρατιᾶς ἐπ' αὐτοὺς ἦγεν. οὕτως
οὐδὲν ἄπορον Ἀλεξάνδρῳ τῶν πολεμικῶν ἦν ἐς ὅ
τι ὁρμήσειε.

4 Κατιόντι δὲ αὐτῷ ἐς Βαβυλῶνα Λιβύων τε πρεσβεῖαι ἐνετύγχανον ἐπαινούντων τε καὶ στεφανούντων ἐπὶ τῇ βασιλείᾳ τῆς Ἀσίας, καὶ ἐξ Ἰταλίας
Βρέττιοί τε καὶ Λευκανοὶ καὶ Τυρρηνοὶ ἐπὶ τοῖς
αὐτοῖς ἐπρέσβευον. καὶ Καρχηδονίους τότε πρεσ-
βεῦσαι λέγεται καὶ ἀπὸ Αἰθιόπων πρέσβεις ἐλθεῖν
καὶ Σκυθῶν τῶν ἐκ τῆς Εὐρώπης, καὶ Κελτοὺς καὶ
Ἴβηρας, ὑπὲρ φιλίας δεησομένους· ὧν τά τε ὀνόματα καὶ τὰς σκευὰς τότε πρῶτον ὀφθῆναι πρὸς

---

[6] Pt./Ar. Chiliarchy: App. XXIV 4.

three thousand performers in all.⁶ Those were the men, it is said, who competed a little later at Alexander's burial.

15. A long time passed in mourning before at last Alexander began to recall his own energies from it; the Companions were more successful in such efforts. It was now then that he made an expedition against the Cossaeans,¹ a warlike race bordering on the Uxians. These Cossaeans are mountaineers, and dwell in village strongholds; whenever a force drew near, they would move off in mass, or each as best he could, to the summits of the mountains, and thereby escape, baffling those who assailed them by force. When the enemy had gone, they would again turn to the brigandage from which they make their livelihood. But Alexander reduced the tribe, although he campaigned in winter. Neither the wintry season nor the difficulties of the country stood in his way; not in his, nor in that of Ptolemy son of Lagus, who led part of the army against them. In fact Alexander found nothing impossible in any military operations he undertook.²

As he was going down to Babylon embassies ³ from the Libyans met him, congratulating him and offering him a crown on his becoming king of Asia; from Italy also Bruttians, Lucanians and Etruscans sent envoys for the same purpose. It is said that the Carthaginians sent envoys at this time, and that others came from Ethiopia and the European Scyths, and Celts and Iberians, to ask for his friendship, and that it was then that Greeks and Macedonians first came to be acquainted with their names and appearances.

---

¹ *Ind.* 40, 6–8; P. 72, **3**; D. 111, 5 f.
² Pt's comment?
³ App. XXII. For Carthage cf. Bosworth on ii 24, 5.

5 Ἑλλήνων τε καὶ Μακεδόνων. τοὺς δὲ καὶ ὑπὲρ
τῶν ἐς ἀλλήλους διαφορῶν λέγουσιν ὅτι Ἀλεξάνδρῳ
διακρῖναι ἐπέτρεπον· καὶ τότε μάλιστα αὐτόν τε
αὐτῷ Ἀλέξανδρον καὶ τοῖς ἀμφ' αὐτὸν φανῆναι γῆς
τε ἁπάσης καὶ θαλάσσης κύριον. Ἄριστος δὲ καὶ
Ἀσκληπιάδης τῶν τὰ Ἀλεξάνδρου ἀναγραψάντων
καὶ Ῥωμαίους λέγουσιν ὅτι ἐπρέσβευσαν· καὶ
ἐντυχόντα ταῖς πρεσβείαις Ἀλέξανδρον ὑπὲρ
Ῥωμαίων τι τῆς ἐς τὸ ἔπειτα ἐσομένης δυνάμεως
μαντεύσασθαι, τόν τε κόσμον τῶν ἀνδρῶν ἰδόντα
καὶ τὸ φιλόπονόν τε καὶ ἐλευθέριον καὶ περὶ τοῦ
6 πολιτεύματος ἅμα διαπυνθανόμενον. καὶ τοῦτο
οὔτε ὡς ἀτρεκὲς οὔτε ὡς ἄπιστον πάντῃ ἀνέγραψα·
πλήν γε δὴ οὔτε τις Ῥωμαίων ὑπὲρ τῆς πρεσβείας
ταύτης ὡς παρὰ Ἀλέξανδρον σταλείσης μνήμην
τινὰ ἐποιήσατο, οὔτε τῶν τὰ Ἀλεξάνδρου γραψάν-
των, οἷστισι μᾶλλον ἐγὼ ξυμφέρομαι, Πτολεμαῖος ὁ Λάγου καὶ Ἀριστόβουλος· οὐδὲ τῷ
Ῥωμαίων πολιτεύματι ἐπεοικὸς ἦν ἐλευθέρῳ δὴ
τότε ἐς τὰ μάλιστα ὄντι, παρὰ βασιλέα ἀλλόφυλον
ἄλλως τε καὶ ἐς τοσόνδε ἀπὸ τῆς οἰκείας πρεσ-
βεῦσαι, οὔτε φόβου ἐξαναγκάζοντος οὔτε κατ' ἐλπίδα
ὠφελείας, μίσει τε, εἴπερ τινὰς ἄλλους, τοῦ τυραν-
νικοῦ γένους τε καὶ ὀνόματος κατεχομένους.

16. Ἐκ τούτου δὴ Ἡρακλείδην τὸν Ἀργαίου
ἐκπέμπει ἐς Ὑρκανίαν ναυπηγοὺς ἅμα οἷ ἄγοντα,
κελεύσας ὕλην τεμόντα ἐκ τῶν ὀρῶν τῶν Ὑρκανίων
ναυπηγεῖσθαι ναῦς μακρὰς ἀφράκτους τε καὶ
2 πεφραγμένας ἐς τὸν κόσμον τὸν Ἑλληνικόν. πόθος
γὰρ εἶχεν αὐτὸν καὶ ταύτην ἐκμαθεῖν τὴν θάλασσαν
τὴν Κασπίαν τε καὶ Ὑρκανίαν καλουμένην ποίᾳ
τινὶ ξυμβάλλει θαλάσσῃ, πότερα τῇ τοῦ πόντου τοῦ
Εὐξείνου ἢ ἀπὸ τῆς ἑῴας τῆς κατ' Ἰνδοὺς ἐκπερι-

Some, it is said, even appealed to Alexander to arbitrate in their differences with each other, and it was then more than ever that both in his own estimation and in that of his entourage Alexander appeared to be master of every land and sea. Aristus and Asclepiades among the historians of Alexander say that even the Romans sent envoys, and that when Alexander met their embassy he prognosticated something of their future power on observing their orderliness, industry and freedom, and at the same time investigating their constitution. This I have recorded as neither true nor wholly incredible, except that no Roman ever referred to this embassy sent to Alexander, nor did the historians of Alexander whom I prefer to follow, Ptolemy son of Lagus and Aristobulus; nor was it suitable for the Roman government, at a time when it enjoyed freedom in the highest degree, to send envoys to a foreign king, especially so far from their own home, without the compulsion of fear or the hope of advantage, given that no other people was so possessed by hatred of despotism and its very name.

16. After this Alexander sent Heraclides son of Argaeus to Hyrcania with shipwrights, with orders to cut wood from the Hyrcanian mountains and build warships, both decked and open, in the Greek style. For he was seized with a longing [1] to discover what other sea is joined by this sea, called both Caspian and Hyrcanian, whether it joins the Euxine, or whether on the east side towards India the great sea

---

[1] App. V 3, *Ind.* 20, 2 n. Geographical problem: App. XII. 'Jaxartes' is not certain (critical note on § 3).

ἐρχομένη ἡ μεγάλη θάλασσα ἀνακεῖται εἰς κόλπον
τὸν Ὑρκάνιον, καθάπερ οὖν καὶ τὸν Περσικὸν
ἐξεῦρε, τὴν Ἐρυθρὰν δὴ καλουμένην θάλασσαν,
3 κόλπον οὖσαν τῆς μεγάλης θαλάσσης. οὐ γάρ πω
ἐξεύρηντο αἱ ἀρχαὶ τῆς Κασπίας θαλάσσης, καίτοι
ἐθνῶν τε αὐτὴν ⟨περι⟩οικούντων οὐκ ὀλίγων καὶ
ποταμῶν πλοΐμων ἐμβαλλόντων ἐς αὐτήν· ἐκ
Βάκτρων μὲν Ὦξος, μέγιστος τῶν Ἀσιανῶν
ποταμῶν, πλήν γε δὴ τῶν Ἰνδῶν, ἐξίησιν ἐς
ταύτην τὴν θάλασσαν, διὰ Σκυθῶν δὲ Ἰαξάρτης [1].
καὶ τὸν Ἀράξην δὲ τὸν ἐξ Ἀρμενίων ῥέοντα ἐς
4 ταύτην ἐσβάλλειν ὁ πλείων λόγος κατέχει. μέγιστοι
μὲν οὗτοι· πολλοὶ δὲ δὴ καὶ ἄλλοι ἔς τε τούτους
ἐμβάλλοντες καὶ αὐτοὶ ἐπὶ σφῶν ἐς τὴν θάλασσαν
ταύτην ἐξιᾶσιν, οἱ μὲν καὶ γινωσκόμενοι πρὸς τῶν
ἀμφ' Ἀλέξανδρον ἐπελθόντων τὰ ἔθνη ταῦτα, οἱ δὲ
κατὰ τὰ ἐπέκεινα τοῦ κόλπου, ὡς εἰκός, κατὰ τοὺς
Σκύθας τοὺς Νομάδας, ὃ δὴ ἄγνωστον πάντῃ ἐστίν.
5 Ἀλέξανδρος δὲ ὡς τὸν Τίγρητα ποταμὸν ξὺν τῇ
στρατιᾷ διέβη ἐλαύνων ἐπὶ Βαβυλῶνος, ἐνταῦθα ἐν-
τυγχάνουσιν αὐτῷ Χαλδαίων οἱ λόγιοι, καὶ ἀπαγαγ-
όντες ἀπὸ τῶν ἑταίρων ἐδέοντο ἐπισχεῖν τὴν ἐπὶ
Βαβυλῶνος ἔλασιν. λόγιον γὰρ γεγονέναι σφίσιν

---

[1] Blancard: Ὀξυαρτής A. Cf. App. XII.

---

[2] A. no doubt held that E. had shown the Caspian to be a
gulf of Ocean.
[3] Like Hdt. i 202 (cf. Wells *ad loc.*), Callisthenes was confused about the Arak (S. xi 14, 13); probably Ar. reported
what in his day was still only ' the majority account', which A.
repeats, as if it had not long been *known* to be true! Stadter
187 offers a lame defence.
[4] Still true in A's day.

circling round pours into a gulf, the Hyrcanian, just
as he had discovered the Persian Sea [Gulf] or, to use
its actual name, the Red Sea, to be only a gulf of the
ocean. For no one had yet discovered the sources of 3
the Caspian sea,[2] though many tribes dwell round it
and navigable rivers flow into it; from Bactria the
river Oxus, the greatest of the Asian rivers, except
for the Indian, has its outlet in this sea; so does the
Jaxartes [Syr Darya] flowing through Scythia, and
the majority account is that the Araxes flowing from
Armenia runs into this sea.[3] These are the greatest 4
rivers; many others, as their tributaries or independently, find their outlet in this sea; some of them
actually became known to Alexander and his men
when they came upon the peoples in these parts, but
probably others flowed into the gulf on its far side, in
the region of the Nomad Scythians, which is in fact
utterly unknown.[4]

When he had crossed the Tigris with his army on 5
his march towards Babylon, Alexander was met by
the Chaldaean seers, who drew him aside from the
Companions and begged him to stop the march to
Babylon; it is said [5] that they had an oracle from their

---

[5] The story in § 5 f. harmonizes with 17, 1–4, but hardly
with the advice recorded in § 6 f., which Al. tried to follow (17,
5); hence the emphatic allusion to Ar. in 17, 5 suggests that he
is *not* the source for the former story. If true, it should rest on
the authority of one in Al's counsels, either Pt. or N.   But N.
figures prominently in D. 112 (cf. P. 73, 1; J. xii 13), where
we hear nothing of Al's suspicions of the Chaldaeans, who also
tell him that he can escape by rebuilding the *tomb* (cf. S. xvi
1, 5), not the *temple* (17, 1), of Belus; this version surely goes
back to N., and A's to Pt.   The mixture of direct and indirect
speech in 5 f. suggests use of a main authority (App. XXVIII
18).   A. offers his own comments in § 7 f. (cf. perhaps ii S. xvi
vii 30, 2), which are not original (cf. D. 116, 1), recalls variants
in 17, 2 and makes a lame attempt in 17, 5 to resolve the
contradictions.

ἐκ τοῦ θεοῦ τοῦ Βήλου μὴ πρὸς ἀγαθοῦ οἱ εἶναι τὴν
6 πάροδον τὴν ἐς Βαβυλῶνα ἐν τῷ τότε. τὸν δὲ ἀπο-
κρίνασθαι αὐτοῖς λόγος τοῦ Εὐριπίδου τοῦ ποιητοῦ
ἔπος· ἔχει δὲ τὸ ἔπος Εὐριπίδη ὧδε·

Μάντις δ' ἄριστος ὅστις εἰκάζει καλῶς.

σὺ δέ, ὦ βασιλεῦ, ἔφασαν οἱ Χαλδαῖοι, μὴ πρὸς
δυσμὰς ἀφορῶν αὐτὸς μηδὲ τὴν στρατιὰν ταύτη
ἐπέχουσαν ἄγων παρελθεῖν, ἀλλὰ ἐκπεριελθὼν πρὸς
7 ἔω μᾶλλον. τῷ δὲ οὐδὲ τοῦτο εὐμαρὲς διὰ δυσ-
χωρίαν ξυνέβη· ἀλλὰ ἦγε γὰρ αὐτὸν ταύτη τὸ δαι-
μόνιον ᾗ παρελθόντα ἐχρῆν ἤδη τελευτῆσαι. καί
που τυχὸν καὶ ἄμεινον αὐτῷ ἦν ἐν ἀκμῇ τῆς τε ἄλλης
δόξης καὶ τοῦ πόθου τοῦ παρ' ἀνθρώπων ἀπηλ-
λάχθαι, πρίν τινα ξυμβῆναι αὐτῷ ξυμφορὰν ἀνθρωπίνην, ἧς ἕνεκα καὶ Σόλωνα Κροίσῳ παραινέσαι
εἰκὸς τέλος ὁρᾶν μακροῦ βίου μηδὲ πρόσθεν τινὰ
8 ἀνθρώπων ἀποφαίνειν εὐδαίμονα. ἐπεὶ καὶ αὐτῷ
Ἀλεξάνδρῳ ἡ Ἡφαιστίωνος τελευτὴ οὐ σμικρὰ
ξυμφορὰ γεγένητο, ἧς καὶ αὐτὸς Ἀλέξανδρος
προαπελθεῖν ἂν δοκεῖ μοι ἐθελῆσαι μᾶλλον ἢ ζῶν
πειραθῆναι, οὐ μεῖον ἢ καὶ Ἀχιλλέα δοκῶ ἂν ἐλέσ-
θαι προαποθανεῖν Πατρόκλου μᾶλλον ἢ τοῦ θανάτου αὐτῷ τιμωρὸν γενέσθαι.

17. Ἦν δέ τι καὶ ὕποπτον αὐτῷ ἐς τοὺς Χαλδαίους, ὡς οὐ κατὰ μαντείαν τι μᾶλλον ἢ ἐς ὠφέλειαν τὴν αὐτῶν φέροι αὐτοῖς ἡ κώλυσις τῆς Ἀλεξάνδρου ἐς Βαβυλῶνα ἐν τῷ τότε ἐλάσεως. ὁ γὰρ
τοῦ Βήλου νεὼς ἐν μέσῃ τῇ πόλει ἦν τῶν Βαβυλωνίων, μεγέθει τε μέγιστος καὶ ἐκ πλίνθου ὀπτῆς
2 ἐν ἀσφάλτῳ ἡρμοσμένης. τοῦτον τὸν νεών, ὥσπερ
καὶ τὰ ἄλλα ἱερὰ τὰ Βαβυλωνίων, Ξέρξης κατέσκαψεν, ὅτε ἐκ τῆς Ἑλλάδος ὀπίσω ἀπενόστησεν·

god Belus [Baal] that his entry into Babylon at that
time would do him harm, but that he answered them 6
with a verse of Euripides the poet; it runs thus:

The best of prophets he who guesses well.

' But, Sire,' the Chaldaeans said, ' do not yourself
look towards the setting sun, and do not enter at the
head of your army facing in that direction, but take a
detour and come in rather on the east side.' How- 7
ever, this course actually turned out not to be so easy
because of the difficulty of the country; the fact was
that divine power led him on the path which once
taken determined his immediate death. And it may
be that it was really better for him to die at the
height of his fame, when men felt most regret for him
and before any ordinary disaster befell him; it was
probably for that reason that Solon advised Croesus
to look to the end of a long life, and not to declare any
man happy till then.[6] In fact the death of Hephaes- 8
tion had proved a great misfortune to Alexander
himself, and Alexander, I believe, would have preferred to have gone first himself rather than experience it during his lifetime, just as I think Achilles
would have preferred to die before Patroclus rather
than to have been the avenger of his death.

17. He was also rather suspicious of the Chaldaeans, thinking that it might be not so much pro-
phetic skill as private advantage that made them try
to prevent his march to Babylon at that time. The
temple of Belus [Baal] was in the centre of the city
of Babylon, unequalled in size, and made of baked
brick with bitumen for mortar; like the other shrines 2
of Babylon, Xerxes had razed it to the ground when
he returned from Greece. and Alexander had it in

[6] Hdt. i 32.

Ἀλέξανδρος δὲ ἐν νῷ εἶχεν ἀνοικοδομεῖν οἱ μὲν
λέγουσιν ὅτι ἐπὶ τοῖς θεμελίοις τοῖς πρόσθεν, καὶ
τούτου ἕνεκα τὸν χοῦν ἐκφέρειν ἐκέλευε τοὺς Βα-
βυλωνίους, οἱ δέ, ὅτι καὶ μείζονα ἔτι τοῦ πάλαι ὄντος.

3 ἐπεὶ δὲ ἀποστάντος αὐτοῦ μαλθακῶς ἀνθήψαντο τοῦ
ἔργου οἷς ταῦτα ἐπετέτραπτο, ὁ δὲ τῇ στρατιᾷ πάσῃ
ἐπενόει τὸ ἔργον ἐργάσασθαι. εἶναι δὲ τῷ θεῷ τῷ
Βήλῳ πολλὴν μὲν τὴν χώραν ἀνειμένην ἐκ τῶν

4 Ἀσσυρίων βασιλέων, πολὺν δὲ χρυσόν. καὶ ἀπὸ
τούτου πάλαι μὲν τὸν νεὼν ἐπισκευάζεσθαι καὶ τὰς
θυσίας τῷ θεῷ θύεσθαι, τότε δὲ τοὺς Χαλδαίους τὰ
τοῦ θεοῦ νέμεσθαι, οὐκ ὄντος ἐς ὅ τι ἀναλωθήσεται
τὰ περιγιγνόμενα. τούτων δὴ ἕνεκα ὕποπτοι
Ἀλεξάνδρῳ ἦσαν οὐκ ἐθέλειν παρελθεῖν εἴσω Βαβυλῶνος Ἀλέξανδρον, ὡς μὴ δι' ὀλίγου τὸν νεὼν
ἐπιτελεσθέντα ἀφελέσθαι αὐτοὺς τὰς ἐκ τῶν

5 χρημάτων ὠφελείας. ὅμως δὲ τά γε τῆς ἐπιστρο-
φῆς τῆς κατὰ τὴν εἴσοδον τὴν ἐς τὴν πόλιν ἐθελῆσαι
αὐτοῖς πεισθῆναι λέγει Ἀριστόβουλος, καὶ τῇ
πρώτῃ μὲν παρὰ τὸν ποταμὸν τὸν Εὐφράτην κατα-
στρατοπεδεῦσαι, ἐς δὲ τὴν ὑστεραίαν ἐν δεξιᾷ
ἔχοντα τὸν ποταμὸν παρ' αὐτὸν πορεύεσθαι,
θέλοντα ὑπερβάλλειν τῆς πόλεως τὸ μέρος τὸ ἐς
δυσμὰς τετραμμένον, ὡς ταύτῃ ἐπιστρέψαντα

6 πρὸς ἕω ἄγειν· ἀλλὰ οὐ γὰρ δυνηθῆναι ὑπὸ
δυσχωρίας οὕτως ἐλάσαι ξὺν τῇ στρατιᾷ, ὅτι τὰ
ἀπὸ δυσμῶν τῆς πόλεως εἰσιόντι, εἰ ταύτῃ πρὸς
ἕω ἐπέστρεφεν, ἑλώδη τε καὶ τεναγώδη ἦν.
καὶ οὕτω καὶ ἑκόντα καὶ ἄκοντα ἀπειθῆσαι τῷ
θεῷ.

18. Ἐπεὶ καὶ τοιόνδε τινὰ λόγον Ἀριστόβουλος
ἀναγέγραφεν, Ἀπολλόδωρον τὸν Ἀμφιπολίτην τῶν

mind to rebuild it, some say on the original foundations, and that for this reason he ordered the
Babylonians to remove the mound of earth; others
say that he wished to make it even larger than the
old one. But since those charged with the work had 3
been slack in handling it after his departure, he
planned to complete it now with the help of his entire
army. The god Belus had a large endowment of
land and gold from the Assyrian kings, from which in 4
old times the temple was kept in repair and the
sacrifices were offered to the god, but at that time the
Chaldaeans were in enjoyment of the revenues of the
god, as there was nothing on which to spend the sur-
pluses. All this made Alexander suspect that they
did not desire him to enter Babylon, so that the rapid
completion of the temple would not deprive them of
the benefit of these moneys. However, Aristobulus 5
states that Alexander was quite ready to follow their
advice for the deviation in his entry into the city, and
that he camped the first day by the river Euphrates,
and the next day marched with the river close on his
right, in the wish to pass by the part of the city with
a western aspect, so as to wheel there and march eastward; but that he was simply unable to proceed this 6
way with his army because of the difficulty of the
ground, since anyone entering the western sector
and wheeling eastwards there found it marshy and
full of pools, so that his disobedience to the god was
both intentional and involuntary.

18. Moreover, Aristobulus records a story as
follows.[1] Apollodorus of Amphipolis, one of Alex-

---

[1] Cf. P. 73 (with other bad omens); Appian, *Civil Wars* ii
152 f. (also with parallels to 16 f. and 22; I doubt if he used
A.: contrast 149 with A. i 26; in 152 he substitutes ' Oxy-
dracan ' for ' Mallian ' town; and 154 cannot come from A.).

ἑταίρων τῶν Ἀλεξάνδρου, στρατηγὸν τῆς στρατιᾶς
ἦν παρὰ Μαζαίῳ τῷ Βαβυλῶνος σατράπῃ ἀπέλιπεν
Ἀλέξανδρος, ἐπειδὴ συνέμιξεν ἐπανιόντι αὐτῷ ἐξ
Ἰνδῶν, ὁρῶντα πικρῶς τιμωρούμενον τοὺς σατράπας ὅσοι ἐπ᾽ ἄλλῃ καὶ ἄλλῃ χώρᾳ τεταγμένοι
ἦσαν, ἐπιστεῖλαι Πειθαγόρᾳ τῷ ἀδελφῷ, μάντιν
γὰρ εἶναι τὸν Πειθαγόραν τῆς ἀπὸ σπλάγχνων
μαντείας, μαντεύσασθαι καὶ ὑπὲρ αὐτοῦ τῆς σωτη-
2 ρίας. ἀντεπιστεῖλαι δὲ αὐτῷ Πειθαγόραν πυνθανό-
μενον τίνα μάλιστα φοβούμενος χρήσασθαι ἐθέλοι
τῇ μαντείᾳ. τὸν δὲ γράψαι αὖθις ὅτι τόν τε
βασιλέα αὐτὸν καὶ Ἡφαιστίωνα. θύεσθαι δὴ τὸν
Πειθαγόραν πρῶτα μὲν ἐπὶ τῷ Ἡφαιστίωνι· ὡς
δὲ ἐπὶ τοῦ ἥπατος τοῦ ἱερείου ὁ λοβὸς ἀφανὴς ἦν,
οὕτω δὴ ἐγγράψαντα καὶ κατασημηνάμενον τὸ
γραμμάτιον πέμψαι παρὰ τὸν Ἀπολλόδωρον ἐκ
Βαβυλῶνος εἰς Ἐκβάτανα, δηλοῦντα μηδέν τι δεδιέναι Ἡφαιστίωνα· ἔσεσθαι γὰρ αὐτοῖς ὀλίγου
3 χρόνου ἐκποδών. καὶ ταύτην τὴν ἐπιστολὴν λέγει
Ἀριστόβουλος κομίσασθαι Ἀπολλόδωρον μιᾷ
πρόσθεν ἡμέρᾳ ἢ τελευτῆσαι Ἡφαιστίωνα. αὖθις
δὲ θύεσθαι τὸν Πειθαγόραν ἐπὶ τῷ Ἀλεξάνδρῳ
⟨καὶ⟩ γενέσθαι καὶ ἐπ᾽ Ἀλεξάνδρῳ ἄλοβον τὸ
ἧπαρ τοῦ ἱερείου. καὶ Πειθαγόραν τὰ αὐτὰ καὶ
ὑπὲρ Ἀλεξάνδρου γράψαι Ἀπολλοδώρῳ. Ἀπολλόδωρον δὲ οὐ κατασιωπῆσαι, ἀλλὰ φράσαι γὰρ
πρὸς Ἀλέξανδρον τὰ ἐπεσταλμένα, ὡς εὔνοιαν
μᾶλλόν τι ἐπιδειξόμενον τῷ βασιλεῖ, εἰ φυλάττεσ-
θαι παραινέσειε μή τις αὐτῷ κίνδυνος ἐν τῷ τότε
4 ξυμπέσοι. καὶ Ἀπολλόδωρόν τε λέγει ὅτι Ἀλέξανδρος ἐπῄνεσε καὶ τὸν Πειθαγόραν, ἐπειδὴ παρ-
ῆλθεν εἰς Βαβυλῶνα, ἤρετο ὅτου γενομένου αὐτῷ

ander's Companions, commander of the force Alexander left behind with Mazaeus the satrap of Babylon,
after he had met Alexander on his return from India
and observed that he was punishing severely the
satraps appointed over various provinces, wrote to
Pithagoras his brother, as he was one of those seers
who prophesy from the flesh of victims, to prophesy
about his own welfare. Pithagoras wrote in answer 2
asking who it was that he chiefly feared that he
wanted the help of prophecy, and he replied that it
was the king himself and Hephaestion. Pithagoras
then sacrificed first in regard to Hephaestion and, as
the lobe could not be seen on the liver of the victim,
he reported this, and sealing his letter sent it to
Apollodorus from Babylon to Ecbatana, showing that
he had nothing to fear from Hephaestion, as in a short
time he would be out of their way. Apollodorus re- 3
ceived this letter, Aristobulus says, on the day before
Hephaestion died. Then Pithagoras sacrificed again
in regard to Alexander, and again the liver of the
victim had no lobe. Pithagoras wrote to Apollodorus in the same terms about Alexander. But
Apollodorus did not keep his counsel; instead he told
Alexander the news he had received, with the idea of
showing loyalty in higher degree to the king by
advising him to beware in case any danger came upon
him at this time. He says that Alexander thanked 4
Apollodorus and, when he reached Babylon, asked
Pithagoras what particular sign caused him to write

σημείου ταῦτα ἐπέστειλεν πρὸς τὸν ἀδελφόν· τὸν δὲ
εἰπεῖν ὅτι ἄλοβόν οἱ τὸ ἧπαρ ἐγένετο τοῦ ἱερείου·
ἐρομένου δὲ ὅ τι νοοῖ τὸ σημεῖον μέγα εἰπεῖν εἶναι
χαλεπόν. Ἀλέξανδρον δὲ τοσούτου δεῆσαι χαλε-
πῆναι τῷ Πειθαγόρᾳ, ὡς καὶ δι' ἐπιμελείας ἔχειν
αὐτὸν πλείονος, ὅτι ἀδόλως τὴν ἀλήθειάν οἱ
5 ἔφρασε. ταῦτα αὐτὸς Ἀριστόβουλος λέγει παρὰ
Πειθαγόρου πυθέσθαι· καὶ Περδίκκᾳ δὲ μαντεύσασθαι αὐτὸν λέγει καὶ Ἀντιγόνῳ χρόνῳ ὕστερον·
καὶ τοῦ αὐτοῦ σημείου ἀμφοῖν γενομένου Περδίκκαν
τε ἐπὶ Πτολεμαῖον στρατεύσαντα ἀποθανεῖν καὶ
Ἀντίγονον ἐν τῇ μάχῃ τῇ πρὸς Σέλευκον καὶ
6 Λυσίμαχον τῇ ἐν Ἰψῷ γενομένῃ. καὶ μὲν δὴ καὶ
ὑπὲρ Καλάνου τοῦ σοφιστοῦ τοῦ Ἰνδοῦ τοιόσδε τις
ἀναγέγραπται λόγος, ὁπότε ἐπὶ τὴν πυρὰν ᾔει
ἀποθανούμενος, τότε τοὺς μὲν ἄλλους ἑταίρους
ἀσπάζεσθαι αὐτόν, Ἀλεξάνδρῳ δὲ οὐκ ἐθελῆσαι
προσελθεῖν ἀσπασόμενον, ἀλλὰ φάναι γὰρ ὅτι ἐν
Βαβυλῶνι αὐτῷ ἐντυχὼν ἀσπάσεται. καὶ τοῦτον
τὸν λόγον ἐν μὲν τῷ τότε ἀμεληθῆναι, ὕστερον δέ,
ἐπειδὴ ἐτελεύτησεν ἐν Βαβυλῶνι Ἀλέξανδρος, ἐς
μνήμην ἐλθεῖν τῶν ἀκουσάντων, ὅτι ἐπὶ τῇ τελευτῇ
ἄρα τῇ Ἀλεξάνδρου ἐθειάσθη.

19. Παρελθόντι δ' αὐτῷ ἐς Βαβυλῶνα πρεσβεῖαι
παρὰ τῶν Ἑλλήνων ἐνέτυχον, ὑπὲρ ὅτων μὲν
ἕκαστοι πρεσβευόμενοι οὐκ ἀναγέγραπται, δοκεῖν
δ' ἔμοιγε αἱ πολλαὶ στεφανούντων τε αὐτὸν ἦσαν
καὶ ἐπαινούντων ἐπὶ ταῖς νίκαις ταῖς τε ἄλλαις καὶ
μάλιστα ταῖς Ἰνδικαῖς, καὶ ὅτι σῶος ἐξ Ἰνδῶν
ἐπανήκει χαίρειν φασκόντων. καὶ τούτους δεξιωσά-
μενός τε καὶ τὰ εἰκότα τιμήσας ἀποπέμψαι ὀπίσω
2 λέγεται. ὅσους δὲ ἀνδριάντας ἢ ὅσα ἀγάλματα

this to his brother. He replied that he found the liver
of his victim without a lobe. When asked what this
sign portended, he said: ' Something very serious.'
However, Alexander was so far from being incensed
against Pithagoras that he actually paid him more
respect for speaking the truth without deceit.
Aristobulus says he learned this at first hand from 5
Pithagoras, and that Pithagoras prophesied later to
Perdiccas and Antigonus; after the same portent had
appeared for both, Perdiccas perished in his campaign against Ptolemy, and Antigonus in the battle
against Seleucus and Lysimachus which took place at
Ipsus.[2] Besides this, a story on these lines [3] had been 6
recorded of Calanus, the Indian sophist: when he was
going to the funeral pyre to die, he greeted all the
Companions, but refused to approach Alexander and
greet him, saying that he would meet him at Babylon,
and greet him there. This saying was ignored at the
time, but later, when Alexander died at Babylon, it
came to the recollection of the hearers that he had
been truly inspired to foretell Alexander's death.

19. When Alexander had entered Babylon, embassies came to meet him from the Greeks; it is not
recorded for what purposes each embassy came, but I
am inclined to think that most of them were to offer
him wreaths and to congratulate him on all his victories, especially those in India, and also to express
their greetings to him at his safe return from India.[1]
He is said to have received them graciously, sent them
home with appropriate honour and given them to 2

---

[2] 301 B.C. (wrong in Introd. 11).
[3] ' Vulgate.'
[1] App. XXII.

ἢ εἰ δή τι ἄλλο ἀνάθημα ἐκ τῆς Ἑλλάδος. Ξέρξης
ἀνεκόμισεν ἐς Βαβυλῶνα ἢ ἐς Πασαργάδας ἢ ἐς
Σοῦσα ἢ ὅπῃ ἄλλῃ τῆς Ἀσίας, ταῦτα δοῦναι ἄγειν
τοῖς πρέσβεσι· καὶ τὰς Ἁρμοδίου καὶ Ἀριστογεί-
τονος εἰκόνας τὰς χαλκᾶς οὕτω λέγεται ἀπενεχθῆναι
ὀπίσω ἐς Ἀθήνας καὶ τῆς Ἀρτέμιδος τῆς Κελκέας [1]
τὸ ἕδος.

3   Κατέλαβε δὲ ἐν Βαβυλῶνι, ὡς λέγει Ἀριστόβουλος, καὶ τὸ ναυτικόν, τὸ μὲν κατὰ τὸν Εὐφράτην
ποταμὸν ἀναπεπλευκὸς ἀπὸ θαλάσσης τῆς Περσι-
κῆς, ὅ τι περ σὺν Νεάρχῳ ἦν, τὸ δὲ ἐκ Φοινίκης
ἀνακεκομισμένον, πεντήρεις μὲν δύο τῶν ἐκ Φοινίκων, τετρήρεις δὲ τρεῖς, τριήρεις δὲ δώδεκα, τριακοντόρους δὲ ἐς τριάκοντα· ταύτας ξυντμηθείσας
κομισθῆναι ἐπὶ τὸν Εὐφράτην ποταμὸν ἐκ Φοινίκης ἐς Θάψακον πόλιν, ἐκεῖ δὲ ξυμπηχθείσας αὖθις
4 καταπλεῦσαι ἐς Βαβυλῶνα. λέγει δὲ ὅτι καὶ ἄλλος
αὐτῷ ἐναυπηγεῖτο στόλος τέμνοντι τὰς κυπαρίσσους
τὰς ἐν τῇ Βαβυλωνίᾳ· τούτων γὰρ μόνων τῶν δένδρων εὐπορίαν εἶναι ἐν τῇ χώρᾳ τῶν Ἀσσυρίων, τῶν
δὲ ἄλλων ὅσα ἐς ναυπηγίαν ἀπόρως ἔχειν τὴν γῆν
ταύτην· πληρώματα δὲ ἐς τὰς ναῦς καὶ τὰς ἄλλας
ὑπηρεσίας πορφυρέων τε πλῆθος καὶ τῶν ἄλλων
ὅσοι ἐργάται τῆς θαλάσσης ἀφῖχθαι αὐτῷ ἐκ
Φοινίκης τε καὶ τῆς ἄλλης παραλίας· λιμένα τε ὅτι
πρὸς Βαβυλῶνι ἐποίει ὀρυκτὸν ὅσον χιλίαις ναυσὶ
μακραῖς ὅρμον εἶναι καὶ νεωσοίκους ἐπὶ τοῦ λιμένος.
5 καὶ Μίκκαλος ὁ Κλαζομένιος μετὰ πεντακοσίων
ταλάντων ἐπὶ Φοινίκης τε καὶ Συρίας ἐστέλλετο,
τοὺς μὲν μισθῷ πείσων, τοὺς δὲ καὶ ὠνησόμενος

---

[1] Κελκαίας may be the right form; see note by Roos.

take back all the statues or images or other votive
offerings Xerxes removed from Greece to Babylon,
Pasargadae, Susa or anywhere else in Asia, and it is
said that the bronze statues of Harmodius and
Aristogiton were taken back to Athens in this way,
as well as the seated figure of Celcean Artemis.[2]

Aristobulus says that Alexander also found the 3
fleet at Babylon; the part which was with Nearchus
had sailed up the Euphrates from the Persian Sea, but
the rest had been brought up from Phoenicia, two
Phoenician quinqueremes, three quadriremes, twelve
triremes and some thirty *triacontoroi*, which had been
broken up and carried across from Phoenicia to the
Euphrates, to the city of Thapsacus,[3] put together
again there, and sailed down to Babylon. Aristo- 4
bulus says that yet another flotilla was being built
for him, by cutting down the cypresses in Babylonia,
as this is the only tree which grows freely in the
Assyrian country, a land bare of everything else
necessary for shipbuilding, that as crews for the ships
and for the other naval services a mass of purple-shell
divers and other sea-faring men reached him from
Phoenicia and the rest of the coast, and that Alexander excavated a harbour at Babylon, large enough
to be an anchorage for a thousand ships of war, with
dockyards in the harbour. Further, Miccalus of 5
Clazomenae was despatched to Phoenicia and Syria
with five hundred Talents, to hire recruits or pur-

---

[2] ' Vulgate '?   Cf. iii 16, 7 f. (where the return of the statues
is not expressly dated), with Bosworth *ad loc.*
[3] App. VII.

ARRIAN

ὅσοι θαλάττιοι ἄνθρωποι. τήν τε γὰρ παραλίαν
τὴν πρὸς τῷ κόλπῳ τῷ Περσικῷ κατοικίζειν
ἐπενόει καὶ τὰς νήσους τὰς ταύτῃ. ἐδόκει γὰρ αὐτῷ
οὐ μεῖον ⟨ἂν⟩ Φοινίκης εὐδαίμων ἡ χώρα αὕτη
6 γενέσθαι. ἦν δὲ αὐτῷ τοῦ ναυτικοῦ ἡ παρασκευὴ
ὡς ἐπὶ Ἄραβας τοὺς πολλούς, πρόφασιν μέν, ὅτι
μόνοι τῶν ταύτῃ βαρβάρων οὔτε πρεσβείαν ἀπέστει-
λαν οὔτε τι ἄλλο ἐπιεικὲς ἢ ἐπὶ τιμῇ ἐπέπρακτο
Ἄραψιν ἐς αὐτόν· τὸ δὲ ἀληθές, ὥς γέ μοι δοκεῖ,
ἄπληστος ἦν τοῦ κτᾶσθαί τι ἀεὶ Ἀλέξανδρος.

20. Λόγος δὲ κατέχει ὅτι ἤκουεν Ἄραβας δύο
μόνον τιμᾶν θεούς, τὸν Οὐρανόν τε καὶ τὸν Διόνυσον, τὸν μὲν Οὐρανὸν αὐτόν τε ὁρώμενον καὶ τὰ
ἄστρα ἐν οἷ ἔχοντα τά τε ἄλλα καὶ τὸν ἥλιον, ἀφ'
ὅτου μεγίστη καὶ φανοτάτη ὠφέλεια ἐς πάντα ἥκει
τὰ ἀνθρώπεια, Διόνυσον δὲ κατὰ δόξαν τῆς ἐς
Ἰνδοὺς στρατιᾶς. οὔκουν ἀπαξιοῦν καὶ αὐτὸν
τρίτον ἂν νομισθῆναι πρὸς Ἀράβων θεόν, οὐ φαυ-
λότερα ἔργα Διονύσου ἀποδειξάμενον, εἴπερ οὖν
καὶ Ἀράβων κρατήσας ἐπιτρέψειεν αὐτοῖς, καθάπερ Ἰνδοῖς, πολιτεύειν κατὰ τὰ σφῶν νόμιμα.
2 τῆς τε χώρας ἡ εὐδαιμονία ὑπεκίνει αὐτόν, ὅτι
ἤκουεν ἐκ μὲν τῶν λιμνῶν τὴν κασίαν γίγνεσθαι
αὐτοῖς, ἀπὸ δὲ τῶν δένδρων τὴν σμύρναν τε καὶ τὸν
λιβανωτόν, ἐκ δὲ τῶν θάμνων τὸ κιννάμωμον τέμνεσθαι, οἱ λειμῶνες δὲ ὅτι νάρδον αὐτόματοι

---

[4] S. xvi 1, 9 ff., also drawing on Ar., says that though Al's
pretext for war was the failure of the Arabians to send an
embassy to him, in truth he desired to be ' lord of all ' (§ 11).
A. adopted Ar's opinion as his own. Cf. *Ind.* 9, 11 (Meg.).

[1] S. (see last note) substitutes Zeus for Uranus and does not
allude to Dionysus' Indian expedition (perhaps because he did

chase men accustomed to seafaring. For Alexander was planning to colonize the coast along the Persian Gulf and the islands there, as he thought that it would become just as prosperous a country as Phoenicia. His naval preparations were directed at the greater number of the Arabs, on the pretext that they alone of the barbarians in these parts had sent no envoys and had taken no other action reasonable or honorific to him. The truth in my own belief is that Alexander was always insatiate in winning possessions.[4]

20. A story is prevalent[1] that he heard that the Arabs honoured only two gods, Uranus[2] and Dionysus, Uranus because he is visible and contains within himself the stars and especially the sun, from which the greatest and most obvious benefit comes to all human affairs, Dionysus in view of his reported expedition to India, and that Alexander therefore thought himself worthy to be regarded as a third god by the Arabs, since his achievements were as magnificent as those of Dionysus, given that he would conquer the Arabians too and permit them, like the Indians, to be governed by their own customs. The prosperity of the country was also an incitement, since he heard that cassia grew in their marshes, that the trees produced myrrh and frankincense, that cinnamon was cut from the bushes,[3] and that spike-

---

not believe in it); he makes Al. assume that after conquest and restoration of their autonomy the Arabians would honour him as a god (the autocrat would let his opinion be known and expect it to be adopted!). Exactly what Ar. wrote is uncertain from the two versions; evidently it was consonant with the ' vulgate.' He remains A's source for 20–22, except for 20, 9 f. (N.) and the last sentence of 22, cf. 20, 5; 21, 1 n.; 22, 2 n. and 4 f. Cf. App. XVI 6 f.; XXIII 2.

[2] Urania in Hdt. iii 8.

[3] But see App. XXV **3**.

ARRIAN

ἐκφέρουσι· τό ⟨τε⟩ μέγεθος τῆς χώρας, ὅτι οὐκ
ἐλάττων ἡ παράλιος τῆς Ἀραβίας ἤπερ ἡ τῆς
Ἰνδικῆς αὐτῷ ἐξηγγέλλετο, καὶ νῆσοι αὐτῇ προσκεῖσθαι πολλαί, καὶ λιμένες πανταχοῦ τῆς χώρας
ἐνεῖναι, οἷοι παρασχεῖν μὲν ὅρμους τῷ ναυτικῷ,
παρασχεῖν δὲ καὶ πόλεις ἐνοικισθῆναι καὶ ταύτας
γενέσθαι εὐδαίμονας.

3   Δύο δὲ νῆσοι κατὰ τὸ στόμα τοῦ Εὐφράτου πε-
λάγιαι ἐξηγγέλλοντο αὐτῷ, ἡ μὲν πρώτη οὐ
πρόσω τῶν ἐκβολῶν τοῦ Εὐφράτου, ἐς ἑκατὸν καὶ
εἴκοσι σταδίους ἀπέχουσα ἀπὸ τοῦ αἰγιαλοῦ τε καὶ
τοῦ στόματος τοῦ ποταμοῦ, μικροτέρα αὕτη καὶ δασεῖα ὕλῃ παντοίᾳ· εἶναι δὲ ἐν αὐτῇ καὶ ἱερὸν
Ἀρτέμιδος καὶ τοὺς οἰκήτορας αὐτῆς ἀμφὶ τὸ
4 ἱερὸν τὴν δίαιταν ποιεῖσθαι· νέμεσθαί τε αὐτὴν
αἰξί τε ἀγρίαις καὶ ἐλάφοις, καὶ ταύτας ἀνεῖσθαι
ἀφέτους τῇ Ἀρτέμιδι, οὐδὲ εἶναι θέμις θήραν
ποιεῖσθαι ἀπ' αὐτῶν, ὅτι μὴ θῦσαί τινα τῇ θεῷ
ἐθέλοντα· ἐπὶ τῷδε γὰρ θηρᾶν μόνον οὐκ [1] εἶναι
5 ἀθέμιτον. καὶ ταύτην τὴν νῆσον λέγει Ἀριστόβουλος ὅτι Ἴκαρον ἐκέλευσε καλεῖσθαι Ἀλέξανδρος
ἐπὶ τῆς νήσου τῆς Ἰκάρου τῆς ἐν τῷ Αἰγαίῳ πόντῳ,
ἐς ἥντινα Ἴκαρον τὸν Δαιδάλου τακέντος τοῦ
κηροῦ ὅτῳ προσήρτητο τὰ πτερὰ πεσεῖν λόγος
κατέχει, ὅτι οὐ κατὰ τὰς ἐντολὰς τοῦ πατρὸς πρὸς
τῇ γῇ ἐφέρετο, ἀλλὰ μετέωρος γὰρ ὑπὸ ἀνοίας
πετόμενος παρέσχε τῷ ἡλίῳ θάλψαι τε καὶ ἀνεῖναι
τὸν κηρόν, καὶ ἀπὸ ἑαυτοῦ τὸν Ἴκαρον τῇ τε νήσῳ
καὶ τῷ πελάγει τὴν ἐπωνυμίαν ἐγκαταλιπεῖν τὴν
6 μὲν Ἴκαρον καλεῖσθαι, τὸ δὲ Ἰκάριον. ἡ δὲ ἑτέρα

---

[1] Castiglioni: ἐπὶ τῷδε θηρᾶν μόνον· ἐπὶ τῷδε γὰρ οὐκ codd.,
Roos (unintelligible).

nard grew self-sown in their meadows. Then there
was also the size of their territory, since he was informed that the sea-coast of Arabia was nearly as
long as that of India, and that there were many islands off-shore and harbours everywhere in the
country, enough to give anchorages for his fleet, and
to permit cities to be built on them, which were
likely to prosper.

He was informed of two islands out at sea near the 3
mouth of the Euphrates. The first was not far from
its outlets about a hundred and twenty stades from
the shore and the river mouth; this one is smaller,
thickly wooded with every kind of tree; it also contained a shrine of Artemis, and the island's inhabitants spent their lives round the shrine; it pas- 4
tured wild goats and deer which were consecrated to
Artemis and could range free, and no one was allowed
to hunt them unless he desired to sacrifice one to the
goddess: only on this condition was hunting not
forbidden. According to Aristobulus, Alexander 5
commanded this island to be called Icarus, after the
island Icarus in the Aegean Sea, upon which according to the prevalent story Icarus, son of Daedalus, fell
when the wax with which his wings had been fastened
melted, because he did not follow his father's in-
junctions and fly low near the ground, but was mad
enough to fly high, allowed the sun to melt and loose
the wax, and left his name to both the island Icarus
and the Icarian sea.[4] The other island was said to be 6

---

[4] Ar. could have told the story (App. XXVIII 22). Islands:
App. XXVI 3.

νῆσος ἀπέχειν μὲν ἀπὸ τοῦ στόματος τοῦ Εὐφράτου
ἐλέγετο ὅσον πλοῦν ἡμέρας καὶ νυκτὸς κατ᾽ οὖρον θε-
ούσῃ νηΐ· Τύλος δὲ αὐτῇ εἶναι ὄνομα· μεγάλη δὲ
εἶναι καὶ οὔτε τραχεῖα ἡ πολλὴ οὔτε ὑλώδης, ἀλλ᾽
οἷα καρπούς τε ἡμέρους ἐκφέρειν καὶ πάντα ὡραῖα.

7   Ταυτὶ ἀπηγγέλθη ᾽Αλεξάνδρῳ τὰ μὲν πρὸς ᾽Αρ-
χίου, ὃς ξὺν τριακοντόρῳ ἐκπεμφθεὶς ἐπὶ κατασκοπὴν τοῦ παράπλου τοῦ ὡς ἐπὶ τοὺς ῎Αραβας
μέχρι μὲν τῆς νήσου τῆς Τύλου ἦλθε, τὸ πρόσω δὲ
οὐκέτι περαιωθῆναι ἐτόλμησεν· ᾽Ανδροσθένης δὲ ξὺν
ἄλλῃ τριακοντόρῳ σταλεὶς καὶ τῆς χερρονήσου τι
τῶν ᾽Αράβων παρέπλευσε· μακροτάτω δὲ τῶν
ἐκπεμφθέντων προὐχώρησεν ῾Ιέρων ὁ Σολεὺς ὁ
κυβερνήτης, λαβὼν καὶ οὗτος παρ᾽ ᾽Αλεξάνδρου
8   τριακόντορον. ἦν μὲν γὰρ αὐτῷ προστεταγμένον
περιπλεῦσαι τὴν χερρόνησον τὴν ᾽Αράβων πᾶσαν
ἔστε ἐπὶ τὸν κόλπον τὸν πρὸς Αἰγύπτῳ τὸν ᾽Αρά-
βιον τὸν καθ᾽ ῾Ηρώων πόλιν· οὐ μὴν ἐτόλμησέ γε
τὸ πρόσω ἐλθεῖν, καίτοι ἐπὶ τὸ πολὺ παραπλεύσας
τὴν ᾽Αράβων γῆν· ἀλλ᾽ ἀναστρέψας γὰρ παρ᾽
᾽Αλέξανδρον ἐξήγγειλεν τὸ μέγεθός τε τῆς χερρονήσου θαυμαστόν τι εἶναι καὶ ὅσον οὐ πολὺ ἀπο-
δέον τῆς ᾽Ινδῶν γῆς, ἄκραν τε ἀνέχειν ἐπὶ πολὺ τῆς
9   μεγάλης θαλάσσης· ἦν δὴ καὶ τοὺς σὺν Νεάρχῳ ἀπὸ
τῆς ᾽Ινδικῆς πλέοντας, πρὶν ἐπικάμψαι ἐς τὸν κόλπον
τὸν Περσικόν, οὐ πόρρω ἀνατείνουσαν ἰδεῖν τε καὶ
παρ᾽ ὀλίγον ἐλθεῖν διαβαλεῖν ἐς αὐτήν, καὶ ᾽Ονησι-
κρίτῳ τῷ κυβερνήτῃ ταύτῃ δοκοῦν· ἀλλὰ Νέαρχος
λέγει ὅτι αὐτὸς διεκώλυσεν, ὡς ἐκπεριπλεύσας τὸν
κόλπον τὸν Περσικὸν ἔχοι ἀπαγγεῖλαι ᾽Αλεξάνδρῳ
10 ἐφ᾽ οἷστισι πρὸς αὐτοῦ ἐστάλη· οὐ γὰρ ἐπὶ τῷ
πλεῦσαι τὴν μεγάλην θάλασσαν ἐστάλθαι, ἀλλ᾽ ἐπὶ

323
B.C.

about a day and night's sail distant from the mouth of the Euphrates for a ship running before the wind; it was called Tylus, and was large and neither rough nor wooded for the most part but of a kind to bear cultivated crops and all things in due season.

This was told to Alexander, partly by Archias,[5] 7 who had been sent with a *triacontor* to reconnoitre the coastal voyage towards Arabia, and reached the island Tylus, though he did not venture further. Androsthenes [6] was despatched with another *triacontor*, and sailed round part of the Arabian peninsula; but of all those sent off, Hieron of Soli the steersman, who also received a *triacontor* from Alexander, went furthest, yet, though his sailing orders 8 were to coast round the whole Arabian peninsula till he reached the Arabian Gulf [Red Sea] on the Egyptian side at Heroonpolis,[7] he did not dare to go further, though he had sailed round the greater part of Arabia, but turned about and reported to Alexander that the peninsula was vast in size and nearly as large as India and that a promontory ran far into the great sea. Nearchus' crews, when sailing 9 from India before they altered course for the Persian Gulf, had seen it stretching out not far away, and they were on the point of putting in there, as advised by Onesicritus the helmsman. But Nearchus says that he himself forbade this; having completed his voyage round the Persian Gulf, he had to report to Alexander on the commission for which he had been despatched, that in fact he had not been sent to 10 navigate the Ocean, but to reconnoitre the coast lying

---

[5] *Ind.* 18, 3; 27 f.; 34 f.; 43, 8 f.
[6] A. evidently did not know his book (Jacoby no. 711). See in general S. xvi 3, 1–6.
[7] In the Suez isthmus.

τῷ καταμαθεῖν τὴν χώραν τὴν προσεχῆ τῇ θαλάσσῃ καὶ τοὺς κατοικοῦντας αὐτὴν ἀνθρώπους, ὅρμους
τε ἐν αὐτῇ καὶ ὕδατα καὶ τὰ νόμαια τῶν ἀνδρῶν καὶ
εἴ τις ἀγαθὴ καρποὺς ἐκφέρειν ἢ εἴ τις κακή· καὶ
οὖν καὶ τοῦτο αἴτιον γενέσθαι ἀποσωθῆναι Ἀλεξάνδρῳ τὸν στρατόν· οὐ γὰρ ἂν σωθῆναι πλεύσαντας
ὑπὲρ τῆς Ἀραβίας τὰ ἔρημα, ἐφ' ὅτῳ καὶ ὁ Ἱέρωι
ἐπιστρέψαι ὀπίσω λέγεται.

21. Ἐν ᾧ δὲ αὐτῷ ἐναυπηγοῦντο μὲν αἱ τριήρεις,
ὁ λιμὴν δὲ πρὸς Βαβυλῶνι ὠρύσσετο, ἐκπλεῖ ἐκ
Βαβυλῶνος κατὰ τὸν Εὐφράτην ὡς ἐπὶ τὸν Πολλακόπαν καλούμενον ποταμόν. ἀπέχει δὲ οὗτος
τῆς Βαβυλῶνος σταδίους ὅσον ὀκτακοσίους, καὶ
ἔστι διῶρυξ αὕτη [ὁ Πολλακόπας] ἐκ τοῦ Εὐφρά-
2 του, οὐχὶ δὲ ἐκ πηγῶν τις ἀνίσχων ποταμός. ὁ
γὰρ Εὐφράτης ποταμὸς ῥέων ἐκ τῶν Ἀρμενίωι
ὀρῶν χειμῶνος μὲν ὥρᾳ προχωρεῖ κατὰ τὰς ὄχθας,
οἷα δὴ οὐ πολλοῦ ὄντος αὐτῷ τοῦ ὕδατος· ἦρος δὲ
ὑποφαίνοντος καὶ πολὺ δὴ μάλιστα ὑπὸ τροπάς,
ἅστινας τοῦ θέρους ὁ ἥλιος ἐπιστρέφει, μέγας τε
ἐπέρχεται καὶ ὑπερβάλλει ὑπὲρ τὰς ὄχθας ἐς τὴι
3 γῆν τὴν Ἀσσυρίαν· τηνικαῦτα γὰρ αἱ χιόνες αἱ
ἐπὶ τοῖς ὄρεσι τοῖς Ἀρμενίοις κατατηκόμεναι
αὔξουσιν αὐτῷ τὸ ὕδωρ ἐπὶ μέγα. ὅτι δὲ ἐπιπολῆς
ἐστιν αὐτῷ καὶ ὑψηλὸς ὁ ῥοῦς, ὑπερβάλλει ἐς
τὴν χώραν, εἰ μή τις ἀναστομώσας αὐτὸν κατὰ τὸν
Πολλακόπαν ἐς τὰ ἕλη τε ἐκτρέψειε καὶ τὰς λίμνας
αἳ δὴ ἀρχόμεναι ἀπὸ ταύτης τῆς διώρυχος ⟨δι-
ήκουσιν⟩ ἔστε ἐπὶ τὴν ξυνεχῆ τῇ Ἀράβων γῇ, καὶ
ἔνθεν μὲν ἐς τέναγος ἐπὶ πολύ, ἐκ δὲ τοῦ ἐς θάλασσαν κατὰ πολλά τε καὶ ἀφανῆ στόματα ἐκδίδωσι
4 τετηκυίας δὲ τῆς χιόνος ἀμφὶ Πλειάδων μάλιστα

on the Ocean, the inhabitants of the coast, its
anchorages, water supplies and the manners and
customs of the people, and to discover if any part of
the coast was fertile or not; and that this was the
reason that Alexander's force came through safely,
for they would have been lost if they had sailed past
the desert parts of Arabia. On this ground Hieron
too is said to have turned about.[8]

21. While his triremes were being built, and the
harbour at Babylon dug out, Alexander sailed from
Babylon down the Euphrates to the so-called river
Pollacopas.[1] This is eight hundred stades away from
Babylon, and it is a canal from the Euphrates, not a
river that rises from its own springs. For the 2
Euphrates river flowing from the Armenian mountains runs within its banks in the winter season, as the
volume of water is not large; but once spring just
shows, and especially about the time of the summer
solstice, its flow is great and it breaks its banks on to
the Assyrian land. For it is then that the snows on 3
the Armenian mountains melt and increase its volume
enormously. Since the bed of the stream is lifted
high up, it would overflow into the surrounding
country unless it were given an outlet along the
Pollacopas and so turned into the marshes and the
lakes, which begin with this canal and continue as far
as the land nearest to Arabia, and thence it runs
mostly into lagoons and thereafter into the sea by
many unnoticed mouths. When the melting of the 4

---

[8] Cf. *Ind.* 32. The final comment probably echoes N.
[1] Ar. *ap.* S. xvi 1, 9 and 11 with further particulars.

δύσιν ὀλίγος τε ὁ Εὐφράτης ῥέει καὶ οὐδὲν μεῖον τὸ
πολὺ αὐτοῦ κατὰ τὸν Πολλακόπαν ἐκδιδοῖ ἐς τὰς
λίμνας. εἰ δή τις μὴ ἀποφράξει⟨ε⟩ τὸν Πολλακόπαν αὖθις, ὡς κατὰ τὰς ὄχθας ἐκτραπὲν
φέρεσθαι τὸ ὕδωρ κατὰ πόρον, ἐκένωσεν ἂν τὸν
Εὐφράτην ἐς αὐτόν, ὡς μηδ' ἐπάρδεσθαι ἀπ'
5 αὐτοῦ τὴν Ἀσσυρίαν γῆν. ἀλλὰ ἀπεφράσσοντο
γὰρ αἱ ἐς τὸν Πολλακόπαν τοῦ Εὐφράτου ἐκβολαὶ
πρὸς τοῦ σατράπου τῆς Βαβυλωνίας πολλῷ πόνῳ,
καίπερ οὐ χαλεπῶς ἀναστομούμεναι, ὅτι ἰλυώδης
τε ἡ ταύτῃ γῆ καὶ πηλὸς ἡ πολλὴ αὐτῆς, οἷα δεχο-
μένη τὸ ὕδωρ τοῦ ποταμοῦ μὴ εὐμαρῆ τὴν ἀποστροφὴν αὐτοῦ παρέχειν· ἀλλὰ καὶ ἐς τρίτον μῆνα
Ἀσσυρίων ἄνδρες ὑπὲρ τοὺς μυρίους ἐν τῷδε τῷ
πόνῳ ξυνείχοντο.

6   Ταῦτα ἀπαγγελθέντα ἐπήγαγεν Ἀλέξανδρον
ὠφελῆσαί τι τὴν χώραν τὴν Ἀσσυρίαν. ἔνθεν μὲν δὴ
ἐς τὸν Πολλακόπαν ἐτρέπετο τοῦ Εὐφράτου ὁ ῥοῦς,
ταύτῃ δὲ ἔγνω βεβαίως ἀποκλεῖσαι τὴν ἐκβολήν·
προελθόντι δὲ ὅσον σταδίους τριάκοντα ὑπόπετρος
ἡ γῆ ἐφαίνετο, οἷα διακοπεῖσα, εἰ ξυναφὴς ἐγένετο
τῇ πάλαι διώρυχι τῇ κατὰ τὸν Πολλακόπαν, οὔτ'
ἂν διαχεῖσθαι παρέχειν τὸ ὕδωρ ὑπὸ στερρότητος
τῆς γῆς, τήν τε ἀποστροφὴν αὐτοῦ τῇ τεταγμένῃ
7 ὥρᾳ μὴ χαλεπῶς γίγνεσθαι. τούτων ἕνεκα ἐπί τε
τὸν Πολλακόπαν ἔπλευσε καὶ κατ' αὐτὸν καταπλεῖ
ἐς τὰς λίμνας ὡς ἐπὶ Ἀράβων γῆν. ἔνθα χῶρόν
τινα ἐν καλῷ ἰδὼν πόλιν ἐξῳκοδόμησέ τε καὶ
ἐτείχισε, καὶ ἐν ταύτῃ κατῴκισε τῶν Ἑλλήνων
τινὰς τῶν μισθοφόρων, ὅσοι τε ἑκόντες καὶ ὅσοι
ὑπὸ γήρως ἢ κατὰ πήρωσιν ἀπόλεμοι ἦσαν.

22. Αὐτὸς δὲ ὡς ἐξελέγξας δὴ τῶν Χαλδαίων

323
B.C.

snow is over about the setting of the Pleiads, the
level of the Euphrates is low, and yet all the same
most of the water flows by the Pollacopas into the
lakes. If, then, the Pollacopas were not dammed in
its turn, so that the water is diverted to run in the
channel between its own banks, it would have
drained off the Euphrates into it, and then it would
never water the Assyrian plain. Hence the satrap 5
of Babylon used to dam the outlets of the Euphrates
into the Pollacopas with considerable effort, even
though they were easily opened, since the earth
there is muddy and mostly soft clay, such as lets
through the river water and makes it none too easy to
turn the river back; for over 2 months more than ten
thousand Assyrians used to be engaged on this task.

When this was reported to Alexander, it incited 6
him to improve the land of Assyria. At the point
where the stream of Euphrates was turned into the
Pollacopas, he determined to close the outlet securely,
but when he had gone about thirty stades he found
the earth appearing rather stony, suggesting that if
it were quarried, and then united with the old canal
along the Pollacopas, it would not permit the water
to pass through because of the solidity of the soil, and
yet the water could easily be diverted at the appointed
season. For these reasons he sailed to the Pollacopas 7
and down it to the lakes in the direction of Arabia.
There, having seen a good site, he built and fortified
a city and settled in it some of the Greek mercenaries,
volunteers and men unfit for service through age or
wounds.

22. As if he had proved the Chaldaeans' prophecy

τὴν μαντείαν, ὅτι οὐδὲν πεπόνθοι ἐν Βαβυλῶνι
ἄχαρι, καθάπερ ἐκεῖνοι ἐμαντεύσαντο, ἀλλὰ ἔφθη
γὰρ ἐλάσας ἔξω Βαβυλῶνος πρίν τι παθεῖν,
ἀνέπλει αὖθις κατὰ τὰ ἕλη θαρρῶν, ἐν ἀριστερᾷ
ἔχων τὴν Βαβυλῶνα· ἵνα δὴ καὶ ἐπλανήθη αὐτῷ
μέρος τοῦ ναυτικοῦ κατὰ τὰ στενὰ ἀπορίᾳ ἡγεμό-
νος, πρίν γε δὴ αὐτὸς πέμψας τὸν ἡγησόμενον
ἐπανήγαγεν αὐτοὺς ἐς τὸν πόρον. λόγος δὲ λέγεται
2 τοιόσδε. τῶν βασιλέων τῶν Ἀσσυρίων τοὺς τάφους ἐν ταῖς λίμναις τε εἶναι τοὺς πολλοὺς καὶ ἐν
τοῖς ἕλεσι δεδομημένους. ὡς δὲ ἔπλει Ἀλέξανδρος
κατὰ τὰ ἕλη, κυβερνᾶν γὰρ αὐτὸν λόγος τὴν τρι-
ήρη, πνεύματος μεγάλου ἐμπεσόντος αὐτῷ ἐς τὴν
καυσίαν καὶ τὸ διάδημα αὐτῇ συνεχόμενον, τὴν μὲν
δὴ οἷα βαρυτέραν πεσεῖν ἐς τὸ ὕδωρ, τὸ διάδημα δὲ
ἀπενεχθὲν πρὸς τῆς πνοῆς σχεθῆναι ἐν καλάμῳ· τὸν
κάλαμον δὲ τῶν ἐπιπεφυκότων εἶναι τάφῳ τινὶ τῶν
3 πάλαι βασιλέων. τοῦτό τε οὖν αὐτὸ πρὸ τῶν μελλόντων σημῆναι καὶ ὅτι τῶν τις ναυτῶν ἐκνηξάμενος ὡς ἐπὶ τὸ διάδημα ἀφελὼν τοῦ καλάμου αὐτὸ
μετὰ χεῖρας μὲν οὐκ ἤνεγκεν, ὅτι νηχομένου ἂν
αὐτοῦ ἐβρέχετο, περιθεὶς δὲ τῇ κεφαλῇ τῇ αὑτοῦ
4 οὕτω διήνεγκε. καὶ οἱ μὲν πολλοὶ τῶν ἀναγραψάντων τὰ Ἀλεξάνδρου λέγουσιν ὅτι τάλαντον μὲν
ἐδωρήσατο αὐτῷ Ἀλέξανδρος τῆς προθυμίας
ἕνεκα, ἀποτεμεῖν δὲ ἐκέλευσε τὴν κεφαλήν, τῶν
μάντεων ταύτῃ ἐξηγησαμένων, μὴ περιιδεῖν σῶαν
ἐκείνην τὴν κεφαλὴν ἥτις τὸ διάδημα ἐφόρησε τὸ
βασίλειον· Ἀριστόβουλος δὲ τάλαντον μὲν ὅτι
ἔλαβε λέγει αὐτόν, ἀλλὰ πληγὰς λαβεῖν τῆς περι-
5 θέσεως ἕνεκα τοῦ διαδήματος. Ἀριστόβουλος μὲν
δὴ τῶν τινα Φοινίκων τῶν ναυτῶν λέγει ὅτι τὸ διά-

false, since he had suffered none of the unpleasantness in Babylon they had prophesied, but had marched out of Babylon again before any misfortune, Alexander himself again sailed up the marsh lands in confidence, with Babylon on his left hand; but here some of his flotilla lost its way in the narrows for want of a pilot, until he himself sent them a pilot and brought them back into the stream. A tale is told 2 as follows. Most of the tombs of the kings of Assyria [1] are built in the lakes and marsh lands. And as Alexander was sailing in the marshes, according to the tale he was steering the trireme himself, a strong breeze struck his cap and the diadem attached to it and, as the hat was heavy, it fell into the stream, while the diadem was carried off by the breeze and caught on one of the reeds which grew on a tomb of the old kings. This in itself seemed to presage his 3 destiny, as did the fact that one of the sailors who had swum off to fetch the diadem, after removing it from the reed, did not carry it in his hands, since it would have become wet as he swam, but bound it round his head and so brought it across. Most of the 4 historians of Alexander say that he gave him a reward of a Talent for his keenness, but ordered his head to be cut off, since the prophets prescribed in their interpretation of the incident that the head which had worn the royal diadem should not be suffered to live. But Aristobulus says that he received the Talent, but was flogged for fastening the diadem about his head. Aristobulus in fact says that it was 5 one of the Phoenician sailors who brought back his

---

[1] Al. inspected them (Ar. *ap.* S. xv 1, 11).

δημα τῷ Ἀλεξάνδρῳ ἐκόμισεν, εἰσὶ δὲ οἳ Σέλευκον
λέγουσιν. καὶ τοῦτο τῷ τε Ἀλεξάνδρῳ σημῆναι
τὴν τελευτὴν καὶ τῷ Σελεύκῳ τὴν βασιλείαν τὴν
μεγάλην. Σέλευκον γὰρ μέγιστον τῶν μετὰ Ἀλέξανδρον διαδεξαμένων τὴν ἀρχὴν βασιλέα γενέσθαι
τήν τε γνώμην βασιλικώτατον καὶ πλείστης γῆς
ἐπάρξαι μετά γε αὐτὸν Ἀλέξανδρον οὔ μοι δοκεῖ
ἰέναι ἐς ἀμφίλογον.

23. Ἐπανελθὼν δὲ ἐς Βαβυλῶνα καταλαμβάνει
Πευκέσταν ἥκοντα ἐκ Περσῶν, ἄγοντα στρατιὰν
Περσῶν ἐς δισμυρίους· ἦγε δὲ καὶ Κοσσαίων καὶ
Ταπούρων οὐκ ὀλίγους, ὅτι καὶ ταῦτα ἔθνη τῶν
προσχώρων τῇ Περσίδι μαχιμώτατα εἶναι ἐξηγγέλλετο. ἦκε δὲ αὐτῷ καὶ Φιλόξενος στρατιὰν
ἄγων ἀπὸ Καρίας καὶ Μένανδρος ἐκ Λυδίας ἄλλους
καὶ Μενίδας τοὺς ἱππέας ἄγων τοὺς αὐτῷ ξυνταχ-
2 θέντας. καὶ πρεσβεῖαι δὲ ἐν τούτῳ ἐκ τῆς Ἑλλάδος
ἧκον, καὶ τούτων οἱ πρέσβεις αὐτοί τε ἐστε-
φανωμένοι Ἀλεξάνδρῳ προσῆλθον καὶ ἐστεφάνουν
αὐτὸν στεφάνοις χρυσοῖς, ὡς θεωροὶ δῆθεν ἐς
τιμὴν θεοῦ ἀφιγμένοι. τῷ δὲ οὐ πόρρω ἄρα ἡ
τελευτὴ ἦν.
3 Ἔνθα δὴ τούς τε Πέρσας ἐπαινέσας τῆς προθυμίας, ὅτι πάντα Πευκέστᾳ ἐπείθοντο, καὶ αὐτὸν
Πευκέσταν τῆς ἐν κόσμῳ αὐτῶν ἐξηγήσεως, κατέ-
λεγεν αὐτοὺς ἐς τὰς Μακεδονικὰς τάξεις, δεκαδάρ-
χην μὲν τῆς δεκάδος ἡγεῖσθαι Μακεδόνα καὶ ἐπὶ
τούτῳ διμοιρίτην Μακεδόνα καὶ δεκαστάτηρον,
οὕτως ὀνομαζόμενον ἀπὸ τῆς μισθοφορᾶς, ἥντινα

---

2 'Vulgate', not from Clitarchus (cf. D. 116, 5 ff.), since
glorification of Seleucus and not Pt. would not be his aim; it

diadem to Alexander. But some say it was Seleucus, and that this portended death to Alexander and his great kingdom to Seleucus. For in my view it is beyond dispute that Seleucus was the greatest king of those who succeeded Alexander, of the most royal mind, and ruling over the greatest extent of territory, next to Alexander himself.[2]

23. On his return to Babylon Alexander found that Peucestas had arrived from Persia with an army of about twenty thousand Persians; he had also brought a number of Cossaeans and Tapurians,[1] because it was reported that these tribes were the most warlike of those bordering on Persia. Alexander was also joined by Philoxenus with an army from Caria, by Menander with other troops from Lydia, and by Menidas with the cavalry which had been placed under his command.[2] Embassies too came from Greece at this juncture and their envoys, crowned themselves, came forward and crowned Alexander with golden crowns, as if actually come on a sacred embassy to honour a god.[3] And yet he was not far from his end.

Then he commended the Persians for their enthusiasm and entire obedience to Peucestas, and Peucestas himself for his orderly government of them, and he enrolled them in the Macedonian battalions, with a Macedonian decadarch to lead each decad and next to him a Macedonian on double pay and a 'ten-stater' man, so called from the pay, which was less

probably postdates 281, when S. briefly re-united most of the empire. Cf. v 13, 1 and 4 nn.; Appian, *Syrian Wars* 56 (probably from a collection of prodigies on Seleucus' future greatness).

[1] If Bosworth is right on iii 8, 4, Ar. called them Topeirians, and A. must here be following Pt.

[2] App. XIX 7.

[3] App. XXII.

μείονα μὲν τοῦ διμοιρίτου, πλείονα δὲ τῶν οὐκ ἐν
4 τιμῇ στρατευομένων ἔφερεν· ἐπὶ τούτοις δὲ δώδεκα
Πέρσας καὶ τελευταῖον τῆς δεκάδος Μακεδόνα,
δεκαστάτηρον καὶ τοῦτον, ὥστε ἐν τῇ δεκάδι τέσσαρας μὲν εἶναι Μακεδόνας, τοὺς μὲν τῇ μισθοφορᾷ
προὔχοντας, τὸν δὲ τῇ ἀρχῇ τῆς δεκάδος, δώδεκα δὲ
Πέρσας, τοὺς μὲν Μακεδόνας τὴν πάτριον ὅπλισιν
ὡπλισμένους, τοὺς δὲ Πέρσας τοὺς μὲν τοξότας,
τοὺς δὲ καὶ μεσάγκυλα ἔχοντας.

5   Ἐν τούτῳ δὲ πολλάκις μὲν τοῦ ναυτικοῦ ἀπε-
πειρᾶτο, πολλαὶ δὲ ἔριδες αὐτῷ τῶν τριήρων καὶ
ὅσαι τετρήρεις κατὰ τὸν ποταμὸν ἐγίγνοντο, καὶ
ἀγῶνες τῶν τε ἐρετῶν καὶ τῶν κυβερνητῶν καὶ
στέφανοι τῶν νικώντων.

6   Ἧκον δὲ καὶ παρὰ Ἄμμωνος οἱ θεωροὶ οὕστινας
ἐστάλκει ἐρησομένους ὅπως θέμις αὐτῷ τιμᾶν
Ἡφαιστίωνα· οἱ δὲ ὡς ἥρωϊ ἔφησαν ὅτι θύειν
θέμις ὁ Ἄμμων λέγει. ὁ δὲ ἔχαιρέ τε τῇ μαντείᾳ καὶ
τὸ ἀπὸ τοῦδε ὡς ἥρωα ἐγέραιρε. καὶ Κλεομένει,
ἀνδρὶ κακῷ καὶ πολλὰ ἀδικήματα ἀδικήσαντι ἐν
Αἰγύπτῳ, ἐπιστέλλει ἐπιστολήν. καὶ ταύτην τῆς
μὲν ἐς Ἡφαιστίωνα καὶ ἀποθανόντα φιλίας ἕνεκα
καὶ μνήμης οὐ μέμφομαι ἔγωγε, ἄλλων δὲ πολ-
7 λῶν ἕνεκα μέμφομαι. ἔλεγε γὰρ ἡ ἐπιστολὴ κατα-
σκευασθῆναι Ἡφαιστίωνι ἡρῷον ἐν Ἀλεξανδρείᾳ
τῇ Αἰγυπτίᾳ, ἔν τε τῇ πόλει αὐτῇ καὶ ἐν τῇ νήσῳ
τῇ Φάρῳ, ἵνα ὁ πύργος ἐστὶν ὁ ἐν τῇ νήσῳ,
μεγέθει τε μέγιστον καὶ πολυτελείᾳ ἐκπρεπέσ-
τατον, καὶ ὅπως ἐπικρατήσῃ ἐπικαλεῖσθαι ἀπὸ
Ἡφαιστίωνος, καὶ τοῖς συμβολαίοις καθ' ὅσα οἱ
ἔμποροι ἀλλήλοις ξυμβάλλουσιν ἐγγράφεσθαι τὸ
8 ὄνομα Ἡφαιστίωνος. ταῦτα μὲν οὐκ ἔχω μέμψασ-

than the men on double pay, but more than the rank and file received, then twelve Persians and last of the decad a Macedonian, also a ' ten-stater ' man. Thus the decad comprised four Macedonians, three on extra pay and one in charge, and twelve Persians; the Macedonians were equipped with their traditional arms and the Persians were either archers or were provided with thonged javelins.

At this time Alexander was testing out the fleet constantly, and there were many competitions between the triremes and such quadriremes as were on the river, and contests between oarsmen and helmsmen and crowns for the victors.

The sacred envoys from Ammon also arrived, whom Alexander had sent to enquire what honour it was lawful to pay Hephaestion; they reported that Ammon said that it was lawful to sacrifice to him as a hero. Alexander was pleased with the oracle and henceforward gave him heroic honours.[4] Cleomenes, a rascal who had been guilty of many wrongful acts in Egypt, was sent a letter which I personally censure, not for its affectionate recollection of Hephaestion even in death but for many other reasons; it said that a hero's shrine was to be built in Egyptian Alexandria, not just in the city itself but actually on the isle of Pharos, where the tower stands on the island; it was to be unparalleled in dimensions and sumptuous splendour, and he was to insist that it be called after Hephaestion, and that his name should be written into the contracts by which traders do business with each other. All this I cannot censure,

---

[4] So P. 72, 2. Perhaps Pt./Ar. reported that Al. asked Ammon if H. should be god or hero (cf. 14, 7). D. 115, 6 and J. xii 12, 12 wrongly say that he was deified. Enforced hero cult at Athens: Hyperides vi 21.

θαι, πλήν γε δὴ ὅτι οὐκ ἐπὶ μεγάλοις μεγάλως διε-
σπουδάζετο. ἐκεῖνα δὲ καὶ πάνυ μέμφομαι. ἢν
γὰρ καταλάβω ἐγώ, ἔλεγε τὰ γράμματα, τὰ ἱερὰ
τὰ ἐν Αἰγύπτῳ καλῶς κατεσκευασμένα καὶ τὰ
ἡρῷα τὰ Ἡφαιστίωνος, εἴ τέ τι πρότερον ἡμάρ-
τηκας, ἀφήσω σε τούτου, καὶ τὸ λοιπόν, ὁπηλίκον
ἂν ἁμάρτῃς, οὐδὲν πείσῃ ἐξ ἐμοῦ ἄχαρι. τοῦτο ἀνδρὶ
ἄρχοντι πολλῆς μὲν χώρας, πολλῶν δὲ ἀνθρώπων
ἐκ βασιλέως μεγάλου ἐπεσταλμένον, ἄλλως τε καὶ
κακῷ ἀνδρί, οὐκ ἔχω ἐπαινέσαι.

24. Ἀλλὰ γὰρ αὐτῷ ἤδη Ἀλεξάνδρῳ ἐγγὺς ἦν
τὸ τέλος. καί τι καὶ τοιόνδε πρὸ τῶν μελλόντων
σημῆναι λέγει Ἀριστόβουλος· καταλοχίζειν μὲν
αὐτὸν τὴν στρατιὰν τὴν σὺν Πευκέστᾳ τε ἐκ Περσῶν καὶ ἀπὸ θαλάσσης ξὺν Φιλοξένῳ καὶ Μενάν-
δρῳ ἥκουσαν ἐς τὰς Μακεδονικὰς τάξεις· διψή-
σαντα δὲ ἀποχωρῆσαι ἐκ τῆς ἕδρας καταλιπόντα
2 ἔρημον τὸν θρόνον τὸν βασίλειον. εἶναι δὲ κλίνας
ἑκατέρωθεν τοῦ θρόνου ἀργυρόποδας, ἐφ᾽ ὧν οἱ
ἀμφ᾽ αὐτὸν ἑταῖροι ἐκάθηντο. τῶν τινα οὖν
ἠμελημένων ἀνθρώπων, οἱ δὲ καὶ τῶν ἐς φυλακὴ
ἀδέσμῳ ὄντα λέγουσιν, ἔρημον ἰδόντα τὸν θρόνον
καὶ τὰς κλίνας, περὶ τῷ θρόνῳ δὲ ἑστηκότας τοὺς
εὐνούχους, καὶ γὰρ καὶ οἱ ἑταῖροι ξυνανέστησαν
τῷ βασιλεῖ ἀποχωροῦντι, διελθόντα διὰ τῶν εὐνού-
χων ἀναβῆναί τε ἐπὶ τὸν θρόνον καὶ καθέζεσθαι.
3 τοὺς δὲ οὐκ ἀναστῆσαι μὲν αὐτὸν ἐκ τοῦ θρόνου
κατὰ δή τινα νόμον Περσικόν, περιρρηξαμένους δὲ
τύπτεσθαι τά τε στήθη καὶ τὰ πρόσωπα ὡς ἐπὶ
μεγάλῳ κακῷ. ταῦτα ὡς ἐξηγγέλθη Ἀλεξάνδρῳ,
κελεῦσαι στρεβλωθῆναι τὸν καθίσαντα, μήποτε ἐξ
ἐπιβουλῆς ξυντεταγμένον τοῦτο ἔδρασε γνῶναι

except in so far as he was showing such great care over matters of no great importance. But what follows I do censure strongly. The letter ran: ' If I find these temples set in good order in Egypt, and these shrines of Hephaestion, whatever wrong you have hitherto done, I pardon it; and for the future, of whatever nature your fault may be, you shall receive no harm at my hands.' I cannot approve this mandate from a great king to a man who was ruling a large and populous area, all the more as the man was wicked.[5]

24. But in fact Alexander's own end was now close. Aristobulus says that there was a further portent of what was to come. Alexander was distributing among the Macedonian battalions the troops who had come with Peucestas from Persia and from the ocean with Philoxenus and Menander and, feeling thirsty, he went away from the tribunal, and left the royal throne empty. On either side of the throne were couches 2 with silver feet, on which the Companions in attendance on him used to sit. Some quite obscure person—some say a prisoner under open arrest—saw the throne and couches vacant, and the eunuchs standing round about the throne (the Companions had all risen with the king when he left), passed through the eunuchs, and went up and sat on the throne. Owing 3 to some Persian custom they did not drag him off the throne but rent their garments and beat themselves on their breasts and faces as if some terrible disaster had happened. When Alexander learned this, he ordered the man who had sat on the throne to be put to the rack, desiring to know if he had done this by

[5] App. XXVII 7.

ἐθέλοντα. τὸν δὲ οὐδὲν ἄλλο κατειπεῖν ὅτι μὴ ἐπὶ
νοῦν οἱ ἐλθὸν οὕτω πρᾶξαι· ᾗ δὴ καὶ μᾶλλον ἐπ'
οὐδενὶ ἀγαθῷ ξυμβῆναι αὐτῷ οἱ μάντεις ἐξηγοῦντο.

4 Ἡμέραι τε οὐ πολλαὶ ἐπὶ τούτῳ ἐγένοντο καὶ
τεθυκὼς τοῖς θεοῖς τάς τε νομιζομένας θυσίας ἐπὶ
ξυμφοραῖς ἀγαθαῖς καί τινας καὶ ἐκ μαντείας
εὐωχεῖτο ἅμα τοῖς φίλοις καὶ ἔπινε πόρρω τῶν
νυκτῶν. δοῦναι δὲ λέγεται καὶ τῇ στρατιᾷ ἱερεῖα
καὶ οἶνον κατὰ λόχους καὶ ἑκατοστύας. ἀπὸ δὲ
τοῦ πότου αὐτὸν μὲν ἀπαλλάττεσθαι ἐθέλειν ἐπὶ
κοιτῶνα εἰσὶν οἳ ἀνέγραψαν· Μήδιον δὲ αὐτῷ
ἐντυχόντα, τῶν ἑταίρων ἐν τῷ τότε τὸν πιθανώτα-
τον, δεηθῆναι κωμάσαι παρὰ οἷ· γενέσθαι γὰρ ἂν
ἡδὺν τὸν κῶμον.

25. Καὶ αἱ βασίλειοι ἐφημερίδες ὧδε ἔχουσιν·
πίνειν παρὰ Μηδίῳ αὐτὸν κωμάσαντα· ἔπειτα
ἐξαναστάντα καὶ λουσάμενον καθεύδειν τε καὶ
αὖθις δειπνεῖν παρὰ Μηδίῳ καὶ αὖθις πίνειν πόρρω
τῶν νυκτῶν· ἀπαλλαχθέντα δὲ τοῦ πότου λούσασ-
θαι· καὶ λουσάμενον ὀλίγον τι ἐμφαγεῖν καὶ καθεύ-
2 δειν αὐτοῦ, ὅτι ἤδη ἐπύρεσσεν. ἐκκομισθέντα δὲ
ἐπὶ κλίνης πρὸς τὰ ἱερὰ θῦσαι ὡς νόμος ἐφ' ἑκάστῃ
ἡμέρᾳ, καὶ τὰ ἱερὰ ἐπιθέντα κατακεῖσθαι ἐν τῷ
ἀνδρῶνι ἔστε ἐπὶ κνέφας. ἐν τούτῳ δὲ τοῖς ἡγεμόσι

---

[1] Al's last days: see also D. 116 f.; P. 73 ff. Note eunuchs
and Oriental ceremony (Ar.), cf. 9, 9 n.

[2] Not Ar., cf. 29, 4; he made Al. drink only after fever had
come on (P. 75, 3), contra the 'journal' (25, 1), which neither
he, nor probably Pt. (26, 2 n.), can have used. A. might have
known of it only through the 'vulgate' source he goes on to
cite for a story also in P. 75, 3, who likewise attaches to it the
record from the 'journal.' I suppose that A. treats as factual
what that source professedly drew from the 'journal.' The

arrangement as part of a plot. He would only say that the idea had come to him to do so. This actually made the seers readier to interpret what had happened as portending no good for Alexander.[1]

Not many days later Alexander offered the gods 4 the customary sacrifices for good fortune as well as some that were enjoined by prophecy and then began feasting with his friends and drinking far into the night.[2] It is said that he also gave the army sacrificial victims and wine by their companies and centuries. Some have recorded that when he was ready to leave the carouse and retire to his bedroom, Medius, one of his most trusted Companions at that time, met him and asked him to come and share his celebration, for it would be a merry party.

25. The royal journals have this account.[1] He drank and made merry with Medius, and then, after rising and bathing, went to sleep; he afterwards dined with Medius, and again drank till late in the night, and then breaking off from the carouse bathed, and after bathing ate a little and slept just where he was, as he was already in a fever. However, he was 2 carried out on a couch to perform the sacrifices custom prescribed for each day; after making the offerings he lay down in the men's apartments till

___

source of D. 117 and J. xii 13 is different, presumably Clitarchus, who wrote too early to bring Sarapis in. Medius of Larissa (Jacoby no. 129) figures in most versions of Al's death, cf. 25; 27, 2.

[1] P's shorter version (76) both omits and adds details; so neither he nor A. quoted *verbatim*. *Contra* Introd. xx 14 their versions are congruent. I regard the ' journal ' as spurious (26, 2 n.). The author might have incorporated authentic evidence (from e.g. Medius and N., who figures prominently). His account is compatible with the theory of excessive potations (14, 1 n.).

παραγγέλλειν ὑπὲρ τῆς πορείας καὶ τοῦ πλοῦ, τοὺς
μὲν ὡς πεζῇ ἰόντας παρασκευάζεσθαι ἐς τετάρτην
ἡμέραν, τοὺς δὲ ἅμα οἱ πλέοντας ὡς εἰς πέμπτην
3 πλευσουμένους. ἐκεῖθεν δὲ κατακομισθῆναι ἐπὶ τῆς
κλίνης ὡς ἐπὶ τὸν ποταμόν, καὶ πλοίου ἐπιβάντα
διαπλεῦσαι πέραν τοῦ ποταμοῦ ἐς τὸν παράδεισον,
κἀκεῖ αὖθις λουσάμενον ἀναπαύεσθαι. ἐς δὲ τὴν
ὑστεραίαν λούσασθαί τε αὖθις καὶ θῦσαι τὰ
νομιζόμενα· καὶ εἰς τὴν καμάραν εἰσελθόντα
κατακεῖσθαι διαμυθολογοῦντα πρὸς Μήδιον·
παραγγεῖλαι δὲ καὶ τοῖς ἡγεμόσιν ἀπαντῆσαι
4 ἕωθεν. ταῦτα πράξαντα δειπνῆσαι ὀλίγον·
κομισθέντα δὲ αὖθις ἐς τὴν καμάραν πυρέσσειν
ἤδη ξυνεχῶς τὴν νύκτα ὅλην· τῇ δὲ ὑστεραίᾳ
λούσασθαι καὶ λουσάμενον θῦσαι. Νεάρχῳ δὲ καὶ
τοῖς ἄλλοις ἡγεμόσι παραγγεῖλαι τὰ ἀμφὶ τὸν πλοῦν
ὅπως ἔσται ἐς τρίτην ἡμέραν. τῇ δὲ ὑστεραίᾳ
λούσασθαι αὖθις καὶ θῦσαι τὰ τεταγμένα, καὶ τὰ
ἱερὰ ἐπιθέντα οὐκέτι ἐλινύειν πυρέσσοντα. ἀλλὰ
καὶ ὣς τοὺς ἡγεμόνας εἰσκαλέσαντα παραγγέλλειν
τὰ πρὸς τὸν ἔκπλουν ὅπως αὐτῷ ἔσται ἕτοιμα·
λούσασθαί τε ἐπὶ τῇ ἑσπέρᾳ, καὶ λουσάμενον ἔχειν
5 ἤδη κακῶς. τῇ δὲ ὑστεραίᾳ μετακομισθῆναι ἐς τὴν
οἰκίαν τὴν πρὸς τῇ κολυμβήθρᾳ καὶ θῦσαι μὲν τὰ
τεταγμένα, ἔχοντα δὲ πονήρως ὅμως ἐσκαλέσαι
τῶν ἡγεμόνων τοὺς ἐπικαιριωτάτους καὶ ὑπὲρ τοῦ
πλοῦ αὖθις παραγγέλλειν. τῇ δ' ἐπιούσῃ μόγις
ἐκκομισθῆναι πρὸς τὰ ἱερὰ καὶ θῦσαι, καὶ μηδὲν
μεῖον ἔτι παραγγέλλειν ὑπὲρ τοῦ πλοῦ τοῖς
6 ἡγεμόσιν. ἐς δὲ τὴν ὑστεραίαν κακῶς ἤδη ἔχοντα
ὅμως θῦσαι τὰ τεταγμένα. παραγγεῖλαι δὲ τοὺς
μὲν στρατηγοὺς διατρίβειν κατὰ τὴν αὐλήν, χιλιάρ-

dark. At this time he gave the officers instructions
for the march and the voyage; the foot were to prepare for departure after three days, and those who
were to sail with him after four. Thence he was 3
carried on his couch to the river, and embarking on a
boat sailed across the river to the garden, and there
again bathed and rested. Next day again he bathed
and offered the usual sacrifices; after going into his
canopied bed he lay down, conversing with Medius.
After instructing his officers to meet him at dawn he
dined lightly, was carried again to the canopied bed 4
and remained in a high fever the whole night.
Next day he bathed, and after bathing sacrificed and
explained to Nearchus and the other officers all about
the voyage, and how it was to be conducted in two
days' time. Next day he bathed again, and offered
the appointed sacrifices, and after making the
offerings he no longer had any respite from fever.
Even so he summoned the officers and ordered them
to see that all was ready for the voyage; he bathed
in the evening, and after bathing was now very ill.
Yet next day he was carried again to the house near 5
the diving place and offered the appointed sacrifices
and, ill though he was, summoned the most important officers and gave them further instructions
for the voyage. Next day he just contrived to be
carried out to the sacrifices and offered them, and yet
still continued giving instructions to his officers for
the voyage. Next day, being now very ill, he still 6
offered the appointed sacrifices but ordered the
generals to wait in the court and the chiliarchs and

χας δὲ καὶ πεντακοσιάρχας πρὸ τῶν θυρῶν. ἤδη
δὲ παντάπασι πονήρως ἔχοντα διακομισθῆναι ἐκ
τοῦ παραδείσου ἐς τὰ βασίλεια. εἰσελθόντων δὲ
τῶν ἡγεμόνων γνῶναι μὲν αὐτούς, φωνῆσαι δὲ
μηδὲν ἔτι, ἀλλὰ εἶναι ἄναυδον· καὶ τὴν νύκτα
πυρέσσειν κακῶς καὶ τὴν ἡμέραν, καὶ τὴν ἄλλην
νύκτα καὶ τὴν ἡμέραν.

26. Οὕτως ἐν ταῖς ἐφημερίσι ταῖς βασιλείοις ἀναγέγραπται, καὶ ἐπὶ τούτοις ὅτι οἱ στρατιῶται ἐπό-
θησαν ἰδεῖν αὐτόν, οἱ μέν, ὡς ζῶντα ἔτι ἴδοιεν, οἱ
δέ, ὅτι τεθνηκέναι ἤδη ἐξηγγέλλετο, ἐπικρύπτεσθαι
δὲ αὐτοῦ ἐτόπαζον πρὸς τῶν σωματοφυλάκων τὸν
θάνατον, ὡς ἔγωγε δοκῶ· τοὺς πολλοὺς ⟨δὲ⟩ ὑπὸ
πένθους καὶ πόθου τοῦ βασιλέως βιάσασθαι ἰδεῖν
Ἀλέξανδρον. τὸν δὲ ἄφωνον μὲν εἶναι λέγουσι
παραπορευομένης τῆς στρατιᾶς, δεξιοῦσθαι δὲ ὡς
ἑκάστους τήν τε κεφαλὴν ἐπαίροντα μόγις καὶ τοῖν
2 ὀφθαλμοῖν ἐπισημαίνοντα. λέγουσι δὲ αἱ ἐφημερίδες αἱ βασίλειοι ἐν τοῦ Σαράπιδος τῷ ἱερῷ Πείθωνά τε ἐγκοιμηθέντα καὶ Ἄτταλον καὶ Δημο-
φῶντα καὶ Πευκέσταν, πρὸς δὲ Κλεομένην τε καὶ
Μενίδαν καὶ Σέλευκον, ἐπερωτᾶν τὸν θεὸν εἰ λῶον
καὶ ἄμεινον Ἀλεξάνδρῳ εἰς τὸ ἱερὸν τοῦ θεοῦ
κομισθέντα καὶ ἱκετεύσαντα θεραπεύεσθαι πρὸς
τοῦ θεοῦ· καὶ γενέσθαι φήμην τινὰ ἐκ τοῦ θεοῦ μὴ
κομίζεσθαι εἰς τὸ ἱερόν, ἀλλὰ αὐτοῦ μένοντι ἔσεσ-
3 θαι ἄμεινον. ταῦτά τε ἀπαγγεῖλαι τοὺς ἐπαίρους
καὶ Ἀλέξανδρον οὐ πολὺ ὕστερον ἀποθανεῖν, ὡς

---

[2] Griffith, *Hist. Maced.* ii 420.

[1] Variants in QC. x 5, 1 ff.; J. xii 15.

[2] The cult of this god was first established (on the best

pentacosiarchs [2] outside the doors. He was now extremely ill and was carried from the garden to the palace. When the officers came in, he knew them, but said no more; he was speechless. He was in high fever that night and day, and also the next night and day.

26. All this is written in the royal journals, which add that his soldiers longed to see him, some simply to see him still alive, and others because it was being put about that he was already dead and they suspected that his death was being concealed by the bodyguards (at least so I think), but the majority pressed in to see Alexander from grief and longing for their king. They say that he was already speechless when the army filed past, but that he greeted one and all, raising his head, though with difficulty, and making a sign to them with his eyes.[1] The royal journals say that Pithon, Attalus, Demophon and Peucestas, with Cleomenes, Menidas and Seleucus, slept in the temple of Sarapis [2] enquiring of the god whether it would be more desirable and better for Alexander to be brought into the temple of the god and after supplication to receive care from the god, but that an oracle was given from the god that he should not be brought into the temple, and that it would be better for him to stay where he was, and that, shortly after the Companions announced this,

evidence) late in Pt's reign (P. M. Fraser, *Ptol. Alexandria* 246 ff.; *Opusc. Athen.* 1967, 23–45). Bosworth, *CQ* 1970, 118 ff. conjectured that an earlier cult of Osiris-Apis could have been equated by contemporaries with that of Bel-Marduk. Let that be so: the *form* Sarapis still proves that the 'journal' has at least been tampered with; if in one point, why not in others? Pt. would hardly have interpolated an appeal to the god whose cult he propagated, where it proved ineffective. Cf. Introd. 14.

τοῦτο ἄρα ἤδη ὂν τὸ ἄμεινον. οὐ πόρρω δὲ τούτων οὔτε Ἀριστοβούλῳ οὔτε Πτολεμαίῳ ἀναγέγραπται. οἱ δὲ καὶ τάδε ἀνέγραψαν, ἐρέσθαι μὲν τοὺς
ἑταίρους αὐτὸν ὅτῳ τὴν βασιλείαν ἀπολείπει, τὸν δὲ
ὑποκρίνασθαι ὅτι τῷ κρατίστῳ· οἱ δέ, προσθεῖναι
πρὸς τούτῳ τῷ λόγῳ ὅτι μέγαν ἐπιτάφιον ἀγῶνα
ὁρᾷ ἐφ᾽ αὑτῷ ἐσόμενον.

27. Πολλὰ δὲ καὶ ἄλλα οἶδα ἀναγεγραμμένα
ὑπὲρ τῆς Ἀλεξάνδρου τελευτῆς, καὶ φάρμακον ὅτι
ἐπέμφθη παρὰ Ἀντιπάτρου Ἀλεξάνδρῳ καὶ ἐκ
τοῦ φαρμάκου ὅτι ἀπέθανε· καὶ τὸ φάρμακον ὅτι
Ἀριστοτέλης μὲν Ἀντιπάτρῳ ἐξεῦρε δεδοικὼς
ἤδη Ἀλέξανδρον Καλλισθένους ἕνεκα, Κάσανδρος [1]
δὲ ὁ Ἀντιπάτρου ἐκόμισεν· οἱ δὲ καὶ ὅτι ἐν
ἡμιόνου ὁπλῇ ἐκόμισε καὶ τοῦτο ἀνέγραψαν.

2 δοῦναι δὲ αὐτὸ Ἰόλλαν τὸν ἀδελφὸν τὸν Κασάνδρου
τὸν νεώτερον· εἶναι γὰρ οἰνοχόον βασιλικὸν τὸν
Ἰόλλαν καί τι καὶ λελυπῆσθαι πρὸς Ἀλεξάνδρου
ὀλίγῳ πρόσθεν τῆς τελευτῆς· οἱ δὲ καὶ Μήδιον
μετασχεῖν τοῦ ἔργου, ἐραστὴν ὄντα τοῦ Ἰόλλα·
καὶ αὐτὸν γὰρ εἶναι τὸν εἰσηγητὴν γενόμενον᾽ Ἀλεξάνδρῳ τοῦ κώμου· ὀδύνην τε αὐτῷ ἐπὶ τῇ κύλικι
γενέσθαι ὀξεῖαν, καὶ ἐπὶ τῇ ὀδύνῃ ἀπαλλαγῆναι ἐκ

3 τοῦ πότου. ἤδη δέ τις οὐκ ᾐσχύνθη ἀναγράψαι ὅτι
αἰσθόμενος οὐ βιώσιμον ὄντα αὐτὸν Ἀλέξανδρος
ἐς τὸν Εὐφράτην ποταμὸν ᾔει ἐμβαλῶν, ὡς ἀφανὴς

---

[1] Κάσσανδρος would be the more correct form.

[3] A's comment?   Or did it stand in the journal?
[4] They supplied no further details; this only shows that
their perhaps brief records did not contradict those in the
'journal'.   Evidently they stopped with Al's death, and
ignored anything such as the following story ('vulgate')

Alexander died; so it was in fact this that was now
' better '.³ Aristobulus and Ptolemy have recorded
no more than this.⁴ Some have also recorded that
his Companions asked him to whom he was leaving
his kingdom, and he replied, ' To the best man ';
others that he added that he saw that there would be
a great funeral contest over him.

27. I am aware, of course, that there are many
other versions recorded of Alexander's death; for
instance, that Antipater sent him a drug, of which he
died, and that it was made up for Antipater by
Aristotle, as he had already come to fear Alexander
on account of Callisthenes' death, and brought by
Cassander, Antipater's son.¹ Others have even said
that it was conveyed in a mule's hoof, and given to 2
Alexander by Iollas, Cassander's younger brother, as
he was the royal cup-bearer and had been aggrieved
by Alexander not long before his death. Others
again hold that Medius had some hand in the business,
as he was Iollas' lover, on the grounds that it was
Medius who suggested to Alexander the drinking-
bout, and that Alexander had a sharp feeling of pain
after quaffing the cup, and on feeling this he retired
from the carouse. One writer has had the impudence 3
to record that Alexander, feeling that he would not
survive, went to throw himself into the Euphrates, so

relating to the succession, or the rumours reported in ch. 27;
more on these topics in D. 117 f.; QC. x 5 and J. xii 14 f.

¹ D. and QC. merely reported, P. rejected, J. accepted the
story of poison, implicating numerous magnates, which probably originated in or before 321 and not first in 318 (P. 77; D.
xix 11), cf. R. Merkelbach, *Die Quellen des Alexanderromans* ²
164 ff., on the ' Testament of Alexander'. Without scientific
post-mortems poisoning could be freely alleged to explain a
sudden death, and neither proved nor disproved. Modern
speculations on the cause of death are futile.

ἐξ ἀνθρώπων γενόμενος πιστοτέραν τὴν δόξαν παρὰ
τοῖς ἔπειτα ἐγκαταλείποι ὅτι ἐκ θεοῦ τε αὐτῷ ἡ
γένεσις ξυνέβη καὶ παρὰ θεοὺς ἡ ἀποχώρησις.
Ῥωξάνην δὲ τὴν γυναῖκα οὐ λαθεῖν ἐξιόντα, ἀλλὰ
εἰργόμενον γὰρ πρὸς αὐτῆς ἐποιμώξαντα εἰπεῖν ὅτι
ἐφθόνησεν ἄρα αὐτῷ δόξης τῆς ἐς ἄπαν, ὡς θεῷ δὴ
γεγενημένῳ. καὶ ταῦτα ἐμοὶ ὡς μὴ ἀγνοεῖν δόξ-
αιμι μᾶλλον ὅτι λεγόμενά ἐστιν ἢ ὡς πιστὰ ἐς
ἀφήγησιν ἀναγεγράφθω.

28. Ἐτελεύτα μὲν δὴ Ἀλέξανδρος τῇ τετάρτῃ
καὶ δεκάτῃ καὶ ἑκατοστῇ Ὀλυμπιάδι ἐπὶ Ἡγησίου
ἄρχοντος Ἀθήνησιν· ἐβίω δὲ δύο καὶ τριάκοντα
ἔτη καὶ τοῦ τρίτου μῆνας ἐπέλαβεν ὀκτώ, ὡς
λέγει Ἀριστόβουλος· ἐβασίλευσε δὲ δώδεκα ἔτη
καὶ τοὺς ὀκτὼ τούτους μῆνας, τό τε σῶμα κάλλισ-
τος καὶ φιλοπονώτατος καὶ ὀξύτατος γενόμενος καὶ
τὴν γνώμην ἀνδρειότατος καὶ φιλοτιμότατος καὶ
φιλοκινδυνότατος καὶ τοῦ θείου ἐπιμελέστατος·
2 ἡδονῶν δὲ τῶν μὲν τοῦ σώματος ἐγκρατέστατος,
τῶν δὲ τῆς γνώμης ἐπαίνου μόνου ἀπληστότατος·
ξυνιδεῖν δὲ τὸ δέον ἔτι ἐν τῷ ἀφανεῖ ὂν δεινότατος,
καὶ ἐκ τῶν φαινομένων τὸ εἰκὸς ξυμβαλεῖν ἐπιτυχ-
έστατος, καὶ τάξαι στρατιὰν καὶ ὁπλίσαι τε καὶ
κοσμῆσαι δαημονέστατος· καὶ τὸν θυμὸν τοῖς
στρατιώταις ἐπᾶραι καὶ ἐλπίδων ἀγαθῶν ἐμπλῆσαι

---

[1] To judge from other archon dates in A., either he or a copyist has omitted the Attic month. A Babylonian document
shows that Al. died on 10/11 June 323 (A. E. Samuel, *Ptol.
Chronology*, 1962, 46 f.).

[2] This puts his birth in October 356 (P. 3, 3 dates it to about
July) and accession in October 336, cf. Bosworth on i 1, 1.

[3] Cf. P. 4. QC. x 5, 26 ff. has a similar list of qualities,
omitting beauty, piety, the technique of generalship and

that he might disappear from the world and make more credible to posterity the belief that his birth was by a god and that it was to the gods that he had departed, but that Roxane, his wife, noticed that he was going out and stopped him, when he groaned and said that she was really grudging him the everlasting fame accorded to one who had been born a god. So much for stories which I have set down to show that I know they are told rather than because they are credible enough to recount.

28. Alexander died in the hundred and fourteenth Olympiad and the archonship of Hegesias at Athens.[1] According to Aristobulus, he lived thirty-two years and eight months; his reign lasted twelve years and the same eight months.[2] He excelled in physical beauty,[3] in zest for exertions, in shrewdness of judgement, in courage, in love of honour and danger, and in care for religion. Over bodily pleasures he 2 exercised the greatest self-control: as for those of the mind, it was praise alone for which he was absolutely insatiate. He had the most wonderful power to discern the right course, when it was still unclear, and was most successful in inferring from observed facts what was likely to follow.[4] His skill in marshalling, arming and equipping a force, in raising the morale of his troops, filling them with

everything in A. § 3, except generosity (shown especially to friends and troops); he adds devotion to his parents, Philip (whom he avenged) and Olympias, and clemency to the conquered; he suggests that his love of danger and glory was excessive, but that he restricted the indulgence of his passions to what was natural.

[4] Reminiscent of Thucydides on Themistocles (i 138, 3). Al. is in general characterized as the good king and the good general by quite conventional criteria. Cf. ii 26, 3 n. for texts that better reveal Al's special qualities.

καὶ τὸ δεῖμα ἐν τοῖς κινδύνοις τῷ ἀδεεῖ τῷ αὐτοῦ
3 ἀφανίσαι, ξύμπαντα ταῦτα γενναιότατος. καὶ οὖν
καὶ ὅσα ἐν τῷ ἐμφανεῖ πρᾶξαι, ξὺν μεγίστῳ θάρσει
ἔπραξεν, ὅσα τε φθάσας ὑφαρπάσαι τῶν πολεμίων,
πρὶν καὶ δεῖσαί τινα αὐτὰ ὡς ἐσόμενα, προλαβεῖν
δεινότατος· καὶ τὰ μὲν ξυντεθέντα ἢ ὁμολογηθέντα
φυλάξαι βεβαιότατος, πρὸς δὲ τῶν ἐξαπατώντων
μὴ ἁλῶναι ἀσφαλέστατος, χρημάτων τε ἐς μὲν
ἡδονὰς τὰς αὐτοῦ φειδωλότατος, ἐς δὲ εὐποιίαν
τῶν πέλας ἀφθονώτατος.

29. Εἰ δέ τι ἐπλημμελήθη Ἀλεξάνδρῳ δι᾽
ὀξύτητα ἢ ὑπ᾽ ὀργῆς, ἢ εἴ τι ἐς τὸ ὑπερογκότερον
προήχθη βαρβαρίσαι, οὐ μεγάλα τίθεμαι ἔγωγε, εἰ
τὴν νεότητά τέ τις τὴν Ἀλεξάνδρου μὴ ἀνεπιεικῶς
ἐνθυμηθείη καὶ τὸ διηνεκὲς τῆς εὐτυχίας καὶ τοὺς
πρὸς ἡδονήν, οὐκ ἐπὶ τῷ βελτίστῳ, τοῖς βασιλεῦσι
ξυνόντας τε καὶ ἐπὶ κακῷ ξυνεσομένους· ἀλλὰ
μεταγνῶναί γε ἐφ᾽ οἷς ἐπλημμέλησε μόνῳ οἶδα τῶν
πάλαι βασιλέων Ἀλεξάνδρῳ ὑπάρξαι ὑπὸ γεν-
2 ναιότητος. οἱ δὲ πολλοί, εἰ καί τι ἔγνωσαν πλημ-
μελήσαντες, οἱ δὲ τῷ προηγορεῖν αὐτοῦ, ὡς καλῶς
δὴ πραχθέντος, ἐπικρύψειν οἴονται τὴν ἁμαρτίαν,
κακῶς γιγνώσκοντες. μόνη γὰρ ἔμοιγε δοκεῖ ἴασις
ἁμαρτίας ὁμολογεῖν τε ἁμαρτόντα καὶ δῆλον εἶναι ἐπ᾽
αὐτῷ μεταγιγνώσκοντα, ὡς τοῖς τε παθοῦσί τι ἄχαρι

---

[5] E.g. iv 27, 3 f.!

[1] Cf. 30, 1; QC. x 5, 26, cf. 29, likewise excuses errors by
youth and fortune.

[2] Cf. ii 6, 4; iv 8, 3 and 9, 7–9 (vii 12, 5 is a little different);
this theme was conventional, see e.g. Seneca, de Beneficiis vi
30 ff.; the model king would choose virtuous and candid
advisers, see Dio Chrysostom i 17; 31; iii 86–129.

confidence and banishing their fear in dangers by
his own fearlessness was altogether most admirable.
In fact, when what was to be done was clear, he dis- 3
played the utmost daring, and whenever he had to
snatch a success from the enemy by anticipation,
before any one could even apprehend what was to
happen, he had a most wonderful ability to strike
first. No one was more reliable in keeping pacts or
agreements, or more secure from being trapped by
the fraudulent.[5] As for money, he was very sparing
in using it for his own pleasures, but most liberal in
employing it for the benefit of others.

29. If Alexander was at all guilty of misdeeds due
to haste or anger, or if he was led on to adopt barbarian practices involving too much pretension, I do
not personally regard it as important; only consider
in charity his youth, his unbroken good fortune,[1] and
the fact that it is men that seek to please and not to
act for the best who are and will be the associates of
kings, exercising an evil influence.[2] But remorse for
his misdeeds [3] was to my knowledge peculiar to Alexander among the kings of old times, and resulted
from his noble nature. Most people, even if they 2
have recognized their guilt, suppose that they will
conceal it by defending their action as actually right.
This shows bad judgement, for in my view there is no
remedy for a misdeed unless a man admits it and
makes his repentance plain; then those who have
sustained some harm would not feel their sufferings

---

[3] iv 9, 2 and 6; vi 13, 4; 30, 1. QC. also illustrates Al's
remorse: v, 7, 11; viii 8, 23; 12, 18. See Brunt, *Athenaeum*
1977, 38.

ARRIAN

οὐ πάντῃ χαλεπὰ τὰ παθήματα φαινόμενα, εἰ ὁ δράσας αὐτὰ ξυγχωροίη ὅτι οὐ καλὰ ἔδρασεν, αὑτῷ τέ τινι ἐς τὸ μέλλον ταύτην ἐλπίδα ἀγαθὴν ὑπολειπομένην, μή ποτε ἂν παραπλήσιόν τι ἁμαρτεῖν, εἰ τοῖς 3 πρόσθεν πλημμεληθεῖσιν ἀχθόμενος φαίνοιτο. ὅτι δὲ ἐς θεὸν τὴν γένεσιν τὴν αὑτοῦ ἀνέφερεν, οὐδὲ τοῦτο ἐμοὶ δοκεῖ μέγα εἶναι αὐτῷ τὸ πλημμέλημα, εἰ μὴ καὶ σόφισμα ἦν τυχὸν ἐς τοὺς ὑπηκόους τοῦ σεμνοῦ ἕνεκα. οὔκουν δοκεῖ ἔμοιγε ἢ Μίνωος γενέσθαι βασιλεὺς ἀφανέστερος ἢ Αἰακοῦ ἢ Ῥαδαμάνθυος, οἷς δὴ ἐς Δία ἀνενεχθεῖσα ἡ γένεσις πρὸς τῶν πάλαι ἀνθρώπων οὐδεμιᾷ αὐτῶν ὕβρει προστίθεται, οὐδὲ Θησέως τοῦ Ποσειδῶνος οὐδὲ Ἴωνος τοῦ 4 Ἀπόλλωνος. ὡς ἔμοιγε καὶ ἡ Περσικὴ σκευὴ σόφισμα δοκεῖ εἶναι πρός τε τοὺς βαρβάρους, ὡς μὴ πάντῃ, ἀλλότριον αὐτῶν φαίνεσθαι τὸν βασιλέα, καὶ πρὸς τοὺς Μακεδόνας, ὡς ἀποστροφήν τινα εἶναι αὐτῷ ἀπὸ τῆς ὀξύτητός τε καὶ ὕβρεως τῆς Μακεδονικῆς· ἐφ' ὅτῳ δὴ καὶ ἐγκαταμίξαί μοι δοκεῖ ταῖς τάξεσιν αὐτῶν τοὺς Πέρσας τοὺς μηλοφόρους καὶ τοῖς ἀγήμασι τοὺς ὁμοτίμους. καὶ οἱ πότοι δέ, ὥς λέγει Ἀριστόβουλος, οὐ τοῦ οἴνου ἕνεκα μακροὶ αὐτῷ ἐγίγνοντο, οὐ γὰρ πίνειν πολὺν οἶνον Ἀλέξανδρον, ἀλλὰ φιλοφροσύνης τῆς ἐς τοὺς ἑταίρους.

30. Ὅστις δὲ κακίζει Ἀλέξανδρον, μὴ μόνον ὅσα ἄξια κακίζεσθαί ἐστι προφερόμενος

---

[4] Cf. Brunt, *op. cit* 45 ff. for P's more thorough-going defence. QC. x 5, 53 f. seems to excuse Al's claim to divinity and adoption of Persian practices by his 'fortune.' A. acknowledges the claim as a historic fact (cf. App. V), but does not concede its truth; even though he thinks Al. enjoyed divine

to be intolerable, if the offender were to concede the
wrongfulness of his action, and he himself would be
left with good hope for the future in the thought that
he would never do like wrong again, if he were
plainly distressed by his former transgressions.
Again even Alexander's practice of referring his own 3
birth to a god was not in my opinion a grave fault on
his part [4]; and perhaps it was no more than an
expedient to make him impressive to his subjects.
Indeed in my own view he was not less distinguished
as a king than Minos or Aeacus or Rhadamanthys,
whose birth was actually referred to Zeus by the men
of old without incurring any imputation of insolence,
or than Theseus, son of Posidon, and Ion, son of
Apollo. So too in my opinion his Persian dress was a 4
device designed for the barbarians, to make the king
not wholly alien from them in appearance, and for the
Macedonians as well, to give him some protection
from the sharpness and insolence of Macedonian behaviour; indeed in my opinion it was also for this
reason that he introduced the Persian ' apple-bearers '
into the Macedonian battalions [5] and the Persian
peers into the *agemas*. His drinking bouts too, as
Aristobulus says, were prolonged not for the sake of
the wine, for he drank little wine, but out of courtesy
to the Companions.[6]

30. Any one who reproaches Alexander should not
do so by merely citing actions that merit reproach,

aid or inspiration (30, 2), the claim can at best be excused,
partly as a means of impressing the ' subjects,' among whom he
may well include here Macedonians as well as Orientals. His
judgement in § 4 is incompatible with iv 7, 4, cf. App. XXVIII
34.

[5] See iii 11, 5; vii 11, 3 nn.
[6] App. XIV 4; vii 14, 1; 24, 4 nn.

κακιζέτω, ἀλλὰ ξύμπαντα τὰ Ἀλεξάνδρου εἰς
ἓν χωρίον ξυναγαγὼν οὕτω δὴ ἐκλογιζέσθω ὅστις
τε ὢν αὐτὸς καὶ ὁποίᾳ τύχῃ κεχρημένος ὅντινα
γενόμενον ἐκεῖνον καὶ ἐς ὅσον εὐτυχίας τῆς
ἀνθρωπίνης ἐλθόντα βασιλέα τε ἀμφοῖν τοῖν
ἠπείροιν ἀναμφιλογώτατα γενόμενον καὶ ἐπὶ πᾶν
ἐξικόμενον τῷ αὐτοῦ ὀνόματι κακίζει, σμικρότερός
τε ὢν αὐτὸς καὶ ἐπὶ σμικροῖς πονούμενος καὶ οὐδὲ
2 ταῦτα ἐν κόσμῳ τιθέμενος. ὡς ἔγωγε δοκῶ ὅτι
οὔτε τι ἔθνος ἀνθρώπων οὔτε τις πόλις ἐν τῷ τότε
ἦν οὔτε τις εἷς ἄνθρωπος εἰς ὃν οὐ πεφοιτήκει τὸ
Ἀλεξάνδρου ὄνομα. οὔκουν οὐδὲ ἐμοὶ ἔξω τοῦ θείου
φῦναι ἂν δοκεῖ ἀνὴρ οὐδενὶ ἄλλῳ ἀνθρώπων ἐοικώς.
καὶ ταῦτα χρησμοί τε ἐπισημῆναι ἐπὶ τῇ τελευτῇ
τῇ Ἀλεξάνδρου λέγονται καὶ φάσματα ἄλλα ἄλλοις
γενόμενα καὶ ἐνύπνια φανέντα ἄλλα ἄλλοις καὶ ἡ
ἐς τοῦτο ἐξ ἀνθρώπων τιμή τε αὐτοῦ καὶ μνήμη
οὐκ ἀνθρωπίνη οὖσα, καὶ νῦν δὲ διὰ τοσούτου
ἄλλοι χρησμοὶ ἐπὶ τῇ τιμῇ αὐτοῦ τῷ ἔθνει τῷ
3 Μακεδόνων χρησθέντες. ἐπεὶ καὶ αὐτὸς ἐμεμψάμην
ἔστιν ἃ ἐν τῇ ξυγγραφῇ τῶν Ἀλεξάνδρου ἔργων,
ἀλλὰ αὐτόν γε Ἀλέξανδρον οὐκ αἰσχύνομαι θαυ-
μάζων· τὰ δὲ ἔργα ἐκεῖνα ἐκάκισα ἀληθείας τε
ἕνεκα τῆς ἐμῆς καὶ ἅμα ὠφελείας τῆς ἐς ἀνθρώπους·
ἐφ' ὅτῳ ὡρμήθην οὐδὲ αὐτὸς ἄνευ θεοῦ ἐς τήνδε
τὴν ξυγγραφήν.

323
B.C.

but should collect all his actions together, and then carefully reflect who he himself is and what kind of fortune he enjoys, that he can condemn Alexander, given what Alexander became and the height of human good fortune he attained, the unquestioned king of both continents whose name reached every part of the world, whereas he is himself a lesser man, whose energies are spent on petty things and who does not even get these things right. In my own 2 view there was no race of men, no city in those days, no single man whom the name of Alexander had not reached. For this reason I do not believe that a man peerless among mankind would have been born without divine agency. Signs of this are said to have been given by oracles on Alexander's death, by various visions seen by different persons and dreams that appeared to different men, and by the honour mankind pay him to this day and the more than human memory preserved of him,[1] and even now after so long a passage of time other oracles in his honour have been given to the Macedonian people. So, 3 while I myself have censured some of Alexander's acts in my history of them, I am not ashamed to express admiration of Alexander himself; I have made those criticisms from my own respect for truth and also for the good of mankind: it was for that purpose that I embarked on this history, and like Alexander not without God's help.

[1] Cults of Al. persisted in Roman times in Greek cities of Asia, where Al. could be seen as a liberator (S. xiv 1, 31; OGIS 3; 222; SEG iv 521), cf. App. XXVIII 29, as in Egyptian Alexandria (Sammelbuch 6611).

INDICA

ΙΝΔΙΚΗ

1. Τὰ ἔξω Ἰνδοῦ ποταμοῦ τὰ πρὸς ἑσπέρην ἔστε
ἐπὶ ποταμὸν Κωφῆνα Ἀστακηνοὶ καὶ Ἀσσακηνοί,
2 ἔθνεα Ἰνδικά, ἐποικέουσιν, ἀλλ᾽ οὔτε μεγάλοι τὰ
σώματα, καθάπερ οἱ ἐντὸς τοῦ Ἰνδοῦ ᾠκισμένοι,
οὔτε ἀγαθοὶ ὡσαύτως τὸν θυμὸν οὐδὲ μέλανες
3 ὡσαύτως τοῖς πολλοῖς Ἰνδοῖσιν. οὗτοι πάλαι μὲν
Ἀσσυρίοις ὑπήκοοι ἦσαν, ἔπει⟨τα Μήδοισιν,
ἐπὶ⟩ δὲ Μήδοισι Περσέων ἤκουον, καὶ φόρους ἀπέ-
φερον Κύρῳ τῷ Καμβύσου ἐκ τῆς γῆς σφῶν, οὓς
4 ἔταξε Κῦρος. Νυσαῖοι δὲ οὐκ Ἰνδικὸν γένος ἐστίν,
ἀλλὰ τῶν ἅμα Διονύσῳ ἐλθόντων ἐς τὴν γῆν τὴν
Ἰνδῶν, τυχὸν μὲν [καὶ] Ἑλλήνων, ὅσοι ἀπόμαχοι
αὐτῶν ἐγένοντο ἐν τοῖς πολέμοις οὕστινας πρὸς
5 Ἰνδοὺς Διόνυσος ἐπολέμησε, τυχὸν δὲ καὶ τῶν
ἐπιχωρίων τοὺς ἐθέλοντας τοῖς Ἕλλησι συνῴκισε,
τήν τε χώρην Νυσαίην ὠνόμασεν ἀπὸ τοῦ ὄρεος [1]
τῆς Νύσης Διόνυσος καὶ τὴν πόλιν αὐτὴν Νῦσαν
6 καὶ τὸ ὄρος τὸ πρὸς τῇ πόλει, ὅτου ἐν τῇσιν

---

[1] I have restored the reading of A. Roos emended to τῆς
τροφοῦ, cf. *Anab.* v 1, 6.

---

* Roos' notes refer to relevant ancient texts and some
modern works. I adopt his spellings of proper names, normally without indicating where he, or other scholars, deviate
from the manuscript. Sources for 1–17: App. XVII 1–9.

[1] A. tries to reconcile E's view that the Indus was the western
boundary of India (App. XVII 7) with the presence of Indians
as far west as the Kabul by differentiating their qualities from
those of Indians east of the Indus and by pointing out that
they had been conquered before Al's time, probably following

INDICA*

1. All the territory that lies beyond the boundary of the river Indus westwards to the river Cophen [Kabul] is inhabited by Astacenians and Assacenians, Indian tribes.[1] But they are not, like the Indians 2 dwelling within the boundary of the river Indus, tall of stature, nor as brave in spirit, nor as black as most Indians. They were subject long ago to the Assy- 3 rians, then to the Medes, and after the Medes to the Persians; and they paid such tribute from their land to Cyrus son of Cambyses as he commanded. The 4 Nysaeans are not an Indian race, but part of those who came with Dionysus to India, perhaps Greeks who became unfit for service in the wars Dionysus waged with the Indians, perhaps also volunteers of 5 the neighbouring tribes whom Dionysus settled there together with the Greeks. He called the country Nysaea from the mountain Nysa,[2] and the city itself Nysa. The mountain near the city, on whose foot- 6

---

[1] Meg. (cf. 5, 4 ff.). There is no other evidence for Assyrian or Median rule even in the Kabul valley, i.e. in Gandara or Gandaritis (*RE* vii 696 ff.), but, already Persian at the accession of Darius I (*c.* 518 BC), it had probably been subdued by Cyrus (*CHI* 329 ff.); the report here is not incongruent with vi 24, 2 (N.) nor with *Ind.* 9, 10 (Meg.), if Meg. thought that the region was not part of ' India'. He and every one had forgotten Darius' conquest of Sind (App. XV). Astaceni (not named in *Anab.*): probably subjects of Astis, who ruled in ' Peucelaotis ' (iv 22, 8); the forms Peucelaitis (cf. Meg. 4, 11) and Massaca (contrast iv 26, 1; 28, 1) show that A. is here following an authority, probably Meg. and not Ar. (App. XVII 5), different from that in *Anab.* iv 22 ff., probably Pt.

[2] See v 1, 2 n.

ὑπωρείῃσιν ᾤκισται ἡ Νῦσα, Μηρὸς κληίζεται ἐπὶ
τῇ συμφορῇ ᾗτινι ἐχρήσατο εὐθὺς γενόμενος.
7 ταῦτα μὲν οἱ ποιηταὶ ἐπὶ Διονύσῳ ἐποίησαν, καὶ
ἐξηγείσθων αὐτὰ ὅσοι λόγιοι Ἑλλήνων ἢ βαρ-
8 βάρων· ἐν Ἀσσακηνοῖσι δὲ Μάσσακα, πόλις
μεγάλη, ἵναπερ καὶ τὸ κράτος τῆς γῆς ἐστι τῆς
Ἀσσακίης· καὶ ἄλλη πόλις Πευκελαῖτις, μεγάλη
καὶ αὐτή, οὐ μακρὰν τοῦ Ἰνδοῦ. ταῦτα μὲν ἔξω
τοῦ Ἰνδοῦ ποταμοῦ ᾤκισται πρὸς ἑσπέρην ἔστε ἐπὶ
τὸν Κωφῆνα· 2. τὰ δὲ ἀπὸ τοῦ Ἰνδοῦ πρὸς ἔω,
τοῦτό μοι ἔστω ἡ Ἰνδῶν γῆ καὶ Ἰνδοὶ οὗτοι ἔστω-
σαν.

ὅροι δὲ τῆς Ἰνδῶν γῆς πρὸς μὲν βορέου ἀνέμου
2 ὁ Ταῦρος τὸ ὄρος. καλέεται δὲ οὐ Ταῦρος ἔτι ἐν
τῇ γῇ ταύτῃ, ἀλλὰ ἄρχεται μὲν ἀπὸ θαλάσσης ὁ
Ταῦρος τῆς κατὰ Παμφύλους τε καὶ Λυκίην καὶ
Κίλικας παρατείνει τε ἔστε τὴν πρὸς ἔω θάλασσαν,
3 τέμνων τὴν Ἀσίην πᾶσαν, ἄλλο δὲ ἄλλῃ καλέεται
τὸ ὄρος, τῇ μὲν Παραπάμισος, τῇ δὲ Ἡμωδός,
ἄλλῃ δὲ Ἴμαον κληίζεται, καὶ τυχὸν ἄλλα καὶ ἄλλα
4 ἔχει οὐνόματα. Μακεδόνες δὲ οἱ ξὺν Ἀλεξάνδρῳ
στρατεύσαντες Καύκασον αὐτὸ ἐκάλεον, ἄλλον τοῦτον Καύκασον, οὐ τὸν Σκυθικόν, ὡς καὶ [τὸν]
ἐπέκεινα τοῦ Καυκάσου λόγον κατέχειν ὅτι
5 ἦλθεν Ἀλέξανδρος. τὰ πρὸς ἑσπέρην δὲ τῆς
Ἰνδῶν γῆς ὁ ποταμὸς ὁ Ἰνδὸς ἀπείργει ἔστε ἐπὶ
τὴν μεγάλην θάλασσαν, ἵναπερ αὐτὸς κατὰ δύο
στόματα ἐκδιδοῖ, οὐ συνεχέα ἀλλήλοισι τὰ στόματα,
6 κατάπερ τὰ πέντε τοῦ Ἴστρου ἐστὶ συνεχέα, ἀλλ'
ὡς τὰ τοῦ Νείλου, ὑπ' ὅτων τὸ Δέλτα ποιέεται τὸ
Αἰγύπτιον, ὧδέ τι καὶ τῆς Ἰνδῶν γῆς Δέλτα ποιέει ὁ
Ἰνδὸς ποταμός, οὐ μεῖον τοῦ Αἰγυπτίου, καὶ τοῦτο

hills Nysa is built, is also called Merus (thigh) because
of the incident at the moment of Dionysus' birth.
All this the poets sang of Dionysus; and I leave in- 7
terpretation to learned Greeks or barbarians. In 8
Assacenian territory lies Massaca, a great city which
has the dominion in the Assacian land, and another
city Peucelaïtis, which is also large, not far from the
Indus. These then are the inhabited places beyond
the Indus west to the river Cophen. 2. It is the parts
east of the Indus that I shall call India, and its inhabitants Indians.

The northern boundary of the land of India is Mount
Taurus. That is not the name given to it in this land: 2
in fact, while Taurus begins from the sea by Pamphylia and Lycia and Cilicia and reaches as far as the
Eastern Ocean, cutting right through Asia, the 3
mountain has different names in different places: in
one Parapamisus, in another Emodus, elsewhere
Imaon, and perhaps it has all sorts of other names.
The Macedonians who fought with Alexander called 4
it Caucasus, a different Caucasus from the Scythian;
so that the story ran that Alexander penetrated
beyond the Caucasus.[1] The western part of India is 5
bounded by the river Indus right down to the Ocean,
where it runs out by two mouths, not joined together
like the five [2] mouths of the Ister, but like those of the 6
Nile which form the Egyptian delta; an Indian delta
is formed in the same way by the river Indus, as large
as the Egyptian, and is called Patala in the Indian

---

[1] Cf. v 5, 1–4; S. xv 1, 11; App. XII 3. This chapter
comes from E. Emodus and Imaon (6, 4), meaning ' snowy '
(Pliny, *NH* vi 64, cf. Sanskrit ' himavat '), represent the
Himalayas.

[2] Evidently from E., cf. i 3, 2; v 4, 1; A. repeats what he
finds in his source, ignorant or oblivious of the 7 mouths known
since Augustus' time (*RE* iv 2117 f.).

309

7 Πάταλα τῇ Ἰνδῶν γλώσσῃ καλέεται. τὸ δὲ πρὸς
νότου τε ἀνέμου καὶ μεσαμβρίης αὐτὴ ἡ μεγάλη
θάλασσα ἀπείργει τὴν Ἰνδῶν γῆν, καὶ τὰ πρὸς ἔω
8 ἡ αὐτὴ θάλασσα ἀπείργει. τὰ μὲν πρὸς μεσημ-
βρίης κατὰ Πάταλά τε καὶ τοῦ Ἰνδοῦ τὰς ἐκβολὰς
ὤφθη πρός τε Ἀλεξάνδρου καὶ Μακεδόνων καὶ
πολλῶν Ἑλλήνων· τὰ δὲ πρὸς ἔω Ἀλέξανδρος μὲν
οὐκ ἐπῆλθε τὰ [δὲ] πρόσω ποταμοῦ Ὑφάσιος,
9 ὀλίγοι δὲ ἀνέγραψαν τὰ μέχρι ποταμοῦ Γάγγεω καὶ ἵνα τοῦ Γάγγεω αἱ ἐκβολαὶ καὶ πόλις
Παλίμβοθρα μεγίστη Ἰνδῶν πρὸς τῷ Γάγγῃ.
3. ἐμοὶ δὲ Ἐρατοσθένης ὁ Κυρηναῖος πιστότερος
ἄλλου ἔστω, ὅτι γῆς περιόδου πέρι ἔμελεν Ἐρατο-
2 σθένει. οὗτος ἀπὸ τοῦ ὄρεος τοῦ Ταύρου, ἵνα τοῦ
Ἰνδοῦ αἱ πηγαί, παρ' αὐτὸν ⟨τὸν⟩ Ἰνδὸν ποταμὸν
ἰόντι ἔστε ἐπὶ τὴν μεγάλην θάλασσαν καὶ τοῦ
Ἰνδοῦ τὰς ἐκβολὰς μυρίους σταδίους καὶ τρισχιλίους τὴν πλευρὴν λέγει ἐπέχειν τῆς γῆς τῆς
3 Ἰνδῶν. ταυτησὶ δὲ ἀντίπορον πλευρὴν ποιέει τὴν
ἀπὸ τοῦ αὐτοῦ ὄρεος παρὰ τὴν ἑώην θάλασσαν,
οὐκέτι ταύτῃ τῇ πλευρῇ ἴσην, ἀλλὰ ἄκρην γὰρ
ἀνέχειν ἐπὶ μέγα εἴσω εἰς τὸ πέλαγος, ἐς τρισχιλίους σταδίους μάλιστα ἀνατείνουσαν τὴν ἄκρην·
εἴη ἂν ὦν αὐτῷ ἡ πλευρὴ τῆς Ἰνδῶν γῆς ⟨ἡ⟩ πρὸς
ἔω μυρίους καὶ ἑξακισχιλίους σταδίους ἐπέχουσα.
4 τοῦτο μὲν αὐτῷ πλάτος τῆς Ἰνδῶν γῆς συμβαίνει,
μῆκος δὲ τὸ ἀπ' ἑσπέρης ἐπὶ ἔω ἔστε μὲν ἐπὶ
πόλιν Παλίμβοθρα μεμετρημένον σχοίνοισι λέγει
ἀναγράφειν καὶ — εἶναι γὰρ ὁδὸν βασιληίην —
τοῦτο ἐπέχειν ἐς μυρίους σταδίους· τὰ δὲ
5 ἐπέκεινα οὐκέτι ὡσαύτως ἀτρεκέα· φήμας δὲ ὅσοι
ἀνέγραψαν, ξὺν τῇ ἄκρῃ τῇ ἀνεχούσῃ ἐς τὸ πέλαγος

tongue. On the south side the Ocean itself bounds 7
the land of India, as also on the east. The southern 8
part near Patala and the mouths of the Indus were
seen by Alexander and Macedonians and many
Greeks; as for the eastern part, Alexander did not
penetrate beyond the river Hyphasis. A few writers 9
have described the parts up to the Ganges and round
its mouths and the city of Palimbothra, the greatest
Indian city near the Ganges. 3. I shall take
Eratosthenes of Cyrene to be more trustworthy than
any other writer, since he concerned himself with a
general chart of the earth. He states that starting 2
from Mount Taurus, where the Indus rises,[1] and
following the course of the river to the Ocean and the
mouths of the Indus, the side of India is thirteen
thousand stades in length. The opposite side from 3
the same mountain to the Eastern Ocean he reckons
as more than equal to this side, since it has a promontory running far out into the sea, stretching to
about three thousand stades. So then he would give
this side of India on the east a total length of sixteen
thousand stades. So this is his estimate of the 4
breadth of India; as for its length, from west to east
as far as the city of Palimbothra, he says that he
records it according to the measurement in *schoinoi* [2]
(for there is a royal road) giving an extent of ten
thousand stades; beyond Palimbothra the information is not so accurate. Those who have followed 5
common talk say that including the promontory that

---

[1] Cf. v 4, 1 n. On what follows see App. XVII 7 f.
[2] Each of 40 stades on E's system, Pliny, *NH* xii 53.

ἐς μυρίους σταδίους μάλιστα ἐπέχειν λέγουσιν·
εἶναι δὲ ἂν ὧν τὸ μῆκος τῆς Ἰνδῶν γῆς σταδίων
6 μάλιστα δισμυρίων. Κτησίης δὲ ὁ Κνίδιος τὴν
Ἰνδῶν γῆν ἴσην τῇ ἄλλῃ Ἀσίῃ λέγει, οὐδὲν λέγων,
οὐδὲ Ὀνησίκριτος, τρίτην μοῖραν τῆς πάσης γῆς.
Νέαρχος δὲ μηνῶν τεσσάρων ὁδὸν τὴν δι᾽ αὐτοῦ
7 τοῦ πεδίου τῆς Ἰνδῶν γῆς. Μεγασθένει δὲ τὸ ἀπὸ
ἀνατολῶν ἐς ἑσπέρην πλάτος ἐστὶ τῆς Ἰνδῶν γῆς ὅ
τι περ οἱ ἄλλοι μῆκος ποιέουσι· καὶ λέγει Μεγα-
8 σθένης μυρίων καὶ ἑξακισχιλίων σταδίων εἶναι
ἵναπερ τὸ βραχύτατον αὐτοῦ. τὸ δὲ ἀπὸ ἄρκτου
πρὸς μεσημβρίην, τοῦτο δὲ αὐτῷ μῆκος γίνεται,
καὶ ἐπέχει ⟨σταδίους⟩ τριηκοσίους καὶ δισχιλίους
9 καὶ δισμυρίους ἵναπερ τὸ στενότατον αὐτοῦ.

ποταμοὶ δὲ τοσοίδε εἰσὶν ἐν τῇ Ἰνδῶν γῇ ὅσοι
οὐδὲ ἐν τῇ πάσῃ Ἀσίῃ. μέγιστοι μὲν ὁ Γάγγης τε
καὶ ὁ Ἰνδός, ὅτου καὶ ἡ γῆ ἐπώνυμος, ἄμφω τοῦ
τε Νείλου τοῦ Αἰγυπτίου καὶ τοῦ Ἴστρου τοῦ
Σκυθικοῦ, καὶ εἰ ἐς ταὐτὸ συνέλθοι αὐτοῖσι τὸ
10 ὕδωρ, μέζονες. δοκέειν δὲ ἔμοιγε, καὶ ὁ Ἀκεσίνης
μέζων ἐστὶ τοῦ τε Ἴστρου καὶ τοῦ Νείλου, ἵναπερ
παραλαβὼν ἅμα τόν τε Ὑδάσπεα καὶ τὸν Ὑδραώ-
τεα καὶ τὸν Ὕφασιν ἐμβάλλει ἐς τὸν Ἰνδόν, ὡς καὶ
τριάκοντα αὐτῷ στάδια τὸ πλάτος ταύτῃ εἶναι· καὶ
τυχὸν καὶ ἄλλοι πολλοὶ μέζονες ποταμοὶ ἐν τῇ
Ἰνδῶν γῇ ῥέουσιν. 4. ἀλλὰ οὔ μοι ἀτρεκὲς ὑπὲρ
τῶν ἐπέκεινα Ὑφάσιος ποταμοῦ ἰσχυρίσασθαι, ὅτι
οὐ πρόσω τοῦ Ὑφάσιος ἦλθεν Ἀλέξανδρος.
2 αὐτοῖν δὲ τοῖν μεγίστοιν ποταμοῖν τοῦ τε Γάγγεω
καὶ τοῦ Ἰνδοῦ τὸν Γάγγεα μεγέθει πολύ τι ὑπερ-
φέρειν Μεγασθένης ἀνέγραψε, καὶ ὅσοι ἄλλοι
3 μνήμην τοῦ Γάγγεω ἔχουσιν· αὐτόν τε γὰρ μέγαν

runs into the sea India extends over about ten thousand stades; but farther north its length is about twenty thousand stades. Ctesias of Cnidus, who says 6 that the land of India is equal to the rest of Asia, is talking nonsense, like Onesicritus, who makes it a third of the entire world. Nearchus states that the journey through the actual plain of India takes four months. Megasthenes would take the breadth of 7 India as running east and west, which others call its length, and says that it is sixteen thousand stades at its shortest stretch; the line from north to south 8 then becomes for him its length, extending twenty-two thousand three hundred stades at its narrowest point.

The Indian rivers are superior to those of all Asia; 9 the greatest are the Ganges and the Indus, whence the land gets its name, both greater than the Nile in Egypt and the Scythian Ister [Danube], even if their streams were to unite [3]; my own idea is that even the 10 Acesines is greater than the Ister and the Nile at the point where, having taken in the Hydaspes, Hydraotes, and Hyphasis, it runs into the Indus, so that its breadth there becomes thirty stades.[4] Possibly also many other greater rivers run through the land of India. 4. But I can make no accurate assertions about lands on the other side of the Hyphasis, since Alexander did not proceed beyond the Hyphasis.[1] As for the two greatest rivers, the Ganges and the 2 Indus, Megasthenes wrote that the Ganges is much greater than the Indus, and so do all others who mention the Ganges; for (they say) the Ganges is 3

---

[3] Still from E., who mentioned the rivers in the same context (S. xv 1, 13); Meg. (ib. 35) ranked Danube before Nile.

[4] E. probably took this from Ar. or N.

[1] A. echoes E., cf. 6, 1; S. xv 1, 37.

ἀνίσχειν ἐκ τῶν πηγέων, δέχεσθαί τε ἐς ἑωυτὸν τόν
τε Καϊνὰν ποταμὸν καὶ τὸν Ἐραννοβόαν καὶ τὸν
Κοσσόανον, πάντας πλωτούς, ἔτι δὲ Σῶνόν τε
ποταμὸν καὶ Σιττόκατιν καὶ Σολόματιν, καὶ τού-
4 τους πλωτούς, ἐπὶ δὲ Κονδοχάτην τε καὶ Σάμβον
καὶ Μάγωνα καὶ Ἀγόρανιν καὶ Ὤμαλιν. ἐμβάλ-
λουσι δὲ ἐς αὐτὸν Κομμινάσης τε μέγας ποταμὸς
καὶ Κάκουθις καὶ Ἀνδώματις ἐξ ἔθνεος Ἰνδικοῦ
5 τοῦ Μαδυανδινῶν ῥέων, καὶ ἐπὶ τούτοισιν Ἄμυστις
παρὰ πόλιν Καταδούπην, καὶ Ὀξύμαγις ἐπὶ
⟨τοῖσι⟩ Παζάλαις καλουμένοισι· καὶ Ἐρέννεσις ἐν
Μάθαις, ἔθνει Ἰνδικῷ, συμβάλλει τῷ Γάγγῃ.
6 τούτων λέγει Μεγασθένης οὐδένα εἶναι τοῦ
Μαιάνδρου ἀποδέοντα, ἵναπερ ναυσίπορος ὁ Μαίαν-
7 δρος. εἶναι ὧν τὸ εὖρος τῷ Γάγγῃ, ἔνθαπερ
αὐτὸς ἑωυτοῦ στεινότατος, ἐς ἑκατὸν σταδίους·
πολλαχῇ δὲ καὶ λιμνάζειν, ὡς μὴ ἄποπτον εἶναι
τὴν πέρην χώρην, ἵναπερ χθαμαλή τέ ἐστι καὶ
8 οὐδαμῇ γηλόφοισιν ἀνεστηκυῖα. τῷ δὲ Ἰνδῷ ἐς
ταὐτὸν ἔρχεται. Ὑδραώτης μὲν ἐν Καμβιστόλοις,
παρειληφὼς τόν τε Ὕφασιν ἐν Ἀστρύβαις καὶ τὸν
Σαράγγην ἐκ Κηκαίων καὶ τὸν Νεῦδρον [1] ἐξ Ἀτ-
9 τακηνῶν ⟨ῥέοντα⟩, ἐς Ἀκεσίνην ἐμβάλλει. Ὑδάσπης δὲ ἐν Συδράκαις [2] ἄγων ἅμα οἷ τὸν Σίναρον
ἐν Ἀρίσπησιν ἐς τὸν Ἀκεσίνην ἐκδιδοῖ καὶ οὗτος.
10 ὁ δὲ Ἀκεσίνης ἐν Μαλλοῖς ξυμβάλλει τῷ Ἰνδῷ·
καὶ Τούταπος δὲ μέγας ποταμὸς ἐς τὸν Ἀκεσίνην
ἐκδιδοῖ. τούτων ὁ Ἀκεσίνης ἐμπλησθεὶς καὶ τῇ
ἐπικλήσει ἐκνικήσας αὐτὸς τῷ ἑωυτοῦ ἤδη ὀνόματι
11 ἐσβάλλει ἐς τὸν Ἰνδόν. Κωφὴν δὲ ἐν Πευκελαΐτιδι,

[1] A: Σύδρον Marquart, Roos.
[2] Marquart: Οὐδράκαις A, Ὀξυδράκαις in most editions.

actually large where it rises, and it receives as tributaries the Caïnas, Erannoboas and Cossoanus, all
navigable; and in addition the Sonus, Sittocatis and
Solomatis, which are also navigable. Besides there 4
are the Condochates, Sambus, Magon, Agoranis and
Omalis; and it is joined by the Comminases, a great
river, and the Cacuthis and Andomatis, flowing from
the Indian tribe of the Madyandini, and afterwards 5
by the Amystis at the city of Catadupe and the
Oxymagis at the place called Pazalae; the Errenesis
also joins the Ganges among the Mathae, an Indian
tribe.[2] Megasthenes says that none of these is in- 6
ferior to the Maeander, where the Maeander is
navigable. The breadth of the Ganges at its nar- 7
rowest is about a hundred stades[3]; often it spreads
into lakes, so that the opposite side cannot be seen
where it is low and does not rise up in hillocks. It 8
is the same with the Indus. The Hydraotes [Ravi]
in the territory of the Cambistholians, after taking
over the waters of the Hyphasis [Beas] in that of the
Astrybae, of the Saranges from the Cecaeans, and the
Neudrus from the Attacenians, flows into the
Acesines [Chenab]. In the territory of the Sydracae 9
the Hydaspes [Jhelum], carrying along the Sinarus
in that of the Arispae, also flows out into the Acesines.
The Acesines joins the Indus in Mallian territory. 10
The Tutapus too, a large river, flows into the Acesines.
All these rivers swell the Acesines, which triumph-
antly keeps its own name till it flows into the Indus.
The Cophen [Kabul] in Peucelaïtis, carrying along 11

---

[2] Not all these rivers can be identified. See O. Stein, *RE*
xv 287 ff.
[3] App. XVII 22.

ἅμα οἷ ἄγων Μαλάμαντόν τε καὶ Σόαστον καὶ
12 Γαροίαν, ἐκδιδοῖ ἐς τὸν Ἰνδόν. καθύπερθε δὲ
τουτέων Πάρεννος καὶ Σάπαρνος, οὐ πολὺ διέχ-
οντες, ἐμβάλλουσιν ἐς τὸν Ἰνδόν. Σόανος δὲ ἐκ τῆς
ὀρεινῆς τῆς Ἀβισσαρέων ἔρημος ἄλλου ποταμοῦ ἐκδιδοῖ ἐς αὐτόν. καὶ τουτέων τοὺς πολλοὺς Μεγα-
13 σθένης λέγει ὅτι πλωτοί εἰσιν. οὔκουν ἀπιστίαν
χρὴ ἔχειν ὑπέρ τε τοῦ Ἰνδοῦ καὶ τοῦ Γάγγεω μηδὲ
συμβλητοὺς εἶναι αὐτοῖσι τόν τε Ἴστρον καὶ τοῦ
14 Νείλου τὸ ὕδωρ. ἐς μέν γε τὸν Νεῖλον οὐδένα
ποταμὸν ἐκδιδόντα ἴσμεν, ἀλλ' ἀπ' αὐτοῦ διώρυχας
15 τετμημένας κατὰ τὴν χώρην τὴν Αἰγυπτίην· ὁ δὲ
Ἴστρος ὀλίγος μὲν ἀνίσχει ἀπὸ τῶν πηγέων,
δέχεται δὲ πολλοὺς ποταμούς, ἀλλὰ οὔτε πλήθει
ἴσους τοῖς Ἰνδῶν ποταμοῖσιν, οἳ ἐς τὸν Ἰνδὸν καὶ
τὸν Γάγγην ἐκδιδοῦσιν, πλωτοὺς δὲ δὴ καὶ κάρτα
ὀλίγους, ὧν τοὺς μὲν αὐτὸς ἰδὼν οἶδα, τὸν Ἔνον τε
16 καὶ τὸν Σάον. Ἔνος μὲν ἐν μεθορίῳ τῆς Νωρικῶν
καὶ Ῥαιτῶν γῆς μίγνυται τῷ Ἴστρῳ, ὁ δὲ Σάος
κατὰ Παίονας. ὁ δὲ χῶρος, ἵναπερ συμβάλλουσιν
οἱ ποταμοί, Ταυροῦνος καλέεται. ὅστις δὲ καὶ
ἄλλον οἶδε ναυσίπορον τῶν ἐς τὸν Ἴστρον ἐκδιδόν-
των, ἀλλὰ οὐ πολλούς που οἶδε.

---

[4] Meg. lists 15 tributaries (cf. v 6, 8; S. xv 1, 32 writes of 15
notable tributaries).   Contrary to fact and A's opinion (vi 14, 5,
cf. *Ind.* 3, 10), he makes the Beas a tributary of the Ravi (§ 8);
evidently he had no personal knowledge of the lower Punjab,
and read his sources carelessly.   If the manuscript text is right,
he also ignored the Sutlej, yet he must have crossed it on his
way to Palimbothra, and it appears as Sydrus in Pliny, *NH* vi
63, ultimately from his account.   Now Al's men never saw
the Sutlej, nor its confluence with the Beas; they did see the
confluence of the united stream with the Chenab, but local
boatmen, as in later times, may have given that stream the same

with it the Malamantus, Soastus [Swat], and the
Garoeas [Panjkora], empties into the Indus.   Above 12
these the Parennus and Saparnus, not far from one
another, flow into the Indus.   The Soanus from the
mountains of the Abissarians, without any tributary, empties into it.   Most of these rivers
Megasthenes reports to be navigable.[4]   It should not 13
then be incredible that neither Nile nor Ister can be
even compared with Indus or Ganges in volume of
water, for we know of no tributary to the Nile; in- 14
stead canals have been cut from it through the land
of Egypt.   As for the Ister, when it rises from its 15
springs it is a feeble stream and, though it receives
many tributaries, they are not equal in number to
the Indian tributaries that empty into Indus or
Ganges, and very few are navigable; from my own
observations I know of the Enus [Inn] and Saus
[Save].[5]   The Enus joins the Ister on the boundary 16
of Noricum and Raetia, the Saus in Pannonia.   The
country where the rivers join is called Taurunus.
Anybody who knows of other navigable tributaries of
the Ister doubtless does not know many.

name as the Beas, whereas modern geographers treat it as the
Sutlej. Meg., for his part, need not have realized that the
Sutlej was a tributary of the Indus at all.   Hence Marquart's
emendation of Neydrus to Sydrus (Sutlej), which would
involve Meg. in the error of making it a tributary of the Ravi,
is not justified. Lassen posited a lacuna after ' Cambistholians,' in which Meg. could have said that Ravi flowed into
Indus and that Sutlej also did so, with tributaries including
the Beas; the confluence of these rivers in the land of the
Astrybae would be plausible, since Ptolemy's map marks
Astrassus (cognate with Astrybae) only 125 stades north of
that confluence, which Ptolemy knew of.   But then the Indus
would have 16 tributaries.   Cf. Kiessling, *RE* ix 230 ff.
Sydracae and Malli: App. XVII 27.
   [5] A's comment here (App. XXVIII 1) follows an argument
which (*contra* Jacoby) I take to be wholly from Meg.

5. τὸ δὲ αἴτιον ὅστις ἐθέλει φράζειν τοῦ πλήθεός τε καὶ μεγέθεος τῶν Ἰνδῶν ποταμῶν, φραζέτω· 2 ἐμοὶ δὲ καὶ ταῦτα ὡς ἀκοὴ ἀναγεγράφθω. ἐπεὶ καὶ ἄλλων πολλῶν ποταμῶν οὐνόματα Μεγασθένης ἀνέγραψεν, οἳ ἔξω τοῦ Γάγγεώ τε καὶ τοῦ Ἰνδοῦ ἐκδιδοῦσιν ἐς τὸν ἐῷόν τε καὶ μεσημβρινὸν τὸν ἔξω πόντον, ὥστε τοὺς πάντας ὀκτὼ καὶ πεντήκοντα λέγει ὅτι εἰσὶν Ἰνδοὶ ποταμοί, ναυσίποροι παντες. 3 ἀλλ' οὐδὲ Μεγασθένης πολλὴν δοκέει μοι ἐπελθεῖν τῆς Ἰνδῶν χώρης, πλήν γε ⟨δὴ⟩ ὅτι πλεῦνα ἢ οἱ ξὺν Ἀλεξάνδρῳ τῷ Φιλίππου ἐπελθόντες· συγγενέσθαι γὰρ Σανδροκόττῳ λέγει, τῷ μεγίστῳ βασιλεῖ Ἰνδῶν, καὶ Πώρου ἔτι τούτῳ μείζονι. 4 οὗτος ὦν ὁ Μεγασθένης λέγει, οὔτε Ἰνδοὺς ἐπιστρατεῦσαι οὐδαμοῖσιν ἀνθρώποισιν, οὔτε Ἰνδοῖσιν 5 ἄλλους ἀνθρώπους, ἀλλὰ Σέσωστριν μὲν τὸν Αἰγύπτιον, τῆς Ἀσίας καταστρεψάμενον τὴν πολλήν, ἔστε ἐπὶ τὴν Εὐρώπην σὺν στρατιῇ ἐλάσαν- 6 τα ὀπίσω ἀπονοστῆσαι, Ἰδάνθυρσον δὲ τὸν Σκύθεα ἐκ Σκυθίης ὁρμηθέντα πολλὰ μὲν τῆς Ἀσίης ἔθνεα καταστρέψασθαι, ἐπελθεῖν δὲ καὶ τὴν Αἰγυπ- 7 τίων γῆν κρατέοντα. Σεμίραμιν δὲ τὴν Ἀσσυρίην ἐπιχειρέειν μὲν στέλλεσθαι εἰς Ἰνδούς, ἀποθανεῖν δὲ πρὶν τέλος ἐπιθεῖναι τοῖς βουλεύμασιν. ἀλλὰ Ἀλέξανδρον γὰρ στρατεῦσαι ἐπ' Ἰνδοὺς μοῦνον. 8 καὶ πρὸ Ἀλεξάνδρου Διονύσου μὲν πέρι πολλὸς λόγος κατέχει ὡς καὶ τούτου στρατεύσαντος ἐς Ἰνδοὺς καὶ καταστρεψαμένου Ἰνδούς, Ἡρακλέος 9 δὲ πέρι οὐ πολλός. Διονύσου μέν γε καὶ Νῦσα πόλις μνῆμα οὐ φαῦλον τῆς στρατηλασίης, καὶ ὁ

---

[1] Seneca *ap.* Pliny vi 60 rounded off the number to 60.

5. Let anyone who desires to explain the cause of the number and size of the Indian rivers do so; my task is to record what I have heard on these matters. Megasthenes has in fact recorded the names of many 2 other rivers beyond the Ganges and the Indus which run into the eastern and southern outer sea, so that he states the total number of Indian rivers to be fifty-eight,[1] all navigable. But even Megasthenes, 3 so far as I can see, did not visit much of India, though he visited more than the followers of Alexander, son of Philip, did; he states that he was in the company of Sandracottus, the greatest of the Indian kings, even greater than Porus.[2] This Megasthenes says 4 that the Indians did not attack any other people, and none attacked them, but as for Sesostris the Egyp- 5 tian, after subduing most of Asia and invading Europe with an army, he returned home again, while 6 Idanthyrsus the Scythian who started from Scythia subdued many tribes of Asia, and traversed even Egypt victoriously[3]; Semiramis[4] the Assyrian 7 woman did attempt an expedition to India, but died before she could carry out her plans; it was in fact Alexander alone who actually invaded India. There 8 is a prevalent report that before Alexander Dionysus too invaded India and subdued the Indians; about Heracles the report is not strong. As for Dionysus, 9 the city of Nysa is a fine memorial of his expedition

---

[2] The text is amended, as Meg. knew that Chandragupta was more powerful than Porus.

[3] For Meg's rejection of these stories S. xv 1, 6, cf. *RE* ii A 1865 ff.

[4] A legendary figure modelled on Schammuramut, queen regent of Assyria (810–806), whose unhistorical invasion of India (Ctesias *ap.* D. ii 4–20) was credited by Al. and N. (vi 24, 2), but denied by Meg., cf. 9, 9 ff. See Lenschau, *RE* vii 1204 ff.

Μηρὸς τὸ ὄρος, καὶ ὁ κισσὸς ὅτι ἐν τῷ ὄρει τούτῳ
φύεται, καὶ αὐτοὶ οἱ Ἰνδοὶ ὑπὸ τυμπάνων τε καὶ
κυμβάλων στελλόμενοι ἐς τὰς μάχας, καὶ ἐσθὴς
αὐτοῖσι κατάστικτος ἐοῦσα, κατάπερ τοῦ Διονύσου
10 τοῖσι βάκχοισιν· Ἡρακλέος δὲ οὐ πολλὰ ὑπομνήματα. ἀλλὰ τὴν Ἄορνον γὰρ πέτρην, ἥντινα Ἀλέξανδρος βίῃ ἐχειρώσατο, ὅτι Ἡρακλέης οὐ δυνατὸς
ἐγένετο ἐξελεῖν, Μακεδονικὸν δοκέει μοί τι κόμπασ-
μα, κατάπερ ὦν καὶ τὸν Παραπάμισον Καύκασον
ἐκάλεον Μακεδόνες, οὐδέν τι προσήκοντα τοῦτον
11 τῷ Καυκάσῳ. καί τι καὶ ἄντρον ἐπιφρασθέντες
ἐν Παραπαμισάδαισι, τοῦτο ἔφασαν ἐκεῖνο εἶναι
τοῦ Προμηθέως τοῦ Τιτῆνος τὸ ἄντρον, ἐν ὅτῳ
12 ἐκρέματο ἐπὶ τῇ κλοπῇ τοῦ πυρός. καὶ δὴ καὶ ἐν
Σίβαισιν, Ἰνδικῷ γένει, ὅτι δορὰς ἀμπεχομένους
εἶδον τοὺς Σίβας, ἀπὸ τῆς Ἡρακλέους στρατηλασίης ἔφασκον τοὺς ὑπολειφθέντας εἶναι τοὺς
Σίβας· καὶ γὰρ καὶ σκυτάλην φορέουσί τε οἱ
Σίβαι καὶ τῇσι βουσὶν αὐτῶν ῥόπαλον ἐπικέκαυται,
καὶ τοῦτο ἐς μνήμην ἀνέφερον τοῦ ῥοπάλου τοῦ
13 Ἡρακλέους. εἰ δέ τῳ πιστὰ ταῦτα, ἄλλος ἂν
οὗτος Ἡρακλέης εἴη, οὐχ ὁ Θηβαῖος ἢ ὁ Τύριος
[οὗτος] ἢ ὁ Αἰγύπτιος, ἤ τις καὶ κατὰ τὴν ἄνω
χώρην οὐ πόρρω τῆς Ἰνδῶν γῆς ᾠκισμένος μέγας
βασιλεύς.

6. ταῦτα μέν μοι ἐκβολὴ ἔστω τοῦ λόγου ἐς τὸ
μὴ πιστὰ φαίνεσθαι ὅσα ὑπὲρ τῶν ἐπέκεινα τοῦ
Ὑφάσιος ποταμοῦ Ἰνδῶν μετεξέτεροι ἀνέγραψαν·
(ἔστε γὰρ ἐπὶ τὸν Ὕφασιν οἱ τῆς Ἀλεξάνδρου
στρατηλασίης μετασχόντες οὐ πάντη ἄπιστοί
2 εἰσιν)· ἐπεὶ καὶ τόδε λέγει Μεγασθένης ὑπὲρ ποταμοῦ Ἰνδικοῦ, Σίλαν μὲν εἶναί οἱ ὄνομα, ῥέειν δὲ

together with Mount Merus and the ivy growing on
this mountain, and the habit of the Indians themselves in setting out to battle to the sound of drums
and cymbals, and their dappled costume, like that
worn by the Bacchanals of Dionysus. But of 10
Heracles there are few memorials; as for the story
that Heracles could not capture Aornos, a rock which
Alexander reduced by force, I am inclined to think it
a Macedonian boast. In the same way the Macedonians called Parapamisus by the name of Caucasus,
though it has nothing to do with Caucasus and, on 11
learning that there was a cave among the Parapamisadae, they said it was the cave of Prometheus
the Titan, in which he was hung up for his theft of the
fire. And after noticing that the Sibae, an Indian 12
tribe, were clad in skins, they actually claimed that
the Sibae had been left behind after Heracles' expedition. What is more, as the Sibae carry a club,
and brand their cattle with a club, they attributed
this too to a recollection of Heracles' club.[5] If any- 13
one believes this, at least it must be a different Heracles, not the Theban, but the Tyrian or Egyptian, or
some great king at home in the upper country near
India.[6]

6. This must be regarded as a digression, so that
too much credence should not be given to the stories
some others have recorded of the Indians beyond the
Hyphasis; up to that limit those who served under
Alexander are not entirely untrustworthy. To take 2
an instance, Megasthenes tells us of an Indian river

---

[5] See v 3, 4; App. XVI. O. Stein (*RE* xv 303 f.) notes that
Indians did brand cattle and that Krishna has a club.

[6] App. XVI 10. *Contra* Jacoby all except § 10–13 (where
A. repeats E's doubts) can come from Meg., who ' proved '
that Heracles and Dionysus had been in India.

ἀπὸ κρήνης ἐπωνύμου τοῦ ποταμοῦ διὰ τῆς χώρης
τῆς Σιλαίων, καὶ τούτων ἐπωνύμων τοῦ ποταμοῦ
3 τε καὶ τῆς κρήνης, τὸ δὲ ὕδωρ παρέχεσθαι τοιόνδε.
οὐδὲν εἶναι ὅτῳ ἀντέχει τὸ ὕδωρ, ⟨καὶ⟩ οὔτε τι
νήχεσθαι ἐπ' αὐτοῦ οὔτε τι ἐπιπλεῖν, ἀλλὰ πάντα
γὰρ ἐς βυσσὸν δύνειν· οὕτω τι ἀμενηνότερον
πάντων εἶναι τὸ ὕδωρ ἐκεῖνο καὶ ἠεροειδέστερον.
4 ὕεται δὲ ἡ Ἰνδῶν γῆ τοῦ θέρεος, μάλιστα μὲν τὰ
ὄρεα, Παραπάμισός τε καὶ ὁ Ἠμωδὸς καὶ τὸ
Ἰμαϊκὸν ὄρος, καὶ ἀπὸ τουτέων μεγάλοι καὶ θολε-
5 ροὶ οἱ ποταμοὶ ῥέουσιν. ὕεται δὲ τοῦ θέρους καὶ τὰ
πεδία τῶν Ἰνδῶν, ὥστε λιμνάζει τὰ πολλὰ αὐτέων.
καὶ ἔφυγεν ἡ Ἀλεξάνδρου στρατιὴ ἀπὸ τοῦ
Ἀκεσίνου ποταμοῦ μέσου θέρεος, ὑπερβαλόντος
6 τοῦ ὕδατος ἐς τὰ πεδία. ὥστε ἀπὸ τῶνδε ἔξεστι
τεκμηριοῦσθαι καὶ τοῦ Νείλου τὸ πάθημα τοῦτο,
ὅτι εἰκὸς [εἶναι] ὕεσθαι τὰ Αἰθιόπων ὄρεα τοῦ
θέρεος, καὶ ἀπ' ἐκείνων ἐμπιπλάμενον τὸν Νεῖλον
ὑπερβάλλειν ὑπὲρ τὰς ὄχθας ἐς τὴν γῆν τὴν Αἰγυπ-
7 τίην. θολερὸς ὢν καὶ οὗτος ῥέει ἐν τῇδε τῇ ὥρῃ,
ὡς οὔτε ἂν ἀπὸ χιόνος τηκομένης ἔρρεεν, οὔτε εἰ
πρὸς τῶν ὥρῃ θέρεος πνεόντων ἐτησίων ἀνέμων
ἀνεκόπτετό οἱ τὸ ὕδωρ· ἄλλως τε οὐδὲ χιονόβλητα
8 εἴη ἂν Αἰθιόπων ὄρεα ὑπὸ καύματος. ὕεσθαι δὲ
κατάπερ τὰ Ἰνδῶν οὐκ ἔξω ἐστὶ τοῦ εἰκότος, ἐπεὶ
καὶ τἆλλα ⟨ἡ⟩ Ἰνδῶν γῆ οὐκ ἀπέοικε τῆς Αἰθιοπίης
καὶ οἱ ποταμοὶ οἱ Ἰνδοὶ ὁμοίως τῷ Νείλῳ τῷ
Αἰθιοπηίῳ τε καὶ Αἰγυπτίῳ κροκοδείλους τε
φέρουσιν, ἔστιν δὲ οἳ αὐτῶν καὶ ἰχθύας καὶ ἄλλα

---

[1] Greeks located such a marvel in several lands, but Meg.
drew on a genuine Indian story (Stein, *RE* xv 244 f.; 307).

named Silas, which flows from a spring of the same
name as the river through the territory of the Sil-
aeans, the people also getting their name from both
the river and the spring; he says that its water mani- 3
fests this phenomenon: nothing is supported by it,
nothing can swim in it or float upon it, but everything goes straight to the bottom, as this water is so
unresisting, and more aery than any other.[1]

Rain falls in India in the summer, especially on the 4
mountains, Parapamisus, Hemodus and the Imaic
mountain, and the flow of the rivers rising there is
great and turbulent. The plains of India also get 5
rain in summer, so that large parts become swamps;
and Alexander's army had an escape from the river
Acesines in midsummer, when the water had over-
flowed on to the plains.[2] From these facts one can 6
then infer that the flooding of the Nile is probably
due to summer rains in the mountains of Ethiopia,
which swell the Nile, so that it overflows its banks on
to the land of Egypt. So in the Nile too the flow is 7
turbid at this time of the year, as it would not be
from melting snow, nor if its stream were dammed up
by the seasonal winds that blow in the summer; and
besides, the mountains of Ethiopia would not be subject to snow-showers on account of the heat.[3] But it 8
is not at all improbable that they receive rain as
India does, since in other respects India is not unlike
Ethiopia, and in the Indian rivers crocodiles are
found, as in the Ethiopian and Egyptian Nile, and in
some of them fish and other large water animals like

---

[2] App. XII 3; XVII 11 and 18. I suspect that Meg. remains
the source throughout this chapter as in 3 and 7, 1, cf. n. 4
below; he could have taken over N's comparison of Nile and
Indus valleys (S. xv 1, 18 and 25).

[3] Cf. vi 1, 3 n.

κήτεα ὅσα ὁ Νεῖλος πλὴν ἵππου τοῦ ποταμίου, —
Ὀνησίκριτος δὲ καὶ τοὺς ἵππους τοὺς ποταμίους
9 λέγει ὅτι φέρουσι — τῶν τε ἀνθρώπων αἱ ἰδέαι οὐ
πάντη ἀπᾴδουσιν αἱ Ἰνδῶν τε καὶ Αἰθιόπων. οἱ
μὲν πρὸς νότου ἀνέμου Ἰνδοὶ τοῖς Αἰθίοψι μᾶλλόν
τι ἐοίκασι μέλανές τε ἰδέσθαι εἰσὶ καὶ ἡ κόμη αὐτοῖς
μέλαινα, πλήν γε δὴ ὅτι σιμοὶ οὐχ ὡσαύτως οὐδὲ
οὐλόκρανοι ὡς Αἰθίοπες. οἱ δὲ βορειότεροι τούτων
κατ' Αἰγυπτίους μάλιστα ἂν εἶεν τὰ σώματα.
7. ἔθνεα δὲ Ἰνδικὰ εἴκοσι καὶ ἑκατὸν τὰ ἅπαντα
λέγει Μεγασθένης, δυοῖν δέοντα. καὶ πολλὰ μὲν
εἶναι ἔθνεα Ἰνδικὰ καὶ αὐτὸς συμφέρομαι Μεγασθένει, τὸ δὲ ἀτρεκὲς οὐκ ἔχω εἰκάσαι ὅπως ἐκμαθὼν ἀνέγραψεν, οὐδὲ πολλοστὸν μέρος τῆς Ἰνδῶν
γῆς ἐπελθών, οὐδὲ ἐπιμιξίης πᾶσι τοῖς γένεσιν
2 ἐούσης ἐς ἀλλήλους. πάλαι μὲν δὴ νομάδας εἶναι
Ἰνδούς, καθάπερ Σκυθέων τοὺς οὐκ ἀροτῆρας, οἳ
ἐπὶ τῇσιν ἁμάξῃσι πλανώμενοι ἄλλοτε ἄλλην τῆς
Σκυθίης ἀμείβουσιν, οὔτε πόληας οἰκέοντες οὔτε
3 ἱερὰ θεῶν σέβοντες. οὕτω μηδὲ Ἰνδοῖσι πόληας
εἶναι μηδὲ ἱερὰ θεῶν δεδομημένα, ἀλλ' ἀμπίσχεσθαι
μὲν δορὰς θηρίων ὅσων κατακάνοιεν, σιτέεσθαι
δὲ τῶν δενδρέων τὸν φλοιόν. καλέεσθαι δὲ τὰ
δένδρεα ταῦτα τῇ Ἰνδῶν φωνῇ τάλα, καὶ φύεσθαι
ἐπ' αὐτῶν, κατάπερ τῶν φοινίκων ἐπὶ τῇσι κορυ-
4 φῇσιν, οἷά περ τολύπας. σιτέεσθαι δὲ καὶ τῶν
θηρίων ὅσα ἕλοιεν ὠμοφαγέοντας, πρίν γε δὴ
5 Διόνυσον ἐλθεῖν ἐς τὴν χώρην τῶν Ἰνδῶν. Διόνυσον δὲ ἐλθόντα, ὡς καρτερὸς ἐγένετο Ἰνδῶν,
πόληάς τε οἰκίσαι καὶ νόμους θέσθαι τῇσι πόλεσιν,
οἴνου τε δοτῆρα Ἰνδοῖς γενέσθαι κατάπερ Ἕλλησι,
καὶ σπείρειν διδάξαι τὴν γῆν διδόντα αὐτὸν σπέρ-

those of the Nile, except for the hippopotamus, though Onesicritus states that this too is found.[4] The [9] appearance of the inhabitants is also not very different in India and Ethiopia: the southern Indians are rather more like Ethiopians as they are black to look on, and their hair is black; only they are not so snub-nosed or woolly-haired as the Ethiopians; the northern Indians are most like the Egyptians physically.

7. Megasthenes states that there are in all one hundred and eighteen tribes. I agree with Megasthenes myself that the Indian tribes are numerous, but I cannot conjecture how he learned and recorded the exact number, since he visited only a small proportion of India, and these peoples do not all mix with each other.[1] The Indians, he says, were [2] originally nomads, like the non-agricultural Scythians, who wander in their waggons and move from one part of Scythia to another, not dwelling in cities and not reverencing shrines of the gods. Just so the [3] Indians had no cities and built no temples, but were clothed with the skins of wild animals they would kill, and ate the bark of trees; these trees were called in the Indian tongue Tala, and what look like clews of wool grew on them, just as on the tops of palm trees.[2] They also fed on what game they had captured, [4] eating it raw, at least until Dionysus reached India. But when he arrived and became master of India, he [5] founded cities, gave them laws, bestowed wine on the Indians as on the Greeks, and taught them to sow

[4] Ar. rightly denied this (S. xv 1, 45). S. xv 1, 13 is so similar to 8 f. that both he and A. evidently followed Meg. No proof that A. read Onesicritus.

[1] E's criticism? 7, 1–9, 8, in indirect speech, is all from Meg. (cf. Jacoby F 12 f. for confirmatory texts), except for A's own comments in 7, 6 (?), 8, 9, and 9, 4–7. Cf. App. XVI 1 f.

[2] A. seems to mix up the cotton plant with another 'tree.'

6 ματα, ἢ οὐκ ἐλάσαντος ταύτῃ Τριπτολέμου, ὅτε περ
ἐκ Δήμητρος ἐστάλη σπείρειν τὴν γῆν πᾶσαν, ἢ πρὸ
Τριπτολέμου τις οὗτος Διόνυσος ἐπελθὼν τὴν
Ἰνδῶν γῆν σπέρματά σφισιν ἔδωκε καρποῦ τοῦ
7 ἡμέρου. βόας τε ὑπ' ἄροτρον ζεῦξαι Διόνυσον
πρῶτον καὶ ἀροτῆρας ἀντὶ νομάδων ποιῆσαι
Ἰνδῶν τοὺς πολλοὺς καὶ ὁπλίσαι ὅπλοισι τοῖσιν
8 ἀρηίοισι. καὶ θεοὺς σέβειν ὅτι ἐδίδαξε Διόνυσος
ἄλλους τε καὶ μάλιστα δὴ ἑωυτὸν κυμβαλίζοντας
καὶ τυμπανίζοντας· καὶ ὄρχησιν δὲ ἐκδιδάξαι τὴν
σατυρικήν, τὸν κόρδακα παρ' Ἕλλησι καλούμενον,
9 καὶ κομᾶν [Ἰνδοὺς] τῷ θεῷ μιτρηφορέειν τε
ἀναδεῖξαι καὶ μύρων ἀλοιφὰς ἐκδιδάξαι, ὥστε καὶ
εἰς Ἀλέξανδρον ἔτι ὑπὸ κυμβάλων τε καὶ τυμπάνων
ἐς τὰς μάχας Ἰνδοὶ καθίσταντο.

8. ἀπιόντα δὲ ἐκ τῆς Ἰνδῶν γῆς, ὡς οἱ ταῦτα
κεκοσμέατο, καταστῆσαι βασιλέα τῆς χώρης
Σπατέμβαν, τῶν ἑταίρων ἕνα τὸν βακχωδέστατον·
τελευτήσαντος δὲ Σπατέμβα τὴν βασιληίην ἐκδέξ-
2 ασθαι Βουδύαν τὸν τούτου παῖδα. καὶ τὸν μὲν
πεντήκοντα καὶ δύο ἔτεα βασιλεῦσαι Ἰνδῶν, τὸν
πατέρα, τὸν δὲ παῖδα εἴκοσιν ἔτεα. καὶ τούτου
3 παῖδα ἐκδέξασθαι τὴν βασιληίην Κραδεύαν, καὶ τὸ
ἀπὸ τοῦδε τὸ πολὺ μὲν κατὰ γένος ἀμείβειν
τὴν βασιληίην, παῖδα παρὰ πατρὸς ἐκδεχόμενον·
εἰ δὲ ἐκλείποι τὸ γένος, οὕτω δὴ ἀριστίνδην καθ-
4 ίστασθαι Ἰνδοῖσι βασιλέας. Ἡρακλέα δέ, ὅντινα
ἐς Ἰνδοὺς ἀφικέσθαι λόγος κατέχει, παρ' αὐτοῖσιν
5 Ἰνδοῖσι γηγενέα λέγεσθαι. τοῦτον τὸν Ἡρακλέα
μάλιστα πρὸς Σουρασηνῶν γεραίρεσθαι, Ἰνδικοῦ
ἔθνεος, ἵνα δύο πόληες μεγάλαι, Μέθορά τε καὶ
Κλεισόβορα· καὶ ποταμὸς Ἰωμάνης πλωτὸς διαρ-

their land, giving them seed. (Either Triptolemus 6
did not come this way when he was sent out by
Demeter to sow the entire earth, or it was earlier
than Triptolemus that this Dionysus, whoever he
was,[3] traversed India and gave the Indians seeds of
domesticated plants.) Dionysus first yoked oxen to 7
the plough and made most of the Indians agricul-
turalists instead of nomads, and equipped them also
with the arms of warfare. He also taught them to 8
reverence various gods, but especially of course himself, with clashings of cymbals and beating of drums;
he instructed them to dance in the Satyric fashion,
the dance called among Greeks the 'cordax', and 9
showed them how to wear long hair in honour of the
god with the conical cap, and instructed them in the
use of perfumed ointments, so that even against
Alexander the Indians came to battle to the sound of
cymbals and drums.[4]

8. When departing from India, after setting all this
in order, Dionysus made Spatembas king of the land,
one of his Companions who was most expert in Bacchic
rites; when Spatembas died, Budyas his son reigned
in his stead; the father was king of India fifty-two 2
years, and the son twenty; his son Cradeuas came to
the throne and his descendants mostly received the 3
kingdom in succession, son succeeding father; if the
succession failed, then Indian kings were appointed
for merit. As for a Heracles reaching India, as the 4
prevalent story goes, the Indians themselves call him
'Indigenous'. This Heracles is chiefly honoured by 5
the Surasenians, an Indian tribe, with two great
cities, Methora and Clisobora; the navigable river

---

[3] It may be A. himself who toys with the idea of a different
Dionysus, cf. App. XVI 10.

[4] See S's criticism in xv 1, 58, doubtless from E.

6 ρεῖ τὴν χώρην αὐτῶν· τὴν σκευὴν δὲ οὗτος ὁ
Ἡρακλέης ἥντινα ἐφόρεε Μεγασθένης λέγει ὅτι
ὁμοίην τῷ Θηβαίῳ Ἡρακλεῖ, ὡς αὐτοὶ Ἰνδοὶ
ἀπηγέονται. καὶ τούτῳ ἄρσενας μὲν παῖδας πολλοὺς κάρτα γενέσθαι ἐν τῇ Ἰνδῶν γῇ — πολλῇσι γὰρ δὴ γυναιξὶν ἐς γάμον ἐλθεῖν καὶ τοῦτον τὸν
Ἡρακλέα —, θυγατέρα δὲ μουνογενέην. οὔνομα
7 δὲ εἶναι τῇ παιδὶ Πανδαίην, καὶ τὴν χώρην, ἵνα τε
ἐγένετο καὶ ἧστινος ἐπέτρεψεν αὐτῇ ἄρχειν Ἡρακλέης, Πανδαίην ⟨καλεῖσθαι⟩ τῆς παιδὸς ἐπώνυμον.
καὶ ταύτῃ ἐλέφαντας μὲν γενέσθαι ἐκ τοῦ πατρὸς ἐς
πεντακοσίους, ἵππον δὲ ἐς τετρακισχιλίην, πεζῶν
8 δὲ ἐς τὰς τρεῖς καὶ δέκα μυριάδας. καὶ τάδε μετεξέτεροι Ἰνδῶν περὶ Ἡρακλέους λέγουσιν, ἐπελ-
θόντα αὐτὸν πᾶσαν γῆν καὶ θάλασσαν καὶ καθ-
ήραντα ὅ τι περ κακόν, καινὸν εἶδος ἐξευρεῖν ἐν τῇ
9 θαλάσσῃ κόσμου γυναικηίου, ὅντινα καὶ εἰς τοῦτο
ἔτι οἵ τε ἐξ Ἰνδῶν τῆς χώρης τὰ ἀγώγιμα παρ'
ἡμέας ἀγινέοντες σπουδῇ ὠνεόμενοι ἐκκομίζουσι,
καὶ Ἑλλήνων δὲ πάλαι καὶ Ῥωμαίων νῦν ὅσοι
πολυκτέανοι καὶ εὐδαίμονες μέζονι ἔτι σπουδῇ
ὠνέονται, τὸν μαργαρίτην δὴ τὸν θαλάσσιον οὕτω
10 τῇ Ἰνδῶν γλώσσῃ καλεόμενον. τὸν γὰρ Ἡρακλέα,
ὡς καλὸν οἱ ἐφάνη τὸ φόρημα, ἐκ πάσης τῆς
θαλάσσης ἐς τὴν Ἰνδῶν γῆν συναγινέειν τὸν
μαργαρίτην δὴ τοῦτον, τῇ θυγατρὶ τῇ ἑωυτοῦ εἶναι
11 κόσμον. καὶ λέγει Μεγασθένης, θηρεύεσθαι τὴν
κόγχην αὐτοῦ δικτύοισι, νέμεσθαι δ' ἐν τῇ θαλάσσῃ
κατὰ ταὐτὸ πολλὰς κόγχας, κατάπερ τὰς μελίσσας.
καὶ εἶναι γὰρ καὶ τοῖσι μαργαρίτῃσι βασιλέα ἢ
12 βασίλισσαν, ὡς τῇσι μελίσσῃσι. καὶ ὅστις μὲν
ἐκεῖνον κατ' ἐπιτυχίην συλλάβοι, τοῦτον δὲ εὐπε-

Iomanes flows through their territory. Megasthenes 6
says that the garb this Heracles wore was like that of
the Theban Heracles by the account of the Indians
themselves [1]; he also had a great many sons in this
country, for this Heracles too wedded many wives,
but he had only one daughter. Her name was 7
Pandaea, and the country in which she was born, the
government of which Heracles entrusted to her, was
called Pandaea after the girl; here she possessed
some five hundred elephants given by her father,
four thousand horsemen, and a hundred and thirty
thousand foot-soldiers. Some other Indians tell of 8
Heracles that, after he had traversed every land and
sea, and purged them of all evil monsters, he found in
the sea a new form of womanly ornament. And 9
thus, even to our day, those who bring merchandise
from India to our country are at pains to purchase
these jewels and export them, and rich and prosperous Greeks in the past, and Romans today, are still
more eager to buy the sea margarita [pearl] as it is
called [2] in the Indian tongue. Heracles was in fact 10
so taken with the beauty of the ornament that he collected this pearl from every sea and brought it to
India to adorn his daughter. Megasthenes also says 11
that the pearl's oyster is caught with nets; and that
many oysters live together in the sea like bees; for
the pearl oysters too have a king or queen, like
bees. Should anyone by chance catch the king, he 12
can easily cast a net around the swarm of the re-

---

[1] Perhaps Meg. left it open whether Heracles was indigenous or Theban.

[2] Apparently untrue, see O. Stein, *RE* xv 299.

τέως περιβάλλειν καὶ τὸ ἄλλο σμῆνος τῶν μαργαρι-
τῶν· εἰ δὲ διαφύγοι σφᾶς ὁ βασιλεύς, τούτῳ δὲ
οὐκέτι θηρατοὺς εἶναι τοὺς ἄλλους. τοὺς ἑλόντας
δὲ περιορᾶν κατασαπῆναί σφισι τὴν σάρκα, τῷ δὲ
13 ὀστέῳ ἐς κόσμον χρῆσθαι. καὶ εἶναι γὰρ καὶ παρ᾽
Ἰνδοῖσι τὸν μαργαρίτην τριστάσιον κατὰ τιμὴν
πρὸς χρυσίον τὸ ἄπεφθον, καὶ τοῦτο ἐν τῇ Ἰνδῶν
γῇ ὀρυσσόμενον.

9. ἐν δὲ τῇ χώρῃ ταύτῃ, ἵνα ἐβασίλευσεν ἡ
θυγάτηρ τοῦ Ἡρακλέος, τὰς μὲν γυναῖκας ἑπταέτεις
ἐούσας ἐς ὥρην γάμου ἰέναι, τοὺς δὲ ἄνδρας τεσσα-
2 ράκοντα ἔτεα τὰ πλεῖστα βιώσκεσθαι. καὶ ὑπὲρ
τούτου λεγόμενον λόγον εἶναι παρὰ Ἰνδοῖσιν.
Ἡρακλέα, ὀψιγόνου οἱ γενομένης τῆς παιδός, ἐπεί
τε δὴ ἐγγὺς ἔμαθεν ἑαυτῷ ἐοῦσαν τὴν τελευτήν,
οὐκ ἔχοντα ὅτῳ ἀνδρὶ ἐκδῷ τὴν παῖδα ἑωυτοῦ
ἐπαξίῳ, αὐτὸν μιγῆναι τῇ παιδὶ ἑπταέτεϊ ἐούσῃ,
ὡς γένος ἐξ οὗ τε κἀκείνης ὑπολείπεσθαι Ἰνδῶν
3 βασιλέας. ποιῆσαι ὦν αὐτὴν Ἡρακλέα ὡραίην
γάμου· καὶ ἐκ τοῦδε ἅπαν τὸ γένος τοῦτο ὅτου ἡ
Πανδαίη ἐπῆρξε, ταὐτὸν τοῦτο γέρας ἔχειν παρὰ
4 Ἡρακλέος. ἐμοὶ δὲ δοκεῖ, εἴπερ ὦν τὰ ἐς τοσόνδε
ἄτοπα Ἡρακλῆς οἷός τε ἦν ἐξεργάζεσθαι, κἂν
αὐτὸν ἀποφῆναι μακροβιώτερον, ὡς ὡραίη μιγῆναι
5 τῇ παιδί. ἀλλὰ γὰρ εἰ ταῦτα ὑπὲρ τῆς ὥρης τῶν
ταύτῃ παίδων ἀτρεκέα ἐστίν, ἐς ταὐτὸν φέρειν
δοκεῖ ἔμοιγε ἐς ὅ τι περ καὶ ⟨τὰ⟩ ὑπὲρ τῶν ἀνδρῶν
τῆς ἡλικίης ὅτι τεσσαρακοντούτεες ἀποθνήσ-
6 κουσιν οἱ πρεσβύτατοι αὐτῶν. οἷς γὰρ τό τε
γῆρας τοσῷδε ταχύτερον ἐπέρχεται καὶ ὁ θάνατος
ὁμοῦ τῷ γήρᾳ, πάντως που καὶ ἡ ἀκμὴ πρὸς λόγον
7 τοῦ τέλεος ταχυτέρη ἐπανθέει. ὥστε τριακοντού-

naining oysters; but should the king slip through,
hen the others cannot be caught.[3] The fishermen
et the flesh rot, but use the skeleton as an ornament.
For among the Indians too the pearl is worth three 13
times its weight in refined gold, and gold is also mined
n India.[4]

9. In this country where Heracles' daughter was
queen, the girls are marriageable at seven years, and
the men do not live longer than forty years. There 2
is a story about this among the Indians, that Heracles, whose daughter was born to him late in life,
realizing that his own end was near, and having no
man of his own worth to whom he might give his
daughter, copulated with her himself when she was
seven, so that their progeny might be left behind as
Indian kings. Thus Heracles made her marriage- 3
able, and thenceforward the whole of this line which
began with Pandaea inherited this very same privilege from Heracles. But I think that if Heracles 4
was able to accomplish anything so extraordinary, he
could have lengthened his own life, so as to copulate
with the girl when mature. But really if this story 5
about the bloom of the girls here is quite true, it seems
to me to tend the same way as what we are told of the
men's age, that the oldest of them die at forty years.[1]
For when old age comes on so much sooner and death 6
along with age, the bloom of maturity will, I suppose,
evidently be earlier in proportion to the end, so that 7

---

[3] Cf. Pliny ix 111.
[4] Contrast v 4, 4.
[1] Meg., cf. § 8. Onesicritus (S. xv 1, 34) credited the
subjects of Musicanus with longevity.

τεες μὲν ὠμογέροντες ἄν που εἶεν αὐτοῖσιν οἱ ἄνδρες,
εἴκοσι δὲ ἔτεα γεγονότες οἱ ἔξω ἥβης νεηνίσκοι,
ἡ δὲ ἀκροτάτη ἥβη ἀμφὶ τὰ πεντεκαίδεκα ἔτεα· καὶ
τῇσι γυναιξὶν ὥρη τοῦ γάμου κατὰ λόγον ἂν οὕτω

8 ἐς τὰ ἑπτὰ ἔτεα συμβαίνοι. καὶ γὰρ τοὺς καρποὺς
ἐν ταύτῃ τῇ χώρῃ πεπαίνεσθαί τε ταχύτερον [μὲν
τῆς ἄλλης αὐτὸς οὗτος Μεγασθένης ἀνέγραψεν καὶ
φθίνειν ταχύτερον.

9 ἀπὸ μὲν δὴ Διονύσου βασιλέας ἠρίθμεον Ἰνδοὶ ἐς
Σανδρόκοττον τρεῖς καὶ πεντήκοντα καὶ ἑκατόν,
ἔπεα δὲ δύο καὶ τεσσαράκοντα καὶ ἑξακισχίλια· ἐν
δὲ τούτοισι τρὶς τὸ πᾶν εἰς ἐλευθερίην . . . . . ,
τὴν δὲ καὶ ἐς τριακόσια, τὴν δὲ εἴκοσίν τε ἐτέων

10 καὶ ἑκατόν. πρεσβύτερόν τε Διόνυσον Ἡρακλέος
δέκα καὶ πέντε γενεῇσιν Ἰνδοὶ λέγουσιν· ἄλλον δὲ
οὐδένα ἐμβαλεῖν ἐς γῆν τὴν Ἰνδῶν ἐπὶ πολέμῳ,
οὐδὲ Κῦρον τὸν Καμβύσεω, καίτοι ἐπὶ Σκύθας
ἐλάσαντα καὶ τἆλλα πολυπραγμονέστατον δὴ τῶν
κατὰ τὴν Ἀσίαν βασιλέων γενόμενον τὸν Κῦρον·

11 ἀλλὰ Ἀλέξανδρον γὰρ ἐλθεῖν τε καὶ κρατῆσαι
[πάντων] τοῖς ὅπλοις ὅσους γε δὴ ἐπῆλθε· καὶ ἂν

12 καὶ πάντων κρατῆσαι, εἰ ἡ στρατιὴ ἤθελεν. οὐ μὲν
δὴ οὐδὲ Ἰνδῶν τινὰ ἔξω τῆς οἰκείης σταλῆναι ἐπὶ
πολέμῳ διὰ δικαιότητα.

10. λέγεται δὲ καὶ τάδε, μνημεῖα ὅτι Ἰνδοὶ τοῖς
τελευτήσασιν οὐ ποιέουσιν, ἀλλὰ τὰς ἀρετὰς γὰρ
τῶν ἀνδρῶν ἱκανὰς ἐς μνήμην τίθενται τοῖσιν ἀποθαν-
2 οῦσι καὶ τὰς ᾠδὰς αἳ αὐτοῖσιν ἐπάδονται. πόλεων
δὲ καὶ ἀριθμὸν οὐκ εἶναι ἂν ἀτρεκὲς ἀναγράψαι

---

¹ Words have clearly fallen out, e.g. ⟨μεταβαλέειν τὴν
πολιτηίην· καὶ ἐς ἔτεα μὲν . . . τὴν πρώτην ὑπάρξαι ἐλευθερίην⟩.

men would be on the threshold of old age at thirty
and young at twenty but passed beyond the first flush
of youth; its prime would be at about fifteen, so that
by analogy the women might be marriageable at
seven. For even the fruits ripen earlier in this 8
country than elsewhere, and decay earlier, as once
again Megasthenes tells us.

From Dionysus to Sandracottus the Indians counted 9
a hundred and fifty-three kings, over six thousand
and forty-two years, and during these years three
times in all of liberty . . .[2] another for three hundred
years, another for a hundred and twenty years. The 10
Indians say that Dionysus was fifteen generations
earlier than Heracles, but no one else ever invaded
India, not even Cyrus son of Cambyses, though he
attacked the Scythians, and in other ways was the
most energetic of the kings in Asia. Only Alex- 11
ander came and conquered by force of arms all the
countries he assailed, and would have conquered the
whole world, had his army been willing. Nor did any 12
Indians ever set out beyond their own country on a
warlike expedition, because of their respect for
justice.

10. It is also said that Indians do not put up
memorials to the dead, but regard their virtues as
sufficient memorials for the departed, together with
songs sung in their honour.[1] As for the cities of 2
India, it would be impossible to record their number

---

[2] The missing words might have this sense: 'was the political
system converted into one of liberty, the first lasting . . .
years, another . . .' A. here uses direct speech but plainly
follows Meg. Cf. 1, 1 n.

[1] S. xv 1, 54: ' their funerals are simple and their mounds
small.' Both he and A. seem to be summarizing Meg., one or
both inexactly.

τῶν Ἰνδικῶν ὑπὸ πλήθεος· ἀλλὰ γὰρ ὅσαι παρα-
ποτάμιαι αὐτέων ἢ παραθαλάσσιαι, ταύτας μὲν ξυλί-
3 νας ποιέεσθαι· οὐ γὰρ ἂν ἐκ πλίνθου ποιεομένας
διαρκέσαι ἐπὶ χρόνον τοῦ τε ὕδατος ἔνεκα τοῦ ἐξ
οὐρανοῦ καὶ ὅτι οἱ ποταμοὶ αὐτοῖσιν ὑπερβάλλοντες
ὑπὲρ τὰς ὄχθας ἐμπιμπλᾶσι τοῦ ὕδατος τὰ πεδία.
4 ὅσαι δὲ ἐν ὑπερδεξίοις τε καὶ μετεώροις τόποισι καὶ
τούτοισι ψιλοῖσιν ᾠκισμέναι εἰσί, ταύτας δὲ ἐκ
5 πλίνθου τε καὶ πηλοῦ ποιέεσθαι. μεγίστην δὲ
πόλιν Ἰνδοῖσιν εἶναι ⟨τὴν⟩ Παλίμβοθρα καλεομέ-
νην, ἐν τῇ Πρασίων γῇ, ἵνα αἱ συμβολαί εἰσι τοῦ τε
Ἐραννοβόα ποταμοῦ καὶ τοῦ Γάγγεω· τοῦ μὲν
Γάγγεω, τοῦ μεγίστου ποταμῶν· ὁ δὲ Ἐραννοβόας
τρίτος μὲν ἂν εἴη τῶν Ἰνδῶν ποταμῶν, μέζων δὲ τῶν
ἄλλῃ καὶ οὗτος, ἀλλὰ ξυγχωρέει αὐτὸς τῷ Γάγγῃ,
6 ἐπειδὰν ἐμβάλῃ ἐς αὐτὸν τὸ ὕδωρ. καὶ λέγει
Μεγασθένης μῆκος μὲν ἐπέχειν τὴν πόλιν καθ'
ἑκατέρην τὴν πλευρήν, ἵναπερ μακροτάτη αὐτὴ
ἑωυτῆς ᾤκισται, ἐς ὀγδοήκοντα σταδίους, τὸ δὲ
7 πλάτος ἐς πεντεκαίδεκα. τάφρον δὲ περιβεβλῆσθαι
τῇ πόλει τὸ εὖρος ἑξάπλεθρον, τὸ δὲ βάθος τρι-
ήκοντα πήχεων· πύργους δὲ ἑβδομήκοντα καὶ
πεντακοσίους ἔχειν τὸ τεῖχος καὶ πύλας τέσσαρας
8 καὶ ἑξήκοντα. εἶναι δὲ καὶ τόδε μέγα ἐν τῇ Ἰνδῶν
γῇ, πάντας Ἰνδοὺς εἶναι ἐλευθέρους, οὐδέ τινα
9 δοῦλον εἶναι Ἰνδόν. τοῦτο μὲν Λακεδαιμονίοισιν
ἐς ταὐτὸ συμβαίνει καὶ Ἰνδοῖσι. Λακεδαιμονίοις
μέν γε οἱ εἵλωτες δοῦλοί εἰσιν καὶ τὰ δούλων
ἐργάζονται, Ἰνδοῖσι δὲ οὐδὲ ἄλλος δοῦλός ἐστι,
μήτι γε Ἰνδῶν τις.

---

[2] S. xv 1, 36; App. XVII 6.

accurately because there are so many. Those on rivers or on the coast are built of wood; if they were 3 built of brick, they could not last long because of the moisture due to rain, and to the fact that the rivers overflow their banks and fill the plains with water. Only where the cities are situated in commanding 4 and lofty places and these are bare, are they built of brick and clay. The greatest of the Indian cities is 5 called Palimbothra,[2] in the district of the Prasians, at the confluence of the Erannoboas [Son] and the Ganges; the Ganges is the greatest of all rivers, while the Erannoboas may be third of the Indian rivers but it is still greater than the rivers of other countries, though it yields precedence to the Ganges after joining it. And Megasthenes says that the 6 length of the city on either side, where it is longest, extends to eighty stades, its breadth to fifteen, and 7 that a ditch has been dug round the city, six plethra in breadth, thirty cubits deep; the wall has five hundred and seventy towers and sixty-four gates. It is also a great thing in India that all Indians are 8 free, and that no Indian at all is a slave.[3] The same 9 is true of the Lacedaemonians, but they have Helots for slaves, who perform the duties of slaves,[4] whereas the Indians have no slaves of any kind, let alone Indian slaves.

[3] Onesicritus *ap.* S. xv 1, 54 (mistranslated in Loeb edition) held that the absence of slavery was peculiar to Musicanus' realm. In fact, slavery is abundantly documented in Sanskrit literature (*CHI*, index *s.v.*).

[4] Helotry lasted only 'till the Roman supremacy' (S. vii 5, 4 f.), perhaps only till Nabis (cf. Polyb. xvi 13, 1). A. is transcribing a statement of Meg., long obsolete.

11. νενέμηνται δὲ οἱ πάντες Ἰνδοὶ ἐς ἑπτὰ
μάλιστα γένεα. ἓν μὲν αὐτοῖσιν οἱ σοφισταί εἰσι,
πλήθει μὲν μείους τῶν ἄλλων, δόξῃ δὲ καὶ τιμῇ
2 γεραρώτατοι· οὔτε γάρ τι τῷ σώματι ἐργάζεσθαι
ἀναγκαίη σφιν προσκέαται οὔτε τι ἀποφέρειν ἀφ'
ὅτων πονέουσιν ἐς τὸ κοινόν. οὐδέ τι ἄλλο ἀνάγκ-
ης ἁπλῶς ἐπεῖναι τοῖς σοφιστῇσιν, ὅτι μὴ θύειν
τὰς θυσίας τοῖσι θεοῖσιν ὑπὲρ τοῦ κοινοῦ ⟨τῶν⟩
3 Ἰνδῶν· καὶ ὅστις δὲ ἰδίᾳ θύει, ἐξηγητὴς αὐτῷ τῆς
θυσίης τῶν τις σοφιστῶν τούτων γίνεται, ὡς οὐκ
4 ἂν ἄλλως κεχαρισμένα τοῖς θεοῖς θύσαντας. εἰσὶ δὲ
καὶ μαντικῆς οὗτοι μοῦνοι Ἰνδῶν δαήμονες, οὐδὲ
ἐφεῖται ἄλλῳ μαντεύεσθαι ὅτι μὴ σοφιστῇ ἀνδρί.
5 μαντεύονται δὲ ὅσα ὑπὲρ τῶν ὡρέων τοῦ ἔτεος καὶ
εἴ τις ἐς τὸ κοινὸν συμφορὴ καταλαμβάνει· τὰ
ἴδια ⟨δὲ⟩ ἑκάστοισιν οὔ σφιν μέλει μαντεύεσθαι,
ὡς οὐκ ἐξικνεομένης τῆς μαντικῆς ἐς τὰ μικρότερα
ἢ ὡς οὐκ ἄξιον ⟨ὂν⟩ ἐπὶ τούτοισι πονέεσθαι.
6 ὅστις δὲ ἁμάρτοι ἐς τρὶς μαντευσάμενος, τούτῳ δὲ
ἄλλο μὲν κακὸν γίνεσθαι οὐδέν, σιωπᾶν δὲ εἶναι
ἐπάναγκες τοῦ λοιποῦ· καὶ οὐκ ἔστιν ὅστις ἐξαναγκάσει τὸν ἄνδρα τοῦτον φωνῆσαι, ὅτου ἡ σιωπὴ
7 κατακέκριται. οὗτοι γυμνοὶ διαιτῶνται οἱ σοφισταί, τοῦ μὲν χειμῶνος ὑπαίθριοι ἐν τῷ ἡλίῳ,
τοῦ δὲ θέρεος, ἐπὴν ὁ ἥλιος κατέχῃ, ἐν τοῖς λειμῶσι
καὶ τοῖσιν ἕλεσιν ὑπὸ δένδρεσι μεγάλοισι, ὧν τὴν
σκιὴν Νέαρχος λέγει ἐς πέντε πλέθρα ἐν κύκλῳ
ἐξικνέεσθαι, καὶ ἂν καὶ μυρίους ἀνθρώπους ὑπὸ
ἑνὶ δένδρεϊ σκιάζεσθαι· τηλικαῦτα εἶναι ταῦτα τὰ
8 δένδρεα. σιτέονται δὲ ⟨τὰ⟩ ὡραῖα καὶ τὸν φλοιὸν
τῶν δένδρων, γλυκύν τε ὄντα τὸν φλοιὸν καὶ τρό-
φιμον οὐ μεῖον ἤπερ αἱ βάλανοι τῶν φοινίκων.

11. All the Indians are divided into generally seven classes.[1]   One consists of the sophists; they are less numerous than the rest, but grandest in reputation and honour, for they are under no necessity to do any 2 bodily labour, nor to contribute from the results of their work to the common store; in fact, no sort of constraint whatever rests on the sophists, save to offer the sacrifices to the gods on behalf of the common weal of the Indians.   Whenever anyone sacri- 3 fices privately, one of the sophists directs him in the sacrifice, on the ground that otherwise it would not prove acceptable to the gods.   Alone of the Indians 4 they are expert in prophecy, and none save a sophist is allowed to prophesy.   They prophesy only about 5 the seasons of the year and any public calamity; it is not their concern to prophesy on private matters to individuals, either because the art of prophecy does not condescend to petty affairs, or because it is undignified for the sophists to trouble about them. Anyone who has made three errors in prophecy does 6 not suffer any harm but must keep silence in future, and no one will ever force the man to speak on whom sentence of silence has been passed.   These sophists 7 spend their time naked, during the winter in the open air and sunshine, but in summer, when the sun is strong, in the meadows and marsh lands under great trees, whose shade, according to Nearchus,[2] reaches five plethra all round, and which are so large that as many as ten thousand men could take shade under one tree.   The sophists eat produce in season 8 and the bark of trees, a bark that is no less sweet and nutritious than palm dates.

[1] Castes and especially Brahmans: App. XVII 9 and XX.
[2] A's insertion in an account otherwise derived from Meg. For the many versions of the marvel see Jacoby on Nearchus F. 6.

9 δεύτεροι δ' ἐπὶ τούτοισιν οἱ γεωργοί εἰσιν, οὗτοι πλήθει πλεῖστοι Ἰνδῶν ἐόντες. καὶ τούτοισιν οὔτε ὅπλα ἐστὶν ἀρήια οὔτε μέλει τὰ πολεμήια ἔργα, ἀλλὰ τὴν χώρην οὗτοι ἐργάζονται, καὶ τοὺς φόρους τοῖς τε βασιλεῦσι καὶ τῇσι πόλεσιν, ὅσαι
10 αὐτόνομοι, οὗτοι ἀποφέρουσι. καὶ εἰ πόλεμος ἐς ἀλλήλους τοῖσιν Ἰνδοῖσι τύχοι, τῶν ἐργαζομένων τὴν γῆν οὐ θέμις σφιν ἅπτεσθαι οὐδὲ αὐτὴν τὴν γῆν τέμνειν, ἀλλὰ οἱ μὲν πολεμοῦσι καὶ κατακαίνουσιν ἀλλήλους ὅπως τύχοιεν, οἱ δὲ πλησίον αὐτῶν κατ' ἡσυχίαν ἀροῦσιν ἢ τρυγῶσιν ἢ κλαδῶσιν ἢ θερίζουσιν.

11 τρίτοι δέ εἰσιν Ἰνδοῖσιν οἱ νομέες, οἱ ποιμένες τε καὶ βουκόλοι. καὶ οὗτοι οὔτε κατὰ πόλῃας οὔτε ἐν τῇσι κώμῃσιν οἰκέουσι· νομάδες τέ εἰσι καὶ ἀνὰ τὰ ὄρεα βιοτεύουσι. φόρον δὲ καὶ οὗτοι ἀπὸ τῶν κτηνέων ἀποφέρουσι, καὶ θηρεύουσιν οὗτοι ἀνὰ τὴν χώρην ὄρνιθάς τε καὶ ἄγρια θηρία.

12. τέταρτον δέ ἐστι τὸ δημιουργικόν τε καὶ καπηλικὸν γένος. καὶ οὗτοι λειτουργοί εἰσι καὶ φόρον ἀποφέρουσιν ἀπὸ τῶν ἔργων τῶν σφετέρων, πλήν γε δὴ ὅσοι τὰ ἀρήια ὅπλα ποιέουσιν· οὗτοι δὲ καὶ μισθὸν ἐκ τοῦ κοινοῦ προσλαμβάνουσιν. ἐν δὲ τούτῳ τῷ γένει οἵ τε ναυπηγοὶ καὶ οἱ ναῦταί εἰσιν, ὅσοι κατὰ τοὺς ποταμοὺς πλώουσι.

2 πέμπτον δὲ γένος ἐστὶν Ἰνδοῖσιν οἱ πολεμισταί, πλήθει μὲν δεύτερον μετὰ τοὺς γεωργούς, πλείστῃ δὲ ἐλευθερίῃ τε καὶ εὐθυμίῃ ἐπιχρεόμενον. καὶ οὗτοι ἀσκηταὶ μόνων τῶν πολεμικῶν ἔργων εἰσίν·
3 τὰ δὲ ὅπλα ἄλλοι αὐτοῖς ποιέουσι καὶ ἵππους ἄλλοι παρέχουσι καὶ διακονοῦσιν ἐπὶ στρατοπέδου ἄλλοι, οἱ τούς τε ἵππους αὐτοῖς θεραπεύουσι καὶ τὰ ὅπλα

Second to them come the farmers, who are the 9
most numerous of Indians; they have no weapons
and no concern in warfare, but they till the land and
pay the taxes to the kings and the self-governing
cities; and if there is internal war among the Indians, 10
it is not lawful for them to touch these land workers,
nor even to devastate the land itself; but while some
are making war and killing each other as opportunity
may serve, others close by are peacefully ploughing
or picking fruits or pruning or harvesting.

The third class of Indians are the herdsmen, who 11
pasture sheep and cattle, and do not dwell in cities or
in villages: they are nomads and get their living on
the hillsides. They too pay taxes from their animals,
and they hunt birds and wild beasts in the country.

12. The fourth class is of artisans and shopkeepers;
they too perform public duties, and pay tax on the
receipts from their work, except for those who make
weapons of war and actually receive a wage from the
community. In this class are the shipwrights and
sailors, who ply on the rivers.

The fifth class of Indians consists of the soldiers, 2
next to the farmers in number; they enjoy the
greatest freedom and most agreeable life. They are
devoted solely to military activities. Others make 3
their arms and provide their horses; others too serve
in the camps, grooming their horses and polishing

ἐκκαθαίρουσι καὶ τοὺς ἐλέφαντας ἄγουσι καὶ τὰ
4 ἅρματα κοσμέουσί τε καὶ ἡνιοχεύουσιν. αὐτοὶ δέ,
ἔστ' ἂν μὲν πολεμεῖν δέῃ, πολεμοῦσιν, εἰρήνης δὲ
γενομένης εὐθυμέονται· καί σφιν μισθὸς ἐκ τοῦ
κοινοῦ τοσόσδε ἔρχεται ὡς καὶ ἄλλους τρέφειν ἀπ'
αὐτοῦ εὐμαρέως.

5 ἕκτοι δέ εἰσιν Ἰνδοῖσιν οἱ ἐπίσκοποι καλεόμενοι.
οὗτοι ἐφορῶσι τὰ γινόμενα κατά τε τὴν χώρην καὶ
κατὰ τὰς πόληας, καὶ ταῦτα ἀναγγέλλουσι τῷ
βασιλεῖ, ἵναπερ βασιλεύονται Ἰνδοί, ἢ τοῖς τέλεσιν,
ἵναπερ αὐτόνομοί εἰσι. καὶ τούτοις οὐ θέμις
ψεῦδος ἀγγεῖλαι οὐδέν, οὐδέ τις Ἰνδῶν αἰτίην ἔσχε
ψεύσασθαι.

6 ἕβδομοι δέ εἰσιν οἱ ὑπὲρ τῶν κοινῶν βουλευόμενοι
ὁμοῦ τῷ βασιλεῖ ἢ κατὰ πόληας ὅσαι αὐτόνομοι
7 σὺν τῇσιν ἀρχῇσι. πλήθει μὲν ὀλίγον τὸ γένος
τοῦτό ἐστι, σοφίῃ δὲ καὶ δικαιότητι ἐκ πάντων
προκεκριμένον. ἔνθεν οἵ τε ἄρχοντες αὐτοῖσιν
ἐπιλέγονται καὶ ὅσοι νομάρχαι καὶ ὕπαρχοι καὶ
θησαυροφύλακές τε καὶ στρατοφύλακες, ναύαρχοί
τε καὶ ταμίαι καὶ τῶν κατὰ γεωργίην ἔργων
ἐπιστάται.

8 γαμέειν δὲ ἐξ ἑτέρου γένεος οὐ θέμις, οἷον τοῖσι
γεωργοῖσιν ἐκ τοῦ δημιουργικοῦ ἢ ἔμπαλιν. οὐδὲ
δύο τέχνας ἐπιτηδεύειν τὸν αὐτὸν οὐδὲ τοῦτο θέμις,
οὐδὲ ἀμείβειν ἐξ ἑτέρου γένεος εἰς ἕτερον, οἷον
γεωργικὸν ἐκ νομέως γενέσθαι ἢ νομέα ἐκ δημιουρ-
9 γικοῦ. μοῦνόν σφισιν ἀνεῖται σοφιστὴν ἐκ παντὸς
γένεος γενέσθαι, ὅτι οὐ μαλθακὰ τοῖσι σοφιστῇσίν
εἰσι τὰ πρήγματα ἀλλὰ πάντων ταλαιπωρότατα.

---

[1] Cf. App. XVII 9. S. is much fuller, but only A. mentions

their arms, driving the elephants, and keeping the chariots in order and driving them. They fight so 4 long as they have to fight, but in time of peace they make merry; and they receive so much pay from the community that they can easily support others from their pay.

The sixth class of Indians are those called over- 5 seers. They supervise everything that goes on in the country and cities, and report it to the king, where the Indians are governed by kings, or to the authorities, where they are self-governing. It is not lawful to make any false report to them; and no Indian was ever accused of such falsification.

The seventh class are those who deliberate about 6 public affairs with the king, or in self-governing cities with the authorities. In number this class is 7 small, but in wisdom and justice it is the most distinguished of all; it is from this class that they select their rulers, nomarchs, hyparchs, treasurers, generals, admirals, comptrollers, and supervisors of agricultural works.[1]

To marry out of any class is unlawful—as, for instance, into the farmer class from the artisans, or the 8 other way; nor again is it even lawful for one man to practise two crafts or to change from one class to another, as to turn farmer from shepherd, or shepherd from artisan. Only a sophist can be drawn from 9 any class; for this way of life is not soft, but the hardest of all.[2]

[1] ' self-governing cities,' as often in *Anab.*; cf. *CHI* 175 ff.; 199 f. Conceivably Meg., concerned only with Chandragupta's kingdom, did not do so, and we have here an insertion made by A. from his recollections of Pt. and Ar., or from N.

[2] But S. xv 1, 49 and D. ii 41 say that only the philosophers could undertake the functions of other castes; we do not know what Meg. really wrote.

13. θηρῶσι δὲ Ἰνδοὶ τὰ μὲν ἄλλα ἄγρια θηρία κατάπερ καὶ Ἕλληνες, ἡ δὲ τῶν ἐλεφάντων σφιν θήρα οὐδέν τι ἄλλῃ ἔοικεν, ὅτι καὶ ταῦτα τὰ θηρία

2 οὐδαμοῖσιν ἄλλοισι θηρίοις ἐπέοικεν. ἀλλὰ τόπον γὰρ ἐπιλεξάμενοι ἄπεδον καὶ καυματώδεα ἐν κύκλῳ τάφρον ὀρύσσουσιν, ὅσον μεγάλῳ στρατοπέδῳ ἐπαυλίσασθαι. τῆς δὲ τάφρου τὸ εὖρος ἐς πέντε

3 ὀργυιὰς ποιέονται, βάθος τε ἐς τέσσαρας. τὸν δὲ χοῦν ὅντινα ἐκβάλλουσιν ἐκ τοῦ ὀρύγματος, ἐπὶ τὰ χείλεα ἑκάτερα τῆς τάφρου ἐπιφορήσαντες ἀντὶ

4 τείχεος διαχρέονται, αὐτοὶ δὲ ὑπὸ τῷ χώματι τῷ ἐπὶ τοῦ χείλεος τοῦ ἔξω τῆς τάφρου σκηνάς σφιν ὀρυκτὰς ποιέονται, καὶ διὰ τουτέων ὀπὰς ὑπολείπονται, δι᾿ ὧν φῶς τε αὐτοῖσιν εἰσέρχεται καὶ τὰ θηρία προσάγοντα καὶ ἐσελαύνοντα ἐς τὸ ἔρκος σκέπ-

5 τονται. ἐνταῦθα ἐντὸς τοῦ ἔρκεος καταστήσαντες τῶν τινας θηλέων τρεῖς ἢ τέσσαρας, ὅσαι μάλιστα τὸν θυμὸν χειροήθεες, μίαν εἴσοδον ἀπολιμπάνουσι κατὰ τὴν τάφρον, γεφυρώσαντες τὴν τάφρον· καὶ ταύτῃ χοῦν τε καὶ πόαν πολλὴν ἐπιφέρουσι τοῦ μὴ ἀρίδηλον εἶναι τοῖσι θηρίοισι τὴν γέφυραν, μή τινα

6 δόλον ὀισθῶσιν. αὐτοὶ μὲν οὖν ἐκποδὼν σφᾶς ⟨ποι⟩έουσι κατὰ τῶν σκηνέων τῶν ὑπὸ τῇ τάφρῳ δεδυκότες, οἱ δὲ ἄγριοι ἐλέφαντες ἡμέρης μὲν οὐ πελάζουσι τοῖσιν οἰκουμένοισι, νύκτωρ δὲ πλανῶνταί τε πάντῃ καὶ ἀγεληδὸν νέμονται τῷ μεγίστῳ καὶ γενναιοτάτῳ σφῶν ἑπόμενοι, κατάπερ αἱ βόες

7 τοῖσι ταύροισιν. ἐπεὰν ὦν τῷ ἔρκει πελάσωσι, τήν τε φωνὴν ἀκούοντες τῶν θηλέων καὶ τῇ ὀδμῇ αἰσθόμενοι, δρόμῳ ἵενται ὡς ἐπὶ τὸν χῶρον τὸν πεφραγμένον· ἐκπεριελθόντες δὲ τῆς τάφρου τὰ χείλεα εὖτ᾿ ἂν τῇ γεφύρῃ ἐπιτύχωσιν, κατὰ ταύ-

13. The Indians hunt wild animals in general in the same way as the Greeks, but their way of hunting elephants is unique, like the animals themselves.[1] They choose a level place, open to the sun's heat, and 2 dig a ditch in a circle, large enough for a great army to camp in, about thirty feet broad and 24 deep. The earth thrown out of the ditch is heaped on either 3 side, and used as a wall; then they make dug-out 4 shelters for themselves beneath the mound on the outside lip of the ditch, and leave small windows in them through which the light reaches them, and they can see the animals coming up to and charging up to the enclosure. Within the enclosure they put 5 three or four of the tamest females and leave only one entrance in the ditch by making a bridge over it, where they heap a great deal of earth and grass so that the animals cannot distinguish the bridge, in case they might suspect a trap. The hunters themselves 6 keep out of the way, hiding in the shelters under the ditch. Now the wild elephants do not approach inhabited places by daylight, but at night they wander everywhere and feed in herds, following the largest and finest of their number, as cows follow bulls. When they get near the enclosure and hear the voice 7 of the females and scent their presence, they charge to the enclosed place and, working round the outside edge of the ditch, find the bridge and shove their way

---

[1] From Meg., cf. S. xv 1, 42 f., cf. D. ii 42 for chs. 13 f. S. adds information from N. and Onesicritus.

8 τὴν ἐς τὸ ἔρκος ὠθέονται. οἱ δὲ ἄνθρωποι αἰσθόμε
νοι τὴν ἔσοδον τῶν ἐλεφάντων τῶν ἀγρίων, οἱ μὲν
αὐτῶν τὴν γέφυραν ὀξέως ἀφεῖλον, οἱ δὲ ἐπὶ τὰς
πέλας κώμας ἀποδραμόντες ἀγγέλλουσι τοὺς ἐλέ
9 φαντας ὅτι ἐν τῷ ἔρκει ἔχονται· οἱ δὲ ἀκούσαντες
ἐπιβαίνουσι τῶν κρατίστων τε τὸν θυμὸν καὶ [τῶν]
χειροηθεστάτων ἐλεφάντων, ἐπιβάντες δὲ ἐλαύν
ουσιν ὡς ἐπὶ τὸ ἔρκος, ἐλάσαντες δὲ οὐκ αὐτίκα
μάχης ἅπτονται, ἀλλ᾽ ἐῶσι γὰρ λιμῷ τε ταλαι
πωρηθῆναι τοὺς ἀγρίους ἐλέφαντας καὶ ὑπὸ τῷ
10 δίψει δουλωθῆναι. εὖτ᾽ ἂν δέ σφισι κακῶς ἔχειν
δοκέωσι, τηνικαῦτα ἐπιστήσαντες αὖθις τὴν γέφυ
ραν ἐλαύνουσί τε ὡς ἐς τὸ ἔρκος, καὶ τὰ μὲν
πρῶτα μάχη ἵσταται κρατερὴ τοῖσιν ἡμέροισι τῶν
ἐλεφάντων πρὸς τοὺς ἑαλωκότας· ἔπειτα κρατέον
ται μὲν κατὰ τὸ εἰκὸς οἱ ἄγριοι ὑπό τε τῇ ἀθυμίῃ καὶ
11 τῷ λιμῷ ταλαιπωρούμενοι. οἱ δὲ ἀπὸ τῶν ἐλεφάν
των καταβάντες παρειμένοισιν ἤδη τοῖσιν ἀγρίοισι
τοὺς πόδας ἄκρους συνδέουσιν, ἔπειτα ἐγκελεύονται
τοῖσιν ἡμέροισι πληγαῖς σφᾶς κολάζειν πολλαῖς,
ἔστ᾽ ἂν ἐκεῖνοι ταλαιπωρεύμενοι ἐς γῆν πέσωσι.
παραστάντες δὲ βρόχους περιβάλλουσιν αὐτοῖσι
κατὰ τοὺς αὐχένας, καὶ αὐτοὶ ἐπιβαίνουσι κειμέ
12 νοισι. τοῦ δὲ μὴ ἀποσείεσθαι τοὺς ἀμβάτας μηδέ
τι ἄλλο ἀτάσθαλον ἐργάζεσθαι, τὸν τράχηλον αὐτοῖ
σιν ἐν κύκλῳ μαχαιρίῳ ὀξεῖ ἐπιτέμνουσι, καὶ τὸν
βρόχον κατὰ τὴν τομὴν περιδέουσιν, ὡς ἀτρέμα
ἔχειν τὴν κεφαλήν τε καὶ τὸν τράχηλον ὑπὸ τοῦ
13 ἕλκεος. εἰ γὰρ περιστρέφοιντο ὑπὸ ἀτασθαλίης,
τρίβεται αὐτοῖσι τὸ ἕλκος ὑπὸ τῷ κάλῳ. οὕτω
μὲν ὦν ἀτρέμα ἴσχουσι καὶ αὐτοὶ γνωσιμαχέοντες
ἤδη ἄγονται κατὰ τὸν δεσμὸν πρὸς τῶν ἡμέρων.

over it into the enclosure. The hunters observe the 8
entry of the wild elephants; some smartly remove the
bridge, others run off to the neighbouring villages
and report that the elephants are caught in the enclosure, and the inhabitants on hearing the news 9
mount the most spirited and manageable elephants
and drive them towards the enclosure, but on arrival
they do not at once join battle, but let the wild
elephants grow distressed by hunger and mastered
by thirst. Only when they think they are in a bad 10
way, do they erect the bridge again, and drive into
the enclosure. At first there is a fierce battle between the tame elephants and the captives, and
then, as one would expect, the wild elephants are
overcome, distressed as they are by sinking of their
spirits and hunger. Then the men dismount from 11
their elephants, tie together the feet of the wild
elephants, which are now exhausted, and then order
the tame elephants to punish the rest by repeated
blows, till in their distress they fall to the ground;
they then stand by them, throw nooses round their
necks and climb on them as they lie there. To pre- 12
vent them tossing their drivers or doing them an in-
jury, they make an incision round their necks with a
sharp knife, and bind the noose round the cut, so that
the sore makes them keep their head and neck still;
if they were to turn round to do mischief, the wound 13
beneath the rope would chafe them. So they keep
quiet and, knowing themselves beaten, they are
roped to the tame elephants and led away.

14. ὅσοι δὲ νήπιοι αὐτῶν ἢ διὰ κακότητα οὐκ ἄξιοι ἐκτῆσθαι, τούτους ἐῶσιν ἀπαλλάττεσθαι ἐς
2 τὰ σφέτερα ἤθεα. ἀγ⟨αγ⟩όντες δὲ εἰς τὰς κώμας τοὺς ἁλόντας τοῦ τε χλωροῦ καλάμου καὶ τῆς πόας
3 τὰ πρῶτα ἐμφαγεῖν ἔδοσαν, οἱ δὲ ὑπὸ ἀθυμίης οὐκ ἐθέλουσιν οὐδὲν σιτέεσθαι, τοὺς δὲ περιστάμενοι οἱ Ἰνδοὶ ᾠδαῖσί τε καὶ τυμπάνοισι καὶ κυμβάλοισιν ἐν κύκλῳ κρούοντές τε καὶ ἐπᾴδοντες κατευνάζουσι.
4 θυμόσοφον γὰρ εἴπερ τι ἄλλο θηρίον ὁ ἐλέφας, καί τινες ἤδη αὐτῶν τοὺς ἀμβάτας σφῶν ἐν πολέμῳ ἀποθανόντας ἄραντες αὐτοὶ ἐξήνεγκαν ἐς ταφήν, οἱ δὲ καὶ ὑπερήσπισαν κειμένους, οἱ δὲ καὶ πεσόντων προεκινδύνευσαν, ὁ δέ τις πρὸς ὀργὴν ἀποκτείνας τὸν ἀμβάτην ὑπὸ μετανοίης τε καὶ
5 ἀθυμίης ἀπέθανεν. εἶδον δὲ ἔγωγε καὶ κυμβαλίζοντα ἤδη ἐλέφαντα καὶ ἄλλους ὀρχεομένους, κυμβάλοιν τῷ κυμβαλίζοντι πρὸς τοῖν σκελοῖν τοῖν ἔμπροσθεν προσηρτημένοιν, καὶ πρὸς τῇ προβοσ-
6 κίδι καλεομένῃ ἄλλου κυμβάλου· ὁ δὲ ἐν μέρει τῇ προβοσκίδι ἔκρουε τὸ κύμβαλον ἐν ῥυθμῷ πρὸς ἑκατέροιν τοῖν σκελοῖν, οἱ δὲ ὀρχεόμενοι ἐν κύκλῳ τε ἐχόρευον, καὶ ἐπαίροντές τε καὶ ἐπικάμπτοντες τὰ ἔμπροσθεν σκέλεα ἐν τῷ μέρει ἐν ῥυθμῷ καὶ οὗτοι ἔβαινον, καθότι ὁ κυμβαλίζων
7 σφίσιν ὑφηγέετο. βαίνεται δὲ ἐλέφας ἦρος ὥρῃ, κατάπερ βοῦς ἢ ἵππος, ἐπεὰν τῇσι θηλέῃσιν αἱ παρὰ τοῖσι κροτάφοισιν ἀναπνοαὶ ἀνοιχθεῖσαι ἐκπνέωσιν. κύει δὲ τοὺς ἐλαχίστους μὲν ἑκκαίδεκα μῆνας, τοὺς πλείστους δὲ ὀκτωκαίδεκα. τίκτει δὲ ἕν, κατάπερ ἵππος, καὶ τοῦτο ἐκτρέφει τῷ γάλακτι ἐς ἔτος
8 ὄγδοον. ζῶσι δὲ ἐλεφάντων οἱ πλεῖστα ἔτεα ζῶντες ἐς διηκόσια, πολλοὶ δὲ νόσῳ προτελευτῶσιν

14. Elephants not yet full grown or not worth acquiring because of a defect are released to their own haunts. The captives are led off to the villages 2 and first of all given green stalks and grass to eat; from want of spirit they are not willing to eat any- 3 thing; so the Indians range themselves round about them and lull them to sleep with songs, drums and cymbals, beating and singing. For if there is an 4 intelligent animal, it is the elephant. Some ele- phants, when their drivers have died in battle, have actually caught them up and carried them to burial; others have protected them where they lay or risked their own lives for the fallen; one indeed, who in a passion killed his driver, died from remorse and grief. I myself have seen an elephant actually clanging the 5 cymbals and others dancing; two cymbals were fastened to the player's forelegs, and another on his trunk, and with his trunk he rhythmically beat the 6 cymbal on either leg in turn; the dancers danced in a circle; raising and bending their forelegs in turn, they too kept in rhythm as their cymbalist gave the beat. The elephants mate in spring, like cattle and 7 horses, when the breathing places by the temples of the females open and exhale; she gives birth after sixteen months at the least, eighteen at most; she has one foal, like a mare, which she suckles till its eighth year.[1] The longest-lived elephants survive to 8 two hundred years, if they reach old age, though

---

[1] Six years in S. xv 1, 43; D. ii 42; probably A. or a copyist is at fault.

9 αὐτῶν· γήρᾳ δὲ ἐς τόσον ἔρχονται. καὶ ἔστιν
αὐτοῖσι τῶν μὲν ὀφθαλμῶν ἴαμα τὸ βόειον γάλα
ἐγχεόμενον, πρὸς δὲ τὰς ἄλλας νόσους ὁ μέλας
οἶνος πινόμενος, ἐπὶ δὲ τοῖσιν ἕλκεσι τὰ ὕεια κρέα
ὀπτώμενα καὶ καταπλασσόμενα· ταῦτα παρ᾽
Ἰνδοῖσίν ἐστιν αὐτοῖσι ἰάματα.

15. τοῦ δὲ ἐλέφαντος τὴν τίγριν πολλόν τι ἀλκι-
μωτέρην Ἰνδοὶ ἄγουσι. τίγριος δὲ δορὴν μὲν
ἰδεῖν λέγει Νέαρχος, αὐτὴν δὲ τίγριν οὐκ ἰδεῖν·
ἀλλὰ τοὺς Ἰνδοὺς γὰρ ἀπηγέεσθαι, τίγριν εἶναι
μέγεθος μὲν ἡλίκον τὸν μέγιστον ἵππον, τὴν δὲ
ὠκύτητα καὶ ἀλκὴν οἵην οὐδενὶ ἄλλῳ εἰκάσαι·
2 τίγριν γὰρ ἐπεὰν ὁμοῦ ἔλθῃ ἐλέφαντι, ἐπιπηδᾶν τε
ἐπὶ τὴν κεφαλὴν τοῦ ἐλέφαντος καὶ ἄγχειν εὐπε-
3 τέως. ταύτας δέ, ἅστινας καὶ ἡμεῖς ὁρέομεν καὶ
τίγριας καλέομεν, θῶας εἶναι αἰόλους καὶ μέζονας
4 ἤπερ τοὺς ἄλλους θῶας. ἐπεὶ καὶ ὑπὲρ τῶν μυρμήκων λέγει Νέαρχος μύρμηκα μὲν αὐτὸς οὐκ ἰδέειν,
ὁποῖον δή τινα μετεξέτεροι διέγραψαν γίνεσθαι ἐν
τῇ Ἰνδῶν γῇ, δορὰς δὲ καὶ τούτων ἰδεῖν πολλὰς ἐς
τὸ στρατόπεδον κατακομισθείσας τὸ Μακεδονικόν.
5 Μεγασθένης δὲ καὶ ἀτρεκέα εἶναι ὑπὲρ τῶν μυρμήκων τὸν λόγον ἱστορέει τούτους εἶναι τοὺς τὸν
χρυσὸν ὀρύσσοντας, οὐκ αὐτοῦ τοῦ χρυσοῦ ἕνεκα,
ἀλλὰ φύσι γὰρ κατὰ τῆς ὀρύσσουσιν, ἵνα φωλεύ-
σαιεν, κατάπερ οἱ ἡμέτεροι οἱ σμικροὶ μύρμηκες
6 ὀλίγον τῆς γῆς ὀρύσσουσιν. ἐκείνους δέ — εἶναι γὰρ
ἀλωπεκέων μέζονας — πρὸς λόγον τοῦ μεγέθεος
σφῶν καὶ τὴν γῆν ὀρύσσειν· τὴν δὲ γῆν χρυσῖτιν
εἶναι, καὶ ἀπὸ ταύτης γίνεσθαι Ἰνδοῖσι τὸν χρυσόν.
7 ἀλλὰ Μεγασθένης τε ἀκοὴν ἀπηγέεται, καὶ ἐγὼ ὅτι
οὐδὲν τούτου ἀτρεκέστερον ἀναγράψαι ἔχω, ἄπίημι

many die before that of disease. A remedy for 9
affections of their eyes is pouring in cows' milk, for
their other sicknesses a draught of dark wine, and for
their wounds swine's flesh roasted and plastered on.
These are remedies the Indians apply to them.

15. The Indians regard the tiger as much stronger
than the elephant. Nearchus says that he had only
seen a tiger's skin but not a tiger, but that by
Indian accounts the tiger is equal in size to the
largest horse, and its swiftness and strength unequalled, for, when a tiger meets an elephant, it 2
leaps on his head and throttles him easily; he adds 3
that the creatures *we* see and call tigers are jackals,
dappled and larger than the other jackals.[1] As for 4
the ants, Nearchus says that he himself saw none of
the sort which some writers have described as native
to India but that he did see many of their skins
brought into the Macedonian camp.[2] Megasthenes, 5
however, recounts that the story told of the ants is
true: these ants do dig up gold, not indeed for the
gold itself, but they naturally burrow in the earth to
make hiding holes, just as our small ants excavate a
little earth; but these ants, which are bigger than 6
foxes, also dig up earth proportionate to their size;
the earth is auriferous, and the Indians get their gold
from it. Megasthenes, however, merely recounts 7
hearsay, and as I have no more accurate information
to record on the subject I readily pass over the tale

---

[1] See Jacoby on Nearchus F. 7, cf. perhaps D. ii 50, 2. A.
ignores the account of Meg., who had seen tigers (S. xv 1, 37).
[2] A. ignores N's statement that they were like leopard skins;
for Meg's account cf. S. xv 1, 44. See v 4, 3 n.; Hdt. iii 102 ff.;
O. Stein, *RE* xv 236 ff.; it was perhaps an Indian legend, cf.
§ 7 (' hearsay ').

8 ἑκὼν τὸν ὑπὲρ τῶν μυρμήκων λόγον. σιττακοὺς
δὲ Νέαρχος μὲν ὡς δή τι θαῦμα ἀπηγέεται ὅτι
γίνονται ἐν τῇ Ἰνδῶν γῇ, καὶ ὁποῖος ὄρνις ἐστὶν ὁ
9 σιττακός, καὶ ὅπως φωνὴν ἵει ἀνθρωπίνην. ἐγὼ δὲ
ὅτι αὐτός τε πολλοὺς ὀπώπεα καὶ ἄλλους ἐπιστα-
μένους ᾔδεα τὸν ὄρνιθα, οὐδὲν ὡς ⟨ὑπὲρ⟩ ἀτόπου
δῆθεν ἀπηγήσομαι· οὐδὲ ὑπὲρ τῶν πιθήκων τοῦ
μεγέθεος, ἢ ὅτι καλοὶ παρ' Ἰνδοῖς πίθηκοί εἰσιν,
οὐδὲ ὅπως θηρῶνται ἐρέω. καὶ γὰρ ταῦτα
γνώριμα ἐρῶ, πλήν γε δὴ ὅτι καλοί που πίθηκοί
10 εἰσιν. καὶ ὄφιας δὲ λέγει Νέαρχος θηρευθῆναι
αἰόλους μὲν καὶ ταχέας, μέγαθος δέ, ὃν μὲν λέγει
ἑλεῖν Πείθωνα τὸν Ἀντιγένεος, πήχεων ὡς ἑκκαίδεκα. αὐτοὺς δὲ τοὺς Ἰνδοὺς πολὺ μείζονας
11 τούτων λέγειν εἶναι τοὺς μεγίστους ὄφεας. ὅσοι δὲ
ἰητροὶ Ἕλληνες, τούτοισιν οὐδὲν ἄκος ἐξεύρητο
ὅστις ὑπὸ ὄφεως δηχθείη Ἰνδικοῦ· ἀλλ' αὐτοὶ γὰρ οἱ
Ἰνδοὶ ἰῶντο τοὺς πληγέντας. καὶ ἐπὶ τῷδε
Νέαρχος λέγει ⟨ὅτι⟩ συλλελεγμένους ἀμφ' αὑτὸν
εἶχεν Ἀλέξανδρος Ἰνδῶν ὅσοι ἰητρικὴν σοφώτατοι,
καὶ κεκήρυκτο ἀνὰ τὸ στρατόπεδον, ὅστις δηχθείη,
12 ἐπὶ τὴν σκηνὴν φοιτᾶν τὴν βασιλέως. οἱ δὲ αὐτοὶ
οὗτοι καὶ τῶν ἄλλων νούσων τε καὶ παθέων ἰητροὶ
ἦσαν. οὐ πολλὰ δὲ ἐν Ἰνδοῖσι πάθεα γίνεται, ὅτι
αἱ ὧραι σύμμετροί εἰσιν αὐτόθι· εἰ δέ τι μεῖζον
καταλαμβάνοι, τοῖσι σοφιστῇσιν ἀνεκοινοῦντο· καὶ
ἐκεῖνοι οὐκ ἄνευ θεοῦ ἐδόκεον ἰῆσθαι ὅ τι περ
ἰήσιμον.

16. ἐσθῆτι δὲ Ἰνδοὶ λινέῃ χρέονται, κατάπερ

---

[3] Yet the stories in Clitarchus F. 19 (cf. D. 90) and S. xv

about the ants.   Nearchus recounts as a kind of mar-   8
vel that parrots are found in India, and describes the
sort of bird a parrot is and how it utters a human
voice.   But as I have seen many myself and know   9
that others are acquainted with the bird, I shall of
course not say anything of it as an oddity, nor shall I
speak of the size of the apes, of the beauty of some
found in India or of the method of capture.   For I
should only say what everyone knows, except perhaps
that there are beautiful apes.[3]   Nearchus also says 10
that snakes were hunted there, dappled and swift;
and that the snake he says Pithon son of Antigenes
caught was about sixteen cubits long, but that the
Indians themselves say that the largest snakes are
much larger.   No Greek physicians discovered a 11
remedy against Indian snakebite, but the Indians
themselves used to cure those who were struck, and
Nearchus adds that Alexander had collected and
kept by him all the Indians most skilled in medicine,
and had it announced in camp that anyone bitten by
a snake was to go to the royal tent.   The same men 12
were physicians for other diseases and injuries as
well.   But there are not many illnesses in India, since
the seasons are temperate there.   If anyone were
seriously ill, they would inform the sophists, who
were thought to use divine help to cure what could
be cured.[4]

16. The Indians wear linen garments according to

1, 29, a chapter probably derived from Ar. (cf. App. XVII
18), are remarkable.   A. now takes no account of Ar.

[4] Cf. S. xv 1, 45 (N.) and 60 (Meg. on Indian medicine).   A.
writes of Indian snakes nowhere else, but see also Onesicritus
and Ar. *ap.* S. xv 1, 28 and 45; 2, 7 (N.); Clitarchus F. 18;
D. 90: they were among the most feared perils of the Indian
campaigns.

λέγει Νέαρχος, λίνου τοῦ ἀπὸ τῶν δενδρέων, ὑπὲρ
ὅτων μοι ἤδη λέλεκται. τὸ δὲ λίνον τοῦτο ἢ λαμπρότερον τὴν χροιήν ἐστιν ἄλλου λίνου παντός, ἢ
μέλανες αὐτοὶ ἐόντες λαμπρότερον τὸ λίνον φαίνεσθαι
2 ποιέουσιν. ἔστι δὲ κιθὼν λίνεος αὐτοῖς ἔστε ἐπὶ
μέσην τὴν κνήμην, εἶμα δὲ τὸ μὲν περὶ τοῖσιν
ὤμοισι περιβεβλημένον, τὸ δὲ περὶ τῆσι κεφαλῆσιν
3 εἱλιγμένον. καὶ ἐνώτια Ἰνδοὶ φορέουσιν ἐλέφαντος ὅσοι κάρτα εὐδαίμονες· οὐ γὰρ πάντες Ἰνδοὶ
4 φορέουσι. τοὺς δὲ πώγωνας λέγει Νέαρχος ὅτι
βάπτονται Ἰνδοί, χροιὴν δὲ ἄλλην καὶ ἄλλην
⟨βάπτονται⟩, οἱ μὲν ὡς λευκοὺς φαίνεσθαι οἵους
λευκοτάτους, οἱ δὲ κυανέους, τοῖς δὲ φοινικέους
εἶναι, τοῖς δὲ καὶ πορφυρέους, ἄλλοις πρασοειδέας·
5 καὶ σκιάδια ὅτι προβάλλονται τοῦ θέρεος ὅσοι οὐκ
ἠμελημένοι Ἰνδῶν. ὑποδήματα δὲ λευκοῦ δέρματος
φορέουσι, περιττῶς καὶ ταῦτα ἠσκημένα· καὶ τὰ
ἴχνη τῶν ὑποδημάτων αὐτοῖσι ποικίλα καὶ ὑψηλά,
τοῦ μέζονας φαίνεσθαι.
6 ὁπλίσιος δὲ τῆς Ἰνδῶν οὐκ ὡυτὸς εἷς τρόπος ἀλλ᾽
οἱ μὲν πεζοὶ αὐτοῖσι τόξον τε ἔχουσι, ἰσόμηκες τῷ
φορέοντι τὸ τόξον, καὶ τοῦτο κάτω ἐπὶ τὴν γῆν θέντες
καὶ τῷ ποδὶ τῷ ἀριστερῷ ἀντιβάντες, οὕτως ἐκτο-
ξεύουσι, τὴν νευρὴν ἐπὶ μέγα ὀπίσω ἀπαγαγόντες·
7 ὁ γὰρ οἰστὸς αὐτοῖσιν ὀλίγον ἀποδέων τριπήχεος,
οὐδέ τι ἀντέχει τοξευθὲν πρὸς Ἰνδοῦ ἀνδρὸς τοξικοῦ,
οὔτε ἀσπὶς οὔτε θώρηξ οὔτε ⟨εἴ⟩ τι ⟨τὸ κάρτα⟩
8 καρτερὸν ἐγένετο. ἐν δὲ τῆσιν ἀριστερῆσι πέλται
εἰσὶν αὐτοῖσιν ὠμοβόιναι, στεινότεραι μὲν ἢ κατὰ
τοὺς φορέοντας, μήκει δὲ οὐ πολλὸν ἀποδέουσαι.
9 τοῖσι δὲ ἄκοντες ἀντὶ τόξων εἰσί. μάχαιραν δὲ
πάντες φορέουσι, πλατείην δὲ καὶ τὸ μῆκος οὐ

Nearchus, the linen coming from the trees of which I have already made mention.[1] This linen is brighter in colour than any other, or else the people's own blackness makes it appear brighter. They wear a 2 linen tunic down to the middle of the calf, one garment thrown about their shoulders, and another wound round their heads. Some wear ivory ear- 3 rings, but only if they are very rich. Nearchus says 4 that they dye their beards but with various colours; some make them look as white as possible, others are dark-blue, crimson, purple or grass-green. All the 5 respectable Indians use sunshades against the summer heat. They have sandals of white skin, and these elaborately fashioned; and the heels of their sandals are of different colours, and high to make them look taller.

Indian war equipment is not all the same; the in- 6 fantry have a bow as tall as the archer, which they base on the ground, and set their left foot on it before shooting, drawing the bowstring a very long way back; for their arrows are little short of three cubits, 7 and an arrow shot by an Indian archer penetrates anything, shield or breastplate or any armour, however strong. In their left hands they carry small shields 8 of raw hide, narrower than their bodies, but not much shorter. Others have javelins in place of bows. All 9 carry a broad sword, not less than three cubits long,

---

[1] Cotton, cf. 7, 3. See Strabo xv 1, 20 (N. and Ar.): Onesicritus F. 23; Theophrastus, *Hist. of Plants* iv, 4, 8; 7, 7; QC. viii 9, 21. A. omits most of what N. and others wrote on Indian plants (S. 20 f.), and selects only a few items from N's account of Indian customs (S. 66 f.); in this ch. he follows N. in preference to Meg. (S. 53–6).

μείω τριπήχεος· καὶ ταύτην, ἐπεὰν συστάδην κατα-
στῇ αὐτοῖσιν ἡ μάχη — τὸ δὲ οὐκ εὐμαρέως Ἰνδοῖσιν ἐς ἀλλήλους γίνεται — ἀμφοῖν τοῖν χεροῖν
καταφέρουσιν ἐς τὴν πληγήν, τοῦ καρτερὴν τὴν
10 πληγὴν γενέσθαι. οἱ δὲ ἱππέες ἀκόντια δύο αὐτοῖσιν ἔχουσιν, οἷα τὰ σαύνια ἀκόντια, καὶ πέλτην
[τὴν] μικροτέρην τῶν πεζῶν. οἱ δὲ ἵπποι αὐτοῖσιν
οὐ σεσαγμένοι εἰσίν, οὐδὲ χαλινοῦνται τοῖσιν
Ἑλληνικοῖσι χαλινοῖσιν ἢ τοῖσι Κελτικοῖσιν ἐμ-
11 φερέως, ἀλλὰ περὶ ἄκρῳ τῷ στόματι τοῦ ἵππου ἐν
κύκλῳ ἔχουσι δέρμα ὠμοβόινον ῥαπτὸν περιηρτη-
μένον, καὶ ἐν τούτῳ χάλκεα κέντρα ἢ σιδήρεα, οὐ
κάρτα ὀξέα, ἔσω ἐστραμμένα· τοῖσι δὲ πλουσίοισιν
ἐλεφάντινα κέντρα ἐστίν. ἐν δὲ τῷ στόματι σίδη-
ρον αὐτοῖσιν οἱ ἵπποι ἔχουσιν, οἷόν περ ὀβελόν,
12 ἔνθεν ἐξηρτημένοι εἰσὶν αὐτοῖσιν οἱ ῥυτῆρες· ἐπεὰν
ὦν ἐπαγάγωσι τὸν ῥυτῆρα, ὅ τε ὀβελὸς κρατέει
τὸν ἵππον, καὶ τὰ κέντρα, οἷα δὴ ἐξ αὐτοῦ ἠρτη-
μένα, κεντέοντα οὐκ ἐᾷ ἄλλο τι ἢ πείθεσθαι τῷ
ῥυτῆρι.

17. τὰ δὲ σώματα ἰσχνοί τέ εἰσιν Ἰνδοὶ καὶ εὐμή-
κεες, καὶ κοῦφοι πολλόν τι ὑπὲρ τοὺς ἄλλους ἀνθρώπους. ὀχήματα δὲ τοῖς μὲν πολλοῖς Ἰνδῶν κάμηλοί
εἰσιν καὶ ἵπποι καὶ ὄνοι, τοῖς δὲ εὐδαίμοσιν ἐλέφαν-
2 τες. βασιλικὸν γὰρ ὄχημα ἐλέφας παρ᾽ Ἰνδοῖς
ἐστι, δεύτερον δὲ τιμῇ ἐπὶ τούτῳ τὰ τέθριππα,
τρίτον δὲ αἱ κάμηλοι. τὸ δὲ ἐφ᾽ ἑνὸς ἵππου ὀχέ-
3 εσθαι ἄτιμον. αἱ γυναῖκες δὲ αὐτοῖσιν, ὅσαι
κάρτα σώφρονες, ἐπὶ μὲν ἄλλῳ μισθῷ οὐκ ἄν τι
διαμάρτοιεν, ἐλέφαντα δὲ λαβοῦσα γυνὴ μίσγεται
τῷ δόντι· οὐδὲ αἰσχρὸν Ἰνδοὶ ἄγουσι τὸ ἐπὶ
ἐλέφαντι μιγῆναι, ἀλλὰ καὶ σεμνὸν δοκέει τῇσι

and when they have a hand to hand fight—and Indians do not readily fight in this way among themselves—they bring it down with both hands in smiting, so as to make the stroke heavy. Their horsemen 10 have two javelins, like lances, and a small shield, smaller than the infantry. Their horses are not saddled nor do they use bits like the Greek or Celtic, but a band of stitched rawhide is fitted round the 11 muzzle of the horse, with bronze or iron goads, not very sharp, turned inwards. The rich use goads of ivory. Inside their mouths their horses have a piece of iron like a spit, to which the reins are attached. And so when the rein is pulled, the spit controls the 12 horse and, since the goads are attached to it, they prick the horse and compel him to obey the rein.

17. Physically the Indians are lean, tall and much lighter in movement than other men.[1] Most of them ride on camels, horses and asses, the rich on elephants. For the elephant in India is a royal mount; second to 2 it in dignity is a four-horse chariot, and camels come third; to ride on a single horse is low. All their very 3 modest women would not misconduct themselves for any reward, except that they have intercourse with anyone who gives them an elephant; nor do the Indians regard intercourse as a disgrace at the price of an elephant, but they actually think it splendid for

---

[1] N. is the source for § 3 f. (S. xv 1, 43 and 66) and presumably throughout the ch. Contrast Meg. (ib. 41; cf. D. ii 36, 1), who wrote perhaps only of Chandragupta's kingdom.

γυναιξὶν ἀξίην τὸ κάλλος φανῆναι ἐλέφαντος.
4 γαμέουσι δὲ οὔτε τι διδόντες οὔτε λαμβάνοντες,
ἀλλὰ ὅσαι ἤδη ὡραῖαι γάμου, ταύτας οἱ πατέρες
προάγοντες ἐς τὸ ἐμφανὲς καθιστᾶσιν ἐκλέξασθαι
τῷ νικήσαντι πάλην ἢ πὺξ ἢ δρόμον ἢ κατ' ἄλλην
5 τινὰ ἀνδρείαν προκριθέντι. σιτοφάγοι δὲ καὶ
ἀροτῆρες Ἰνδοί εἰσιν, ὅσοι γε μὴ ὄρειοι αὐτῶν·
οὗτοι δὲ τὰ θήρεια κρέα σιτέονται.

6 ταῦτά μοι ἀπόχρη δεδηλῶσθαι ὑπὲρ Ἰνδῶν, ὅσα
γνωριμώτατα Νέαρχός τε καὶ Μεγασθένης, δοκίμω
7 ἄνδρε, ἀνεγραψάτην, ἐπεὶ οὐδὲ ἡ ὑπόθεσίς μοι
τῆσδε τῆς συγγραφῆς τὰ Ἰνδῶν νόμιμα ἀναγράψαι
ἦν, ἀλλ' ὅπως γὰρ παρεκομίσθη Ἀλεξάνδρῳ ἐς
Πέρσας ἐξ Ἰνδῶν ὁ στόλος· ταῦτα δὲ ἐκβολή μοι
ἔστω τοῦ λόγου.

18. Ἀλέξανδρος γάρ, ἐπειδή οἱ παρεσκεύαστο τὸ
ναυτικὸν ἐπὶ τοῦ Ὑδάσπεω τῇσιν ὄχθῃσιν, ἐπιλεγόμενος ὅσοι τε Φοινίκων καὶ ὅσοι Κύπριοι ἢ
Αἰγύπτιοι εἴποντο ἐν τῇ ἄνω στρατηλασίῃ, ἐκ
τούτων ἐπλήρου τὰς νέας, ὑπηρεσίας τε αὐτῇσι καὶ
ἐρέτας ἐπιλεγόμενος ὅσοι τῶν θαλασσίων ἔργων
2 δαήμονες. ἦσαν δὲ καὶ νησιῶται ἄνδρες οὐκ
ὀλίγοι ἐν τῇ στρατιῇ οἷς ταῦτα ἔμελε, καὶ Ἴωνες
3 καὶ Ἑλλησπόντιοι. τριήραρχοι δὲ αὐτῷ ἐπεστά-
θησαν ἐκ Μακεδόνων μὲν Ἡφαιστίων τε Ἀμύντορος
καὶ Λεόννατος ὁ Εὔνου [1] καὶ Λυσίμαχος ὁ Ἀγαθοκλέους καὶ Ἀσκληπιόδωρος ὁ Τιμάνδρου καὶ Ἄρχων

---

[1] See textual note on *Anab.* iii 5, 5. Jacoby proposed ὁ
⟨ . . . καὶ Ἀσκληπιόδωρος ὁ⟩ Εὐ⟨νί⟩κου.

---

[2] Cf. 11, 9 f. A. is deficient on the economy (App. XVII 9).

the women that their beauty should seem to be as
valuable as an elephant. They marry without 4
giving or receiving anything; all girls at the marriageable age are brought out by their fathers and
exposed to the public choice of victors in wrestling,
boxing or running, or anyone distinguished for any
other manly quality. The Indians eat grain and till 5
the ground, except the mountaineers, who eat the
flesh of game.[2]

This must be enough by way of description of the 6
Indians; I have given the most notable things recorded by Nearchus and Megasthenes, men worthy of
credit, but as it was not even my main subject in this 7
work to record Indian customs but the way in which
Alexander's navy reached Persia from India, this
must all be accounted a digression.

18. When the fleet was made ready for Alexander 326
on the banks of the Hydaspes, he picked out all the B.C.
Phoenicians, Cypriotes and Egyptians who had followed the expedition up-country and used them to
man his ships, picking out for their crews and rowers
all who were skilled in seafaring. There were also a 2
good many islanders in the army, practised in these
things, and Ionians and Hellespontines.[1] As tri- 3
erarchs [2] he appointed the following Macedonians:
Hephaestion son of Amyntor, Leonnatus son of
Eunous,[3] Lysimachus son of Agathocles, Asclepio-
dorus son of Timander, Archon son of Clinias,

---

[1] For 18 f. (N.) see vi 1–4 (mainly Pt.) with notes. Crews:
vi 1, 6; App. XXV 1 f.
[2] The title is presumably honorific; no triremes are mentioned in the flotilla or in the Ocean fleet (contrast vii 19, 3).
The men named include many of the most eminent Companions, some of whom marched by land throughout.
[3] So the MS reads, but cf. critical note.

ὁ Κλεινίου καὶ Δημόνικος ὁ ᾿Αθηναίου καὶ ᾿Αρχίας
ὁ ᾿Αναξιδότου καὶ ᾿Οφέλλας Σειληνοῦ καὶ Τιμάν-
4 θης Παντιάδου. οὗτοι μὲν Πελλαῖοι· ἐκ δὲ
᾿Αμφιπόλεως ἦγον οἵδε· [ἐκ Κρήτης] ² Νέαρχος
᾿Ανδροτίμου, ὃς τὰ ἀμφὶ τῷ παράπλῳ ἀνέγραψε, καὶ
Λαομέδων Λαρίχου, καὶ ᾿Ανδροσθένης Καλλιστρά-
5 του· ἐκ δὲ ᾿Ορεστίδος Κρατερός τε ὁ ᾿Αλεξ-
άνδρου καὶ Περδίκκας ὁ ᾿Ορόντεω· ᾿Εορδαῖοι δὲ
Πτολεμαῖός τε ὁ Λάγου καὶ ᾿Αριστόνους ὁ
Πεισαίου. ἐκ Πύδνης δὲ Μήτρων τε ὁ ᾿Επιχάρμου
6 καὶ Νικαρχίδης ὁ Σίμου. ἐπὶ δὲ ῎Ατταλός τε ὁ
᾿Ανδρομένεος Τυμφαῖος καὶ Πευκέστας ᾿Αλεξάν-
δρου Μιεζεὺς καὶ Πείθων Κρατεύα ᾿Αλκομενεὺς καὶ
Λεόννατος ᾿Αντιπάτρου Αἰγαῖος καὶ Πάνταυχος
Νικολάου ᾿Αλωρίτης καὶ Μυλλέας Ζωίλου Βε-
ροιαῖος. οὗτοι μὲν οἱ σύμπαντες Μακεδόνες·
7 ῾Ελλήνων δὲ Μήδιος μὲν ᾿Οξυθέμιδος Λαρισαῖος,
Εὐμένης δὲ ῾Ιερωνύμου ἐκ Καρδίης, Κριτόβουλος
δὲ Πλάτωνος Κῷος, καὶ Θόας Μανδροδώρου ¹ καὶ
8 Μαίανδρος Μανδρογένεος Μάγνητες, ῎Ανδρων δὲ
Καβήλεω Τήιος. Κυπρίων δὲ Νικοκλέης Πασι-
κράτεος Σόλιος καὶ Νιθάφων Πνυταγόρεω Σαλα-
μίνιος. ἦν δὲ δὴ καὶ Πέρσης αὐτῷ τριήραρχος,
9 Βαγώας ὁ Φαρνούχεος. τῆς δὲ αὐτοῦ ᾿Αλεξ-

² See historical note.
¹ Μηνοδώρου codd., Roos, but cf. Anab. vi 23, 2; Berve ii 181
n. 1.

---

⁴ The MS here reads ' from Crete Nearchus ' (cf. § 10), but
this is clearly a gloss; N. classes himself among the Macedonians (cf. § 3 and 6), along with other Companions who were not
of Macedonian blood, Laomedon a Mitylenaean (Berve no. 464)
and Androsthenes a Thasian (ib. 80); they had all (we must
infer) received fiefs in Amphipolis, a Greek city but now part

Demonicus son of Athenaeus, Archias son of Anaxi-
dotus, Ophellas son of Silenus, Timanthes son of
Pantiades, all from Pella. The following com- 4
manders came from Amphipolis [4]: Nearchus son of
Androtimus, who recorded the coastal voyage,
Laomedon son of Larichus, Androsthenes son of
Callistratus; the following from Orestis: Craterus 5
son of Alexander, and Perdiccas son of Orontes.
Ptolemy son of Lagos and Aristonous son of Pisaeus
were Eordaeans; Metron son of Epicharmus and
Nicarchides son of Simus came from Pydna. In 6
addition, Attalus son of Andromenes came from
Tympha, Peucestas son of Alexander from Mieza,
Pithon son of Crateuas from Alcomenae, Leonnatus
son of Antipater from Aegae, Pantauchus son of
Nicolaus from Aloris, Mylleas son of Zoilus from
Beroea. All these were Macdonians. As for Greeks, 7
Medius son of Oxythemis came from Larisa, Eumenes
son of Hieronymus from Cardia, Critobulus son of
Plato from Cos, Thoas son of Mandrodorus and
Maeander son of Mandrogenes from Magnesia,
Andron son of Cabeleus from Teos; Nicocles son of 8
Pasicrates from Soli, and Nithaphon son of Pnyta-
goras [5] from Salamis were Cypriotes. Alexander
also even appointed a Persian, Bagoas son of Phar-
nuches, trierarch. The helmsman of Alexander's own 9

of Macedon; it contributed a squadron to the Companion
cavalry (i 2, 5). Cf. Introd. 25 and n. 43 (vol. I). Greek
feoffees held high posts in Al's army and administration: e.g.
Laomedon's brother, Erigyius (iii 6, 5), now dead. Lysimachus is probably wrongly reported elsewhere to be a
Thessalian (Berve no. 480). Oddly Eumenes (§ 7) had
apparently not been ' naturalized', but like Medius (vii 24 ff.)
he must have ranked as a Companion (v 24, 6 n.). See also vi
28, 4 n. 4.

[5] King of Salamis (ii 22, 2).

ἄνδρου νεὼς κυβερνήτης ἦν Ὀνησίκριτος Ἀστυ-
παλαιεύς, γραμματεὺς δὲ τοῦ στόλου παντὸς
10 Εὐαγόρας Εὐκλέωνος Κορίνθιος. ναύαρχος δὲ
αὐτοῖσιν ἐπεστάθη Νέαρχος Ἀνδροτίμου, τὸ γένος
μὲν Κρὴς ὁ Νέαρχος, ᾤκει δὲ ἐν Ἀμφιπόλει τῇ
11 ἐπὶ Στρυμόνι. ὡς δὲ ταῦτα ἐκεκόσμητο Ἀλεξάνδρῳ, ἔθυε τοῖς θεοῖσιν ὅσοι τε πάτριοι ἢ μαντευτοὶ
αὐτῷ καὶ Ποσειδῶνι καὶ Ἀμφιτρίτῃ καὶ Νηρηίσι
καὶ αὐτῷ τῷ Ὠκεανῷ, καὶ τῷ Ὑδάσπῃ ποταμῷ,
ἀπ᾽ ὅτου ὡρμᾶτο, καὶ τῷ Ἀκεσίνῃ, ἐς ὅντινα
ἐκδιδοῖ ὁ Ὑδάσπης, καὶ τῷ Ἰνδῷ, ἐς ὅντινα ἄμφω
12 ἐκδιδοῦσιν· ἀγῶνές τε αὐτῷ μουσικοὶ καὶ γυμνι-
κοὶ ἐποιεῦντο, καὶ ἱερεῖα τῇ στρατιῇ πάσῃ κατὰ
τέλεα ἐδίδοτο.

19. ὡς δὲ πάντα ἐξήρτυτο αὐτῷ ἐς ἀναγωγήν,
Κράτερον μὲν τὰ ἐπὶ θάτερα τοῦ Ὑδάσπεω ἰέναι
σὺν στρατιῇ [πεζῇ] ἐκέλευσε πεζικῇ τε καὶ ἱπ-
πικῇ· ἐς τὸ ἐπὶ θάτερα ⟨δὲ⟩ Ἡφαιστίων αὐτῷ
παρεπορεύετο σὺν ἄλλῃ στρατιῇ πλείονι ἔτι τῆς
Κρατέρῳ συντεταγμένης. καὶ τοὺς ἐλέφαντας
Ἡφαιστίων αὐτῷ ἦγεν, ὄντας ἐς διακοσίους.
2 αὐτὸς δὲ τούς τε ὑπασπιστὰς καλεομένους ἅμα οἷ
ἦγε καὶ τοὺς τοξότας πάντας καὶ τῶν ἱππέων τοὺς
ἑταίρους καλεομένους, τοὺς πάντας ἐς ὀκτακισ-
3 χιλίους. τοῖσι μὲν δὴ ἀμφὶ Κράτερον καὶ Ἡφαιστίωνα ἐτέτακτο ἵνα προπορευθέντες ὑπομένοιεν τὸν
4 στόλον. Φίλιππον δέ, ὃς αὐτῷ σατράπης τῆς
χώρης ταύτης ἦν, ἐπὶ τοῦ Ἀκεσίνου ποταμοῦ τὰς
ὄχθας πέμπει, ἅμα στρατιῇ πολλῇ καὶ τοῦτον·
5 ἤδη γὰρ καὶ δώδεκα μυριάδες αὐτῷ μάχιμοι εἵπον-
το σὺν οἷς ἀπὸ θαλάσσης τε αὐτὸς ἀνήγαγε καὶ
αὖθις οἱ ἐπὶ συλλογὴν αὐτῷ στρατιᾶς πεμφθέντες

ship was Onesicritus from Astypalaea [6]; and the secretary for the whole fleet was Evagoras son of Eucleon
from Corinth. As admiral he appointed Nearchus, 10
son of Androtimus, a Cretan by lineage, who lived in
Amphipolis on the Strymon. When Alexander had 11
made all these dispositions, he sacrificed to his an-
cestral gods and those designated by oracle,[7] to
Posidon, Amphitrite, the Nereids, to Ocean himself,
to the river Hydaspes, whence he started, to the
Acesines, into which the Hydaspes runs, and to the
Indus, into which both run; and he instituted 12
musical and athletic games, and victims for sacrifice
were given to all the army, regiment by regiment.

19. When everything had been made ready for
him to start the voyage, he ordered Craterus to
march along one side of the Hydaspes with an army
of cavalry and infantry; Hephaestion had already
started along the other, with another army even
bigger than that under Craterus. Hephaestion took
with him the elephants, numbering about two
hundred. Alexander himself took with him the so- 2
called hypaspists, all the archers, and that part of the
cavalry called ' Companions ', in all about eight
thousand. Craterus and Hephaestion with their 3
forces had been instructed where they were to await
the fleet after marching ahead. Philip, whom he 4
had made satrap of this country, was sent to the
banks of the river Acesines, and he too had a considerable force; for by this time a hundred and 5
twenty thousand fighting men were following him,
including those he had himself brought up from
the sea-coast and those whom his officers, sent to re-

[6] App. XVII 4.
[7] Ammon? Cf. vi 3, 2 n.

ἧκον ἔχοντες, παντοῖα ἔθνεα βαρβαρικὰ ἅμα οἷ
6 ἄγοντι καὶ πᾶσαν ἰδέην ὡπλισμένα. αὐτὸς δὲ
ἄρας ταῖς ναυσὶ κατέπλει κατὰ τὸν Ὑδάσπεα ἔστε
ἐπὶ τοῦ Ἀκεσίνου τε καὶ τοῦ Ὑδάσπεω τὰς
7 συμβολάς. νῆες δὲ αἱ σύμπασαι αὐτῷ ὀκτακόσιαι
ἦσαν, αἵ τε μακραὶ καὶ ὅσα στρογγύλα πλοῖα καὶ
ἄλλαι ἱππαγωγοὶ καὶ σιτία ἅμα τῇ στρατιῇ ἄγουσαι.
8 ὅπως μὲν δὴ κατὰ τοὺς ποταμοὺς κατέπλευσεν
αὐτῷ ὁ στόλος, καὶ ὅσα ἐν τῷ παράπλῳ ἔθνεα κατεστρέψατο, καὶ ὅπως διὰ κινδύνου αὐτὸς ἐν Μαλλοῖς ἧκε, καὶ τὸ τρῶμα ὃ ἐτρώθη ἐν Μαλλοῖς, καὶ
Πευκέστας τε καὶ Λεόννατος ὅπως ὑπερήσπισαν
αὐτὸν πεσόντα, πάντα ταῦτα λέλεκταί μοι ἤδη ἐν
9 τῇ ἄλλῃ τῇ Ἀττικῇ ξυγγραφῇ. ὁ δὲ λόγος ὅδε
τοῦ παράπλου μοι ἀφήγησίς ἐστιν, ὃν Νέαρχος
σὺν τῷ στόλῳ παρέπλευσεν ἀπὸ τοῦ Ἰνδοῦ τῶν
ἐκβολέων ὁρμηθεὶς κατὰ τὴν θάλασσαν τὴν μεγάλην
ἔστε ἐπὶ τὸν κόλπον τὸν Περσικόν, ἣν δὴ Ἐρυθρὴν
θάλασσαν μετεξέτεροι καλέουσι.

20. Νεάρχῳ δὲ λέλεκται ὑπὲρ τούτων ὅδε ὁ
λόγος. πόθον μὲν εἶναι Ἀλεξάνδρῳ ἐκπεριπλῶσαι
τὴν θάλασσαν τὴν ἀπὸ Ἰνδῶν ἔστε ἐπὶ τὴν Περσι-
2 κήν, ὀκνέειν δὲ αὐτὸν τοῦ τε πλόου τὸ μῆκος καὶ
μή τινι ἄρα χώρῃ ἐρήμῳ ἐγκύρσαντες ἢ ὅρμων
ἀπόρῳ ἢ οὐ ξυμμέτρως ἐχούσῃ τῶν ὡραίων, οὕτω
δὴ διαφθαρῇ αὐτῷ ὁ στόλος, καὶ οὐ φαύλη κηλὶς
αὕτη τοῖς ἔργοισιν αὐτοῦ τοῖσι μεγάλοισιν ἐπιγενο-
μένη τὴν πᾶσαν εὐτυχίην αὐτῷ ἀφανίσῃ· ἀλλὰ

---

[1] App. XIII 8; XIX 3. Cf. vi 2 (with some divergencies).
In particular N. omits the Agrianians but includes all the Companions in § 2. A's reference to two chilarchies of archers (iv

cruit forces, had brought with them; at the same
time he led all sorts of barbarian tribes, armed in
every fashion.[1] He himself raised anchor and 6
sailed down the Hydaspes to the confluence of the
Acesines and Hydaspes. His whole fleet of ships 7
was eight hundred,[2] including ships of war, merchant-
men and horse transports, besides others carrying
provisions as well as troops. I have already told in 8
my other history in the Attic dialect of his fleet's
voyage down the rivers, of all the tribes he conquered on the way, and of the danger he himself ran
among the Mallians, the wound he received there,
and the way in which Peucestas and Leonnatus protected him with their shields when he had fallen.
My present work, however, is a story of the coastal 9
voyage that Nearchus successfully undertook with
his fleet, starting from the mouths of the Indus by the
great sea to the Persian Gulf, which others indeed
call the Red Sea.

20. Of this Nearchus has given the following
account: Alexander had a longing to sail out into the
sea and round from India to Persia, but was appre- 2
hensive of the length of the voyage and the risk that
they would find a land uninhabited or destitute of
roadsteads or inadequately provided with natural
products, so that his whole fleet might be actually
destroyed; such a sequel to his great achievements
would be a serious stain on them and would obliterate

24, 10) was held by Berve (133) to imply that there were at
least three. With 3000 hypaspists (Introd. 61), this leaves
about 2000 Companions, not incompatible with vi 14, 4.

[2] App. XXV 2. Emendation to ' 1800 ' is unnecessary.

ἐκνικῆσαι γὰρ αὐτῷ τὴν ἐπιθυμίην τοῦ καινόν τι
3 αἰεὶ καὶ ἄτοπον ἐργάζεσθαι. ἀπόρως δὲ ἔχειν
ὅντινα οὐκ ἀδύνατόν τε ἐς τὰ ἐπινοούμενα ἐπιλέξ-
αιτο καὶ ἅμα τῶν ἐν νηὶ ἀνδρῶν, ὡς καὶ [τῶν]
τοιοῦτον στόλον στελλομένων, ἀφελεῖν τὸ δεῖμα
τοῦ δὴ ἠμελημένως αὐτοὺς ἐς προῦπτον κίνδυνον
4 ἐκπέμπεσθαι. λέγει δὴ ὁ Νέαρχος ἑωυτῷ ξυνοῦσ-
θαι τὸν Ἀλέξανδρον ὅντινα προχειρίσηται ἐξηγέεσ-
θαι τοῦ στόλου. ὡς δὲ ἄλλου καὶ ἄλλου ἐς μνήμην ἰόντα τοὺς μὲν ὡς οὐκ ἐθέλοντας κινδυνεύειν
ὑπὲρ οὗ ἀπολέγειν, τοὺς δὲ ὡς μαλακοὺς τὸν
θυμόν, τοὺς δὲ ὡς πόθῳ τῆς οἰκηίης κατεχομένους,
5 τοῖς δὲ ἄλλο καὶ ἄλλο ἐπικαλέοντα, τότε δὴ αὐτὸν
ὑποστάντα εἰπεῖν ὅτι "ὦ βασιλεῦ, ἐγώ τοι ὑποδέκ-
ομαι ἐξηγήσεσθαι τοῦ στόλου, καὶ εἰ τὰ ἀπὸ τοῦ
θείου ξυνεπιλαμβάνοι, περιάξω τοι σῶας τὰς νέας
καὶ τοὺς ἀνθρώπους ἔστε ἐπὶ τὴν Περσίδα γῆν, εἰ
δὴ πλωτός τέ ἐστιν ὁ ταύτῃ πόντος καὶ τὸ ἔργον
6 οὐκ ἄπορον γνώμῃ ἀνθρωπηίῃ." Ἀλέξανδρον δὲ
λόγῳ μὲν οὐ φάναι ἐθέλειν ἐς τοσήνδε ταλαιπωρίην
καὶ τοσόνδε κίνδυνον τῶν τινα ἑαυτοῦ φίλων
ἐμβάλλειν, αὐτὸν δὲ ταύτῃ δὴ καὶ μᾶλλον οὐκ ἀν-
7 ιέναι ἀλλὰ λιπαρεῖν. οὕτω δὴ ἀγαπῆσαί τε Ἀλέξανδρον τοῦ Νεάρχου τὴν προθυμίην, καὶ ἐπιστῆσαι
8 αὐτὸν ἄρχειν τοῦ στόλου παντός. καὶ τότε δὴ ἔτι
μᾶλλον τῆς στρατιῆς ὅ τι περ ἐπὶ τῷ παράπλῳ
τῷδε ἐτάσσετο καὶ τὰς ὑπηρεσίας ἵλεω ἔχειν

---

[1] App. V 3. This passage shows best of all that whatever
Herodotean echoes the allusions to *pothos* may have (Bosworth
on i 3, 5), they remain significant for Al's personality as seen by
those who knew him. Cf. also App. XXV 1 f.

[2] N's story is dishonest, if the work of Scylax was known,

his good fortune. Yet his perpetual desire to do
something new and extraordinary won the day.[1]
But he was in a quandary whom to choose capable of 3
carrying out his plans and removing the fear of the
men on board ship, despatched on an expedition of
this kind, that they were being sent off without due
thought into manifest danger. Nearchus says that 4
Alexander discussed with him whom he should select
as admiral of the fleet; but as he thought of one after
another, Alexander rejected them on the ground
that they were not willing to risk themselves for his
sake, or as chickenhearted, or as mastered by a
yearning for home, and accused each of them of different faults.[2] Then Nearchus spoke and made his 5
offer: ' I undertake, Sire, to lead your fleet myself,
and, if heaven grants its aid, I will bring ships and
men safe to Persia, if this sea is navigable at all and
the task is not impracticable for human intelligence.'
Alexander replied in word [3] that he would not allow 6
one of his own friends to endure such hardships and
incur such danger, but Nearchus did not give up for
that reason but pressed more urgently, and so Alex- 7
ander, well pleased with his eagerness, appointed him
admiral of the entire fleet. The men in the army and 8
the rowers detailed to sail on this coastal voyage were
then more ready to take a favourable opinion of it, on

but that is unproven and unlikely (App. XXV 1). The objections of Badian (*Yale Cl. St.* 1975, 160 ff.) do not convince
me; Al. had found his officers mostly craven at the Beas, and
would perhaps not have considered sparing some whom he did
trust, such as Hephaestion. Of course we cannot check what
N. tells of a private conversation.

[3] The Greek λόγῳ μέν seems to require an antithesis, e.g.
' but he really wished N. to proceed;' hence a copyist has left
out some of A's words, or (less probably) A. has left out a
phrase in N.

τὴν γνώμην, ὅτι δὴ Νέαρχόν γε οὔποτε ἂν ᾿Αλέξαν-
δρος προήκατο ἐς κίνδυνον καταφανέα, εἰ μή
9 σφι σωθήσεσθαι ἔμελλεν. λαμπρότης τε πολλὴ τῇ
παρασκευῇ ἐποῦσα καὶ κόσμος τῶν νεῶν καὶ
σπουδαὶ τῶν τριηράρχων ἀμφὶ τὰς ὑπηρεσίας τε
καὶ τὰ πληρώματα ἐκπρεπέες καὶ τοὺς πάντ᾿ ἤδη
πάλαι κατοκνέοντας ἐς ῥώμην ἅμα καὶ ἐλπίδας
χρηστοτέρας ὑπὲρ τοῦ παντὸς ἔργου ἐπηρκότα ἦν.
10 πολὺ δὲ δὴ συνεπιλαβέσθαι ἐς εὐθυμίην τῇ στρατιῇ
τὸ δὴ αὐτὸν ᾿Αλέξανδρον ὁρμηθέντα κατὰ τοῦ
᾿Ινδοῦ τὰ στόματα ἀμφότερα ἐκπλῶσαι ἐς τὸν
πόντον σφάγιά τε τῷ Ποσειδῶνι ἐντεμεῖν καὶ ὅσοι
ἄλλοι θεοὶ θαλάσσιοι, καὶ δῶρα μεγαλοπρεπέα
11 τῇ θαλάσσῃ χαρίσασθαι. τῇ τε ἄλλῃ τῇ ᾿Αλεξ-
άνδρου παραλόγῳ εὐτυχίῃ πεποιθότας οὐδὲν ὅ τι οὐ
τολμητόν τε ἐκείνῳ καὶ ἐρκτὸν ἡγέεσθαι.

21. ὡς δὲ τὰ ἐτήσια πνεύματα ἐκοιμήθη, ἃ δὴ
τοῦ θέρεος τὴν ὥρην πᾶσαν κατέχει ἐκ τοῦ
πελάγεος ἐπιπνέοντα ἐπὶ τὴν γῆν καὶ ταύτῃ
ἄπορον τὸν πλοῦν ποιέοντα, τότε δὴ ὡρμῶντο ἐπὶ
ἄρχοντος ᾿Αθήνησι Κηφισοδώρου, εἰκάδι τοῦ
Βοηδρομιῶνος μηνός καθότι ᾿Αθηναῖοι ἄγουσιν,
ὡς δὲ Μακεδόνες τε καὶ ᾿Ασιανοὶ ἦγον ⟨μηνὸς
῾Υπερβερεταίου, ἔτος⟩ τὸ ἑνδέκατον βασιλεύοντος
2 ᾿Αλεξάνδρου. θύει δὲ καὶ Νέαρχος πρὸ τῆς
ἀναγωγῆς Διὶ Σωτῆρι καὶ ἀγῶνα ποιέει καὶ οὗτος

---

[4] Cf. iii 6, 5.
[5] Cf. vi 19, 4 f. Sacrifices and games (which were also
religious celebrations), so often mentioned in the *Anabasis*,
were evidently important for morale. Good fortune was often
viewed as proof of divine favour. Cf. 21, 2.

the ground that Nearchus was the last person Alexander would have exposed to an obvious danger unless they were likely to come through safe.[4]   Then 9 the great splendour incidental to the preparations, the fine equipment of the ships and the conspicuous energy of the trierarchs in providing for the rowers and other personnel had raised the courage of men who were previously full of apprehension and made them more hopeful of the whole enterprise; and 10 really it contributed much to the good spirit of the force that Alexander himself had started down both outlets of the Indus and sailed out into the sea, and had offered victims to Posidon and all the other sea gods, and given splendid gifts to the sea.   Trusting 11 in Alexander's incalculable good fortune in other ventures, they thought that there was nothing that he might not both dare and carry through.[5]

21. When the seasonal winds had sunk to rest, which continue blowing from the Ocean on to the land all the summer season, thus making it impossible to sail, they at last set out, in the archonship at Athens of Cephisodorus, on the twentieth day of the month Boedromion, as the Athenians reckon it; but as the Macedonians and Asians counted it, it was in the month of Hyperberetaeus and the eleventh year of Alexander's reign.[1]   Nearchus too sacrificed, be- 2 fore weighing anchor, to Zeus the Saviour, and he too

---

[1] Sept. 325, cf. App. XVII 24 and, on the archon date, 15, but cf. vii 28, 1 n.   According to S. xv 2, 5 N. said that he started (a) when Al. was completing his Gadrosian march; (b) in autumn, at the western rising of the Pleiads, though the winds were not yet favourable (cf. n. 5; vi 21, 1–3), since the Indians on Al's departure attacked and tried to drive him out. Here (a) is clearly a misunderstanding.   The Indian attack, or a delusive lull in the S.W. monsoon, can explain a premature start.

γυμνικόν. ἄραντες δὲ ἀπὸ τοῦ ναυστάθμου τῇ
πρώτῃ ἡμέρῃ κατὰ τὸν Ἰνδὸν ποταμὸν ὁρμίζονται
πρὸς διώρυχι μεγάλῃ, καὶ μένουσιν αὐτοῦ δύο
ἡμέρας· Στοῦρα δὲ ὄνομα ἦν τῷ χώρῳ· στάδιοι
3 ἀπὸ τοῦ ναυστάθμου ἐς ἑκατόν. τῇ τρίτῃ δὲ
ἄραντες ἔπλεον ἔστε ἐπὶ διώρυχα ἄλλην σταδίους
τριάκοντα, ἁλμυρὴν ἤδη ταύτην τὴν διώρυχα· ἀνῄει
γὰρ ἡ θάλασσα ἐς αὐτήν, μάλιστα μὲν τῇσι πλημ-
μυρίῃσιν, ὑπέμενε δὲ καὶ ἐν τῇ⟨σιν⟩ ἀμπώτεσι τὸ
ὕδωρ μεμιγμένον τῷ ποταμῷ· Καύμανα δὲ
4 οὔνομα ἦν τῷ χώρῳ. ἐνθένδε εἴκοσι σταδίους
καταπλώσαντες ἐς Κορέεστιν ὁρμίζονται ἔτι κατὰ
5 τὸν ποταμόν. ἐνθένδε ὁρμηθέντες ἔπλεον οὐκ ἐπὶ
πολλόν· ἕρμα γὰρ ἐφάνη αὐτοῖσι κατὰ τὴν
ἐκβολὴν τὴν ταύτῃ τοῦ Ἰνδοῦ καὶ τὰ κύματα ἐρρόχ-
θει πρὸς τῇ ἠιόνι, καὶ ἡ ἠιὼν αὕτη τραχεῖα ἦν.
6 ἀλλὰ ἵναπερ μαλθακὸν ἦν τοῦ ἕρματος, ταύτῃ
διώρυχα ποιήσαντες ἐπὶ σταδίους πέντε, διῆγον
τὰς νέας, ἐπειδὴ ἡ πλήμμυρα ἐπῆλθεν ἡ ἐκ τοῦ
7 πόντου. ἐκπεριπλώσαντες δὲ σταδίους πεντήκοντα
καὶ ἑκατὸν ὁρμίζονται ἐς Κρώκαλα νῆσον ἀμμώδεα
καὶ μένουσιν αὐτοῦ τὴν ἄλλην ἡμέραν. προσοικέει
δὲ ταύτῃ ἔθνος Ἰνδικόν, οἱ Ἀράβιες καλεόμενοι,
8 ὧν καὶ ἐν τῇ μέζονι ξυγγραφῇ μνήμην ἔσχον, καὶ
ὅτι εἰσὶν ἐπώνυμοι ποταμοῦ Ἀράβιος, ὃς διὰ τῆς
γῆς αὐτῶν ῥέων ἐκδιδοῖ ἐς θάλασσαν, ὁρίζων τού-
9 των τε τὴν χώρην καὶ τὴν Ὠρειτέων. ἐκ δὲ
Κρωκάλων ἐν δεξιᾷ μὲν ἔχοντες ὄρος τὸ καλεόμενον
αὐτοῖσιν Εἶρον, ἐν ἀριστερᾷ δὲ νῆσον ἀλιτενέα
ἔπλεον· ἡ δὲ νῆσος παρατεταμένη τῇ ἠιόνι κόλπον
10 στεινὸν ποιέει. διεκπλεύσαντες δὲ ταύτην ὁρμί-

held athletic games. Then, moving out from the
ship-station, they anchored on the first day in the
Indus river near a great canal, and remained there
two days; the place was called Stura and was about
100 stades from the shipstation.[2] On the third day 3
they started out and sailed to another canal, 30
stades' distance; this canal was already salt, as the
sea came up into it, especially at full tide, and then
at the ebb the sea water remained there, mixed with
the river. The place was called Caumana. Thence 4
they sailed 25 stades down to Coreëstis, and anchored
still in the river. Thence they started and sailed a 5
little way, for they saw a reef at the outlet of the
river Indus here, and the waves were breaking
violently on the shore, and the shore itself was
rough. But in a softer part of the reef they dug a 6
channel 5 stades long, and brought the ships through
it, when the flood tide came up from the sea. Then 7
sailing round 150 stades, they anchored at a sandy
island called Crocala, and stayed there the next day.
The people living there were an Indian tribe called
Arabies, mentioned in my larger treatise, where I 8
stated that they take their name from the river Arabis
[Hab], which runs through their country and finds
its outlet in the sea, forming a boundary between
their country and that of the Oritans.[3] From 9
Crocala they sailed on, keeping the hill they call Irus
on the right, and a low-lying island on the left; the
island running parallel with the shore makes a narrow
bay. When they had sailed through this, they an- 10

[2] Where this was is disputed. Onesicritus *ap.* Pliny vi 96
is also vague. As N. does not describe the coast of the Indus
delta, he evidently did not sail down the eastern branch, as at
first intended (vi 20, 3–5), perhaps because it ceased to be so
easily navigable as the water-level sank.

[3] See vi 21, 4, where A. writes 'Arabitae' and 'Arabius'.

ζονται ἐν λιμένι εὐόρμῳ. ὅτι δὲ μέγας τε καὶ
καλὸς ὁ λιμήν, Νεάρχῳ ἔδοξεν ἐπονομάζειν αὐτὸν
11 Ἀλεξάνδρου λιμένα. νῆσος δέ ἐστιν ἐπὶ τῷ
στόματι τοῦ λιμένος ὅσον σταδίους δύο ἀπέχουσα·
Βίβακτα ὄνομα τῇ νήσῳ, ὁ δὲ χῶρος ἅπας Σάγ-
γαδα. ἡ δὲ νῆσος καὶ τὸν λιμένα, προκειμένη πρὸ
12 τοῦ πελάγεος, αὐτὴ ἐποίεεν. ἐνταῦθα πνεύματα
μεγάλα ἐκ τοῦ πόντου ἔπνεε καὶ συνεχέα, καὶ
Νέαρχος δείσας τῶν βαρβάρων μή τινες συνταχ-
θέντες ἐφ' ἁρπαγὴν τοῦ στρατοπέδου τραποίατο,
13 ἐκτειχίζει τὸν χῶρον λιθίνῳ τείχει. τέσσαρες δὲ
καὶ εἴκοσιν ἡμέραι τῇ μονῇ ἐγένοντο. καὶ λέγει ὅτι
μύας τε ἐθήρων τοὺς θαλασσίους οἱ στρατιῶται, καὶ
ὄστρεια δὲ καὶ τοὺς σωλῆνας καλεομένους, ἄτοπα
τὸ μέγεθος, ὡς τοῖσιν ἐν τῇδε τῇ ἡμετέρῃ θαλάσσῃ
συμβαλέειν· καὶ ὕδωρ ὅτι ἁλμυρὸν ἐπίνετο.

22. ἅμα τε ὁ ἄνεμος ἐπαύσατο καὶ οἳ ἀνήγοντο.
καὶ περαιωθέντες σταδίους ἐς ἑξήκοντα ὁρμίζονται
πρὸς αἰγιαλῷ ψαμμώδεϊ· νῆσος δὲ ἐπῆν τῷ
2 αἰγιαλῷ ἐρήμη. ταύτην δὲ πρόβλημα ποιησάμενοι
ὡρμίσθησαν· Δόμαι οὔνομα τῇ νήσῳ. ὕδωρ δὲ οὐκ
ἦν ἐν τῷ αἰγιαλῷ, ἀλλὰ προελθόντες ἐς τὴν μεσογαίην ὅσον εἴκοσι σταδίους ἐπιτυγχάνουσιν ὕδατι
3 καλῷ. τῇ δὲ ὑστεραίῃ ἐς νύκτα αὐτοῖς ὁ πλόος
ἐγίνετο ἐς Σάραγγα σταδίους τριακοσίους, καὶ
ὁρμίζονται πρὸς αἰγιαλῷ, καὶ ὕδωρ ἦν ἀπὸ τοῦ
4 αἰγιαλοῦ ὅσον ὀκτὼ σταδίους. ἐνθένδε πλώσαντες
ὁρμίζονται ἐν Σακάλοισι, τόπῳ ἐρήμῳ. καὶ
διεκπλώσαντες σκοπέλους δύο, οὕτω τι ἀλλήλοις
πελάζοντας, ὥστε τοὺς ταρσοὺς τῶν νεῶν ἅπτεσθαι

---

⁴ See 22, 4 n.   ⁵ He had to await the end of the S.W. monsoon (22, 1); the N.E. trade wind seems not to have blown
strongly till later (24, 1).

chored in a harbour with good anchorage; and as the
harbour was fine and large Nearchus decided to call
it Alexander's haven.[4]   An island, about 2 stades 11
away, called Bibacta, lies at the mouth of the harbour;
the whole area is called Sangada.   This island, forming a barrier to the sea, of itself makes a harbour.
There constant strong winds were blowing off the 12
ocean, and Nearchus, fearing that some of the
natives might collect to plunder the camp, fortified
the place with a stone wall.   He stayed there 13
twenty-four days [5]; and through that time, he says,
the soldiers hunted for mussels, oysters, and *solenes*,
as they are called, of unusual size by comparison with
those of our seas, and they also drank briny water.

22. As soon as the wind fell, they weighed anchor,
and after sailing 60 stades moored off a sandy shore;
there was a desert island near the shore.   They used 2
this, therefore, as a breakwater and moored there;
the island was called Domai.   On the shore there
was no water, but after proceeding some 20 stades
inland they found good water.   Next day they 3
sailed till nightfall 300 stades to Saranga, and moored
off the beach, and water was found about 8 stades
from the beach.   Thence they sailed and moored at 4
Sacala, a desert spot, and, making their way between
two rocks so close together that the oar-blades of the
ships touched the rocks to port and starboard, they
moored at Morontobara,[1] after sailing some 300

---

[1] A. omits distance to Sacala; for similar omissions see
21, 9; 26, 4 f.; 27, 2; 29, 2 f.; 32, 2–5; 37, 8. Note resort to
oars. Very short voyages could be due to lack of favouring
winds or currents, need for foraging, ship-repairs, perhaps
reconnoitring in advance or out at sea (cf. 31, 3), matters that
N. may have recorded in his report to Al. and in his book.
H. T. Lambrick, *Sind* 117 ff. argues convincingly that Moron-
tabara is Karachi, and Alexander's harbour near the village
of Gujo, the sea having receded since.

ἔνθεν καὶ ἔνθεν τῶν πετρέων, καθορμίζονται ἐν
Μοροντοβάροις, σταδίους διελθόντες ἐς τριακοσίους·
5 ὁ δὲ λιμὴν μέγας καὶ εὔκυκλος καὶ βαθὺς καὶ
ἄκλυστος, ὁ δὲ ἔσπλους ἐς αὐτὸν στεινός. τοῦτον
τῇ γλώσσῃ τῇ ἐπιχωρίῃ Γυναικῶν λιμένα ἐκάλεον,
6 ὅτι γυνὴ τοῦ χώρου τούτου πρώτη ἐπῆρξεν. ὡς δὲ
διὰ τῶν σκοπέλων διεξέπλεον, κύμασί τε μεγάλοις
ἐνέκυρσαν καὶ τῇ θαλάσσῃ ῥοώδει. ἀλλὰ ἐκπεριπλῶσαι γὰρ ὑπὲρ τοὺς σκοπέλους μέγα ἔργον ἐφαί-
7 νετο. ἐς δὲ τὴν ὑστεραίην ἔπλεον νῆσον ἐν ἀριστερᾷ ἔχοντες πρὸ τοῦ πελάγεος οὕτω τι τῷ
αἰγιαλῷ συναφέα ὥστε εἰκάσαι ἂν διώρυχα εἶναι τὸ
μέσον τοῦ τε αἰγιαλοῦ καὶ τῆς νήσου· στάδιοι οἱ
πάντες ἑβδομήκοντα τοῦ διέκπλου. καὶ ἐπί τε τοῦ
αἰγιαλοῦ δένδρεα ἦν πολλὰ καὶ δασέα, καὶ ἡ
8 νῆσος ὕλῃ παντοίῃ σύσκιος. ὑπὸ δὲ τὴν ἕω ἔπλεον
ἔξω τῆς νήσου κατὰ ῥηχίην στενήν· ἔτι γὰρ ἡ
ἀνάπωτις κατεῖχε. πλώσαντες δὲ ἐς ἑκατὸν καὶ
εἴκοσι σταδίους ὁρμίζονται ἐν τῷ στόματι τοῦ
Ἀράβιος ποταμοῦ· καὶ λιμὴν μέγας καὶ καλὸς
πρὸς τῷ στόματι, ὕδωρ δὲ οὐκ ἦν πότιμον· τοῦ
γὰρ Ἀράβιος αἱ ἐκβολαὶ ἀναμεμιγμέναι τῷ πόντῳ
9 ἦσαν. ἀλλὰ τεσσαράκοντα σταδίους ἐς τὸ ἄνω
προχωρήσαντες λάκκῳ ἐπιτυγχάνουσι, καὶ ἔνθεν
10 ὑδρευσάμενοι ὀπίσω ἀπενόστησαν. νῆσος δὲ ἐπὶ
τῷ λιμένι ὑψηλὴ καὶ ἔρημος, καὶ περὶ ταύτην
ὀστρείων τε καὶ ἰχθύων παντοδαπῶν θήρα.
μέχρι μὲν τοῦδε Ἀράβιες, ἔσχατοι Ἰνδῶν ταύτῃ
ᾠκισμένοι, τὰ δὲ ἀπὸ τοῦδε Ὠρεῖται ἐπεῖχον.

---

[2] Cf. 24, 2 f. and 9; D. 105, 1 f.; Clitarchus F 27. The
Oritans on the coast resembled the Fish-Eaters, cf. vi 23, 3
(Ar.?). N. and Onesicritus (Pliny vi 95) distinguished them

stades. The harbour is spacious, circular, deep and 5   325
calm, but its entrance is narrow. It was called in the   B.C.
local language ' Woman's harbour ', since a woman
was the first sovereign of this district. When they 6
had got safe through the rocks, they met great waves,
and the sea running strong, but it seemed very
hazardous to sail seaward of the rocks. For the next 7
day, however, they sailed with an island on their left
breaking the sea, so close indeed to the beach that
one would have conjectured that the space between
the island and the coast was an artificial channel.
The entire passage was of some 70 stades. On the
beach were many trees, set thick, and the island was
shaded with a forest of every variety. About dawn, 8
they sailed outside the island, by a narrow rough
passage, as the tide was still falling. When they had
sailed some 120 stades they anchored in the mouth of
the river Arabis [Hab]. There was a fine large
harbour by its mouth but no drinking water, as the
outlets of the Arabis were mixed with sea-water.
However, after proceeding 40 stades inland they 9
found a pool, and after drawing water thence returned back again. By the harbour was a lofty 10
desert island, and round it one could catch oysters
and all kinds of fish. Up to this point the country
of the Arabies extended; they are the last Indians
settled here; from here on the territory of the Oritans
begins.[2]

from Indians (cf. 25, 2), *contra* manuscript text of vi 21, 3
(probably Pt., who was indifferent to ethnography; no need
then to emend); linguistic evidence confirms their view. A.
does not make clear how long N. stayed at the mouth of the
Arabis. Pliny vi 96 makes him found a town there, perhaps
misunderstanding Onesicritus' account of the wall at Alexander's harbour (21, 12). But a march inland of 40 stades
and back implies more than a night's stay.

23. ὁρμηθέντες δὲ ἐκ τῶν ἐκβολῶν τοῦ Ἀράβιος παρέπλεον τῶν Ὠρειτέων τὴν χώρην. καὶ ὁρμίζονται ἐν Παγάλοισι, πλώσαντες σταδίους ἐς διακοσίους, πρὸς ῥηχίῃ. ἀλλὰ ἀγκύρῃσι γὰρ ἐπήβολος ἦν ὁ χῶρος. τὰ μὲν οὖν πληρώματα ἀπεσάλευον ἐν τῇσι νηυσίν, οἱ δὲ ἐφ᾽ ὕδωρ ἐκβάντες ὑδρεύοντο.

2 τῇ δ᾽ ὑστεραίῃ ἀναχθέντες ἅμα ἡμέρῃ καὶ πλώσαντες σταδίους ἐς τριάκοντα καὶ τετρακοσίους κατάγονται ἑσπέριοι ἐς Κάβανα, καὶ ὁρμίζονται πρὸς αἰγιαλῷ ἐρήμῳ. καὶ ἐνταῦθα ῥηχίη τραχεῖα ἦν, καὶ ἐπὶ τῷδε μετεώρους τὰς νέας ὡρμίσαντο.

3 κατὰ τοῦτον τὸν πλόον πνεῦμα ὑπολαμβάνει τὰς νέας μέγα ἐκ πόντου, καὶ νέες δύο μακραὶ διαφθείρονται ἐν τῷ πλόῳ, καὶ κέρκουρος· οἱ δὲ ἄνθρωποι σώζονται ἀπονηξάμενοι, ὅτι οὐ πόρρω τῆς γῆς ὁ

4 πλόος ἐγίνετο. ἀμφὶ δὲ μέσας νύκτας ἀναχθέντες πλέουσιν ἔστε ἐπὶ Κώκαλα, ⟨ἃ⟩ τοῦ αἰγιαλοῦ, ἔνθεν ὡρμήθησαν, ἀπεῖχε σταδίους διακοσίους· καὶ αἱ μὲν νῆες σαλεύουσαι ὥρμεον, τὰ πληρώματα δὲ ἐκβιβάσας Νέαρχος πρὸς τῇ γῇ ηὐλίσθη, ὅτι ἐπὶ πολλὸν τεταλαιπωρηκότες ἐν τῇ θαλάσσῃ ἀναπαύσασθαι ἐπόθεον· στρατόπεδον δὲ περι-

5 εβάλετο τῶν βαρβάρων τῆς φυλακῆς ἕνεκα. ἐν τούτῳ τῷ χώρῳ Λεόννατος, ὅτῳ τὰ Ὠρειτῶν ἐξ Ἀλεξάνδρου ἐπετέτραπτο, μάχῃ μεγάλῃ νικᾷ Ὠρείτας τε καὶ ὅσοι Ὠρείταις συνεπέλαβον τοῦ ἔργου. καὶ κτείνει αὐτῶν ἑξακισχιλίους, καὶ τοὺς

325
B.C.

23. Leaving the outlets of the Arabis they coasted along the territory of the Oritans and anchored at Pagala after a voyage of some 200 stades, near a breaking sea, but they were able all the same to cast anchor. The crews rode out the rough water in their vessels, while some disembarked in search of water, and procured it. Next day they set off at dawn and, 2 after making about 430 stades, put in towards evening at Cabana and moored on a desert shore. There too the breakers were rough, so they anchored their vessels well out to sea. It was on this part of the voyage 3 that a heavy squall from seaward caught the fleet, and two warships and one galley were lost on the voyage; the men swam off and got to safety, as they were sailing quite near the land. About midnight [1] they 4 weighed anchor and sailed as far as Cocala, which was 200 stades from the beach off which they had anchored. The ships were tossing at anchor, but Nearchus disembarked the crews and bivouacked on shore, since after all these hardships they longed to rest awhile. The camp was surrounded with defences against barbarian attack. In this place 5 Leonnatus, who had been charged by Alexander with operations against the Oritans, beat them in a great battle, along with others who had joined their enterprise. He killed some six thousand of them, in-

---

[1] Schiwek thinks night voyages too risky without local pilots, but he ignores the possibility of reconnoitring voyages (22, 4 n.). Surely N. had no pilots before Mosarna (27, 1). His knowledge of place names etc. shows only that he had local interpreters.

ἡγεμόνας πάντας· τῶν δὲ σὺν Λεοννάτῳ ἱππεῖς
μὲν ἀποθνήσκουσι πεντεκαίδεκα, τῶν δὲ πεζῶν
ἄλλοι τε οὐ πολλοὶ καὶ Ἀπολλοφάνης ὁ Γαδρωσίων
6 σατράπης. ταῦτα μὲν δὴ ἐν τῇ ἄλλῃ ξυγγραφῇ
ἀναγέγραπται, καὶ ὅπως Λεόννατος ἐπὶ τῷδε
ἐστεφανώθη πρὸς Ἀλεξάνδρου χρυσῷ στεφάνῳ ἐν
7 Μακεδόσιν. ἐνταῦθα σῖτος ἦν νενημένος κατὰ
πρόσταγμα Ἀλεξάνδρου ἐς ἐπισιτισμὸν τῷ στρατῷ,
καὶ ἐμβάλλονται σιτία ἡμερέων δέκα ἐς τὰς νέας.
8 καὶ τῶν νεῶν ὅσαι πεπονήκεσαν κατὰ τὸν πλόον
μέχρι τοῦδε ἐπεσκεύασαν, καὶ τῶν ναυτέων ὅσοι
ἐν τῷ ἔργῳ βλακεύειν ἐφαίνοντο Νεάρχῳ, τούτους
μὲν πεζῇ ἄγειν Λεοννάτῳ ἔδωκεν, αὐτὸς δὲ ἀπὸ
τῶν σὺν Λεοννάτῳ στρατιωτῶν συμπληροῖ τὸ ναυτικόν.

24. ἐνθένδε ὁρμηθέντες ἔπλεον ἀκραεῖ, καὶ διελθόντες σταδίους ἐς πεντακοσίους ὡρμίζοντο πρὸς
ποταμῷ χειμάρρῳ· Τόμηρος ὄνομα ἦν τῷ ποταμῷ.
2 καὶ λίμνη ἦν ἐπὶ ταῖς ἐκβολαῖς τοῦ ποταμοῦ, τὰ δὲ
βράχεα τὰ πρὸς τῷ αἰγιαλῷ ἐπῴκεον ἄνθρωποι ἐν
καλύβαις πνιγηραῖς. καὶ οὗτοι ὡς προσπλέοντας
εἶδον, ἐθάμβησάν τε καὶ παρατείναντες σφᾶς παρὰ
τὸν αἰγιαλὸν ἐτάχθησαν ὡς ἀπομαχούμενοι πρὸς
3 τοὺς ἐκβαίνοντας. λόγχας δὲ ἐφόρεον παχέας,
μέγεθος ὡς ἑξαπήχεας· ἀκωκὴ δὲ οὐκ ἐπῆν
σιδηρέη, ἀλλὰ τὸ ὀξὺ αὐτῇσι πεπυρακτωμένον
4 ταὐτὸ ἐποίεε. πλῆθος δὲ ἦσαν ὡς ἑξακόσιοι. καὶ
τούτους Νέαρχος ὡς ὑπομένοντάς τε καὶ παρατεταγ-
μένους κατεῖδε, τὰς μὲν νέας ἀνακωχεύειν κελεύει
ἐντὸς βέλους, ὡς τὰ τοξεύματα ἐς τὴν γῆν ἀπ'
αὐτῶν ἐξικνεῖσθαι· αἱ γὰρ τῶν βαρβάρων λόγχαι
παχέαι φαινόμεναι ἀγχέμαχοι μέν, ἄφοβοι δὲ ἐς τὸ

cluding all the leaders; fifteen of his cavalry, a few footsoldiers, and Apollophanes satrap of Gadrosia were lost. I have related this in my other treatise, 6 and told how Leonnatus was crowned by Alexander for this exploit with a golden crown in the presence of the Macedonians.[2] Corn had been piled up there 7 by Alexander's orders to victual the expedition, and they took on board ten days' rations. The ships that 8 had suffered in the voyage so far were repaired, and Nearchus handed over to Leonnatus' command for infantry service any of his sailors whom he thought slack at their work, while he himself filled the gaps in his fleet from Leonnatus' soldiers.

24. Thence they set sail, and sailed with a fresh wind, and after a passage of about 500 stades they anchored by a torrential river called Tomerus.[1] There was a lagoon at the outlets of the river, and on 2 the shallows near the shore men were living in stifling cabins. Seeing the ships approaching they were astounded, and lined the shore in battle array to repel the landing. They carried thick spears, about 3 six cubits long, which had no iron tips, but were just as sharp through hardening the point with fire. They numbered about six hundred. Nearchus, observing 4 them standing firm and drawn up in order, instructed the ships to ride at anchor within range, so that their arrows might reach the shore, for the natives' spears, whose thickness was apparent, were good for close fighting but had no terrors in a battle

---

[2] In fact there is only the allusion in vii 5, 5. Cf. also vi 22, 2 f.; 27, 1 n.; D. 105, 8; QC. ix 10, 19. N. is now near the mouth of the Purali (App. XVIII 4). A. surely omits his record of the duration of the stay.

[1] Presumably the Hingol, falsely described as navigable, like other rivers, in Pliny vi 96 ff. (Onesicritus).

5 ἐσακοντίζεσθαι ἦσαν. αὐτὸς δὲ τῶν στρατιωτῶν
ὅσοι αὐτοί τε κουφότατοι καὶ κουφότατα ὡπλισ-
μένοι τοῦ τε νεῖν δαημονέστατοι, τούτους δὲ
6 ἐκνήξασθαι κελεύει ἀπὸ ξυνθήματος. πρόσταγμα
δέ σφισιν ἦν, ὅπως τις ἐκνηξάμενος σταίη ἐν τῷ
ὕδατι, προσμένειν τὸν παραστάτην οἱ ἐσόμενον,
μηδὲ ⟨ἐμ⟩βάλλειν πρόσθεν ἐς τοὺς βαρβάρους,
πρὶν ἐπὶ τριῶν ἐς βάθος ταχθῆναι τὴν φάλαγγα,
7 τότε ⟨δὲ⟩ δρόμῳ ἤδη ἰέναι ἐπαλαλάξαντας. ἅμα
δὲ ἐρρίπτουν ἑωυτοὺς οἱ ἐπὶ τῷδε τεταγμένοι ἐκ
τῶν νεῶν ἐς τὸν πόντον, καὶ ἐνήχοντο ὀξέως, καὶ
ἵσταντο ἐν κόσμῳ, καὶ φάλαγγα ἐκ σφῶν ποιησάμενοι δρόμῳ ἐπῄεσαν αὐτοί τε ἀλαλάζοντες τῷ
Ἐνναλίῳ καὶ οἱ ἐπὶ τῶν νεῶν ξυνεπήχεον, τοξεύ-
ματά τε καὶ ἀπὸ μηχανῶν βέλεα ἐφέροντο ἐς τοὺς
8 βαρβάρους. οἱ δὲ τήν τε λαμπρότητα τῶν ὅπλων
ἐκπλαγέντες καὶ τῆς ἐφόδου τὴν ὀξύτητα καὶ πρὸς
τῶν τοξευμάτων τε καὶ τῶν ἄλλων βελῶν βαλλό-
μενοι, οἷα δὴ ἡμίγυμνοι ἄνθρωποι, οὐδὲ ὀλίγον ἐς
ἀλκὴν τραπέντες ἐγκλίνουσι. καὶ οἱ μὲν αὐτοῦ
φεύγοντες ἀποθνήσκουσιν, οἱ δὲ καὶ ἁλίσκονται·
9 ἔστι δὲ οἳ καὶ διέφυγον ἐς τὰ ὄρεα. ἦσαν δὲ οἱ
ἁλόντες τά τε ἄλλα σώματα δασέες καὶ τὰς
κεφαλάς, καὶ τοὺς ὄνυχας θηριώδεες· τοῖς γὰρ δὴ
ὄνυξιν ὅσα σιδήρῳ διαχρᾶσθαι ἐλέγοντο καὶ τοὺς
ἰχθύας τούτοισι παρασχίζοντες κατεργάζεσθαι καὶ
τῶν ξύλων ὅσα μαλακώτερα. τὰ δὲ ἄλλα τοῖς
λίθοισι τοῖσιν ὀξέσιν ἔκοπτον· σίδηρος γὰρ αὐτοῖσιν οὐκ ἦν. ἐσθῆτα δὲ ἐφόρεον δέρματα θήρεια, οἱ
δὲ καὶ ἰχθύων τῶν μεγάλων [τε] τὰ παχέα.

25. ἐνταῦθα νεωλκοῦσι τὰς νέας, καὶ ὅσαι πεπονη-
κυῖαι αὐτῶν ἐπισκευάζουσι. τῇ δὲ ἕκτῃ ἡμέρῃ

of missiles. Nearchus took all the nimblest and light- 5   325
est-armed troops, who were also the most experi-   B.C.
enced swimmers, and bade them swim off as soon as
the signal was given. Their orders were that as soon 6
as any swimmer found bottom he should wait for
the man who was to stand alongside him and not
attack the barbarians till they had their phalanx
three deep, but that they should then raise their
battle cry and charge at the double. All together, 7
those detailed for this service dived from the ships
into the sea, swam smartly, found their footing in
proper order and, having formed a phalanx, charged
at the double, raising their battle cry to the God of
War, while those on shipboard raised the cry along
with them; and arrows and other missiles from the
engines were hurled at the natives. Panic-stricken 8
by the flash of the armour and the swiftness of the
charge, and attacked by showers of arrows and other
missiles, half naked as they were, they never stopped
to resist but gave way. Some were killed there in
flight, others were captured, but some escaped to the 9
hills. The prisoners had thick hair on their heads as
on the rest of their bodies; their nails were rather
like beasts' claws; they used their nails (according to
report) as if they were iron tools, and prepared fishes
with them for use by tearing them in pieces, as they
also did with the softer kinds of wood; everything
else they cut with sharp stones, for they did not
possess any iron. As clothes they wore skins of
animals and in some cases thick skins of large fishes.

25. Here the crews beached their ships and repaired those which had been damaged.[1] On the sixth

---

[1] The wind in 24, 1 had been a little too fresh!

ἐστέλλοντο, καὶ πλώσαντες σταδίους ἐς τριακοσίους
ἀφικνέονται ἐς χῶρον, ὃς δὴ ἔσχατος ἦν τῆς
2 Ὠρειτῶν γῆς· Μάλανα τῷ χώρῳ ὄνομα. Ὠρεῖται
δὲ ὅσοι ἄνω ἀπὸ θαλάσσης οἰκέουσιν, ἐσταλμένοι
μὲν κατάπερ Ἰνδοί εἰσι, καὶ τὰ ἐς πόλεμον ὡσαύτως
παραρτέονται· γλῶσσα δὲ ἄλλη αὐτοῖσι καὶ ἄλλα
3 νόμαια. μῆκος τοῦ παράπλου παρὰ μὲν χώρην
τὴν Ἀραβίων ἐς χιλίους μάλιστα σταδίους, ἔνθενπερ ὡρμήθησαν, παρὰ δὲ τὴν Ὠρειτῶν γῆν
4 ἑξακόσιοι καὶ χίλιοι. παραπλεόντων δὲ τὴν Ἰνδῶν
γῆν (τὸ ἐντεῦθεν γὰρ οὐκέτι Ἰνδοί εἰσι) λέγει
Νέαρχος ὅτι αἱ σκιαὶ αὐτοῖσιν οὐ ταὐτὸ ἐποίεον·
5 ἀλλὰ ὅπου μὲν ἐπὶ πολὺ τοῦ πόντου ὡς πρὸς
μεσημβρίαν προχωρήσειαν, αἱ δὲ καὶ αὐταὶ [αἱ
σκιαὶ] πρὸς μεσημβρίην τετραμμέναι ἐφαίνοντο·
ὁπότε δὲ τὸ μέσον τῆς ἡμέρης ἐπέχοι ὁ ἥλιος, ἤδη
6 δὲ καὶ ἔρημα σκιῆς πάντα ὤφθη αὐτοῖς. τῶν τε
ἀστέρων ὅσους πρόσθεν μετεώρους κατεώρων, οἱ
μὲν ἀφανέες πάντη ἦσαν, οἱ δὲ πρὸς αὐτῇ τῇ
γῇ ἐφαίνοντο, καταδύνοντές τε καὶ αὐτίκα ἀνατέλ-
7 λοντες οἱ πάλαι ἀειφανέες. καὶ ταῦτα οὐκ ἀπεικότα
δοκέει μοι ἀναγράψαι Νέαρχος· ἐπεὶ καὶ ἐν Συήνῃ
τῇ Αἰγυπτίῃ, ἐπὰν τροπὰς ἄγῃ θέρεος ὥρῃ ὁ ἥλιος,
φρέαρ ἀποδεδειγμένον ἐστί, καὶ τοῦτο ἄσκιον ἐν
μεσημβρίῃ φαίνεται· ἐν Μερόῃ δὲ πάντα ἄσκια
8 τῇ αὐτῇ ὥρῃ. εἰκὸς ὦν καὶ ἐν Ἰνδοῖσιν, ἅτε πρὸς
μεσαμβρίην ᾠκισμένοισι, τὰ αὐτὰ δὴ πάθεα ἐπέχειν,
καὶ μάλιστα δὴ κατὰ τὸν πόντον τὸν Ἰνδικόν, ὅσῳ
μᾶλλον αὐτοῖσιν ἡ θάλασσα πρὸς μεσαμβρίην
κέκλιται. ταῦτα μὲν δὴ ὧδε ἐχέτω.

26. ἐπὶ δὲ Ὠρείτῃσι κατὰ μὲν μεσογαίην
Γαδρώσιοι ἐπεῖχον, ὧν τὴν χώρην χαλεπῶς διεξ-

day from this they set sail and, after voyaging about
300 stades, they came to a place that was the last
point in the territory of the Oritans, called Malana.[2]
The Oritans who live inland, away from the sea, are 2
dressed like Indians and equipped similarly for warfare, but their language and other customs differ.
The length of the coasting voyage along the ter- 3
ritory of the Arabies was about 1000 stades from the
point of departure, but along the Oritan land 1600.[3]
Nearchus states that when men were sailing along 4
the land of India (from that point the people were no
longer Indians) their shadows were not always cast
in the same way; wherever they were sailing a long 5
distance by sea on a southerly course, their shadows
were seen to fall southerly too; but whenever the sun
was at midday, then everything appeared to them
shadowless. Further, of the stars they had seen 6
hitherto in the sky, some were completely hidden,
others showed themselves low down towards the
earth; those which had never set before were now
observed both setting and at once rising again.[4] I 7
think Nearchus' record here not implausible, since in
Egyptian Syene, when the sun is at the summer solstice, people show a well where at midday one sees
no shadow; and in Meroë, at the same season, no
shadows are cast. So it seems reasonable that the 8
same natural phenomena occur among the Indians
too, since they are far south, and especially in the
Indian Ocean, since the sea falls still further south.
But here I must leave this subject.

26. Next to the Oritans in the interior dwelt the
Gadrosians, whose country Alexander and his army

[2] Ras Malan.
[3] App. XXV 7.
[4] Ib. 3. A's comment comes from E., cf. S. ii 5, 7.

ἦλθεν ἅμα τῇ στρατιῇ Ἀλέξανδρος, καὶ κακὰ τοσαῦτα ἔπαθεν, ὅσα οὐδὲ τὰ σύμπαντα τῆς συμπάσης
στρατηλασίης. ταῦτά μοι ἐν τῇ μέζονι συγγραφῇ
2 ἀναγέγραπται. κάτω δὲ Γαδρωσίων παρὰ τὴν
θάλασσαν αὐτὴν οἱ Ἰχθυοφάγοι καλεόμενοι οἰκοῦσι·
παρὰ τούτων τὴν γῆν ἔπλεον. τῇ μὲν πρώτῃ
ἡμέρῃ περὶ τὴν δευτέρην φυλακὴν ἀναχθέντες
καταίρουσιν εἰς Βάγισαρα· στάδιοι τοῦ παράπλου
3 ἑξακόσιοι. λιμήν τε ἔνι αὐτόθι εὔορμος, καὶ κώμη
Πάσιρα, ἀπέχουσα ἀπὸ θαλάσσης ἑξήκοντα στα-
4 δίους, καὶ οἱ πρόσοικοι αὐτῆς Πασιρέες. ἐς δὲ τὴν
ὑστεραίαν πρωΐτερον τῆς ὥρης ἀναχθέντες περιπλέ-
ουσιν ἄκρην ἐπὶ πολύ τε ἀνέχουσαν ἐς τὸν πόντον
5 καὶ αὐτὴν ὑψηλὴν καὶ κρημνώδεα. φρέατα δὲ
ὀρύξαντες, ὕδωρ [οὐκ] ὀλίγον καὶ πονηρὸν ἀρυσά-
μενοι ταύτῃ μὲν τῇ ἡμέρᾳ ἐπὶ ἀγκυρέων ὥρμεον,
6 ὅτι ῥηχίη κατὰ τὸν αἰγιαλὸν ἀνεῖχεν· ἐς δὲ τὴν
ὑστεραίην καταίρουσιν ἐς Κόλτα, σταδίους ἐλθόντες
διακοσίους. ἐνθένδε ἔωθεν πλεύσαντες σταδίους
ἑξακοσίους ἐν Καλίμοισιν ὁρμίζονται. κώμη πρὸς
τῷ αἰγιαλῷ, φοίνικες δὲ περὶ αὐτὴν ὀλίγοι πεφύκεσαν, καὶ βάλανοι ἐπ' αὐτοῖσι χλωραὶ ἐπῆσαν. καὶ
νῆσος ὡς ἑκατὸν σταδίους ἀπὸ τοῦ αἰγιαλοῦ
7 ἀπέχουσα, Καρνίνη ὄνομα. ἐνταῦθα ξένια Νεάρχῳ
προσφέρουσιν οἱ κωμῆται πρόβατα καὶ ἰχθύας· καὶ
τῶν προβάτων τὰ κρέα λέγει ὅτι ἦν ἰχθυώδεα, ἴσα
τοῖς τῶν ὀρνίθων τῶν πελαγίων, ὅτι καὶ αὐτὰ
8 ἰχθύων σιτέεται· πόα γὰρ οὐκ ἔνι ἐν τῇ χώρῃ. ἀλλὰ
τῇ ὑστεραίῃ πλεύσαντες ἐς σταδίους διακοσίους
ὁρμίζονται πρὸς αἰγιαλῷ καὶ κώμῃ ἀπὸ θαλάσσης
ἐς σταδίους τριάκοντα ἀπεχούσῃ· ἡ μὲν κώμη
Κύσα ἐκαλέετο, Καρβὶς δὲ τῷ αἰγιαλῷ ὄνομα ἦν.

had much difficulty in traversing; they suffered more here than during all the rest of his expedition; all this I have related in my larger treatise. Below the Gadrosians, as you follow the actual coast, dwell the people called the Fish-eaters. The fleet sailed past their country. On the first day they hove anchor about the second watch and put in at Bagisara, a voyage along the coast of 600 stades. There is a safe harbour for anchoring there, and a village called Pasira 60 stades from the sea; the inhabitants of the neighbourhood are called Pasireans. The next day they weighed anchor and very early in the morning sailed round a promontory which jutted far out into the sea and was itself high and precipitous. They dug wells and obtained a little water of poor quality; that day they rode at anchor, because there was heavy surf on the beach. Next day they put in at Colta after a voyage of 200 stades. Thence they departed at dawn, and after sailing 600 stades anchored at Calima. A village is near the shore, a few date-palms grew round it, bearing dates, still green. About 100 stades from the beach is an island called Carnine. There the villagers brought gifts to Nearchus, sheep and fishes; the mutton, he says, had a fishy taste like the flesh of sea-birds, since even the sheep feed on fish as there is no grass in the country. On the next day they sailed 200 stades and moored off a beach and a village about 30 stades from the sea, called Cysa; Carbis was the name of the

2

3

4

5

6

7

8

9 ἐνταῦθα πλοίοις ἐπιτυγχάνουσι σμικροῖσιν, οἷα
ἁλιέων εἶναι πλοῖα οὐκ εὐδαιμόνων· αὐτοὺς δὲ
οὐ καταλαμβάνουσιν, ἀλλ᾽ ἔφυγον γὰρ καθορμιζο-
μένας κατιδόντες τὰς νέας. σῖτός τε αὐτόθι οὐκ
ἐνῆν, καὶ ἐπιλελοίπει τὴν στρατιὴν ὁ πολλός·
ἀλλὰ αἶγας ἐμβαλόμενοι ἐς τὰς νέας, οὕτω δὴ
10 ἀπέπλεον. καὶ περιπλώσαντες ἄκρην ὑψηλὴν ὅσον
πεντήκοντα καὶ ἑκατὸν σταδίους ἀνέχουσαν ἐς τὸν
πόντον, κατάγονται ἐν λιμένι ἀκλύστῳ. καὶ ὕδωρ
αὐτόθι ἦν, καὶ ἁλιέες ᾤκεον· Μόσαρνα ὄνομα ἦν
τῷ λιμένι.

27. ἐνθένδε καὶ ἡγεμὼν τοῦ πλόου λέγει Νέαρχος
ὅτι συνέπλωσεν αὐτοῖσιν, Ὑδράκης ὄνομα, Γαδρώ-
σιος· ὑπέστη δὲ Ὑδράκης καταστήσειν αὐτοὺς
μέχρι Καρμανίης. τὸ δὲ ἀπὸ τοῦδε οὐκέτι χαλεπὰ
ἦν, ἀλλὰ μᾶλλόν τι † ὀνομαζόμενα,[1] ἔστε ἐπὶ
2 τὸν κόλπον τὸν Περσικόν. ἐκ δὲ Μοσάρνων νυκτὸς ἐπάραντες πλώουσι σταδίους ἑπτακοσίους
καὶ πεντήκοντα ἐς Βάλωμον αἰγιαλόν· ἐνθένδε
ἐς Βάρνα κώμην σταδίους τετρακοσίους, ἵνα φοίνικές τε πολλοὶ ἐνῆσαν καὶ κῆπος, καὶ ἐν τῷ κήπῳ
μύρριναι ἐπεφύκεσαν καὶ ἄλλα ἄνθεα, ἀφ᾽ ὅτων
στεφανώματα τοῖσι κωμήτῃσιν ἐπλέκοντο· ἐνταῦθα
πρῶτον δένδρεά τε εἶδον ἥμερα, καὶ ἀνθρώπους οὐ
3 πάντῃ θηριώδεας ἐποικέοντας. ἐνθένδε ἐς διακοσίους σταδίους περιπλώσαντες καταίρουσιν ἐς
Δενδρόβοσα, καὶ αἱ νέες ἐπ᾽ ἀγκυρέων ἐσάλευσαν.
4 ἐνθένδε ἀμφὶ μέσας νύκτας ἄραντες ἐς Κώφαντα
λιμένα ἀπίκοντο, τετρακοσίους μάλιστα σταδίους

---

[1] See historical note.

[1] Pasni(?).

shore. There they found some small boats, the sort 9
that poor fishermen might use, but they did not find
the fishermen, who fled as soon as they saw the ships
anchoring. There was no corn there, and the expedition had used most of its supply, but they embarked some goats and then started away. Round- 10
ing a high cape jutting some 150 stades into the sea,
they put into a calm harbour; there was water there,
and fishermen inhabitants; the harbour was called
Mosarna.[1]

27. Nearchus tells us that from this point a pilot
sailed with them, a Gadrosian called Hydraces.[1] He
promised to take them as far as Carmania; from there
the difficulties ceased but there were more . . . up
to the Persian Gulf.[2] From Mosarna they started 2
at night and sailed 750 stades to the beach of Balomus.
Thence again 400 stades to Barna, a village, where
there were many date-palms and a garden, with
myrtles and flowers growing in it, of which wreaths
were woven by the natives. There for the first time
they saw cultivated trees, and inhabitants not quite
like animals.[3] Thence they coasted a further 200 3
stades and put in at Dendrobosa where the ships
tossed at anchor. Thence starting out about mid- 4
night they reached a harbour, Cophas, after a voyage

---

[1] He was only the chief pilot, cf. 30, 3; 31, 4; 32, 7(?); S.
xv 2, 12.
[2] Roos thought the text corrupt. Emendations to mean
' with better harbours (anchorages) ' or ' better populated '
give good sense, but are not palaeographically plausible.
Schiwek keeps the manuscript reading, which means literally
' rather more named ' and understands ' whose names were
rather better known'. I doubt (a) if this is tolerable Greek;
(b) if the names were known (as he thinks) from the Persian
archives (App. XXV 3).
[3] Perhaps Gwadar, now the chief place on the coast.

5 διεκπλώσαντες· ἐνταῦθα ἁλιέες τε ᾤκεον, καὶ
πλοῖα αὐτοῖσιν ἦν μικρὰ καὶ πονηρά· καὶ ταῖς
κώπαις οὐ κατὰ σκαλμὸν ἤρεσσον ὡς ὁ Ἑλλήνων
νόμος, ἀλλ' ὥσπερ ἐν ποταμῷ [1] τὸ ὕδωρ ἐπιβάλ-
λοντες ἔνθεν καὶ ἔνθεν, κατάπερ οἱ σκάπτοντες
τὴν γῆν. ὕδωρ δὲ πολύ τε ἦν ἐν τῷ λιμένι καὶ
6 καθαρόν. περὶ δὲ πρώτην φυλακὴν ἄραντες καταίρουσιν ἐς Κύιζα, ἐς ὀκτακοσίους σταδίους διεκπλώσαντες, ἵνα αἰγιαλός τε ἔρημος ἦν καὶ ῥαχίη.
αὐτόθι ὦν ἐπ' ἀγκυρέων ὥρμεον, κατὰ ναῦν τε
7 ἐδειπνοποιέοντο. ἐνθένδε διεκπλώσαντες σταδίους
πεντακοσίους ἀπίκοντο ἔς τινα πόλιν μικρήν,
οἰκεομένην ἐπὶ γηλόφου οὐ πόρρω τοῦ αἰγιαλοῦ.
8 καὶ Νέαρχος ἐπιφρασθεὶς ὅτι σπείρεσθαι τὴν
χώρην εἰκός, λέγει πρὸς Ἀρχίην, ὃς ἦν Ἀναξιδότου
μὲν παῖς, Πελλαῖος, συνέπλει δὲ Νεάρχῳ, τῶν ἐν
αἴνῃ ὦν Μακεδόνων — πρὸς τοῦτον λέγει ὅτι κατα-
9 ληπτέον σφίσιν εἴη τὸ χωρίον· ἑκόντας τε γὰρ
οὐκ ἂν οἴεσθαι δοῦναι τῇ στρατιῇ σιτία, βίῃ τε οὐχ
οἷόν τε εἶναι ἐξαιρέειν, πολιορκίης δὲ καὶ τριβῆς
δεήσειν, σφᾶς δὲ ἐπιλελοιπέναι τὰ σιτία. ὅτι δὲ ἡ
γῆ σιτοφόρος, τῇ καλάμῃ τεκμηριοῦσθαι, ἥντινα οὐ
10 πόρρω τοῦ αἰγιαλοῦ ἀφεώρων βαθέην. ταῦτα ἐπεί
σφισιν ἐδόκεε, τὰς μὲν ἄλλας νέας κελεύει παραρτέ-
εσθαι ὡς ἐς πλόον, καὶ ὁ Ἀρχίης αὐτῷ ἐξήρτυε
τὰ ἐς τὸν πλόον· αὐτὸς δὲ ὑπολειφθεὶς μετὰ μιῆς
νεὼς ἐπὶ θέαν δῆθεν τῆς πόλιος ᾔει.

28. προσάγοντι δὲ αὐτῷ πρὸς τὰ τείχεα φιλίως
ξένια ἔφερον ἐκ τῆς πόλιος θύννους τε ἐν κριβά-
νοισιν ὀπτούς — οὗτοι γὰρ ἔσχατοι τῶν Ἰχθυοφά-

---

[1] I see no reason to suspect the reading, *contra* Roos.

325
B.C.

of about 400 stades; here fishermen dwelt, with 5
wretched small boats; and they did not row with
their oars in a tholepin in the Greek way; but as you
do in a river, propelling the water on this side and
that, like labourers digging the soil. Water in the
harbour was abundant and pure. About the first 6
watch they weighed anchor and, after a passage of
some 800 stades, put in at Cyiza, where there was a
desert beach and a heavy surf. Here then they rode
at anchor and made their supper aboard the ships.
Thence they voyaged 500 stades and reached a small 7
town built near the shore on a hill. Noting that the 8
land was probably cultivated, Nearchus told Archias
of Pella, son of Anaxidotus, a Macedonian of distinction who was sailing with him,[4] that they must
surprise the place, since he did not suppose that the 9
natives would willingly give the army provisions, and
he could not capture it by force; this would require a
siege and delay, while their provisions had failed.
That the land produced corn he gathered from the
straw they saw lying deep near the beach.[5] After 10
they reached this decision, he ordered the rest of the
ships to get ready as if to put to sea, and Archias made
the preparations for him, while Nearchus himself was
left behind with a single ship and went off as if merely
to look at the town.

28. As he approached the walls, the natives
brought him in a friendly way gifts from the city,
tunny-fish baked in earthen pans (for these people

---

[4] Cf. 18, 3; **34**; vii 20, 7.
[5] Probably the coast of Gwatar bay, enriched by the rivers
Dasht and Silup.

γων οἰκέοντες πρῶτοι ἐν αὐτοῖσιν ὤφθησαν οὐκ
ὠμοφαγέοντες — καὶ πέμματα ὀλίγα καὶ βαλάνους
2 τῶν φοινίκων. ὁ δὲ ταῦτα μὲν ἀσμένως δέκεσθαι
ἔφη, ἐθέλειν δὲ θεήσασθαι τὴν πόλιν· οἱ δὲ εἴων
3 παρελθεῖν. ὡς δὲ εἴσω πυλῶν παρῆλθε, δύο μὲν
τῶν τοξοτῶν κατέχειν κελεύει τὴν πυλίδα, αὐτὸς
δὲ μετὰ δύο ἄλλων καὶ τοῦ ἑρμηνέως ἐπὶ τὸ τεῖχος
τὸ ταύτῃ ἀνελθὼν ἐσήμηνε τοῖς ἀμφὶ τὸν Ἀρχίην
ὅπως συνέκειτο. συνέκειτο γὰρ τὸν μὲν σημῆναι,
4 τὸν δὲ συμβαλόντα ποιέειν τὸ τεταγμένον. ἰδόντες
δὲ τὸ σημήιον οἱ Μακεδόνες ἐπώκελλόν τε κατὰ
τάχος τὰς νέας καὶ ἐξεπήδων σπουδῇ ἐς τὴν
θάλασσαν, οἱ δὲ βάρβαροι ἐκπλαγέντες τοῖς γινο-
5 μένοις ἐπὶ τὰ ὅπλα ἔθεον. ὁ δὲ ἑρμηνεὺς ὁ σὺν
Νεάρχῳ ἐκήρυσσε σῖτον διδόναι τῇ στρατιῇ, εἰ
σώαν ἐθέλουσιν ἔχειν τὴν πόλιν· οἱ δὲ ἠρνοῦντο
εἶναι σφίσι, καὶ ἅμα προσέβαλλον τῷ τείχει.
ἀλλὰ ἀνέστελλον αὐτοὺς οἱ τοξόται οἱ ἀμφὶ τὸν
6 Νέαρχον, ἐξ ὑπερδεξίου τοξεύοντες. ὡς δὲ ἔμαθον
ἐχομένην τε ἤδη καὶ ὅσον οὔπω ἀνδραποδισθησο-
μένην σφίσι τὴν πόλιν, τότε δὲ δὴ ἐδέοντο τοῦ
Νεάρχου τὸν μὲν σῖτον ὅσπερ ἦν αὐτοῖσι λαβόντα
7 ἀπάγειν, τὴν πόλιν δὲ μὴ διαφθεῖραι. Νέαρχος δὲ
τὸν μὲν Ἀρχίην κελεύει καταλαβεῖν τὰς πύλας καὶ
τὸ κατ' αὐτὰς τεῖχος, αὐτὸς δὲ συμπέμπει τοὺς
κατοψομένους τὸν σῖτον εἰ ἀδόλως δεικνύουσιν.
8 οἱ δὲ τὸ μὲν ἀπὸ τῶν ἰχθύων τῶν ὀπτῶν ἀληλεσμέ-
νον ἄλευρον πολὺ ἐδείκνυσαν, πυροὺς δὲ καὶ κριθὰς
ὀλίγας· καὶ γὰρ καὶ ἐτύγχανον σίτῳ μὲν τῷ ἀπὸ
τῶν ἰχθύων, τοῖσι δὲ ἄρτοισιν ὅσα ὄψῳ διαχρεό-
9 μενοι. ὡς δὲ τὰ ὄντα ἐπεδείκνυον, οὕτω δὴ ἐκ
τῶν παρόντων ἐπισιτισάμενοι ἀνήγοντο, καὶ ὁρμί-

325
B.C.

were the last of the Fish-eaters and the first they
saw who did not eat fish raw) and a few cakes and
dates from the palms. He said that he accepted these 2
gratefully, but wished to view the town, and they
permitted him to enter. As soon as he had passed 3
inside the gates, he ordered two of the archers to
occupy the postern, while he himself with two others
and the interpreter mounted the wall on the near side
and signalled to Archias and his men as had been
arranged; the arrangement was that Nearchus should
send the signal and Archias should note it and act as
instructed. On seeing the signal the Macedonians 4
beached their ships with all speed and leapt in haste
into the sea, while the natives, astounded at what was
happening, ran to their arms. The interpreter with 5
Nearchus proclaimed that they should give corn to
the army, if they wanted to save their city; the
natives replied that they had none, and at the same
time attacked the wall. But the archers with
Nearchus, shooting from above, easily held them
back and, when the natives saw that their town was 6
already occupied and almost on the way to being enslaved, they then at last begged Nearchus to take
away what corn they had and retire, but not to des-
troy the town. Nearchus ordered Archias to seize 7
the gates and the neighbouring wall, while he himself
sent some soldiers with the natives to see whether
they would reveal their corn without trickery. They 8
showed plenty of meal ground from baked fish, but
only a little corn and barley. In fact their staple
food came from the fish, and they consumed bread
loaves as a delicacy. When they had shown him 9
what they had, the Greeks provisioned themselves
from what was available and put to sea, anchoring by

ζονται πρὸς ἄκρην, ἥντινα οἱ ἐπιχώριοι ἱρὴν Ἡλίου
ἦγον· οὔνομα τῇ ἄκρῃ Βάγεια.

29. ἐνθένδε ἀμφὶ μέσας νύκτας ἄραντες διεκ-
πλώουσι σταδίους ἐς χιλίους ἐς Τάλμενα λιμένα [1]
εὔορμον. ἐνθένδε ἐς Κανασίδα πόλιν ἐρήμην
σταδίους ἐς τετρακοσίους, ἵνα τινὶ φρέατι ὀρυκτῷ
ἐπιτυγχάνουσι, καὶ φοίνικες ἄγριοι ἐπεφύκεσαν.
τούτων τοὺς ἐγκεφάλους κόπτοντες ἐσιτέοντο·
2 σῖτος γὰρ ἐπελελοίπει τὴν στρατιήν. καὶ κακῶς
ἤδη ὑπὸ λιμοῦ ἔχοντες ἔπλεον τήν τε ἡμέρην καὶ
τὴν νύκτα, καὶ ὁρμίζονται πρὸς αἰγιαλῷ ἐρήμῳ.
3 Νέαρχος δὲ καταδείσας μὴ ἄρα ἐς τὴν γῆν ἐκβάντες ἀπολίποιεν τὰς νέας ὑπὸ ἀθυμίης, ἐπὶ τῷδε
4 μετεώρους ἔσχε τὰς νέας ἐπ᾽ ἀγκυρέων. ἐνθένδε
ἀναχθέντες ἐς Κανάτην ὁρμίζονται, σταδίους ὡς
ἑπτακοσίους καὶ πεντήκοντα διεκπλώσαντες. ἔστι
δὲ καὶ αἰγιαλὸς ἐνταῦθα καὶ διώρυχες βραχεῖαι.
5 ἐνθένδε σταδίους ὀκτακοσίους πλώσαντες ἐν Ταοῖσιν
ὁρμίζονται, κῶμαι δὲ μικραὶ καὶ πονηραὶ ἐπῆσαν.
καὶ οἱ μὲν ἄνθρωποι ἐκλείπουσι τὰ οἰκία, αὐτοὶ δὲ
σίτῳ τινὶ ὀλίγῳ ἐπιτυγχάνουσι, καὶ βαλάνοις ἐκ
φοινίκων. καὶ καμήλους ἑπτὰ ὅσαι ἐγκατελήφ-
θησαν κατακόψαντες, ἀπὸ τούτων τὰ κρέα ἐσιτέον-
6 το. ὑπὸ δὲ τὴν ἕω ἀναχθέντες σταδίους τριακοσίους πλώουσι, καὶ καθορμίζονται ἐς Δαγάσειρα·
7 ἔνθα νομάδες τινὲς ἄνθρωποι ᾤκεον. ἐνθένδε
ἄραντες τήν τε νύκτα καὶ τὴν ἡμέρην οὐδέν τι
ἐλινύοντες ἔπλεον, ἀλλὰ διελθόντες γὰρ σταδίους
χιλίους τε καὶ ἑκατὸν ἐξέπλωσαν τὸ ἔθνος τῶν
Ἰχθυοφάγων, πολλὰ κακὰ ταύτῃ παθόντες ἀπορίῃ

[1] Tomaschek proposed ἐς Τεῖσα λιμένα, cf. Ptolem. vi 8,
p. 414, 7 W.

a headland which the inhabitants regarded as sacred to Helios (the Sun), called Bagia.

29. Thence, weighing anchor about midnight,[1] they voyaged another 1000 stades to Talmena,[2] a harbour giving good anchorage, and to Canasis, a deserted town, 400 stades further, where they found a well sunk, and wild date-palms growing near by. They cut out the hearts of these and ate them, for the expedition had run short of food. In fact they were 2 now really distressed by hunger and sailed on for the day and night, and anchored off a desolate shore. Afraid that they would disembark and leave their 3 ships from faint-heartedness, Nearchus purposely kept the ships anchored at sea. They sailed thence 4 and anchored at Canate, after a voyage of 750 stades. Here there is a beach with shallow channels. Thence 5 they sailed 800 stades, anchoring at Taa; there were small wretched villages on the coast. The inhabitants deserted their homes and they found a little corn there, and dates from the palms. They slaughtered the seven camels captured there and ate their flesh. About daybreak they weighed anchor and 6 sailed 300 stades, and anchored at Dagasira; there some wandering tribe dwelt. Starting thence, they 7 sailed without rest all night and day, and after a voyage of 1100 stades they got past the people of Fish-eaters, in whose land they had been much dis-

---

[1] N. must have recorded the name of the town and length of stay; to fit Onesicritus' statement (Pliny vi 97) that the voyage on the Fish-eaters' coast lasted 20 days, N. left on the second night.

[2] Probably read: ' to Tis, a harbour '.

8 τῶν ἀναγκαίων. ὁρμίζονται δὲ οὐ πρὸς τῇ γῇ —
ῥηχίη γὰρ ἦν ἐπὶ πολλὸν ἀνέχουσα —, ἀλλὰ μετέωροι ἐπ' ἀγκυρέων· μῆκος τοῦ παράπλου τῶν
Ἰχθυοφάγων τῆς χώρης ὀλίγῳ πλεῦνες στάδιοι
μύριοι.

9 οὗτοι οἱ Ἰχθυοφάγοι σιτέονται, κατ' ὅ τι περ καὶ
κληΐζονται, ἰχθύας, ὀλίγοι μὲν αὐτῶν ἁλιεύοντες
τοὺς ἰχθύας — ὀλίγοισι γὰρ καὶ πλοῖα ἐπὶ τῷδε
πεποίηται καὶ τέχνη ἐξεύρηται ἐπὶ τῇ θήρῃ τῶν
ἰχθύων —, τὸ πολὺ δὲ ἡ ἀνάπωτις αὐτοῖσι παρέχει.

10 οἱ δὲ δίκτυα ἐπὶ τῷδε πεποίηνται, μέγαθος καὶ ἐς
δύο σταδίους τὰ πολλὰ αὐτῶν. πλέκουσι δὲ αὐτὰ
ἐκ τοῦ φλοιοῦ τῶν φοινίκων, στρέφοντες τὸν

11 φλοιὸν ὥσπερ λίνον. ἐπεὰν δὲ ἡ θάλασσα ὑπονοσ-
τήσῃ καὶ γῆ ὑπολειφθῇ, ἵνα μὲν ξηρὴ ἡ γῆ ὑπολείπεται, ἐρήμη τὸ πολύ ἐστιν ἰχθύων· ἔνθα δὲ βαθέα
ἐστίν, ὑπολείπεταί τι τοῦ ὕδατος καὶ ἐν τῷδε κάρτα
πολλοὶ ἰχθύες, οἱ μὲν πολλοὶ σμικροὶ αὐτῶν, οἱ δὲ καὶ
μέζονες· τούτοις περιβάλλοντες τὰ δίκτυα αἱρέουσι.

12 σιτέονται δὲ ὠμοὺς μέν, ὅπως ἀνειρύουσιν ἐκ τοῦ
ὕδατος, τοὺς ἁπαλωτάτους αὐτῶν· τοὺς δὲ
μέζονάς τε καὶ σκληροτέρους ὑπὸ ἡλίῳ αὐαίνοντες,
εὖτ' ἂν ἀφανανθῶσι, καταλοῦντες ἄλευρα ἀπ'
αὐτῶν ποιέονται καὶ ἄρτους, οἱ δὲ μάζας ἐκ τού-

13 των τῶν ἀλεύρων πέσσουσι. καὶ τὰ βοσκήματα
αὐτοῖσι τοὺς ἰχθύας ξηροὺς σιτέονται· ἡ γὰρ

14 χώρη ἔρημος λειμώνων οὐδὲ ποίην φέρει. θηρεύ-
ουσι δὲ καὶ καράβους πολλαχῇ καὶ ὄστρεια καὶ τὰ
κογχύλια· ἅλες δὲ αὐτόματοι γίνονται ἐν τῇ

15 χώρῃ· ἀπὸ τούτων ἔλαιον ποιέουσιν. οἱ μὲν δὴ

---

[3] App. XXV 7.

tressed by want of necessaries. They did not moor 8 325 B.C.
near shore, as there was a long line of surf, but at
anchor in the open sea. The length of the voyage
along the coast of the Fish-eaters is a little above
10,000 stades.[3]

These Fish-eaters [4] live on fish, hence their name; 9
only a few of them are active fishing, as only a few
have made boats for the purpose and acquire any
skill in the art of catching fish, but for the most part
the receding tide supplies them. They have nets 10
made for this purpose mostly about two stades in
length.[5] They plait them from bark of the date-palm,
twisting the bark like twine. When the sea recedes 11
and exposes the land, the fish are not found as a rule
where the earth is left dry, but where there are hol-
lows some water is left, containing a very large number of fish, mostly small, but some large ones too,
which they catch by throwing nets over them. They 12
eat the tenderest raw, just as they pull them out of
the water; larger and tougher fish are dried in the
sun till they are desiccated, and then pounded and
made into meal and bread; some even make cakes
of this flour. Even their flocks are fed on the dried 13
fish, for the country has no meadows and produces no
grass. In many places they also catch crayfish, 14
oysters and mussels; there are many natural salts in
the country, and from these ingredients they make an
oily sauce. Some of them inhabit desert tracts, 15

---

[4] Cf. 22, 11 n.; 26, 7–9; 27, 2, 5 and 9; 28, 1 and 7 f.; 29,
5; S. xv 2, 2 (with further details from N.) and 13; D. 105,
3–5; QC. ix 10, 8 ff. (who wrongly calls the Fish-eaters
Indians).
[5] Whatever the length of N's stade (App. XXV 7 f.), N.
probably wrote that the nets extended altogether for two
stades.

αὐτῶν ἐρήμους τόπους οἰκέουσιν ἄδενδρόν τε τὴν
χώρην καὶ ἄφορον καρπῶν ἡμέρων, τούτοισιν ἀπὸ
τῶν ἰχθύων ἡ πᾶσα δίαιτα πεποίηται· ὀλίγοι δὲ
αὐτῶν σπείρουσιν ὅσον τῆς χώρης, καὶ τούτῳ
κατάπερ ὄψῳ, χρῶνται πρὸς τοὺς ἰχθύας· ὁ γὰρ
16 σῖτος αὐτοῖσίν εἰσιν οἱ ἰχθύες. οἰκία δὲ πεποίηνται
οἱ μὲν εὐδαιμονέστατοι αὐτῶν ὅσα κήτεα ἐκβάλλει
ἡ θάλασσα τούτων τὰ ὀστᾶ ἐπιλεγόμενοι ⟨καὶ⟩
τούτοισιν ἀντὶ ξύλων χρεόμενοι, καὶ θύρας τὰ
ὀστέα ὅσα πλατέα αὐτῶν ἁλίσκεται ἀπὸ τούτων
ποιέονται· τοῖσι δὲ πολλοῖς καὶ πενεστέροισιν
ἀπὸ τῶν ἀκανθῶν τῶν ἰχθύων τὰ οἰκία ποιέεται.

30. Κήτεα δὲ μεγάλα ἐν τῇ ἔξω θαλάσσῃ βόσ-
κεται, καὶ ἰχθύες πολὺ μέζονες ἢ ἐν τῇδε τῇ εἴσω.
2 καὶ λέγει Νέαρχος, ὁπότε ἀπὸ Κυΐζων παρέπλεον,
ὑπὸ τὴν ἕω ὀφθῆναι ὕδωρ ἄνω ἀναφυσώμενον τῆς
θαλάσσης οἷά περ ἐκ πρηστήρων βίᾳ ἀναφερόμενον,
3 ἐκπλαγέντας δὲ σφᾶς πυνθάνεσθαι τῶν κατηγεομέ-
νων τοῦ πλόου ὅ τι εἴη καὶ ἀπ' ὅτου τὸ πάθημα·
τοὺς δὲ ὑποκρίνασθαι ὅτι κήτεα ταῦτα φερόμενα
κατὰ τὸν πόντον ἀναφυσᾷ ἐς τὸ ἄνω τὸ ὕδωρ. καὶ
τοῖσι ναύτῃσιν ἐκπλαγεῖσιν ἐκ τῶν χειρῶν τὰ
4 ἐρετμὰ ἐκπεσεῖν, αὐτὸς δὲ ἐπιὼν παρακαλεῖν τε
καὶ θαρσύνειν, καὶ κατ' οὕστινας παραπλέων ἐγένετο, ἐς μέτωπόν τε κελεῦσαι καταστῆσαι ὡς ἐπὶ
ναυμαχίῃ τὰς νέας, καὶ ἐπαλαλάζοντας ὁμοῦ τῷ
ῥοθίῳ πυκνήν τε καὶ ξὺν κτύπῳ πολλῷ τὴν εἰρε-
5 σίην ποιέεσθαι. οὕτως ἀναθαρσήσαντας ὁμοῦ δὴ
πλέειν ἀπὸ ξυνθήματος. ὡς δὲ ἐπέλαζον ἤδη τοῖσι
θηρίοισιν, ἐνταῦθα αὐτοὺς μὲν ὅσον αἱ κεφαλαὶ
αὐτοῖσιν ἐχώρεον ἐπαλαλάξαι, τὰς δὲ σάλπιγγας
σημῆναι, καὶ τὸν κτύπον ἀπὸ τῆς εἰρεσίης ὡς ἐπὶ

country without trees and fruits produced by cultivation, and their whole diet consists in fish, but a few sow a little land, using the corn as a relish to the fish, for fish forms their staple. The richest among them 16 have built huts by collecting the bones of any large sea animal [6] the sea casts up, and using them in place of beams, with doors made from any flat bones which they get hold of. But the majority, and the poor, have huts made from the backbones of ordinary fishes.

30. Monstrously large sea animals feed in the outer ocean, much larger than those in our inland sea. Nearchus says that when they were sailing along the 2 coast from Cyiza, about daybreak they saw water being blown upwards from the sea as it might be shot upwards by the force of a waterspout. They were 3 astonished, and asked the pilots what it might be and how it was caused; they replied that it was these great animals spouting up the water as they moved about in the sea. The sailors were so startled that the oars fell from their hands. Nearchus went along 4 the line encouraging and cheering them, and whenever he sailed past them he signalled them to turn the ships in line towards the animals as if to give them battle, to raise their battle cry in time with the plash of oars and to row with rapid strokes and with a great deal of noise. So they all took heart and 5 sailed together according to signal. But when they were actually nearing the beasts, then they shouted with all the power of their throats, the trumpets gave the signal, and the rowers made the utmost splash-

[6] Whales.

ARRIAN

6 μήκιστον κατασχεῖν. οὕτω δὴ ὁρώμενα ἤδη κατὰ
τὰς πρώρας τῶν νεῶν τὰ κήτεα ἐς βυθὸν δῦναι
ἐκπλαγέντα, καὶ οὐ πολλῷ ὕστερον κατὰ τὰς
πρύμνας ἀναδύντα ἀνασχεῖν καὶ τῆς θαλάσσης
7 αὖθις ἀναφυσῆσαι ἐπὶ μέγα. ἔνθεν κρότον τε ἐπὶ
τῇ παραλόγῳ σωτηρίᾳ γενέσθαι τῶν ναυτέων, καὶ
αἶνον ἐς τὸν Νέαρχον τῆς τε τόλμης καὶ τῆς σοφίης.
8 τούτων μετεξέτερα τῶν κητέων ἐποκέλλειν πολλαχοῦ τῆς χώρης, ἐπειδὰν ἀνάπωτις κατάσχῃ, ἐν
τοῖσι βράχεσιν ἐχόμενα, τὰ δὲ καὶ ὑπὸ χειμώνων
σκληρῶν ἐς τὴν χέρσον ἐξωθέεσθαι, καὶ οὕτω δὴ
καὐτὰ σηπόμενα ἀπόλλυσθαί τε καὶ τὰς σάρκας
αὐτοῖσι περιρρεούσας ὑπολείπειν τὰ ὀστέα χρῆσθαι
9 τοῖσιν ἀνθρώποισιν ἐς τὰ οἰκία. εἶναι ὦν τὰ μὲν
ἐν τῇσι πλευρῇσιν αὐτῶν ὀστέα δοκοὺς τοῖσιν
οἰκήμασιν ὅσα μεγάλα, τὰ δὲ μικρότερα στρωτῆρας·
τὰ δὲ ἐν τῇσι σιαγόσι, ταῦτα δὲ εἶναι τὰ θύρετρα,
οἷα δὴ πολλῶν καὶ εἰς εἴκοσι καὶ πέντε ὀργυιὰς
ἀνηκόντων τὸ μέγεθος.

31. εὖτε δὲ παρέπλεον τὴν χώρην τῶν Ἰχθυοφάγων, λόγον ἀκούουσι περὶ νήσου τινός, ἣ κεῖται
μὲν ἀπέχουσα τῆς ταύτῃ ἠπείρου σταδίους ἐς
2 ἑκατόν, ἐρήμη δέ ἐστιν οἰκητόρων. ταύτην ἰρὴν
Ἡλίου ἔλεγον εἶναι οἱ ἐπιχώριοι καὶ Νόσαλα
καλέεσθαι, οὐδέ τινα ἀνθρώπων καταίρειν ἐθέλειν
ἐς αὐτήν· ὅστις δ᾽ ἂν ἀπειρίῃ προσχῇ, γίνεσθαι
3 ἀφανέα. ἀλλὰ λέγει Νέαρχος κέρκουρόν σφι ἕνα
πλήρωμα ἔχοντα Αἰγυπτίων οὐ πόρρω τῆς νήσου
ταύτης γενέσθαι ἀφανέα, καὶ ὑπὲρ τούτου τοὺς
ἡγεμόνας τοῦ πλόου ἰσχυρίζεσθαι ὅτι ἄρα κατάραν-

ings with their oars. So the animals, now visible at 6 ³²⁵
B.C.
the bows of the ships, were scared and dived into the
depths; then not long afterwards they came up to
the surface astern and again spouted water over a
great expanse of sea. The sailors clapped at their 7
unexpected escape from destruction and praised
Nearchus for his courage and cleverness. Some of 8
these large fishes go ashore at many parts of the coast,
and when the ebb comes are caught in the shallows,
while some are cast on the dry land by heavy storms
and as a result putrefy and die; their flesh rots away
and the bones are left, to be used by the natives for
their huts. In fact the bones in their ribs served for 9
the larger beams of their dwellings, the smaller for
rafters and the jawbones for doorposts, since many of
these creatures reached a length of five-and-twenty
fathoms.[1]

31. While they were coasting along the territory of the Fish-eaters, they heard a story of an uninhabited island which lies some 100 stades from
the mainland here.[1] The local people said that it was 2
sacred to Helios and called Nosala, and that no human being put in there of his own will, but that anyone who touched there in ignorance disappeared.
However, Nearchus says that when one of his *kerkouroi* with an Egyptian crew disappeared with all 3
hands not far fom this island, and the pilots explained

---

danger from the whales (xv 2, 12 f.), S. gives ' 23 '; one or the
other figure is corrupt. Cf. 39, 3 n.; other figures in Onesicritus F 28 and 31; D. 106, 6 f.; QC. x 1, 12.

[1] S's version of N. (xv 2, 13) shows that he landed with an
escort. QC. x 1, 13 f., who confuses the island with that in
37, 3, like Pliny, vi 97, purporting to summarize N. and
Onesicritus, does not reveal that N. refuted the legend. For
modern speculations on island and legend see Schiwek 58.

τες ὑπ᾽ ἀγνοίης εἰς τὴν νῆσον γένοιντο ἀφανέες.
4 Νέαρχος δὲ πέμπει κύκλῳ περὶ τὴν νῆσον τρι-
ηκόντορον, κελεύσας μὴ κατασχεῖν μὲν ἐς τὴν
νῆσον, ἐμβοᾶν δὲ τοῖς ἀνθρώποις ὡς μάλιστα ἐν
χρῷ παραπλέοντας, καὶ τὸν κυβερνήτην ὀνομάζον-
5 τας καὶ ὅτου ἄλλου οὐκ ἀφανὲς τὸ οὔνομα. ὡς δὲ
οὐδένα ὑπακούειν, τότε δὲ αὐτὸς λέγει πλεῦσαι
ἐς τὴν νῆσον καὶ κατασχεῖν δὴ προσαναγκάσαι τοὺς
ναύτας οὐκ ἐθέλοντας, καὶ ἐκβῆναι αὐτὸς καὶ
ἐλέγξαι κενὸν μῦθον ἐόντα τὸν περὶ τῆς νήσου
6 λόγον. ἀκοῦσαι δὲ καὶ ἄλλον λόγον ὑπὲρ τῆς
νήσου ταύτης λεγόμενον, οἰκῆσαι τὴν νῆσον ταύτην
μίαν τῶν Νηρηίδων· τὸ δὲ οὔνομα οὐ λέγεσθαι τῆς
Νηρηίδος. ταύτῃ δὲ ὅστις πελάσειε τῇ νήσῳ,
τούτῳ συγγίνεσθαι μέν, ἰχθὺν δὲ αὐτὸν ἐξ ἀνθρώπου
7 ποιέουσαν ἐμβάλλειν ἐς τὸν πόντον. Ἥλιον δὲ
ἀχθεσθέντα τῇ Νηρηίδι κελεύειν μετοικίζεσθαι
αὐτὴν ἐκ τῆς νήσου· τὴν δὲ ὁμολογεῖν μὲν ὅτι
ἐξοικισθήσεται, δεῖσθαι δέ οἱ τὸ πάθημα ⟨παυ-
8 θῆναι⟩. καὶ τὸν Ἥλιον ὑποδέξασθαι, τοὺς δὲ δὴ
ἀνθρώπους οὕστινας [ἂν] ἰχθύας ἐξ ἀνθρώπων
πεποιήκει κατελεήσαντα ἀνθρώπους αὖθις ἐξ
ἰχθύων ποιῆσαι, καὶ ἀπὸ τούτων τῶν Ἰχθυοφάγων
9 τὸ γένος καὶ εἰς Ἀλέξανδρον κατελθεῖν. καὶ
ταῦτα ὅτι ψεύδεα ἐξελέγχει Νέαρχος, οὐκ ἐπαινῶ
αὐτὸν ἔγωγε τῆς σχολῆς τε καὶ σοφίης, οὔτε κάρτα
χαλεπὰ ἐξελεγχθῆναι ἐόντα, ταλαίπωρόν τε ὂν
γιγνώσκων τοὺς παλαιοὺς λόγους ἐπιλεγόμενον
ἐξελέγχειν ὄντας ψευδέας.

32. ὑπὲρ τοὺς Ἰχθυοφάγους Γαδρώσιοι ἐς τὸ
ἄνω οἰκέουσι γῆν πονηρὴν καὶ ψαμμώδεα, ἔνθεν καὶ
τὰ πολλὰ κακὰ ἡ στρατιά τε Ἀλεξάνδρῳ ἔπαθεν

325
B.C.

this by asserting that it was because they had touched
ignorantly on the island that they had disappeared, he 4
sent a triacontor to sail round the island, with orders
that they should not put in, but that the crew should
shout loudly, while coasting round as near as they
dared, and should call on the lost helmsman by name,
or on any of the crew whose name they knew. He 5
tells us that as no one answered he himself sailed up to
the island, and compelled his crew to put in against
their will; he went ashore and exploded this island
fairy-tale. They heard another story current about 6
this island, that one of the Nereids dwelt there, whose
name was not told; she would have intercourse with
anyone who approached the island, but then turn him
into a fish and throw him into the sea. Helios became 7
irritated with the Nereid and ordered her to leave the
island, and she agreed to move, but begged that the
misery she caused be ended; Helios consented and in 8
compassion for the men she had turned into fishes
turned them back again into human beings; they
were the ancestors of the people of Fish-eaters down
to Alexander's day. Nearchus shows that all this is 9
false, but I do not commend him for his learned discussion, as in my judgement the stories are easy
enough to refute and it is tedious to relate the old
tales and then prove them false.

32. Beyond the Fish-eaters the Gadrosians inhabit
the interior, a poor and sandy territory, where Alexander's army and Alexander himself suffered so ser-

καὶ αὐτὸς Ἀλέξανδρος, ὥς μοι ἤδη ἐν τῷ ἄλλῳ
2 λόγῳ ἀπήγηται. ὡς δὲ ἐς τὴν Καρμανίην ἀπὸ
τῶν Ἰχθυοφάγων κατῆρεν ὁ στρατός, ἐνταῦθα ἵνα
πρῶτον τῆς Καρμανίης ὡρμίσαντο, ἐπ᾽ ἀγκυρέων
ἐσάλευσαν, ὅτι ῥηχίη παρετέτατο ἐς τὸ πέλαγος
3 τρηχείη. ἐνθένδε οὐκέτι ὡσαύτως πρὸς ἡλίου
δυομένου ἔπλωον, ἀλλὰ τὸ μεταξὺ δύσιός τε ἡλίου
καὶ τῆς ἄρκτου μᾶλλόν τι αἱ πρῷραι αὐτοῖσιν
4 ἐπεῖχον, καὶ ἡ Καρμανίη ¹ τῶν Ἰχθυοφάγων τῆς
γῆς καὶ τῶν Ὠρειτῶν εὐδενδροτέρη τε καὶ εὐκαρπο-
τέρη ἐστὶ καὶ ποιώδης μᾶλλόν τι καὶ ἔνυδρος.
5 ὁρμίζονται δὲ ἐν Βάδει χώρῳ τῆς Καρμανίης
οἰκουμένῳ, δένδρεά τε πολλὰ ἥμερα πεφυκότα
ἔχοντι πλὴν ἐλαίης, καὶ ἀμπέλους ἀγαθάς, καὶ
6 σιτοφόρῳ. ἐνθένδε ὁρμηθέντες καὶ διεκπλώσαντες
σταδίους ὀκτακοσίους πρὸς αἰγιαλῷ ὁρμίζονται
ἐρήμῳ, καὶ καθορῶσιν ἄκρην μακρὴν ἀνέχουσαν
ἐπὶ πολλὸν ἐς τὸ πέλαγος· ἀπέχειν δὲ ἐφαίνετο ἡ
7 ἄκρη πλόον ὡς ἡμέρης. καὶ οἱ τῶν χώρων ἐκείνων
δαήμονες τῆς Ἀραβίης ἔλεγον τὴν ἀνίσχουσαν ταύτην ἄκρην, καλέεσθαι ⟨δὲ⟩ Μάκετα· ἔνθεν τὰ
κιννάμωμά τε καὶ ἄλλα τοιουτότροπα ἐς Ἀσσυρίους
8 ἀγινέεσθαι. καὶ ἀπὸ τοῦ αἰγιαλοῦ τούτου, ἵναπερ
ὁ στόλος ἐσάλευε, καὶ τῆς ἄκρης, ἥντινα καταντικρὺ ἀφεώρων ἀνέχουσαν ἐς τὸ πέλαγος, ὁ κόλπος
— ἐμοί τε δοκεῖ καὶ Νεάρχῳ ὡσαύτως ἐδόκεεν —
ἐς τὸ εἴσω ἀναχεῖται, ὅπερ εἰκὸς ἡ Ἐρυθρὴ
9 θάλασσα. ταύτην τὴν ἄκρην ὡς κατεῖδον, Ὀνησίκριτος μὲν ἐπέχοντας ἐπ᾽ αὐτὴν πλέειν ἐκέλευεν,

_____

¹ οὕτω μᾶλλον . . . οὕτω ἡ Καρμανίη codd. I follow
Hercher in deleting οὕτω in both cases.

iously, as I have already related in my other book.
But when the fleet, leaving the Fish-eaters, put in at 2
Carmania, at the point where they first touched
Carmania, they rode at anchor, since the surf extended
along the coast out to sea and was rough. From 3
there they sailed no further due west, but steered
with their bows pointing rather between north and
west.[1] Carmania is better wooded than the country 4
of the Fish-eaters and the Oritans and bears more
fruits; it has more grass and is well watered. They 5
moored at an inhabited place called Badis in Carmania with many cultivated trees growing (but not
the olive), and good vines; it also produced corn.
Setting out from there, they voyaged 800 stades and 6
moored off a desert shore, where they sighted a long
cape jutting out far into the ocean; it seemed as if
the headland itself was a day's sail away. Those who 7
had knowledge of the district said that this jutting
promontory belonged to Arabia, and was called
Maceta,[2] and that it was from there that cinnamon
and other such commodities were imported into
Assyria.[3] From this beach, off which the fleet an- 8
chored in the open roadstead, and from the promontory which they sighted opposite them jutting out
into the sea, the bay (in my opinion, and that of
Nearchus) runs back into the interior, and would seem
to be the Red Sea.[4] When they sighted this cape, 9
Onesicritus urged them to make for it in their voyage,

---

[1] They had turned the Ras el Kuh headland; § 1 repeats
26, 1.

[2] Ras Masandam; A. omits N's estimate of the distance to
the Carmanian coast as a day's sailing (S. xv 2, 14, with
description of Carmania from N. or Onesicritus).

[3] I.e. Mesopotamia (*RE* ii 2701; Ar. *ap.* vii 19, 4; 21, 5 for
parallels). See App. XXV 3.

[4] App. XXV 1.

ὡς μὴ κατὰ τὸν κόλπον ἐλαστρέοντας ταλαιπωρέεσ-
10 θαι. Νέαρχος δὲ ὑποκρίνεται νήπιον εἶναι Ὀνησί-
κριτον, εἰ ἀγνοέει ἐπ᾽ ὅτῳ ἐστάλη πρὸς Ἀλεξ-
11 άνδρου ὁ στόλος. οὐ γὰρ ὅτι ἀπορίη ἦν πεζῇ
διασωθῆναι πάντα αὐτῷ τὸν στρατόν, ἐπὶ τῷδε
ἄρα ἐκπέμψαι τὰς νέας, ἀλλὰ ἐθέλοντα αἰγιαλούς
τε τοὺς κατὰ τὸν παράπλουν κατασκέψασθαι καὶ
ὅρμους καὶ νησῖδας, καὶ ὅστις κόλπος ἐσέχοι
ἐκπεριπλῶσαι τοῦτον, καὶ πόλιας ὅσαι ἐπιθαλάσ-
σιαι, καὶ εἴ τις ἔγκαρπος γῆ καὶ εἴ τις ἐρήμη.
12 σφᾶς ὧν οὐ χρῆναι ἀφανίσαι τὸ ἔργον, πρὸς τέρματι
ἤδη ἐόντας τῶν πόνων, ἄλλως τε οὐδὲ ἀπόρως ἔτι
τῶν ἀναγκαίων ἐν τῷ παράπλῳ ἔχοντας. δεδιέναι
τε, ὅτι ἡ ἄκρη ἐς μεσημβρίην ἀνέχει, μὴ ἐρήμῳ τε
τῇ ταύτῃ γῇ καὶ ἀνύδρῳ καὶ φλογώδει ἐγκύρσειαν.
13 ταῦτα ἐνίκα, καί μοι δοκέει περιφανέως σῶσαι τὴν
στρατιὴν τῇδε τῇ βουλῇ Νέαρχος· τὴν γὰρ δὴ
ἄκρην ἐκείνην καὶ τὴν πρὸς αὐτῇ χώρην πᾶσαν
ἐρήμην τε εἶναι λόγος κατέχει καὶ ὕδατος ἀπορίη
ἔχεσθαι.

33. ἀλλὰ ἔπλωον γὰρ ἀπὸ τοῦ αἰγιαλοῦ ἄραντες
τῇ γῇ προσεχέες, καὶ πλώσαντες σταδίους ὡς
ἑπτακοσίους ἐν ἄλλῳ αἰγιαλῷ ὡρμίσαντο· Νεό-
2 πτανα ὄνομα τῷ αἰγιαλῷ. καὶ αὖθις ὑπὸ τὴν ἔω
ἀνήγοντο, καὶ πλεύσαντες σταδίους ἑκατὸν ὁρμίζονται κατὰ ποταμὸν Ἄναμιν· ὁ δὲ χῶρος Ἁρμό-
ζεια ἐκαλέετο. δαψιλέα δὲ ἤδη καὶ πάμφορα ⟨τὰ⟩

---

[5] A's alternative paraphrase in vii 20, 10 shows that here
too he is simply endorsing N's self-justification; 'the prevalent
story' was doubtless based on the reports of voyages in vii 20,
7–9, to which N. appealed. Schiwek 72 f. argues that Onesi-

325
B.C.

to avoid the hardship of rowing right round the bay.
Nearchus replied that he was childish, if he was 10
ignorant of Alexander's purpose in despatching the
expedition; it was certainly not because he was un- 11
equal to bringing all his force safely through on foot
that he had despatched the fleet: he desired to reconnoitre the coasts that lay on the line of the voyage
and the roadsteads and islets, to explore thoroughly
every bay which they found, to learn about all the
cities on the sea-coast, and to discover which land was
fruitful and which desert. They must therefore not 12
nullify the enterprise when they were almost at the
close of their hardships, especially as they no longer
had any problem about necessities on the coasting
voyage. His own fear was that, since the cape ran
southward, they would find the land there desert,
waterless and sun-scorched. This view prevailed; 13
and I think that Nearchus manifestly saved the
expedition by this decision, for it is the prevalent
story that this cape and the country near it are
entirely desert and denuded of water.[5]

33. So on leaving the shore they hugged the land
in their voyage, and after some 700 stades they anchored off another beach, called Neoptana. At dawn 2
they put off again and, after sailing 100 stades,
moored by the river Anamis at a place called Harmozia.[1] Here there was an abundance of products of

critus merely proposed a short cut across the Straits of Hormuz
to the Carmanian coast, not sailing up the Arabian coast to the
Euphrates mouth. This course would still have contravened
Al's instructions and N. would then have by-passed Harmozia.
[1] At the Minab mouth. Badian, *Yale Cl. St.* 1975, 160 ff.
justifiably doubts N's veracity here. It is odd to find Greeks
wandering about (§ 5) and small Macedonian parties safely
traversing (34) an unpacified region (36, 8 f.).

3 ταύτῃ ἦν, πλὴν ἐλαῖαι οὐ πεφύκεσαν. ἐνταῦθα
ἐκβαίνουσί τε ἐκ τῶν νεῶν καὶ ἀπὸ τῶν πολλῶν
πόνων ἄσμενοι ἀνεπαύοντο, μεμνημένοι ὅσα κακὰ
κατὰ τὴν θάλασσαν πεπονθότες ἦσαν καὶ πρὸς τῇ
γῇ τῶν Ἰχθυοφάγων, τήν τε ἐρημίην τῆς χώρης
καὶ τοὺς ἀνθρώπους ὅπως θηριώδεες καὶ τὰς σφῶν
4 ἀπορίας ἐπιλεγόμενοι. καί τινες αὐτῶν ἀπὸ θαλάσσης ἐς τὸ πρόσω ἀνῆλθον, ἀποσκεδασθέντες τῆς
5 στρατιῆς κατὰ ζήτησιν ἄλλος ἄλλου. ἐνταῦθα
ἄνθρωπός σφισιν ὤφθη χλαμύδα τε φορῶν Ἑλληνικὴν καὶ τὰ ἄλλα ὡς Ἕλλην ἐσκευασμένος, καὶ
φωνὴν Ἑλλάδα ἐφώνεε. τοῦτον οἱ πρῶτοι ἰδόντες
δακρῦσαι ἔλεγον· οὕτω τι παράλογόν σφισι φανῆναι ἐκ τῶν τοσῶνδε κακῶν Ἕλληνα μὲν ἄνθρωπον
6 ἰδεῖν, Ἑλλάδος δὲ φωνῆς ἀκοῦσαι. ἐπηρώτων τε
ὁπόθεν ἥκοι καὶ ὅστις ὤν· ὁ δὲ ἀπὸ τοῦ στρατοπέδου τοῦ Ἀλεξάνδρου ἀποσκεδασθῆναι ἔλεγε, καὶ
εἶναι οὐ πόρρω τὸ στρατόπεδον καὶ αὐτὸν Ἀλέξ-
7 ανδρον. τοῦτον τὸν ἄνθρωπον βοῶντές τε καὶ
κροτέοντες ἀνάγουσι παρὰ τὸν Νέαρχον· καὶ
Νεάρχῳ πάντα ἔφρασε, καὶ ὅτι πέντε ἡμερέων
ὁδὸν ἀπέχει τὸ στρατόπεδον καὶ ὁ βασιλεὺς ἀπὸ
8 τῆς θαλάσσης. τόν τε ὕπαρχον τῆς χώρης ταύτης
δείξειν ἔφη Νεάρχῳ, καὶ ἔδειξε· καὶ μετὰ τούτου
Νέαρχος γνώμην ποιέεται, ὅπως ἀναβήσεται πρὸς
9 βασιλέα. τότε μὲν δὴ ἐπὶ τὰς νέας ἀπῆλθον· ὑπὸ
δὲ τὴν ἔω τὰς νέας ἐνεώλκεεν, ἐπισκευῆς τε
εἵνεκα, ὅσαι αὐτῶν κατὰ τὸν πλοῦν πεπονήκεσαν,
καὶ ἅμα ὅτι ἐν τῷ χώρῳ τούτῳ ὑπολείπεσθαί οἱ
10 ἐδόκεε τὸν πολλὸν στρατόν. χάρακά τε ὦν περι-
βάλλεται διπλοῦν περὶ τῷ ναυστάθμῳ, καὶ τεῖχος
γήϊνον καὶ τάφρον βαθείην, ἀπὸ τοῦ ποταμοῦ τῆς

all kinds, except that olives did not grow. They 3 $\substack{325 \\ \text{B.C.}}$
disembarked, and had a welcome rest from their num-
erous hardships, remembering the miseries they had
endured by sea and on the coast of the Fish-eaters
and reflecting on the desolation of the country, the
bestial nature of the men, and their own difficulties.
Some of them went off inland from the sea and dis- 4
persed from the main force with varying quests.
There they met a man in a Greek cloak, dressed in 5
other ways like a Greek, and also speaking Greek.
Those who first sighted him said that they burst into
tears, so contrary to expectation did it seem after all
these miseries to see a Greek, and to hear Greek
spoken. They asked where he came from and who he 6
was; and he said that he had strayed from Alexander's
camp and that the camp, and Alexander himself, were
not very far distant. Shouting and clapping, they 7
brought him to Nearchus, and he told Nearchus
everything, and that the camp and the king himself
were five days' journey distant from the coast. He 8
also promised to show Nearchus the hyparch of this
district, and did so. With his help Nearchus decided
how to go inland to the King. For the moment in- 9
deed they returned to the ships, but at dawn he had
them drawn up on shore, to repair any that had been
damaged on the voyage, and also because it was in
his mind to leave the greater part of the force behind
here. So he had a double stockade built round the 10
ships' station, and an earthen wall with a deep trench,

ὄχθης ἀρξάμενος ἔστε ἐπὶ τὸν αἰγιαλόν, ἵνα αἱ νέες
αὐτῷ ἀνειρυσμέναι ἦσαν.

34. ἐν ᾧ δὲ ὁ Νέαρχος ταῦτα ἐκόσμεε, τῆς χώρης
ὁ ὕπαρχος πεπυσμένος ὅπως ἐν μεγάλῃ φροντίδι
ἔχοι Ἀλέξανδρος τὰ ἀμφὶ τὸν στόλον τοῦτον, μέγα
δή τι ἀγαθὸν ἐξ Ἀλεξάνδρου ἂν ἔγνω πείσεσθαι,
εἰ πρῶτός οἱ ἀπαγγείλειε τοῦ στρατοῦ τὴν
σωτηρίην καὶ τὸν Νέαρχον ὅτι οὐ πολλῷ ὕστερον
2 ἀφίξεται ἐς ὄψιν τὴν βασιλέος. οὕτω δὴ τὴν
βραχυτάτην ἐλάσας ἀπαγγέλλει Ἀλεξάνδρῳ ὅτι
Νέαρχος οὗτος προσάγει ἀπὸ τῶν νεῶν. τότε μὲν
δὴ καίπερ ἀπιστέων τῷ λόγῳ Ἀλέξανδρος ἀλλὰ
3 ἐχάρη γε κατὰ τὸ εἰκὸς τῇ ἀγγελίῃ· ὡς δὲ ἡμέρη τε
ἄλλη ἐξ ἄλλης ἐγίνετο, καὶ ξυντιθέντι αὐτῷ τῆς
ἀγγελίης τὸν χρόνον οὐκέτι πιστὰ τὰ ἐξηγγελμένα
4 ἐφαίνετο, πεμπόμενοί τε ἄλλοι ἐπ᾽ ἄλλοισιν ὡς ἐπὶ
κομιδῇ τοῦ Νεάρχου οἱ μέν τινες ὀλίγον τῆς ὁδοῦ
προελθόντες καὶ οὐδενὶ ἐγκύρσαντες κενοὶ ἐπανήεσαν, οἱ δὲ καὶ πορρωτέρω ἐλθόντες καὶ διαμαρ-
τόντες τῶν ἀμφὶ τὸν Νέαρχον οὐδὲ αὐτοὶ ἐπανήεσαν,
5 ἐνταῦθα δὴ τὸν μὲν ἄνθρωπον ἐκεῖνον, ὡς κενά τε
ἀγγείλαντα καὶ λυπηρότερά οἱ τὰ πρήγματα ποιή-
σαντα τῇ ματαίῃ εὐφροσύνῃ, συλλαβεῖν κελεύει
Ἀλέξανδρος, αὐτὸς δὲ τῇ τε ὄψει καὶ τῇ γνώμῃ
6 δῆλος ἦν μεγάλῳ ἄχει βεβλημένος. ἐν τούτῳ δὲ
τῶν τινες κατὰ ζήτησιν τοῦ Νεάρχου ἐσταλμένων
ἵππους τε ἐπὶ κομιδῇ αὐτῶν καὶ ἀπήνας δὲ ἄγοντες
ἐντυγχάνουσι κατὰ τὴν ὁδὸν αὐτῷ τε Νεάρχῳ καὶ
τῷ Ἀρχίῃ καὶ πέντε ἢ ἐξ ἅμα αὐτοῖσιν· μετὰ
7 τοσούτων γὰρ ἀνήει. καὶ ἐντυχόντες οὔτε αὐτὸν
ἐγνώρισαν οὔτε τὸν Ἀρχίην — οὕτω τοι κάρτα
ἀλλοῖοι ἐφάνησαν, κομόωντές τε καί ῥυπόωντες καὶ

beginning from the bank of the river and going on to
the beach where his ships had been dragged ashore.

34. While Nearchus was making these arrangements, the hyparch of the country, who had been told
that Alexander felt the deepest concern about this
expedition, concluded that he would receive a great
reward from Alexander if he were the first to tell him
of the safety of the expedition, and that Nearchus
would soon appear before the king. So he rode by 2
the shortest route and announced that Nearchus was
coming from the ships. On this Alexander, though
sceptical of the report, was naturally pleased by the
news. But when day succeeded day and Alexander, 3
reckoning the time when he received the news, could
not any longer believe it, when, moreover, relay after 4
relay sent to escort Nearchus either went a little way
and, meeting no one, came back unsuccessful, or went
on further, missed Nearchus' party and did not themselves return at all, Alexander at last ordered the 5
man to be arrested for bringing an idle tale, and
aggravating his distress with false happiness, and
showed by both his looks and decision the great pain
he was suffering. Meanwhile, however, some of 6
those sent to search for Nearchus, with horses and
chariots to convey him, did meet Nearchus himself
on the way with Archias and five or six others; so
small was his party on his journey inland. On this 7
meeting they did not recognize either Nearchus or
Archias; so greatly altered did they appear, with
their hair long, unwashed, covered with brine, wiz-

ARRIAN

μεστοὶ ἅλμης καὶ ῥικνοὶ τὰ σώματα καὶ ὠχροὶ ὑπὸ
8 ἀγρυπνίης τε καὶ τῆς ἄλλης ταλαιπωρίης — ἀλλὰ
ἐρομένοις γὰρ αὐτοῖς ἵναπερ εἴη Ἀλέξανδρος,
ὑποκρινάμενοι τὸν χῶρον οἱ δὲ παρήλαυνον.
9 Ἀρχίης δὲ ἐπιφρασθεὶς λέγει πρὸς Νέαρχον "ὦ
Νέαρχε, τούτους τοὺς ἀνθρώπους δι᾽ ἐρημίας
ἐλαύνειν τὴν αὐτὴν ἡμῖν ὁδὸν οὐκ ἐπ᾽ ἄλλῳ τινὶ
συντίθημι [ἢ] ὅτι μὴ κατὰ ζήτησιν τὴν ἡμετέρην
10 ἀπεσταλμένους. ὅτι δὲ οὐ γιγνώσκουσιν ἡμέας,
οὐκ ἐν θώματι ποιέομαι· οὕτω γάρ τι ἔχομεν κακῶς
ὡς ἄγνωστοι εἶναι. φράσωμεν αὐτοῖσιν οἵτινές
εἰμεν, καὶ αὐτοὺς ἐρώμεθα καθότι ταύτῃ ἐλαύνου-
11 σιν." ἔδοξε τῷ Νεάρχῳ ἐναίσιμα λέγειν· καὶ
ἤροντο ὅποι ἐλαύνουσιν· οἱ δὲ ὑποκρίνονται ὅτι
κατὰ ζήτησιν Νεάρχου τε καὶ τοῦ στρατοῦ τοῦ
12 ναυτικοῦ. ὁ δέ "οὗτος" ἔφη "ἐγώ εἰμι Νέαρχος,
καὶ Ἀρχίας οὗτος. ἀλλ᾽ ἄγετε ἡμέας· ἡμεῖς δὲ τὰ
ὑπὲρ τῆς στρατιῆς Ἀλεξάνδρῳ ἀπηγησόμεθα."

35. ἀναλαβόντες ⟨ὧν⟩ αὐτοὺς ἐπὶ τὰς ἀπήνας
ὀπίσω ἤλαυνον. καί τινες αὐτῶν τούτων ὑποφθά-
σαι ἐθελήσαντες τὴν ἀγγελίην, προδραμόντες
λέγουσιν Ἀλεξάνδρῳ ὅτι "οὗτός τοι Νέαρχος, καὶ
σὺν αὐτῷ Ἀρχίης καὶ πέντε ἄλλοι κομίζονται παρὰ
σέ," ὑπὲρ δὲ τοῦ στρατοῦ παντὸς οὐδὲν εἶχον
2 ὑποκρίνασθαι. τοῦτο ἐκεῖνο συνθεὶς Ἀλέξανδρος,
τοὺς μὲν παραλόγως ἀποσωθῆναι, τὴν στρατιὴν δὲ
πᾶσαν διεφθάρθαι αὐτῷ, οὐ τοσόνδε τοῦ Νεάρχου τε
καὶ τοῦ Ἀρχίου τῇ σωτηρίῃ ἔχαιρεν, ὅσον ἐλύπει
3 αὐτὸν ἀπολομένη ἡ στρατιὴ πᾶσα. οὔπω πάντα
ταῦτα εἴρητο, καὶ ὁ Νέαρχός τε καὶ ὁ Ἀρχίης
προσῆγον. τοὺς δὲ μόγις καὶ χαλεπῶς ἐπέγνω
Ἀλέξανδρος, ὅτι τε κομόωντας καὶ κακῶς ἐσταλ-

ened, pale from sleeplessness and their other hardships; when they asked where Alexander might be, 8
the search party told them the place and were driving
on. Archias, however, had a thought and said to 9
Nearchus: ' I suspect, Nearchus, that these persons
who are traversing the same road as we through
desert country have been sent for the express purpose
of finding us; as for their failure to recognize us, I do 10
not wonder at that; we are in such bad condition
as to be unrecognizable. Let us tell them who we
are, and ask them why they are driving this way.'
Nearchus approved; they did ask where they were 11
driving, and had the reply: ' To look for Nearchus
and his naval force.' Then Nearchus said: ' I am 12
Nearchus and this is Archias. Lead on; we ourselves
will report to Alexander about the expedition.'

35. The soldiers took them up in their cars and drove
back again. Some of them, anxious to be beforehand with the news, ran ahead and told Alexander:
' Here is Nearchus with Archias and five others being
brought before you.' They could not, however,
answer any questions about the fleet as a whole.
Fastening on this, Alexander concluded that these 2
few had been miraculously saved, but that his whole
expedition had been lost, and did not feel so much
pleasure at the safe arrival of Nearchus and Archias
as pain at the loss of all his force. Hardly had the 3
soldiers told him this much, when Nearchus and
Archias approached; Alexander recognized them

μένους καθεώρα, ταύτῃ μᾶλλόν τι βεβαιότερον αὐτῷ
τὸ ἄχος ὑπὲρ τῆς στρατιῆς τῆς ναυτικῆς ἐγίνετο.
4 ὁ δὲ τὴν δεξιὰν τῷ Νεάρχῳ ἐμβαλὼν καὶ ἀπαγαγὼν
μόνον αὐτὸν ἀπὸ τῶν ἑταίρων τε καὶ τῶν ὑπασ-
5 πιστῶν, πολλὸν ἐπὶ χρόνον ἐδάκρυεν· ὀψὲ δὲ
ἀνενεγκὼν "ἀλλὰ ὅτι σύγε ἡμῖν ἐπανήκεις σῶος"
ἔφη "καὶ Ἀρχίης οὗτος, ἔχοι ἂν ἔμοιγε ὡς ἐπὶ
συμφορῇ τῇ ἁπάσῃ μετρίως· αἱ δέ τοι νέες καὶ ἡ
6 στρατιὴ κοίῳ τινὶ τρόπῳ διεφθάρησαν;" ὁ δὲ ὑπολαβὼν "ὦ βασιλεῦ," ἔφη "καὶ αἱ νέες τοι σῷαί εἰσι
καὶ ὁ στρατός· ἡμεῖς δὲ οὗτοι ἄγγελοι τῆς σωτη-
7 ρίας αὐτῶν ἥκομεν." ἔτι μᾶλλον ἐδάκρυεν Ἀλέξανδρος, καθότι ἀνέλπιστός οἱ ἡ σωτηρίη τοῦ
στρατοῦ ἐφαίνετο, καὶ ὅπου ὁρμέουσιν αἱ νέες
ἀνηρώτα. ὁ δὲ "αὗται" ἔφη "ἐν τῷ στόματι τοῦ
Ἀνάμιδος ποταμοῦ ἀνειρυσμέναι ἐπισκευάζονται."
8 Ἀλέξανδρος δὲ τόν τε Δία τὸν Ἑλλήνων καὶ τὸν
Ἄμμωνα τὸν Λιβύων ἐπόμνυσιν, ἦ μὴν μειζόνως
ἐπὶ τῇδε τῇ ἀγγελίῃ χαίρειν ἢ ὅτι τὴν Ἀσίην πᾶσαν
ἐκτημένος ἔρχεται. καὶ γὰρ καὶ τὸ ἄχος οἱ ἐπὶ τῇ
ἀπωλείῃ τῆς στρατιῆς ἀντίρροπον γενέσθαι τῇ
ἄλλῃ πάσῃ εὐτυχίῃ.

36. ὁ δὲ ὕπαρχος τῆς χώρης, ὅντινα συνειλήφει
Ἀλέξανδρος ἐπὶ τῆς ἀγγελίης τῇ ματαιότητι,
παρόντα κατιδὼν τὸν Νέαρχον, πίπτει τε αὐτῷ πρὸς
2 τὰ γόνατα, καὶ "οὗτός τοι" ἔφη "ἐγώ εἰμι, ὃς
ἀπήγγειλα Ἀλεξάνδρῳ ὅτι σῷοι ἥκετε· ὁρᾷς ὅπως
διάκειμαι." οὕτω δὴ δεῖται Ἀλεξάνδρου Νέαρχος
3 ἀφεῖναι τὸν ἄνδρα, καὶ ἀφίεται. Ἀλέξανδρος δὲ
σωτήρια τοῦ στρατοῦ ἔθυε Διὶ Σωτῆρι καὶ Ἡρακλεῖ καὶ Ἀπόλλωνι Ἀλεξικάκῳ καὶ Ποσειδῶνί τε καὶ
ὅσοι ἄλλοι θαλάσσιοι θεοί, καὶ ἀγῶνα ἐποίεε γυμνι-

only with great difficulty and, seeing them as he did
long-haired and ill-clad, his grief for the whole naval
expedition received further confirmation. Giving 4
his right hand to Nearchus and leading him aside
from the Companions and hypaspists, he wept for a
long time, but at last recovered himself and said: 5
' Your safe return and that of Archias may mitigate
my pain at the whole disaster, but how were the ships
and the force destroyed ? ' ' Sire,' he replied, ' your 6
ships and force are both safe; we are come to tell
with our own lips of their safety.' On this Alexander 7
wept still the more, since the safety of the force had
seemed too good to be true, and enquired where the
ships were anchored. Nearchus replied: ' They are
all hauled up at the mouth of the river Anamis, and
are being refitted.' Alexander then swore by Zeus 8
of the Greeks and the Libyan Ammon [1] that he really
rejoiced more at the news than at having come as a
conqueror through all Asia, since the distress he had
felt at the supposed loss of the fleet actually bal-
lanced all his other good fortune.

36. The hyparch of the province, whom Alexander
had arrested for a false report, seeing Nearchus there
on the spot, fell at his knees and said: ' I am the man 2
who reported your safe arrival to Alexander; you see
my plight.' So at Nearchus' intercession he was
released. Alexander then engaged in sacrificing 3
thank-offerings for the safety of the expedition, to
Zeus the Saviour, Heracles, Apollo the Averter of
Evil, Posidon and all the gods of the sea, and holding

[1] App. V 7.

ARRIAN

κόν τε καὶ μουσικόν, καὶ πομπὴν ἔπεμπε· καὶ Νέαρχος ἐν πρώτοισιν ἐπόμπευε ταινίῃσί τε καὶ ἄνθεσι
4 πρὸς τῆς στρατιῆς βαλλόμενος. ὡς δὲ ταῦτά οἱ
τέλος εἶχε, λέγει πρὸς Νέαρχον "ἐγώ σε, ὦ
Νέαρχε, οὐκέτι θέλω τὸ πρόσω οὔτ' οὖν κινδυνεύειν οὔτε ταλαιπωρέεσθαι, ἀλλὰ ἄλλος γὰρ τοῦ
ναυτικοῦ ἐξηγήσεται τὸ ἀπὸ τοῦδε ἔστε καταστῆσαι
5 αὐτὸ ἐς Σοῦσα." Νέαρχος δὲ ὑπολαβὼν λέγει
"ὦ βασιλεῦ, ἐγὼ μέν τοι πάντα πείθεσθαι ἐθέλω
τε καὶ ἀναγκαίη μοί ἐστιν. ἀλλὰ εἰ δή τι καὶ σὺ
ἐμοὶ χαρίζεσθαι ἐθέλοις, μὴ ποιήσῃς ὧδε, ἀλλά με
ἔασον ἐξηγήσασθαι ἐς ἅπαν τοῦ στρατοῦ, ἔστε σοι
6 σώας καταστήσω ἐς Σοῦσα τὰς νέας, μηδὲ τὰ μὲν
χαλεπὰ αὐτοῦ τε καὶ ἄπορα ἐμοὶ ἐπιτετραμμένα ἐκ
σοῦ ἔστω, τὰ δὲ εὐπετέα τε καὶ κλέους ἤδη ἑτοίμου
ἐχόμενα, ταῦτα δὲ ἀφαιρεθέντα ἄλλῳ ἐς χεῖρας
7 διδόσθω." ἔτι λέγοντα παύει αὐτὸν Ἀλέξανδρος,
καὶ χάριν προσωμολόγει εἰδέναι. οὕτω δὴ καταπέμπει αὐτόν, στρατιὴν δοὺς ἐς παραπομπὴν ὡς διὰ
8 φιλίας ἰόντι ὀλίγην. τῷ δὲ οὐδὲ τὰ τῆς ὁδοῦ τῆς
ἐπὶ θάλασσαν ἔξω πόνου ἐγένετο, ἀλλὰ συλλελεγ-
μένοι γὰρ οἱ κύκλῳ βάρβαροι τὰ ἐρυμνὰ τῆς χώρης
τῆς Καρμανίης κατεῖχον, ὅτι καὶ ὁ σατράπης αὐτοῖσι τετελευτήκει κατὰ πρόσταξιν Ἀλεξάνδρου, ὁ δὲ
νεωστὶ καθεστηκὼς Τληπόλεμος οὔπω βέβαιον τὸ
9 κράτος εἶχε. καὶ δὶς ὢν καὶ τρὶς τῇ αὐτῇ ἡμέρῃ
ἄλλοισι καὶ ἄλλοισι τῶν βαρβάρων ἐπιφαινομένοισιν
ἐς χεῖρας ᾔεσαν, καὶ οὕτως οὐδέν τι ἐλινύσαντες
μόλις καὶ χαλεπῶς ἐπὶ θάλασσαν ἀπεσώθησαν.
ἐνταῦθα θύει Νέαρχος Διὶ Σωτῆρι καὶ ἀγῶνα ποιεῖ
γυμνικόν.

athletic and musical games and a procession; Near- chus was one of the first in the procession, and the troops showered on him ribbons and flowers.[1]   At the 4 end of the procession Alexander said to Nearchus: ' I will not let you in future, Nearchus, run risks or suffer hardships again; some one else shall com- mand the navy from this time till he brings it to Susa.' Nearchus took him up by saying: ' I am ready and 5 indeed bound, Sire, to obey all your orders, but if you were really disposed to show me favour, do not do this, but let me command your fleet right up to the end, till I bring the ships safe to Susa for you.   Let it not 6 be said that you entrusted me with the difficult and desperate work, but that the easy task, with fame sure to follow, was taken away and put into another's hands.'   Alexander checked his speaking further 7 and acknowledged that he deserved gratitude; so he sent him back again, giving him a force as escort, but a small one, as he was going through friendly ter- ritory.

Yet his journey to the sea was not untroubled; 8 the barbarians round about had mustered and were in possession of the strong places of Carmania, since their satrap had been put to death by Alexander's orders, and his successor recently appointed, Tle- polemus, had not yet established his authority.[2]   On 9 one and the same day they came to blows two or even three times with different bodies of barbarians who kept coming up, and thus without resting they only just managed to get safe to the sea-coast.   Then Nearchus sacrificed to Zeus the Saviour and held athletic games.

[1] vi 28, 5 n.
[2] vi 27, 1 n. 3.

37. ὡς δὲ αὐτῷ τὰ θεῖα ἐν κόσμῳ πεποίητο,
οὕτω δὴ ἀνήγοντο. παραπλώσαντες δὲ νῆσον
ἐρήμην τε καὶ τραχείην ἐν ἄλλῃ νήσῳ ὁρμίζονται,
μεγάλῃ ταύτῃ καὶ οἰκουμένῃ, πλώσαντες σταδίους
2 τριηκοσίους ἔνθενπερ ὡρμήθησαν. καὶ ἡ μὲν ἐρήμη
νῆσος Ὀργάνα ἐκαλέετο, ἐς ἣν δὲ ὡρμίσθησαν
Ὀάρακτα, ἄμπελοί τε ἐν αὐτῇ ἐπεφύκεσαν καὶ
φοίνικες, καὶ σιτοφόρος ⟨ἦν⟩· τὸ δὲ μῆκος [ἦν]
τῆς νήσου στάδιοι ὀκτακόσιοι. καὶ ὁ ὕπαρχος τῆς
νήσου Μαζήνης συνέπλει αὐτοῖσι μέχρι Σούσων
3 ἐθελοντὴς ἡγεμὼν τοῦ πλόου. ἐν ταύτῃ τῇ νήσῳ
ἔλεγον καὶ τοῦ πρώτου δυναστεύσαντος τῆς χώρης
ταύτης δείκνυσθαι τὸν τάφον· ὄνομα δὲ αὐτῷ
Ἐρύθρην εἶναι, ἀπ' ὅτου καὶ τὴν ἐπωνυμίην τῇ θαλάσσῃ ταύτῃ εἶναι [Ἐρυθρὴν καλέεσθαι].[1] ἐνθένδε
4 ἐκ τῆς νήσου ἄραντες ἔπλεον· καὶ τῆς νήσου αὐτῆς
παραπλώσαντες ὅσον διακοσίους σταδίους ὁρμίζονται ἐν αὐτῇ αὖθις, καὶ καθορῶσιν ἄλλην νῆσον,
ἀπέχουσαν τῆς μεγάλης ταύτης τεσσαράκοντα
μάλιστα σταδίους. Ποσειδῶνος ἱρὴ ἐλέγετο εἶναι
5 καὶ ἄβατος. ὑπὸ δὲ τὴν ἔω ἀνήγοντο, καὶ καταλαμβάνει αὐτοὺς ἀνάπωτις οὕτω τι καρτερή, ὥστε
τρεῖς τῶν νεῶν ἐποκείλασαι ἐν τῷ ξηρῷ ἐσχέθησαν,
αἱ δὲ ἄλλαι χαλεπῶς διεκπλώουσαι τὰς ῥηχίας ἐς
6 τὰ βάθεα ἀπεσώθησαν. αἱ δὲ ἐποκείλασαι τῆς
πλημμυρίδος ἐπιγενομένης αὖθις ἐξέπλωσάν τε καὶ
7 δευτεραῖαι κατήγοντο ἵναπερ ὁ πᾶς στόλος. ὁρμίζονται δὲ ἐς νῆσον ἄλλην, διέχουσαν τῆς ἠπείρου

---

[1] A gloss (Hercher).

---

[1] Red (erythraios) Sea is in A. our 'Persian Gulf,' though it
could also refer to our 'Arabian Sea' (S. xvi 3, 1); origin of

37. When he had duly performed his religious duties, they weighed anchor. Coasting along a rugged and deserted island, they anchored at another large, inhabited island after sailing 300 stades from their point of departure. The desert island was 2 called Organa, and that where they moored Oaracta. Vines and date-palms grew there, and it produced corn; its length was 800 stades. The hyparch of the island, Mazenes, sailed with them as far as Susa as a volunteer pilot. They said that in this island the 3 tomb of the first ruler of this territory was shown; his name was Erythres, and hence came the name of the sea.[1] Then they weighed anchor and sailed 4 onward, and when they had coasted about 200 stades along the island itself, they anchored there once more and sighted another island, about 40 stades from this large one. It was said to be sacred to Posidon, and not to be trod by foot of man.[2] About dawn they 5 put out to sea, and found themselves in the grip of so violent an ebb-tide that three of the ships ran ashore and were held hard and fast on dry land, and the rest only just sailed through the surf and got safe into deep water. However the ships which ran aground 6 were floated off when the next flood came, and next day overtook the main fleet. They moored at another 7

[1] name: ib. 4, 20; Pliny vi 107. Our 'Red Sea' is A's 'Arabian Gulf' (ch. 43). N. and Orthagoras both told that the grave of Erythres was on Ogyris (*RE* xvii 2080 f. for possible identification with Masira, 2000 stades from Carmania, of which they heard from a banished Persian grandee (S. xvi 3, 5 and 7; cf. QC. x 1, 14). A. is grossly inaccurate in summarizing N.

[2] Hengam. N. equated native gods of traders and seafarers (cf. § 10 f.; Ones. *ap.* Pliny vi 111) with appropriate Greek gods (Schiwek 76). However, Organa [Hormuz] and Cataea [Qeys] were not yet thriving commercial centres, as later (Tomaschek).

ὅσον τριακοσίους σταδίους, πλώσαντες τετρακο-
8 σίους. ἐντεῦθεν ὑπὸ τὴν ἔω ἔπλεον, νῆσον ἐρήμην
ἐν ἀριστερᾷ παραμείβοντες· ὄνομα δὲ τῇ νήσῳ
Πύλωρα. καὶ ὁρμίζον⟨ται⟩ πρὸς † ἰδωδώνῃ, πολ-
ιχνίῳ σμικρῷ καὶ πάντων ἀπόρῳ ὅτι μὴ ὕδατος
καὶ ἰχθύων· ἰχθυοφάγοι γὰρ καὶ οὗτοι ὑπ' ἀναγκ-
9 αίης ἦσαν, ὅτι πονηρὰν γῆν νέμονται. ἐνθένδε
ὑδρευσάμενοι καταίρουσιν ἐς Ταρσίην ἄκρην ἀνατείνουσαν ἐς τὸ πέλαγος, πλώσαντες σταδίους τριακο-
10 σίους. ἔνθεν ἐς Καταίην, νῆσον ἐρήμην, ἁλιτενέα·
αὕτη ἱερὴ Ἑρμέω καὶ Ἀφροδίτης ἐλέγετο· στάδιοι
11 τοῦ πλόου τριηκόσιοι. ἐς ταύτην ὅσα ἔτη ἀφίεται
ἐκ τῶν περιοίκων πρόβατα καὶ αἶγες ἱρὰ τῷ Ἑρμῇ
καὶ τῇ Ἀφροδίτῃ, καὶ ταῦτα ἀπηγριωμένα ἦν
ὁρᾶν ὑπὸ χρόνου τε καὶ ἐρημίης.

38. μέχρι τοῦδε Καρμανίη· τὰ δὲ ἀπὸ τοῦδε
Πέρσαι ἔχουσι. μῆκος τοῦ πλόου παρὰ τὴν
Καρμανίην χώρην στάδιοι τρισχίλιοι καὶ ἑπτακόσιοι. ζώουσι δὲ κατάπερ Πέρσαι, ὅτι καὶ ὅμοροί
εἰσι Πέρσῃσι, καὶ τὰ ἐς τὸν πόλεμον ὡσαύτως
2 κοσμέονται. ἐνθένδε ἄραντες ἐκ τῆς νήσου τῆς
ἱρῆς παρὰ τὴν Περσίδα ἤδη ἔπλεον, καὶ κατάγονται ἐς Ἴλαν χῶρον, ἵνα λιμὴν πρὸς νήσου σμικ-
ρῆς καὶ ἐρήμης γίνεται· οὔνομα τῇ νήσῳ Καΐκαν-
3 δρος, ὁ δὲ πλόος στάδιοι τετρακόσιοι. ὑπὸ δὲ τὴν
ἔω ἐς ἄλλην νῆσον πλεύσαντες ὁρμίζονται οἰκουμ-
ένην, ἵνα καὶ μαργαρίτην θηρᾶσθαι λέγει Νέαρχος
κατάπερ ἐν τῇ Ἰνδῶν θαλάσσῃ. ταύτης τῆς νήσου
τὴν ἄκρην παραπλώσαντες σταδίους ὡς τεσσαράκοντα, ἐνταῦθα ὡρμίσθησαν. ἐνθένδε πρὸς ὄρει
4 ὁρμίζονται ὑψηλῷ — Ὦχος ὄνομα τῷ ὄρει — ἐν
5 λιμένι εὐόρμῳ, καὶ ἁλιέες αὐτοῦ ᾤκεον. καὶ ἔνθεν

island, about 300 stades from the mainland, after a
voyage of 400. They sailed off about dawn, and 8
passed on the left a desert island named Pylora.
Then they anchored at . . . . . ., a desolate little
township, destitute of everything but water and fish;
here again the natives were fish-eaters of necessity,
as their soil was wretched. They got water there 9
and reached Cape Tarsias, which runs right out into
the sea, after a voyage of 300 stades, and next came to 10
Cataea, a desert, low-lying island, said to be sacred to
Hermes and Aphrodite; the voyage was of 300
stades. Every year the people round about send
sheep and goats consecrated to Hermes and Aphrodite, which could be seen, quite wild from lapse of
time and want of handling.

38. So far Carmania extends; beyond this is Persia.
The length of the voyage along the Carmanian coast
is 3700 stades.[1] The people live like the Persians, as
they are their neighbours, and have the same military
equipment.[2] Starting from the sacred island, and 2
sailing along the Persian coast, they put in at a place
called Ilas, where a harbour is formed by a small
desert island, called Caïcandrus; the voyage is 400
stades. At daybreak they sailed to another island, 3
inhabited, and anchored there; according to Nearchus there is pearl fishing here, as in the Indian
Sea.[3] They sailed past the point of this island, about
40 stades, and moored there. Next they anchored 4
off a high mountain, called Ochus, in a safe harbour
inhabited by fishermen. From there they sailed 450 5

---

[1] App. XXV 7. As he passed south of Qeshm, N. did not in
fact sail along the Carmanian coast throughout.

[2] N. also said that their language was the same (S. xv 2, 14).

[3] Cf. Pliny vi 110 (Ones.); Athenaeus iii 92 F–94 B. A.
omits some other information from N. hereabouts (S. xvi 3, 7).

πλώσαντες σταδίους τετρακοσίους τε καὶ πεντήκοντα ὁρμίζονται ἐν Ἀποστάνοισι· καὶ πλοῖα πολλὰ
αὐτόθι ὥρμεε, κώμη τε ἐπῆν ἀπέχουσα ἀπὸ
6 θαλάσσης σταδίους ἑξήκοντα. νυκτὸς δὲ ἐπάραντες
ἔνθεν ἐσπλώουσιν ἐς κόλπον συνοικεόμενον πολλῇσι
κώμῃσι. στάδιοι τοῦ πλόου τετρακόσιοι· ὁρμίζονται δὲ πρὸς ὑπωρείην. ταύτῃ φοίνικές τε
πολλοὶ ἐπεφύκεσαν καὶ ὅσα ἄλλα ἀκρόδρυα ἐν τῇ
7 Ἑλλάδι γῇ φύεται. ἔνθεν ἄραντες ἐς Γώγανα
παραπλέουσι σταδίους μάλιστα ἐς ἑξακοσίους ἐς
χώρην οἰκουμένην· ὁρμίζονται δὲ τοῦ ποταμοῦ
τοῦ χειμάρρου — ὄνομα δὲ Ἀρεών — ἐν τῇσιν
ἐκβολῇσιν. ἐνταῦθα χαλεπῶς ὁρμίζονται· στεινὸς
γὰρ ἦν ὁ ἔσπλους κατὰ τὸ στόμα, ὅτι βράχεα τὰ
8 κύκλῳ αὐτοῦ ἡ ἀνάπωτις ἐποίεε. καὶ ἔνθεν αὖ ἐν
στόματι ἄλλου ποταμοῦ ὁρμίζονται, διεκπλώσαντες
σταδίους ἐς ὀκτακοσίους· Σιτακὸς ὄνομα τῷ ποταμῷ ἦν· οὐδὲ ἐν τούτῳ εὐμαρέως ὁρμίζονται, καὶ
ὁ πλόος ἅπας οὗτος ὁ παρὰ τὴν Περσίδα βράχεά τε
9 ἦσαν καὶ ῥηχίαι καὶ τενάγεα. ἐνταῦθα σῖτον κατα-
λαμβάνουσι πολὺν ξυγκεκομισμένον κατὰ πρόσταξιν βασιλέως, ὡς σφίσιν εἶναι ἐπισιτίσασθαι·
ἐνταῦθα ἔμειναν ἡμέρας τὰς πάσας μίαν καὶ εἴκοσι,
καὶ τὰς ναῦς ἀνειρυσάμενοι, ὅσαι μὲν πεπονήκεσαν
ἐπεσκεύαζον, τὰς δὲ ἄλλας ἐθεράπευον.

39. ἐνθένδε ὁρμηθέντες εἰς Ἱέρατιν πόλιν ἀφίκοντο, ἐς χῶρον οἰκούμενον. ἑπτακόσιοι καὶ πεντήκοντα στάσιοι ὁ πλόος· ὡρμίσθησαν δὲ ἐν διώρυχι ἀπὸ τοῦ ποταμοῦ ἐμβεβλημένῃ ἐς θάλασσαν,
2 ᾗ ὄνομα ἦν Ἡράτεμις. ἅμα δὲ ἡλίῳ ἀνίσχοντι
παραπλέουσιν ἐς ποταμὸν χειμάρρουν, ὄνομα
Πάδαργον, ὁ δὲ χῶρος χερρόνησος ἅπας. καὶ ἐν

stades, and anchored at Apostana; many boats were anchored there, and there was a village about 60 stades from the sea. They weighed anchor at night 6 and sailed thence to a gulf with many village settlements. This was a voyage of 400 stades, and they anchored near foothills, on which grew many date-palms and all the other fruit-trees that flourish in Greece. There they unmoored and sailed along to 7 Gogana, about 600 stades, to an inhabited district and anchored off the torrential river called Areon at its outlet. The anchorage was uncomfortable; the entrance was narrow at the mouth, since the ebb tide made shallows all round. After this they anchored 8 again at another river-mouth, after a voyage of about 800 stades. The river was called Sitacus.[4] Even here, however, they did not find easy anchorage; in fact this whole voyage along Persia was shallows, surf and lagoons. They found in the place a great 9 supply of corn conveyed by the king's orders for their provisioning, and stayed twenty-one days in all; they hauled the ships ashore, and spent the time refitting those which were damaged, while maintaining the rest.

39. Starting from this point, they reached a city called Hieratis, an inhabited place, after a voyage of 750 stades; they anchored in a channel running from the river to the sea and called Heratemis. At sun- 2 rise they sailed along the coast to a torrential river called Padargus; the whole place forms a peninsula.

---

[4] Perhaps the Mand.

αὐτῷ κῆποί τε πολλοὶ καὶ ἀκρόδρυα παντοῖα
3 ἐφύετο· ὄνομα τῷ χώρῳ Μεσαμβρίη. ἐκ Μεσαμβρίης δὲ ὁρμηθέντες καὶ διεκπλώσαντες σταδίους
μάλιστα ἐς διακοσίους ἐς Ταόκην ὁρμίζονται ἐπὶ
ποταμῷ Γράνιδι. καὶ ἀπὸ τούτου ἐς τὸ ἄνω ⟨τὰ⟩
Περσῶν βασίλεια ἦν, ἀπέχοντα τοῦ ποταμοῦ τῶν
4 ἐκβολέων σταδίους ἐς διακοσίους. κατὰ τοῦτον
τὸν παράπλουν λέγει Νέαρχος ὀφθῆναι κῆτος
ἐκβεβλημένον ἐς τὴν ἠιόνα, καὶ τοῦτο προσπλώσ-
αντάς τινας τῶν ναυτῶν ἐκμετρῆσαι καὶ φάναι εἶναι
5 πήχεων πεντήκοντα· δέρμα δὲ αὐτῷ εἶναι φολι-
δωτόν, οὕτω τι ἐς βάθος ἧκον ὡς καὶ ἐπὶ πῆχυν
ἐπέχειν, ὄστρειά τε καὶ λοπάδας καὶ φυκία πολλὰ
ἔχειν ἐπιπεφυκότα. καὶ δελφῖνας λέγει ὅτι καθ-
ορᾶν ἦν πολλοὺς ἀμφὶ τῷ κήτει, καὶ τῶν ἐν τῇ ἔσω
6 θαλάσσῃ μείζονας τοὺς δελφῖνας. ἐνθένδε ὁρμηθέντες κατάγονται ἐς Ῥώγονιν ποταμὸν χειμάρρουν
ἐν λιμένι εὐόρμῳ· μῆκος τοῦ παράπλου στάδιοι
7 διακόσιοι. ἐνθένδε τετρακοσίους σταδίους διεκπλώσαντες αὐλίζονται ἐν ποταμῷ χειμάρρῳ
Βρίζανα τῷ ποταμῷ ὄνομα. ἐνταῦθα χαλεπῶς
ὡρμίσαντο, ὅτι ῥηχίη ἦν καὶ βράχεα, καὶ χοιράδες
8 ἐκ τοῦ πόντου ἀνεῖχον. ἀλλ' ὅτε ἡ πλήμμυρα
ἐπῄει, τότε ὡρμίσαντο· ὑπονοστήσαντος δὲ τοῦ
ὕδατος, ἐπὶ ξηρῷ ὑπελείφθησαν αἱ νῆες. ἐπεὶ δὲ ἡ
πλημμυρὶς ἐν τάξει ἀμείβουσα ἐπῆλθε, τότε δὴ
9 ἐκπλώσαντες ὁρμίζονται ἐπὶ ποταμῷ· ὄνομα δὲ
τῷ ποταμῷ Ἄροσις, μέγιστος τῶν ποταμῶν, ὡς
λέγει Νέαρχος, ὅσοι ἐν τῷ παράπλῳ τῷδε ἐμβάλλουσιν ἐς τὸν ἔξω πόντον.

---

[1] Bushêhr.

There were many gardens, and all sorts of fruit trees were growing there; the name of the place was Mesambria.[1] From Mesambria they set out and after a **3** voyage of about 200 stades anchored at Taoce on the river Granis. Inland from here there was a Persian royal residence, about 200 stades from the mouth of the river. Nearchus says that on this coastal voyage **4** a great sea animal (whale) was seen stranded on the shore, that some of the sailors sailed up to it, measured it and reported its length as 50 cubits,[2] that its **5** hide was scaly and actually as much as a cubit thick, and that it had many oysters, shell-fish and seaweeds growing on it. Nearchus adds that they could see many dolphins round the animal, larger than those of the inner sea. Going on from there, they put in at **6** the torrential river Rogonis in a good harbour; the length of this voyage was 200 stades. From there **7** they sailed 400 stades and bivouacked on a torrential river named Brizana, where it was difficult to anchor, with surf and shallows and reefs showing above the sea. When the flood tide came in, they **8** were at anchor, but when the water went out again the ships were left high and dry. However, when the flood duly returned, they sailed out and anchored in a river called Arosis (?), the greatest, **9** according to Nearchus, of all the rivers which on this coastal voyage run into the Ocean.[3]

[2] I.e. 76 feet, or on Tarn's view (ii 169 f.) 60: credible, unlike the measurements in 30, 9 (150 or 120 feet). The largest recorded specimen was 110 feet.

[3] The MS. may be corrupt, cf. Oroatis in S. xv 3, 1 (from N.); Ptol. vi 4, 2; Oratis, Pliny vi 111; 136, though Ones. or Juba wrote Zarotis (ib. 99). This should be the Jarrāhi, the only considerable river on the whole coast, with outlet at Bandar e Mashur (Herzfeld, *Klio* 1908).

40. μέχρι τοῦδε Πέρσαι οἰκέουσι, τὰ δὲ ἀπὸ τούτων Σούσιοι. Σουσίων δὲ ἔθνος αὐτόνομον κατ-
ύπερθε προσοικέει· Οὔξιοι καλοῦνται, ὑπὲρ ὅτων
λέλεκταί μοι ἐν τῇ ἄλλῃ συγγραφῇ ὅτι λῃσταί εἰσι.
μῆκος τοῦ παράπλου τῆς Περσίδος χώρης στάδιοι
2 τετρακόσιοι καὶ τετρακισχίλιοι. τὴν δὲ Περσίδα
γῆν τρίχα νενεμῆσθαι τῶν ὡρέων λόγος κατέχει.
τὸ μὲν αὐτῆς πρὸς τῇ Ἐρυθρῇ θαλάσσῃ οἰκεόμενον
3 ἀμμῶδές τε εἶναι καὶ ἄκαρπον ὑπὸ καύματος, τὸ δὲ
ἐπὶ τῷδε ὡς πρὸς ἄρκτον τε καὶ βορέην ἄνεμον
ἰόντων καλῶς κεκρᾶσθαι τῶν ὡρέων, καὶ τὴν
χώρην ποιώδεά τε εἶναι καὶ λειμῶνας ὑδρηλούς, καὶ
ἄμπελον πολλὴν φέρειν καὶ ὅσοι ἄλλοι καρποὶ
4 πλὴν ἐλαίης, παραδείσοις τε παντοίοισι τεθηλέναι
καὶ ποταμοῖσι καθαροῖσι διαρρέεσθαι καὶ λίμνῃσι,
καὶ ὄρνισιν ὁκόσοισιν ἀμφὶ ποταμούς τε καὶ
λίμνας ἐστὶ τὰ ἤθεα ἱπποισί τε ἀγαθὴν εἶναι καὶ
τοῖσιν ἄλλοισιν ὑποζυγίοισι νέμεσθαι, καὶ ὑλώδεά
5 τε πολλαχῇ καὶ πολύθηρον. τὴν δὲ πρόσω ἔτι ἐπ'
ἄρκτον ἰόντων χειμερίην τε καὶ νιφετώδεα * * *,
ὥστε πρέσβεις τινὰς ἐκ τοῦ Εὐξείνου πόντου
λέγει Νέαρχος κάρτα ὀλίγην ὁδὸν διελθόντας ἐντυχεῖν κατ' ὁδὸν ἰόντι τῆς Περσίδος καὶ θῶμα
γενέσθαι Ἀλεξάνδρῳ καὶ εἰπεῖν Ἀλεξάνδρῳ τῆς
6 ὁδοῦ τὴν βραχύτητα. Σουσίοις δὲ πρόσοικοι ὅτι
εἰσὶν Οὔξιοι λέλεκταί μοι, κατάπερ Μάρδοι μὲν
Πέρσαισι προσεχέες οἰκέουσι, λῃσταὶ καὶ οὗτοι,
7 Κοσσαῖοι δὲ Μήδοισι. καὶ ταῦτα πάντα τὰ ἔθνεα

---

[1] Not explicit in iii 17.   N. so classified them, cf. § 6.
[2] App. XXV 7.
[3] The account is perhaps that of E., rather than N., cf. S. xv
3, 1 (which suggests a lacuna).

324
B.C.

40. The Persians dwell up to this point and the Susians beyond. Above the Susians on their border lives another independent tribe called Uxians, and in my earlier history I have described them as brigands.[1] The length of the voyage along the Persian coast was 4400 stades.[2] The Persian land is divided 2 on the prevalent account into three climatic zones. The inhabited part which lies by the Red Sea is sandy and sterile owing to the heat. The next zone, going 3 northward, has a temperate climate; the country is grassy with water meadows, many vines and all other fruits except the olive; it is rich with all sorts 4 of gardens, has pure rivers running through and lakes, and is good for all sorts of birds that haunt rivers and lakes, and for horses; it provides pasture for the other domestic animals, is well wooded, and has plenty of game. The next zone, still going north- 5 ward, is wintry and snowy . . .[3] Nearchus tells us of some envoys from the Black Sea who after quite a short journey met Alexander traversing Persia and caused him no small astonishment by telling him how short the journey was.[4] The Uxians are neighbours 6 to the Susians, as I have said, as the Mardians who are also brigands live next to the Persians,[5] and the Cossaeans next to the Medes. Alexander pacified all 7

[4] In fact (say) 1800 km. from Trabzon by air. E. knew better (S. xv **3**, 1).

[5] S. xi 13, 6 shows that A. omits the Elymaeans (cf. xv 3, 12; xvi 1, 8) from N's list, perhaps because (as N. may have said) Al. did not attack them. N. also said that all four tribes exacted tribute from the Persian kings; Al. made his attacks in winter on the Cossaeans in Luristan (vii 15), the Uxians in Khuzistan (iii 17) and the Persian Mardians in the Zagros range near Persepolis (QC. v 6, 17, cf. App. VIII 6), doubtless because the tribesmen could not then take refuge in the heights.

ἡμέρωσεν Ἀλέξανδρος, χειμῶνος ὥρῃ ἐπιπεσὼν
8 αὐτοῖσιν, ὅτε ἄβατον σφῶν τὴν χώρην ἦγον. καὶ
πόληας ἐπέκτισε τοῦ μὴ νομάδας ἔτι εἶναι ἀλλὰ
ἀροτῆρας καὶ γῆς ἐργάτας, καὶ ἔχειν ὑπὲρ ὅτων
δειμαίνοντες μὴ κακὰ ἀλλήλους ἐργάσονται. ἐνθένδε τὴν Σουσίων γῆν παρήμειβεν ὁ στρατός.
9 καὶ ταῦτα οὐκέτι ὡσαύτως ἀτρεκέως λέγει
Νέαρχος ὅτι ἔστιν οἷ ἐκφράσαι, πλήν γε δὴ τοὺς
10 ὅρμους τε καὶ τὸ μῆκος τοῦ πλόου· τὴν χώρην γὰρ
τεναγώδεά τε εἶναι τὴν πολλὴν καὶ ῥηχίῃσιν ἐπὶ
μέγα ἐς τὸν πόντον ἐσέχουσαν καὶ ταύτῃ σφαλερὴν
ἐγκαθορμίζεσθαι· πελαγίοισιν ὧν σφίσι τὴν κομι-
11 δὴν τὸ πολὺ γίνεσθαι. ὁρμηθῆναι μὲν δὴ ἐκ τοῦ
ποταμοῦ τῶν ἐκβολέων, ἵναπερ ηὐλίσθησαν ἐπὶ
τοῖσιν οὔροισι τῆς Περσίδος, ὕδωρ δὲ ἐμβαλέσθαι
καὶ πέντε ἡμερέων· οὐκ ἔφασκον γὰρ εἶναι ὕδωρ
οἱ καθηγεμόνες τοῦ πλόου.

41. σταδίους δὲ πεντακοσίους κομισθέντες ὁρμίζονται ἐπὶ στόματι λίμνης ἰχθυώδεος, ᾗ οὔνομα
Κατάδερβις· καὶ νησὶς ἐπῆν τῷ στόματι· Μαργά-
2 στανα τῇ νησῖδι οὔνομα. ἐνθένδε ὑπὸ τὴν ἔω
ἐκπλώσαντες κατὰ βράχεα ἐκομίζοντο ἐπὶ μιᾶς
νεώς· πασσάλοις δὲ ἔνθεν καὶ ἔνθεν πεπηγόσιν
ἀπεδηλοῦτο τὰ βράχεα, κατάπερ ἐν τῷ μεσσηγὺς
Λευκάδος τε νήσου ἰσθμῷ καὶ Ἀκαρνανίης
ἀποδέδεικται σημεῖα τοῖσι ναυτιλλομένοισι τοῦ μὴ
3 ἐποκέλλειν ἐν τοῖσι βράχεσι τὰς νέας. ἀλλὰ τὰ μὲν
κατὰ Λευκάδα ψαμμώδεα ὄντα καὶ τοῖσιν ἐποκεί-
λασι ταχεῖαν τὴν ὑπονόστησιν ἐνδιδοῖ· κεῖθι δὲ
πηλός ἐστιν ἐφ' ἑκάτερα τοῦ πλεομένου βαθὺς καὶ
ἰλυώδης, ὥστε οὐδεμιᾷ μηχανῇ ἐποκείλασιν ἦν
4 ἀποσωθῆναι. οἵ τε γὰρ κοντοὶ κατὰ τοῦ πηλοῦ

these tribes, falling upon them in winter-time, when they thought their country unapproachable. He also founded cities so that they should no longer be nomads but cultivators and tillers of the ground and, having a stake in the country, might be deterred from injuring one another.[6] From here the fleet passed along the Susian land. Nearchus says that he cannot describe this part of the voyage in accurate detail, except for the roadsteads and the length of the voyage. This is because the country is mostly marshy and runs out well into the sea, with breakers, and is very hard to get safe anchorage in. So their voyage was mostly in the open sea. They sailed out from the outlets of the river, where they had encamped on the Persian border, and took on board water for five days, as the pilots said that water was lacking.[7]

41. After traversing 500 stades, they anchored at the mouth of a lake, full of fish, called Cataderbis, off which lay a small island called Margastana. From there, they sailed about daybreak and in single line ahead passed the shallows, which were marked on either side by poles driven in, just as in the strait between the island of Leucas and Acarnania signposts have been set up for navigators to prevent the ships grounding in the shallows.[1] However, the shallows round Leucas are sandy and allow those aground to get off quickly; but here there is mud on both sides of the channel, both deep and viscous; and no device could save them once aground there, as the

---

[6] But cf. P. 72, **3**. D. xix 19 shows that Al. did not permanently pacify them.

[7] I.e. Mazenes and followers; N. said that he could obtain no local pilots (S. xv **3**, 11).

[1] An interpolation by A. in N's account?

δύνοντες αὐτοὶ οὐδέν τι ἐπωφέλουν, ἀνθρώπῳ τε
ἐκβῆναι τοῦ ἀπῶσαι τὰς νέας ἐς τὰ πλεόμενα
ἄπορον ἐγίνετο· ἔδυνον γὰρ κατὰ τοῦ πηλοῦ ἔστε
5 ἐπὶ τὰ στήθεα. οὕτω δὴ χαλεπῶς διεκπλώσαντες
σταδίους ἑξακοσίους κατὰ ναῦν ἕκαστοι ὁρμισθέντες
6 ἐνταῦθα δείπνου ἐμνήσθησαν. τὴν νύκτα δὲ ἤδη
κατὰ βάθεα ἔπλεον καὶ τὴν ἐφεξῆς ἡμέρην ἔστε ἐπὶ
βουλυτόν· καὶ ἦλθον σταδίους ἐνακοσίους, καὶ
καθωρμίσθησαν ἐπὶ τοῦ στόματος τοῦ Εὐφράτου
πρὸς κώμῃ τινὶ τῆς Βαβυλωνίης χώρης — ὄνομα
7 δὲ αὐτῇ Διρίδωτις —, ἵνα λιβανωτόν τε ἀπὸ τῆς
Γερραίης γῆς οἱ ἔμποροι ἀγινέουσι καὶ τὰ ἄλλα
8 ὅσα θυμιήματα ἡ Ἀράβων γῆ φέρει. ἀπὸ δὲ τοῦ
στόματος τοῦ Εὐφράτου ἔστε Βαβυλῶνα πλοῦν
λέγει Νέαρχος σταδίους εἶναι ἐς τρισχιλίους καὶ
τριακοσίους.

42. ἐνταῦθα ἀγγέλλεται Ἀλέξανδρον ἐπὶ Σούσων
στέλλεσθαι. ἔνθεν καὶ αὐτοὶ τὸ ὀπίσω ἔπλεον, ὡς
κατὰ τὸν Πασιτίγριν ποταμὸν ἀναπλώσαντες συμ-
2 μῖξαι Ἀλεξάνδρῳ. ἔπλεον δὴ τὸ ἔμπαλιν ἐν
ἀριστερᾷ τὴν γῆν τὴν Σουσίδα ἔχοντες, καὶ
παραπλέουσι λίμνην, ἐς ἣν ὁ Τίγρης ἐσβάλλει
3 ποταμός, ὃς ῥέων ἐξ Ἀρμενίης παρὰ πόλιν Νίνον,
πάλαι ποτὲ μεγάλην καὶ εὐδαίμονα, τὴν μέσην
ἑωυτοῦ τε καὶ τοῦ Εὐφράτου ποταμοῦ γῆν Μεσο-
4 ποταμίην ἐπὶ τῷδε κληίζεσθαι ποιέει. ἀπὸ δὲ
τῆς λίμνης ἐς αὐτὸν τὸν ποταμὸν ἀνάπλους

---

[2] S. xvi 3, 2 and others call the place Teredon; it was in
Babylonia (Jacoby 122 F 3), hence on the right bank of the Eu-
phrates, which was the boundary of Susiana. See also App.
XXVI.

punt-poles sank into the mud and gave them no help, and it became impossible for the men to disembark and push the ships off into the sailable water, for they sank up to their breasts in the ooze. So they sailed 5 out with difficulty, traversed 600 stades, and after anchoring attended to supper on board, each in their own ships. During the night, however, they were 6 sailing in deep water and next day also till the evening; they made 900 stades and anchored in the mouth of the Euphrates near a village of Babylonia, called Diridotis; here the merchants gather together 7 frankincense from the land of Gerrha and all the other sweet-smelling spices Arabia produces.[2] Nearchus 8 says it is a voyage of about 3300 stades from the mouth of the Euphrates to Babylon.[3]

42. There they heard that Alexander was on his way to Susa. They therefore sailed back themselves in order to sail up the Pasitigris and meet him.[1] They sailed back with the land of Susia on their left 2 and went along the lake into which the Tigris runs. It flows from Armenia past the city of Ninus [Nine-3 veh], once great and prosperous, and gives the region between itself and the Euphrates the name of Mesopotamia (between the rivers). The voyage is 4 600 stades from the lake up to the river itself at a

---

[3] N. made the voyage, vii 19, 3. For the distance cf. Pliny vi 124, citing N. and Onesicritus (412 m. = 3296 stades); E. *ap.* S. ii 1, 26 (rounded off as 3000). These estimates correspond fairly well to the distance from Babylon (near Hilla) to the coast at Qasr as Subiya (about 600 km.), if the stade is taken to be 185 m. (cf. App. XXV 8).

[1] Topography: App. XXVI. It is impossible to suppose that the length of the Susian coast (§ 4) could have much exceeded 200 km.

στάδιοι ἑξακόσιοι, ἵνα καὶ κώμη τῆς Σουσίδος, ἣν
καλέουσιν Ἄγινιν· αὕτη δὲ ἀπέχει Σούσων
σταδίους ἐς πεντακοσίους. μῆκος τοῦ παράπλου τῆς
Σουσίων γῆς ἔστε ἐπὶ ⟨τὸ⟩ στόμα τοῦ Πασιτίγριδος
5 ποταμοῦ στάδιοι δισχίλιοι. ἐνθένδε κατὰ τὸν
Πασιτίγριν ἄνω ἀνέπλεον διὰ χώρης οἰκουμένης καὶ εὐδαίμονος. ἀναπλώσαντες δὲ σταδίους
ὡς πεντήκοντα καὶ ἑκατὸν αὐτοῦ ὁρμίζονται,
προσμένοντες οὕστινας ἐστάλκει Νέαρχος σκεψομέ-
6 νους ἵνα ὁ βασιλεὺς εἴη. αὐτὸς δὲ ἔθυε θεοῖς τοῖς
σωτῆρσι, καὶ ἀγῶνα ἐποίεε, καὶ ἡ στρατιὴ ἡ
7 ναυτικὴ πᾶσα ἐν εὐθυμίῃσιν ἦν. ὡς δὲ προσάγων
ἤδη Ἀλέξανδρος ἠγγέλλετο, ἔπλεον ἤδη αὖθις ἐς
τὸ ἄνω κατὰ τὸν ποταμόν· καὶ πρὸς τῇ σχεδίῃ
ὁρμίζονται, ἐφ᾿ ᾗ τὸ στράτευμα διαβιβάσειν
8 ἔμελλεν Ἀλέξανδρος ἐς Σοῦσα. ἐνταῦθα ἀνεμίχθη
ὁ στρατός, καὶ θυσίαι πρὸς Ἀλεξάνδρου ἐθύοντο
ἐπὶ τῶν νεῶν τε καὶ τῶν ἀνθρώπων τῇ σωτηρίῃ,
καὶ ἀγῶνες ἐποιέοντο· καὶ Νέαρχος ὅποι παρα-
φανείη τῆς στρατιῆς, ἄνθεσί τε καὶ ταινίῃσιν ἐβάλ-
9 λετο. ἔνθα καὶ χρυσᾷ στεφάνῳ στεφανοῦνται ἐξ
Ἀλεξάνδρου Νέαρχός τε καὶ Λεόννατος, Νέαρχος
μὲν ἐπὶ τοῦ ναυτικοῦ τῇ σωτηρίῃ, Λεόννατος δὲ
ἐπὶ τῇ νίκῃ, ἣν Ὠρείτας τε ἐνίκησε καὶ τοὺς
10 Ὠρείταις προσοικέοντας βαρβάρους. οὕτω μὲν
ἀπεσώθη Ἀλεξάνδρῳ ἐκ τοῦ Ἰνδοῦ τῶν ἐκβολέων
ὁρμηθεὶς ὁ στρατός.

43. τὰ δὲ ἐν δεξιᾷ τῆς Ἐρυθρῆς θαλάσσης ὑπὲρ
τὴν Βαβυλωνίην Ἀραβίη ἡ πολλή ἐστι, καὶ
ταύτης τὰ μὲν κατήκει ἔστε ἐπὶ τὴν θάλασσαν τὴν
κατὰ Φοινίκην τε καὶ τὴν Παλαιστίνην Συρίην,
πρὸς δυομένου δὲ ἡλίου ὡς ἐπὶ τὴν εἴσω θάλασσαν

point where a village of Susia lies, called Aginis, 500
stades from Susa. The length of the coastal voyage
along Susian territory to the mouth of the Pasitigris is
2000 stades. From there they sailed up the Pasi- 5
tigris through inhabited and prosperous country.
When they had sailed up about 150 stades, they
moored, waiting for the scouts whom Nearchus had
sent to see where the king might be. Nearchus him- 6
self sacrificed to the Saviour gods and held games,
and the whole naval force made merry. And when 7
news was brought that Alexander was actually
approaching, they again sailed up river, and moored
near the pontoon bridge on which Alexander intended to take his army over to Susa.² There the 8
two forces met; Alexander offered sacrifices for the
preservation of his ships and men, and games were
held, and, wherever Nearchus appeared in the
camp, the troops pelted him with ribbons and
flowers. Thereupon too Nearchus and Leonnatus 9
were crowned by Alexander with a golden crown,
Nearchus because of the safety of the ships, Leonnatus for the victory he had achieved among the
Oritans and the barbarians who dwelt next to them.³
This was how Alexander received back in safety the 10
navy which had started from the mouths of the Indus.

43. On the right side of the Red Sea beyond
Babylonia lies the main part of Arabia; some of it
extends to the sea of Phoenicia and Palestinian
Syria,¹ while on the west towards the inner sea the

² A. omits the distance, sc. to Ahwaz.
³ Contrast vii 5, 6. If A. has correctly reported N., he misplaced the festivities and exaggerated the extent to which they
celebrated his own success.
¹ It was not usual to make Arabia extend to the Mediterranean (on the coast south of Gaza?). This chapter is an
addendum by A., the purpose and sources of which are obscure.

ARRIAN

2 Αἰγύπτιοι τῇ Ἀραβίῃ ὁμουρέουσι. κατὰ δὲ Αἴγυπτον εἰσέχων ἐκ τῆς μεγάλης θαλάσσης κόλπος δῆλον
ποιέει ὅτι ἕνεκά γε τοῦ σύρρουν εἶναι τὴν ἔξω
θάλασσαν περίπλους ἂν ἦν ἐκ Βαβυλῶνος ἐς τὸν
κόλπον τοῦτον ⟨τὸν⟩ ἐπέχοντα ὡς ἐπ' Αἴγυπτον.
3 ἀλλὰ γὰρ οὔ τις παρέπλωσε ταύτῃ οὐδαμῶν ἀνθρώπων ὑπὸ καύματος καὶ ἐρημίης, εἰ μή τινές γε
4 πελάγιοι κομιζόμενοι. ἀλλὰ οἱ ἀπ' Αἰγύπτου γὰρ
ἐς Σοῦσα ἀποσωθέντες τῆς στρατιῆς τῆς Καμβύσεω
καὶ οἱ παρὰ Πτολεμαίου τοῦ Λάγου παρὰ Σέλευκον
τὸν Νικάτορα σταλέντες ἐς Βαβυλῶνα διὰ τῆς
5 Ἀραβίης χώρης ἰσθμόν τινα διαπορευθέντες ἐν
ἡμέρῃσιν ὀκτὼ ταῖς πάσαις ἄνυδρον καὶ ἐρήμην
χώρην ἐπῆλθον ἐπὶ καμήλων σπουδῇ ἐλαύνοντες
ὕδωρ τέ σφιν ἐπὶ τῶν καμήλων φέροντες καὶ νυκτο-
πορέοντες· τὰς γὰρ ἡμέρας ὑπαίθριοι ἀνέχεσθαι
6 διὰ καῦμα ἀδύνατοι ἦσαν. τοσούτου δεῖ τά γε
ἐπέκεινα ταύτης τῆς χώρης, ἥντινα ἰσθμὸν ἀπεφαί-
νομεν ἐκ τοῦ κόλπου τοῦ Ἀραβίου κατήκοντα ἐς
τὴν Ἐρυθρὰν θάλασσαν, οἰκεόμενα εἶναι, ὁπότε τὰ
πρὸς ἄρκτον μᾶλλον αὐτῶν ἀνέχοντα ἔρημά τέ
7 ἐστι καὶ ψαμμώδεα. ἀλλὰ γὰρ ἀπὸ τοῦ Ἀραβίου
κόλπου τοῦ κατ' Αἴγυπτον ὁρμηθέντες ἄνθρωποι
ἐκπεριπλώσαντες τὴν πολλὴν Ἀραβίην ἐλθεῖν ἐς
τὴν κατὰ Σοῦσά τε καὶ Πέρσας θάλασσαν, ἐς
τοσόνδε ἄρα παραπλώσαντες τῆς Ἀραβίης ἐς
ὅσον σφίσι τὸ ὕδωρ ἐπήρκεσε τὸ ἐμβληθὲν ἐς τὰς
8 νέας, ἔπειτα ὀπίσω ἀπενόστησαν. ἐκ Βαβυλῶνός

---

² A. reflects the state of knowledge in E's time, when the
Arabian coasts were known only in the Red Sea and in the
Persian Gulf as far as Cape Maceta (S. xvi **3** f.). In the

Egyptians are on the Arabian borders.   A gulf [the   2
Red Sea] running from the Great Sea [the Arabian
Sea] by Egypt makes it clear that, as the gulf is connected with the outer sea, it is possible to sail round
from Babylon into this gulf which runs up to Egypt.
Yet, in point of fact, no one has yet sailed round the   3
coast this way because of the heat and desert, if we
disregard any who cross the open water.[2] But the   4
survivors from the army of Cambyses who reached
Susa from Egypt [3] and the troops who were sent by
Ptolemy son of Lagus to Seleucus Nicator at Babylon
through Arabia crossed an isthmus in eight days in all,   5
a waterless and desert country, riding fast upon
camels, carrying water for themselves on their
camels; they travelled by night, as during the day
they could not come into the open air because of the
heat.[4] So far from being inhabited is the region on   6
the other side of this stretch of land, which we des-
scribe as an isthmus from the Arabian gulf [Red Sea]
running into the Red Sea [Arabian Sea], inasmuch
as its more northerly parts are a sandy desert.   Yet   7
people have started from the Arabian gulf in its
Egyptian sector [Red Sea] and have circumnavigated
the main part of Arabia hoping to reach the sea by
Susa and Persia but, after sailing as far round the
Arabian coast as the amount of fresh water taken
aboard their vessels permitted, have then returned
home again.   And though the men Alexander sent   8

Periplous of the Red Sea, perhaps best dated to A's time (*Oxf.
Class. Dict.*[2] 802 for bibliography), there was trading all round
the coast. This was already known to Pliny. A. is out-of-
date, but is vaguely aware of the direct sea-voyages to India
(App. XVII 8).
   [3] The story is wholly incompatible with all known accounts
of Cambyses' Egyptian campaign.
   [4] Date and circumstances are unknown.

τε οὕστινας ἔστειλεν Ἀλέξανδρος ὡς ἐπὶ μήκιστον
πλέοντας ἐν δεξιᾷ τῆς Ἐρυθρῆς θαλάσσης γνῶναι
τοὺς ταύτῃ χώρους, οὗτοι νήσους μέν τινας κατε-
σκέψαντο ἐν τῷ παράπλῳ κειμένας, καί που καὶ

9 τῆς ἠπείρου τῆς Ἀραβίης προσέσχον, τὴν δὲ ἄκρην,
ἥντινα καταντικρὺ τῆς Καρμανίης ἀνέχουσαν λέγει
φανῆναι σφίσι Νέαρχος, οὐκ ἔστιν ὅστις ὑπερβαλὼν
ἐπικάμψαι ἐς τὸ ἐπὶ θάτερα δυνατὸς ἐγένετο.

10 δοκέω δὲ ὡς εἴπερ πλωτά τε ἦν καὶ βαδιστὰ ⟨τὰ⟩
ταύτῃ, ὑπ᾽ Ἀλεξάνδρου ἂν τῆς πολυπραγμοσύνης

11 ἐξελήλεγκτο πλωτά τε καὶ βαδιστὰ ἐόντα. καὶ
Ἄννων δὲ ὁ Λίβυς ἐκ Καρχηδόνος ὁρμηθεὶς ὑπὲρ
μὲν Ἡρακλείας στήλας ἐξέπλωσεν ἐς τὸν ἔξω
πόντον, ἐν ἀριστερᾷ τὴν Λιβύην γῆν ἔχων, καὶ
ἔστε μὲν πρὸς ἀνίσχοντα ἥλιον ὁ πλόος αὐτῷ

12 ἐγένετο τὰς πάσας πέντε καὶ τριάκοντα ἡμέρας· ὡς
δὲ δὴ ἐς μεσημβρίην ἐξετράπετο, πολλῆσιν ἀμηχανί-
ῃσιν ἐνετύγχανεν ὕδατός τε ἀπορίῃ καὶ καύματι
ἐπιφλέγοντι καὶ ῥύαξι πυρὸς ἐς τὸν πόντον ἐμβάλ-

13 λουσιν. ἀλλ᾽ ἡ Κυρήνη γὰρ τῆς Λιβύης ἐν τοῖς
ἐρημοτέροις πεπολισμένη ποιώδης τέ ἐστι καὶ
μαλθακὴ καὶ εὔυδρος καὶ ἄλσεα καὶ λειμῶνες, καὶ
καρπῶν παντοίων καὶ κτηνέων πάμφορός ⟨ἐστι⟩
ἔστε ἐπὶ τοῦ σιλφίου τὰς ἐκφύσεις· ὑπὲρ δὲ τὸ
σίλφιον τὰ ἄνω αὐτῆς ἔρημα καὶ ψαμμώδεα.

14 οὗτός μοι ὁ λόγος ἀναγεγράφθω, φέρων καὶ
αὐτὸς ἐς Ἀλέξανδρον τὸν Φιλίππου, τὸν Μακεδόνα.

from Babylon, to sail as far as they could on the right of the Red Sea [Persian Gulf] and discover the regions there, sighted certain islands lying on their coastal course, and doubtless put in at places on the mainland of Arabia, yet the cape which Nearchus 9 says his party sighted running out into the sea opposite Carmania has never been rounded, and no one has been able to turn inwards on the far side. I 10 think that, had it been possible to proceed by sailing this way, it would have been proved possible so to proceed and sail by the indefatigable energy of Alexander. Hanno the Libyan started out from 11 Carthage and sailed beyond the pillars of Heracles [Gibraltar] into the outer sea, with Libya on his left, and sailed on towards the east, five-and-thirty days all told. But when at last he turned southward, he fell 12 in with every sort of difficulty, want of water, blazing heat, and fiery streams running into the sea. However, Cyrene, though it is a city lying in the 13 more desert parts of Africa, is grassy, mild and well-watered with groves and meadows and bears all sorts of fruits and animals, up to the region where the silphium grows; beyond this silphium belt its upper parts are bare and sandy.[5]

Let this be the end of my record, which also bears 14 on Alexander of Macedon, son of Philip.

---

[5] The sequence of thought is puzzling. What has an inaccurately reported voyage on the west coast of Africa (*Oxf. Class. Dict. s.v.* Hanno), or the fertility of Cyrene, to do with the circumnavigation of Arabia?

APPENDIX XVI

DIONYSUS, HERACLES AND INDIA

1. A. reports tales that Heracles (iv 28–30; v 3, 5; *Ind.* 5, 10) and Dionysus (v 1 f.; vi 3, 4; 14, 2) had invaded India and that at Aornus (as previously in his journey to Siwah, iii 3, 2) Al. had set out to rival Heracles. These tales certainly appeared in the ' vulgate ' (§ 4 below), on which A. could have drawn when he made Al. himself allude to them in v 26, 5; vii 10, 6. However, I shall argue that he found them in Ar. They were certainly accepted by Megasthenes, whose accounts are found probably in *Ind.* 1, 4–7, and in 5 (where ' proofs ' of the historicity of the tales are adduced, cf. *Ind.* 5, 12; 7, 8; S. xv 1, 8, 33 and 58; D. ii 38, 3–6, and for Nysa A. v 1, 6; 2, 5; *Ind.* 5, 9), certainly in 7–9, where A. summarizes his pseudo-history of early India. A. himself expresses doubts whether the stories were true (iv 28, 1 f.; v 3, 1–4; *Ind.* 5; 7, 6; 8, 3). These doubts were clearly inspired chiefly by Eratosthenes (v 3); S. xv 1 urges that little was known of India and least of all about its early history (1–4), and that ' most writers ' including E. considered the stories untrustworthy (7); he subjects the ' proofs ' to detailed criticism (8), and observes that the ' most reliable ' authorities did not mention them and that those who did contradicted each other (9); he concludes that they were fabrications to flatter Al. Comparison of his sceptical

comments with those of A. shows that both were following E. (cf. also App. XVII 6–8; App. XII 1). But
A. is much less decisive than S., and in *Ind.* 1, 4 f. and
7–9 he writes as if the reports about Dionysus at
least were acceptable. He certainly thought better
of Meg. than E. did, and it may be significant that he
does not appeal to ' the most reliable ' authorities
against them; contrast vi 11, 5; 28; vii 13, 2; 15, 6),
where he treats the silence of *both* Pt. *and* Ar. as
decisive or nearly so.

2. Glorification of Al. was certainly an inadequate
explanation of the stories; Meg. elaborated them
when Al. was dead, and related them to parts of India
which Al. never traversed. It is also plain that he
professed to derive his pseudo-history from Indian
traditions, citing variants (*Ind.* 8, 4, 6 and 8; 9, 9 ff.);
D. ii 38, 3 may reflect what he wrote in ascribing the
stories to ' the most learned ' of the Indians. It
speaks for his good faith, though not for his sense of
coherence, that he told that the Brahmans wor-
shipped Dionysus in the mountains and Heracles in
the plains (S. xv 1, 58) as among the Sydraci, A's
Oxydracae, in the Punjab (ib. 8 and 33) and yet made
D. as well as H. rule in the Ganges plain. Following
Ar. (*infra*), A. too implies that the Indians ' remembered ' Dionysus (vi 3, 4; 14, 2), cf. QC. viii 10,
1; 14, 11; ix 8, 5.

3. What can have put these persons into the minds
of the flatterers? Heracles was a reputed ancestor of
Al. (App. IV), and so was Dionysus, but perhaps only
by a construction due to Ptolemaic genealogists (A.
D. Nock, *Essays on Religion and the Ancient World* 134
ff. = *JHS* xlviii, 1928, 21 ff.), and it has been argued,

speculatively, that Al. showed him special veneration (A. Piganiol, *REA* xliii, 1940, 285 ff.). But ancient Greeks and Romans were always ready to identify foreign gods with their own on the basis of the most slender similarities of myth, cult or function, and it was surely such similarities in what they saw or heard of Indian practices and legends that suggested to them that Dionysus and Heracles had been active in India. With Dionysus there was the less difficulty, since Euripides (*Bacchae* 13 ff., quoted by Strabo xv 1, 7, perhaps from a writer who sought to authenticate the story) had already represented him as coming west from Bactria. The ' proofs ' of the stories, however fallacious they appeared to Eratosthenes, can have seemed persuasive to Al. and his men. A. himself is less sceptical about Dionysus. As for Heracles, whom Greek legend had hitherto not taken to the east, we can readily assume that the confusion of the Hindu-Kush with the Caucasus (App. XII), the discovery there of a cave that fitted the legend of Prometheus (D. 83; QC. vii 3, 22) and the misinterpretation of local legends, both in this case and in that of Aornus, created a genuine conviction, which the practices of the Sibae (*Ind.* 5, 12 n.) later seemed to confirm. Many experts in Indian studies have in fact held that the Macedonians equated Çiva with Dionysus (but O. Stein, *RE* xv 301 ff. would substitute Manu) and Krishna with Heracles (e.g. *CHI* 408).

4. The vulgate not only alludes to the Indian conquests of H. and D. (e.g. QC viii 9, 1; ix 8, 5), but makes much of Al. emulating them. In particular the drunken frolic in which Persepolis was allegedly burned down (App. X 1) was construed by D. 72, 4

(but not by QC.) as a Dionysiac victory procession; and similar revels were depicted at Nysa (QC. viii 10, 17; A. v 2, 7) and in Carmania (D. 106, 1; QC. ix 10, 24 ff.; A. vi 28), where vines grew according to S. xv 1, 58. If Clitarchus was the common source where D. and QC. agree, these accounts can be ascribed to him; he certainly told of the drunken frolic (F. 11), and of Dionysus at Nysa (F. 17). Attribution to Clitarchus is, however, not enough to discredit the stories, even when coupled with the silence of Pt. and Ar., which is implicit (but explicable on grounds other than their veracity) in the first case and stressed by A. in the third. However, one of A's main sources seems to record a procession in Dionysus' honour at Nysa, through less extravagant than in the vulgate. Here (and in Carmania too) the most hard-headed general might have welcomed an occasion to give his troops relaxation from campaigning by the most exuberant festivities. Nor was Clitarchus necessarily the only source. He alone held that the mountain as well as the city was called Nysa and that it was not ivy that grew there but a plant like it called *skindapsos* (F 17; Pearson 215). It is not proven that QC. followed him here (D's account is lost).

5. Dionysus' foundation at Nysa is represented as a prototype of Al's cities (cf. v 1, 5 and *Ind.* 1, 4 with iv 4, 1; 22, 5; 24, 7 and v 29, 3). S. iii 5, 5 says that in setting up altars on the Hyphasis (A. v 29, 1) Al. imitated H. and Dionysus. Pliny, *N.H.* vi 49 is no doubt right that he had also set up altars on the Jaxartes, as (it was held) Heracles, Dionysus, Cyrus and Semiramis had done before him. By his foray beyond that river Al. could be said to have gone beyond Dionysus (QC. vii 9, 15). QC. elsewhere re-

presents him as anxious to emulate or outdo these
divine figures in a context which sometimes relates
to his supposed design of world-conquest (iii 10, 5;
12, 18; ix 2, 29 and 4, 21); the same *motiv* appears in
speeches in A. (v 26, 2; vii 10, 6), see App. XXVII 5.
QC. viii 5, 11 and 17, cf. A. iv 10, 6 (vulgate), also
make H. and D. models for Al's deification. Presumably S's view that the stories of their exploits in
India were invented for Al's glory is based on the
known fact that it was suggested that Al. would earn
the same reward after ' world ' conquest. Those
who hold that Al. did in reality aspire to world-rule
and apotheosis may readily credit that all this was
agreeable to him, even though there is no evidence
that he ever claimed to be a re-incarnation of Dionysus
(Nock, cited in § 3); he did on Ephippus' hostile
testimony pose as Heracles (Athenaeus xii 537 E),
and gave H's name to his son by Barsine (Brunt, *Riv.
Fil.* 1975, 22 ff.).   But in any event there is no reason
to think that Al. was himself more sceptical about the
stories than Meg. was to be.

6. Allusions to these stories actually appear in A's
factual narrative, which should come from one or both
of his main sources (iv 28, 4; 30, 4; vi 3, 4; 14, 2).
So too in the Nysa narrative, probably under the influence of Eratosthenes' scepticism, he begins by
saying that it is a mere story that Dionysus founded
Nysa (v 1, 1) but then tells it in a mixture of direct
speech (1, 3; 2, 1 f. and 4 f.) and indirect (1, 4; 2, 3
and 5 f.); the narrative is consecutive throughout till
the ' vulgate ' is cited in 2, 7; for Acuphis' speech see
App. XXVII 4.   This procedure points to use of at
least one of his main sources, see App. XXVIII 18.
Here the reference to the Nysaean horsemen in 2, 4 is

corroborated by the factual narrative in vi 2, 3, the *pothos motiv* in 2, 1 is characteristic of the best sources (App. V 3), and the slightly cynical observation that Al. hoped to raise morale by building on the Dionysus myth is reminiscent of iii 3, 4, cf. perhaps vii 29, 3; if accepted, it would confirm (like iv 28, 4) that Al. did seek or pretend to rival Heracles and Dionysus, cf. iii 3, 2 and his desire to outstrip Cyrus and Semiramis (Nearchus, vi 24, 3 n.). I suggest that Ar. alone is his source.

7. Like QC. viii 10, 7 ff., D., whose account is lost, placed the Nysa incident, as we know from the table of contents, between the episode in A. iv 23, 3 and the operations A. describes in the rest of book iv, relying mainly on Pt., to judge from Pt's prominence in the account. S. xv 1, 27 puts Nysa further west than Masoga, A's Massaga (iv 26; *Ind.* 1) and he probably drew here on Ar. (App. XVII 18). Some would identify Nysa with Nagara or Dionysopolis in the *Geography* of Claudius Ptolemy (viii 1, 43), which was near modern Jalalabad. The opening words of v 1 indicate that A's story is loosely tied to what precedes, and point to a change of source; on other occasions (App. XXVIII 25) such a change breaks the chronological sequence. If he now turns to Ar., that does not, however, show that Ar. did not himself narrate events in due order, cf. vi 22 ff. (App. XVIII) for a sequence of two narratives (Pt. and N.) covering the same events. Now A. told that Al. later wished to be honoured by the Arabians as a god like Zeus and Dionysus after equalling the latter's exploits in India (vii 20, 1 n); he probably held that Al. professed belief that Dionysus had been active in India and that Al. emulated him. Yet ' the most reliable

authorities ' ignored this theme (§ 1). The plural
could be rhetoric for the singular, and though Strabo
had apparently not read Pt. (Pearson 188) he is
surely repeating E., and the latter, librarian at
Alexandria, would naturally have studied the work
written by the ancestor of his patron and sovereign,
and have treated it with the same respect as he
accorded to Patrocles, on the ground that he was a
high official of the Seleucids (S. ii 1, 2 and 6)! On this
view the later allusions to Nysa or Dionysus in the
factual narrative (vi 2, 3; 3, 4; 14, 2) must also come
from Ar.

8. P. 58, 4 f. (though he has something close to A. v
2, 3 f.) and QC. viii 10, 7 ff. differ radically from A. in
making Nysa surrender after attack, and in some
other particulars, not agreeing *inter se*; they are, for
instance, topographically incompatible. Thus A's
account down to 2, 7 could not be the same version of
the vulgate as they knew, whereas 2, 7 corresponds to
QC. viii 10, 15 ff; J. xii 7, 8 f. If it comes from Ar.,
we should not with O. Stein (*RE* xvii 1640 ff., who
produces no cogent reasons in an exhaustive discussion) reject the Nysa incident altogether as unhistorical. A. K. Narain, *The Indo-Greeks*, 1957, ch. I
argues that the Nysaeans were in fact a people of
Greek descent, settled by the Persians in the far
east. Whatever else may be said of this hypothesis,
Ind. 1, 4 is not good support for it; the Nysaeans are
necessarily non-Indian, if descended from Dionysus'
men, and the suggestion that they *might* be Greeks
plainly implies that there was no other evidence of
their Greekness (contrast D. 110, 5).

9. Whoever ignored the legends deserves some cre-

441

dit, if he thought the identification of Indian gods
or heroes with Greek unsound, but he suppressed a
fact of some importance, if Al. and most of his entourage accepted it. The rational good sense
Eratosthenes commended was by no means the same
as the candour of the good historian, a virtue for
which Pt. is not notable.

10. A. himself was more interested in the question
whether the Heracles and Dionysus of Greek myth
had indeed visited India than whether Al. believed
that they had. He could not make up his mind to
reject the stories; the usual criteria of historical probability hardly applied where gods were concerned
(v 1, 2). He was ready to think that the Heracleses of
Greece, Tyre and Egypt were three different persons (ii 16; iv 28, 2; *Ind.* 5, 13) and that there might
be more than one Dionysus (v 1, cf. *Ind.* 7, 6, where it
may be either A. or Meg. who hints at this possibility;
Meg. certainly noted that the Indians held ' Heracles '
to have been born in their land, ib. 8, 4, cf. D. ii 39, 1).
Others distinguished three or five persons of that
name (D. iii 63 f., who has a Dionysus born and perhaps dying in India; Cicero, *Nat. Deor.* iii 58). This
pseudo-rationalization, muddle-headed, since the
identifications made certainly did not rest on homo-
nymity, was obviously intended to resolve incoher-
encies in the legends; it did not originate with A.
Nothing did!

APPENDIX XVII

INDIAN QUESTIONS

Bibliography. See J. Seibert, *Alexander der Grosse* 145 ff. The works he cites by B. Breloer may be neglected with special advantage: they are marked by unwarranted assumptions, and disregard and distortion of A's meaning. Anspach carefully examined the literary accounts and the topographical speculations of earlier scholars.

1. In the *Anabasis* A. provides few geographical descriptions, although they were thought to diversify historical narratives with the pleasures of the picturesque (*e.g.* Tacitus, *Annals* iv 33) or to be sometimes necessary for the explication of events (*e.g.* Polyb. xii 25 (e); Cicero, *de Oratore* ii 63). For A. this necessity should have been more rather than less evident, given the remoteness of the regions in which Al's campaigns were conducted, at any rate after 331. Military operations could not indeed be made easily intelligible in detail without adequate maps, but a general account of the unfamiliar conditions in which Al. had to march and fight was required for the full understanding of his campaigns in Mesopotamia, Iran, the Hindu-Kush, Turkestan and India. Ar. at least, as we know from S's citations, provided much relevant material (§ 10 f.), though perhaps he himself did not make its significance readily apparent, but inserted digressions merely to vary the tedium of a military narrative. Yet A. made little use of it. In the *Anabasis*, except for his comments on the Punjab rivers, he chose to say hardly anything even on climate

APPENDIX XVII

and topography. India, however, was to Greeks a
wonderland, and for once A. could not entirely resist
the opportunity to retail part of what he read of the
country in his sources, but he reserved this subject
(v 5, 1) for a special monograph, the *Indica*.

2. This monograph does not exactly correspond to his
advertisement. More than half of it is a narrative of
Nearchus' voyages. The general account of Indian
geography and customs (1–17) is expressly characterized as ancillary (17, 7). A's main purpose is clear:
the romantic story of N's exploration was to accompany
the *Anabasis* as a small scale Odyssey to A's Iliad.

3. Nearchus, a Cretan by birth, was one of those
Greeks who had been enrolled among the Companions (Introd. 34) with a fief at Amphipolis (*Ind.* 18,
4 and 10). He counted himself as a Macedonian. A
boyhood friend of Al. and banished by Philip on that
account (iii 6, 5), he had been appointed satrap of
Lycia and Pamphylia (i 24, 4), but rejoined the army
in 329/8 (iv 7, 2), and became chiliarch of the hypaspists (iv 30, 5), i.e. of Macedonian troops, commander
of the river flotilla in 326 (vi 2, 3) and finally admiral
of the fleet. The warmth of Al's feelings for him no
doubt loses nothing in his telling (*Ind.* 20, cf. 35). It
probably much impressed A. His marriage at Susa
to a daughter of Al's former mistress (vii 4, 6) is
objective proof of his importance while Al. was alive.
He played only a subordinate part in the conflicts that
ensued on Al's death; he last appears in Antigonus'
service in 314. His book evidently came out after
Onesicritus of Astypalaea had published his account,
partly as a correction, but its date cannot be precisely fixed.

4. Such was A's confidence in N's veracity that he apparently did not consult this rival account. O. was pilot of Al's own ship in the river flotilla (*Ind.* 18, 9; vi 2, 3) and ' chief pilot ' (S. xv 2, 4) or ' commander of the pilots ' (Plut. 331 E) on the coastal voyage, probably in N's flagship. This was clearly an important position, since he was decorated, like N., for his services (vii 5, 6); Badian (*Yale Cl. Studies* 1975) adduces a parallel from D. xx 50, 4, which shows that such an officer could be given a tactical command in battle. No doubt O. exaggerated his role, calling himself navarch or admiral of the river flotilla; the repudiation of this claim (vi 2, 3) may come from Pt., there A's main source (2, 4). It is true that A. cites O. in *Ind.* 3, 6 and 6, 8, but (it seems) from the works of E. and Meg.; he never refers to the information he gave about the coastal voyage, which was not always congruent with N's, as we can tell from Pliny (who regarded him as ' classis praefectus ', *NH* vi 81). A. had learned from his other sources to view him as mendacious (vi 2, 3). That was also the opinion of S., who none the less held that he had some plausible and noteworthy things to say (xv 1, 28, cf. ii 1, 9); moreover, S's, or E's, harsh judgement applied to N. too, not without reason, for he retails fables and is given to exaggerations (E. Badian, *op. cit.* is too severe). A. condemned O. unread (cf. also § 8 at end), although he had much to tell about Al's whole expedition, and particularly about India and its people, and one might have expected the pupil of Epictetus to take some interest in the work of a pupil of Diogenes the Cynic. Some modern scholars, Pearson and Truesdell S. Brown (*Onesicritus*, 1949), have come to his defence, yet he was among those who said that Al. met the queen of the Amazons. Whatever his merits or

faults, A. lacked the curiosity to discover them for himself, or perhaps the energy to attempt so much collation of rival accounts as in the *Anabasis*; in the *Indica* he generally follows one authority at a time. As for the versions of N's voyage given by Androsthenes (vii 20, 7; *Ind.* 18, 4), cited by E., Theophrastus and Athenaeus (Jacoby no. 711), and of Orthagoras, apparently one of N's men (ib. no. 713, cf. *RE* xviii 1424 ff.), A. may not have known that they existed; he did not necessarily study E. with care.

5. N., like Onesicritus, did more than simply describe the river and Ocean voyages; he also gave at least brief accounts of other events connected with them, see vi 13, 4; 24, 2; cf. *Ind.* 23, 5 and 40. Jacoby supposed that he was A's main source for vi 1–5 (he is used but not cited in 1, 2 f.) and 18, 2–21, 2 (A. silently prefers his view to that of Ar. in 20, 3); but as to the former passage, though A. may have taken graphic details from N., e.g. 4, 4–5, 4, it seems unlikely that he used the same source for two accounts of the same transactions, which are indeed sometimes complementary but sometimes divergent; 2, 4 plainly indicates that he was mainly following Pt., and where the accounts agree it is doubtless because both Pt. and N. reported the facts accurately. By contrast 18, 2–21, 2 fills a gap in the *Indica* and may well be from N. A. also follows him in vi 24, 4–25, 6 (App. XVIII 2), and cites him in vii 3, 6, perhaps from his general account of the Brahmans, ignored in *Indica*; probably it is N. he has in mind, when he refers to the silence of good witnesses other than Pt. and Ar. (vi 28, 2; vii 13, 3, cf. 3, 6). However, N's evidence is not fully integrated, except in vi 18 f., into the general narrative (cf. vi 21, 3 with *Ind.* 22,

10 n.; vi 27, 1; vii 4, 1 and 7, 1 nn.; 15, 1 with *Ind*. 40, 6–8; 16, 5 nn.). Again, Nearchus, like Onesicritus, Ar. (F 35–42), and indeed Clitarchus (F 17–23), had much to say (F 12–28) on the land, people, animals and plants of India (cf. also *Ind*. 38; S. xv 2, 4 on Carmania), but A. made no such attempt as S. did to collate different accounts, and found it convenient to rely chiefly on Meg. Jacoby (no. 715) prints as fragments of Meg. *Ind*. 4, 1–15, 7, omitting only a few sections as comments of A. or insertions from N. But I would add the first chapter (see note); cf. nn. on 4, 15; 5, 13; 10, 9 restricting A's comments; I do not know why 10, 1 is not credited to Meg., and I suspect that 6, 4–9, though ultimately derived from N., who is not named, was taken by A. from Meg., just as in 3, 6 N. is mediated through E. (11, 6 is doubtless a direct citation). A. turns to N. in 15, 1, and with a single addition from Meg. in 15, 5–7 may then keep to him (though this cannot be proved for every item) for the small remaining part of his description of India. (The source of A's information, when not expressly recorded, can generally be ascertained by comparison with S., who is liberal with citations.) A's procedure thus suggests that he took little pains in collation, and preferred to follow first one of his authorities and then the other. Ar., who also provided comparable information on many points, he now totally ignores. Nor did it occur to him that Meg. was describing a quite different region in India from that which the historians of Al. had known.

6. Meg. was associated with Sibyrtius (v 6, 2), appointed by Al. satrap of Arachosia and Gadrosia (vi 27, 1), where he is last found in 316 (D. xix 48), and

was sent to the court of ' Sandrocottus ' as ambassador (S. ii 1, 9), probably by Seleucus (Jacoby no. 715 T. 1); he often referred to this mission in his work, the *Indica*, which filled probably four books (ib. F. 1–3), and mentioned his presence in Sandracottus' army, estimated at 400,000 (!) men (S. xv 1, 53), cf. v 6, 2; *Ind.* 5, 3; *contra* O. Stein, *RE* xv 231 ff., there is no proof that he visited Sandracottus more than once, or stayed long (cf. Strabo xv 1, 2). Sandracottus is his name for Chandragupta (*CHI* ch. XVIII), whose capital was Pali(m)bothra, i.e. Patna, but who was able after Porus' murder in 317 (§ 32) to subdue all the lands east of Indus; in 303 Seleucus had to cede to him Parapamisus, Arachosia and part of Gadrosia, perhaps also Areia (P. 62, 2 with Hamilton's notes); he died in the next decade. Meg. thus penetrated to the Ganges; he gave measurements of the distance by the royal road from the Indus to Palibothra, but could only report what he was told about the length of voyages thence to the Ganges mouth (S. xv 1, 11, cf. *Ind.* 3, 4; Pliny, *NH* vi 63 f.). There is no evidence that he himself knew the lower Punjab or Sind. His account concerns Chandragupta's kingdom, so far as it rests on autopsy. It is cited (apart from A.) chiefly by S. (O. Stein, *RE* xv 267 ff., proved that D. ii 35–42, which Jacoby prints as F. 4, derives in part from different sources, though it seems to me unlikely on general grounds that it was D. himself who combined the data of Meg. and other writers.) Much of what Meg. reported clearly came from what Indians told him (App. XVI 2; cf. *Ind.* 9, 2; 15, 7; S. xv 1, 59; perhaps D. ii 37, 5 f.; 38, 2 f.), including the stories of marvels (O. Stein, *op. cit.* 236–45; 301 ff.) that E. adduced to prove his mendacity; doubtless, like Onesicritus (S. xv 1, 64), he found it hard to ascertain through interpreters what his informants really meant. Under E's influence, A. almost ignores such stories in Meg. (S. ii 1, 9; xv 1, 56 f.; F 27–30); elephants apart, he also repeats little of what Meg. wrote on Indian plants and animals (F 8; 21–5; 30). But he uses him to supplement E. on Indian geography, and Meg. is his chief source for Indian ' history '. S. is fuller especially on political institutions (xv 1, 39–41; 45–55), as also on the Brahmans (ib. 58–60), and A. does not bring out the way in which Meg. idealized the simple and virtuous life of the Indians (ib. 53–5). Perhaps v 4, 4 contains a reminiscence of this. D. ii 39, 5 probably followed Meg. in claiming that the Indians respected equality, and Meg's account of the seven ' castes ' (*Ind.* 11 f.) was perhaps designed to show how each contributed to the common weal. Much of this, e.g. his claim that slavery was unknown, was wide of the truth. Meg. seems to have interpreted what he heard and saw to make it fit Greek philosophical models, just as he also employed perhaps inapposite Greek political terms in describing the government (O. Stein, *op. cit.* 273–84).

7. A. also cites (v 3; 5 f.) the geographical work of the great scientist, Eratosthenes of Cyrene (*c.* 280–200), who was librarian at Alexandria (see P. M. Fraser, *Ptolemaic Alexandria* 197; 456 f.; 529 ff., and esp. 535). E. took the Indus to be the western boundary of India (v 4, 3; 6, 3; *Ind* 2, 1); this conception apparently went back to Meg. (cf. v 6, 2 f.; *Ind*. 1 n.). It was hardly that of Al's other sources; in iv 22–30, as in iii 8 etc. he freely speaks of Indians west of Indus, a view justified by the linguistic evidence of proper names, and Pliny, *NH* vi 78 says that the Kabul was

commonly taken as the boundary. As in his use of the names Caucasus and Tanais (App. XII), A. oscillated between the nomenclature of his main sources and later theory. In v 3, 1 f. and 5 f. he seems to be following E., as (without citing him) in *Ind.* 2 f., cf. S. ii 1, 4 ff.; xv 1, 10 ff. So too he follows E. on the mouth of the Danube (*Ind.* 2, 5 n.). Cf. also *Ind.* 3, 9 and 10 nn. The incorrect estimates of India's dimensions and the polemic in *Ind.* 3 come from E., more fully summarized by Strabo *ll. cc.* (see diagrams in *CHI* 400 f.). Both A. and Strabo xv 1, 12 reject the opinions of Ctesias, Onesicritus, Nearchus and Megasthenes in identical order, which shows that even when they had read these authors for themselves, they here drew the citations from E., just as A. presumably cites Ctesias from E. on the breadth of the Indus in v 3, 2, not correlating it with an estimate (Ar?) in v 20, 10; S. xv 1, 32 has yet other figures, together with material from Meg. Embedded in v 6, there is a comparison (4 ff.) between the Indus and Anatolian rivers which was drawn by N. (S. xv 1, 16 f.); it was he who quoted Homer (cf. vi 1, 3 n.) to show that the Nile had once been called Aegyptus. But E., who read and cited N., is presumably again the intermediate source. I doubt if N. also referred to Hdt. If he had read Hdt., he was in ill faith in never referring to the voyage of Scylax (App. XV). Moreover one can hardly dissociate the allusion to Hdt. from that to Hecataeus (Jacoby no. 1 F. 301), and the authenticity of the work that went under his name was first questioned by E's elder contemporary at Alexandria, Callimachus (Athenaeus ii 70 A); these doubts, expressed by A., are too early for N., and (in my judgement) too learned for an independent insertion by A. himself, but should come from E.

APPENDIX XVII

(That they are not mentioned by S. is evidence that A. did not get his knowledge of E. from S.) E. was of course quite capable of adding comments to N. So was S., and in xv 1, 32 the allusion to Hdt., in direct speech, looks like his own gloss on N., reported in indirect. I am not persuaded by the other proofs of N's imitation of Hdt. in Pearson ch. V. For instance, the similarity of the alluvial plain of India and Egypt was evident to many eye-witnesses (v 4, 4 n. 7).

8. S. xv 1, 2 remarks that few Greeks had visited India, and none for long, that their accounts rested largely on hearsay, and that the Alexander-historians often contradicted each other on what they had seen; he treats Meg. and, still more, Daimachus as even greater liars (ii 1, 9). These criticisms were probably in part unfair, in so far as the writers concerned did not pretend to do more than relate what they had been told. They evidently spring from E. (cf. A. v 3; S. ii 1, 9 and 19), who set a higher value on the geographical evidence of Patrocles (App. XII 2), but this hardly impinged on India (Jacoby no. 712). It is surely from recollection of E's criticisms that A. expresses some reservations on Meg's reliability, at least when he is reporting hearsay (*Ind.* 4, 1; 5, 1–3; 6, 1 ff.; 7, 1; 15, 7) and refuses to tell or accept some of the tall stories he found in his sources (v 3, 3; 4, 3; *Ind.* 9, 4–6; 15, 4 ff.). Yet he still regards Meg. as well as E. as a reputable source (v 5, 1; *Ind.* 17, 6), even through he had seen little of India (*Ind.* 5, 3). He also oscillates between E. and the tradition on the tales of Dionysus and Heracles (App. XVI). In fact, the stock of information about India had increased but little even in S's time (xv 1, 3 f.); E. had had no

option but to map the country by applying his mathematical and astronomical knowledge to the data supplied by authorities he despised, and S. had to judge between his and rival theories (book ii *passim*) on the same basis. Despite the increased sea-borne trade between Egypt and India (ii 5, 12), which supplied a little new information (xv 1, 3 and 72 f.; 2, 13), S. mistrusting merchants' reports (xv 1, 4) still turned in the main to the Alexander-historians and to Meg. (xv 1 *passim*) for a detailed description. (This was probably not provided by E., who could anyhow only have given it at second hand.) In S. this was perhaps excusable, but between his time and A's the discovery of the trade-winds in the Indian Ocean had facilitated navigation, and geographical knowledge had accumulated, some of which appears in a jumbled form in Pliny's *Natural History* and in the *Geography* of A's eminent contemporary, the scientist Ptolemy (Claudius Ptolemaeus). See further J. O. Thomson, *Hist. of Ancient Geography*, 1948 (index *s.v.* India); *RE* ix 1264 ff. (Wecker). A. was perhaps vaguely aware of this, but indifferent to it (cf. *Ind.* 43, 3). He repeats only what had been said three or more centuries earlier, even transcribing from his source an anachronistic analogy between India and Hellenistic Sparta (*Ind.* 10, 9 n.). Hence he is as ignorant of south India as they were, more ignorant than Onesicritus, who had heard of Taprobane or Ceylon (S. xv 1, 15): another proof that he never read O.

9. A's survey in *Ind.* 1—17 is neither as full nor as well-proportioned an account of what he read in Meg. and N. as that of S. xv 1 (where Ar. and O. are also used). Thus S. has much more on the system of

castes (§ 39–49, cf. D. ii 40 ff., which they both call *mere*; A's *genea* better brings out their hereditary character); in fact there were only four, not seven (*CHI* 53 f. etc., cf. 409 on Meg's error). The author of a treatise on hunting could not resist the impulse to give a lengthy description of Indian methods of catching elephants (13), yet he says relatively little on the Brahmans (11, 8 n. but cf. vii 1–3), though they played some part in the resistance to Al. (vi 7, 4; 16, 5; 17, 2), and long continued to fascinate Greeks with philosophic interests, as they had fascinated Ar., N., O. and Meg. (S. xv 1, 39, 59–61, 63–6, 68, 70 f.). He omits most of what Meg. reported on the government of Chandragupta's realm and says little of the powers of the Indian kings or the Republican system of peoples named in the *Anabasis*. There are only brief allusions to the economy (11, 9; 17, 5), nothing of the astonishing fertility of the river plains with two harvests a year which had excited the attention of Ar. and N. (S. xv 1, 18) as well as Meg. and Eratosthenes (ib. 20, cf. D. ii 35 f.), or of rice as the staple diet (Ar. and Meg. *ap.* S. 18 and 53), or of the cultivation of sugar, which was imported from India in A's day (ib. 20, from N., cf. Pliny, *NH* xii 32). Yet Indian productivity enabled Al. to obtain supplies for an army, which was certainly larger, with native auxiliaries, than ever before, even though estimates in our sources may be exaggerated (App. XIII 8); note v 9, 3; 21, 1 and 4; vi 20, 5.

10. What most impressed A. was the number and size of the Indian rivers. Accustomed to torrential streams, which often dried up in summer, Greeks and Romans were fascinated by the broad, perennial and navigable rivers of other lands, cf. Hdt. iv 47–58; S.

iv 1, 2, 11, 14 and 32 f. A's account in *Ind.* 4–6 comes mainly from Meg. and v 4–6 from E., but he reverts to the subject in v 9; 20, 8 f., 21, 4 and 6, vi 1; 3, 1 and 3, 4, 2 and 4, 4–5, 4; 12, 2; 14, 5. Since the rivers formed obstacles to Al's advance in summer 326 and carried his forces down to the Indian Ocean in 326–5, descriptions of them were highly relevant, but the way in which A. harps on them and the details he gives notably contrast with the general sparseness of geographical material. Pt. commented only on the greatness of the Acesines (v 20, 8 f.). Ar., perhaps supplemented by N., must be the source for A's account of Indian, and probably of all other rivers (cf. App. XXVIII 23).

11. It is unfortunate that A. did not follow Ar. more often in his attention to geography (App. XXVII 23). As for India, Ar. remarked that rain fell at Taxila, and that there were continuous rains after Porus' defeat all the way to the Beas (S. xv 1, 17); this agrees well with D's statement (94, 3) that at that point it had been raining heavily for 70 days (cf. § 13). D. gives plausible particulars of the misery caused and says that it had done much to undermine the troops' morale, which Al. tried to raise by ravaging expeditions, and that this contributed to the ' mutiny '. S. xv 1, 27 confirms this, and he is probably following Ar. (§ 18 below). Of course Ar. too described the Acesines in spate, and N. told how Al's camp there was all but swept away (S. 18, cf. *Ind.* 6, 4 ff.); no wonder that for once Pt. broke his silence. But A. has nothing of the hardships; he merely records the thunderstorm at the Hydaspes (v 12, 3; 13, 3; cf. 15, 5), the swollen rivers (9, 4) and the damage to Al's colonies (29, 5). A. was at fault in keeping too

closely to Pt's dry record of military operations, cf. App. XVIII; XXVIII 23.

12. Pliny, *NH* vi 62 f., shows that the bematists (App. VIII 1) continued to record the stages of Al's march in India; their data combined with those procured by Seleucus, doubtless through Meg., were the basis for the computations made by Meg. and others of the total distance from the Indus to the mouth of the Ganges (*Ind.* 3, 4; S. xv 1, 11). Pt. himself may well have recorded with the help of these data the marches of Al's army. Vestiges of such ' log-book ' documentation appear, when A. tells how many days Al. took over particular marches (v 22, 3; vi 4, 1 and 4; 6, 2; 8, 1 f.; 9, 1; 20, 4; 24, 1). But he gives no distances, and these scattered data lack any clear chronological context. A. is also vague about precise locations or direction of marches. The lack of maps was an almost insuperable problem; still Ar. had something of value which he neglects.

13. Sir Aurel Stein conjecturally assigned the capture of Aornos to April 326 (iv 29, 1 n.); this fits all the reliable chronological data for later operations. From Aornos Al. might have returned to Embolima (iv 28, 7), whence QC. viii 12, 1–4 takes him on the 16th day to the Indus; for such ' log-book ' information in QC. cf. App. VIII 4–6; 10 etc. He crossed, near Peucelaotis (Charsadda), cf. iv 22, 7; S. xv 1, 27 (probably Ar., cf. § 18), probably just above the confluence with the Kabul (Anspach, n. 98, cf. § 17). D. 86, 3 makes him wait there 30 days *before* crossing. This is implausible, since he could only expect the Indus to rise as the snows melted. The same figure occurs where it is certainly incor-

rect (App. VIII 11) or again questionable (*infra*); it is probably conventional, as also in 110, 6. On the other hand, the Alexander-historians had much to tell of Taxila (§ 31), where there may have been a longish pause; there is no reason to reject QC's report (viii 13, 2) that Al. sent an envoy to demand submission, and he may have waited some time for the adverse reply, as he had waited in Afghanistan for news of the attitude of Taxilas etc. (App. VIII 19).

14. Pliny, *NH* vi 61, gives the distance from Taxila to the Hydaspes as 120 Roman miles, i.e. 960 stades or about 178 km. (App. VIII 1 and 12). The march need not have taken Al's army long, but that he had to have the boats constructed for crossing the Indus conveyed in sections to the Hydaspes (v 8, 4 f.). The rafts also used to ferry his troops over that river may have been made on the spot, but this work would also have taken time. We do not know the interval between his leaving Taxila and the battle, which one or both of A's main sources put, very precisely, just after the summer solstice (v 9, 4), i.e. in late June. On this basis Al. might have left Taxila in May. The rain that Ar. mentions as falling there (S. xv 1, 17) must have been one of the occasional spring storms of the N. Punjab; the rainy season *normally* lasts from about mid-June to mid-September, and the rivers, already high from the Himalayan snows, are in full spate from mid-July. The Hydaspes, despite 9, 4, was obviously not so swollen as the Acesines was later on (v 20). D. once again reports a pause of 30 days after Porus' defeat, but N. *ap.* S. xv 1, 18 dates the arrival at the Acesines to ' *about* the time of the summer solstice '. We must believe N.; his expression, like our ' midsummer ', is vaguer than v

9, 4 and could fit mid, perhaps even late, July, but if we accept D's testimony, the army could hardly have already got so far after fighting at the end of June. Once again we should reject D. There is no need to posit a long pause even for the foundation of the colonies, cf. 20, 1 with 19, 4. The great storm in the night before the battle was doubtless the earnest of the monsoon rains, which could have begun a little late and which on Ar's testimony went on continuously from the time of the victory to the return of the army to the Hydaspes at the rising of Arcturus, say early October. D's 70 days of heavy rains down to the arrival at the Beas would date that to early September, as a month seems adequate for the pause there, and the return march, which was not (like the advance) punctuated by military operations.

15. The battle is wrongly dated earlier in v 19, 3, as the Attic month Munichion corresponds to April/May, i.e. at latest, mid-May. This can easily be combined with D. and N., but not with A. v 9, 4. A. draws from an unknown chronographer seven dates by Athenian reckoning in the *Anabasis*, of which those in ii 11, 10 and iii 15, 7 have the wrong months (see notes); there is, I think, no way of testing the accuracy of ii 24, 6; and in vii 28, 1 the name of the month is lost. There remain two further dates (iii 7, 1 and 22, 2), which may be correct. In *Ind.* 21, 1 A. has the wrong archon, Cephisodorus (323/2) in place of Anticles (325/4); the error can hardly be blamed on a copyist! Chronological indications A. found in his main sources should always have more authority than these dates. For inaccuracies in chronographic sources see Jacoby's tables in his notes on no. 239 B 1–27.

16. It had long been noted that a spot for the crossing of the Hydaspes at or near Jalalpur best fitted S's statement (xv 1, 32), taken from Ar. (§ 18), that Al. marched south to that river and Pliny's figure for the distance. Sir Aurel Stein (*Archaeol. Reconnaissances in N.W. India*, 1937, improving on *Geogr. Journal* lxxx, 1932, 31 ff.) argued that he reached the river at Haranpur after defeating an attempt (Polyaenus iv 3, 21) by Porus' kinsman and general ' Pittacus ' (perhaps Spitaces, v 18, 2) to hold him up in a defile that can be placed in the Salt Range. He crossed upstream (cf. Frontinus, *Stratagems* i 4, 9) at Jalalpur, 17½ miles away, a distance that corresponds to A's 150 stades (v 11, 2), by a road out of Porus' sight. At Jalalpur there is a bend in the river, admittedly slight, and a headland jutting out from the Salt Range (which prevents in this sector any westward shift in the river's course, cf. § 25); the island opposite is properly described (by QC. viii 13, 17) as the largest in the river, and a ravine with a stream, which runs down just above Jalalpur, and in which the troops could have been covertly embarked, corresponds to QC's *praealta fossa*. (As often, QC. preserves good topographical information.) Jalalpur, where Greek coins have been found, would thus be the ancient Bucephala (v 19, 4 n.). Some scholars continue to prefer to place the crossing at Jhelun, but there the terrain is totally unsuited to the manoeuvres on the opposite side of the river.

17. For the battle itself see D. 87–9 (who abbreviates his source to the point of not recording the crossing); QC. viii 13, 5–xiv 46; P. 60, partly based on a ' letter ' of Al., which some think authentic (*contra* Introd. 15); Polyaenus iv 3, 22, cf. 9 and 21, who certainly drew on

the vulgate (ib. 6 and 17 for use of ' Arbela '). A.
14, 3 ff. notes discrepancies between Ar., the vulgate
and Pt. The suggestion by Schwartz (*RE* ii 917)
that Ar. (14, 3) simply modified the vulgate version
recorded in 14, 4 is wanton, especially as there is no
evidence that 14, 4 represents Clitarchus rather than
some later version of the vulgate, such as A. normally
seems to use (App. XXVIII 13). It is clear that Porus
must have had scouts at the point of crossing, who
sent word to Porus of Al's movement, as a result of
which Porus despatched his son, but too late to prevent the crossing. Ar. perhaps had a false impression of the strength of the scouts and confused it with
that brought up by Porus' son. A. was right to prefer Pt's evidence, since Pt. was actually with Al.
(13, 1), and Ar. presumably was not; his own reasons
for rejecting Ar. are not cogent, since he assumes
without warrant that Porus realized Al's strength and
must have taken the most appropriate measures; in
fact, the chariots he sent stuck in the mud (15, 2).
Modern reconstructions of the battle usually start
from A., but as his description is sometimes careless,
sometimes ambiguous (see notes), they often end in
fantasies like Tarn's, in which more or less coherent
fictions are invested with the habiliments of historical truth. Fuller, 180 ff., is at least sensible, but
I doubt if the full truth can ever be ascertained.

18. S. xv 1, 26 says that at the outset of his Indian
campaign Al. decided to take a northerly route, since
he had learned that the mountainous region was more
habitable, fertile and cool, and that the rivers would
be easier to cross nearer their sources and above the
confluences. Though he marched southwards to the
Hydaspes, he then took a more easterly direction,

keeping to the foothills rather than to the plains (ib.
32). S. probably did not read Pt. (Pearson 188) and
thought ill of Onesicritus; he seldom cites Clitarchus;
N. is unlikely to have described the land route in the
north, and Ar., the only historian of Al. S. never expressly decries, was his named authority elsewhere
(ib. 17) for Al's route in India. So too his account of
Al's route from Hyrcania to Bactria (xv 2, 10) seems
to come from Ar., cf. A. iii 28, 5–7. On this ground
alone we may agree with Tarn (ii 32 f.) that Ar. gave
all the particulars about Al's march that S. mentions
in xv 1, 17–33, as distinguished from digressions in
which he names other authorities as well. Though
Ar. wrote of the continuous summer rains, he held
also (unlike N.) that the Indian plains, as distinct
from the mountains and foothills, were free from rain
as well as snow in the summer (S. 17 f.); he would not
have classified the terrain of Al's marches in summer
326 in or close to the foothills as ' plains '. It is not
inconsistent with his account that when Al. actually
reached the Acesines (fairly far to the north) he found
it best to cross at a point where the stream was wider
but less rapid (A. v 20, 9). In the foothills timber was
already being cut for shipbuilding, in preparation for
the voyage to the Indus mouths (App. XXV 2).

18a. Tarn ii 32 also argues plausibly that S's use of
Hypanis for Beas comes from Ar., whereas A. usually
preferred Pt's Hyphasis; he adduces probable parallels. (His argument from S. xv 1, 3 and 33 is not
cogent, since Onesicritus, cited in 33, certainly did
come from Astypalaea near Cos, and he rather than
Ar. could be S's source for the comparison in size
between Cos and Indian cities.) Hypanis may indeed have been the form preferred by other writers

APPENDIX XVII

S. used (xi 11, 1; xv 1, 3; 33; 37), e.g. Meg. (cf. perhaps D. ii 37); in that case A. has deliberately substituted Hyphasis in *Ind.* 4, where he follows Meg., though he normally simply adopts the usage of his source. If Tarn is right, Hyarotis (S.) for Hydraotes (A.) should also come from Ar. A. himself preserves one instance of divergence between Ar. and Pt. on proper names (v 20, 2). For other cases see Bosworth on iii 8, 4 (Topeirians); 24, 7 (Autophradates); 25, 7 (see my notes on vi 15, 5; vii 6, 2); such divergences indicate how A. turned from one main source to another more often than has sometimes been allowed. Ar. perhaps noted the local name for the Syr-Darya, and for the Zeravshan, though he certainly used for the latter the name that the Macedonians attached to it (App. XII 4; iii 30, 7; vii 16, 3; S. xi 11, 5). For other divergences in nomenclature in which A. reflects different sources see App. XXVI 2; *Ind.* 1, 1 n.

19. The general course of Al's route makes it plausible that the Glausai (v 20, 2) were to be found near Bember (Anspach 62), though there is no proof, and this actually involves a northward, not an eastward, route from Jalalpur. Al. would then have been threatening Abisares. Anspach further supposes (66) that Al. crossed the Chenab (Acesines) between Sialkot and Wezirabad, where the river normally flows in several streams that unite in flood, leaving rocky islands (v 20, 8), and (67) that he reached the Ravi (Hydraotes) a little below Nainakot, and (77) the Beas (Hyphasis) near Gurdaspur. Some such route must be posited, but precision is delusive, especially for those operations which could have taken detachments of the army south of the main

route that Ar. described. Our sources contain only vague and sometimes contradictory data, and the identification of peoples by their Sanskrit names seems precarious, and topographically unrewarding.

20. The territory of the ' bad ' Porus lay between the Chenab and the Ravi, and probably south of the route that Al. himself took (v 21, 2 and 5). The Adraestae and Cathaeans are placed by A. (21, 6 ff.) beyond the Ravi. D. 90 puts the operations against them after only one river crossing (90, 4); he has simply left another out, if his source is that of QC., who refers first to an unnamed rapid river, evidently the Acesines, and then to the Hydraotes by name (ix 1, 8 and 13), before narrating the operations against Adraestae and Cathaeans; QC. names neither, and has but one resemblance to A's story; still that is sufficient; the ' marsh ' by the city captured in ix 1, 18 is A's ' lake ' near Sangala (v 23, 6 ff.). Thus all three writers agreed on the location of the Cathaeans, but D. and QC. go on to recount the surrender of their neighbour, the ' king ' Sopithes, whom A. places somewhere near the east bank of the Hydaspes (vi 2, 2), though the reference in S. xv 1, 30 to the ' mountain of mineral salt ' suggests that he also ruled in the Salt Range on the other side. None thinks that Sopithes ruled over the Cathaeans, whom A. calls ' self-governing ' or Republican (v 22, 1), but Onesicritus *ap.* S. (1, 2) says that they chose the handsomest man as king, and he may be responsible for what S. probably reports (the text is uncertain), that Sopithes ruled over them; thence, knowing that Sopithes by some accounts had his territory between Hydaspes and Acesines, he thought this a possible location for the Cathaeans too,

while also noting that others made them neighbours
of the ' bad ' Porus. To add to the confusion, he says
that Porus (not Sopithes, as Anspach misconstrues
the Greek) ruled in Gandaris (a name otherwise un-
attested in this region), whereas D. 91, 1 makes him
flee to the ' Gandaridae ', i.e. to the Ganges (§ 22).
Alii alia; Anspach believed in two lots of Cathaeans
and two kings called Sopithes. I think it futile to
affirm more than what A. and the source of D. and
QC. concur in: the bad Porus ruled between Chenab
and Ravi, and the Cathaeans lived between Ravi and
Beas.

21. D. 93 gives the breadth of the Hyphasis, where
Al. reached it, as over 7 stades. This would fit a
point near Gurdaspur (§ 19) and the place where it
debouches into the plain. This again agrees with
the hypothesis that Al. kept close to the foothills.
Pliny, *NH* vi 62, makes it 390 miles from Hydaspes to
Hyphasis, twice the true distance (Kiessling, *RE* ix
230 ff.), but all would be in order, if Pliny confused
this distance with that from Peucelaotis, an error
precisely similar to that which I traced in App. VIII
13.

22. A. says that Al. was told that beyond the Beas
the country was fertile (cf. S. xv 1, 37) and inhabited
by good fighting men with more elephants than he
had so far met (v 25, 1). D. 93 and QC. ix 1, 36–2, 4
relate that before he reached it a ruler called Phegeus
(whose name Anspach, n. 245, connected with the
local river Begas-Ganga) submitted to Al. and told
him that after a 12 days' march across desert he would
come to the Ganges. This was of course nonsense;
if Al. kept to the north, there was no desert, but the

Sutlej (*Ind.* 4, 13 n.) and Jumna lay between him and the upper Ganges, and the distance was far greater. On the Ganges, Phegeus allegedly said, there lived the Gandaridae (D.; 'Gangaridae', QC.) and Tabraesii (D.; 'Prasii', QC.) under king Xandrammes (D.; 'Aggrammes', QC.) with 20,000 cavalry, 200,000 foot, 200 chariots and 4000 (D.; 3000 QC.) elephants. P. 62 (not mentioning Phegeus) speaks of kings of the Gandarites and Praesii with 80,000 horse, 20,000 foot, 8000 chariots and 6000 elephants, and adds that this was no 'idle boast', since 'Androcottus' (Chandragupta, cf. § 6) gave Seleucus 500 elephants and overran India with 600,000 men; presumably these last figures came from Meg. Chandragupta was in fact heir to a kingdom with its centre at Patna, which he greatly aggrandised (*CHI* ch. XIII; p. 469). D. and QC. say that Porus confirmed Phegeus' reports but alleged that the king was of low birth and character and could easily be conquered. It is inherently likely that Al. obtained information from Phegeus and Porus and that he heard of this kingdom and of the Ganges. 'Prasii' or 'Praesii' reflects the Sanskrit word for 'easterners' and was thus the name given in the Punjab to the people round Patna. 'Gangaridae', for which there is no Sanskrit equivalent, probably means 'dwellers on the Ganges'; Pliny (vi 66), probably following Meg., puts them ('Gangaridae Calingae') in the Ganges delta. The name was sometimes written 'Gandaridae' by assimilation to Gandaritis in NW India; see Kiessling, *RE* VII 694 ff. But what Al. learned and what the 'vulgate' reports are two different things, cf. perhaps S. ii 1, 6. Clitarchus, for instance, may have retailed camp gossip, which was then modified (as the discrepancies

show) by later writers according to taste. The
' vulgate ' differed from Meg. (S. xv 1, 35; *Ind.* 4, 7),
making the Ganges only 32 stades broad (100, Meg.)
but 100 fathoms deep (minimum of 20, Meg.).

23. Ar. (App. XXVII 5) made it clear that Al. was
prevented from going beyond the Hyphasis by
opposition in the army, voiced by Coenus; Pt. indeed
tried to suggest that unfavourable omens were decisive (28, 4). The speeches are A's invention
(App. XXVII 5 f.), in which he uses material perhaps
from Ar., perhaps from elsewhere; so 26, 1 is not good
authority that Al. had heard of the Ganges (though he
surely had) or that he designed to reach the Bay of
Bengal. But where would he have wished to stop
except at the Ocean stream? In later legend he
turned back only at the Ganges! See e.g. D. ii 37,
which cannot come from Meg.

24. Al. had returned to the Hydaspes (by the same
route, D. 95, 3; QC. ix 3, 20) in early October (§ 14). I
Ar. made him start downstream a few days before the
morning setting of the Pleiads and reach Patalene
about the rising of the dog-star (S. xv 1, 17). I
assume that here and elsewhere historians intended
such astronomical marks of time to be intelligible to
Greek readers and refer to the visibility of stars in
Greece, for which cf. *RE* xxi 2505 ff. The dates are
thus early Nov. 326 and July 325. But Ar. also made
the voyage last ten months (ibid.), perhaps rounding
its length upwards; we must also allow for the stay
in Patalene. P. 66, 1 gives only seven months.
The voyage was of course prolonged by Al's convalescence (vi 14, 4). Pliny, *NH* vi 60, makes it last only a
little over 5 months, but on the Indus alone, and he

may include the time in the Indus delta; in any event we must prefer Ar's testimony. He also said that no rain fell throughout the voyage; such droughts are well attested in Sind. Al. left for Gadrosia while Nearchus was still awaiting the favourable winds that blow from early winter and the morning setting of the Pleiads (vi 21, 2). In fact N. sailed by his own account at the time of the evening rising of the Pleiads (S. xv 2, 5), in late September or early October and not in November; this fits *Ind.* 21, 1 (Boedromion = September/October; the archon year is erroneous) but, as the monsoon began to blow again, he made hardly any progress till late October or November. Al. probably left in early September, and thus reached Pura in early December (App. XVIII 6). N., as abbreviated by S., says that he was completing his march when N. sailed; this was not far from the truth if N. really referred to the time when the winds at last enabled him to proceed. Cf. also App. XXIII 1; Beloch III 2, 321: there is no ground for pushing Al's departure back to July (Engels 135 f.), against Ar's evidence.

25. In the plains the Indus and its tributaries have been continuously shifting their courses westwards (Stein, *op. cit.* in § 16, 1 ff.), except where there is any such obstacle as the Salt Range: Ar. himself observed how such a change in the course of the Indus had turned a once populous country into a desert (S. xv 1, 19); hence the waterless country of v 6, 1 and the desert of 8, 1 cannot safely be identified. The continuous deposit of silt has extended the delta and lengthened the course of the rivers, and their points of confluence will have changed. Thus Patala must have lain much to the north of the present delta and

east of the modern river course, perhaps at Bahmana-
bad east of Hyderabad. But the alluvial plain has
few marked features except the rivers. Hence from
the ancient accounts, which anyhow contain little
topographical description, and which are not fully
consistent, we cannot precisely locate the peoples and
cities they mention. The equations of Mallians and
Oxydracae with Sanskrit Malavas and Kshudrakas
give no aid. Modern conjectures hardly illuminate
A's narrative.

26. From Jalalabad (§ 16) the fleet proceeded downstream, with Craterus on the west bank and Hephaestion and Philip on the east (vi 2, 2 f.); Philip was
soon despatched to the west bank of the Chenab
(4, 1). Modern experience does not confirm the
terrors of the confluence reported in 5, perhaps
because it is now in a different place. A's account
in 5, 4–7 is not perspicuous. The flotilla first anchors
on the west bank; Nearchus is ordered downstream;
Al. conducts some raids, evidently east and south of
the confluence, since they were to deter support for
the Mallians (§ 27) and rejoins the fleet, and then puts
Philip across the Jhelum. Obviously Philip had just
reached the confluence, and Al. had returned there;
Philip was shipped over the Jhelum rather than over
the Chenab, so as to march down the west bank of
that river with Craterus, while Hephaestion, Ptolemy
and Alexander himself operated on the east side.
Either then Nearchus had been sent ahead or (more
probably) his instructions have been antedated. At
this point D. (96, 2–5) interposes the peaceful submission of the Sibae (v 3, 4 n.), a riverain people,
whereas S. xv 1, 33 puts them between Indus and
Hydaspes, and Al's attack on the Agalasseis (QC.

ix 4, 2 ff.) makes Al. reduce the Sibae by force, as well as another unnamed people (Agalasseis?) with a city surrounded by the waters of the Indus, Jhelum and Chenab! (No doubt there is some basis in truth for this nonsense, see Anspach n. 304.) QC. ix 4, 5 says that Al. crossed the Chenab, and I suspect that this means that he is describing one of the raids Al. conducted before leaving the confluence (*supra*).

27. S. xv 1, 33 puts the Mallians and Sydracae (A's Oxydracae) vaguely south of Taxilas' and Porus' dominions; Meg., who could have been ill-informed about a region he did not visit, places the former at the confluence of Indus and Chenab, and the latter at that of Jhelum and Chenab (*Ind.* 4, 9 n.; A. does not notice the incongruity with his own account); and D. 97 ff., and probably QC. ix 4, 15 ff. with 8, date the operations in which Al. was nearly killed after the confluence of Chenab and Indus had been reached. No doubt we should prefer to locate the Mallians from A's narrative: Al. crosses and recrosses the Ravi in attacking them; evidently their cities lay on both sides of that river and the stronghold where Al. was wounded on the western. A. gives no clue to the whereabouts of the Oxydracae, who in his story submitted without a fight. QC. ix 4, 26, and probably D., held that it was they who wounded Al., and that he sailed down to Mallian territory after obtaining their submission (7, 12 ff.; 8, 3). A's own account of events after the wounding is not perspicuous. Boats had been assembled on the Ravi to convey Al. downstream towards the confluence with the Chenab, where Hephaestion and Nearchus had arrived (13, 1); 14, 4 may be a muddled reference to this *new* flotilla; Nearchus can hardly have moved upstream.

APPENDIX XVII

In 13, 2 and 14, 4 Al. twice reaches the confluence. No doubt A. has unskillfully combined his sources. It is also not clear, as a consequence, at just what point the Mallians and Oxydracae capitulated (14, 1 ff.).

28. The operations described in vi 15–17 took place between Al's arrival on the Indus and his reaching its bifurcation at Patala (v 4, 1; cf. § 25). D. 102 f. and QC. ix 8, 4–28 give other particulars, often discordant with A. The locations of the rulers and peoples mentioned are merely conjectural. The capital of Musicanus, who (like other Indian princes) seems to have borne a title derived from the name of his people (QC. 8, 8), is commonly fixed at Alor near Sukkur, where there are ancient ruins. In that case, since the land was exceptionally fertile, channels that are now dry must then have carried abundant water, cf. Lambrick (cited vi 18, 3 n.) 108. Onesicritus, who idealized the kingdom's institutions (Pearson 100 ff.), placed it far to the south. Sambus evidently ruled in the hill country (16, 3) west of the Indus. Detailed analysis is futile, but movement must have been impeded by numerous water-courses, even though the river was probably not yet in full flood when Al. reached it, as it probably was by the time Al. sailed down to the Ocean; hence the operations may have occupied some weeks.

29. From Patala or earlier, if vi 15, 5 be accepted (see note), Al. despatched Craterus to Carmania (vi 17, 3); S., probably following Ar. as usual (§ 18), says that he went via Chaarene, probably modern Kharan, and Arachosia; he was to subdue Ariana (used in a wide sense, cf. xv 2, 1), and did in fact subdue those who

would not submit (2, 4 and 11). In N's version (2, 5, cf. App. XVIII 2) he started from the Hydaspes (Cr's march did in a sense begin there, cf. A. vi 2, and the bematists may have measured his march from Bucephala), and went through the lands of the Arachotians and Drangae. His route lay via the Bolan or Mullah pass, Kandahar and the Helmund. We need not assume that Cr. had only the units with him that A. mentions; there is no proof that all the numerous mercenaries remained with the main army. A. also refers to his quelling a ' revolt ' (27, 3 with n.). Al. had of course not traversed these regions.

30. A. never defines Al's purpose in invading India, and consequently cannot say how far he fulfilled it. He constituted three satrapies there (iv 28, 6; v 8, 3, cf. vi 15, 2; vi 15, 4), and another in Gadrosia (vi 22, 2). No doubt the people were everywhere expected to pay tribute (cf. vi 14, 2); that was so much the normal practice of an imperial power that it hardly needed saying. The Indians, it was said, had paid more tribute to Darius than any other province (Hdt. iii 97). If they submitted, Republics or princes were (as in the west) recognized as units of local government (iv 22, 8; 30, 4; v 2, 1; vi 15, 5–7; 16, 3), and as elsewhere local customs were naturally respected (vii 20, 2). If they refused submission, it was a *casus belli* (v 22; vi 4, 3; 5, 4; 16, 1; 21, 3), and resistance was savagely repressed (iv 22, 8; 23, 5; 24, 2; 27, 2–4; vi 16, 5; 17, 1; 22, 2), yet revolts still broke out in Al's rear (v 20, 7; *Ind.* 23, 5; S. xv 2, 5). Within a generation there was no vestige of Macedonian rule beyond the Indus. A. tells a heroic story of Al's skill and valour. To the people he temporarily conquered his progress was like a destructive

hurricane. Torn by internecine rivalries, his successors had to acquiesce, as he would hardly have done, in the independence of the Indians, notably of three vassal princes.

31. Taxila (Sanskrit, Takshaçila), near Rawalpindi (for excavations see J. Marshall, *A Guide to Taxila* 1960), was the centre of a large and fertile state between Indus and Hydaspes, v 3, 6, cf. S. xv 1, 28; *RE* v A 75 ff. The ruler had submitted to Al. in 327, evidently in hope of aid against Abisares and Porus (iv 22, 6 n.), cf. QC. viii 12, 4 ff., who tells also that his son had succeeded before the arrival of Hephaestion on the Indus (iv 22, 7; 30, 9), to whom he had sent free grain, and that he formally renewed his submission to Al. when Al. reached the Indus, and only took his official name (Taxilas) on receiving back his ' kingdom ' from Al. (D. 86, 4 ff; QC. *l.c.*): A., however, never calls him anything but ' hyparch ' (v 8, 2 and 5), cf. App. XV 2. S. (*l.c.*) says that his gifts to Al., variously reported in v 3, 5 and D. and QC., were more than requited by Al., cf. QC. viii 12, 17. Al's appointment of a satrap and installation of a garrison (v 8, 3) implies that Taxilas was to be a vassal prince. He was present at the battle of the Hydaspes (v 18, 6), and then reconciled (20, 4) and connected by marriage (QC. ix 3, 22) with Porus. On the murder of Philip in 325 Al. provisionally left Taxilas, together with a Macedonian general Eudamus, in charge of the satrapy (vi 27, 2; QC. x 1, 21 is presumably wrong in saying that ' Eudaemon ' was made satrap). This represented an extension of Taxilas' *de facto* dominion, since Philip's satrapy ran south to the confluence of Indus and Acesines (vi 15, 2), and eastwards over the Mallians and Oxy-

dracae (14, 3), and probably over the Abastanes, Xathrians and Ossadians (15, 1–2). Moreover Al. in fact never appointed a successor to Taxilas.

32. Porus (Paurava), i.e. the ruler of the Purus, whose fertile lands, abutting on those of Taxilas, lay between Hydaspes and Acesines and were said to contain 300 cities (S. xv 1, 29), is the only Indian ruler A. calls a king (App. XV 2). He was allied with Abisares against both Taxilas and the Cathaeans (v 20, 5; 22, 2; QC. viii 12, 13). After capturing him, Al. confirmed him in his realm (v 19, 3), presumably then, as later (vi 2, 2), with the title of king (v 19, 2), though P. 60, 8 makes him a satrap. He could still have been a vassal; compare the status of Thracian and Illyrian kings (Berve I 227, e.g. A. i 9, 1 f.), perhaps of Phoenician and Cypriot (ib. 284 ff., e.g. A. ii 13, 7; 20, 1). He was under Al's orders (v 21, 1; 24, 8), and A. treats his dominions as subject to Al. (v 21, 1). But in return for his loyal services and reconciliation with Taxilas (v 20, 4), Al. extended his realm progressively to include all the territory he had conquered up to the Hyphasis; see v 29, 2 and vi 2, 2, perhaps a doublet, which says that he was to rule over 7 nations and 2000 cities; P. 60, 8 gives 15 and 5000 respectively while S. xv 1, 33 and Pliny, *NH* vi 59 respectively report 9 nations and 5000 cities as (a) lying between Jhelum and Beas or (b) as conquered by Al. The statements in v 19, 3 and 21, 3 are, perhaps, anticipatory; could Al. make grants of lands he had not yet subdued, and would he have done so until assured of Porus' fidelity? No European troops in his realm are mentioned, and he was allowed to put in his own garrisons (v 24, 8). Still, he was a vassal; the cities founded in his kingdom (v 19, 4; 29, 3) were

surely independent of him, and it need not be significant that we hear no more of the tribute which Al.
originally demanded (QC. viii 13, 2). QC. ix 3, 22
draws no distinction between his position and that of
Taxilas and, though his was certainly more honorific,
in the arrangements made for the government of the
empire on Al's death, and again in 321, the dominions of both were treated as parts of it; see Arrian,
Successors fr. 1, 36 in Roos' edition and D. xviii 3,
3; 39, 6; both are presumably following Hieronymus.
Here too A. calls only Porus a king, and is doubtless
technically correct, even though D. says that in 323
both were left as ' masters of their own kingdoms, as
Al. himself had arranged.' A. explains that it was
impossible to dispossess them, and D. repeats this
explanation, when he comes to 321. But in point of
power no distinction is drawn between them. Taxilas disappears from history after 321, while Porus was
treacherously killed in or before 317 by the Macedonian general, Eudamus, who then marched west
with his forces (D. xix 14); as a result the realms of
both fell into the hands of Chandragupta (§ 6).

33. Abisares, the ruler of the Abhisara (cf. *Ind.* 4,
12), called Embisarus by D. 87, 2, who says he had an
army little inferior to that of Porus, ruled north of
Taxilas (S. xv 1, 28) in mountainous country (A.
v 8, 3), which may have comprised most of Kashmir
(iv 27, 7 n. is too limiting, cf. *CHI* 468 n. 2). An ally
of Porus (§ 32), who expected his aid at the Hydaspes
(D. 87; QC. viii 14, 1), he had shown his hostility to
Al. (A. iv 30, 7), yet made some sort of submission by
an embassy to Taxila (v 8, 3; QC. viii 13, 1) and again
after Porus' defeat, when Al. demanded his personal
appearance and threatened to march against him (v

APPENDIX XVII

20, 5 f.; QC. ix 1, 7 f.). QC. ignores the final agreement (A. v 29, 4 f.), which D., now calling him Sasibares (90, 4), seems to associate with the second embassy; QC. implies later that he became a vassal. Although he had not fulfilled Al's requirement, he was made a ' satrap '(!), and subjected to annual tribute, yet his territory was actually enlarged like that of Porus, though he had given no proof of true loyalty (A. v 29). On his death in 325 Al. approved the succession of his son (QC. x 1, 20 f.), of whom nothing is heard in the arrangements made in and after 323 for the government of the empire, perhaps because it was recognized that Abisares' realm had never been effectively annexed. QC's account (with the same name as A's) fits and amplifies A's.

APPENDIX XVIII

FROM PATALA TO PURA (vi 21, 1–27)

1. A's account of the march from Patala to Carmania is a mosaic from different sources. The narrative in 21, 3–22, 3 comes from his main authorities. Then follows a digression on Gadrosian plants explicitly drawn from Ar. (22, 4–8). In 23, 1 he must then have turned to Pt.; ' from there ' is obscure in his text, referring to Ora, which Pt. had evidently mentioned in a previous sentence, reproduced by A. in 22, 3. Now comes the ' official ' version (23–24, 1) of the march through Gadrosia (Makran) to Pura, minimizing its hardships. Struck by its discordance with most accounts, which showed the army suffering unprecedented distress (24, 1–3), A. then adds the

' pathetic account ' of the march, which again brings the reader to Pura in 27, 1. It begins in indirect speech, but turns almost at once (24, 4) to direct and so continues to the end of 25. We then have one anecdote in indirect speech (26, 1–3), and another (26, 4 f.) in which direct and indirect speech alternate. The partial use of direct speech in itself suggests that A. thought his source reliable (cf. App. XVI 6): he was not just repeating a story, but relating facts. Moreover, there is an almost exact parallel to 24, 4–25 (but not to 26) in S. xv 2, 5 f.; now S. seldom cites Clitarchus, and Onesicritus mostly on local customs, plants and animals; he generally follows Ar. for Al's marches (App. XVII 18), though here his source is more probably N. (§ 2). Comparison with S. does not then suggest that A's pathetic account comes from the ' vulgate ', and although QC. ix 10, 8 ff. and (much more briefly) D. 105 and P. 66 agree as to the army's sufferings, there are few detailed resemblances between their versions and A's pathetic account; such as there are can be explained by the assumption that the facts were truly recorded by independent authorities. Only in 26, 1–3 does A. seem to be using the ' vulgate ' for a fictitious anecdote, and then (as usual) in a version different from that known to the writers who are deemed to be reproducing Clitarchus.

2. Jacoby identified the common source of A. and S. as Ar., H. Strasburger in his classic study (*Hermes* lxxx, 1952, 456 ff.) as N. It is clear from 24, 1–3 (not from *Ind.* 26, 1; 32, 1, which can be A's own insertions) that N. recognized the fearful sufferings of the army. Like Pt. and probably Ar. (21, 3; 22, 3; 23, 1 and 4 f.), he explained Al's decision partly by

his anxiety to provide supplies of water and food for
the fleet (24, 3); still he agreed with other writers
that Al. desired to outdo Cyrus and Semiramis, who
were said to have come to total disaster in Gadrosia
(24, 3 n.); if then he also denied that Al. was unaware of the difficulty of the route, he can only have
meant that Al. believed in his own ability to overcome natural obstacles (cf. ii 26, 2 n.). (In a sense he
did overcome them: his army was not entirely destroyed.) N. could certainly have described the
march (App. XVII 5), and the graphic character of
A's pathetic account is in his manner. Strasburger
has many arguments for his attribution, not all compelling. But an analysis of S. proves his case. Ar.
seems to be S's usual authority for Al's marches
(App. XVII 18), and should then be his source in xv
2, 3 f. and again at the end of § 7 and in § 11, where
he briefly reports the itineraries of Al. and Craterus.
But in § 5 there is an emphatic initial allusion to N's
account, marking a change of source, and followed
by a doublet account of Craterus' route; the description of the hardships of Al's march follows without a break, and adds data on noxious plants (§ 7)
quite different from those supplied by Ar. (A. 22,
4–8). Some indeed think that A. 25, 4 points de-
cisively to Ar., and not N., since N., *contra* Ar., held
that it rained in the summer on the Indian plains (S.
xv 1, 18), and Strabo says (§ 3), where he is surely
drawing on Ar., that Al. started in the summer, when
the rains in the mountains could be expected to fill
the rivers and wells. (Al. was in fact accurately informed about rainfall in Gadrosia.) However, the
worst of the march actually took place in October and
November (§ 6), and N. too held that there was no
rainfall in the plains in winter.

APPENDIX XVIII

3. But if the pathetic account is based on N., 22, 4–8
need not represent A's only debt to Ar.: Strasburger
himself conjectured that 26, 4 f. (no parallel in
S.) came from Ar. The ' official ' version too need
not be only Pt's. Such ethnographic data as we
have in 23, 3 are unexampled in Pt's attested fragments, but for Ar. cf. iii 28, 5–7; S. xv 1, 62; xvi
3, 3. The record of two missions in 23, 4 f. looks to
me like a doublet on Al's effort to victual the fleet;
we may suppose that only one of his sources (Pt. ?)
gave the name of Cretheus, and only the other (Ar. ?)
added that the effort failed; hence A. did not realize
that each was recounting the same incident. If 23,
3–4 comes from Ar., then Pt. perhaps never alluded
to the shortage of food, as distinct from water (23,
1). It may be significant that Ar., and not Pt., recorded Al's thank-offerings for his safety in Carmania (28, 3). If Strasburger rightly ascribes 26, 4 f.
to Ar., that would again show that he did not wholly
conceal the army's distress. Pt. even contrived to
suggest that Al. fulfilled his plan to dig wells and
establish supply depots for the fleet (23, 1 and 5),
though N's silence shows that no such depots existed
beyond the Oritan country (*Ind.* 23, 7). A. never
observed this; he did not collate N's story of the
voyage with Pt's account of the march. Cf. 18, 3;
20, 5 nn. for misleading statements on other impracticable plans. Pt. also noted Al's (eventual)
success in obtaining provisions (23, 6). Curiously it
is D. 105 and QC. ix 10, 22 alone who say that the
supplies that reached Al. in Carmania arrived on his
directions and not (A. 27, 6) on the initiative of the
satraps. Above all, there was nothing in Pt. of
heavy losses of men or (except for an incidental
allusion to their replacement in 27, 6) of animals.

APPENDIX XVIII

4. For the topography of the march see Sir Aurel Stein, *Geogr. Journal* cii, 1943, 193 ff. Al. left Patala in summer (S. xv 2, 3), probably in early September (App. XVII 24), crossed the Arabius near the coast and then encamped, in Stein's view, near Lake Siranda (21, 5 n.)—the map in vol. I is inaccurate—and attacked the Oritans. For Stein the Arabius is the Hab, and the Arabii, who plainly lived round the river, fled to hills in the north, A's desolate country. Other scholars have identified the Arabius with the Purali, but in that case not only would Stein's identification of Lake Siranda be wrong, but the Arabii, located on the Purali, would naturally have fled to its upper valley, the modern Welpat, one of the few relatively fertile and populous parts of Baluchistan. But the Oritans were evidently a more formidable tribe, and there is no suitable terrain further west than Welpat for them to inhabit. There is no mention of Al. crossing the Purali in A.; after crossing the Hab he advanced ' further ' (21, 5), sc. up the valley; here D. 104 is helpful in telling that Al. divided his force and himself ' devastated the foothills and mountainous country ', whereas A. just says that he advanced ' further '. The defile into which Al. pursued the Oritans (22, 1) was in the north and led to Jhau in the upper Hingol valley; Al. entered that tract and thence pursued the caravan route along the Kolwa basin and Kech valley, the natural line through Makran to Kerman (Carmania). See now Engels, Appendix 4.

5. On Stein's theory the ' halting place nearest the sea ' (23, 4) was the oasis of Turbat, where Al. could have received supplies from the ' upper parts ' (23, 6), i.e. from Panjgur, the best cultivated part of

Makran, north of the central range. Thence he will have turned south to the small port of Pasni by a route that traverses a ' maze of low sandy hillocks ', which explains how the army lost its way (26, 4), and marched along the coast for 7 days (26, 5) to Gwadar. It seems to me that the army will have turned inland again a little west of Gwadar, on the track which now leads north-west to Suntsar and rejoins the route to Bampur which Al. had deserted at Turbat, in the hope that he could progress along the coast; presumably he soon found supplies quite inadequate. Stein thought that he continued along the coast to Gabd, but the total distance from Pasni to Gabd (about 120 miles) is too long for a march of 7 days, given the average rate of progress (§ 6). Pura, as all agree, lies in the alluvial Bampur basin (see Stein, *op. cit.* in App. XVII 15, pp. 105, 113, 136). Strasburger (*Hermes* lxxxii, 1954, 251 ff.), with whom Hamilton agreed, argued that Stein's route took A. too far inland, as much as 140 km. by air in the upper Hingol valley; S. (xv 2, 3) says that he always kept within 500 stades from the sea. *Contra* Strasburger, S. should here be following Ar. and not N., and even if N. used a very short stade (App. XXV 7), there is no reason to think that Ar. did so; hence his estimate is about 90 km. However, on Stein's theory the army, separated from the sea by the coastal Makran range, could not know the distance, except when they could measure the route followed by the reconnoitring party (23, 2) or that from Turbat to Pasni; and the length of the latter route corresponds to S's 500 stades. S. also says that the army was much closer at times: so it was, between Pasni and Gwadar! In the Bampur basin it was some 200 km. (by air) from the sea, and Strasburger does not dispute its arrival there, though this alone exposes S's error. From Pura it proceeded to the Carmanian capital, which cannot be located but was clearly far south of modern Kerman, perhaps near Golashkerd, but at any rate five days' march from the mouth of the Minab (*Ind.* 33, 7). So Al. had to abandon his plan of keeping near the shore. The ' official ' version also confirms that he was often far from it, whereas Strasburger's route is within 15–20 km. throughout up to Gwadar. The barrier of the coastal range made it necessary to choose between routes to the south, very close to the sea between the Purali outlet and Pasni, and to the north, rather distant. Autopsy convinced Stein that the former was *totally* impracticable for a large army to pass along the coast at least between the Purali and the Hingol; hence Al. was committed from the first to the route via Welpat and Jhau, and reconnaissance of the ' Fish-Eaters'' country showed him that he must continue inland to Turbat. Strasburger objects that Stein's route is too easy. But Stein describes it as mostly through desert with rare and limited areas of cultivation, but for which no army could have got through at all. He found every detail of the ' pathetic ' account true to life, except that the shifting sands of 24, 4 could only have been encountered in the very last stage approaching Bampur; an incident like that in 25, 4 f. was repeated in his own experience.

6. The march from Ora to Pura lasted 60 days (24, 1, cf. S. xv 2, 7; P. 66, no doubt given by Ar. as well as Pt.). On Stein's estimate the distance would have been between 410 and 470 miles; it would not have been greater if the coastal route could have been taken. Thus on average the army covered only 11–

12 km. a day. The marches only seemed long (24, 5) because of their difficulty. QC. ix 10, 4–18 makes Al. take 20 days (not 23, as Stein says) from Patala to the Hab, a distance of about 120 miles. Stein doubted if he would have taken so long, but I am reluctant to discard this ' log-book ' information (App. XVII 12), and the average marching rate is about the same as in Gadrosia. Al. can hardly have spent *less* than 10 days in the Oritan country. Probably then, leaving Patala in early September, he did not enter Gadrosia till early October nor reach Pura till early December, and the water supply in Gadrosia was less than he had expected, because the march began later and lasted longer than he had planned.

7. Strasburger had shown before Stein wrote, from comparative material, that the pathetic account must have underrated rather than exaggerated the sufferings of the army (*op. cit.* in § 2). Great losses of men and animals must have occurred. But they cannot be precisely estimated. P. 66 says that not a fourth part of Al's army survived. But then he had an exaggerated total for the forces of India, 120,000 foot and 15,000 horse (App. XIII 8), and those forces, whatever their true number, included (a) local levies who doubtless never left India; (b) men who went homewards with Craterus, Nearchus and Leonnatus (who presumably followed later in Al's tracks). We can only be sure that the march was a disaster, and that Pt. at least concealed its magnitude. Even A. evidently doubted if the versions of Pt. and Ar. revealed the truth. He must have thought the divergent accounts ' not entirely untrustworthy ' (preface), no doubt because they were confirmed by

N. Lacking any independent knowledge of Makran, such as Strasburger culled from mediaeval and modern descriptions, he could perhaps do no more than bring the contradictions to his readers' notice.

8. Engels 110 ff. and 137 ff. rejects the irrational motivation given by N. (vi 14, 2; S. xv 1, 5) for the Gadrosian march, and conjectures that Al. wished to secure his southern boundary and open up the sea route from Indus to Euphrates; although N. says that the army was to supply the fleet (vi 24, 3; S. xv 2, 4), the truth is that the fleet was to supply the army, except that the army was to water the fleet. N. only sought to obscure his own responsibilities. But on Engels' own showing he was not to blame for the failure of Al's imputed plan, and clearly he was not blamed by Al. Disaster on Engels' view resulted because the monsoon delayed N's departure. Engels exonerates both Al. and N. for not knowing when the winds would be favourable, by supposing that they could get no information, but see *contra* vi 21, 2. Moreover, if no information could be obtained on this matter, Al. could also have had no certainty that the coast would permit supply ships to put in to land, where required. Engels compounds Al's blunder by dating his departure to July (*contra* App. XVII 24), and by estimating his force at 150,000, of whom one third would be non-combatants. Like all the running totals Engels gives (146 ff.) for Al's forces, this estimate is worthless, since Engels simply takes the totals of all who are ever known to have served with Al. and deducts recorded numbers of casualties and garrisons; but the sources understate casualties in fighting and ignore deaths from disease, and seldom state how many were left behind in garrisons and

colonies.   Of course, for the purpose Engels imputes
to Al., there was no reason why he should have taken
with him the greater part of his army.

APPENDIX XIX

MILITARY QUESTIONS

1. In his *Tactica* A. described old Greek and Macedonian methods of warfare for Greek readers without
experience of soldiering and unfamiliar with the old
technical terms (1, 2; 32, 2; see e.g. 13, 6 on the
Macedonian phalanx).   The *Anabasis* does not cite
this work and, even if it was written earlier, A. could
not assume that his new readers would be acquainted
with it.   Polybius had thought it necessary to explain the organization and fighting methods of the
Roman army, so different from those of the Greek
world (vi 19 ff.), and an intelligent historian of Al's
campaigns should have seen the same need, especially as Al's army had peculiarities that distinguished
it from earlier and later Greek or Macedonian
armies.   *Pezetairoi* and *asthetairoi*, *agema* and hypaspists: most of his readers would have found these
terms meaningless.   Did A. understand them himself?   To say nothing of the perhaps corrupt expression ' hypaspists of the Companions ' (i 14, 2, cf.
Bosworth *ad loc.*), he writes ' *agema* and hypaspists '
(i 1, 11; i 8, 3 (misinterpreted in Introd. 58); ii 8, 3;
vii 7, 1) or ' (royal) bodyguards and hypaspists ' (iii
17, 2; iv 3, 2; 30, 3); only in iii 11, 9 does he imply
that the (infantry) *agema* was part of the hypaspists,
and ' royal hypaspists and royal *agema* ' (v 13, 4)

suggests that he did not realize that these two ex-
pressions had the same reference; one must also
doubt if he understood that the ' silvershields ' were
the hypaspists (vii 11, 3 n.). His readers at least are
not apprised of this, nor of the identity of *prodromoi*
and *sarissophoroi* (Introd. n. 84); until they reached
vi 28, 4, they would not know that individuals called
' bodyguards ' (e.g. ii 12, 2) were not simply soldiers in
the royal *agema* (if indeed they understood that ' royal
bodyguards ' designated that unit), or that a man
named as ' one of the Companions ' was more than a
trooper in the Companion cavalry. There was merit
in retaining such technical terms, if they had been
explained, but D. was more sensible in describing
the aristocratic Companions (Introd. 30) as ' friends '.
If A. was aware of the distinct meanings of Companions and bodyguards (Introd. 30 f.), he did not
convey them to his readers. He seems to have delighted in mechanically transcribing technical terms
which gave an air of scholarly authenticity to his
account. Nor did he always give full and accurate
excerpts of what he found in his sources on military
matters.

2. Evidently they provided details of Al's battle
formations, unit by unit, naming commanders, but in
A. there are omissions probably due to his carelessness. Thus, at the Granicus the light troops played
an important part (i 16, 1), but none except the
Agrianians are named in the battle-order (i 14).
Here too A. does not name all the commanders of the
units he does mention, whereas at Issus and Gaugamela he records even the rather unimportant
ilarchs. At the Granicus he altogether omits the
allied and Thracian foot and the mercenary regi-

ments. The lists for Issus and Gaugamela are much fuller, but of what nation were the archers under Antiochus, as distinguished from the Cretan archers arrayed with Attalus (ii 9, 2 f.)? Only at Gaugamela do we hear of Macedonian archers (iii 12, 2). A. does not make clear that Sitalces' regiment (ii 9, 3; iii 12, 4) consisted of javelin-men (i 28, 4). At Gaugamela again one force of archers is not fully designated, the nationality of Balacrus' javelin-men is not stated (iii 12, 3), and no commander is named for the Thracian foot (12, 5).

3. For the battle of the Hydaspes A. is still more confusing. Al. divided his forces into three (v 11, 3–12, 2). Of Macedonian units Craterus, commanding the first division, had ' his own' hipparchy and the foot battalions of Alcetas and Polyperchon. The second division is stated to have comprised only the mercenary foot and horse; it is by inference from the names of the commanders, Meleager, Attalus and Gorgias, that we can assign to it the three foot battalions of Macedonians of which they were taxiarchs. Alexander himself is said to have had the *agema*, three hipparchies (Hephaestion's, Perdiccas' and Demetrius'), the hypaspists and two Macedonian battalions of foot, those of Coenus and Clitus. Among other troops A. ignores the javelin-throwers who appear later (13, 4). On the face of it there were only four hipparchies *plus* the *agema*, and seven foot battalions (three not specifically recorded). Yet in the battle we hear of Coenus' own hipparchy (16, 3), and later of one commanded by Clitus (22, 6). Hammond, *CQ* 1980, 469 f., supposes that Coenus was in the battle the effective commander of Perdiccas' hipparchy, and that Clitus was the effective

commander of Craterus' hipparchy; on this view, when A. writes 'his own hipparchy', he refers in one case to the nominal commander (11, 3), in another to the actual commander (16, 3), though we should surely expect him to have written that Coenus was in charge of Perdiccas' as well as Demetrius' hipparchy. Of course a man might have remained the nominal colonel of a regiment, when he had in fact been transferred to other duties, and an acting colonel had taken his place; on the orthodox view Coenus and Clitus were colonels nominally of foot and in fact of cavalry in this very battle, cf. App. XXIV 4 for another parallel. Hammond's view makes sense of vii 6, 4, from which it appears that in 324 a fifth hipparchy had recently been added to the pre-existing four. Hammond concedes that there had been seven hipparchies in the operations of 327/6 (cf. Introd. 58; Bosworth *JHS* 1980 n. 130 alleges that I miscounted, but A's curious expression in iv 24, 1 surely means that, with half the Companions detached (22, 7), Al. had with him the equivalent of four hipparchies counting the *agema*). Hence Hammond assumes a reorganization on the Indus. But this neglects the implication of vi 6, 1 and 4: Al. was able to detach two hipparchies from a force including only half the Companion, the rest being evidently with Hephaestion and Ptolemy (5, 6; 11, 8; 13, 1); this detachment could have rejoined him, when he once again detached two hipparchies (7, 2). We must conclude that A. has omitted three hipparchies from his initial account of Al's dispositions at the Hydaspes.

4. Has he also omitted phalanx battalions? In spring 327 Al. sent three forward to the Indus, those

of Gorgias, Clitus and Meleager (iv 22, 7), all present at the Hydaspes; with Al. there remained battalions of Craterus (? cf. 23, 5 with 22, 1), Coenus (24, 1; 25, 6; 28, 8), Attalus (24, 1 and 10), Balacrus (24, 10), Philip (ibid.), Philotas (ibid., cf. iii 29, 7), Polyperchon (25, 6), Alcetas (27, 1); of these Alcetas, Polyperchon, Meleager, Attalus, Gorgias, Clitus and Coenus re-appear at the Hydaspes, and in Introd. 61 I inferred that the phalanx still consisted of 7 battalions (plus the hypaspists). To reconcile this view with the attestation of ten or eleven taxiarchs in 327, we should have to suppose that some of those named were merely acting taxiarchs. But there is a difficulty: in 24, 10 Al. divided his forces in three, one including two of the battalions, the second two more plus one third of the hypaspists; it is hard to believe that his own division with the hardest fighting to do comprised only the two remaining thirds of the hypaspists; moreover Alcetas, Coenus and Polyperchon are not among the commanders here named. Hence the inference from A's defective account of dispositions at the Hydaspes, that there were then only seven phalanx battalions, must be doubted.

5. On any view A. failed to record any increase in the number of these battalions from the original six, or the constitution of seven hipparchies plus the *agema*, or except by allusion in vii 6 their reduction to four, and the subsequent addition of a fifth, just as he also fails to tell when Orientals were first embodied in the hipparchies. And yet his sources enabled him to report the formation of companies within each cavalry squadron in 331 (iii 16, 11) and the appointment of two hipparchs to command the Companions in 330 (iii 27, 4), as well as the projected remodelling

487

of the phalanx in 323 (vii 23, 3). It is highly improbable that they omitted the other changes, which A. passes over.

6. Certainly they listed the units engaged in battles. This did little to promote a reader's understanding of the tactics, if he had no clue to the strength of any of the units. D. inserted a summary of the numbers of Al's expeditionary force, nation by nation (Introd. 56). A. does not even supply this, but Pt./Ar. probably furnished still fuller particulars, which would have shown their readers how many men were deployed in each part of the line, when the units were simply listed. One at least of them may have recorded where each Macedonian regiment was recruited (Introd. n. 30). Of course it was also necessary, in order to understand the campaigns, to know something of Al's losses, and of his reinforcements; the latter are more fully but not completely reported by D. and QC. (Introd. 57; App. XIII). I find it incredible that (i) what they tell us is fiction and (ii) that it was all omitted by both Pt. and Ar. Cf. § 7.

7. After the arrival of the last reinforcements ever reported from Macedon in 330 (iii 16), the total number of Macedonians, including *prodromoi* but excluding archers, who had ever served under Alexander was 21,000 foot and probably 3400 horse (App. XIII 1 and 4). Menidas and others were sent for new drafts in 328/7 (iv 18, 3). Such drafts *could* have reached Al. in or before 326/5, since other troops did reach him from the west in early autumn 326. D. 95 speaks of 30,000 allied and mercenary foot from Greece and nearly 6000 horse, QC. ix 3, 21 of 5000

men from Thrace and 6000 (mercenaries?) sent by
Harpalus. Perhaps their common source gave D's
total, specifying contingents of which QC. misleadingly selected only two. Macedonians might
then be included in D's total, or they might have
arrived on another unrecorded occasion. Al. would
hardly have condoned neglect of his orders, yet
Menidas at least suffered no penalty: in 323 he
brought cavalry to Al. at Babylon, at the same time
as Philoxenus and Menander brought troops from
Caria and Lydia (vii 23, 1). The nationality of these
forces is not stated: were they then the new drafts
from Macedon? Their arrival would surely have
been too tardy, even if we suppose that Al. had never
intended that these drafts should join him before his
return from India. And it looks as if they were not
all Macedonian (vii 24, 1).

8. In 324 Craterus was ordered home with rather
more than 10,000 Macedonian foot and 1500 horse,
presumably Macedonian; of the former 6000 were
survivors of the original expeditionary force and 4000
of the men who had joined Al. later (vii 12, 1; D. 109,
1; Hieronymus *ap.* D. xviii 4, 1; 12, 1; 16, 4). QC.
x 2, 8 alleges that at the same time Al. selected
13,000 foot and 2000 horse to hold down Asia. If
this is correct, it is obvious that Al. must have had
previous reinforcements from Macedon that are not
reported, unless QC's figure includes Greek mercenaries; otherwise Craterus' departure would have
left in the grand army only two or three thousand
Macedonian foot and virtually no Companions (cf. vi
14, 4; *Ind.* 19, 5 n.); the number of men lost from
fighting and disease and left behind in colonies and
garrisons must have been large. Schachermeyr has

in fact conjectured that mercenaries had been gradually incorporated in the Macedonian regiments (*Alex. der Grosse*, 1973, 359). But in 323, after Al's death, Perdiccas was able to detach from the grand army 3000 Macedonian foot and 800 horse to suppress a revolt of 20,000 mercenary foot and 3000 horse in the eastern satrapies (D. xviii 7), obviously without denuding himself of Macedonian soldiers. D's narrative seems to show that the fusion of Greeks and Macedonians assumed by Schachermeyr had not occurred. It is indeed clear that in 323–1 the grand army remained powerful, though the troops that Antipater had been ordered to bring out (vii 12, 4) had never come. We must conclude that A. has omitted somewhere between 326 and 323 the arrival of a very considerable force of Macedonian recruits.

9. I take this opportunity to retract my contention in the introduction (§ 62) that the hypaspists were less heavily armed than the phalanx regiments; the Greek words which I have occasionally rendered as 'lighter' or 'lightest armed' should be translated 'nimblest' or the like (i 27, 8; iii 23, 3; iv 6, 3), see R. D. Milns, *Entretiens Hardt* xxii 118 ff. Milns 89 ff. also has new suggestions on *pezetairoi* and *asthetairoi* (cf. Introd. 30 and n. 99; on the former, Brunt, *JHS* 1976, 151 ff.), see also Griffith, *Hist. of Macedon* ii 709 ff., whose views in general on *hctairoi* and *pezetairoi* I find unconvincing, not least because they imply that a doubtless encomiastic history of Philip by Anaximenes began by suggesting that there was no well organized Macedonian cavalry or infantry until the reign of his son.

APPENDIX XX

ALEXANDER AND THE INDIAN SOPHISTS

1. A. reports as a fact that Al. saw and admired naked sophists at Taxila, and desired that one of them should join him (vii 2, 2), and as stories that he saw them in a meadow and learned of their views of his conduct (1, 5 f.) and that ' Dandamis ' refused to join him (2, 2–4) and Calanus agreed (as Meg. recorded) (2, 4); he then relates his death as a tale, which was, however, vouched for by competent writers, including N. (3, 1 and 6); in fact, according to S. xv 1, 68, all writers recorded it, though differing in details (e.g. Chares F. 19, Onesicritus F. 18, Meg. cited by S. and presumably Ar., whom S. consulted on the ' sophists ', xv 1, 61, as well as N.; D. 107 presumably goes back to Clitarchus). A. vii 2, 2 might come from Ar., though A. ignores his general account *ap.* S. with the tale of two sophists, evidently Calanus and another, who appeared at Al's table. According to Onesicritus *ap.* S. xv 1, 63–5 (cf. P. 65), Al. had heard about the sophists, who lived 20 stades from the city (i.e. Taxila), and sent O. to invite them to his presence; except for Calanus they declined, but O. professed to have learned of their views and practices from Calanus and ' Mandanis '; that is the name S. gives to the sophist whom P. (also citing O.) and A. call ' Dandamis,' probably adopting the usage of Meg. (cf. xv 1, 68) and not that of O. himself, which was more generally followed. Neither S. nor P. represents O. as reporting that the sophists expressed the disdain for Al's conduct and pretensions we find in A. vii 1, 5 f. and 2, 3, but there is a close parallel

APPENDIX XX

to the second passage in Meg. *ap*. S. xv 1, 68. Since A. goes on immediately to cite Meg. in 2, 4, we might conclude that 2, 3 also derives directly from him, though there is no other proof that A. read Meg. before he embarked on the *Indica*; however, *Ind*. 3 supplies an example of A. citing an authority at second hand, and the whole of ch. 2 may come from a late version of the vulgate, in which Meg. was named as an authority, but in which the name Mandanis was replaced by Dandamis.

2. A. evidently thought Calanus' self-immolation a laudable example of resolution, though as a Stoic he should have taken this view only if the resolution was itself rational (cf. Epict. ii 15). He implies a different valuation of Calanus from that of Meg., who held that he acted impetuously and violated the rule of his sect against suicide (*contra* Ones. *ap*. S. xv 1, 65), just as he had shown lack of self-control in attaching himself to Al. in the first place (ib. 68). S. was also impressed with the discord on details among the writers who recorded the death; A. hints at this (3, 2). A's own source or sources cannot be determined. The prominence of Ptolemy is no proof that he even mentioned the event, since Clitarchus liked to bring his sovereign in (vi 11, 8; 16, 5 nn.), and even if A. never used Clitarchus (App. XXVII 12 f.), the reference to Pt. in a later version of the vulgate which A. did read may go back to him. Calanus fell ill at Pasargadae (S.) and died in Persia (A. 3, 1; P. 69, 3), on the border of Susiana according to D. Hence N., whom A. does cite, was not an eye-witness, nor was Onesicritus, as he claimed to be (F. 18; perhaps he transposed the suicide to Babylon, cf. Aelian, *Varia Historia* v 6). Like Chares (F. 19), Onesicritus also

wrote of Calanus throwing himself on the pyre; A.
3, 5 does not seem to know this version. I incline
to the view that he followed in the main some late
account.

APPENDIX XXI

ARRIAN AND THE AMAZONS (vii 13)

1. In antiquity virtually everyone believed that
there were or had been Amazons somewhere at some
time (Grote, *Hist. of Greece* ch. xi). They were
originally located on the river Thermodon in N.E.
Asia Minor. As A. remarks, Xenophon did not find
them in this region (*Anab.* iv 6–v 6), though he too
retained his faith in their existence somewhere (iv
4, 16). Xenophon's evidence did not at once lead to
their transposition. The Chorasmian Pharasmanes
was understood to say that he was a neighbour of the
Colchians and the Amazons, which surely means that
they were still placed in N.E. Asia Minor by Pt./Ar.,
whom A. is here following (iv 15, 4). Al's men had
no conception of the distance between the ' Tanais '—
Jaxartes (App. XII)—and the Black Sea. Onesicritus and others after him told that the queen of the
Amazons visited Al. in Hyrcania (P. 46; D. 77 with
Welles' notes; QC. vi 5, 24); in Clitarchus' version
she came from the Thermodon and the Caspian Gates,
which he thought were quite close (S. xi 5, 4, cf.
1, 5)! But, as N.E. Asia Minor became more
generally familiar, the Amazons had to be transposed
to lands still unknown, so writers in the first century
B.C. put them in the foothills of the northern Cau-

casus in modern Daghestan (S. xi 5, 1). Even Hdt. iv 110 ff. had made them migrate to a land east of Don and north of the Sea of Azov. Other locations may well have been conjectured.

2. S. thought it odd that it was usual to exclude the Amazons from history, which aimed at the truth and could hardly contain any ' monstrous ' element, and yet to credit their existence in mythical times (xi 5, 3); he probably wrote under the influence of Eratosthenes, since he goes on to report E's criticisms of the introduction of marvels into the histories of Al., including the visit of the queen of the Amazons (§ 3 f., cf. App. XII 1; XVII 8). This scepticism about the very existence of the Amazons is not shared by A. The unanimity of belief in the legend, and such ' testimony ' as Hdt. iv 110 ff. and Athenian funeral speeches (e.g. Lysias ii 4–6; Demosthenes lx 8, cf. Hdt. ix 27 and How *ad loc.*), deter him from rejecting a tale as totally untrustworthy (cf. preface 3) on the simple ground that it is impossible. His history of Bithynia was rich in myths, including Heracles' war with the Amazons, once more in their old home on the Thermodon (fr. 48–50 Roos)! A. is one of those half-hearted rationalists decried by S. He can believe in marvels, if they are not intruded into history (cf. v 4, 3), and he tries to find some factual basis for a tale he rejects.

3. Curiously, he never alludes to the more famous story (P. 46) of the visit paid to Al. by the queen of the Amazons. It was denied by Pt. and Ar. *expressly* (P. 46, which need not be doubted, *contra* Hamilton *ad loc.*). By contrast, they merely ignored the story he alone purveys. This is not surprising.

APPENDIX XXI

It was evidently of late origin. The Amazons are brought by the satrap of Media: they cannot then come from the Thermodon region, but perhaps from near the S.E. angle of the Caspian, in his satrapy, rather than Daghestan. The story must have been invented after they had been transposed from the region where Clitarchus' generation still placed them. Once again A. is using a late version of the vulgate.

APPENDIX XXII

THE EMBASSIES AT BABYLON

1. D. 113 places at Babylon the arrival of embassies from ' almost the whole world '. According to A. envoys arrived from ' Libya ' and Italy when Al. was still on the way to Babylon after the winter-campaign of 324/3 (vii 15, 4), whereas Greek embassies reached him at Babylon, both before and after his excursion to the Pollacopas (19, 1; 23, 2). No doubt in his more summary narrative D. grouped all embassies together, and, though A. is somewhat more precise, probably embassies were always arriving (cf. 14, 6). Still, there is a puzzle about the Greek embassies.

2. How did the second differ from the first, which A. supposes to have been merely congratulatory? Is it a mere doublet? Both passages come from A's main sources, but he might perhaps have taken one from Pt. and one from Ar. This explanation is possible, but unnecessary. On the second occasion the envoys are described as *theoroi*, engaged on a sacred mission (cf. 23, 6). A. correctly adds that this

implied that they had come to honour a god, cf. Plut. *Demetrius*, 10, 3–11, 1: it was after Antigonus the One-Eyed and Demetrius had been proclaimed Saviour Gods at Athens that it was decreed there that ambassadors to them should be styled *theoroi*, which incidentally implies that this would be their appellation, even if they had secular business to transact. Now divine honours were certainly proposed and presumably voted to Al. in 324 at Athens and Sparta and, as these cities were among the most hostile to Macedon, the practice was surely wide-spread, perhaps universal, in Greece, see A. D. Nock, *Essays on Religion and the Anc. World* 134 f. with further discussion by J. P. V. D. Balsdon, *Historia* i, 1950, 383 ff.; E. Bickermann, *Athenaeum* 1963, 70 ff.; C. Habicht, *Gottmenschentum u. gr. Städte* [2] 28 ff., revised in 246 ff. Al's order that Hephaestion be honoured as a hero, issued even before Ammon had given his sanction (vii 14, 7; 23, 6), cannot formally have applied to the ' autonomous ' Greek cities, but they had evident reasons for complying with his known wishes, and Hyperides' *Epitaphios* 21 seems to attest such a hero-cult; this in turn will have stimulated moves to accord still higher status to Al. himself. But as the death of H. occurred perhaps as late as autumn 324, all the necessary measures had not perhaps been taken in Greek cities at the time when earlier embassies were despatched: *theoroi* might have started and arrived later. (I need not discuss here whether divine honours were voted to Al. at his behest; my own view is that these honours were far more extraordinary than they were to become in the next generation, and that, as they cannot have sprung in places hostile to him from genuine reverence or gratitude to Al., they must have been prompted by the belief that they were welcome to an autocrat whom it was expedient to please and who aspired to deification, cf. vii 20, 1 n.)

3. A. suggests that, as Pt./Ar. said nothing of the purpose of the first Greek embassies, they were merely sent to congratulate Al. on his victories and safe return from India—twelve months earlier! This is puerile. Pt. and Ar. probably had little interest in Greek affairs (App. II and VI), and did not explain *theoroi*. D. says of all the embassies, Greek and barbarian, that they not only brought congratulations, crowns and gifts but negotiated treaties, answered charges against their states, and sought decisions on their disputes and in particular on difficulties that arose from the exiles' decree (App. XXIII 6). This is what we should assume, even in default of testimony. D. tells us something of the order which Al. prescribed for hearing different kinds of business they brought before him. This cannot be invention, and could come from Chares, as chief of protocol.

4. Pt. and Ar. also did not mention an embassy from Rome. A. rejects it partly on that ground, partly because it was not attested in Roman annals, and adds that it was unnecessary and inappropriate for Rome to send one. These arguments are worthless. Whatever Al's true designs were, no one in the west could be confident that he would not turn there (App. XXIII 5). Already the strongest state in central Italy, Rome had as good reason to seek his friendship as e.g. the Etruscans. We do not need to think that a Roman embassy offered submission. As nothing came of it, the embassy could easily

have been forgotten in the very defective annalistic tradition. Now Clitarchus alluded to the Roman embassy; he wrote too early to be influenced by the later importance of Rome. It would have been incumbent on A. to discredit this contemporary evidence, if he had known of it. Instead, he refers only to Aristus and Asclepiades, who also made Al. predict Rome's future greatness. Aristus of Salamis wrote before S., who says that he was much later than Ar. and Onesicritus (xv 3, 8). It is an unwarranted conjecture that he is the Cyprian Aristus (Athenaeus x 438 D) who served Antiochus II (261–46); the date is too early for the *post factum* prediction; to put him two or three generations before S. would fit S's vague indication. Asclepiades is otherwise unknown. I infer that A. did not read Clitarchus. Of course Clitarchus could not have had the prediction, but it is the embassy itself that interests A. and stirs his scepticism. What he knows of the vulgate is (as usual) a much later version. Aristus and Asclepiades may have recorded the Roman embassy in the same spirit as ' levissimi ex Graecis ', who held that had Al. lived he would easily have subdued the Romans (Livy ix 18, 6), cf. A. vii 1, 3 (from the same sources?); in their judgement it showed how terrified the Romans were, an imputation that A. loyally repudiates.

5. Tarn ii 374 ff. is quite right that the vulgate in A. vii 15, 4 and J. xii 13 with the references to Celts (obviously Gauls) and Iberians, hitherto unknown to the Greek world (J. adds Sardinians), is very late and designed to make 'Al. *seem* to be lord of the whole earth.' But his assumption that all this is in D. is false. D's Celts are neighbours of the Thracians, not

unknown peoples; this can be a true statement from
Clitarchus, wilfully transformed in later versions.   D.
mentions Macedonian embassies: Tarn objects that
the Macedonians had as yet no corporate organization
to make this possible; but we know far too little of
Macedonian institutions to deny that individual
cities and tribes (Pydna, Orestae etc.) could have sent
deputies to their king.   Similarly the Greek ambassadors are not just representatives of the League of
Corinth; D. 113, 3 implies the contrary, cf. A. vii 14,
6 (vulgate).   D's reference to ' envoys from the
tribes and cities of Asia and many of the dynasts' is
said to be a Seleucid formula.   What of that?   Of
course D. could use the *language* of a later day, but it
is absurd to deny the possibility that these tribes,
cities and dynasts sent ambassadors to Al.   Pt./Ar.
themselves referred to envoys from ' Libya.'   What
could that mean except for Greek and Phoenician
places, from Cyrene eastwards, including Carthage
and perhaps as far as Gades (as D. says)?   D's list
is itself defective; he ignores not only the Roman
embassy but all from Italy (even those which Pt./Ar.
mentioned), perhaps to spare Roman susceptibilities.
Only J. refers to Sicily, yet one can hardly believe
that the Greek cities there were less concerned to
establish good relations with Al. than the Etruscans.
None of our sources is complete, and least of all those
on which A. relied.   Clitarchus (whence D.), in
particular, supplied valuable data they omitted.

APPENDIX XXIII

THE LAST PHASE

1. Al. cannot have reached the Carmanian capital before late December 325 (App. XVIII 6). He was joined by N. at Susa ' in the seventh month ' after N. left the Indus, i.e. not earlier than the end of March (cf. *Ind.* 21 with notes); we cannot check this statement of Pliny vi 100 (presumably from Onesicritus), since in the *Indica* A. does not report the length of all intermissions in the voyage. The next dateable event is the winter campaign against the Cossaeans (A. vii 15), which occupied 40 days at most (D. 111) at any time between December 324 and March 323. Thus A. is very sparse (as in books v and vi) with chronological information. Even his extracts from the *ephemerides* (vii 25) omit datings by the Macedonian month Daisios which P. inserts in his shorter version (76). Al's death can be fixed on 10/11 June 323 (vii 28, 1 n.). He had probably reached Babylon less than two months earlier, since that was the time required to clear the site of the temple of Baal, work still unfinished at his death (S. xvi 1, 5).

2. Except in winter 324/3, there were no military operations. For the first time Al. paused. But he was preparing an expedition against the Arabians. He planned the circumnavigation of Arabia (*Ind.* 43), but more than that, he intended to found colonies on the coast, which presupposed conquest (vii 19, 5), even though the Arabians would be allowed local self-government (20, 1); he evidently hoped for substantial revenue (20, 2). The failure of the Arabians

to send him embassies was to be a pretext for war, if they would not submit (Ar. *ap.* 19, 6; S. xvi 1, 11, cf. 4, 27); hence an army was required (vii 25, 2), as well as a fleet. To supplement N's flotilla, ships were brought to the Euphrates from Phoenicia and built at Babylon (vii 19, 3 f.); the preparations must have begun in 324, since they were nearly complete in spring 323 (19, 3; 21, 1; 23, 5). Al. was evidently to command in person. There is no sign that he intended, as in 329/8 (iv 15, 6), to return to the Caspian, but the fleet he ordered for that sea included warships and was presumably not designed for mere exploration (vii 16, 1).

3. A. (vii 1, 2 f.) notes that some historians alleged that Al. meant to circumnavigate Africa and subdue Carthage on his way back through the Mediterranean (cf. P. 68), or to make an expedition to the Black Sea, or to go to Sicily and Italy (cf. QC. x 1, 17–19, who mentions the subjugation of Carthage) and to assail Rome; the last point betrays the lateness of A's vulgate source, since Rome, though already powerful (App. XXII 4), had not yet engaged much attention in the Greek world. In iv 7, 5 A. had accepted the first plan as authentic and in v 26, 2 he makes Al. himself outline it, but none of these passages come from Pt./Ar. Because of their silence many modern scholars pronounce all such plans to be fictitious.

4. However, it was the manner of Pt./Ar. not to mention Al's plans until they were ready, or almost ready, for execution. His intention to invade Asia is first incidentally revealed in i 10, 6; his plan to sail down to the Indus delta (App. XXV 2) only when the

flotilla was ready; if we hear of the project of conquering India in iv 15, 6, it was probably because Al. had then decided to carry it out at once, though resistance in Sogdiana was to postpone it. The mobilization of the fleet in spring 334 (i 11, 6) must have been ordered in 335, cf. § 2 on the preparations for the Arabian expedition. If Al. had lived to assail Carthage in 322 or 321, they would probably have been content to defer to that very moment any account of his decision and of the prior preparations, and if he had died in 324 we should have heard nothing of the Arabian project. Their story ended with his death, and his unfulfilled plans were not their concern. Indeed, if their silence meant anything, it would mean that Al. had no further plans of any kind except those which were already operational, and not, for instance, that he intended to devote his energy to organizing his ramshackle empire! But Ar. (who did not know his mind) was sure that he was insatiate for conquest (vii 19, 6 n.), and his promise to reward veterans so handsomely that other Macedonians would desire to share in the same dangers and toils (vii 8, 2 from Pt./Ar.) clearly implies that the new troops Antipater was commanded to bring out (12, 4) were not to form a peaceful army of occupation, nor were they needed for the Arabian expedition, which was to go forward at once.

5. No project is more likely to have appealed to Al. than a western expedition; assistance to the Greeks of Italy would have been a plausible pretext, if he needed one, especially as his uncle, Alexander of Epirus, had died while aiding Taras (iii 6, 7 n.). The prospect of the Pillars of Heracles and the western Ocean must also have allured him. According to D.

xviii 4 he gave Craterus instructions relating to his future plans; memoranda of these (*hypomnemata*) were found by Perdiccas among his papers and disclosed to the army, which decided, obviously at Perdiccas' instigation, not to proceed with them; they included a great western expedition. There is no agreement about D's source. Some suppose it to have been the reliable Hieronymus; others think that it was Clitarchus. But even in the latter case we cannot conclude that the story is fiction; Clitarchus *could* record the facts! And as for Hieronymus Badian (*Harvard St. in Class. Phil.* 1968, 183 ff.) is probably right in holding that he need have known no more than what Perdiccas chose to give out (though I do not find Badian's further conjectures compelling). Whether Clitarchus or Hieronymus was D's source, it emerges that a contemporary writer could believe that Al. meditated a western expedition. Of course, if the *hypomnemata* were genuine, it becomes certain that he did. As to these, we have only D's version; he does not purport to give a full text, and we cannot depend on the verbal accuracy of his summary; objections resting on his precise language are invalid. For many scholars most of the plans are too grandiose or absurd to be authentic (e.g. Tarn ii 378 ff; F. Hampl, *Studies presented to D. M. Robinson* 819 ff. = G. T. Griffith, *Alexander the Great* 308 ff.); to my mind they have been answered by F. Schachermeyr, *Jahrb. der oesterreich.-arch. Instituts* 1954, 118 ff. = Griffith 322 ff. and by Badian (*op. cit.*). One objection at least should not be heard: the silence of A. No doubt, if he had read of the *hypomnemata*, he would hardly have been capable of the subtle scepticism of modern scholars, and they would have resolved his doubts about Al's plans (vii 1). But Pt. and Ar.

APPENDIX XXIII

stopped at Al's death; genuine or forged, the *hypomnemata* lay beyond their scope. A. did not consult Clitarchus (App. XXVIII 13), and there is no reason to think that he read Hieronymus before composing his later work on Al's Successors. A's ignorance proves nothing.

6. Had Al. lived, he might well have been delayed or thwarted in a western enterprise by other pre-occupations. For what follows in this Appendix see especially E. Badian, *JHS* 1961, 16 ff. Al. had provoked discontent in Greece, of which A. tells even less than of earlier opposition there to Al. (App. II and VI). His reports of the Greek embassies rather suggest that Al. was beloved in Greece. This was false, cf. App. XXII 2 f. A. passes over Al's decree of early 324 (D. xvii 109; xviii 8; QC. x 2, 4 ff.; J. xiii 5) that all exiles except for certain criminals were to be restored to Greek cities. At the Olympic festival in early August 324, no less than 20,000 of them were present to hear with joy a letter publishing the decision. But the surviving ordinance of Tegea· (Tod 202) illustrates the embarrassing legal problems that it must have created everywhere, since restoration included recovery of some property rights. Tegea gave effect to the ordinance herself, but Antipater had been instructed to enforce it, and it is absurd to deny that it was a gross infraction of the autonomy of the Greek cities. Above all, it dismayed the Athenians and Aetolians, who feared that they would be compelled to give back to the people of Samos (cf. Dittenberger, *SIG* [3] 312) and Oeniadae respectively the lands on which they had settled their own colonists; they were to lead to the great anti-Macedonian movement which ensued on Al's death,

known as the Lamian war, far more widespread and dangerous than those of 334–1. For Hieronymus (D. xviii 8) the exiles' decree was the main cause. The underlying explanation was surely attachment to the old ideal of the freedom of Greek cities.

7. Another of Al's measures, of which our text of A. says nothing, was to make the Greek insurrection more formidable. In Carmania Al. directed his generals and satraps to disband the mercenary forces they had raised (D. 106). Since they could hardly maintain royal authority without armed force, this must mean that they were to have no troops except those which he himself sanctioned (cf. D. xviii 7 for the continued presence of mercenaries in Asia). Large numbers of discharged mercenaries began to assemble at Taenarum. Some were doubtless exiles whom Al's decree would return to their homes. Others remained to serve the Greek cause against Macedon. Money to pay them was provided in part out of the 5000 Talents which Harpalus brought with him (as well as 6000 mercenaries) on his flight from Babylon (D. 108). There he had been treasurer, with responsibilities whose extent we cannot define, but D. calls him satrap; perhaps he had usurped the office (Stamenes is not heard of after the appointment in 328/7, A. iv 18, 3), like Orxines in Persia (vi 30, 1) and perhaps Cleomenes in Egypt (App. XXIV 6). We are told that he feared punishment for mal-administration; probably then his flight occurred when he heard of the executions in Carmania (vi 27), i.e. early in 324. He temporarily took refuge in Athens in summer 324, and some of his money came into Athenian hands. The details do not concern us here; availability of a substantial force of

mercenaries gave the Greeks initial superiority in numbers over Antipater in the Lamian war.

8. There is a lacuna equivalent to about two pages of this edition in vii 12, 7, in which (as we know from Photius' epitome) the flight of Harpalus with the royal treasures was mentioned. The missing pages must also have recorded the march from Opis to Ecbatana (D. 110) and something of a dispute between Hephaestion and Eumenes (13, 1). There may also have been other matter, and there cannot have been space for a full treatment of the transactions summarized in § 6 f. The reserve with which Pt./Ar. alluded to Harpalus' much earlier flight (iii 6, 7) suggests that neither would have had much to say of his new defection. Why was it mentioned at just this point, some months after its occurrence? A. has previously told (12, 4) how Antipater had been ordered to bring Macedonian reinforcements to Al., and has discussed the supposed deterioration of relations between Al. and Antipater. In fact Antipater had not complied with the order at Al's death, after about twelve months. Perhaps he pleaded dangers in Greece, if not in Thrace (QC. x 1, 43 ff.) as an excuse, and this was mentioned by Pt./Ar. The origins of the Lamian war they probably regarded as lying outside their subject (App. XXVIII 29).

9. Al's decree disbanding mercenaries suggests that he feared revolts if his generals had troops attached to their own persons. In Carmania and later he removed and often executed satraps and generals for maladministration or disloyalty. Pt./Ar. evidently ascribed these actions to his concern for justice to his subjects (vi 27, 5), though they also hinted (vii 4,

APPENDIX XXIII

2) that he thought it treasonable if men had simply
despaired of his safe return from India. The same
favourable explanation sometimes appears in other
sources (P. 68; QC. x 1, 1–9). Yet doubts super-
vene. Al's later indulgence to Cleomenes (vii 23, 7
f.) is inconsistent with whole-hearted care for the
subjects. The supersession of Apollophanes (vi 27, 1
n.) was unjust; Orxines was probably the victim of
calumny (vi 30, 2 n.); the mode of Oxathres' execution (vii 4, 1 n.) suggests that Al. acted in passion.
In the vulgate (vii 4, 3; QC. x 1, 39 ff.; P. 42) he is
depicted as too prone to receive malicious accusations
and inexorably cruel in punishment; P. 57, 2 traces
this back to 327. A. thinks it necessary to defend
him on the charge of barbaric arrogance by referring
among other things to the evil influence of flatterers
(vii 29, 1, cf. ii 6, 4; iv 8, 3; 9, 7 f.). Even Pt. or Ar.
remarked that by 324 he had become more irascible
and that Oriental subservience had made him less
kindly to the Macedonians (vii 8, 3). Anecdotes told
by N. (*Ind.* 34, 5) and Ar. (vii 18) unintentionally
reveal his harshness and the terror he inspired. At
times he could still call forth the affection of the
army (vi 12; vii 11, 5 f.; 26, 1; cf. QC. x 5), but he
could no longer rely on it, as the resistance on the
Hyphasis and the mutiny at Opis showed. His
officers had opposed his will on the first occasion; they
had not accepted *proscynesis* (App. XIV 5), and Al.
must have sensed that they did not approve of his
Orientalism, or of his honouring Iranians, any more
than the common soldiers did (vii 6 and 8); yet he
persisted relentlessly in his policy, marrying the
Macedonian magnates willy-nilly to Persian ladies
(vii 4, 6 n.) and enrolling Orientals in the Macedonian
foot regiments (23, 2; 29, 4), as previously in the

Companion cavalry (vii 6 and 8). A's defence of his Orientalism as statesmanlike policy (29, 4) implies that men continued to censure him for it; A. does not ponder how far it was prudent to alienate the Macedonian nobility. The rumour that he was poisoned by Antipater's sons with the complicity of many of his chief officers arose soon after his death (27, 1 n.) and, false as it doubtless was, it could hardly have had any currency, but that they were thought to fear and detest him in their hearts. A's own opinion that he died ' when men felt most regret for him ' (16, 7) is hardly justified, but may betray a suspicion that his supposed popularity would inevitably have waned.

10. Pt. or Ar. felt obliged to refer to the rumour that Olympias' continual calumnies on Antipater had induced Al. to summon him from Macedon and appoint Craterus in his place; the same authority (who did not profess to kn(w Al's mind) supposed that Al. thought it best to prevent the conflict becoming irreconcilable by removing Antipater from the scene, on the ground that he continued to speak of Antipater with honour (12, 4–7), as if he were not capable of dissimulation. Badian (op. cit. § 6) argues that Antipater, fearing that obedience to the summons would be the prelude to his execution, not only did not comply (that is beyond question), but began to intrigue with the malcontents in Greece, of whom he had long been the oppressor. Why then did he place another of his sons, Cassander, as a hostage in Al's hands (P. 74 etc.)? See the reply by G. T. Griffith, *Proc. of Afr. Class. Associations* 1965, 12 ff. The relations between Al., Antipater and Craterus remain extremely obscure. One would naturally

APPENDIX XXIII

infer from vii 12, 4 that Craterus set off in summer 324; his men must have been anxious to return home quickly, and yet he was still in Cilicia a year later (D. xviii 12, 1); moreover, though his troops were desperately needed to repress the Greeks later in 323, he did not leave Cilicia to assist Antipater till spring 322 (ib. 16, 4). The local rising in which the satrap Balacrus had been killed (ib. 22) perhaps furnished a reason, or pretext, for delay. How much, if any part, of the explanation may have been given in the lacuna in vii 12 we cannot guess. If A. himself at this time read no detailed account of events after Al's death, he could have been unaware of Craterus' curious behaviour. It looks as if Pt. was very brief on Al's last year (the subject was delicate), while Ar., from whom A. draws much of his material, would have known nothing of high politics.

APPENDIX XXIV

PROSOPOGRAPHICAL DATA IN ARRIAN

1. A. names many of Al's military and civil officers but, though some were of great note in Al's reign or later, they all remain lay figures. Their services on the expedition, when they were given independent commands, are generally passed over in silence (ii 4, 2 n.) or in a few words, see ii 11, 10; iii 2, 3–7 with ii 2, 3; iii 27, 3; 28, 2 f. (contrast D. 83, 6); iv 16, 2 f.; 16, 4–17, 2 and 17, 4–7 (both exceptional); 22, 7 with 30, 9; v 20, 7; 21, 5; 24, 6; vi 5, 5–7; 6, 4 and 6; 15, 1; 20, 1; 27, 2 f.; vii 5, 5 with *Ind.* 23, 5; cf. App. XI 4 on Parmenio. So too Antipater's suppression

of Agis is neglected. Only Pt.'s courage and ability make some impression on the reader; this needs no explaining. (Even he gets a bare mention in vii 15, 3.) Scholars have recently been zealous to discern signs of Pt's bias towards those who were his enemies (notably Perdiccas) or friends in the struggles that followed Al's death. But the depreciation of Perdiccas (e.g. i 8, 1 n.), if such it be, is very veiled, or wholly lacking (vi 15, 1); to be effective, obloquy has to be laid on more heavily. If A. faithfully represents his main sources, it looks as if their aim was to keep the spotlight almost always focussed on Al. A. himself also betrays no interest in the future greatness of any officer except Seleucus (v 13, 1; vii 22, 5 n.).

2. From the information on appointments A. supplies we can attempt to trace Al's policy in trusting Orientals with high posts. But A. merely provides the facts without interpretation. He does not connect these appointments with other evidence for Al's policy towards Orientals: his marriage with Roxane, in which A. discerns no political significance (iv 19, 5 f.), and the marriages at Susa (vii 4, cf. 6, 2), for which he offers no explicit explanation; the prayer at Opis (vii 11, 8); the introduction of Orientals into Macedonian units (vii 6, 3–5; 8, 2; 23, 3 f.); the training of the Epigoni (vii 6, 1); the mixture of population in new cities (iii 1, 5 n.); Al's adoption of the style of a Persian king (iv 7, 4; 9, 9; vii 6, 2 and 5; 8, 2 f.; 29, 4); his commendation of Peucestas (vi 30, 2 f; vii 6, 3); and other honours paid to the Persians (vii 11, 1–3); it is indeed only implicit in his narrative that Al. regarded himself as Darius' legitimate successor, and no longer as simply Macedonian

APPENDIX XXIV

king. It may be said that he lets the facts speak for themselves, but in vii 29, 4 he offers an apology for just one or two elements in Al's Orientalism. I do not believe that he had thought about the subject as a whole.

3. Very seldom does A. advert to any policy that Al. had in making appointments (iii 5, 7; 27, 4); he sometimes explains why particular individuals were retired (iv 17, 3) or promoted (iii 6, 6; 23, 7; vi 28, 3; 30, 2 f.; vii 12, 4 ff.), more often why they were deposed or punished (i 25; iii 6, 8; iv 18, 2 f.; vi 27, 1; 28, 4 f.; 29, 2; vii 4, 1). Again his prosopographical data enable modern scholars to offer conjectures on the strength of factions in Al's Macedonian entourage. A. himself only alludes to such factions in vii 12, 4 ff.; 14, 9. QC., if reliable, is sometimes more useful (as in his account of the conspiracy against Philotas).

4. In particular, A. does not make clear the special position obtained by Hephaestion (Berve no. 357). The reader can only infer his growing importance from the independent commands he held from 328, and his ultimate primacy from his marriage at Susa to a sister of Al's bride and from the behaviour of Al. when he died (vii 14; 23, 6). In A's account this is naïvely treated as a mere manifestation of personal grief: Al. mourns for him rather like Achilles for Patroclus (cf. i 12, 1; vii 16, 8), though A. is concerned to defend his hero against the imputation of uncontrolled emotion. No doubt a unique affinity was the basis of H's influence—he was Al's *alter ego* (ii 12, 6–8, vulgate)—though he must also have been competent as a commander. Only P. (47) tells us

that he was enthusiastic for Al's Orientalizing policy and that this brought him into conflict with Craterus, whose disapproval of it was probably one reason why Al. decided in 324 to pack him off to Macedon; for their hostility cf. D. 114. Al's commendation of Craterus to the troops (vii 12, 3) need not be taken as wholly sincere. H's enmity with Eumenes (vii 13, 1, cf. Plut., *Eum.* 2) was apparently reported by Pt./Ar. (vii 14, 9). Perhaps of all his officers H. was at the last the only one whom Al. could fully trust. A. alludes to his being chiliarch over the Companion horse, a post to which no successor was appointed on his death (14, 10). This is quite obscure in the context. Previously we have heard only of hipparchs, among them H. (Introd. 58). Evidently H. was still in command of a regiment of horse (hipparchy), which was to preserve his name; Plut. *Eum.* 1 shows that *de facto* Perdiccas took it over, transferring his own ' hipparchy ' to Eumenes; D. xviii 3, 4 suggests that general command of all the Companion horse went with it and also belonged to Perdiccas at the time of Al's death, which would explain A's phraseology. But the title chiliarch corresponds to the Persian *hazārapatis* (commander of a thousand), who had been a sort of grand vizier under the Achaemenids, and D. xviii 48, 5 (Hieronymus) expressly says that Al. re-established the post, evidently for H's benefit. On Al's death Perdiccas at last acquired H's chiliarchy, and therewith ' the stewardship of the entire kingdom ' (Hieronymus *ap.* Arrian, *Succ.* 1, 3). With no king capable of governing, Perdiccas' position was even stronger than H's, though unlike H. he did not also hold the command over the Companions, which he relinquished to Seleucus. However, H. had at least become formally Al's chief minister (cf. F. Schachermeyr, *Alex. in Babylon*, 1970, 31 ff.). Was not the appointment recorded in its due place by either Pt. or Ar.?

5. Since Ar. listed the bodyguards (vi 28, 4) and N. trierarchs of the Indus flotilla (*Ind.* 18), we should not assume that Pt. was A's sole source of prosopographical data. They are also provided by QC. and, to a less extent, no doubt because he is much briefer, by D., evidently from their common source, presumed to be Clitarchus. Very likely it was the practice of the Alexander-historians to show Al. surrounded by his paladins, whose names (even those later forgotten) must often have been resonant to readers in their own day. The list of satraps in post at Al's death given by D. xviii 3 and Arrian in his *Successors*, together with the summary of that work by Dexippus (Roos ii 255 f.), is believed to come from the reliable Hieronymus, and also shows that in the *Anabasis* A. failed to record all the changes made in Al's lifetime. QC. and D. actually supply information not to be found in A. Discrepancies in names occur. Some may be due to textual errors or mere variations in the transcription of foreign names, e.g. Phradates for Autophradates; others, e.g. Terioltes for Tyriaspes (vi 15, 3 n.), can be explained by slips of memory; and it is probably unjustified without supporting reasons (e.g. iii 16, 9 n. on Xenophilus) to suppose that where A. and QC. differ (e.g. ii 4, 2 n.) one of them has inadvertently substituted the second for the first holder of a post. Though sometimes careless (v 20, 7 n.), A. is probably more accurate than D. or QC., but he confirms them often enough to justify us in accepting their *supplementary* information. A. himself sometimes reveals in later allusions appointments

he has not mentioned in their due place. His
omissions show that though it was his practice to
transcribe mechanically from his sources data of little
interest or meaning to himself or his readers, which
perhaps served the purpose of demonstrating the
fullness of his acquaintance with his subject, his
diligence failed at times.

6. *Satraps*. A. records the *first appointments* when
made, except for Nearchus in Lycia (omitted in i 24,
but cf. iii 6, 6) and Astaspes in Carmania (vi 27, 1 n.).
Replacements are often neglected, or incompletely
reported, e.g. iii 6, 8 (the previous satrap of Lydia,
Asander, re-appears without explanation in iv 7, 2).
It is a conjecture that Lycia was attached to Great
Phrygia, when Nearchus came east (iv 7, 2). Ad-
ministrative changes in Syria and Cilicia are unclear
(iii 6, 8 and 16, 9 nn.). A's account of the original
arrangements for Egypt is perplexing (iii 5, 6 n.),
and we do not find in the *Anabasis* what he recorded
in the sequel (*Successors* fr. 1, 5, cf. Dexippus fr. 1, 2
in Roos vol. ii), that Al. at some time put Cleomenes
in charge of Egypt, which would mean that the
apparent division of authority devised in 331 had
been abandoned. See J. Seibert, *Untersuch. zur
Gesch. des Ptol. I*, 39 ff.; J. Vogt and Seibert in
Chiron 1971, 153 ff. and 1972, 99 ff. On Al's death
Cleomenes became hyparch to Pt., who soon put him
to death. It is hard to believe that Pt. did not record
changes in the government of Egypt affecting Cleomenes, especially if vii 23, 6–8 comes from his
account (App. XXVII 7). Again, A. does not
mention that Black Clitus was to succeed Artabazus in
Bactria (QC. viii 1, 19); he is not explicit on the death
of Nicanor in N.W. India (v 20, 7 n.); he overlooks

the death of Menon in Arachosia and, as he ignores
Astaspes, he does not record that Sibyrtius was his
successor in Carmania (vi 27, 1 n.). He does not
name the successor of Abulites in Susiana (vii 4, 1)—
who it was is disputed (cf. Berve nos. 107 and 440,
not perhaps right)—nor tell us why and when
Philoxenus (Berve no. 794) had taken over Caria (vii
23, 1; 24, 2; cf. i 23). He does not report the death
in Al's lifetime of Balacrus in Cilicia at the hands of
local tribesmen (D. xviii 22, 1). Only D. xviii 3 shows
that when Al. died Philip (Berve no. 785) and not
Amyntas (iv 22, 3 n.) was satrap of Bactria, and
Archon (*Ind.* 18), and not Stamenes (iv 18, 3), of
Babylon, and that Mesopotamia had become a
separate province under Arcesilaus. By 323 Demar-
chus had replaced Calas in Hellespontine Phrygia
(Arrian. *Succ.* fr. 1, 6; p. 257 Roos). Badian, *JHS*
1961, 16 ff. conjectures that Amyntas, Calas and
Stamenes may have been victims of the purge Al.
carried out in 324. But A's authorities did not
hesitate to record, however apologetically, Al's
removal of men who incurred his displeasure, whereas
they showed virtually no interest in transactions
where he was not present (cf. the case of Balacrus);
the common view is more likely, that Amyntas and
Calas at least died fighting rebels.

7. *Generals and commandants of citadels.* Among the
generals in Media (iii 26, 3) the position of Heracon
(vi 27) is unexplained, and Agathon (QC. x 1, 1) is
perhaps carelessly omitted. The satrap was the
Persian Atropates; one can hardly suppose that after
324 no European troops were stationed in Media, but
we are not told who succeeded to the command.
Commandants are mentioned in i 17, 7; iii 5, 3; 16, 9;

APPENDIX XXIV

29, 1; iv 28, 6; 30, 4, but not at Babylon and Persepolis (QC. v 1, 43, cf. D. 64, 5, and v 6, 11).

8. *Financial officials.* The roles of those in Egypt (iii 5, 4), Phoenicia and Asia this side of Taurus (iii 6, 4) and indeed of Harpalus (App. XXIII 7) are not clearly defined. It seems unlikely that Lydia and Babylonia were the only satrapies in which there were officials corresponding to Roman procurators (i 17, 7; iii 16, 4). QC. (cf. D. 69, 1) mentions financial officials, not necessarily of the same kind, at Susa and Persepolis, see iii 16, 9 n.; App. X 1. Harpalus' successor, perhaps Antimenes (Berve no. 89), is not named, unless in the lacuna (vii 12).

9. *The seven Bodyguards.* A. copied out Ar's list for 325, when an eighth was added (vi 28, 4). They were then, as earlier, staff officers of high eminence. Apparently no one retained the post once he had received another appointment which *permanently* separated him from the royal person. Altogether 14 names are attested for Al's reign (Berve i 27). A. intermittently notes changes (ii 12, 2; iii 5, 5; 27, 5). Surely his sources did not fail to record others, especially when the context made this natural, e.g. the death of one Ptolemaeus (Berve no. 672) in battle (i 22, 7), the removal of another man of that name (i 24, 1; Berve no. 670) to command of a phalanx regiment (ii 8, 4; 10, 7), and the appointment of Menes to a high post (iii 16, 9, cf. ii 12, 2). By 325 the bodyguards included Hephaestion, Lysimachus, Perdiccas and Pithon, men of great importance, who cannot *all* have enjoyed this rank from the first, yet in *no* case are we told when they were first appointed (contrast iii 5, 5 for Leonnatus and 27, 5 for Ptolemy).

APPENDIX XXIV

10. *Commanders of military units.* On Philotas' execution the command of the Companions was divided between Hephaestion and Black Clitus (iii 27, 4), but only incidental allusions indicate that after Clitus' murder there were seven hipparchs, of whom six are casually named (Introd. 58). Nicanor, son of Parmenio, held a great post as commander of the hypaspists; did he have a successor on his death (iii 25, 4), or was the command divided between three chiliarchs (cf. iv 30, 5)? At the Hydaspes Seleucus was perhaps in command (v 13, 4 n.). At first Calas commanded the Thessalian cavalry (i 14, 3); we are told that Alexander the Lyncestian replaced him when he became a satrap (i 25, 2), but only in connection with the Lyncestian's arrest, and his successor must be identified, conjecturally, from a subsequent allusion in iii 11, 10. Yet these changes were more important than those in the commands of Greek allies or mercenaries recorded in i 29, 3; iii 5, 6; 6, 8. The colonels of the phalanx regiments too were men of note; in 334 they included Coenus, Perdiccas and Craterus. Just one new appointment is registered (ii 12, 2); other changes must be inferred from A's accounts of battle-orders and other casual references.

11. It is theoretically possible that A's sources omitted what he omits. But it appears in several instances that they are likely to have recorded new appointments that he mentions later or not at all; the evidence is cumulative that his excerpts from their histories was in this respect, as in others, incomplete.

APPENDIX XXV

NEARCHUS' VOYAGES

1. At one time Al. thought that the Indus was the Nile in its upper course (vi 1); even then he could have supposed that India was connected with Persia and Egypt by an inner sea, into which one branch of the Indus flowed, while the main stream ran south of this sea through deserts, taking first a westward and then a northward course to become the Nile (Schachermeyr, *Alex. der Grosse*, 1973, 443–51). No doubt this illusion did not long persist; he must surely have acquired better information about the lower course and delta of the Indus even before reaching the Acesines. He was ultimately in no doubt that at the outlets of the Indus he had come to the great encompassing Ocean. By then he knew that the Ocean linked India with Persia, though he had no detailed information about the sea route, and N. was specifically directed to report on the coastline and off-shore islands, the inhabitants and their manners and customs, anchorages, water supplies and products (*Ind.* 20; 32, 11; vii 20, 10). N. also rightly supposed that the Persian Gulf was connected by water with Egypt, but he seems to have thought that there was a passage into the Red Sea from a bay north of the Oman promontory (*Ind.* 32, 8); this was only refuted by Hieron in 324 or 323 (vii 20, 8).

2. The availability of seamen from the Mediterranean (vi 1, 6; *Ind.* 18, 2; 31, 3), who had no role to perform earlier in Al's expedition, suggests that they

had been summoned for the purpose; they could have arrived as late as autumn 326 under escort of reinforcements (App. XIX 3), and in that case must have been sent for before Al. entered India, when he still did not realize that India was washed by the Ocean and thought of reaching Egypt by river (S. xv 1, 25); he had been detained in Sogdiana long after he had decided on the invasion of India in 329/8 (iv 15, 6). Cutting of timber for the river flotilla began soon after Porus' defeat (D. 89, 4; QC. ix 1, 4, confirmed by S. xv 1, 29, which should come from Ar., cf. App. XVII 18). This does not prove that Al. was not as yet bent on penetrating to the mouth of the Ganges, since (as D. and QC. supposed) he could have intended to go down to the mouths of the Indus later. He had some boats already (v 3, 5; 8, 5; 13, 1), and commandeered others from natives, doubtless with crews, but he added to the number ships of a Greek type by new construction (vi 2, 4). Pt. gave the whole number as 2000 (ibid.), which might be a round number for 1800, if we amend '800' in the text of *Ind.* 19. 7 (N.). However, D. 95, 5 speaks of 200 *aphractoi* and 800 'service' vessels, and QC. ix 3, 22 of 1000 in all. It may be (a) that D's 200 *aphractoi* (cf. Casson, *op. cit.* v 3, 6 n., p. 134) includes the 80 triacontors and other larger vessels to which Pt. alluded (*l.c.*), and that this figure has fallen out of A's excerpt of N.; (b) that Pt. included about 1000 very small boats, which all the other writers ignored. For further constructions cf. vi 14, 4; 15, 1. Schiwek rightly emphasizes that Al. could call on local shipwrights and rivermen, citing evidence from Meg. *ap.* *Ind.* 12, 1 and S. xv 1, 46 and 50 f. and from Indian sources; for river pilots note vi 20, 3; QC. ix 8, 30–9, 3. Patala means 'ship-station'. We have no data for the fleet of the coastal voyage (*contra* Engels 111, who is also inaccurate on the river flotilla).

3. There was also some seafaring activity on the Indian coast. This explains how O. heard of Ceylon (S. xv 1, 15). The phenomena described in *Ind.* 25, 4 ff. (cf. S. ii 1, 20; Orthagoras, Jacoby no. 713, F. 2) could not have been observed north of the Tropic of Cancer, some 70 km. south of the existing eastern mouth of the Indus and much further from the outlet in Al's day. There is nothing to show that Al. ventured so far into the open sea or passed down the Ran of Kutch, while N. himself hugged the coast. N. must then be reporting what local sailors had told him. Even in A's version, which may have been less clear than the original, it is not implied (as often alleged) that N. and his men claimed to have seen the phenomena for themselves; and the coastal voyage can have been that undertaken by those who traded with Ceylon (as A. doubtless failed to discern). Local sailors could inform N. in advance of the on-coming of the N.E. monsoon (vi 21, 2). As cinnamon grows only in India and further east (*RE* xi 481 f.), *Ind.* 32, 7 implies the existence of seaborne trade between India and Arabia; Schiwek (68) seems also to have proved that the Arabians imported certain woods from India. But they may have had the carriage in their own hands (cf. *Ind.* 41, 6 ff.; Ar. *ap.* S. xvi 3, 3 for their voyages in the Persian Gulf). N's mission and instructions would have been super-fluous if Al. could have obtained, while in Sind, detailed information about the coast between the mouths of the Indus and Euphrates. Many scholars argue that he and N. had access to Scylax' book, but their ignorance of the existence and the extent of

APPENDIX XXV

Darius' rule in India (App. XV) seems to me decisive against this; it is a wanton assumption that Aristotle, who refers to it (*Politics* 1332 b 24), had imparted his miscellaneous erudition to the princely teenager. The brief allusion to Scylax in Hdt. iv 44 could easily have been overlooked. Still stranger are notions that Al. was carrying round the Persian archives and found relevant data in them, or that they could be obtained from Persian nobles in his court, landlubbers to a man.

4. N's book was obviously based on the reports he made to Al., and ultimately on the log-book in which he must have recorded data for those reports, but such passages as A. paraphrases in 20; 34–6; 41, 8–10 were clearly added on publication, together with much other matter not concerned with the voyages at all (App. XVII 5; XVIII). If it was to have been useful as sailing directions, the report should have had more information than A. provides on winds, currents, coastal features etc., but N. himself may have left out of his book much in his report that would not interest the reading public. However, A. certainly did not reproduce the entire substance of N's book; this we know from the incidental and generally briefer paraphrases or summaries of N. in S. (21, 1; 29, 9; 31, 1; 32, 3; 37, 3; 38, 1 and 3; 40, 6 and 11 nn.); and it is probable that he carelessly omitted in a few places data which N. normally supplied on the length of voyages (22, 4; 42, 7 nn.) and other such matters (21, 2; 22, 11; 23, 6; 29, 1 nn.); he was grossly inaccurate in at least one case (37, 3 n.) and probably misunderstood N. in 25, 4 (cf. § 3) and 29, 10. The language is of course always his own (App. XXVIII 7).

APPENDIX XXV

5. A. did not collate other accounts of the voyages (App. XVII 4). We know little of them. Pliny cites both N. and O. (vi 96), but his language shows that he knew O. only through Juba (*c.* 50 B.C.–A.D. 23), and he, and perhaps Juba (but cf. vi 107), had not actually read N. at all, since Pliny alleges that neither account recorded the names of stopping places and the distances between them. In vi 96–100, cf. 109–11; 124, he then gives a second hand summary of O., a jumble and nearly useless, with some manifest falsehoods, such as the repeated allusions to navigable rivers, one reaching across the watershed to Pasargadae, which must go back to O. himself. Very little is preserved of Androsthenes and Orthagoras (Jacoby nos. 711; 713). Theophrastus used all these accounts for his botanical work. Philostratus' life of Apollonius describes a fictitious voyage of his hero and contains some reminiscences of them (iii 53 ff.), but a writer who makes the Hyphasis discharge into the sea (52) is totally unreliable. The brief summaries of N's report to Al. in D. and QC. no doubt go back to Clitarchus, who presumably read N. and O., but they add almost nothing.

6. The frequent vagueness in the topographical descriptions preserved in our sources, and the lack of good modern accounts of the coast, have made the identification of the places N. mentions generally insecure, and I have been sparing in offering suggestions in the commentary. The principal modern studies are those of W. Tomaschek (*SB Wien*, 1890), M. Neubert (*Petermanns Geogr. Mitteilungen*, 1928, 136 ff.) and H. Schiwek, cf. also E. Herzfeld, *Klio* 1908, 1 ff.

7. A. usually gives the number of stades for each day's sailing; his occasional omissions explain why his totals for the length of coastlines do not tally with the sums of the individual voyages. The totals, in *Ind.* 25, 3; 29, 8; 38, 1; 40, 1; 42, 4 are as follows:

A	Coast of Arabies (Indus to Hab)	about 1000 stades
B	Coast of Oritans (Hab to Ras Malan)	„ 1600 „
C	Coast of Fisheaters (Ras Malan to Ras el Kuh)	over 10,000 „
D	Coast of Carmania (Ras el Kuh to near Qeys)	3700 „
E	Coast of Persis (near Qeys to Bandar e Mashur)	4400 „
F	Coast of Susiana (Bandar e Mashur to mouth of Euphrates)	not given
G	(mouth of Karun to mouth of Euphrates)	2000 „

S. xv 2, 1 gives the same figures for A and D, but 1800 for B (this is not a corruption in his text, but N's figure may have been wrongly transmitted to him or to us) and 7400 for C.; probably E. had arbitrarily reduced the figure, to make the coastline equal to his measurement for the northern boundary of 'Ariana', and S. followed him. Neubert remarked that the total distance from the mouth of the Indus to Harmozia (including over 1600 stades of the Carmanian coast) was over 14,200 stades, corresponding to about 1300 km, and argued that N. consistently used a stade a little less than 100 metres long. He then identified many places simply on the basis of sailing distances between them and places which could be securely identified on other grounds. By contrast, Tomaschek held that N's stade varied in length between 75 and 150 metres.

8. Neubert was led by his thesis into false identifications (e.g. Arabis with Purali) and had to admit that later N. sometimes used a longer stade. To take clear instances, N's estimate of the length of Qeshm (37, 2) implies a stade of about 150 m. and that of the distance up the Euphrates to Babylon one of about 185 m. (41, 8); yet that for the coast of Persis still requires one of no more than 100 m. In my judgement Lehmann-Haupt (*Klio Beiheft* 37, 117 ff.), whose views I adapt, rightly explained these inconsistencies on the footing that N's stade is estimated from sailing times. Even the bematists indeed probably based their estimates on hours of marching but, when the conditions of a march made an average rate unlikely, they could resort to pacing short sectors. No such control was possible at sea. Probably N. assumed that the fleet traversed 50 stades an hour, so that a voyage lasting all day and night, perhaps 22 hours rather than 24, was deemed to be one of 1100 stades (29, 7). But variations of wind or current, and changes of course occasioned by shoals, reefs, and indentations in the coastline, must have greatly affected speed and made calculations of the length of a coast-line unreliable. Thus speed must have been reduced when N. was negotiating the shoals of the Susian coast without local pilots (40, 9–11; 41, 2; cf. 42, 1–4). No doubt over longer distances these variations averaged out, and this explains the degree of consistency Neubert noted. Whether N. was conscious of using such a stade, little more than half of the bematists', is another matter. He may have

overrated his average speed. In fact his estimate in 41, 8 (above) implies adoption of the bematists' stade, but here he may have actually given their measurement, and not calculated the distance up to Babylon from his own voyage-times. Other reports of land-distances must have come from unreliable estimates by natives (e.g. in 26, 3), while in his account of the Gadrosian march (App. XVIII), when he wrote of Al. camping 20 stades from water-courses (vi 25, 6) or effecting marches of up to 600 stades (S. xv 2, 6), he clearly repeated exaggerated stories told him by the survivors. To make sense of them, it has been suggested that the stade was here only 40 m., for which there is no parallel, in his work or elsewhere. Since Neubert's theory that his stade was about half the normal stade does not remove the absurdity of these statements, they afford no proof of the theory.

APPENDIX XXVI

MESOPOTAMIAN RIVERS

1. The ancient accounts of the lower courses of the rivers that flow into the Persian Gulf, including A's, are confused and contradictory. At present the Euphrates and Tigris unite nearly 200 km. from the sea to form the Shatt al Arab, into which the Karun flows. In antiquity hydrographic conditions varied and this was not always true.

2. One confusion in A. can be elucidated. In vii 7, 1 Al. sails down the Eulaeus from Susa to the sea, but in *Ind.* 42 N. sails up the Pasitigris to meet him. The

Pasitigris is certainly the Karun, but the river that flows close to Susa is the Kharkeh (Choaspes), which now loses itself in swamps east of Tigris. Evidently a canal connected the Kharkeh with the Karun, probably at Ahvaz, below the rapids which barred navigation on the Karun; there Al's pontoon bridge (*Ind.* 42, 7) may be placed. At Susa this name was sometimes applied to the whole waterway, viz. the upper course of the Choaspes, the canal and the lower course of the Pasitigris, while that river was given its proper name by people living at its mouth. Thus Ar. and Pt. adopted the first usage and N. the second, and A. follows the practice of whichever source he used. See G. le Rider, *Suse sous les Séleucides*, 1965, 262 ff. with map.

3. Following N., A. speaks of the mouth of the Euphrates with the mart of Diridotis nearby (*Ind.* 41, 7 n.), whence N. could sail up to Babylon (41, 8; vii 19, 3). Ar. too wrote of two islands near the mouth (vii 20, 3–6); he absurdly over-estimated the close-ness of Tylos, one of the Bahrain islands (S. xvi 3, 4; *RE* vii A 1732 f.), but could be roughly right in making Icarus 120 stades distant, cf. S. xvi 3, 2. It should then be the modern Failaki, and the Euphrates must have flowed into the sea in one of the present creeks above the island of Waraba. Cf. E. *ap.* S. xvi 3, 2; ii 1, 26. However, in Polybius' time the irrigation canals had so far reduced the stream of Euphrates in its lower course that it never reached the sea (ix 43). A. describes how it was lost in swamps (v 5, 5; vii 7, 3–5). It is clear that he is not in the second passage following any of the historians of Al., for whom the Euphrates had an outlet into the sea; in the first he is otherwise following E. and,

unless for once he has silently corrected his source
from more up-to-date information, we must suppose
that the change had occurred in E's time and was
intermittently recognized in his work. Cf. *RE* vi
1200 ff.

4. In 324 the Karun too had its own outlet into the
sea (N. *ap. Ind.* 42; S. xv 3, 5); S's report (xv 3, 4)
that it flowed into the Tigris doubtless reflects later
conditions; this outlet was separated by the Susian
coast from the so-called mouths of the Euphrates and
Tigris (cf. also vii 7, 6; Pliny, *NH.* vi 130); the lake
into which the Tigris flowed and which N. ' sailed
past ' (*Ind.* 42, 2) was evidently separated from the
sea by a strip of land. But according to Polyclitus
the Choaspes (Kharkeh), Eulaeus (Karun) and Tigris
all met in the lake and then emptied into the sea;
Onesicritus said that the Euphrates also did so, but
had its own outlet into the sea (S. xv 3, 4 f.). To
make sense of all this, we must suppose that the lake
had various outlets into the sea, which were respectively identified as the mouths of the Euphrates,
Tigris and Karun. From the evidence about this
lake and Aginis and from modern discussions (e.g.
RE i 810 ff.; 1877 ff.), I can get no clear picture of its
precise location, dimensions or relation to the numerous lakes which still exist. The hand of man has
obviously made great changes in the appearance of
the region. The figures for distances along the coast
or for internal waterways given by N. and others
seem to be inconsistent and unreliable.

APPENDIX XXVII

ARRIAN'S SPEECHES AND LETTERS

1. Instructions issued by generals, debates in a council or assembly which took decisions, diplomatic communications and the like were an important part of the historical record. In principle their substance could be as well remembered and as accurately reported as other events. Naturally no one could recollect the exact words used, except perhaps for some striking phrase, and even that might be *ben trovato*. If then A., like Xenophon, chooses at times (e.g. i 13; ii 12, 4; v 11, 4; *Ind.* 20; 34–6) to report dialogues or military orders wholly or partly in direct speech, it is for variety and vividness; it is naïve to suppose that he is then giving, or purporting to give, the *ipsissima verba*, but absurd to hold that as the *words* are A.'s, the *substance* is less authentic than if A. had employed indirect speech (as in e.g. i 18, 6 ff.). However, the longer a speech is, and the more elaborate, the less easy it becomes to assume its complete ' authenticity ' even in substance. Complex arguments were harder to recall in their exact tenor and order. Thucydides had admitted to supplementing what he knew had been said by what was appropriate to speaker and occasion (i 22). Lucian recommended this procedure (*How to Write History* 58). In so far as any ancient historian adopted this method with success, we cannot distinguish truth from plausible fiction. Exaggerations, half-truths and lies offer no criterion, for they might all be ' authentic '. Invention can only be proved where the speaker is credited with statements, true or false,

that *he* could not have uttered. The rhetoric of the historian may also clothe utterances that are in substance ' authentic '. It is of course another matter when there is reason to think that the historian *could* not have known that a speech was delivered or what it contained. Beyond doubt many speeches in classical histories are nothing but literary embellishments. In any event all allowed the historian to display his own eloquence (Lucian *loc. cit.*).

2. A. of course knew nothing of Al's time except what he read in his sources. The substance of the speeches and conversations in his works must come from them, or be his own invention. But in the former case we must not assume that where A. inserts a speech he necessarily found one in his source; he could himself have worked up relevant material. No one, however, can doubt that the dialogues in the *Indica* go back to N. himself. In any case, convinced as he was of his mastery of style (App. XXVIII 6 ff.), A. would naturally have rewritten a speech he had before him; knowing that it could not represent, any more than his own composition, the actual *words* of the speaker, he was free to improve on it. He could then, consciously or unconsciously, have inserted what he believed to be true and appropriate to the speaker, even though the additions were not guaranteed either by the speech in his source or by data which that source supplied. In his own personal reflections A. accepts from the ' vulgate ' Al's adoption of the dress and style of a Persian king (iv 7, 4; vii 29, 4), his claim to be of divine birth (vii 29, 3) and his ambitions of world-conquest (iv 7, 5; vii 1), though Pt. and Ar. at most hinted at these things (vii 8, 2 f.; 19, 6; 22, 4). In the same way

speeches written by A. could be coloured by what he found credible in inferior authorities, even when their setting was given by Pt. or Ar. and though they may be derived in part from speeches composed by one of those writers. Thus the speeches in A. cannot be *more* reliable than the contextual narrative, and they may be *less*. The speeches and discourse in iv 10 f. must be dismissed at once, as they are part of a story that is pure fiction (App. XIV 7 ff.), but this does not imply that their substance is A's own invention: the sharp distinction drawn in iv 11, 8 between Greeks and Macedonians (cf. Introd. 25) shows that he was using fairly early source material. The other speeches are all attached to a narrative derived from Pt./Ar.

3. Tarn accepted some of them as authentic but not others, in accordance with his personal prepossessions (App. 15); of the typically learned sophistry with which he defended his arbitrary distinctions one general argument merits refutation. He thought it proof of fiction that the speakers at the Beas are made to say ' these things and the like ' or to speak ' somewhat as follows ' or ' in such terms ' (v 27, 1; 28, 1), whereas in authentic speeches (ii 18, 1; vii 11, 1) we have ' these things ' (cf. also ii 15, 1); Tarn actually thought that Al's speech at Opis included some of his actual words! However, A's model, Xenophon, makes these formulae correspond (*Anabasis* i 3, 2 and 7; 9 and 13; ii 5, 3 and 15). Moreover, the formula Tarn takes to signify authenticity occurs also in ii 7, 6, in a speech to which he took unwarranted objection; and the introductory ' thus ' prefaces Al's speech at the Beas (v 25, 2) as well as those at Tyre (ii 16, 8) and Opis (vii 8, 3).

APPENDIX XXVII

Finally Tarn himself held some parts of the Opis speech to be fiction, because Al. could not have said it. But if any part is demonstrably fiction, no reliance can be placed on the rest except on the implausible premise that all fiction must be *patently* false.

4. In substance Al's speech before Issus, partly in direct speech, seems as likely to come from Pt./Ar. as that in indirect speech before Gaugamela (iii 9, 5 ff., cf. ii 7, 3 n.); at most the addendum in ii 7, 8 f. is suspect. In ii 17 A. takes the opportunity to explain Al's strategy in the siege of Tyre, perhaps following Pt., whereas Ar. may be his source for what immediately precedes (App. XXVIII 25). (The reference to Sparta (§ 2) is a venial exaggeration, and § 3 inspires confidence precisely because the Phoenicians and Cypriotes joined Al. earlier than here predicted.) It is quite possible that A. had authority for supposing that on each occasion Al. spoke in the sense he conveys. On the other hand, Acuphis could have known nothing of Al's city foundations, so that v 5 f. certainly includes invention, which may, however, be due to Ar. rather than to A. (App. XVI). None of these speeches is characterized by the rhetoric of those at the Beas and at Opis.

5. The discontent of the army at the Beas, the convening of the officers and the delivery of speeches by Al. and Coenus are reported by A. as facts (v 25, 1 f.; 27, 1). Tarn had no right to hold that Coenus could not even have been present (v 27, 1 n.). But in A's description of the effects of Coenus' speech (28, 1–4) there is that alternation of direct and indirect

531

speech which in other cases seems to reflect dependence on some good source other than Pt., usually Ar. (App. XXVIII 18). The emphatic allusion to Pt. in 28, 4, as stating that Al. found the omens for crossing the Beas unfavourable, suggests that Pt. was used here for the first time and only recorded that Al. decided to turn back after and because of this sign of divine will, without even hinting that the army was not prepared to go further. This would be characteristic of Pt's apologetic reticence. In that case the whole context of the speeches is due to Ar. We know that he had said something of the hardships of the march to the Beas, and probably of the demoralization they caused (App. XVII 11). All this gives no ground for doubting the historicity of the setting of the speeches. What of the content? Of the proofs that Tarn adduces of the lateness of the speech none is inconsistent with derivation from Ar., who wrote not earlier than 301. He believed that Al. was insatiate in conquest (vii 19, 6 n.) and could easily have ascribed to him the vast plan in v 26, 2. He might have forgotten (26, 1 f.) that Al. was not certain that the Caspian was a gulf of the Ocean (vii 16, 2); probably Al. was already inclining to that view (Schachermeyr, *Al. der Grosse* 541) and the theory may have gained ground before E. made it the accepted dogma. The allusion to Dionysus (26, 5) reflects Ar's narrative (App. XVI 6 f.). The error in 27, 5 (which A. could have corrected by reference to his own narrative) can be set down to an old man's imperfect memory.

6. *Contra* Tarn, lack of authenticity is much more evident in the speech at Opis, though not all the objections of F. R. Wüst, *Historia* ii 177 ff. are well-

founded. Once again the setting is guaranteed by
one or both of A's main sources, yet neither Ar. (vii
9, 6 n.) nor Pt. can be the sole source of the material
A. incorporates. A. is so much influenced by the
vulgate that he presupposes the scene to be Susa
(10, 7). There are also exaggerations and absur-
dities (see notes) which are not only inappropriate for
Al. but unlikely to have been fathered on him by a
well-informed writer, either Pt. or Ar. This is an
epideictic display by A., and the same is then
probably true of the speeches at the Beas, though
they are less open to criticism. QC. (who indeed
embellishes his work with many more speeches) has
the same pair at the Beas and Al's at Opis. They
probably belong to the traditional declamations of
the rhetorical schools.

7. The letters in ii 14 and vii 23 do not seem to be
drawn from the collection of fictitious letters (Introd.
15), with which A. elsewhere shows no acquaintance.
The context in each case is the ' factual ' narrative of
Pt./Ar. In ii 14 we have first a summary of Darius'
letter in indirect speech, and then Al's reply in direct.
A single phrase (Introd. n. 33) shows that the words
are A's, just as Thucydides (vii 10 ff.) supplies the
words for a letter of Nicias ; but the substance may be
authentic ; even the mendacities can well represent
Al's propaganda. As for the letter to Cleomenes,
part is summarized in the factual narrative (vii 23, 7),
and then A. adds a single sentence in direct speech,
which looks like an actual verbatim quotation. Pt.
could of course have found it in the provincial
archive of Egypt. Why he chose to quote something
that A. regarded as unworthy of Al. can only be
conjectured. He was to put Cleomenes to death, as

he suspected him of favouring Perdiccas against himself (Pausanias i 6, 3). But perhaps he thought that Al's attitude could be construed as clemency and was admirable in him, but not deserved by Cleomenes, whom Pt. may have *charged* with neglecting to perform Al's orders; the shrines of Hephaestion are not known to have been completed.

APPENDIX XXVIII

THE DATE AND CHARACTER OF ARRIAN'S WORK

1. Of A's writings only the three tracts composed when he was governor of Cappadocia, probably 130–137 (*contra* Introd. 1), can be dated with any precision, though his memorials of Epictetus were presumably written when he was sitting at the master's feet (but published much later). In *Cynegetica* 1, 4 he claims to have practised hunting, generalship and philosophy since youth; we must infer that his military career in Roman service began early and that both the *Anabasis* and *Indica* were composed after it commenced. The *Indica* was designed while he was writing the *Anabasis* and written later (v 5, 1; 6, 8; vi 28, 6; *Ind.* 19, 8; 21, 8; 23, 6; 26, 1; 32, 1; 43, 14), perhaps not immediately; his neglect of relevant data in Ar. (App. XVII 5) and occasional incongruities with the earlier narrative (*Ind.* 4, 13; 19, 5 and 7; 42, 7 nn.) might suggest that he had had time to forget what he had learned for the *Anabasis*, were it not that he was capable of similar faults within the compass of the *Anabasis* itself. From *Ind.* 41, 15 f.

we know that he had seen the Inn and Save, probably when serving in equestrian or senatorial office in the Danubian provinces (P. A. Stadter, *Arrian of Nicomedia* 15 f.), though his familiarity with the area is not wide: he ignores the Morava and Drave. In the *Bithynica* he stated that he had always purposed to write the history of his native land, but had postponed the work till he was better equipped, and that his works on Timoleon and Dion were compositions of the necessary apprenticeship (Roos ii p. 197). Photius, who reports this, thought that the *Anabasis* also preceded the *Bithynica*; Stadter 179 ff. argues that he was mistaken, and certainly A's boast in i 12, 5 shows that he cannot have viewed the *Anabasis* as an immature work at the time when he gave it to the world. Photius clearly supposed that A's other historical works, the *Parthica* and *Affairs after Alexander* (obviously a sequel to the *Anabasis*), were subsequent to the *Bithynica*. What evidence he had is unknown. All A's other tracts, including those written in Cappadocia, belonged to genres different from history, and A. would not have mentioned them in the *Bithynica*, when referring to his development as a historian.

2. For Schwartz it was ' irrefutably established that A., the soldier and official, with true vision took Pt's official account as the best and purest source for the history of Al.' (*RE* ii 1238); many other scholars concurred (Strasburger, *Ptolemaios und Alexander* 9), and dated the *Anabasis* and all the historical works to his retirement. However, A's explicit reasons for trusting Pt. do not include his political and military experience, nor even his close connection with Al., and Schwartz' confidence in the reliability of official

history is as naïve as A's belief that Pt. as a king would not lie. A. prides himself not on the insight that participation in public affairs might have given him but on the literary merits of his work (§ 6). For Lucian, though he briefly acknowledged the utility to the historian of practical experience, political understanding was a natural gift, style the craft that had to be learned (*How to Write History* 34 and 37). I find no proof in the *Anabasis* of political or military expertise. The merits of his military narrative may be due entirely to his sources. His specific reference to Roman statecraft reveals no comprehension of Al's or Roman arrangements for the government of Egypt (iii 5, 6). His allusions to court life are conventional (vii 29, 1 n.). It is likely but not certain that his judgement on Callisthenes reflects the outlook of a senator (App. XIV 11). Naturally it is absurd to assume that he had no leisure to write history in the course of his public career (Bosworth, *Commentary* 4 f.), or that his allusion to Athenian topography (iii 16, 8) implies that he had already retired to Athens; it might as well be inferred from *Ind.* 41, 2 that he was still resident at Nicopolis, and thus near Leucas and Acarnania, and A. had no doubt visited Athens long before he settled there, and could expect readers to be familiar with a tourist centre.

3. Stadter 183 would place the *Anabasis* after both the *Bithynica* and the *Parthica*, which went down to 117 (fr. 1 Roos, cf. Stadter 135 ff.). It is often supposed that the description in v 7 of Roman methods of bridging the Euphrates and Tigris alludes to Trajan's operations. But A. himself says that these methods were used ' as often as ' the Romans crossed these rivers; such crossings of the Euphrates had been

common, and the upper Tigris had been bridged by
Lucullus and perhaps by generals engaged in later
and ill-recorded operations in Armenia. In the
Parthica A. must have described Trajan's crossing,
and one would expect a cross-reference in v 7 to his
account of the incident, if it had been written earlier,
and perhaps other allusions to Trajan's campaigns,
especially if A. had been present himself (as might be
inferred from an inaccurate statement by Lydus *ap.*
Roos ii p. LXII). Dio's narrative of Trajan's march
(lxviii 26), which probably derived from A's, alludes
to Al's campaign of 331, and that suggests that in
writing the *Parthica* A. referred back to the *Anabasis.*
Bosworth (*Commentary* 9) discerns stylistic similarities
between fragments of the *Parthica* and the *Anabasis*;
however, even if A. is echoing what he had written
earlier, we could not determine which work came first.
Still, I agree with him for the reasons I have given
that the *Parthica* was the later work.

4. Bosworth may also be right in thinking that the
Ectaxis contra Alanos presupposes the *Anabasis*
(*Commentary* 10). In that case the *Anabasis* predates
A's command in Cappadocia. I find no cogency,
however, in Bosworth's inference from i 16, 4 that A.
was still unfamiliar with Rome (even a Roman senator had not necessarily inspected and noted all Greek
works of art in the city); moreover A. was always
prone to copy what he found in his sources, and this
habit (rather than Stadter's explanation, 184 f.) may
account also for various instances of geographical
ignorance adduced by Bosworth to show that the
Anabasis predates his tenure of Cappadocia or the
proconsulate of Baetica, which is made probable by an
inscription (see Bosworth, *Gr., Roman and Byz.*

Studies 1976, 55 f.), of which I made no mention in
Introd. 1; cf. § 33. Bosworth guesses that A.
owed his promotion at Rome to his literary reputation.
This was what late writers, Themistius, Heliconius
and Photius (Roos ii pp. LVIII–LXII) supposed, but
that may have been an undocumented assumption,
natural for men who remembered A. primarily as an
author. Though it is clear that A. owed to Hadrian
his advancement to the consulship and to command of
a great province, there is of course nothing to show
that his official career did not begin under Trajan, and
that is what *Cyn.* 1, 4 should compel us to believe.
Even if the *Anabasis* precedes A's Cappadocian years,
it is in my judgement the product of a man who had
already held offices at Rome.

5. The crucial text is surely i 12, 5. Here A. says
that his name, fatherland, lineage and the offices he
has held in his own country are nothing in comparison
with ' these *logoi* ', not ' tales ' as I rendered it, but his
writings, and clearly the *Anabasis* above all, from
which he expects recognition as one of the masters of
Greek literature. What fatherland has he in mind?
Nicomedia was his birthplace, proudly recorded in
the *Bithynica*; there he was certainly a priest (Roos ii
197), and may have held magistracies. Once he had
settled in Athens, where he became *archon*, he could
claim to be of the same city as Xenophon (*Cyneg.*
1, 4). But Rome too was the ' common fatherland '
of Roman citizens, and the proper domicile of
senators (*Digest* i 9, 11; 1 1, 22, 6). It is true that
Greek senators like Cassius Dio, another Bithynian,
could continue to speak of their native homes as their
fatherlands (lxxx 5, 2, cf. *ILS* 8821), though Dio
could also speak of Rome as ' the land we dwell in '

(fr. 1). Some would therefore hold that A. could not have meant that Rome was his fatherland. However, high rank at Rome shed more lustre than any offices in a Greek city. A contemporary of A., C. Iulius Severus, is honoured at Ancyra as a descendant of kings and tetrarchs, and his offices and munificence in his fatherland are celebrated (*OGIS* 544), but, once he had entered the Roman senate, all this is dismissed in a couple of lines, in a subsequent honorific inscription (ib. 543), which gives greater emphasis to his Roman career. It seems to me inconceivable that if A. had already held senatorial offices he would have merely referred to those which he had held in either Nicomedia or Athens as those high social distinctions, which were still to be ranked below his literary achievements. This argument seems to me conclusive against the identification of his ' own country ' or fatherland with Athens, since his Roman career is antecedent to his Athenian. But there is also a difficulty in supposing Nicomedia to be meant. A. of course wrote his name into the title of his work, even though he chose (as he tells us here) not to repeat it in the body of the work. But he thinks that his name is ' not at all unknown among men '; i.e. it is celebrated. In the context this means that he is celebrated for rank. How many of his readers would have known of a mere local magnate in Nicomedia? It is most natural to infer that he has an imperial renown for his position in the Roman state. This by no means implies that he had yet reached the consulship, but only that like the *Indica* the *Anabasis* was composed when he had held at least other posts of importance. This view also fits the fact that the influence of Epictetus had faded, cf. Brunt, *Athenaeum* 1977, 30 ff.

6. A's claims in i 12 are more significant in another way. He says that Al's deeds had never been worthily celebrated in prose or verse. His preface shows that he regarded the histories of Pt. and Ar. as reliable, yet he now implies that they did not do justice to their theme, as he hopes to do. But how could his account be superior not only to the many other histories of Al. based on untrustworthy sources but to the primary authorities which he himself commended? No doubt he could have improved on both Pt. and Ar. by combining their complementary evidence or by more acute interpretation of events that they merely recorded. But what A. claims is something quite different: his history is to place him among the masters of Greek speech, as a modern Xenophon, indeed to make him an Alexander of literature; this was evidently a rhetorical commonplace (cf. Aristides, *Sacred Tales* iv 49). In the same way, while convinced of the reliability of N., he intended in his *Indica* to report his voyage in good Greek (vi 28, 6). By implication N. had failed in that point. We may be sure that Pt. and Ar. were equally unsatisfactory. Of the early Alexander-historians only Callisthenes (Polyb. vi 45, 1; D. iv 1, 2, f.), and Clitarchus to a lesser extent (Pliny, *NH* x 136; Quintilian x 1, 74), had ever enjoyed great reputation, which they owed to admiration for their theatrical style, but from the first century BC fashion was turning against them, and both were condemned by the author of the treatise *On the Sublime* (3, 2; cf. Cicero, *de oratore* ii 58; *ad Quintum fratrem* ii 11, 4; *Brut.* 42; *de legibus* i 7). Writing in the 160s, Lucian insists that the main function of the historian is to recount events as they actually happened (*op. cit.* 7; 9; 61; 63 etc.); none the less, it must also be his

aim to give pleasure (9; 13; 48), and the greater part of Lucian's exposition concerns not the methods of ascertaining the truth but matters of diction and arrangement. The acknowledged models in Lucian's day were Herodotus, Thucydides and Xenophon (2; 15; 18; 23; 25). Their influence can be detected in A's composition (cf. Bosworth's *Commentary*, index under their names). His programme and practice illustrate the same attitude as Lucian's to historical writing.

7. The *Indica* is in Herodotus' Ionic dialect. This was surely A's choice. Of his two authorities for this work N. at least is unlikely to have adopted a dialect not his own; he was not a literary man by profession, and indeed even Theopompus of Chios, who was an Ionian, had not used it for his history, though Herodotus perhaps inspired his proclivity to geographic and ethnographic excursuses; of Meg's origins, career and dialect nothing is known. In A's time there was something of an archaizing revival of Ionic (Hiller von Gärtringen, *Sitzungsberichte Berlin Akad.* 1918, 760). Ionic gave the old material a new look and suited A's essentially literary pretensions.

8. Diction was evidently all-important. In his *Tactica* A. followed Aelian, who had written only a generation earlier (H. Köchly, *Gr. Kriegsschriftsteller*, ii 1), or at any rate Aelian's source, differing in substance only by trivial additions or more frequent omissions, but restyling the original by alterations of words or of their order and rhythm (cf. Stadter 41 ff. and works he cites). The ' log-book ' passages in the *Indica* illustrate the same procedure. Indeed N's artless gift of story-telling, in which he was

plainly more vivid than Pt. or Ar., shines through A's narrative in the *Indica*, as in one or two passages of the *Anabasis* where he drew on N. (App. XVII 5; XVIII 2). But the language will be that of A. He can paraphrase the same original in two different ways (*Ind.* 32, 11 f. with vii 20, 10). Comparison of the ' fragments ' of N. in A. and S. (App. XVIII; XXV 4) shows that each made his own version, sometimes omitting or misunderstanding something found in the original; they treated Ar. in the same way (ii 5, 4 n.; iv 6, 6 with S. xi 11, 5; vi 29 with S. xv 3, 7; vii 19–22 with S. xvi 1, 9–11), and A's excerpts from the so-called royal journals are again not verbally exact (vii 25, 1 n.). And A. could no doubt import into a passage in which he is mainly following one authority some detail derived from another, with acknowledgement (vii 4, 4) or without.

9. Literary excellence was of course not the only claim that A. made for the special value of his own history. In his very first words he emphasizes, in a manner unparalleled in ancient historiography, his dependence on the best authorities. So too Lucian was to prescribe that, if the historian was not himself an eye-witness, he should follow those who knew the facts and reported them impartially and credibly (*op. cit.* 47 f.). In A's judgement this was what Pt. and Ar. had done. Unlike current histories derived from inferior sources, his work would thus describe events as they had actually occurred. But just because the story it told would be markedly different, it would also have a new literary appeal to readers, who would find it fresh and original.

10. This was the more requisite as there was no

dearth of works on Al. in antiquity. To say nothing of general histories, Jacoby lists ten writers of monographs between Ar. and A. Some are mere names; of fourteen authorities mentioned by P. 46, three are totally and a fourth almost unknown to us. Only A. (vii 16, 5) refers to Asclepiades. The eight books on Al's virtues composed by the famous Dio of Prusa (Jacoby no. 153 F 6) are never cited. QC's extant work is not mentioned by any ancient author. Some fragments survive of histories by authors whose names are lost (Jacoby nos. 148; 151). So there were probably far more books on Al. than we happen to know of. Why were they continually produced? There were no archives from which new evidence could be elicited, and in any case, as the younger Pliny implies (*ep.* v 8, 12), research was only thought necessary when a historian attempted to describe contemporary events for the first time; otherwise it was enough to collate the old accounts. New writers, therefore, usually aimed at dressing up the facts in a form that would give pleasure. They might of course also offer a different interpretation, as A. did, by following forgotten authorities. But, like A., they all hoped to win esteem by their literary merits. They included rhetoricians like Hegesias, Polemo and Dio. Under Marcus Aurelius, Amyntianus, like A., asserted his ability to write worthily of Al., though in Photius' judgement he lamentably failed (Jacoby no. 150 T 1). Of the original accounts some had always lacked a literary flavour; others were disfigured by a style that had come to appear bombastic (§ 6, cf. also Jacoby no. 142 T 4 f.; F 5 for Hegesias). Changes in literary fashion incited new treatments of the old story. A. owed his survival to the *continuing* approval of his Greek style (Introd. 6).

11. A. refers to the plurality of accounts of Al. in his preface (i 12 1; iv 9, 3; vi 24, 1; 26, 1; vii 1, 1–3; 3, 2; 13, 2; 22, 4 f.; 27); though he can write of the majority or prevalent story (i 11, 6; iv 9, 9 contrasted with 9, 7; 10, 5 contrasted with 12, 2; 13, 2; 14, 1; vii 11, 9), or ' the whole tradition ' (vi 11, 3 f.), he expressly refers to variants (e.g. iv 14, 4; vii 14), and we can supply additional instances (e.g. App. XIV 5; XVI; XX; XXI). *Prima facie* A's language suggests that he collated numerous other accounts with those of Pt. and Ar. But this is improbable. The younger Pliny thought the collation of earlier histories a heavy task (*ep.* v 8, 12). He had in mind the exemplary diligence of his uncle (iii 5; v 8, 5), who claimed to have consulted 2000 volumes in compiling his *Natural History* (*pr.* 17), including no less than 15 historians of Alexander, besides the bematists and Al. himself (i.e. his supposed letters), all cited chiefly for geographical and botanical matters. But F. Münzer seems to have shown that even Pliny rarely went back to the primary sources, but generally cited them from relatively recent works (*Beiträge zur Quellenkritik der Naturalgeschichte*, esp. pp. 8–25; 128 ff.; cf. Kroll, *RE* xxi 304 ff.). Thus Pliny knew N. and Onesicritus indirectly and imperfectly (App. XXV 5). A's method in the *Tactica* (§ 8) and in the *Indica* do not encourage us to think that he was more diligent in the *Anabasis*. He did not even integrate into his narrative what he had read in N. (App. XVII 5). Did he not write out one authority at a time? On occasions he does merely juxtapose conflicting accounts (§ 17). Still there is probably some interweaving of Pt. and Ar. As for the vulgate, he had doubtless read more of the histories current in his day than he consulted when writing, and his

recollections would permit him to refer to an account as prevalent or to the existence of variants, to which there could have been allusions in relatively recent works, including monographs on particular subjects like the Amazons (vii 14, 1 n.). Even Plutarch, though exceptionally well read, had hardly inspected for himself all the authors he names in ch. 46, cf. Hamilton *ad loc*.

12. A. exalts the authority of Pt. and Ar. because both accompanied Al., yet wrote after his death. He *could* then have treated as inferior accounts given by contemporaries of Al., who wrote like Callisthenes before his death, or who did not accompany him. Anaximenes, who is said to have recorded all Al's deeds, though he is seldom cited (Jacoby no. 72 T 6; F 15–17; 29), might come in the second category, and so might Clitarchus. He was certainly a contemporary (Jacoby, *RE* xi 622 f.; E. Badian, *Proc. Afr. Class. Ass.* 1965, 5 ff., cf. § 20), and he wrote a full historical narrative, but there is no clear evidence that he was with Al. at any rate throughout the expedition. However, A. also depreciates or neglects Chares, Onesicritus, Medius (Jacoby no. 129) and Polyclitus; the first three, and probably the last (Pearson 70 ff.), took part in the expedition, and Onesicritus (F 1), and presumably Chares (F 4 on the marriages at Susa), wrote after Al's death, as the others may have done. Thus A's explicit criteria are insufficient to explain his preference for Pt. and Ar. Still less do they justify it. He no doubt means to suggest that only participants in the expedition had direct knowledge of events, but in fact neither Pt. (see, for instance, vi 5–11) nor Ar. can have been an eye-witness of all transactions they described, and a

contemporary like Clitarchus who did not accompany
Al. *could* have obtained as accurate information from
witnesses. It was also naïve to think (as A. surely
did) that contemporary accounts composed after Al's
death would be written without bias, or that apparent
bias was reason enough to neglect the evidence of a
well-informed writer like Callisthenes. In my view
Pt. and Ar. themselves relied in part on his detailed,
official narrative, cf. App. I 6; III; V; iii 11, 3 n.,
and their record, on which A. drew, deteriorated
after 330, when this source was no longer available.
The fact that Callisthenes wrote when events were
still fresh in men's minds may well have limited his
mendacity. If A. had been truly seized of the value
of primary evidence, he should have consulted
Callisthenes for himself. There is reason to think
that he never did so. He omits salient points in C's
version of the Siwah march (App. V 2 f.), and does
not cite him to authenticate the story of the two crows
(iii 3, 6), nor indeed anywhere else. He appears
unfamiliar with the very character of C's history
(App. XIV 11). In his day C. was no longer admired
as a stylist (§ 6), and it would have been inconvenient
to use a narrative that remained incomplete.

13. So too he never names Chares; he overlooks his
testimony at times (ii 11, 4; vii 4, 4 n.; App. XIV
13), and gives it elsewhere as a mere tale (App. XIV
5), which he had probably read in one of his inferior
authorities, who did not name Chares as the source.
He cites Onesicritus only at second hand (App.
XVII 4, cf. XX). He is still less likely to have collated works like those of Medius and Polyclitus which
were less commonly read. I do not believe that he
used Clitarchus, who was no longer esteemed in his

own day (§ 6). A's ' vulgate ' is sometimes manifestly of origin later than Clitarchus' time (vi 11, 8;
28, 2; vii 2, 1; 22, 5; 24, 4 nn.; App. XXI; XXII 4;
XXIII 3), to say nothing of its other divergences
from the authors, D., QC. and J., whose accounts
ultimately stem from Clitarchus (cf. now J. R.
Hamilton, *Greece and the Eastern Mediterranean* . . .,
ed. K. H. Kinzl, 1977, 126 ff.). Not indeed that we
can be sure that any particular statement in one of
these authors comes from Clitarchus. QC. may not
have read Clitarchus for himself; J. summarized
Trogus; and D., whose usual practice was to summarize a history of repute, which Clitarchus still
enjoyed in his time, compressed at least twelve
books (Jacoby no. 137 F 6) into one. For the distortions that could result in the process of epitomiz-
ing and excerpting, see Brunt, *CQ* 1980, 477 ff.; D.
14, 4 compared with Athen. iv 30 (Clitarchus F 1)
provides an illustration. It is not then surprising
that the ' Clitarchean ' sources often differ *inter se*.
What Clitarchus wrote can at best sometimes be
inferred from their agreement.

13a. A. would perhaps never have discovered Pt. and
Ar. without rummaging in a library and becoming
aware of the existence of other contemporary works,
some of which were certainly not less accessible to
writers of his time. I do not contend that he had
never looked into any of them, only that he did not
collate them for his own history. Probably his aim
was to discredit and supplant the account or accounts
of Al. which were current in his day, and which had
probably been composed long after Clitarchus wrote,
like those of Aristus and Asclepiades, the only inferior authorities he ever names (App. XXII 4);

even Aristus was perhaps known to him from a
citation in a much more modern work, conceivably
that of Asclepiades, whose date is unknown. Reliance on Pt. and Ar. enabled him to supply a story
that seemed and was much fresher as well as more
authentic than the then popular versions of Al's
expedition, which must often have been corrupted by
the inventions of many writers later than Clitarchus,
e.g. QC.

14. A. may indeed have had other reasons for disregarding the works of other contemporaries of Al.
Perhaps they did not all furnish the detailed, continuous narrative of military and political transactions
that he required. The mysterious title of Onesicritus' work (Pearson 89 f.) might suggest that his
theme did not demand such a narrative; Truesdell
Brown (*Onesicritus* ch. V) thinks that he did not even
supply one for N's voyages. The fragments of
Chares, Polyclitus and Medius are as consistent as
those of Onesicritus with the hypothesis that they
did not write histories, but they are too meagre to
demonstrate its truth, being mostly citations by
later writers who were themselves not historians (like
Athenaeus). Moreover, Polyclitus is said to have
written ' Histories ', and Chares is, like Clitarchus,
credited with ' Histories about Al.' (Pearson 51 is
perverse). Perhaps A. neglected the historical
information they must anyhow have contained, after
merely casual inspection, for reasons that are only
implicit in his preface. There he promised that
where Pt. and Ar. gave different versions of events
(Introd. 19) he would select that which was more
trustworthy and better worth telling, and that he
would also insert statements from other histories

which seemed worth telling and not entirely untrustworthy. Undefined criteria of what was credible
and notable, which permitted him to adjudicate even
between Pt. and Ar., may have led him to scorn all
the other early authorities (Clitarchus perhaps included), on the footing that they contained too much
that was in his estimation too trivial or implausible
to justify the effort of continuous collation.

15. It is not hard to discern what A. meant by noteworthy. The exploits and personality of Al. were
his theme. But most of the early writers on Al.,
including Ar., expatiated on the physical features,
climate, customs, antiquities, flora and fauna of the
regions he traversed, especially of India. A.
omitted most of this material, even from Ar. (§ 22 f.).
Some of his most extensive interpolations from the
vulgate (App. XIV 1; cf. vii 1 and 27) relate to
incidents or reports of manifest significance to his
theme, of which his preferred authorities said too
little or nothing at all. In addition he could not
resist referring to a story so piquant to his readers as
that of the Roman embassy (vii 15), or to Calanus'
death, because it had made such a lasting impression
on men's minds (App. XX). But here he is apologetic
about recounting a tale that cast little or no light on
Al., whereas he cannot forbear to write of Bucephalas ' for Al's sake ' (v 19, 6), or of his marriage
with Roxane, not as an act of political importance,
but as proof of the king's self-restraint (iv 20, 6). In
these two cases he could follow at least one of his
main authorities, but he could also recount anecdotes
from the vulgate (ii 4; vi 26; vii 1 f.) which illustrated facets of Al's personality, if they fitted his own
conception of it (§ 17) Still, he has relatively few

anecdotes, and can relate them far more briefly than D. does in a much shorter history (cf. ii 12 with D. 35–8), whereas not only Clitarchus but the other early writers seem to have indulged themselves freely and discursively in tales which A. doubtless regarded as beneath the dignity of history. I append a list of anecdotes in A. which are not essential (at least in his interpretation) to the narrative of Al's expedition, though Al's experience at Gordium and Nysa (if we accept the reports) may in fact be significant for an assessment of his aims; I have omitted geographical excursuses and descriptions, and A's own digression (*contra* Bosworth *ad loc.*) in ii 16, and have placed in square brackets those few passages which do not bear on Al's personality:

(a) Pt.: [i 4, 7 f.]; iv 15, 8; 25, 4;

(b) Ar.: [ii 5, 2–4]; v 1 f.; vi 29, 4–11; perhaps we may include the stories of portents in vii 17 f. and 22; for a curious omission see i 7, 1 n.;

(c) both Pt. and Ar.: ii 12, 3–5;

(d) either or both Pt. and Ar.: i 11, 5; 16, 4; ii 3 (primarily Ar.?); iv 19, 5 f.; v 19, 4–6;

(e) N.: vi 13, 4 f.; vii 3, 6;

(f) vulgate: i 9, 10 and 11, 6–8 (though both passages might be from Pt./Ar.); 12, 1; ii 4, 7–11; 12, 6–8; iii 2, 1 f.; iv 20, 1–3; vi 26, 1 f.; vii [13] and parts of 14;

(g) debateable sources: vii 1, 4–2; [3].

16. The division of the *Anabasis* into seven books suggests conscious imitation of Xenophon's work with that title. A. had to be selective to keep his history within that compass. This may help to explain his omission of material furnished by Ar. and Pt. (§ 22 f.;

26). Conceivably the works of Chares, Polyclitus and Clitarchus, in at least ten, eight and twelve books respectively, were longer than theirs. In any case it was natural for A. to neglect authorities who dilated more on matters peripheral to his theme.

17. His concept of credibility is less easy to grasp. He was clearly aware of the importance of autopsy (App. XVII 8), and prepared to reject reports for which there was no first hand evidence (vi 28, 2; vii 13, 3; contrast 3, 6): he relied on Pt., Ar. and N. just because they were ' adequate witnesses '. Perhaps he ignores some well-known stories in the ' vulgate ', like the personal confrontations between Al. and Darius at Issus and Gaugamela and between Al. and Porus, the massacre of the Branchidae (QC. vii 5, 28 ff.), the drunken riot at Persepolis (App. X 1), and many details of the visit to Siwah (App. V 4), chiefly because they were inadequately authenticated (but cf. ii 11, 4 n.) or, in the case of the tale of the queen of the Amazons, directly denied by Pt. and Ar. Perhaps he mentions one or two tales which they contradicted or neglected, partly to illustrate his critical principle (esp. vi 11 and 28). The principle, it may be added, did not apply to ancient traditions (App. XXI).

17a. But what if ' adequate witnesses ' disagreed? Sometimes he merely juxtaposed the rival versions, even when we should naturally have preferred Pt. to Ar. (§ 24 ii). On only one occasion does he *expressly* decide between them, giving a reason for holding Pt's account more plausible (v 14). N's evidence seems to have made him doubt whether Pt. told the whole truth about the Gadrosian march (App.

XVIII). Cf. also App. XIV 13. Believing, like Ar. (vii 19, 6 n.), that Al. was insatiate for conquest (vii 1), he seems to have preferred Ar's account of events at the Hyphasis (App. XXVI 5). This illustrates how he could make his conception of Al. a test of truth. Stories in the vulgate were credible if they did him honour (ii 4, 7 ff.; 12, 6 ff.; iv 20, 1–3; vi 26, 1–3), but not otherwise (vi 28, 1 f.; vii 14, 5; 27, 3), cf. perhaps the omission from Ar. noted at ii 12, 8. As Al. was loved to the last (vii 17, 6), and there was no proof of a quarrel with Antipater (12, 5 f.), he could not have been poisoned at Antipater's instigation (27, 1). Macedonians (v 2, 7) and Romans (vii 15, 6) would hardly have acted out of character. Modern scholars of course utter judgements no more firmly based. A. was also sceptical of marvels (v 4, 3 f.; vii 13; App. XVII 8), and, though he properly reports instances of Al's religiosity, his own piety hardly colours his account. It makes little difference that he admits that the ' divine ' upsets all human calculations of probability (v 1, 2; 3, 2–4); that he was evidently impressed by omens that were apparently fulfilled (i 9, 8; iii 7, 6; iv 4; vii 17 f.; 22; 24) and that he thought some divine influence required to account for Al's success (vii 30, 2, cf. ii 6, 6) and for the ruin of Thebes (i 9, 6). The hints at divine interposition are very hesitant in i 26, 2; ii 3, 8 and even in iii 3, 5 f.; other writers made more of it. In general A. was faithful to the long tradition of Greek historiography, which excluded the supernatural from historical explanation.

18. A. then wrote his *Anabasis* in the light of a general knowledge of current accounts of Al. and perhaps of inspection of *some* of the early authorities,

but he probably collated only one or two modern histories with the works of Pt. and Ar. (for N. see App. XVII 5), and then chiefly when he remembered that many different accounts were current or that the common version was discrepant from that of his authorities, or from one of them. In the preface he distinguishes the ' factual ' part of his account, which he says is derived from Pt., Ar. or both, from mere tales (*legomena*). However, as Schwartz observed (*RE* ii 1241 ff.), A. sometimes introduces material which really comes from one of his main sources with such words as ' it is said that . . .'. See i 9, 10 (?); ii 12, 3–6; iii 10, 1 (?); 27, 1, cf. App. XI; iv 19, 5; 28, 2; vii 6, 2 (?); 13, 1; 18; 20 with notes. In particular an alternation of direct with indirect speech in a wholly consecutive and consistent narrative (cf. App. XVI 6; XVIII 3; XXVII 5; i 1, 1 n.; iii 26 f.; vii 16, 5 n.) seems to show that A. is following a trusted authority throughout. When Ar. seems to be his source for such reports, we sometimes find that his account more or less coincided with the ' prevalent story ' (iii 3, 6; iv 28, 2 n.; vii 20, 1 n.), cf. App. XVIII for N.; but on other such occasions it differed from versions in the vulgate (e.g. ii 3; App. XVI). It should hardly need saying that the testimony of Ar. (or N.) is not discredited by such a coincidence; not everything in the ' vulgate ' must be deemed false, unless confirmed by Pt. No doubt A's resort to indirect speech may indicate that he will not take full responsibility for it (see App. XVI, but cf. i 1, 1 n.). Sometimes inconsistencies between Pt. and Ar. may provide the explanation (e.g. App. XXVII 5). This kind of reservation is implicit when he actually notes their contradictions without arbitrating between them, and sometimes when he cites the account of only one (e.g. probably iii 26). In any case, not every ' tale ' is necessarily from the vulgate; my notes on i 11, 6 (cf. vi 10, 2 with i 11, 8); 12, 1 (one version might be from a good source); ii 7, 8; 25, 3 are too dogmatic. *Some* of the tales in vii 14, 2–7 could also be from Pt./Ar. One can only feel confident in ascribing a tale to the vulgate when it is contrasted with what A. treats as factual or ascribes to Pt./Ar. (e.g. v 2, 7) or when he contradicts it (e.g. vi 11), or when this can be shown in other ways (App. XIV). On the other hand it is mere caprice to assert, disregarding A's preface, that a ' factual ' statement rests on the vulgate (e.g. App. XXVII 5). There is very little of the vulgate in A.

19. Throughout the commentary I have used the formula ' Pt./Ar.' to mean that factual statements come from either or both of A's main authorities but that I cannot decide between the alternatives. Most scholars assume that A. kept close to Pt. A's normal manner is then taken to be Pt's, and particular statements are confidently ascribed to Pt. without evidence for the ascription (cf. Pearson ch. VII for a more prudent procedure). Yet the preface gives only one reason for special respect for Pt., which is quite absurd and which A. himself never adduces later as a ground for preferring Pt. to Ar. when he notes their disagreements. Can we determine his practice with less dogmatism? What follows is supplementary to Introd. 19 f.

20. Something must first be said about the relation of the works of Pt. and Ar. to each other and to other early histories. Most of them cannot be dated even relatively. Onesicritus probably wrote in or before

APPENDIX XXVIII

321 (R. Merkelbach, *Die Quellen des Alexanderromans*[2], 187), and N. surely to correct him. It is clear that Clitarchus, who sought to glorify his sovereign, would not have reported that Pt. had been present in the Mallian town if he had known that Pt's own account excluded this (vi 11, 8 n.). But, since Clitarchus was an Alexandrian, he would surely have read Pt. if the latter's work had already been published. Hence, the publication (but not necessarily the composition) of Pt's history was later than that of Clitarchus'. I know no better argument for more precisely dating Clitarchus' history than Schachermeyr's (*Alexander in Babylon* 211 ff.); assuming that D. xvii depends on him, and noting that D. 118 illustrates Cassander's hatred for Al. by events of 316 but not by his murder of Al's wife and son, which occurred in 310 or 309 but was not acknowledged officially in Egypt until 305, he infers that Clitarchus wrote between 316 and 305. This is not really conclusive, since D. could be a slipshod summarizer (§ 13). But if it be accepted, Clitarchus' publication-date would have been not before but not necessarily much after 316. We do not know when Pt. published (Introd. 11). Ar. certainly finished after 301 (vii 18, 5): perhaps he would not have ventured to *publish* an eulogistic book on Al. before the death of his sovereign, Cassander, in 297; and most of his work may have been *written* far earlier.

21. Modern scholars have decried Ar., in comparison with Pt., on various grounds. He was certainly an apologist for Al., but so was Pt. Some texts which have been adduced to convict him of absurd flattery, or of being a rhetorical writer, have no evidentiary value (Brunt, *CQ* 1974, 65 ff.). He is

555

known to have had some technical qualifications (vi 29, cf. perhaps S. xv 1, 19), but (*contra* Pearson 151) this does not imply that he was not a soldier too. Undoubtedly he had not the same chance of knowing Al's thoughts as Pt. or N., nor experience of command, but all understanding of military affairs need not be denied him. To Schwartz he was essentially a secondary authority who combined Clitarchus and Pt., adding a few reminiscences. Now he may well have read Clitarchus, whose history was probably admired from the start and widely circulated, but he would hardly have deliberately contradicted Pt. about transactions in which Pt. was engaged, without giving reasons, and, if he gave reasons, A. would surely have reported them in iii 30, 5; v 14 (other contradictions are less probative). We have no evidence that Pt. published first, or that, if he did, his book was accessible to Ar. I actually see no way of refuting a hypothesis that Pt. wrote later, and used Ar. (sometimes correcting him), but no reason to believe it (cf. v 14, 5 n.). It is mere dogma that, if Ar. and Clitarchus agreed against Pt., we must still prefer Pt. as the one primary source, and that, if Ar. more commonly concurred with Pt., it was because he generally chose to follow him, paring away Clitarchus' extravagances. In my judgement Pt. too was at times a secondary authority (following Callisthenes), but both Ar. and he could control existing accounts from their own recollections; and they could agree independently, when each recorded the truth, or the official version of the truth.

22. There is no reason to think that A. *could* not have obtained a full account of Al's expedition from Ar. alone. Ar. provided details of military operations

(ii 27, 3 n.; iii 11, 3 ff.; 13, 3 n.; iv 3, 5; 6, 1 f.; v 14, 3; 20, 2; F. 5 and 46), finances (F 4), which Pt. perhaps ignored, political events (iii 26 f.; 30, 5; iv 8, 9; 13 f.; F. 32); he mentioned appointments (vi 28, 5) and festivals (vi 28, 3). Cf. App. XVII 18a; v 20, 3 n.; vi 15, 5 n. for more indirect evidence of his use by A. He gave at least an outline of Al's itinerary with indications of space and time, which A. sometimes failed to incorporate, without substituting any equally clear information culled from Pt. (App. XVII 11; 18; 24; XVIII 2). The greater part of A's narrative of Al's last activities (vii 16–22) comes from him. Above all, in several instances A. treats his silence as significant (v 7, 1; vi 28, 2; vii 13, 1 f.; 15, 6). This is enough to refute the theory (G. Wirth, *Historia* 1964, 209 ff.) that his book was merely anecdotal, though (like Pt.) he did include anecdotes (§ 15); A. had read it, and Wirth has not. Very probably he was more discursive than Pt. He digressed on legendary antiquities (ii 5, 4 n.), and we may refer to him all references to such matters (i 26, 4; ii 5, 9; vii 20, 5), including the Gordium legend (ii 3); this may explain his interest in the stories of Heracles and Dionysus in India (App. XVI), and perhaps the heroic *motiv* in ii 15 f. (apart from A's own rationalizing); 18, 1; 24, 5 f. (cf. 5, 4; vi 29, 8 for his use of inscriptions); iii 3, 1 f. are all due to him. Some, though not all (e.g. i 18, 3 n.), of his geographical excursuses were of high historical value and unwisely neglected by A.

23. Since Pt. described only one of the Indian rivers (v 20, 8) we may infer *a fortiori* (cf. App. XVII 10) that Pt. indulged little in geographical disquisitions, and still less in ethnography, which was less relevant

to a military narrative; no doubt this was why S.
ignored his work. By contrast, Ar. was fascinated by
rivers (iii 30, 7; iv 6, 6 f. with S. xi 7, 3; vii 19–21
with S. xvi 1, 9–11); we may then ascribe to him not
only most of what A. says on the Indian rivers (App.
XVII 10 f., cf. also S. xv 1, 17–19; 21) but also
probably i 3, 1; iii 29, 1–3 (cf. F. 20); vii 7, 7; likewise other geographical material (cf. iii 28, 5–7): i
29, 1 and 5; iii 4 (with one insertion from Pt.); vii 16,
1–4. S. of course preserves several geographical and
ethnographical fragments of Ar. If A. had made
more use of such material, we should have been told
more of the conditions of terrain and climate, knowledge of which is indispensable to comprehension of
Al's problems in the winter campaigns of 334/3 (cf.
Bosworth on i 26, 2), 331/0, 330/29 and 328/7, or in
the blazing heat in which he pursued Darius and
conducted operations in Turkestan. Bosworth indeed accuses Ar. of merely displaying interest in
botanical curiosities and the like (*Commentary* 27 ff.);
in particular he contrasts A's citation of Ar. on
silphium (iii 28, 6) with S's evidence that the troops
had to eat it out of hunger (xv 2, 10). But the fault
is surely A's: S. seems to have relied on Ar. for Al's
marches, and what he tells us there probably came
from Ar. Similarly, it was probably Ar., who certainly described the monsoon rains in Punjab (S. xv 1,
17 f.), from whom S. learned that the demoralization
they caused forced A. to turn back at the Beas (ib. 27).
Cf. App. XVII 18. Ar. also, unlike Pt., had something, though less than N., on the army's sufferings
in Gadrosia, cf. App. XVIII. Probably A. derived
from him his few allusions to earlier hardships (iii
28, 1; 30, 6; iv 21, 10). To judge from D. and QC.
(the latter is often very valuable on geographical

matters), Clitarchus had far more on such matters than Pt., whom no doubt A. chiefly followed for campaigns; if (as some think) Ar. here imitated or borrowed from Clitarchus, the more credit to him.

24. A's neglect of Ar. in this regard perhaps in itself tends to confirm the orthodox view that he relied chiefly on Pt.   Other arguments can be adduced.

(i) A. twice says that he is mainly following Pt., but in v 14, 5 he gives reasons for preferring him to Ar. in a particular instance, and in vi 2, 4 he may be contrasting Pt. with N.

(ii) A. implicitly prefers Pt. to Ar. in iii 26, and adopts his account against Ar. on details in three or four other cases (i 10, 4; 11, 3; 16, 4; vi 11, 7 nn.). But he probably follows Ar. against Pt. in v 25 ff. (App. XXVII 5), a more important matter, and in iii 3, 5 f.; 4, 5; 30, 5; iv 3, 5; 5 f.; 14, 3; v 20, 2 he juxtaposes their rival accounts without choosing between them; in some of these cases he could justifiably have accepted Pt's account as that of an eye-witness.

(iii) A. names Pt. first in the preface perhaps as the greater man, and in ii 12, 6; iii 3, 5 f.; 26; 30, 5; iv 3, 5; vi 11, 5; 28, 2; vii 15, 6, but Ar. first in eight instances, probably because Ar. was uppermost in his mind as the authority he had been consulting. Thus iii 4, 5 follows a geographical description; as to iv 14, 1 and 3, A. had had to follow Ar. rather than Pt. on the death of Clitus; v 7, 1 comes soon after the Nysa story (App. XVI 6 f.) and perhaps A. expected more from Ar. on the Indus crossing; as to v 14, 3–5 and 20, 2, Ar. may have been his source for the terrors of the Hydaspes, and for the digression on Bucephalas and the games; vii 13, 3 follows a tale Ar.

might have told; and as for vii 26, 3, Ar. had for some time been the chief source (vii 16 ff.). I do not indeed think that Pt. is named first for a similar reason; in iii 3, 6 the allusion to a statement of his is inset in an excerpt from Ar.; rather Pt. naturally takes pride of place. Moreover, in iii 30 Pt's account is first given in detail, and Ar's rival version briefly appended; similarly Ar's story in iv 6 is a variant on iv 5, which must therefore be from Pt., and Ar's description of the Persian battle-order in iii 11 is a sort of doublet of iii 13; the latter must therefore be attributed to Pt. and it is more fully integrated into the narrative of Gaugamela (but cf. iii 13, 3 n.). Pt's narrative of the Gadrosian march also has precedence (App. XVIII). It thus seems probable that A. relies primarily on Pt. for military operations.

(iv) A. would have trusted Pt. more, because as a high ranking officer he knew more of the facts than Ar. and was a better judge of military strategy and tactics. There is in fact no evidence that A. valued him especially on these counts, but it may well be that Pt's special advantages enabled him to furnish a fuller account of many transactions, which A. therefore preferred.

(v) Pt. himself has a large, perhaps too large a role in some parts of the narrative, while the services of his later enemy, Perdiccas, are depreciated; but cf. App. XXIV 1. At best this argument shows that A. used Pt. where Pt. is prominent (but cf. vi 11, 8 n. and perhaps iv 8, 9 for the influence of Clitarchus in magnifying his importance) or in passages which betray bias against his later enemies.

24a. These arguments have some cumulative force. Others are worthless. It is immaterial that we do

not *know* of major omissions from Pt., since he is
hardly ever cited elsewhere; cf. also § 26. It is true
that A. supposed that as a king Pt. would be vera-
cious, but he never employs this consideration to
decide between him and Ar. And it is a mere *petitio
principii* to suppose that the ' bulletin style ' in much
of A. is that of Pt. (who need not, any more than
Thuc. or A. himself, have had one unvarying manner).
On the other hand, the fact that Ar. was an apologist
for Al. does not imply that A's own predilection for
apology stems from his work; Pt. was probably no
less biased for Al.

25. Granted that Pt. was A's chief source, we still
may not attribute to Pt. any particular statement
without specific reasons. A. could cite Ar. for
complementary information within a context which
(on the orthodox view) depends on Pt. (iii 11, 3;
vii 4, 4), and, as he also uses Ar. without naming him
(ii 5, 4; iv 6, 4; vii 19, 6; 20, 1 nn., cf. § 22 f.), we
cannot say how often he intruded Ar's evidence into
narratives based on Pt. Some incongruities in A.,
probable repetitions (ii 27, 3 n.; iii 11 with 13; 13, 3
n.; vi 15, 5; 28, 3 with 30, 2 f.; vii 6, 2 n.; App.
XVII 27 and 32; XVIII 3; see also Bosworth, *JHS*
1981, 19 ff. on iv 7, 2 and 18, 1), divergencies in
nomenclature (App. XVII 18a) and in military technical terms (App. XIX 1; v 20, 3 n.), may point to
such interpolations. When A. changed source, his
chronology could become disordered (App. XIV 3;
cf. Bosworth *op. cit.*; App. XVI 7; vi 28, 5; vii 4, 1
nn.). Now the account of naval operations in ii 1 f.
is in this and other respects very loosely tied to the
narrative of Al's doings; conceivably it stems from
Ar., who like Clitarchus (to judge from D. and QC.)

561

could have given more attention than Pt. to Greek affairs. We must not, of course, assume that incongruities or badly seamed joins always occurred, whenever A. turned from one source to another.

26. Nor can we properly hold that what is not in A. was not in Pt. (e.g. vii 9, 8 n.). Pt. may have furnished just the kind of succinct military and political record that A. desiderated. But when parallel versions make it possible to check A's excerpts from Ar. and N., we find that they can be incomplete, or inaccurate, cf. § 22 f.; App. XVII 5; XXV 4. It is unlikely that Pt. fared better. One might wonder if he had no more to say of his own prowess than A. allows in vi 11, 8; vii 15, 3; cf. also vi 16, 5 n. Far more important omissions are probable under the following heads:

(a) army numbers and reinforcements (Introd. 56 f., App. XIII and XIX);
(b) battle-orders, military reorganisations etc. (App. XIX 2);
(c) appointments (App. XXIV).

A. also gives an incomplete record of the siege of Tyre (Bosworth, *Commentary* 245), of operations in Turkestan (Bosworth, *JHS* 1981), and of many itineraries (App. III 3; VIII *passim*; XVII 11–15; 24; XVIII 6; cf. Bosworth on i 5, 3); in the last case we have to reckon with omissions from Ar. too, as he was doubtless S's authority that Al. crossed the Hindu-Kush to Bactria in 14 days (xv 2, 10, not in A.). Hence chronological vagueness. (A. would have done better to transcribe Ar's indications of time than to intrude sometimes inaccurate data from a chronographic source, cf. iii 15, 7 n.; App. XVII 15.) The comparable gaps, though fewer, in the narrative of N's voyages (App. XXV 4) are significant. QC. supplements Ar. not only on the length of marches, but also by giving valuable topographical information, which Ar., if not Pt., probably supplied (App. VIII 15 f.; 18; 20; XVII 15; cf. Bosworth, *JHS* 1981, who shows *inter alia* that, *contra* App. VIII 17, QC. did not make the mistake of taking Al. to Merv). The arguments that A. omitted much important material from Pt. as well as Ar. have cumulative force. He could also be vague and careless in use of his sources. I now believe that Bosworth (on iii 19, 5) is right in thinking that he misunderstood them in taking Al. to Ecbatana in 330. Cf. also App. III 5; XIII 5 and 9; i, 6, 9; ii 8, 4; iii 21, 5; iv 3, 6; v, 7, 1; 12, 1; 13, 1; 14, 3–5; 15, 5; 17, 3; 20, 7; 29, 3; vi 5, 5; perhaps 18, 3 and 20, 4 with notes; Bosworth on iii 11, 3. Some obscurities that vex scholars in reconstructing Al's marches and battles may be blamed on A. rather than on his authorities.

27. Like Lucian (*op. cit.* 7–13; 40), A. was conscious that flattery would probably mar the history of a ruler written in his own lifetime. It did not occur to him that Pt. and Ar. could have been unduly favourable to Al., out of personal friendship or genuine admiration, even though they published only after his death. No doubt they abstained from ostentatious panegyric. Moreover, though Al. was often condemned by moralists, the historical tradition from Callisthenes and Clitarchus seems to have consistently glorified him, so that A's suspicions would not have been awakened by comparison with any more critical account. (On Clitarchus cf. E. J. Bickermann, *Cl.*

Phil. xliii 42; the portrait in QC. of a ruler corrupted by power was surely not due to Clitarchus but suggested by Roman experience.) It seems too that Pt. and Ar. commonly confirmed or complemented each other (Introd. 19) and their general concurrence would have supported A. in his estimate of their reliability. Since neither need have used the other's work (§ 21), and since, alternatively, the later writer could control the earlier's account from his own recollections, we may think that their record of *overt* transactions was on the whole trustworthy, so far as it went. Exceptions must, however, be made, such as exaggerations in enemy numbers (App. III 5; IX 3; v 24, 5; vi 8, 6), the falsifications Bosworth has recently detected in A's stories of the sieges of Halicarnassus, Tyre and Gaza (*Entretiens Hardt* xxii ch. 1), the fables about the march to Siwah, and (I would add) distortions in the account of Gaugamela (App. IX 4–6), cf. also Bosworth, *JHS* 1981.

28. Certainly we must not assume that their interpretations of events were impartial or correct, or that they told the whole truth, nor reject a story just because it was not in Pt., or in Pt./Ar. Probably both traduced Parmenio (App. I 6); they imputed treason to Philotas on insufficient evidence, as perhaps to Alexander the Lyncestian and Callisthenes (App. XI; XIV 12); they may have put too favourable a colouring on the harshness of Al. to his officials in 324 (App. XXIII 9). Parmenio's execution was extenuated by Pt. as a necessary act of state. Both were reticent on some actions of Al. which provoked censure or which did him (in their judgement) no credit. Thus Pt. (unlike Ar.) did no more than allude to Clitus' murder, and neither said anything of

proscynesis (App. XIV). An embarrassed silence descended over Al's relation to Ammon (App. V) and his partial adoption of the style of a Persian king (App. XIV 1 f.); at most incidental allusions betray the truth.   Pt., but not Ar., seems to have concealed the successful resistance of Al's officers at the Beas (App. XXVII 5).   They did not indeed pass over the mutiny at Opis, and could not avoid explaining why it occurred; but on that occasion Al. showed his indomitable will, and the opposition he overcame had arisen not among the magnates (like Pt.) but among the common soldiers.   Presumably they omitted all mention of the executions and murders by which Al. had made his throne safe (Introd. 45 ff.), as of the factions in his entourage (App. XXIV 3); they denied the deterioration of his relations with Antipater (App. XXIII 10), and tacitly discounted the rumours that he was poisoned (vii 27).   To the last Al. remained a beloved hero (App. XXIII 9).   Perhaps they wished to avoid defacing that image if they said nothing of the mercenaries' decree (ib. 7 ff.).   Their technique consisted above all in the art of omission.   Pt. was the more consistent practitioner.   His masterpiece was the record of the Gadrosian march (App. XVIII); he concealed a disaster without uttering a falsehood. Here A. had his doubts, as about their testimony on Callisthenes (iv 14); and he was forced to turn to the vulgate for the murder of Clitus, *proscynesis* and Al's Orientalism (App. XIV).   But in general he was uncritical of their versions.

29. Devoid of sympathy for the old Greek ideal of freedom (cf. Bosworth on i 7, 4), A. could believe that the Greeks were sincerely devoted to Al. (App. XXII); this was very probably true of many of those

in Asia whom he had freed from Persia and oligarchs, but not of the homeland (vii 30, 2 n.). Perhaps in exculpating the Macedonians and Al. in particular for the destruction of Thebes and transferring the blame to Thebes' Greek enemies, he was guided by Pt. (cf. Bosworth, *Commentary* 79–81, who argues that here, as elsewhere, Pt's bias also places Perdiccas in an unfavourable light); Polybius xxxviii 2, 14 thought that no one approved the atrocity, but cf. D. xix 61 for persistent Macedonian rancour against Thebes. It is also possible that neither Pt. nor Ar. had much to say on Greek affairs after 335, and that this not only explains A's omissions (App. II; VI; XXIII 6 ff.), but also his failure to understand feelings in Greece. This would be a reasonable assumption if the *Anabasis* reflects the scope of their works. Though not a life of Al., since it starts only with his accession, and the title ' History of Alexander ', which Bosworth gives it (pp. 7 f.), if correct, is a misnomer, it is focused almost entirely on his own actions; his personal prowess, most notably at the Mallian town, occupies a disproportionate part in the work (cf. App. IV 2), and important operations that others conducted, even on occasion those conducted by Pt. (vi 11, 8), are mentioned briefly or not at all, and usually when they were reported to Al., to show his instructions had been fulfilled (App. XXIV 1); the treatment of N's expedition in vi 28, 5 f. is probably typical of the procedure of Pt./Ar. As Philip began the Persian war (Polyb. iii 6; xxii 8, 10), they had no need to explain its causes, nor to refer to its pretexts until Al. himself had occasion to parade them (ii 14), nor to relate operations before Philip's death, which A. almost ignores (Introd. 45; 56). They could also have passed over the origins of the Lamian war, since

it broke out only after Al's death; A. can at most have
alluded briefly to those acts of Al. which precipitated
it, in the lacuna after vii 12 (App. XXIII).

30. In general they too may have merely chronicled
events without explaining them, as A. normally does.
His objectives in invading Asia were not necessarily
Philip's, and they may have expanded with success;
what they became is only implicit in ii 3; 14; 25.
Again A's authorities do not seem to have disclosed
how far he intended to go in India, and they certainly
had nothing on his final plans (App. XVII 23; 30–3;
XXIII), unless we assume that A. himself left out
their interpretative comments. At most Ar. held
that Al. was insatiate for conquests, a view A.
endorsed (vii 19, 6 n.). This conception of Al.,
which was universal in antiquity, may have made both
them and A. regard it as unnecessary to define his
purposes at any stage in his career. Readers would
take it for granted that he meant to go as far as he
could. Very likely it was Pt. who suggested that the
more difficult an enterprise seemed, the more Al. was
determined to undertake it (ii 26, 3 n.). N's ex-
planations of his motives (vi 24, 3; *Ind.* 20, 2 n.), and
the emulation of Heracles and Dionysus, which Ar.
as well as the vulgate apparently imputed to him
(App. XVI), coincide with such an interpretation of
Al., which is remote from that of a statesman guided
mainly by rational considerations (cf. also App. V 3).
But all this was at best implicit in A's sources and
therefore in his own work.

31. Al's strategy was necessarily determined not
only by his aims, which A. does not define, but also by
the resources available to each side, the dispositions

of the enemy and the geographical conditions in the theatres of war. Pt./Ar. probably supplied far more detailed information of Al's resources than A. has preserved (App. XIX), but they exaggerated enemy numbers (§ 27) and (so far as we can tell) did not fully bring out the qualitative superiority of his army in training and equipment (Introd. 55–65). They also seem to have said less than Clitarchus (cf. D. 5–7; 23; 29–32; 39; 53) about the situation and plans of Darius. Despite the analyses in i 18, 6–9; ii 6, 3–7 and 17, A. is inadequate even on Al's naval inferiority (App. II 1), and much remains totally unexplained even in the early campaigns (for which Callisthenes was surely helpful), cf. i 24, 3 n.; App. VIII 3 f. and 19. These deficiencies are compounded in A. by the inadequacy of topographical descriptions, sometimes even for battles (App. III 5); hence the operations in Sogdiana and India are virtually unintelligible in his narrative, without the benefit of modern information on climate and terrain. No doubt A. could have improved his account if he had drawn more on Ar. (§ 23), even if Ar. himself inserted regional descriptions to give variety to his work rather than to show how Al's operations were adapted to, or defeated by, the geographical conditions of the lands he traversed. But A. lacked the reflective insight required. As for Pt., it puzzles me that scholars who produce widely discrepant reconstructions of the great battles can still extol his merits as a military historian, unless it be assumed that all the obscurities are due to A's carelessness. What really happened at Gaugamela and the Hydaspes is conjectural. Moreover, neither A. nor presumably his authorities made it clear what Al. had achieved. It was not only in India that his conquests were imperfect (App.

APPENDIX XXVIII

XVII 30). Parts of Anatolia had never submitted, or been truly pacified (ii 4, 2 n.; App. XXIV 6), and he had not himself ended all resistance in Iran (vi 27, 3; *Ind.* 36, 8); a great revolt of mercenaries in Bactria was impending (Introd. n. 66), and Al. did not fully trust his own generals (App. XXIII 9).

32. Incidental data in A. reveal Al's claim to be the legitimate heir of the Achaemenids, his efforts to use Iranians as well as Macedonians in army and government, his respect for local customs and religions and so forth. But only in his obituary notice (vii 29, 3 f.) does he explicitly attempt to explain Al's 'Orientalism,' on which see now Bosworth, *JHS* 1980. Even then he does not correlate all the various types of action relevant to it (App. XXIV 2). His concern is rather to portray his hero's personality than to illuminate his statecraft, or lack of it: his supposed magnanimity and justice to subjects and defeated enemies (i 17; iii 27, 5; vi 27; vii 20, 1), of which the treatment of Porus was the most conspicuous example (App. XVII 32); the desire for fame which partly inspired his city foundations (iii 1, 5 n.); the piety reflected not only in his regular sacrifices but in his reverence for foreign gods (iii 1, 4; 16, 4 f.; vii 17), notably Ammon (App. V); the chivalry and self-control evinced in his respect for the Achaemenid family and in his marriage to Roxane; the comradely spirit illustrated in the marriages at Susa (vii 4, 7). Perhaps the listing of appointments serves chiefly to set the king among his paladins, whom he rewards for valour and other services: certainly his policy in making them is seldom explained (App. XXIV 1–4). A. does not try to trace Al's changing relationship with the Macedonians (App. XXIII 9).

APPENDIX XXVIII

We look in vain for any political analysis comparable
with that which Hieronymus, a contemporary of Pt.
and Ar., provided in his history of Al's successors (cf.
D. xviii–xx *passim*). This deficiency surely arises
from the character of A's chief sources. In general
they were content to stress Al's indomitable will and
his persistent longing to see and do new things; for
instance, the visit to Siwah illustrates this aspect of
their hero, along with his reverence for Ammon
(App. V, esp. 3; cf. N. *ap. Ind.* 20, 2). Whether this
interpretation of Al. was adequate or not, A. was
incapable of criticizing it and supplying his own.
The independent scrutiny that Polybius brought to
bear on the pretexts for the Persian war (Introd. 42),
or somewhat captiously on Callisthenes' account of
Issus (App. III), was outside his range. Instead he
transcribed more or less what he found in his sources,
including what he did not understand (App. XIX 1).
Therein lies his usefulness!

33. This slavish reliance on his sources is most clearly
apparent in geographical matters. He seldom
imports new information or contemporary usages;
for exceptional cases see Bosworth, *Commentary* pp.
60; 225. He writes out obsolete statements of E.
(v 3, 1; *Ind.* 2, 5; 43, 3 nn.), just as he repeats an
out-of-date historical statement he read in Meg.
(*Ind.* 10, 9 n.), cf. App. XVII 8. He treats a con-
troversy that had long been settled as if it were still
alive, merely following Ar. (vii 16, 3 n.). He uses
names which he knows to be misleading because Pt.
used them (App. XII). He reproduces contradictory
or confusing testimony from different sources (App.
XXVI). It is very improbable that he showed more
independence in his historical narrative. All this

was common enough among writers of the Roman period. Even the conscientious Pliny purveyed out-of-date information (Münzer and Kroll, cited in § 11). It would hardly be worth stressing but that critical judgement has often been claimed on A's behalf. Like Pliny, A. is capable of expressing as his own views what he had really borrowed without acknowledgement from his authorities, see iii 10, 2 ff.; vii 19, 6; *Ind.* 32, 13 nn. Of course he was sincerely endorsing them, but subject to that proviso there is nothing absurd in principle in Kornemann's thesis (Introd. n. 24) that many of A's personal judgements were really those of Pt.

34. Kornemann went too far, notably in his inference from the similarity of the obituary notices in vii 28 f. and QC. x 5, 26–37, all the more remarkable, since QC. here obliterates his earlier portrait of a deteriorating tyrant, and A. contradicts his verdict in iv 7 on Al's Orientalism. Still (*contra* Kornemann) Pt. can hardly be the common source: he preferred to veil that Orientalism, not to defend it; and the list of Al's virtues in vii 28 is little more than an enumeration of the qualities conventionally credited to the good king and general. Perhaps we should rather invoke the influence of traditional encomia in the rhetorical schools, of which P's first essay on *The Fortune or Virtue of Alexander* is a far more intelligent specimen. At any rate, the contradiction between vii 29 and iv 7 (vulgate) shows how A. could readily adopt as his own opinion whatever he read last (cf. App. XIV 10). Most of his other commendations or censures of Al. (ii 12, 8; iv 9, 1 f.; 12, 6; 19, 6; vi 13, 4 f.; 26, 1 f.; vii 23, 8) are in a conventionally moralizing vein, with no hint of practical experience underlying them.

APPENDIX XXVIII

Few, if any, need be original, any more than his comments on the burning of Persepolis (iii 18, 12; cf. vi 30, 1), or on Callisthenes (iv 10, 1; 12, 6; cf. P. 54, 1) or on Al's lust for conquest (vii 1 f.). In criticizing Ar. in v 14, he rejects his account for the wrong reasons. The semi-rationalism of ii 16 (App. XVI 10) or of vii 13 (App. XXI) and the muddle of *Ind.* 43 attest the limits of his own mental resources.

35. Like Pt. and Ar. (vii 26, 3 n.) A. did not go beyond Al's death: his sources had run out. He did not ask himself whether the break-up of Al's empire was inevitable (so QC.), or whether (as the practical Augustus held, Plut. 207 D) Al. should have been devoting himself to its organisation. He thought that a divinity had promoted Al's success (vii 30, 2), but he did not speculate on the purposes of providence, and only adduced in confirmation the fact that Al. enjoyed undying fame. Yet A's own world had been shaped by Al's conquests, and he lived late enough to have discerned more of their historic significance than Pt. or Ar. could have done. But for him the tale is still that which they told: essentially one of epic adventure. His methods and outlook are all too typical of the intellectual poverty of an age of which he was (and, perhaps, still is) regarded as one of the greatest adornments.

INDEXES

References are to book and chapter. Some names, e.g. of fathers of Companions, are omitted. Numbers in brackets after a name refer to the numbers in Berve, *Das Alexanderreich* vol. ii.

I ANABASIS

Abastani, vi 15.
Abdera, i 11.
Abian Scythians, iv 1.
Abisares (2), iv 27; v 8; 20; 22; 29.
Abreas (6), vi 9; 10; 11.
Abulites (5), iii 8; 16; 19; vii 4.
Abydus, i 11.
Acesines, v 4; 5; 20; 25; 29; vi 1; 3; 4; 13; 14; 15; vii 10.
Acuphis (36), v 1; 2.
Ada (20), i 23.
Adaeus (22), i 22.
Admetus (24), ii 23 f.
Adraïstae, v 22.
Aeacidae, ii 27; iv 11.
Aeacus, vii 29.
Aegae, i 11.
Aegean Sea, vii 20.
Aegina, vi 11.
Aegobares (32), vii 6.
Aeolis, i 18; iii 22; vii 9.
Aeschylus (35), iii 5.
Aetolians, i 7; 10.
Agamemnon, i 11.
Agathon (8), i 14; iii 12.

Agesilaus (11), ii 13.
Agis (15), ii 13. (16), iv 9.
Agrianians, i 5; and often, cf. Introd. p. lxxxii.
Alcetas (45), iv 22; 27; v 11.
Alcias (46), i 29.
Alcimachus (47), i 18.
Alcmene, ii 16.
Alexander (37), i 7; 17; 25.
Alexander, king of Epirus (38), iii 6.
Alexander, son of Philip, *passim.*
Alexandria (Egypt), iii 1; v 1; vii 23. (Caucasus), iii 28; v 1. (Parapamisus), iv 22. (Tanais), iv 1; 4.
Alinda, i 23.
Amanian Gates, ii 7.
Amastrine (50), vii 4.
Amazons, iv 15; vii 13.
Ambracia, ii 16.
Amminapes (55), iii 22.
Ammon, iii 3; 4; iv 9; vi 3; 19; vii 8; 14; 23.
Amphilochus, Amphilochians, ii 5; 16.

INDEX

INDEX

INDEX

577

INDEX

INDEX

INDEX

INDEX

581

INDEX

INDEX

INDEX

INDEX

INDEX

INDEX

Printed in Great Britain
by Richard Clay (The Chaucer Press), Ltd,
Bungay, Suffolk

THE LOEB CLASSICAL LIBRARY

VOLUMES ALREADY PUBLISHED

Latin Authors

AMMIANUS MARCELLINUS. Translated by J. C. Rolfe. 3 Vols.

APULEIUS: THE GOLDEN ASS (METAMORPHOSES). W. Adlington (1566). Revised by S. Gaselee.

ST. AUGUSTINE: CITY OF GOD. 7 Vols. Vol. I. G. E. McCracken. Vols. II and VII. W. M. Green. Vol. III. D. Wiesen. Vol. IV. P. Levine. Vol. V. E. M. Sanford and W. M. Green. Vol. VI. W. C. Greene.

ST. AUGUSTINE, CONFESSIONS OF. W. Watts (1631). 2 Vols.

ST. AUGUSTINE, SELECT LETTERS. J. H. Baxter.

AUSONIUS. H. G. Evelyn White. 2 Vols.

BEDE. J. E. King. 2 Vols.

BOETHIUS: TRACTS and DE CONSOLATIONE PHILOSOPHIAE. Rev. H. F. Stewart and E. K. Rand. Revised by S. J. Tester.

CAESAR: ALEXANDRIAN, AFRICAN and SPANISH WARS. A. G. Way.

CAESAR: CIVIL WARS. A. G. Peskett.

CAESAR: GALLIC WAR. H. J. Edwards.

CATO: DE RE RUSTICA. VARRO: DE RE RUSTICA. H. B. Ash and W. D. Hooper.

CATULLUS. F. W. Cornish. TIBULLUS. J. B. Postgate. PERVIGILIUM VENERIS. J. W. Mackail.

CELSUS: DE MEDICINA. W. G. Spencer. 3 Vols.

CICERO: BRUTUS and ORATOR. G. L. Hendrickson and H. M. Hubbell.

[CICERO]: AD HERENNIUM. H. Caplan.

CICERO: DE ORATORE, etc. 2 Vols. Vol. I. DE ORATORE, Books I and II. E. W. Sutton and H. Rackham. Vol. II. DE ORATORE, Book III. DE FATO; PARADOXA STOICORUM; DE PARTITIONE ORATORIA. H. Rackham.

CICERO: DE FINIBUS. H. Rackham.

CICERO: DE INVENTIONE, etc. H. M. Hubbell.

CICERO: DE NATURA DEORUM and ACADEMICA. H. Rackham.

CICERO: DE OFFICIIS. Walter Miller.

CICERO: DE REPUBLICA and DE LEGIBUS. Clinton W. Keyes.

2

Minucius Felix. Cf. Tertullian.

Ovid: The Art of Love and Other Poems. J. H. Mosley. Revised by G. P. Goold.

Ovid: Fasti. Sir James G. Frazer

Ovid: Heroides and Amores. Grant Showerman. Revised by G. P. Goold

Ovid: Metamorphoses. F. J. Miller. 2 Vols. Vol. 1 revised by G. P. Goold.

Ovid: Tristia and Ex Ponto. A. L. Wheeler.

Persius. Cf. Juvenal.

Pervigilium Veneris. Cf. Catullus.

Petronius. M. Heseltine. Seneca: Apocolocyntosis. W. H. D. Rouse. Revised by E. H. Warmington.

Phaedrus and Babrius (Greek). B. E. Perry.

Plautus. Paul Nixon. 5 Vols.

Pliny: Letters, Panegyricus. Betty Radice. 2 Vols.

Pliny: Natural History. 10 Vols. Vols. I–V and IX. H. Rackham. VI.–VIII. W. H. S. Jones. X. D. E. Eichholz.

Propertius. H. E. Butler.

Prudentius. H. J. Thomson. 2 Vols.

Quintilian. H. E. Butler. 4 Vols.

Remains of Old Latin. E. H. Warmington. 4 Vols. Vol. I. (Ennius and Caecilius) Vol. II. (Livius, Naevius Pacuvius, Accius) Vol. III. (Lucilius and Laws of XII Tables) Vol. IV. (Archaic Inscriptions)

Res Gestae Divi Augusti. Cf. Velleius Paterculus.

Sallust. J. C. Rolfe.

Scriptores Historiae Augustae. D. Magie. 3 Vols.

Seneca, The Elder: Controversiae, Suasoriae. M. Winterbottom. 2 Vols.

Seneca: Apocolocyntosis. Cf. Petronius.

Seneca: Epistulae Morales. R. M. Gummere. 3 Vols.

Seneca: Moral Essays. J. W. Basore. 3 Vols.

Seneca: Tragedies. F. J. Miller. 2 Vols.

Seneca: Naturales Quaestiones. T. H. Corcoran. 2 Vols.

Sidonius: Poems and Letters. W. B. Anderson. 2 Vols.

Silius Italicus. J. D. Duff. 2 Vols.

Statius. J. H. Mozley. 2 Vols.

Suetonius. J. C. Rolfe. 2 Vols.

Tacitus: Dialogus. Sir Wm. Peterson. Agricola and Germania. Maurice Hutton. Revised by M. Winterbottom, R. M. Ogilvie, E. H. Warmington.

Tacitus: Histories and Annals. C. H. Moore and J. Jackson. 4 Vols.

TERENCE. John Sargeaunt. 2 Vols.
TERTULLIAN: APOLOGIA and DE SPECTACULIS. T. R. Glover. MINUCIUS FELIX. G. H. Rendall.
TIBULLUS. Cf. CATULLUS.
VALERIUS FLACCUS. J. H. Mozley.
VARRO: DE LINGUA LATINA. R. G. Kent. 2 Vols.
VELLEIUS PATERCULUS and RES GESTAE DIVI AUGUSTI. F. W. Shipley.
VIRGIL. H. R. Fairclough. 2 Vols.
VITRUVIUS: DE ARCHITECTURA. F. Granger. 2 Vols.

Greek Authors

ACHILLES TATIUS. S. Gaselee.
AELIAN: ON THE NATURE OF ANIMALS. A. F. Scholfield. 3 Vols.
AENEAS TACTICUS. ASCLEPIODOTUS and ONASANDER. The Illinois Greek Club.
AESCHINES. C. D. Adams.
AESCHYLUS. H. Weir Smyth. 2 Vols.
ALCIPHRON, AELIAN, PHILOSTRATUS: LETTERS. A. R. Benner and F. H. Fobes.
ANDOCIDES, ANTIPHON. Cf. MINOR ATTIC ORATORS.
APOLLODORUS. Sir James G. Frazer. 2 Vols.
APOLLONIUS RHODIUS. R. C. Seaton.
APOSTOLIC FATHERS. Kirsopp Lake. 2 Vols.
APPIAN: ROMAN HISTORY. Horace White. 4 Vols.
ARATUS. Cf. CALLIMACHUS.
ARISTIDES: ORATIONS. C. A. Behr. Vol. I.
ARISTOPHANES. Benjamin Bickley Rogers. 3 Vols. Verse trans.
ARISTOTLE: ART OF RHETORIC. J. H. Freese.
ARISTOTLE: ATHENIAN CONSTITUTION, EUDEMIAN ETHICS, VICES AND VIRTUES. H. Rackham.
ARISTOTLE: GENERATION OF ANIMALS. A. L. Peck.
ARISTOTLE: HISTORIA ANIMALIUM. A. L. Peck. Vols. I.–II.
ARISTOTLE: METAPHYSICS. H. Tredennick. 2 Vols.
ARISTOTLE: METEOROLOGICA. H. D. P. Lee.
ARISTOTLE: MINOR WORKS. W. S. Hett. On Colours, On Things Heard, On Physiognomies, On Plants, On Marvellous Things Heard, Mechanical Problems, On Indivisible Lines, On Situations and Names of Winds, On Melissus, Xenophanes, and Gorgias.
ARISTOTLE: NICOMACHEAN ETHICS. H. Rackham.

4

Aristotle: Oeconomica and Magna Moralia. G. C. Armstrong (with Metaphysics, Vol. II).

Aristotle: On the Heavens. W. K. C. Guthrie.

Aristotle: On the Soul, Parva Naturalia, On Breath. W. S. Hett.

Aristotle: Categories, On Interpretation, Prior Analytics. H. P. Cooke and H. Tredennick.

Aristotle: Posterior Analytics, Topics. H. Tredennick and E. S. Forster.

Aristotle: On Sophistical Refutations.
On Coming to be and Passing Away, On the Cosmos. E. S. Forster and D. J. Furley.

Aristotle: Parts of Animals. A. L. Peck; Motion and Progression of Animals. E. S. Forster.

Aristotle: Physics. Rev. P. Wicksteed and F. M. Cornford. 2 Vols.

Aristotle: Poetics and Longinus. W. Hamilton Fyfe; Demetrius on Style. W. Rhys Roberts.

Aristotle: Politics. H. Rackham.

Aristotle: Problems. W. S. Hett. 2 Vols.

Aristotle: Rhetorica Ad Alexandrum (with Problems. Vol. II). H. Rackham.

Arrian: History of Alexander and Indica, 2 Vols. Vol. II 1983). New version P. Brunt.

Athenaeus: Deipnosophistae. C. B. Gulick. 7 Vols.

Babrius and Phaedrus (Latin). B. E. Perry.

St. Basil: Letters. R. J. Deferrari. 4 Vols.

Callimachus: Fragments. C. A. Trypanis. Musaeus: Hero and Leander. T. Gelzer and C. Whitman.

Callimachus, Hymns and Epigrams, and Lycophron. A. W. Mair; Aratus. G. R. Mair.

Clement of Alexandria. Rev. G. W. Butterworth.

Colluthus. Cf. Oppian.

Daphnis and Chloe. Thornley's Translation revised by J. M. Edmonds: and Parthenius. S. Gaselee.

Demosthenes I.: Olynthiacs, Philippics and Minor Orations I.–XVII. and XX. J. H. Vince.

Demosthenes II.: De Corona and De Falsa Legatione. C. A. Vince and J. H. Vince.

Demosthenes III.: Meidias, Androtion, Aristocrates, Timocrates and Aristogeiton I. and II. J. H. Vince.

Demosthenes IV.–VI: Private Orations and In Neaeram. A. T. Murray.

Demosthenes VII: Funeral Speech, Erotic Essay, Exordia and Letters. N. W. and N. J. DeWitt.

Dio Cassius: Roman History. E. Cary. 9 Vols.

DIO CHRYSOSTOM. J. W. Cohoon and H. Lamar Crosby. 5 Vols.

DIODORUS SICULUS. 12 Vols. Vols. I.–VI. C. H. Oldfather. Vol. VII. C. L. Sherman. Vol. VIII. C. B. Welles. Vols. IX. and X. R. M. Geer. Vol. XI. F. Walton. Vol. XII. F. Walton. General Index. R. M. Geer.

DIOGENES LAERTIUS. R. D. Hicks. 2 Vols. New Introduction by H. S. Long.

DIONYSIUS OF HALICARNASSUS: ROMAN ANTIQUITIES. Spelman's translation revised by E. Cary. 7 Vols.

DIONYSIUS OF HALICARNASSUS: CRITICAL ESSAYS. S. Usher. 2 Vols. Vol. I.

EPICTETUS. W. A. Oldfather. 2 Vols.

EURIPIDES. A. S. Way. 4 Vols. Verse trans.

EUSEBIUS: ECCLESIASTICAL HISTORY. Kirsopp Lake and J. E. L. Oulton. 2 Vols.

GALEN: ON THE NATURAL FACULTIES. A. J. Brock.

GREEK ANTHOLOGY. W. R. Paton. 5 Vols.

GREEK BUCOLIC POETS (THEOCRITUS, BION, MOSCHUS). J. M Edmonds.

GREEK ELEGY AND IAMBUS with the ANACREONTEA. J. M. Edmonds. 2 Vols.

GREEK LYRIC. D. A. Campbell. 4 Vols. Vol. I.

GREEK MATHEMATICAL WORKS. Ivor Thomas. 2 Vols.

HERODES. Cf. THEOPHRASTUS: CHARACTERS.

HERODIAN. C. R. Whittaker. 2 Vols.

HERODOTUS. A. D. Godley. 4 Vols.

HESIOD AND THE HOMERIC HYMNS. H. G. Evelyn White.

HIPPOCRATES and the FRAGMENTS OF HERACLEITUS. W. H. S. Jones and E. T. Withington. 4 Vols.

HOMER: ILIAD. A. T. Murray. 2 Vols.

HOMER: ODYSSEY. A. T. Murray. 2 Vols.

ISAEUS. E. W. Forster.

ISOCRATES. George Norlin and LaRue Van Hook. 3 Vols.

[ST. JOHN DAMASCENE]: BARLAAM AND IOASAPH. Rev. G. R. Woodward, Harold Mattingly and D. M. Lang.

JOSEPHUS. 10 Vols. Vols. I.–IV. H. Thackeray. Vol. V. H. Thackeray and R. Marcus. Vols. VI.–VII. R. Marcus. Vol. VIII. R. Marcus and Allen Wikgren. Vols. IX.–X. L. H. Feldman.

JULIAN. Wilmer Cave Wright. 3 Vols.

LIBANIUS. A. F. Norman. 3 Vols. Vols. I.–II.

LUCIAN. 8 Vols. Vols. I.–V. A. M. Harmon. Vol. VI. K. Kilburn. Vols. VII.–VIII. M. D. Macleod.

LYCOPHRON. Cf. CALLIMACHUS.

LYRA GRAECA, J. M. Edmonds. 2 Vols.

LYSIAS. W. R. M. Lamb.

MANETHO. W. G. Waddell.

MARCUS AURELIUS. C. R. Haines.

MENANDER. W. G. Arnott. 3 Vols. Vol. I.

MINOR ATTIC ORATORS (ANTIPHON, ANDOCIDES, LYCURGUS, DEMADES, DINARCHUS, HYPERIDES). K. J. Maidment and J. O. Burtt. 2 Vols.

MUSAEUS: HERO AND LEANDER. Cf. CALLIMACHUS.

NONNOS: DIONYSIACA. W. H. D. Rouse. 3 Vols.

OPPIAN, COLLUTHUS, TRYPHIODORUS. A. W. Mair.

PAPYRI. NON-LITERARY SELECTIONS. A. S. Hunt and C. C. Edgar. 2 Vols. LITERARY SELECTIONS (Poetry). D. L. Page.

PARTHENIUS. Cf. DAPHNIS and CHLOE.

PAUSANIAS: DESCRIPTION OF GREECE. W. H. S. Jones. 4 Vols. and Companion Vol. arranged by R. E. Wycherley.

PHILO. 10 Vols. Vols. I.–V. F. H. Colson and Rev. G. H. Whitaker. Vols. VI.–IX. F. H. Colson. Vol. X. F. H. Colson and the Rev. J. W. Earp.

PHILO: two supplementary Vols. (*Translation only.*) Ralph Marcus.

PHILOSTRATUS: THE LIFE OF APOLLONIUS OF TYANA. F. C. Conybeare. 2 Vols.

PHILOSTRATUS: IMAGINES; CALLISTRATUS: DESCRIPTIONS. A. Fairbanks.

PHILOSTRATUS and EUNAPIUS: LIVES OF THE SOPHISTS. Wilmer Cave Wright.

PINDAR. Sir J. E. Sandys.

PLATO: CHARMIDES, ALCIBIADES, HIPPARCHUS, THE LOVERS, THEAGES, MINOS and EPINOMIS. W. R. M. Lamb.

PLATO: CRATYLUS, PARMENIDES, GREATER HIPPIAS, LESSER HIPPIAS. H. N. Fowler.

PLATO: EUTHYPHRO, APOLOGY, CRITO, PHAEDO, PHAEDRUS, H. N. Fowler.

PLATO: LACHES, PROTAGORAS, MENO, EUTHYDEMUS. W. R. M. Lamb.

PLATO: LAWS. Rev. R. G. Bury. 2 Vols.

PLATO: LYSIS, SYMPOSIUM, GORGIAS. W. R. M. Lamb.

PLATO: Republic. Paul Shorey. 2 Vols.

PLATO: STATESMAN, PHILEBUS. H. N. Fowler; ION. W. R. M. Lamb.

PLATO: THEAETETUS and SOPHIST. H. N. Fowler.

PLATO: TIMAEUS, CRITIAS, CLITOPHO, MENEXENUS, EPISTULAE. Rev. R. G. Bury.

PLOTINUS: A. H. Armstrong. 7 Vols. Vols. I.–III.

PLUTARCH: MORALIA. 16 Vols. Vols I.–V. F. C. Babbitt. Vol. VI. W. C. Helmbold. Vols. VII. and XIV. P. H. De Lacy and B. Einarson. Vol. VIII. P. A. Clement and H. B. Hoffleit. Vol. IX. E. L. Minar, Jr., F. H. Sandbach, W. C. Helmbold. Vol. X. H. N. Fowler. Vol. XI. L. Pearson and F. H. Sandbach. Vol. XII. H. Cherniss and W. C. Helmbold. Vol. XIII 1–2. H. Cherniss. Vol. XV. F. H. Sandbach.

PLUTARCH: THE PARALLEL LIVES. B. Perrin. 11 Vols.

POLYBIUS. W. R. Paton. 6 Vols.

PROCOPIUS. H. B. Dewing. 7 Vols.

PTOLEMY: TETRABIBLOS. F. E. Robbins.

QUINTUS SMYRNAEUS. A. S. Way. Verse trans.

SEXTUS EMPIRICUS. Rev. R. G. Bury. 4 Vols.

SOPHOCLES. F. Storr. 2 Vols. Verse trans.

STRABO: GEOGRAPHY. Horace L. Jones. 8 Vols.

THEOCRITUS. Cf. GREEK BUCOLIC POETS.

THEOPHRASTUS: CHARACTERS. J. M. Edmonds. HERODES, etc. A. D. Knox.

THEOPHRASTUS: ENQUIRY INTO PLANTS. Sir Arthur Hort, Bart. 2 Vols.

THEOPHRASTUS: DE CAUSIS PLANTARUM. G. K. K. Link and B. Einarson. 3 Vols. Vol. I.

THUCYDIDES. C. F. Smith. 4 Vols.

TRYPHIODORUS. Cf. OPPIAN.

XENOPHON: CYROPAEDIA. Walter Miller. 2 Vols.

XENOPHON: HELLENICA. C. L. Brownson. 2 Vols.

XENOPHON: ANABASIS. C. L. Brownson.

XENOPHON: MEMORABILIA AND OECONOMICUS. E. C. Marchant. SYMPOSIUM AND APOLOGY. O. J. Todd.

XENOPHON: SCRIPTA MINORA. E. C. Marchant. CONSTITUTION OF THE ATHENIANS. G. W. Bowersock.